ISBN 978-0-282-50254-6
PIBN 10853993

Forgotten Books is a registered trademark of FB &c Ltd.
Copyright © 2018 FB &c Ltd.
FB &c Ltd, Dalton House, 60 Windsor Avenue, London, SW19 2RR.
Company number 08720141. Registered in England and Wales.

For support please visit www.forgottenbooks.com

1 MONTH OF
FREE
READING

at

www.ForgottenBooks.com

By purchasing this book you are eligible for one month membership to ForgottenBooks.com, giving you unlimited access to our entire collection of over 1,000,000 titles via our web site and mobile apps.

To claim your free month visit:

www.forgottenbooks.com/free853993

English
Français
Deutsche
Italiano
Español
Português

www.forgottenbooks.com

Mythology Photography **Fiction**
Fishing Christianity **Art** Cooking
Essays Buddhism Freemasonry
Medicine **Biology** Music **Ancient**
Egypt Evolution Carpentry Physics
Dance Geology **Mathematics** Fitness
Shakespeare **Folklore** Yoga Marketing
Confidence Immortality Biographies
Poetry **Psychology** Witchcraft
Electronics Chemistry History **Law**
Accounting **Philosophy** Anthropology
Alchemy Drama Quantum Mechanics
Atheism Sexual Health **Ancient History**
Entrepreneurship Languages Sport
Paleontology Needlework Islam
Metaphysics Investment Archaeology
Parenting Statistics Criminology
Motivational

SERIES OF 1922
THE HALE LECTURES
WESTERN THEOLOGICAL SEMINARY
CHICAGO, ILL.

SOME ASPECTS OF
CONTEMPORARY GREEK ORTHODOX THOUGHT

G

THE HALE LECTURES 1922

Some Aspects of
Contemporary Greek Orthodox Thought

By the

REV. FRANK GAVIN, B. H. L., M. A., TH. D.
Professor of New Testament
Nashotah House
Nashotah, Wisconsin

18 11 70.
7. 6. 2

Milwaukee
MOREHOUSE PUBLISHING CO.
London
A. R. MOWBRAY AND CO.
1923

EXISTS

EXTRACTS

FROM THE WILL OF THE RT. REV. CHARLES REUBEN HALE, D.D., LL.D., BISHOP COADJUTOR OF SPRINGFIELD, *born* 1837; *consecrated July* 26, 1892; *died December* 25, 1900.

 In the Name of the Father, and of the Son, and of the Holy Ghost. Amen.

I, CHARLES REUBEN HALE, BISHOP OF CAIRO, BISHOP COADJUTOR OF SPRINGFIELD, of the City of Cairo, Illinois, do make, publish, and declare this, as and for my Last Will and Testament, hereby revoking all former wills by me made.

First, First of all, I commit myself, soul and body, into the hands of Jesus Christ, my Lord and Saviour, in Whose Merits alone I trust, looking for the Resurrection of the Body and the Life of the World to come.

.   .   .   .

Fourteenth. All the rest and residue of my Estate, personal and real, not in this my Will otherwise specifically devised, wheresoever situate, and whether legal or equitable, I give, devise, and bequeath to "THE WESTERN THEOLOGICAL SEMINARY, CHICAGO, ILLINOIS," above mentioned, but nevertheless *In Trust*, provided it shall accept the trust by an instrument in writing so stating, filed with this Will in the Court where probated, within six months after the probate of this Will—for the general purpose of promoting the Catholic Faith, in its purity and integrity, as taught in Holy Scripture, held by the Primitive Church, summed up in the Creeds, and affirmed by the undisputed General Councils, and, in particular, to be used only and exclusively for the purposes following, to-wit:—

.   .   .   .

(2) The establishment, endowment, publication, and due circulation of Courses of Lectures, to be delivered annually forever, to be called "The Hale Lectures."

The lectures shall treat of one of the following subjects:
    (a) Liturgies and Liturgics.
    (b) Church Hymns and Church Music.
    (c) The History of the Eastern Churches.
    (d) The History of National Churches.

    (e)   Contemporaneous Church History: *i.e*, treating of events happening since the beginning of what is called "The Oxford Movement," in 1833.

It is the aim of the Seminary, through the Hale Lectures, to make from time to time some valuable contribution to certain of the Church's problems, without thereby committing itself to agreement with the utterances of its own selected Preachers.

GUILIELMO ET LAURAE GAVIN

PARENTIBUS CARISSIMIS

FILIUS

CARITATIS EXEMPLIS

SACERDOS

PRIMIS MAGISTRIS

DISCIPULUS

HAS PRIMITIAS

AUCTOR

D. D. D.

TABLE OF CONTENTS

1. *Dogma and Dogmatic*: three uses of the word *dogma* p. 4) ; Androutsos on *dogma*,—objective and subjective aspects; his definition descriptive rather than analytic; Rhôsse,—his definition relates to its content (p. 5) ; R. on Christianity (p. 6) and on Dogmatic: four notes of its scientific character (p. 7). Organizing and unitary principle of Orthodox Dogmatic: Androutsos (p. 8), and Rhôsse (p. 9) ; comparison of the two methods (p. 10).

2. *Revelation*: (a) inspiration,—internal or subjective r., —and (b) miracle,—external or objective r.; criteria of valid r. (p. 11) ; notes: (1) creative and new quality, (2) consistency and supplementary character (p. 12),—"natural" and "supernatural" are relative terms, valid for human experience (p. 13),—and (3) progressive development (p. 14).

3. *Revelation and Miracle*: the conception of m.; (a) neither violation nor suspension of natural law, (b) but result of the introduction of a new cause; (c) not derogatory to the unchangeableness of God, (d) nor 'impossible' scientifically (p. 15). Inspiration and miracle; the Incarnation as the complete and final revelation (p. 16).

4. *The Sources of Dogmatic*: definitions (p. 17).

5. (1) *The Bible*: (a) the Church as infallible interpreter p. 18) ; (b) Canon and Text; O. T. and Deutero-canonica; N. T. (p. 19) ; status of LXX; condemnation of vernacular N. T. (p. 20) ; (c) Inspiration of B.: definition; degrees of inspiration (p. 21) ; canonicity not dependent upon authorship; *fact* of inspiration, but no definite *theory* accepted; inspiration—not literal (p. 22), not simply subjective, or result of delusion, hallucination, or imagination, nor limited to dogma and morals (p. 23) ; Orthodox view of i.; (d) Biblical teaching in relation to Dogma; rule of faith (p. 24).

6. (2.) *Tradition*: (a) origin and relation to Bible; oral preceded written word (p. 25) ; N. T. first formulation of T.; relation of Bible to T. (p. 26) ; (b) content and formula-

PREFACE

The Primitive Church extended its message to all parts of the world. Secure in the commission and promise of its Founder, it presented to the common needs of mankind a gospel in which was embodied an answer universal in its scope and character. Just in proportion as the Faith took deep root in different places it underwent certain inevitable transformations. The Gospel must needs be translated, and as the process of translation involves more than merely turning a meaning in one language into its nearest equivalent in another, the translation of the Church's message effected certain differences in emphasis, brought to light new aspects of its meaning, and involved subtle variations in the kind and degree of its apprehension on the part of different peoples. That such a process should come about is both a result of and a testimony to the inherently universal character of the Church's Faith, the intrinsic value and appeal it possessed, and the power of the assimilative faculties of the three dominant types of Catholic Christianity which emerged. These three resultant presentations had almost the distinctness of personalities; Semitic, Greek, and Latin Catholicism were in essence fundamentally the same, but strongly marked and almost personal in their own individuality of character.

Semitic Catholicism, which has long ceased to exist as a correlative and collateral branch of Catholic Christendom, in a very true sense approximated most closely to Apostolic Christianity, since for it no process of translation had been necessary. It may best be studied, in the few remaining vestiges of a once mighty Church, in the writings of Aphraates. Its history is instructive. Beginning with St. Ephraim, Semitic Catholicism attempted the impossible task of Hellenization; while St. Ephraim and his successors concerned themselves with the translation into Semitic terms of contemporaneous Greek thought, this process later degenerated into a kind of thought transliteration, which did violence to both Greek and Syriac, and resulted in the lamentable mediocrity which is the distinguishing mark of its subsequent literature. The true Semitic Catholicism was so thoroughly erased from history that we have become accustomed to think of early Christianity as of two types only—Eastern and Western, Greek and Latin.

Each of these two great surviving types has its own strongly marked character, and throughout history it has been the bane of Christianity that neither has succeeded in understanding the other. The differences between East and West are fundamental, and the divergences spring, so to speak, farther up the stream of corporate consciousness than at the point of Christianization. Much as we may emphasize our identity of Faith in fundamental matters, we must yet make allowance for deep-rooted differences of temperament. East and West not only differ in their essential character and viewpoint, but also have had these underlying differences protracted and exaggerated by the underlying experiences of the East and the West. Our history, both before and after the Schism of the eleventh century, has been different; our code and table of values has been different; external conditions have been different. Finally, from the days of the first Ecumenical Councils until to-day, there has been the almost insuperable barrier of the difference in language.

When we come to scrutinize and analyze these fundamental differences we are met with other problems of no slight difficulty. To set off in a phrase the essential character of Eastern Orthodox Christianity would indeed have a certain worth and value. Kattenbusch speaks of its "essentially mystagogic character," passing over other fundamental characteristics; Dorner makes this one of three essential notes, of which the others are its emphasis on "knowledge" and the strong bond between ethics and religion. Most Orthodox writers, such as Eugenius Bulgaris and Rhôsse, put special accent on the intimate union of the moral life—that is, religion as conduct—with true faith—religion as right belief.[1] According to

---

[1] Kattenbusch in *Confessionskunde;* Dorner, *Grundriss der Dogmengeschichte*, pp. 613-614; Eugenius Bulgaris, Θεολογικόν (translated into Greek by Agathangelos Leontopoulos, Venice, 1872); Rhôsse, Δογματική, pp. 35-36; Mesolora, Πρακτικὴ Θεολογία, pp. 16-18.

Androutsos, "authenticity and freedom" are the chief notes of Orthodoxy.[1] In Dr. Frere's very illuminating but brief paper on *The Eastern Orthodox Church* he characterizes the Westernizing process as a movement animated by two main forces, "legalism" and "regimentation".[2] The impress and effects of these two tendencies on all Western Christianity has so greatly influenced our way of looking at Church matters and theological questions that a certain process of un-westernizing must be undertaken before we can attain to any measure of sympathetic understanding of Orthodoxy. Familiar and almost axiomatic preconceptions, which are all but universal in the Western point of view, must be laid aside if we are to comprehend the genius of Eastern Christianity. The process is not so difficult if we read history carefully, and thereby become conscious of certain presuppositions, from which we must divest ourselves.

Two examples which illustrate the difficulty in the way of the West understanding the East come to mind immediately: we may find it almost impossible to rid ourselves of the effect of the sixteenth century Reformation, which as a movement of thought has so profoundly influenced all of Western Christendom as to color our views of all theological and ecclesiastical matters. In the East, however, this movement had nothing like so far-reaching an influence. It did indeed affect Eastern thought, both directly and indirectly, but it did not impinge on all Church life in the East. As an instance of this effect of the Reformation on our thinking, we have all been infected in varying degrees by the notion of the Church as invisible, so when we come to study Orthodoxy we see everywhere, with a significance which it perhaps does not deserve, the so-called "Erastian character" of the national Orthodox Churches. Some of the difficulties which these conditions impose on us the writer has briefly pointed out elsewhere.[3] Again, the westerner is confronted, not only with the problem of the nationalistic character of Orthodoxy, but with that of its seemingly prepon-

[1] Androutsos, Συμβολική, p. 350.
[2] In the *Report of the First Anglo-Catholic Congress*, 1920, S P C K, 1920, pp. 98-99.
[3] *Some Aspects of Greek Church Life Today*, in the *Church Quarterly Review*, July, 1921, pp. 236-251.

derant emphasis on conservatism. Western Catholicism is conservative, but this conservatism is hardly an end in itself; the Western Catholic is actuated by some motive usually practical and pragmatic. Even a cursory study of the Liturgy in the East and West will show how changes in the West were usually in the nature of abbreviation and curtailment, while the Eastern Liturgy has grown by accretion and amplification. The Mass of the Catechumens has long since disappeared as a distinct entity in the Western Liturgy, while it is retained in full in the East. In both East and West the institution of the Catechumenate has long been lost. But when we remember the vast differences in Church history in East and West we are reminded of the circumstances and conditions of Orthodox life. Under Turkish tyranny survival and the preservation of the type became the fundamental evidence of life. The greatest proof of the "life" of Orthodoxy for centuries lay in this evidence of its power to survive: "to live" meant "to exist", and conservatism as a principle was the index of life.

So, naturally, we should conclude that Orthodoxy is static, and that our conceptions of development and growth in theology and thought in general, would be entirely foreign to it, especially to that type of Orthodoxy which has most poignantly suffered from the Turk. While the iron has entered into the soul of the Greek Church, the living soul has been able to outgrow the wound. The vitality and dynamic power of Orthodox thought may be seen in such a modern conception as is developed in these words of Dyobouniotes: "In Holy Scripture is contained the loftiest revelation, but this revelation exists in germ and stands in need of development. Individual (believers) and especially the Church (in which the Holy Spirit dwells to guide it and preserve it from every error), must concern themselves with the development of the religious truths and moral ideas contained in germ in Holy Writ, keeping in mind the fact . . that this has infinite value as well for the Church as for the individual. The profundity of these ideas is such that the Church can succeed in understanding them only at the price of great effort. . . . The more warm and vigorous is the religious sense in the individual and in the Church, the more vigorous and warm will be the interest of individual and Church in a deeper penetration into, and de-

velopment of the religious and ethical truths contained in
Holy Scripture . . . Unfortunately this work of dogmatic development, begun in the Eastern Church with such marvelous
insight and such unlimited enthusiasm, was cut off short by
unhappy circumstances beyond her control, and the work she
had undertaken with diligence and zeal, and not by mere
chance, was only half done."[1] In another connection the same
writer says: "It is obvious that the early Church had the
right and duty to develop dogmas; thus too the later Church
has both the right and the duty as well to develop dogmas not
developed by the early Church. This development is prepared
in advance by the work of theological writers, since theological
opinion can rightly enter into dogmatic," [2] as Androutsos observes.[3] The modern ring of such a passage, and its underlying thought, will do much to disabuse us of the notion that
Orthodoxy is sterile and static, that it views the Church as
mechanical rather than as living, or that Orthodoxy is a prone
corpse, incapable of manifesting energy of thought or living
action.[4] It is significant that from the history of its external
affairs of the past six centuries one would scarcely expect what
he actually finds in the study of present-day Orthodoxy. In
the case of the student of this subject, happy indeed is the
man who finds himself wrong in his expectations!

The following lectures have as their purpose the study of
a limited field of Orthodox literature—the writings of some
of the conspicuous present-day Greek Orthodox theologians. The
subject matter includes the treatment by these writers of some
of the cardinal doctrines of the Orthodox Church. No attempt could have been made to deal, even briefly, with all of the
Greek-Orthodox theologians of the modern school, and certainly
it would have been impossible within the compass of these
lectures to attempt a resume of the whole of present Orthodox
teaching. Strangely enough, Slavic Orthodoxy has had more

[1] Dyobouniotes, 'Οφειλομένη ἀπάντησις, pp. 155-156.
[2] Ibid., Δογματική τοῦ κ. 'Ανδρούτσου κρινομένη, p. 62.
[3] Δογματική, p. 3.
[4] Interesting in this connection is the complacently depreciatory
tone of certain Roman Catholic writers on Orthodoxy—e. g., S.
Vailhé, s. v. "Greek Church", in the Catholic Encyclopedia, VI,
p. 769.

attention from Anglican writers than that of the Greek-speaking sections of the Church of the East. The initial difficulties of language are much less in the case of the Greek writers than in that of the Russian, and it is to be hoped that an ever increasing number of Anglican readers will interest themselves in the fruitful and stimulating literature of the modern thinkers of the Greek Church.

Contemporary with the liberation from the Turk, the Church of Greece especially (and in fact all other parts of the Orthodox Church where Greek is the language spoken,) shook off the lethargy of centuries and began to develop a theological and philosophical literature which is modern, living, genuinely true to native genius, and loyal to the Orthodox heritage of the ages. The intrinsic worth of some of the writers of this school is such that any company of modern scholars would gladly and gratefully admit them to their fellowship. Passing over the earlier generation, some of the writers of which exercise a profound influence to-day, we have a number of eminent theologians who are all but unknown to the Anglican world: Philippos Papadopoulos, the Archimandrite Chrysostom Papadopoulos, Constantine Rhalle, Zekos Rhôsse, P. Comnenos, Constantine Dyobouniotes, I. E. Mesolora, Antoniades, and the most distinguished theological writer of the present day—Chrestos Androutsos. Of the above a preponderant number obtained much from their German education—exactness, accuracy, exhaustiveness of research, and acquaintance with and grasp of modern problems in philosophy and theology. All of them are "modern" in their point of view, alive to present-day difficulties, keenly interested in the progress of European scholarship, broad in the horizon of their sympathies, and utterly antagonistic to narrow insularity, complacency, and to the position called "obscurantist". If the present lectures serve but to introduce such men to American Churchmen they will not have been entirely in vain. If they serve to discount the venerable and deeply-rooted calumny that Orthodoxy is "intellectually sterile", "barren in the results of modern scholarship and theological research", "static", "out of touch with modern thought and conditions", and "not alive to the problems of the day", their purpose will have been fulfilled. The following lectures attempt to present the results of the writer's studies in the works of modern Greek-Orthodox theologians. In so doing the writer has confined himself to a very limited portion of the field, and to a few outstanding theologians. The scheme is largely due to the arrangement in Androutsos', Δογματική, and, as far as has been possible, the presentation has been purely objective.

The work of a modern Greek theologian has not been easy. Damalas admits that outside theologians could justly speak of a kind of relative stagnation and torpor of the Orthodox Church,[1] and the signs of intellectual life were not always greeted with due acclamation and sympathy. Furthermore, besides the accusations of "innovating" and "perverting true Orthodoxy" with which the earlier attempts to create a scientific theology were met, there are intrinsic difficulties which face the modern theologian. In many cases he cannot transcribe statements of belief, but must speak in the spirit of Orthodoxy, on matters not explicitly defined.[2] Androutsos' great work[3] is a conspicuous evidence both to the depth and to the keenness of the writer's thought; it is brilliantly written, concise, lucid, fearless, and alive to difficulties, which are always faced and never shirked or summarily disposed of. It provoked several bitter attacks—notably those of Dyobouniotes,[4] and Balanos,[5] the first numbers in a veritable pamphlet campaign.[6] Androutsos was harried and irritated by his critics, and, despite the sharpness in the remark, there is undoubtedly some basis for his comment: "getting into print is the surest way to advancement".[7] An interesting review of the work of Androutsos and his difficulties with his critics appeared in the *Echos d' Orient.*[8] None of the writings of this eminent theologian have appeared in English except

[1] Περὶ ἀρχῶν, Leipzig, 1865, p. 5.
[2] Androutsos, Δογματική, *preface*, p. 10.
[3] Δογματικὴ τῆς Ὀρθοδόξου Ἀνατολικῆς Ἐκκλησίας, Athens, 1907.
[4] Ἡ Δογματικὴ τοῦ κ. Ἀνδρούτσου κρινομένη, Athens, 1907.
[5] Κρίσις τῆς Δογματικῆς τοῦ κ. Ἀνδρούτσου, in Νέα Σιών, 1907, vol. V, pp. 669-705.
[6] Δογματικαὶ Μελέται, Α', Athens, 1907; Dyobouniotes, Ὀφειλομένη ἀπάντησις; Androutsos, Δογματικαὶ Μελέται, Β', Athens, 1908.
[7] Δογματικαὶ Μελέται, Β', p. 5.
[8] Jugie, *Une nouvelle dogmatique orthodoxe, trois théologiens grecs en présence*, vol. XI, 1908, pp. 146-154, 257-264.

his monograph on Anglican Orders,[1] which in its translated form[2] is not altogether accurate.[3]

Another work of conspicuous merit is Rhôsse's Δογματική,[4] of which the first volume only has appeared. Both of these works, Dyobouniotes *On the Sacraments*,[5] Mesolora's Συμβολική, and in fact most of these modern works in general, owe much to European scholarship. In their effort to refute the allegation that Orthodoxy is intellectually moribund, present-day writers have availed themselves extensively of what non-Orthodox thinkers have done. Thus Rhôsse's words in his *preface*:[6] "The Orthodox theologian in his scientific investigation and orderly presentation of dogma stands in need of the study of dogmatic theologians, both Latin and Protestant—especially the latter," and Dyobouniotes' frank admission of the fact that he had used "such Roman teaching as in his judgment is based on a sound interpretation of Holy Scriptures and Sacred Tradition"[7] as well as Protestant works chiefly of a historical nature, suggest the indebtedness of theologians of the modern school to Continental scholarship, especially German.[8] In fact Dorner commented on Rhôsse's Δογματική in the words: "Die Schrift zeigt sich von der spekulativen deutschen Theologie des vorigen Jahrhunderts auf das Stärkste beeinflusst."[9] Most of the knowledge of things Anglican which contemporary Greek-Orthodox writers possess has been gained at

---

[1] Τό κῦρος τῶν 'Αγγλικῶν Χειροτονιῶν, Constantinople, 1903.

[2] *The Validity of English Ordinations, from an Orthodox Catholic point of view*, by the Most Rev. Chrestos Androutsos (sic), translated by F. W. Groves Campbell, London, 1909.

[3] On which cf. *The Relations of the Anglican Churches with the Eastern Orthodox*, the Rev. J. A. Douglas, London, 1921, p. 98, note 3.

[4] Σύστημα Δογματικῆς τῆς ὀρθοδόξου 'Εκκλησίας, vol. I, Athens, 1903.

[5] Τὰ Μυστήρια τῆς 'Ανατολικῆς 'Ορθοδόξου 'Εκκλησίας, Athens, 1913.

[6] Σύστημα Δογματικῆς, p. 6.

[7] Τὰ Μυστήρια, preface, pp. 3-4.

[8] For example, Androutsos frequently refers to Möhler's *Symbolik*, Martensen's *Dogmatik*, Nitzsch's *Lehrbuch der evangelischen Dogmatik*, Scheeben's *Handbuch der katholischen Dogmatik*, Schmidt's *Christliche Dogmatik*, Simar's *Lehrbuch der Dogmatik;* Rhôsse, to the works of Martensen, Trendelenburg, Dorner, etc., and Dyobouniotes' bibliographies contain a preponderance of non-Orthodox works.

[9] *Eine neue griechische Dogmatik*, Z W T, vol. XLVIII, 1905, p. 153. *Theologischer Jahresbericht*, Berlin, vol. XXIII, 1904, p. 692.

second hand—through French, Latin, or German translations of our formularies, or interpretations and studies of our Church written in these languages. Yet the Greek Orthodox are not a whit different in this regard from most of us, who know so little about the Greek Church of to-day from its own official teaching and its own representative scholars.

In conclusion, the writer desires to thank most sincerely the Committee of the Hale Lectureship Foundation for extending to him the invitation to deliver these lectures. Especially are his thanks due the Dean of the Western Theological Seminary for many courtesies extended to him in the course of the preparation and delivery of the lectures. He desires to acknowledge with gratitude the care, interest, and suggestions of the Rev. Prof. F. J. Hall, and the Rev. Chrysostom Trahatheas. His wife has been of great assistance in the preparation and correction of the manuscript. Finally his thanks are due Miss Anne Venus for her careful and painstaking work in the typing of the lectures. F. GAVIN.

St. Agnes by the Lake, Algoma, Wisconsin,
Feast of the Nativity of Our Lady, 1921.

BIBLIOGRAPHY

The Sources¹ of Orthodox Teaching

(I)   *The Holy Bible;* the Old Testament in the Septuagint Version, and the New Testament in the original Greek.²

(II) *Sacred Tradition;* which includes the

(a)   Decrees and Definitions of the seven *Ecumenical Councils,*³ namely, those of: (1) Nicaea, (325) ; (2) I Constantinople, (381) ; (3) Ephesus, (431) ; (4) Chalcedon, (451) ; (5) II Constantinople, (553) ; (6) III Constantinople, (680) and the Synod *in Trullo* (Σύνοδος πενθέκτη), (691) ; (7) II. Nicaea (787).

(b)   Ecumenical Creeds,⁴ namely: (1) the *Apostles' Creed;* (2) the *Niceno-Constantinopolitan Creed;* and (3) the *Athanasian Creed.*

(c)   Writings of the Fathers of the Undivided Church, both Eastern and Western, with a special preëminence accorded the works of the "Doctors", particularly St. John Damascene.

(d)   Symbolic Books;⁵ including the following:

(1)   Ἡ ὁμολογία Γενναδίου τοῦ σχολαρίου.

(The Confession of Gennadius Scholaris.)

(2)   Αἱ τρεῖς ἀποκρίσεις Ἱερεμίου τοῦ Β΄. πατριάρχου Κωνσταντινουπόλεως πρὸς τοὺς διαμαρτυρομένους θεολόγους τῆς Τυβίγγης.

(The Three Answers of Jeremiah II, Patriarch of Constantinople, to the Protestant Theologians of Tübingen.⁶)

¹ On which cf. Lecture I, pp. 17-30; IV, pp. 206-218.

² Cf. Lecture I, pp. 19-20; Mesolora, Συμβολική, III, pp. 34-63.

³ Cf. Mesolora, *ibid.*, pp. 31-32; Nicholas Bulgaris, Θεολογικόν, (Greek translation) p. 68; Diomede Kyriakos, Ἑλληνικὴ Ἱστορία.

⁴ Cf. Androutsos, Συμβολική, pp. 17-31; Mesolora, *op. cit.*, I, pp. 1-64; IV, pp. 458-459.

⁵ Text in Kimmel, *Monumenta Fidei Ecclesiae Orientalis*, Jena, 1850, vols. I & II; Mesolora, *op. cit.*, vols I & II, and cf. *ibid.*, IV, pp. 457-458; Cf. Androutsos, *op. cit.*, 31-38; Lecture IV, pp. 206 ff.

⁶ *Acta et Scripta theologorum Wirtembergensium et Patriarchae Constantinopolitani, D. Hieremiae*, Würtemberg, 1633.

(3) Ἡ ὁμολογία Μητροφάνους τοῦ Κριτοπούλου, πατριάρχου Ἀλεξανδρείας.
(*The Confession of Metrophanes Kritopoulos,
Patriarch of Alexandria.*)
(4) Ἡ ὀρθόδοξος ὁμολογία Πέτρου τοῦ Μογίλα, μητρο-
πολίτου Κιέβου.
(*The Orthodox Confession of Peter Mogila,
Metropolitan of Kiev.*)
(5) Τὰ πρακτικὰ τῶν ἐν Κωνσταντινουπόλει (1638), ἐν
Ἰασίω (1641-2), ἐν Ἱεροσολύμοις (1672), καὶ ἐν
Κωνσταντινουπόλει (1672) συνόδων.
(*The Acts of the Synods* (held) *in Constan-
tinople,* (1638), *Jassy* (1641-1642), *Jerusalem*
(1672), *and Constantinople* (1672).
(6) Ἡ ὁμολογία τοῦ Δοσιθέου, πατριάρχου Ἱεροσολύμων.
(*The Confession of Dositheus, Patriarch of
Jerusalem.*)

List of some of the most important theological works of the Greek Orthodox Church

(a) Works of the earlier periods:
St. John Damascene, Ἡ ἔκθεσις (ἔκδοσις) ἀκριβὴς τῆς
ὀρθοδόξου πίστεως.
(*The Exposition of the Precious Orthodox Faith.*)
This work, as Palmieri notes, is the "sole compen-
dium of dogmatic theology up until the
seventeenth century."[1]

---

[1] *Theologia Dogmatica Orthodoxa* (*Ecclesiae Graeco-Russiae*) *ad
lumen Catholicae Doctrinae examinata et discussa, Tomus I, Prolegomena,* Florence, 1911, p. 140, and pp. ff. Dyobouniotes' monograph on
St. John (Ἰωάννης ὁ Δαμασκηνός, Athens, 1903,) is of very considerable
value. Rangabé writes: "Le manque de fécondité théologique chez
les Grecs tient à l'esprit même de l'Église grecque, qui repoussant toute
innovation, n'admet plus les discussions dogmatiques après le septième
Synode et depuis la scission de l'Église; le droit d'examiner et d'in-
tepréter les dogmes ne pouvait appartenir, selon ses principes con-
servatifs, qu'à totalité de la chrétienté, lorsqu'elle était réunie"
(*Histoire littérarie de la Grèce moderne,* Paris, 1877, vol. I, pp. 217,
218.) Few present-day theologians, however, would endorse this statement.

Coursoulas, Nicholas, (1653)Σύνοψις τῆς ἱερᾶς θεολογίας φιλοπονηθεῖσα εἰς ὠφέλειαν τῶν ὀρθοδόξων φιλομαθῶν, edited by Sergius Raftanis, vols. I. &II. Zacynthus, 1862.

Athanasius of Paros, (1813) Ἐπιτομὴ εἴτε συλλογὴ τῶν θείων τῆς πίστεως δογμάτων μετὰ πάσης ἐπιμελείας, κατ᾽ ἐπιτομὴν φιλοπονηθεῖσα, edited by the Most Rev. Macarius Notara, Leipzig, 1806.

Damodos, Vincent, θεία καὶ ἱερὰ διδασκαλία, ἤτοι ὀρθόδοξος δογματικὴ θεολογία τῆς ἁγίας, καθολικῆς, ἀποστολικῆς καὶ ὀρθοδόξου Ἐκκλησίας τῆς Ἀνατολῆς, τῆς ὁποίας ἡ διδασκαλία θεμελιοῦται ἐν τῇ ἱερᾷ ἀποκαλύψει, ἐν τῇ θεοπνεύστῳ Γραφῇ, ἐν ταῖς παραδόσεσι τῶν Ἀποστόλων, ἐν ταῖς οἰκουμενικαῖς καὶ τοπικαῖς ὀρθοδόξοις συνόδοις, καί ἐν τοῖς θείοις πατράσι τῆς Ἐκκλησίας. 1730.

Eugenius Bulgaris, (1716-1806) Θεολογικόν, translated and edited by the Archimandrite Agathangelos Lontopoulos, Venice, 1872.

Moschopoulos, Anthony (1713-1788), Ἐπιτομὴ τῆς δογματικῆς καὶ ἠθικῆς θεολογίας, published by the Rev. G. Solomos, Cephalonia, 1851.

(b) Later and contemporaneous works.[1]

Ambraze, Nicholas, Δοκίμιον περὶ ἑνώσεως τῶν Ἀγγλικῶν ἐπισκοπιανῶν μετὰ τῆς ὀρθοδόξου ἀνατολικῆς Ἐκκλησίας, Athens, 1891.

......, Ἡ ὀρθόδοξος Ἐκκλησία ἐν σχέσει πρὸς ὅλας τὰς χριστιανικὰς Ἐκκλησίας ἐξεταζομένη,..Athens, 1902.

Amphiteatrov, Antonius (of Kiev), Δογματικὴ θεολογία τῆς ὀρθοδόξου καθολικῆς καὶ ἀνατολικῆς Ἐκκλησίας, revised according to the sixth edition, of 1856, and translated from the Russian by Col. Theodore Ballianos, Athens, 1856.

----

[1] For fuller bibliographical notes, cf. Legrand, *Bibliographie hellénique du XVIIe siècle*, especially vol. V, (Paris, 1903) ; Demetracopoulos Ἡ ὀρθόδοξος Ἐκκλησία, Leipzig, 1870; on the minor works of the earlier period, *e. g.*, those of Theoklytos of Polyide, Theophilus of Campania, Cyril of Lisinitze,—cf. Palmieri, *op. cit.*, I, p. 146, note 2; *Wiederanfänge der theologischen Literatur in Griechenland*, in *Theologische Studien und Kritiken*, vol. I, 1841, pp. 7-53; the brief history of Dogmatic, in Androutsos, Δογματικὴ, pp. 28, ff.

Androutsos, Chrestos, Ἕν Μάθημα περὶ προπατορικοῦ ἁμαρτήματος, Constantinople, 1896.

......, Δεύτερον Μάθημα περὶ προπατορικοῦ ἁμαρτήματος, Constantinople, 1896.

......, Δοκίμιον Συμβολικῆς ἐξ ἐπόψεως ὀρθοδόξου, Athens, 1901.

......, Τὸ κῦρος τῶν Ἀγγλικῶν χειροτονιῶν ἐξ ἐπόψεως ὀρθοδόξου, Constantinople, 1903.[1]

......, Αἱ βάσεις τῆς ἑνώσεως τῶν Ἐκκλησιῶν κατὰ τὰ ἀρτιφανῆ τῶν ὀρθοδόξων Ἐκκλησιῶν γράμματα, Constantinople, 1905.

......, Δογματικὴ τῆς ὀρθοδόξου ἀνατολικῆς Ἐκκλησίας, Athens, 1907.

......, Δογματικαὶ Μελέται, Α΄. ὁ Ὑφηγητὴς τῆς θεολογίας κ. Δυοβουνιώτης ἐξεταζόμενος εἰς τὴν Δογματικὴν καὶ εἰς τὴν Λογικήν, Athens, 1907.

......, Δογματικαὶ Μελέται, Β΄. Ἡ μετὰ τὰς ἐξετάσεις δικαιολογία τοῦ κ. Κ. Δυοβουνιώτου, καὶ ἡ κρίσις τοῦ κ. Μπαλάνου, Athens, 1908.

......, Ἐκκλησία καὶ Πολιτεία ἐξ ἐπόψεως ὀρθοδόξου, Athens, 1920.

Balanos, D., Κρίσις τῆς δογματικῆς τοῦ κ. Χρήστου Ἀνδρούτσου, in Νέα Σιών, 1907, vol. V., 669-705.

......, Πολιτεία καὶ Ἐκκλησία, Athens, 1920.

Basil, Metropolitan of Smyrna, Πραγματεία περὶ τοῦ κύρους τῆς χειροτονίας τῶν ὑπὸ ἐπισκόπου καθῃρημένου καὶ σχισματικοῦ χειροτονηθέντων, Smyrna, 1887.

Bulgakov,[2] Macarius, (of Moscow) Ἐγχειρίδιον τῆς κατὰ τὴν ὀρθόδοξον εἰς Χριστὸν πίστιν δογματικῆς θεολογίας, translated by the Archimandrite Neophytes Pagida, Athens, 1883.

Christodoulos, Apostolos, Δοκίμιον ἐκκλησιαστικοῦ δικαίου, Constantinople, 1896.

---

[1] English translation by F. W. Groves Campbell, *The Validity of English Ordinations from an Orthodox Catholic point of view*, London, 1909; an excellent review of this work by the Rev. Dr. Severin-Salaville, in the *Révue Augustinienne*, vol. III, 1903.

[2] Two other works of this writer are very much used: *Introduction à la théologie orthodoxe*, Paris, 1857; and *Théologie dogmatique orthodoxe*, vols. I & II, Paris, 1860.

Damalas, N., Περὶ ἀρχῶν, Leipzig, 1865.

......,Περὶ τῆς σχέσεως τῆς Ἀγγλικῆς Ἐκκλησίας πρὸς τὴν ὀρθόδοξον, London, 1867.

Delikanis, Τὰ ἐν τοῖς κώδιξι τοῦ πατρ. ἀρχαιοφυλακίου σωζόμενα ἐπίσημα ἐκκλησιαστικὰ ἔγγραφα τὰ ἀφορῶντα εἰς τὰς σχέσεις τοῦ οἰκουμενικοῦ πατριαρχείου πρὸς τὰς Ἐκκλησίας Ῥωσσίας, Βλαχίας, καὶ Μολδαβίας, κ. τ. λ., Constantinople, 1905.

Dyobouniotes, Constantine, Ἰωάννης ὁ Δαμασκηνός, Athens, 1903.

......,Ἡ δογματικὴ τοῦ κ. Χρήστου Ἀνδρούτσου κρινομένη, Athens, 1907.

......,Ὀφειλομένη ἀπάντησις, Athens, 1908.

......,Τὰ Μυστήρια τῆς ἀνατολικῆς ὀρθοδόξου Ἐκκλησίας ἐξ ἐπόψεως δογματικῆς, Athens, 1912 (1913).

Eutaxia, Τοῦ κανονικοῦ δικαίου τῆς ὀρθοδόξου ἀνατολικῆς Ἐκκλησίας τὰ περὶ ἱερατικῆς ἐξουσίας, Athens, 1872.

Gedeon, Κανονικαὶ διατάξεις, ἐπιστολαί, λύσεις, θεσπίσματα, τῶν ἁγιωτάτων πατριαρχῶν Κ. ἀπὸ Γρηγορίου τοῦ θεολόγου μέχρι Διονυσίου τοῦ ἀπὸ Ἀδριανουπόλεως, Constantinople, vol. 1. 1888; vol. II. 1889.

Ghiannopoulos, Συλλογὴ τῶν ἐγκυκλίων τῆς ἱερᾶς συνόδου τῆς Ἐκκλησίας τῆς Ἑλλάδος μετὰ τῶν οἰκείων νόμων, β. διαταγμάτων, ὑπουργικῶν ἐγγράφων, ὁδηγιῶν κ.τ.λ., ἀπὸ τοῦ 1883 μέχρι σήμερον ἐκδιδομένη ἐντολῇ τῆς ἱερᾶς συνόδου, Athens, 1901.

Kephala, Nectarius, Χριστολογία, Athens, 1900.

Komnenos, P. Συμβολαὶ εἰς τὰς προσπαθείας πρὸς ἕνωσιν τῶν Ἐκκλησιῶν, Τεῦχος Α΄, Αἱ ἀγγλικανικαὶ χειροτονίαι, Constantinople, 1921.

Mesolora, I. E. Συμβολικὴ τῆς ὀρθοδόξου ἀνατολικῆς Ἐκκλησίας; Τὰ συμβολικὰ βιβλία, Athens, vol. I. 1883; II. 1893;—III. 1901; IV. 1904.

......,Πρακτικὴ Θεολογία,—Εἰσαγωγή, Athens, 1911.

Papadopoulos, Chrysostom, Ἀπόπειρα τῶν Ἄγγλων ἀνωμότων μετὰ τῶν ὀρθοδόξων, Alexandria, 1911.

Petrakakos, Τινὰ περὶ τοῦ κύρους τῶν χειροτονιῶν in Ἐκκλησιαστικὴ Ἀλήθεια, vol. XXX., 1910, pp. 134-408.

Rhalle and Potle, Σύνταγμα τῶν θείων καὶ ἱερῶν κανόνων τῶν τε ἁγίων καὶ πανευφήμων ἀποστόλων, καὶ τῶν ἱερῶν οἰκουμενικῶν καὶ τοπικῶν συνόδων, . . . Athens, Vols. I-II, 1852; III. 1853; IV. 1854; V. 1855; VI. 1859.

Sakellaropoulos, Ἐκκλησιαστικὸν δίκαιον τῆς ἀνατολικῆς ὀρθοδόξου Ἐκκλησίας μετὰ τοῦ ἰσχύοντος νῦν ἐν τῇ Ἐκκλησίᾳ τοῦ πατριαρχείου καὶ ἐν Ἑλλάδι, Athens, 1898.

Severus, Gabriel (of Philadelphia) Τὰ ἱερὰ ἑπτὰ τῆς καθολικῆς Ἐκκλησίας μυστήρια.

Technopoulos, N., Ἡ δογματικὴ θέσις τῆς ἀγγλικῆς Ἐκκλησίας καθ' ἑαυτὴν ἐξεταζομένη in Ἕνωσις τῶν Ἐκκλησιῶν, London, 1904, no. 40, pp. 635, ff.

Theotokas, Νομολογία τοῦ οἰκουμενικοῦ πατριαρχείου, ἤτοι τῆς ἱερᾶς συνόδου καὶ τοῦ Δ. Ε. Μ. συμβουλίου, Constantinople, 1897.[1]

---

[1] For additional bibliographical material, cf, Palmieri, *op. cit.*, vols. I. & II, passim; Mesolora. Συμβολική, II., pp. 150-153; Douglas, *The Relations of the Anglican Churches with the Eastern-Orthodox*, London, 1921, pp. 187-194.

LECTURE I.
PROLEGOMENA

LECTURE I.

PROLEGOMENA

CONTENTS

1. DOGMA AND DOGMATICS

The word "dogma" in its general meaning signifies an "opinion", a "precept", a "decree", a "law". As an "opinion" the word was applied to the teachings of the great philosophical schools founded by Pythagoras, Plato, Socrates, and Aristotle. These "opinions" had for the members of the schools the binding force of a precept or law. This may be distinguished as the philosophical use of the word, as Cicero[1] uses it: *Sapientia neque de se ipsa disputare debet, neque de suis decretis, quae philosophi vocant dogmata, quorum nullum sine scelere prodi potest.* In this notion of dogma as a fundamental philosophical principle there is present as the essential note that of validity or authenticity. The use of "dogma" in a political sense is akin to this, for it is applied to the decrees, laws, or mandates of a king or a realm, always with the essential connotation of authority and validity. We find the word so used in the Bible, e. g., Dan. 6, 8-9; 2, 13; St. Luke 2, 1; Acts 17, 7. In the Bible the word is also applied to the precepts of the Jewish Law, as in Col. 2, 14, and Eph. 2, 15, and the decrees of Jewish courts, as in 2 Mac. 10, 8; 15, 36. To this quasi-legal use of the word belongs the reference in Acts 16, 4 (cf. Acts 15, 28).

Nowhere in the New Testament has the word "dogma" taken on the ecclesiastical meaning which has prevailed from the time of the Fathers[2] until the present day. According to Androutsos, "dogmas, in the ecclesiastical meaning of the word, are the ethical ordinances and truths regulating the Christian life, and more especially the theoretical doctrines of the Faith, which are

---

[1] Cicero, *Quaestiones academicae,* IV, 9; cf. Rhôsse, Δογματική, p. 45.
[2] Cf. Socrates, *Eccl. Hist.* 2, 44; Greg. Nyss. *Epist.* 6; Cyril Jeru. *Cat.* 4, 2, etc.; cf. n. 2, p. 24, of Mesolora, Πρακτικὴ Θεολογία.

contained in the Bible and Tradition, and have been defined and explained by the Church, and formulated in part by her holy Synods."[1]

The essential characteristic is the same note of validity and authenticity which is the fundamental significance of dogma in its wider meaning. Dogma as such is the authentic declaration of the faith necessary to salvation, and contained in the Bible and Tradition. This may be called its objective aspect.[2] But the Church "as the authentic interpreter of Revelation, explaining authoritatively Scripture and Tradition, formulates the teaching of our Lord necessary to salvation in unchangeable terms and statements called dogmas."[3] The Church acts in this way through a reflective process of human insight and human reasoning, whereby she presents that which has been defined and taught by herself as the infallible Interpreter of the Bible and Tradition and the supreme Arbiter in questions concerning the Faith. Under this aspect dogma is "the explanation of the content of the Faith . . . . as the mind of the Church investigates, compares, and correlates dogmas with each other and with the whole body of her teaching." This is the subjective and theoretic aspect of dogma.[4]

Both of these aspects of dogma, as (a) resident in and deducible from the double sources of Bible and Tradition (which may be called the objective view), and that of dogma as (b) the product of the reflective action of the infallible Church (subjective view) are descriptive rather than analytic. Dogma is thus definable without a further investigation into its content, though, as we shall see, Androutsos proceeds to analyze the content of dogma and to orientate it about one central idea. According to Rhôsse, it is impossible to define dogma without reference to its content, and to him this core and heart of dogmatic truth is the "teaching of the Faith concerning the operations of God."[5] "The dogmas of the Christian religion are

[1] Androutsos, Δογματική, pp. 1-2.
[2] Ibid., p. 2.
[3] Ibid., p. 9.
[4] Ibid., p. 2.
[5] Rhôsse, Δογματική, p. 28.

those teachings of the Faith about the energies of God, together
with the premises or conditions involved in them and their consequences or results, which are contained essentially and in germ
in the Holy Scripture and Sacred Tradition, and have been
unfolded, defined, and in part formulated through legitimate
theological speculation in local, ecumenical, and general councils
of the true (genuine) Catholic and Orthodox Church of Christ,
under the inspiration and guidance of the Holy Spirit abiding
in the Church, and are authoritative and binding upon every true
member of that Church."[1] "The Christian Religion is the removal of discord between God and man made possible by and
functioning through the religious fellowship (κοινωνία) founded
by Jesus Christ, and the reëstablishment of the right relation
of man to God."[2] This new relationship is reciprocal, since it
was initiated by the loving act of God, and yet depends upon
the response of man and his coöperation in it. Hence the inevitably ethical character of Christianity.[3] The whole heart of
Christianity is then the establishment of a new status of man
with God, the maintainance of which is conditioned as well by
the continuous action on the part of God as it is by a continuous response on the part of man. So Rhôsse would analyze
the content of dogma on the basis of God's energies—e. g.,
(a) in relation to Himself: His energies in eternity—His eternal Being, Life, Knowledge of Himself as Absolute Truth,
Love of Himself as Absolute God, the Eternal Generation of
the Son, the Eternal Procession of the Holy Spirit, and the
like; (b) in relation to the world, and created things: His
energies in time—creating, governing, and sustaining His creation; the angels and man—creation, fore-knowledge, redemption, sanctification; (c) the constitution of man—his free will
as coöperating agency with the energy of God in effecting his
regeneration, redemption, justification, sanctification, and the
operations of God in relation to Him.[4]

[1] *Ibid.*, p. 23.

[2] *Ibid.*, p. 21.

[3] *Ibid.*, p. 21; cf. Mesolora's definition in his Πρακτικὴ Θεολογία,
pp. 1-18; "theology may be termed the science of religion", p. 14. *ibid;*
cf. his Συμβολική, III. pp. 1-33.

[4] Rhôsse, *op. cit.*, pp. 23-25, especially note (1) pp. 24-25.

Dogmatic theology[1] is "the scientific presentation of the teaching of the Christian Faith," and its scientific character, according to Androutsos, is constituted by the four following notes: (a) the consideration of the nexus of dogmatic truths each in relation to the whole content of dogma, and in the relation of each dogma to the other; (b) the explanation and exposition of the meaning of each dogma; (c) the recognition of the historical background and development of doctrine; (d) the presentation of the dogmatic truths in opposition to the refuted errors which were often the occasion of their definition.[2] Dogmas are simply the statement of the content of the Faith, but dogmatic is a science which is characterized by the four notes above mentioned. Since Rhôsse has included several of these characteristics in his definition of dogma, he defines dogmatic simply as a scientific presentation of dogma in the sense which his definition of dogma demands: ("about the operations of God, and their premises and consequences.") "Dogmatic is the science which methodically presents these truths."[3] Both deny the name of "scientific dogmatic" to the purely catechetical presentations of the Orthodox Faith which have appeared from the middle ages on, for such manuals lack the ordered and systematic character of a science, they are deficient in historical method, and they are not analytic.[4] Dogmatic, according to Androutsos, does not profess to prove dogmas, but simply presents the faith of the Church as an organic whole. Hence the so-called "philosophic dogmatic" is outside the province of true dogmatic, and belongs rather to apologetic, or to the philosophy of Christianity. In the same way the scholastic dogmatic manuals of the Western Church are not true dogmatic, since in practice, though not in theory, they conceive "the purpose of dogmatic to be the exaltation of faith into knowledge."[5]

[1] On the relation of Dogmatic to the other branches of theology, cf. additional note at end of Lecture I, p. 50.
[2] Androutsos, *op. cit.*, pp. 2, 3, 21-25, cf. T. D. Balanos, Εἶναι ἡ θεολογία ἐπιστήμη; Athens, 1906; Skaltsoune, Θρησκεία καὶ 'Επιστήμη.
[3] Rhôsse, *op. cit.*, pp. 23-25.
[4] *E. g.*, the works of Damodos, Eugenius Bulgaris, Athanasius of Paros, Moschopoulos, Ballianos (Δογματικὴ Θεολογία τῆς 'Ορθοδόξου Καθολικοῦ καὶ 'Ανατολικῆς 'Εκκλησίας, Athens, 1858), Macarius, etc.
[5] Androutsos, *op. cit.*, pp. 23-24.

From what has been said it is apparent that a dogmatic system should be orientated about some single fundamental principle, from which the various truths are developed and to which they are all related. In his sketch of the history of the dogmatic, Androutsos[1] divides it into two periods—the patristic, up till the time of St. John Damascene, and the modern, from St. John till the present day. Much of the patristic work was apologetic rather than dogmatic, though the early works serve as sources for dogmas afterwards enunciated by the Church. Most of the early works lacked the systematic grouping of dogmas about a central principle, yet Origen had as his central idea the principle that "God is all in all". Subsequent theologians did not group their dogmatic presentation about a single well-defined and central conception, and in consequence lack unity. The theological output of the middle ages was scholastic, barren, devoid of originality, and lacking in any living and vivid appreciation of the value of the content of dogmatic truth; much of the modern Orthodox work has been satisfied to follow the same course of stereotyped reproduction[2] of ancient dogmas, without regard to their living value or their systematic arrangement. St. John Damascene arranged his theology by topics,[3] a useless and unscientific method for modern times. Attempts have been made by various schools of philosophy and by various non-orthodox theologians to discover the unitary principle of Christian dogma and of Christian Faith. Since the Revelation was made not to satisfy a philosophical necessity, but for a practical end, Hegel, Strauss, Schleiermacher, Harnack, and others are only partially successful in attempting to discover in the data of Christianity such a unitary principle, from the standpoint of philosophy.[4] Androutsos develops the following proposition as the central dogma of the Orthodox Faith: "the Church founded on earth by Christ is the treasure house of Salvation." He regards it as a satisfactory principle, uniting Orthodoxy on the common ground it has with Roman Catholic Christendom, and separating it

[1] Introductory Chapter, Sect. 9.
[2] Androutsos, pp. 28-31.
[3] Cf. his Ἔκδοσις τῆς ὀρθοδόξου Πίστεως.
[4] Androutsos, op cit., pp. 25-26.

from the essential principle of Protestantism. Furthermore, all the dogmas of the Faith are involved in this principle— those about Christ, the Church's Founder, the Church and Salvation, the sacraments as means of Grace, the completion of salvation in the teaching of Eschatology. "The foundation of the Church and the nature of salvation cannot be understood without the doctrine of God, the world, the nature and constitution of man, the fore-knowledge of God, His creation of the world, angels, and man."[1] So he divides his dogmatic into two parts—(1) the premises involved in the Redemption wrought by Christ, and (2) the redeeming work of Christ. The articulation of his whole system is made on this basis, and his dogmatic is adequately orientated about the principle enunciated above, that the "Church is the treasury of Salvation," which is the central truth of Orthodox dogmatic.[2]

Rhôsse, as we have seen, develops the arrangement of his material in accordance with the analytical definition of dogma, as the teaching of the Christian Faith about the operations of God, together with the related premises, conditions, and the conclusions involved. So among the "premises" he discusses the eternal acts of God, and as "conditions" he treats of the nature of man, the sin of Adam, original sin, and the like. As "consequences" of God's operations are the following: Creation out of nothing of man, angels, the world; the Incarnation, Redemption of man, the sacrifice on the Cross; the actualizing of the Kingdom of God in His Church, a conception which before its realization was only an abstract idea; the relation of the Church visible to the Church invisible; and the doctrine of saints and angels.[3] The whole content of Christian dogma, according to Rhôsse, is marshalled about this central idea. "This conception of dogma is most fundamental, since it contains in germ or bud the conceptions of all the several dogmas, which are developed and unfolded from this fundamental conception. It contains the absolute or highest principle out of which all others proceed."[4] Androutsos regards his principle

[1] Cf. Androutsos, ibid., p. 27.
[2] Cf. Androutsos, pp. 27, 32-33; 165-167.
[3] Cf. Rhôsse, op. cit., pp. 24-27, notes and 124-5.
[4] Rhôsse, ibid., pp. 25-26, note (1); for the articulation of his system cf. especially pp. 23-27.

as the one which "pervades"[1] all portions of the dogmatic edifice, while Rhôsse regards his as the source from which all other dogmas are derived.[2] It is typical of the point of view of the two works that Androutsos should develop his system on an inductive basis, and that Rhôsse should articulate his dogmatic system on a deductive basis. The former is chiefly concerned with the practical bearings of dogmatic truth, its clear exposition, and the articulation of his system according to the plan he set himself for his work. The latter's interest is philosophical and theoretical. His single tome of five hundred pages, the only portion of his Dogmatic that has appeared, only treats of the content of dogma as far as the creation of man, with its corollary truths regarding immortality, free will, and the relation of man's will to divine Revelation. Androutsos' criticism of Rhôsse's work is that it is "rather a scientific justification of dogmas than a systematic presentation of them. His Dogmatic has, rather, the character of polemic and apologetic, in the style of some of the German conservative theologians, particularly J. A. Dorner, who hold that the aim of dogmatic theology as a science is to demonstrate the logical necessity of dogmas"[3] which, Androutsos says, subverts the true conception of dogmatic.

Any conception of dogmatic in its Orthodox sense, involves three elements,—(a) the principle of a Revelation made by God to man, (b) embodied in the Holy Scriptures and Tradition, and (c) in part formulated and defined by the Church. We shall proceed to examine the conception of Revelation in Orthodox Theology, as preliminary to a survey of the sources of Dogmatic, and of its developed content.

[1] Androutsos, op cit., p. 27.
[2] Rhôsse, pp. 26, 114-124.
[3] Androutsos, op. oit., p. 31.

2. REVELATION[1]

Since God is not only above His universe, but also working in it, in His Might, Wisdom, and Goodness, it is in accordance with His nature and character to reveal Himself to man. Man is created in His image and likeness, and is capable of receiving His revelations concerning Himself, the more so as God's Spirit quickens and energizes the part of man which is in His likeness. The content of the revelation is a truth which man by his own unaided powers would be incapable of discovering, but which, when revealed, takes its place along with other truths which man has discovered, as it were to advance, complement, and complete them. The action of the spirit of God communicating directly with the human spirit in a revelation, is called "inspiration," or "internal revelation". It does not preclude the action of man's free will, for man acts as an agent or organ of the Holy Spirit, in full possession of his faculties and consciously, and not as an automaton. When the spirit of God acts along with the human understanding, and as it were with a parallel effect upon matter or by material agencies, the revelation is called "external". Such manifestations of God's power act as validating and guaranteeing the inner revelation made to the spirit of man.[2]

There are definite criteria by which the data of revelation may be examined and judged, and these are two, external and internal. The external criterion is that of miracle, as an indication of the will, power, and love of God.[3] The internal criterion is both positive and negative; positive, in that the truth is demonstrably "one which satisfies the religious and ethical ideals of man, and makes for his holiness and happiness;"[4] negative, in that it is capable of being shown consistent with other

[1] "Religion in man consists not only of a certain subjective energy on his own part, but also of a certain energy of God Himself, by which He makes Himself and His Will known to man. This act whereby God makes Himself known is called Divine Revelation."—Rhôsse, *op. cit.*, p. 447, and cf. his treatment of the subject of religion, pp. 438-444; Mesolora, Συμβολική, III, pp. 17-21, 26-32.

[2] Rhôsse, *op. cit.*, pp. 444-5, 462.

[3] Cf. 1 Cor. 2, 4; Origen, *Contra Celsum*, 1, 2.

[4] Rhôsse, *ibid.*, p. 446.

revelation, and not repugnant to reason. There is also the powerful argument for validity in the demonstration of power, the proving of the authenticity of Christian revelation by its fruits.[1] There are, however, three fundamental notes of a genuine revelation, which render it worthy of credence and belief. These are: (1) a creative, original, and new quality, (2) its consistency with itself, and with the whole complex of known, experienced, and revealed truth, and (3) its positive character as part of a gradual and progressive development.

(1) God works along with man in his religious life, and His spirit shares with the human soul the activity of reaching Godward. Yet this coöperation of God's spirit with ours may be neither inspiration nor revelation. The term *revelation* may be applied to the discovery, by means of a new and creative act of God's spirit operating in man's, of something new, which was not known before, though man's spirit might have been capable of receiving it.[2] Furthermore, this distinct and new act of God's revelation to man is not of the sort that is to be appropriated by the individual to whom the revelation is made, but it must be proclaimed abroad, as it is a truth for mankind. The individual acts as agent for the promulgation of the new revelation, and his guarantee is the evidence of miracle. There is an exact correlation and parallel between the revelation to a human soul from without, through God's inspiration, and the occurrence of a miracle in the order of natural phenomena. Both are supernatural.

(2) At first it would seem that this note of the catastrophic and apocalyptic character of revelation would clash with the second note—consistency with itself and with the whole content of knowledge, natural and supernatural. But each several new revelation serves but to explain better and unify the content of religious truth; it comes to supplement and complete, and not to subvert. It must form part of an ordered whole, yet the method of its introduction is always by some such extraordinary subjective and objective declaration of God's

[1] Rom. 1, 16; 1 Cor. 1, 27; 2 Cor. 4, 15; Eph. 2, 1-6-14; Gal. 3, 18. This same argument is used by Eusebius, St. Chrysostom, and St. Athanasius.
[2] Mesolora, *op. cit.*, III, p. 31.

Will. Every step in the process of revelation is initiated by inspiration and miracle.

Nevertheless it is only from our limited point of view that such extraordinary events may be regarded as even apparent contradictions of the order of nature. The terms natural and supernatural, rational and supra-rational, are only relative, and coined by man with the limited experience of his own finite plane. "The terms 'above nature' and 'above reason' are only applicable to the 'nature' and 'reason' of *human beings* for they are 'according to reason' and 'according to nature' in God's sight. They are never 'unreasonable' or 'unnatural' even according to human reason."[1]

So for convenience we use the word "supra-rational" to describe the illumination of the mind of man by God as a means of the revelation of a truth to which man's unaided reason could not attain. We apply the term "supernatural" to an extraordinary occurrence in the realm of the tangible and physical, the causes of which are not the ordinary secondary causes resident in the world of experience.[2] Inasmuch as the two spheres of natural and supernatural, rational and supra-rational, are actually only one unified plane of being, such distinctions are not absolutely valid, yet may be logically helpful and legitimately useful because of our limited and finite range of knowledge. Yet the great fact remains that each addition, by means of supra-rational illumination verified by miracle in the external order, to the stock of man's knowledge is in the way of an increment to it, the new fact being of necessity of a sort to complement, complete, and further the scope of that knowledge, of which it becomes an integral and constituent part. Thus the second note of self-consistency and harmony with the previously ascertained body of knowledge is a criterion of the validity of revelation. It must dovetail into the past experience of man as well as into the corporate body of knowledge developed by revelation. It can never abrogate a truth once for all given, nor supplant it, but must supplement, complement, and complete it. This is what is meant by the self-consistency of the content of a new revelation and its agreement with the preceding.

[1] Rhôsse, *op. cit.*, pp. 449-450.
[2] *Ibid.*, p. 451.

(3) "Inasmuch as the religious receptivity of man allows only of a gradual process of inspiration and revelation by God through new acts and works in history, by means of which something new is imparted which supplements and fulfills what has gone before, divine Revelation has also the characteristic note of a gradual and progressive development."[1] This does not violate the finality or positive character of any previous revelation. Each successive step in the[2] process is conditioned by the will of God foreordaining the given sequence of gradual illumination on God's part, and of response, acceptance, and appropriation on the part of man. The double characteristic of conservation and progress is predicable of every vital and genuine religion. The relation of the two functioning properly forbids the refusal of a hearing to a new revelation by a too literal adherence to the letter of past revelation, and at the same time inhibits an unregulated and unfettered evolution of novel and uninspired developments by means of the fixed content of past revelation. The proper relation of the conservative and progressive principles of true religion is perhaps best expressed in the thought that Christianity has the duty of conserving a growing thing: the better it fulfills its conservative purpose, the more opportunity does it give for the nascent life and constant development of the great revelation committed to it. "The higher degree of the new divine revelation, preserving the fundamental features of the foregoing lower degree, fulfills and perfects it, while the lower degree of divine revelation, preparing the place for the higher, raises expectation and desire for it, and renders man ready and capable to receive the higher degree."[3]

3. REVELATION AND MIRACLE

Of the two-fold form of revelation we have already treated of the first—that of "internal revelation," or "inspiration". As we have seen, the external manifestation of the will of God in

---

[1] Rhôsse, *op cit.*, p. 452.

[2] Mesolora, *op. cit.*, p. 33. (vol. III.)

[3] Rhôsse, *op. cit.*, p. 453. Mesolora's definition embodies these elements: "Revelation is the Divine, supernatural, and graduated action of God's energy upon man" (*op. cit.*, III, p. 29).

the order of natural phenomena acts as a validation and guarantee of a subjective inspiration vouchsafed to man. There is a close and intimate relation between the external and the internal, the objective and subjective forms of revelation. "A miracle is an extraordinary and perceived phenomenon, taking place in the world of matter or sense, which is not attributable to nor explicable by the natural constitution of the world, but only attributable to a new exercise of God's energy in the physical world."[1] A miracle is neither a suspension nor violation of natural law, nor can it be said to be an impossibility, save on the principle of the denial of the existence of any causes save the resident causes in the cosmos. Since physical causes working in a certain way produce certain fixed results, we codify the results of the observations made by natural science in a "natural law," a statement of the sequence of cause and effect. In the ordered hierarchy of natural order certain definite planes of action are discernible—inorganic, physical, organic, chemical, and the like. We do not say of the general law governing the action of inorganic bodies that it is either suspended or violated when they are acted upon by organic bodies, functioning according to the law of their being. Neither does the occurrance of miracle, the presence of a Cause not generally active in that way among the forces of nature, postulate the suspension or temporary abrogation of natural law.[2] A new Element has come in as a new cause, and the new effect is a miracle. So the miracle does not suspend or violate natural law. Nor is a miracle a violation of the immutability of God's character, for He does not change even though He seems to us to adopt different ways of working in His world. The change is something we attribute to Him, not something belonging to His Essence. Neither is it scientific to say that miracles are impossible, except on the premise which involves the

---

[1] Rhôsse, op. cit., p. 454.

[2] Ibid., p. 456. On the whole subject, cf. the chapter on miracles in N. Kephala's Χριστολογία, (Athens, 1901) pp. 100-115 & ff., and Androutsos, op. cit., pp. 119-120: "The possibility of miracle rests partly in the Creation of the world not of necessity but of God's free-will, and partly in the dependence of natural forces and beings on the Will and Might of God." cf. Lecture II, p. 91, III, pp. 148-152.

denial of everything save the resident physical forces of the universe.[1]

As revelation to the spirit of man acts upon that which in creation is nearest akin to God, subjective revelation or inspiration is of a higher order than external or objective revelation, or miracle. External revelation seals, guarantees, validates, and authenticates the subjective revelation given to man's spirit directly from God. Inspiration, or the direct illumination of man's spirit by God, by as it were a temporary union with Him, is not a mechanical, magical, or automatic domination of man by the Divine Spirit. The inspired man coöperates with God in order that the Revelation may become a fact to mankind. He abandons neither reason, conscience, nor will.[2]

The most complete Revelation of God to man is in the Person of Him who was both God and Man, Who was always God from eternity, and from the instant of His conception in the womb of our Lady, was perfectly one with the Father. He is the climax of Revelation. Prophets and seers were only for the time being united with God when He used them as vehicles of Revelation. Jesus was always united with Him. The Incarnation then is the perfect and final revelation of God to man— perfect and final as well in the Vehicle of the Revelation as in the content of what is revealed. He is the acme of human perfections completing the edifice of man's spiritual development, who was at it were a "super-man," the example and type of the Ideal Man. The Revelation of Perfect Man in the Incarnation is also the means of man's attainment of that perfection. As the development of God's plan made necessary the appearance of the perfect and ultimate Revelation, completing and unifying the whole process so the nature of this perfect Revelation demanded a perfect Vehicle. "So the idea of the God-man and His actual appearance in the historic Person of Jesus Christ, is at once the Miracle and the greatest of all the miracles, and is not in opposition to the mind of mankind in its healthful state, but is rather demanded by it as necessary for the perfection of man."[3]

[1] Cf. Rhôsse, op. cit., § 310, pp. 457-458. ·
[2] Ibid., p. 461-62.
[3] Cf. Eph. 4, 13; Rhôsse, op. cit., pp. 463-466. · Cf. St. Irenaeus' doctrine of the ἀνακεφαλαίωσις.

4. THE SOURCES OF DOGMATIC

"We derive our knowledge of the teaching of the Christian Religion from Holy Scripture and Sacred Tradition, which we therefore call the *sources of our Religion*."[1] This concise statement embodies the Orthodox position as to the sources from which all the dogmas of the Faith are obtained. They are of equal weight. The Orthodox standpoint is neither that of the Roman Church, which does not found its dogma entirely upon the Bible and Tradition, nor that of Protestantism, which casts tradition completely aside.[2] Besides the dogmas of the Faith there are "pious opinions," which are allowed to circulate freely among members of different schools of thought as their own personal conclusions and speculations, provided they do not violate or oppose any of the dogmas of the Faith.[3] Tradition "in its widest meaning includes Revelation, or the teaching of our Lord and the Apostles," handed down from generation to generation, and treasured up in the Holy Scriptures and other monuments of the past.[4] In its narrower or restricted meaning it is applied to the teaching of the Church not set down in Holy Scripture. The Bible takes for granted the oral tradition, for the Faith was preached by word of mouth.[5] It was never meant to be self-explanatory, for it needs the interpretation of a living tradition.[6] Furthermore, it was not meant to contain explicitly all that is necessary to salvation, for the oral tradition supplements, completes, and develops its doctrines. "The Holy Scriptures, from their avowed purpose, neither were written nor purported to be a full and systematic presentation of the Faith first imparted by living voice."[7] In the words

[1] *Orthodox Cat.* of Balanos, Athens, 1920, p. 4.

[2] Androutsos, *op. cit.*, pp. 2-3.

[3] *Ibid.*, p. 3. These are called "theological opinions", Θεολογικαὶ γνῶμαι or Θεολογούμενα (*dubia*).

[4] *Ibid.*, note 7, pp. 6-7. Rhôsse, *op. cit.*, p. 57.

[5] Cf. 2. Thes. 2, 14; 1 Cor. 11, 2; 2 Tim. 1, 13-14, 2, 2; 2, St. John 12.

[6] Androutsos, *op. cit.*, p. 8. "Holy Tradition is not only the continuation of the Word of God contained in Holy Writ, but also the trustworthy guide and interpreter of it."—Mesolora, Πρακτικὴ Θεολογία, p. 29, note.

[7] *Ibid.*, and Rhôsse, *op. cit.*, p. 58, and note. Compare Dyobouniotes Ὀφέιλ. ἀπάντησις, pp. 154-156.

of St. Basil the Great "of the doctrines and teachings preserved
in the Church, we have some from the written word, and others
we have received handed down from the apostolic tradition as
it were in secret (ἐν μυστηρίῳ), both of which have equal force
for our religion."[1]

5. THE BIBLE:

(a) The Church as Interpreter

"The Church is that holy Foundation made by the Incarnate Word of God for the salvation and sanctification of men,
having divine authenticity and bearing His authority, consisting of men holding one Faith, bound to Christ and each other
by the bonds of Faith, Hope, and Love, believing the same dogmas, having the same worship, and governed by Bishops who
are genuine successors of the Apostles."[2] "As the authentic
interpreter of Revelation, authoritatively explaining Holy Scripture and Sacred Tradition, she formulates the teaching of our
Lord."[3] As such she is infallible, for "the Saviour founded the
Church as the centre as well as the vehicle of His Redemptive
Work,"[4] since she is "inseparably united with her Head, Christ,
the Living Centre of Redemption. . . . and exercises His priestly
and prophetic office."[5] She has "preserved pure and undefiled
both sources of dogmatic truth, and by her they are rightly interpreted, defined, and infallibly formulated through the Holy
Spirit."[6] By the Catholic Church, Orthodox writers understand the undivided Church up to the time of the Schism in
the 11th century, and the Orthodox Church since that day. As
will be shown later, they regard the Orthodox Church as the
only true Church. Rome is in heresy and schism, and all Protestant Communions are separated from the unity of Christendom. Neither Protestant bodies nor the whole Western Church
is part of the Catholic Church, which consists solely of the Or-

[1] *De Spiritu Sancto*, 27, 2, with which cf. the 8th Canon of the
VII Ecum. Coun.

[2] Androutsos, *op. cit.*, p. 262; Rhôsse, *op. cit.*, p. 56; Mesolora
op. cit., IV, pp. 5-13.

[3] Androutsos, *ibid.*, p. 9.

[4] Androutsos, *op. cit.*, p. 264, Rhôsse, *op. cit.*, p. 57.

[5] Androutsos, *ibid.*, pp. 260, 277.

[6] Rhôsse, *op. cit.*, p. 58; Mesolora, *op. cit.*, IV, pp. 17-39.

thodox Church.[1] Endowed by her Founder with the inerrant faculty of "rightly dividing the word of truth" she fixed the canon of Holy Scripture,[2] being guided thereto by the Holy Spirit. The Holy Scriptures are "the collection of books written by inspired men in which the divine revelations are contained."[3]

(b) Canon and Text of Holy Scripture[4]

To the 24 books, written in Hebrew and Aramaic, of the Hebrew Canon were added the books of Baruch, Tobit, Wisdom of Solomon, Ben Sirach, and the Maccabees. These books together with the others in the Greek version of the LXX, made in the 3d century B. C., form the Old Testament of the Orthodox Church. As they were regarded by the Fathers—for example, St. Athanasius—as not quite on a par with the books of the Jewish Canon, and were called by them "useful to be read," they were included in the councils of Hippo (393) and Carthage (397) as "deutero-canonical". Questions were still raised regarding their canonicity, so in later councils (post-Reformation) they were styled "good and excellent" yet lacking the validity of the other books, which only were recognized by such Fathers as St. Gregory the Theologian, St. Amphilochios, and St. John Damascene.[5] The New Testament canon of the Council of Laodicea, (350) [canon 60] left out the Apocalypse, but the subsequent councils mentioned above (Hippo, 393, canon 36, and Carthage, 397, canon 47), and the decrees of the 6th Ecumenical Council decided on the canonicity of all of the books of the New Testament, including the Apocalypse.

[1] Cf. Rhôsse, op. cit., pp. 24, 56, 489-91, etc.; Mesolora, op cit., vol. III, pp. 21-26, 17; Androutsos, op. cit., pp. 268, 282, et al. Androutsos, Αἱ βάσεις τῆς Ἑνώσεως τ. Ἐκκλησ., Athens, 1905, esp. pp. 22 ff.; Monumenta Fidei Ecclesiae Orientalis, Kimmel, Jena, 1850, vol. II; Ἡ Ὀρθόδοξος Ἐκκλησία, Nicholas Ambraze, Athens, 1902, pp. 17, 280, et. al.; also Lecture IV, § II. especially 5.

[2] Rhôsse, op. cit., p. 467.

[3] Ibid., p. 466.

[4] Mesolora, op. cit., III, pp. 42-49.

[5] For Council of Constantinople, 1675, cf. Kimmel, II, 225; and Kritopoulos' summary of the Orthodox position, ibid., pp. 105-6; in extenso, in Mesolora, op. cit., I, pp. 265-361; so too Eugenius Bulgaris, Θεολογικόν, § 29, and Macaire, Introduction à la théologie, p. 489 (cf. Art VI in B. C. P.).

Though the original text of the Old Testament was not Greek, yet the Septuagint translation has the same authority as the original. The LXX was the text used by the Apostles. Moreover it had equal authority with the original text practically from the time of its translation. Furthermore, the Masoretic text may not be taken as a faithful transmission of the Hebrew original, as is apparent from the critical study of its text.[1] While some Orthodox theologians have attempted to assign a kind of Divine authority to the LXX translation, and thereby have much overstated the case,[2] still it is true that the Orthodox Church treats the LXX as of paramount value, and accords it canonical standing.[3] She has never disavowed the careful work of competent ecclesiastical scholars who correct the text of the LXX by the Hebrew. She does not tolerate any translation of the Bible into the current idiom of vernacular Greek, whether of the Old or the New Testaments. For example, the translation made by Maximus of Kallipolis, revised and published by Seraphim of Mytilene, was banned by Gabriel, the Patriarch of Constantinople, in 1704. The translation of Hilarion was condemned in 1823, and the Holy Synod of Greece Sept. 7-9, 1901, forbade any translation being made, sold, or used, and excommunicated any who disobeyed. All of the translations into modern Greek made by various Protestant bodies, are forbidden to be used by a faithful Orthodox, as for example, that by Palle. The reasons for this attitude are: the impossibility of conveying the exact meaning of the original in a modern language without the use of paraphrases, notes, or commentaries; such commentaries and notes, even when based on good authorities, tend to be utterly misleading; the translations which have appeared are crude, inexact, and irreverent; any Greek who takes the trouble to study can read the original texts without difficulty; furthermore, many of the texts have been published for propaganda and proselytizing purposes, on the Protestant principle of the sufficiency for salvation of the Bible only.[4]

[1] Rhôsse, op. cit., p. 456-6; Mesolora, op. cit., III, pp. 54-63.

[2] Androutsos, op. cit., p. 6, note 7.

[3] "It is of the greatest ecclesiastical authority." (Mesolora, op. cit., III. p. 63.)

[4] Cf. Rhôsse, op. cit., pp. 476-480; Androutsos, op. cit., pp. 6-8, note 7.

(c) Inspiration of the Bible

The writers of the Holy Scripture were men, "illuminated by the Holy Spirit."[1] "Since the Holy Spirit illuminated the writers of the Holy Scripture we say that the Bible is inspired."[2] The fact of inspiration of the Scriptures is clear from internal evidence of the text—cf. St. Matt. 5, 17-18; 22, 43; Rom. 16, 25-26; 2 St. Peter 1, 19-21. All these passages imply the inspiration of the Old Testament, and their witness is best summarized in 2 Tim. 3, 16. St. Paul's conviction of having the Spirit of God, and of being taught by Him "comparing spiritual things with spiritual" (1 Cor. 2, 12-13) is evidence of the consciousness of inspiration on the part of the writers of the New Testament. Inspiration means the imparting of the Divine and supernatural truths to men by the Holy Spirit, who gives grace to set them down in writing or to give them adequate and meet expression.[3] The understanding of the writer was illuminated and his thought exalted to the fellowship of Divine things, so that the devout human spirit became the bearer and sharer of Divine truths, receiving thoughts and ofttimes even words, directly from God.[4] There are different degrees of inspiration. Bulgaris distinguishes between *inspiration* (ἔμπνευσις) "an internal energy operating in man's mind by which he is divinely impelled to write or enact something supernaturally revealed", and *illumination* (φωτισμός) "the assistance and help of the Holy Spirit, guarding man from error in speech and writing."[5] So Rhôsse speaks of this lower degree, the preservation from error in writing, as being under the oversight of Holy Spirit, and the higher, as that "whereby truths are imparted which exceed the bounds of the finite spirit of man, and which have their origin only in the Divine Revelation."[6]

It was because of the inspiration of the various books of

[1] *Orthodox Cat.* p. 4; *Conf.* of Dositheus, ch. 2, and quest. 1, in Mesolora, *op. cit.*, vol. 1, pp. 103-4, 120.
[2] *Orthodox Cat.* p. 5, cf. *Conf.* of Kritopoulos, ch. 7.
[3] Rhôsse, *op. cit.*, p. 469.
[4] Mesolora Συμβολική, III, p. 38.
[5] *Theologikon*, p. 24, yet without the abrogation of man's free will or mental functioning; quoted in Mesolora, III, pp. 38-9, note 2.
[6] *Op. cit.*, p. 470.

the Bible that they received a place in the Canon. Canonicity does not depend upon the personality of the writers. "Even if it should be shown that certain of the writings in Holy Writ were not by those holy men to whom authorship has been commonly ascribed, and that they were actually written by unknown writers, the passages in question would not be regarded as unauthentic."[1]   The integrity of the Bible is assured by reason of the great care and solicitude with which the Jews preserved the Old Testament, and the Christian Church the New Testament.   Variant readings are never significant, nor are the minor errors which have crept into the text; for inspiration "has reference only to the fundamentals and essentials, and these concern the revealed truth and dogmas of the Faith, and the ethical teachings."[2]

Of the fact of Inspiration there is no doubt, but there is no dogmatic definition of its nature.   It is certain, however, that it is not "literal" inspiration.   The personal peculiarities and idiosyncrasies of each writer are apparent everywhere.   There are differences of style and content in   the various writers, even when they are dealing with the same subject matter, as St. John Chrysostom and St. Jerome noted.[3] The fact of authorized translations, for example, and the use by St. Paul of the LXX, militates against the theory of literal inspiration.[4]   Inspiration was not "ecstasy".   Plato, following Greek theories of inspiration, such as those of the oracles, mystery cults, and the like, regards it as consisting of a passive and automatic surrender to the direction of the Spirit.   So did some of the early apologists, for example, St. Justin Martyr, who said that the inspired men were "as harps under the energy of the Holy Spirit", and Athenagoras, "as a flute in the hands of a flute player".   This view developed into heresy when Montanism claimed this type of inspiration, and held that it was the same as that under which the writers of Holy Scripture had written: "as passive instruments" of the Holy Spirit. The Fathers rejected this view and combated it strenuously,—

[1] Rhôsse, op. cit., p. 468.
[2] Ibid., p. 469.
[3] E. g., St. Jerome on Gal. 6, I.
[4] Androutsos, op. cit., pp. 4-5.

Miltiades, Clem. Alex., Athanasius, Basil, Chrysostom, and Epiphanius. Inspiration was "the imparting of conceptions and truths which the holy writers could not have discovered by means of unaided human spirit[1] . . . It did not preclude the exercise of the faculties of an individual, and cannot be understood as ecstatic rapture, with its loss of self-consciousness and self-direction".[2] It was not "automatic writing" at the dictation of the Holy Spirit.

Closely akin to the view of inspiration as ecstasy or rapture, is that of the "rationalists", who hold that it was simply subjective, a result of a heightened degree of faith,[3] and that the content of revelation, being shown by reason, "the critic and judge of the truths of revelation,"[4] to abound in errors, reason should pass on what purports to be revelation, selecting what is good and rejecting what is valueless. There can be then nothing supernatural in the content of Holy Writ, and its "inspiration" is merely the subjective illusion of the writers. Whatever good there is in it is solely of human origin. When human reason is at its highest and noblest, and functions with its clearest insight, it may be called "inspiration".[5] This view is untenable, since it denies the possibility of supernatural revelation, and puts reason above faith as the means of apprehending religious truth.[6]

The definition of inspiration which limits its range to the dogmatic and ethical content of Holy Scripture, is also unsatisfactory. Such a view of inspiration divides the Holy Scriptures into two parts—human and divine; but as there is no way of deciding where one begins and the other leaves off, the way is left open for a purely rationalistic conception of inspiration, making reason the arbiter and judge over the content of revela-

[1] Rhôsse, op. cit., pp. 470, 472.

[2] Ibid., p. 473; cf. Bulgaris in Mesolora, op. cit., p. 38, note 2.

[3] Mesolora, ibid., III, p. 36, note 3.

[4] Ambraze, op. cit., p. 191.

[5] Mesolora, III, p. 4, note 2, and p. 36-7. Rhôsse, (op. cit., p. 451, note 2) prefers "λογοφροσύνη" for "rationalism", to the usual word, "ὀρθολογισμός".

[6] Additional note A, The Relation between Faith and Knowledge, pp. 45-49, ff.

tion.[1] This view logically leads to the preceding one, which is absolutely incompatible with the Orthodox position.

The Orthodox view of inspiration involves these elements: (a) the illumination of the writer by the Holy Spirit, for the purpose of (b) imparting religious or ethical truths, (c) not within the range of discovery by ordinary human faculties, (d) together with the grace adequately to set these down in writing, and (e) protection from error and mistake in fundamental and significant matters, (f) with due regard for individuality and the fullest exercise of all human faculties.[2] As internal proofs of the Revelation contained in Holy Writ imparted by the Holy Spirit inspiring the writers, Mesolora cites the following: (a) the dogmatic content of Holy Scripture, with its supernatural truths about God, creation, redemption, salvation, and the like, (b) the lofty ethical content of the Holy Scriptures, (c) the subject matter, substance, and manner of construction of Holy Writ, as, for example, the relation of prophecy to fulfillment, of type to anti-type, and the like; (d) the reception of it by mankind, the tremendous value put upon it in the estimation of men, and its effect on human life.[3]

(d) Biblical Teaching in Relation to Dogma

Since the Bible cannot be understood by itself, and the only adequate test for its interpretation is the standard of the Church's teachings, it follows that it may not be used by each individual as a store house from which to derive any doctrine which he seeks to find in it, and which may commend itself to him. It must be read in the light of the living teaching of the Church. The rule of interpretation is the "mind of the Church,"[4] the *secundum ecclesiastici et catholici sensus normam* of St. Vincent of Lerins.[5] The *Confession* of Dositheus expli-

[1] Androutsos, *op. cit.*, p. 5.
[2] Mesolora, *op. cit.*, III. pp. 36-38; Rhôsse, *op. cit.*, pp. 468-473; Ambraze, *op. cit.*, pp. 190-191; Androutsos, *op. cit.*, p 5.—"God the Holy Spirit speaks in Holy Scripture, and there is no falsehood nor contradiction in it."
[3] Mesolora, *op. cit.*, III. pp. 39-40.
[4] Hippolytus, in Euseb. *Hist. E.*, V, 28.
[5] *Commonitorium*, 2. Mesolora, *op. cit.*, III. pp. 49-54. On the importance of St. Vincent's Canon according to Orthodox opinion, cf. Palmieri, *Il Progresso Dommatico*, pp. 255-274.

citly states that Holy Scripture is to be understood "not otherwise than as the Catholic Church has interpreted and transmitted it".[1] Any other standard than this would subvert the constitution of the Church, and make her essential teachings subject to the exegetical and hermeneutic whims of the day.[2] For "as it is One and the selfsame Holy Spirit who is the Author of both, it is the same whether one be taught by the Bible or by the Catholic Church".[3]

6. (2) TRADITION:

(a) Origin and Relation to Bible

Since the Bible takes for granted the existence of oral tradition, and there is "no evidence that the Apostles wrote all that was necessary for the Faithful to know, or all that they taught them by word of mouth, or that their written words should be the sole canon of Christian faith and life,"[4] we find that in the earliest times the oral tradition held a unique place in Christian teaching.[5] For more than twenty years the Church had no written New Testament, and "Tradition was the standard of faith first in time as well as in importance."[6] When converts were made they were not sent to study from a book, but given instruction by word of mouth.[7] The Church taught them herself, pointing to the Bible for corroboration of her teaching when such a course would aid in clearing up difficulties, or explain her tradition. Her tradition of teaching was passed down from generation to generation, but it did not at first have a systematic form. When first a formulation was made it was as a corporate witness of the mind of the Church, and an evidence of the common faith of communities of Christians scattered in different

[1] Cf. proceedings of the Council of Jerusalem, Mesolora, II, pp. 61-88. ch. 2 of Dositheus, *ibid.*, 11, p. 103.

[2] Rhôsse, *op. cit.*, p. 474.

[3] Rhôsse, *ibid.*, p. 475.

[4] *Ibid.*, p. 481.

[5] *Ibid.*, p. 58, note 1; Cf. *Orth. Cat.* pp. 6-7.

[6] Rhôsse, *ibid.*, p. 481, and Mesolora, *op. cit.*, III, pp. 63-77.

[7] For an illustration of this method and its developments, cf. the History of the Catechetical School of Alexandria, P. M. Papadopoulos Τὸ ἐν τῇ ἀρχαίᾳ οἰκουμενικῇ Ἐκκλησίᾳ κρατῆσαν Κατηχητικὸν Σύστημα; Papadoupoulos, Ὁ Ἅγιος Διονύσιος ὁ Μέγας, Alexandria, 1918,

localities. Their common agreement was a testimony to a common tradition received unchanged from the past. Such an early formulation of the content of Tradition in relation to the dogmas of the Faith is embodied in the Roman baptismal formula, the so-called Apostles' Creed. Other typical examples are to be found in St. Irenaeus, *adv. Haer.* 1, 1, 10; Tertullian, *De virg. vel.* 1; *de praescrip. Haer*; 13; *adv. Prax. c.* 2; and Origen, *De principiis,* 4 and 5.

As a matter of fact, the New Testament itself is the first example of the same type of formulated oral teaching. The construction of the synoptics, the character of the epistles, and the Church's seal upon the whole collection, demonstrate the first codification of oral into written teaching.[1] It was first in time, the prototype of other formulation of the teaching of the Church, and in this sense may be called the first canon of faith. But oral Tradition, wider, fuller, and earlier than the written word, the Tradition "written not with pen and ink upon parchment but in the hearts of the Faithful by the Holy Spirit, may more properly be called the first canon of Faith."[2]

Since every true revelation has as one of its essential characteristics the note of gradual development, we may expect to find progressive development when we investigate the history of Tradition. The principle of development[3] is as fully present in the New Testament as it is in later formulations of Christian teaching. Under the guidance of the Holy Spirit the teaching of our Lord set down in the Gospels is developed and unfolded in the Epistles. The same Spirit who should "lead them into all truth" is He who directed and guided the further developments of Christian doctrine in Holy Tradition. "As proceeding from the One and same Divine Spirit, there appears in a different form, more or less amplified, one and the same Gospel. There is consequently no essential difference, but solely a superficial one"[4] between Gospels and Epistles, and between the New Testa-

---

[1] Rhôsse, Δογματική, p. 483.

[2] *Ibid.,* pp. 57, 485—cf. St. Irenaeus, *adv. Haer.* III. 3; "The Holy Scriptures are the first written formulation of Tradition".

[3] On which, cf. subsequent section, pp. 35-45, "Faith and Reason in relation to Dogma."

[4] Rhôsse, *op. cit.,* p. 484.

ment and Christian Tradition. The continuity of a stable and unswerving Tradition, varying its form with the ages, at once preserves the Church from heresy, false doctrine, and novel opinions, and also presents a living and vital interpretation, characterized by insight and complete understanding of the content of Holy Writ.[1]

(b) Content and Formulation of Tradition

Of this Tradition which forms a continuous chain from the Apostles to the end of time, the Scriptures form the first link of its written and formulated expression.[2] Scripture and Tradition are one in orgin, since the Holy Spirit is Author of both; one in content, since they teach the same faith; and one in essence, since they are substantially the same identical entity. From the time of the earliest heresies, of the Gnostics, Monarchians, Sabellians, Arians, Pelagians, and Nestorians, to those of the present day, heresies have attempted to found their divergent interpretations of Christian truth on the word of Holy Scripture. The Bible, being so intimately bound up with Tradition, if it be rightly interpreted by it, presents one single true conception, in any given case.[3] Thus Tradition is the protection and shield for the true interpretation of Holy Writ. Heretics, in consequence, cast Tradition aside. "Though the two sources of dogma may be logically defined and distinguished, yet they cannot be separated from each other, nor from the Church".[4] As Tradition is essential to the right interpretation of Holy Writ, so is Holy Writ essential as a proper criterion to determine the value and weight of any specific Tradition.[5]

The formulation of Christian doctrine from the Bible to the present day is the work of the Church. She possesses the Holy Spirit and is an infallible teacher, as well as the mouthpiece and organ of His expression. What she defines is the same Faith as

[1] Rhôsse, op. cit., pp. 486-488. Cf. Gavin, The Greek Orthodox Church and Biblical Criticism, in The Christian East, December 1922 (vol. III, no. 4), pp. 162-172.

[2] Rhôsse, ibid., p. 485.

[3] Ibid., p. 488.

[4] Ibid., p. 59.

[5] Androutsos, op. cit., p. 7.

she has always taught, formulated with a view to some contingency or emergency, usually the attacks of heretics on a cardinal doctrine of that Faith. Her act of definition or formulation is only the expression of her mind, not the creation of a new doctrine. Universality[1] is the great test: *quod apud multos invenitur unum, non est erratum sed traditun,* in the words of Tertullian.[2] This is the Orthodox definition of the canon of St. Vincent: *quod semper, quod ubique, quod ab omnibus creditum est.* Representative universality and consent are all that is necessary, not a numerical majority.[3] Consequently, all the definitions, decrees, confessions, and formulations of the Church from the earliest days until now form the content of the Faith for an Orthodox Churchman. Such include :[4] (1) the Creeds—the Niceno-Constantinopolitan (without the *Filioque* clause), which alone has a place in the Orthodox Liturgy and service books, the Apostles' Creed, that of St. Gregory of Neocaesarea, and that of St. Athanasius (given place in an appendix to the 'Ευχολόγιον); (2) the decrees and canons of the Ecumenical Councils, and all the definitions and formularies of the Undivided Church; (3) decrees of councils and synods subsequent to the separation of the Eastern and Western Churches, especially those held since the Reformation[5]—Jassy, 1638, Constantinople, 1672, Jerusalem, 1672; (4) the Orthodox *Confessions,* such as that of Peter of Mogila, Metropolitan of Kieff, examined, edited, and ratified by a committee of Greek and Russian theologians and published with the imprimatur of four Eastern Patriarchs; (5) Encyclicals and synodical letters—such as those of the Patriarch Jeremiah II to the Tübingen theologians, Kroustos and Andreas (1570; the Encyclical of the Orthodox Church, published by the Patriarchs in the year 1848; that *On Unity and the State of the Autocephalous Churches of the East,* published by all of them in 1902; (6) the authorized

[1] On the relation of Tradition to the Church, cf. Mesolora, *op. cit.,* III. pp. 63-67.

[2] Androutsos, *op. cit.,* pp. 10-11.

[3] *Ibid.,* pp. 10-15.

[4] Cf. Palmieri, *Theologia Dogmatica Orthodoxa,* vol. 1. (Prolegomena), pp. 138-183, 267-660.

[5] For a fuller discussion of all the later sources, cf. Lecture IV, pp. 206-218 following.

Catechisms of the Eastern Church, such as those of Kephala
(1899) and D. S. Balanos, published in 1920.[1]

"The full Tradition of the true Catholic Church contains
not only the decrees of the Ecumenical Synods, but also
those dogmas which had not encountered the opposition of
heretical teaching in the ancient Catholic Church previous to
the Schism, but which were potentially and essentially part of
the genuine and full Tradition, and, though not formulated in
local or ecumenical synods before the Schism, were afterwards defined in the Holy Synods of the Eastern Church from
the 16th century on . . . These have authority and binding
force upon every true member of the Orthodox Catholic
Church."[2] If such dogmatic decrees are not to be counted as
binding,[3] then "all dogmatic character is removed from the
teaching of the Orthodox Church on such points as the au-

---

[1] All are treated and discussed in Androutsos' Συμβολική, given in
Mesolora's Συμβολική, vol. I. and II.; in *Monumenta Fidei Ecclesiae
Orientalis*, Kimmel; cf. Ambraze, Ἡ ὀρθόδοξος Ἐκκλησία, etc.
p. 16-19; Androutsos' essay on the "Basis of Reunion"; Rhôsse,
Θεμελιώδεις δογματικαὶ Ἀρχαὶ τῆς Ὀρθοδόξου Ἀνατολικῆς Ἐκκλησίας and his
report to the Holy Synod, 1874.

[2] Rhôsse, *op. cit.*, p. 59.

[3] Older writers, such as *e. g.*, Mesolora, do not seem quite to follow
this course of reasoning to this conclusion. Mesolora distinguishes
apostolic from *ecclesiastical* tradition. The former is the "tradition
not written in the Gospels, which completes and develops the teaching of Our Lord", which he further subdivides. The latter, "ecclesiastical tradition, is the teaching of Our Saviour and His Apostles
as expounded, developed, and defined officially and unanimously by
the Fathers of the One Catholic Church in ecumenical synods" (III.
op. cit., pp. 69-70). Tradition has equal weight with the Bible, for
the ecumenical synods so regarded it (*ibid*, p. 76). The Bible is
"the first source and canon of true religious knowledge" (*ibid.*, p.
35), and Tradition is the second (*ibid.*, p. 65). Yet he seems to imply that the Vincentian standard of universality, antiquity, and consent is applicable only to the decrees of the Undivided Church, out of
the whole content of Orthodox Tradition (*ibid.*, pp. 63-64 and p. 71,
note 2, pp. 75-76). So the canons of the seven ecumenical councils, together with the Bible, form the double source of authorized
Orthodox dogma. "Subsequent formulations have not the obligatory
character of the creed and the decrees of the seven ecumemical councils", but only illustrative and secondary value (vol. I, pp. 12-13). For
a fuller discussion, compare Lecture IV. pp. 206-218.

thenticity of the Church, the Seven Sacraments, the doctrine of Justification",[1] and the way will be left open for proselytism of the Orthodox.

7. FAITH AND REASON

(1) In Relation to Religion

The theory of Revelation stated above, as well as that of biblical inspiration, involves the interrelation and interaction of two elements—faith and knowledge. Certain facts belong to the domain of knowledge and are within the range of human experience. These form the material of science. Philosophy develops its speculations and inductions by means of the data of experience and by the use of the reason. Ideas based upon experience, developed by the exercise of reason, compared, correlated and arranged into order and form, constitute the material of philosophy. But theology claims as its sphere a field which includes the data of man's experience and thinking, yet the peculiar content of which is neither attributable alone to human experience as such, nor based ultimately upon the conclusions of human thought. It is constituted of material offered and presented, as it were, from without the circumscribed area of purely human experience and reasoning, imparted to man through the inspiration the Holy Spirit, and guaranteed and validated by phenomena in the external world of experience, called miracles. Thus Revelation transcends and extends beyond human experience which furnishes the data for the physical sciences, and human thought, which, operating on the data of experience, evolves a system of ideas which form a philosophy. The content of Revelation stands in the same relation both to human experience and human thinking: what it offers us is not within the scope of the circumscribed range of ordinary human powers.[2]

[1] Rhôsse, *ibid.*, note 1, pp. 59-60, *q. v.* Androutsos gives: "Dogmatic decrees of the ecumenical councils, and the creed; and the decrees of local synods ratified by ecumenical synods; as secondary authorities: all presentations of the faith made in local synods, which agree with Church teaching,—such as the "symbolic books" on the occasion of the Calvinistic confession of Lucar, among which are conspicuous the *Confession of Dositheus*" (p. 20); cf. Sect. 5 of his *Introduction*.

[2] Rhôsse, pp. 36-38, 39-44.

In both science and philosophy, human reason is the organ for the appropriation, investigation, and codification of the data. Experience is codified into conclusions, and conclusions are correlated and developed into a philosophic system. But any philosophic system makes certain assumptions, just as certainly as does any science—geometry, mathematics, physics, or chemistry. Such axioms, or truths assumed without proof or demonstration, are fundamentally dogmatic in character. They are not demonstrated, yet they are fundamental. They are essentially dogmas, whether in the domain of science or philosophy, and they are vital dogmas. Every philosophical system assumes, for example, the validity of human reason. Even Pyrrhonism, while it denies this axiom, is as essentially dogmatic in its denial of this principle, as all other systems are in affirming it. It is no less dogmatic to say "the human mind cannot know anything" than to assert the opposite, for the two positions have in common the idea of knowing, and the fact of something to be known. "Every system of philosophy which accepts the possibility of knowledge has therefore a certain dogmatic character."[1] In this connection Origen observed the necessity of faith in the possibility of knowing and in the validity of human reason, as an essential pre-requisite of any system of philosophy.[3]

So, in a sense, philosophy and theology have a history which presents common, analogous, and parallel features. Philosophical speculation is reflected in theological thought, which in its turn follows a similar course of development. The alternate phases of aprioristic reasoning, empiricism, and materialism have parallels in the history of theological speculation.[4] There is, however, a fundamental difference between the history of Christian dogmatic theology, and that of speculative philosophy.[5]

[1] Rhôsse, op. cit., pp. 44-47.
[2] Ibid., p. 48.
[3] Contra Celsum, 1, 10, 11.
[4] Rhôsse, pp. 50-55. On this topic, cf. Palmieri, op. cit., I, pp. 252-266.
[5] Rhôsse, op. cit., p. 63. (in note) "Christianity was destined to accomplish a much loftier achievement than philosophy . . . both from the religious and ethical, as well as from the intellectual point of view . . The Gospel contained in essence from the beginning . . . everything that was to be developed and formulated from it in time to come . . . without change in its substance" (and cf. p. 64).

Philosophy has changed, abrogated, alternated, and discarded its systems. In each such case there was an evolution, not a development—a creation of a fundamentally and essentially different type, resting on different premises and developing different conclusions. In Christian thought, on the contrary, there was undoubtedly a development, but no evolution, in the sense of the emergence of an essentially different type. While a given philosophical system rests on the dogmas of its founder, it is destroyed when their authority is questioned and denied. The data of Christian theology are the content of the teaching of its Founder, the Incarnate God, and His authority is always accepted and affirmed.[1] Consequently the *development* of Christian theology is a fact, while the *evolution* of its content is an impossibility, for it remains the same "faith once for all delivered to the Saints," once for all claiming the constant allegiance of all true followers of Him.[2]

Faith is the means to the knowledge of the revelation of supernatural truth in Jesus Christ.[3] It is the point of departure for a type and kind of knowledge which would otherwise not be available to man. "Faith comes from hearing and hearing by (through) the word of God."[4] It may be then defined as "the assent of man, generated on the basis of their authenticity, to the truths of the teaching of the Christian Religion, and the Divinity of Christ."[5] It is based on the reasonableness, probability, and validity of these claims, for all the truths of Christianity are founded on the authenticity of God's own word.[6] Faith then has in this respect a totally different foundation from that of human reason. It has an objective and external basis, independent and outside of man himself. Reason leads man outside of himself to appropriate the content of Revelation through faith. Faith will never change into knowledge, for the basis of it always remains something es-

---

[1] Rhôsse, p. 50.
[2] *Ibid.*, p. 54.
[3] *Ibid.*, p. 70.
[4] Rom. 10, 17.
[5] Rhôsse, p. 66, and on knowledge, p. 133.
[6] "Reason is the organ, not the source" of Religious Truth,—Mesolora, *op. cit.*, III. p. 81.

sentially outside the range and origination of human speculation—the authenticity of God's own word.[1]

The Fathers have always asserted this relation of Faith to
knowledge. It is indispensable, for *fides praecedit intellectum
. . . credo ut intelligam,* as St. Augustine says. "Faith
under the influence of reason disposes (lit. "pulls along") the
soul to consent."[2] "Neither faith without reason, nor reason
without faith would be of any value: faith leads reason, and
reason follows faith. . . . It is necessary first to believe,
thereafter to know."[3] Faith is then, in the first instancce,
a means to knowledge. It is essentially a moral and spiritual
matter, not simply an activity of the intellect. It primarily concerns the will, which in turn is induced to choose its path on the
basis of probability. Reason furnishes the motive power whereby
the will accepts and consents to the objective validity of the Revelation given by God, as possessing His authenticity and guarantee. The assent of the will makes a man capable of acquiring
knowledge. Experiment follows this state of the soul, and conviction ensues upon such experiment. "Only through experience
can the soul of man be made receptive for truth."[4] His understanding digests the material made available to his experience.

---

[1] Androutsos, *op. cit.,* pp. 12-13. "Most of the dogmas become accessible to the human reason through different arguments, showing
their plausibility and logical coherence, their practical religious and
ethical value, and their application to our needs. So human reason
was early recognized as a necessary and indispensable help" (*ibid.,*
p. 19). On relation of faith and knowledge in regard to the Being
and Existence of God, cf. *ibid.,* pp. 34-41. But Dyobouniotes says
('Η Δογμ. 'Ανδρ. κριν., pp. 6-7): "Faith must be elevated into knowledge. Thus says Rhôsse in his Dogmatic, thus teach the Holy Scriptures and the Fathers of the Church, and thus demands the logical
constitution of man's mind . . . Man as a logical entity tends from
his nature to lift faith into knowledge, and the denial of this resolution of faith entirely into knowledge is a denial of the logical character
of man."—on Androutsos' answer, cf. his Δογματικαὶ Μελέται, Α', pp. 13-21
and the note at end of this Lecture on "The Relation between Faith and
Knowledge", pp. 46-49.

[2] St. Basil, on Ps. 116, 1.

[3] Theodoret, quoted in Androutsos, *op. cit.,* p. 17; Rhôsse, *op.
cit.,* pp. 70-72, and note.

[4] Rhôsse, *op. cit.,* p. 69.

While faith never changes into knowledge,[1] yet it is the means of knowledge. It is an act of the will inclining toward the acceptance of the divinely guaranteed revelation made by God, and makes possible an ever developing progress in knowledge. It never loses its character of faith, for the foundation of the objective guarantee of God's revelation never serves as a scaffolding for another foundation. It is always essentially a moral and spiritual fact, and never declines to the level of the merely rational. Nevertheless, through it man is so disposed as to be capable of experiences of a more than simply rational order, and the resulting experience brings certainty. Religious certainty is actually, and in practice, an inductive process, as it is inevitably bound up with the experience of the Christian life in the Church.[2] The types of certainty which follow the practice of the Christian religion may be considered under their (a) objective and (b) subjective aspects.

(a) The objective certainty which is generated in the practice of the Christian Religion is a conviction "of Christianity as religious and ethical truth founded upon the authenticity of the Church."[3] It is the reflection of experience and reason on the weight of the evidence of the Church's history, of her claims, of her doctrines as being one with those of her Master, and as the result of this, the redoubled force of these claims in the case of the individual.[4] Furthermore, it is not only as religious and ethical truth that the individual perceives the force of the Church's teaching, but also as power and life. Christianity is not only the Truth, but also dynamic and vital contact with God. The Church is the means of the dissemination of supernatural truth, the gigantic unit transmitting and communicating power, and the living organism begetting life.[5]

(b) In his own life the Christian comes to realize these facts as something not outside himself, but as intimately connected with him. Experience of the Christian life generates the con-

---

[1] Androutsos, *op. cit.*, pp. 12-14 and the controversy between him and Dyobouniotes, particularly Androutsos' response and 'exposition of his position, in Δογματικαὶ Μελέται, A', Athens, 1907, pp. 8-18.

[2] Rhôsse, *op. cit.*, pp. 72-73.

[3] *Ibid.*, p. 73.

[4] *Ibid.*, pp. 74-77.

[5] Rhôsse, *op. cit.*, pp. 78-9.

viction of the truth and living power of Christianity in his own case. It shows the practicability and necessity of all the dogmas of the Church and their application to the needs of his every day experiences.[1] "Spiritual experience" and "personal religion" prove to him the claim of the Church as the means by which they are made available to him. His appropriation of the means of Grace, the teaching of the Church, and the discipline and standards of life she inspires, bring him to a realization of his own sin, his need of redemption, the fact of his redemption in the person of Jesus, and its realization in His Mystical Body, his sanctification through the Church and his gradual appropriation of all the truths of the Faith.[2]

So the objective and subjective experiences of a Christian in the life of the Church develop and strengthen his faith. Realization by experience on the one hand, of the Church as containing and presenting him the truth and the living power of Jesus, and on the other, the knowledge of the Person, work, and teaching of Jesus in His Church, continue to generate a certainty about the Revelation made by God in Christ, which, while it may seem to attain almost the character of knowledge, is yet of faith. It is of the same quality, character, and essence as that by which he set forth on his pilgrimage, but developed, strengthened, and reinforced through experience and knowledge. As such, the faith of "the profound theologian does not differ from that of the simple believer."[3]

(2) In Relation to Dogma

The place of reason in the province of dogma is no less important than it is in the domain of religon. Much of what has been said in the preceding section will apply equally here, if the conception of faith and reason be transferred to the corporate life of the Church instead of being limited to that of the individual. Theologians of the Orthodox Church repudiate the accusation that Orthodox Theology looks with disfavor upon scientific theological research, and upon the theory of the development of doctrine. "We do not repudiate legitimate

[1] *Ibid.*, p. 80.
[2] *Ibid.*, pp. 81-84.
[3] Androutsos, *op. cit.*, p. 13.

scientific development, but on the contrary regard reason as the indispensable organ of acquiring the knowledge of Christian Truth, and of applying it."[1] That the Eastern Church is "static and in a state of torpor" so far as the development of its theology is concerned is an accusation which Androutsos admits as in a certain degree true. This static character does not, however, reflect the true spirit of Orthodoxy and is rather the consequence of external conditions.[2] "No one can dispute the fact that in the history of Dogmas there is a development or progress,"[3] and the fact that this development has gone on throughout the history of the Church, and is discernible in the Orthodox Church since the Schism and after the Reformation, without "the introduction of change or innovations"[4] is a testimony to the vitality and life of the Orthodox Church.[5]

A living thing must develop and grow or else it belies its fundamental character. An essential quality of the Christian message is this capacity for growth. Because it is alive it must needs develop. We find a development in the understanding and in the implications of the Faith even in the New Testament. St. John's *Prologue,* with its developed theology, sets the scheme for his Gospel. St. Paul's appreciation of the significance and bearing of the Sacrifice of the Cross,[6] is a true and legitimate development of the Gospel message. "The inspired writers of the New Testament . . . . offer us the prototype and basis of all subsequent legitimate theological speculation".[7] "There is latent in the Faith itself a certain capacity for the fuller development of its content . . . . so that what is contained in the Bible and Tradition as it were compactly and in general terms, issues (later) in explicit statements."[8] "What is contained in the Bible and Tradition in a vague, undeveloped form, ... is capable of classification and development, by which

[1] Mesolora, Συμβολική, III, p. 80.
[2] *Op. cit.,* p. 16, note.
[3] Rhôsse, *op. cit.,* in note, p. 101.
[4] *Ibid.,* p. 94.
[5] *Ibid.,* p. 93.
[6] Rhôsse, *op. cit.,* p. 91.
[7] Rhôsse, *op. cit.,* p. 91.
[8] Androutsos, *op. cit.,* p. 15; so also Dyobouniotes in 'Οφειλ. ἀπάντ., pp. 154 ff.

the same teaching . . . ., as a whole, is resolved into its several parts, each of which is defined and developed in the Church . . . . and formulated by her in a definite statement."[1] Such false developments as those of the Judaisers and of the Hellenistic schools, departed from the essential character of Christian teaching, and changed the matter of its message. The Church incorporated all that was of value to her from Judaism, the Greek cults, and the mystery religions,[2] but never altered the *matter* but only the *manner* of her message.

The fundamental character of true development consists in this, that the substance of the Faith remain unchanged, while its expression and formulation may be changed with different times and circumstances. "We must distinguish between the kernel, the content of the Faith, and its integument, the form it receives in the more explicit definition of dogmas in the course of time, under the surveillance of the Holy Spirit."[3] The form of the definition of the faith depends upon the state of knowledge of the time. "The more the knowledge of the content of the Faith is rightly developed . . .. the more perfect its expression becomes."[4] There is always then a parallel between the state of theological knowledge and the degree and quality of theological statement: "the more developed theological science is, the more complete and clear will be the formulation of the content of the Faith."[5] Theological science can add nothing to the content of the Faith, but continually derives new truths from it. "There is no question of Revelation fulfilling its foreordained course and, with the passing years, giving way before the advent of new dogmas." There can be no change in content. No new dogmas are enunciated, but the personal appropriation and realization of the truths of the Faith in all their various aspects, naturally results in the more perfect formulation of them by the Church.[6] "The dogmas contained in the Bible and

[1] Rhôsse, p. 92, cf. also pp. 116-118.
[2] *Ibid.*
[3] Androutsos, *op. cit.*, p. 14. cf. Dyobouniotes in 'Οφειλομένη ἀπάντησις, pp. 154-156, quoted in the preface to these Lectures (pp. ix-x, above).
[4] Rhôsse, *op. cit.*, p. 86.
[5] Androutsos, *op. cit.*, p. 14.
[6] *Ibid.*, p. 15.

Tradition....being essentially the same as those developed
in the Church, formulated through her regular channels, and
defined under the guidance of the Holy Spirit, differ from those
only in form or expression."[1]

The Church defines, formulates, and enunciates the dogmas
of the Faith, and her infallibility preserves her from any error
or mistake in the process.[2] In so doing she employs human
reason, operating through the theological speculation and investigation of her children. Her "corporate mind" is the result
of a reflective, analytic, and synthetic intellectual activity.
It is reason actuated by and operating in faith, which is always the foundation of theological knowledge.[3] As St. John
Chrysostom said: "through faith, knowledge; no knowledge
without faith."[4] "The more we believe, the more we seek to
understand both the cause and the reason for its coming to
pass."[5] "Human reason operating in faith is . . . . the organ,
but not the source, nor alone the safe criterion, of religious
truths."[6] "It is the means to the formulation of the content
of the Faith."[7] If it be objected that "the so-called knowledge
built on faith....has no validity, weight, or worth", it may be
answered that faith is the one means to make the experience
possible by which alone the data of Christianity become accessible.[8] Others object to this relationship of faith and dogma, by saying, "if faith be all important, then knowledge is
superfluous." "The knowledge of the inner truth of Christianity comes through reason scientifically applied....and it
is not only not superfluous but most essential" to this end.[9]
It is an all important adjunct in receiving and appropriating
the truths of the Faith.[10] Furthermore, it refutes wrong con-

---

[1] Rhôsse, pp. 60-61, p. 93.

[2] "Infallibility" then does not mean "inspiration", Androutsos,
op. cit., p. 14.

[3] Mesolora, III, p. 80, and cf. p. 79, and Clem. Alex., Strom.,
there quoted.

[4] On Philippians, in Migne, XI, p. 265 b.

[5] Quoted by Mesolora, op. cit., III, p. 80.

[6] Ibid., p. 81, and cf. Androutsos, op. cit., pp. 13-14.

[7] Rhôsse, op. cit., pp. 86-87.

[8] Rhôsse, p. 88.

[9] Ibid., p. 89.

[10] Mesolora, 111, p. 81.

ceptions of the Faith, and fills in the gaps in the dogmatic system, by attempting a more thorough articulation of its members. Theological knowledge "is not repugnant to dogmas which are authentic....but completes, clarifies, and develops them."[1] Reason is then the organ for the formulation of the doctrines of the Faith. The occasion of such formulation is in many cases the rise of heresies which prompt "the Church to go more deeply into the truths of the Faith and enunciate them in more explicit terms, in a way which allows neither of doubt nor of misinterpretation."[2]

As we saw above, every true Revelation has three characteristics: a dynamic and creative character, the quality of consistency with itself and with the whole body of revealed truths, and the note of progressive development. Revelation, then, is contingent upon the development and capacity of mankind. What was said applied more properly to the Revelation made by God in the Old Testament, yet may be most clearly illustrated from the New. Our Lord is the final Revelation of God to man. Yet if His Coming were prepared for by a gradual and careful process, a progressive development of the capacity of humanity to receive this final Revelation, we should expect that the full significance and bearing of His Life, Work, and Teaching should not be realized in the short span of one human life. All the implications, consequents, and the full meaning of the teaching of the God-Man were to be apprehended and appropriated by successive generations of His followers, bound to Him in His Church. The appropriation and realization of the fuller significance of the Faith by means of human reason[3] is the work of every generation of believers. An in-

---

[1] Rhôsse, pp. 90-91; Androutsos, pp. 13-14, cf. his definition: "Dogmas as the expression and formulations of the Faith are constituted through the action of the mind, distinguishing the identical and essential (and putting them) into brief statements, which include the important content of the Faith and protect it from all false views and adulteration".

[2] Androutsos, *op. cit.*, p. 15.

[3] Androutsos, *op. cit.*, pp. 16-17. On the relation of faith to theological knowledge, cf. 1 Cor. 2, 8; 2 Cor. 8, 9; St. John 7, 18; 2, 32; 14, 20-31; 2 St. John 1.

finite message cannot be comprehended in all its bearings and aspects in any single generation. Rather do successive generations work gradually towards the full appreciation of the Revelation made in Jesus Christ, and while they develop by faith and reason the implications of that teaching, they never exhaust the infinite and many-sided aspects of its content. It remains ever the same infinite and final Revelation. Mankind but grows in the appreciation of its meaning. As the Church grows more fully cognizant of its content, she expresses her mind; growing in appreciation of her priceless heritage, she developes and formulates more exactly the implications and bearings of the same Faith she received from the Incarnate Son of God.

Dogma develops and changes its form with the successive generations of the Faithful, as they grow in appreciation of the meaning of their faith and express this realization and apprehension in new formulations. Such a development of dogma, inevitable[1] where there is true theological and spiritual life, is a testimony both to the vitality of the Church and to that of its faith. Dogmatic development means the more definite and concrete exposition of the content of Christian teaching. It is not an evolution,[2] a change in substance. Nor is it a development by accretion, or the addition to the original deposit of alien and foreign elements. The test of a right development is the Vincentian formula[3], *quod semper, quod ubique et quod ab omnibus creditum est.* It is St. Vincent himself who first explicitly treats of the phenomena of genuine "development" (*profectus*—πρόοδος), as opposed to evolution, or "change" (*permutatio*—μεταβολή).[4] He uses the figure of growth to illustrate his conception of right development. A boy does not change his identity when he becomes a man. As a human life develops and grows so does the Church: *sed in suo dumtaxat genere, in eodum scilicet dogmate, eodem sensu,*

---

[1] Cf. Dyobouniotes, in 'Οφειλομένη ἀπάντησις, pp. 154-156.
[2] Androutsos, *op. cit.*, p. 15; Rhôsse, *op. cit.*, p. 93 *et al.* .. .. ..
[3] St. Vincent of Lerins, *Commonitorium*, 2.
[4] *Ibid.*, c. 23; cf. St. Irenaeus, *adv. Haer*, 1, 10, 2-3; St. Greg. Naz., *Discourse against Julian*, 1, 100; Rhôsse, *op. cit.*, pp. 97 ff.; Androutsos, *op. cit.*, pp. 15-16.

eademque sententia. A child growing into a man does not add new members to his body,—*quot parvulovum artus, tot virorum; eadem ipsa sunt tamen.* His advice to Timothy summarizes his conception of dogmatic development, *ut cum dicas nove, non dicas nova.*[1]

The position of Greek theology on the subject of the development of doctrine may best be made clear by distinguishing it from the views of Rationalists, Protestants, and Roman Catholics. "Rationalists" regard dogmatic development as evolution, and the several dogmas in their formulated character as having a certain intrinsic worth or validity, but only in each instance as examples of a (claimed) spiritual knowledge[2] historically interesting, and as illustrations of the conceptions developed by certain Christian thinkers. Liberal Protestant scholarship tends to discover a change in intrinsic character and essential content in the course of the Church's dogmatic development. Harnack regards the formulation of Christian dogma as the consequence of the action of the Hellenic spirit in the Church.[3] He finds an antithesis between the Gospel and dogma, for the latter imported an alien and foreign element from Greek philosophy.[4] Dogmatic development is for him not a change in form but a change in the content of Christian teaching. He, and, in common with him, the scholars of the Tübingen school, proceeded on certain premises or theories, according to which they include in their evidence not only the teachings of Orthodox Christianity, but those of all the sects. So Harnack regards Ebionism as being nearest to Gospel Christianity.[5] While the representatives of the German School acknowledge the element of development in the history of Christian dogma, they make two mistakes: they attempt to seek order in chaos without assuming any point of view from which to orientate themselves in relation to the evidence,[6] and in consequence of this, they attempt

[1] C. 22, 23, quoted by Rhôsse, p. 98; cf. p. 54. n. 2, of this Lecture.

[2] Androutsos, p. 16; Rhôsse, p. 107, note.

[3] *Dogmengeschichte*, 3d ed. 1894, 1, p. 12, pp. 16-18.

[4] *D.G.* 3, 1, p. 18 and p. 22, note 1: "Dogma in its conception and formulation is the work of the Greek spirit."

[5] Rhôsse, *op. cit.*, pp. 98-99 (note).

[6] *Ibid.*, p. 101 (note).

to discover the central and essential teaching of Christianity
by analyzing the data till they discover the common teachings
of all bodies calling themselves Christian.[1] Such is the case,
for example, in Dorner's *Dogmatik,* and the author is driven
to regard this central idea of Christianity as being subject
not only to change in form, but more or less in essence also.[2]
Since dogmas are a result purely of the human effort to intel-
lectualize the teaching of Christianity, they have no permanent value.[3]

In answer to Harnack, who speaks of the superstructure of
Christian dogma being built "on the ground of the Gospel",[4]
Rhôsse claims that the phrase is absolutely misleading. Christianity is not built up as an edifice on the foundation of a Book,
but it has, on the contrary, used a totally different figure; it
has always regarded the Gospel as the germ or bud in which
Christian doctrine is contained, awaiting full development
and growth.[5] Harnack's figure is unhappy, as it bespeaks a
mechanistic instead of a biological conception of the life of
Christianity. Furthermore, it is so loosely employed in different connections[6] as to empty it of real value. Biological meta-
phor is the most appropriate vehicle to describe a vital process.
A mechanical figure is one which proceeds on the premise that
the subject which it is used to describe is not living, but dead—
not organic, but mechanical. So the Liberal School reads the
history of Christianity as a succession of phases, a continuous
series of acts and deeds and thoughts having no essential organic
relationship one with the other, and not being the various manifestations of a single stream of vital and living truth. "The
denial of the legitimacy and truth (of dogmatic formulations)
proceeds from the philosophical and theoretical preconceptions
and presuppositions of Harnack and the theological school of
Ritschl, to which he belongs;....from these results a denial

[1] Pp. 103-4 (note.
[2] *Ibid.,* p. 107, (note).
[3] *Ibid.,* p. 108, (note) and p. 112.
[4] *D.G.* 3, 1, p. 18, note 1, p. 22.
[5] Rhôsse, *op. cit.,* p. 62, note.
[6] Cf. *D.G.* 3, 1, pp. 18, 22 (note), 46, 50, etc.

of all true development and progress in history, and most of all in the history of dogmas."[1]

As instances of false development, Rhôsse gives: the addition of the *Filioque* clause to the ancient Nicene-Constantinopolitan creed, the change in the essential character of baptism as practised in the Roman Church, and the utterly arbitrary and unhistorical dogma of Papal Infallibility.[2] "While the Western theologians in theory have never taught that the Church is justified in creating new dogmas, yet in practice they regard tradition as a *depositum fidei* from which they bring forth new dogmas, manipulating them arbitrarily, and apparently not concerned whether or not they are founded on Holy Scripture and Tradition."[3] The Roman Church, while holding a proper theory of development,[4] still "remodels"[5] and "manipulates" the material at her disposal, to issue new and novel teachings, which, not having the authority of the true sources of dogmatic, are without validity, void, and instances of vicious and false development of doctrine. In fact, the false development of doctrine in the Roman Church, which in reality is a change in the substance of dogmatic content, does not proceed from true theological insight and speculation, and is not founded upon the Bible and Tradition. It is arbitrary and self-

---

[1] Rhôsse, *op. cit.*, p. 63. In regard to the position of conservative Protestantism in relation to the Development of Doctrine, Androutsos says: "Protestants, dating from the 16th century and splitting away from the Church, are incapable of having the Faith which was taught throughout the years, for they deny in principle the equal validity of Tradition as a source of Christian Truth, and reject the Church as supreme interpreter of Holy Scripture." They attempted to restore the ancient *form* of Christianity, and inevitably lost contact with its *matter*, (*op. cit.*, p. 16).

[2] Rhôsse, *op. cit.*, pp. 95-96, Mesolora, *op. cit.*, IV, pp. 17-56; Ambraze, Ἡ Ὀρθόδοξος Ἐκκλησία, pp. 19-57; Anastasius, *On the Unity of the Churches*, gives a list of other departures of Rome from true biblical teaching and traditional doctrine and practice.

[3] Androutsos, *op. cit.*, p. 16.

[4] Cf. Newman's *Essay on the Development of Doctrine*, chapter I, and V; discussion of "profectus" or "progressus secundum quid" in Tanqueray, Wilhelm and Scannell, and other standard works of Roman Catholic theology.

[5] Androutsos, *op. cit.*, note, p. 16.

willed, and is on a par with other rationalistic systems.[1] It
follows, then, that the only ecclesiastical system which qualifies
according to the test of the Vincentian canon, is that of the
Orthodox Church, which alone has kept the true Tradition,
and the full teaching of the Holy Scriptures. It alone has formulated them according to the true standard of legitimate doctrinal development.[2]

Reason is, then, the organ for the formulation of Christian
doctrine, as well as the means of its appropriation and realization by the mind both of the individual and the Church. It
has a third function. It is preëminently useful in the vindication of Christian truth from attack. Its function is primarily negative, in that reason can never demonstrate the necessity of the dogmas of the Faith,—either theoretically, logically,
or practically. They are beyond the compass of the intellect,
as they are supernaturally revealed. No matter how far legitimate theological speculation may be developed, the dogmas of
the Faith "always bear their mysterious character" in this life.
Many futile attempts have been made to put the dogmas on a
rational basis, so that they may seem to be inevitable and necessary. Such attempts have never succeeded, nor can they succeed. "Even though the dogmas (of the Faith) cannot be
shown to be inevitable and of binding obligation logically upon
all rational human beings, yet they may be demonstrated as
possible and probable."[3] Reason can show that it is not inconsistent either with science or philosophy to be a devout
Christian. "Christian truths issue from supernatural Revelation, and exceed man's comprehension, yet at the same time
they are not antagonistic to human reason.... While reason can
never show dogmas as necessary and of universal obligation....
it can demonstrate that they are consonant with rational thought;
....nor can Unbelief show them to be impossible, by substitut-

---

[1] Rhôsse, op. cit., p. 96.
[2] Ibid., pp. 102-104, and p. 491. "Die Orientalische Kirke be-
streitet die Continuität der Tradition in der römischen Kirche nach
dem Schisma",—note 1, in Bericht (Reusch) for 1874, p. 34; cf. also
pp. 24, 56, 101, ibid., and the Letter of Timothy Anastasios On the
Union of the Churches, Περὶ τῆς ἐνώσεως τῶν Ἐκκλησιῶν, to Max, Prince
of Saxony, Athens, 1910.
[3] Androutsos, op. cit., p. 18.

ing for the teachings of the Faith something of human origin only, Unbelief cannot claim such substitutes as probable, or logically necessary, much as it may reject the dogmas of the Faith as not obligatory, and logically contingent."[1]

The three functions of reason in relation to dogma are then, (a) that it is the organ for the formulation of dogma, (b) the means for the realization and appropriation of Christian Truth by the individual and the Church, and (c) the protagonist for dogma, defending it from assault, and vindicating it in the face of hostile, insidious, and subversive attacks.

(A) ADDITIONAL NOTE ON

THE RELATION BETWEEN FAITH AND KNOWLEDGE

The three writers, Androutsos, Rhôsse, and Dyobouniotes, all seem to disagree on the relation of faith and knowledge. Mesolora does not deal directly with this problem, but by indicating the necessity of the moral element in theological knowledge[2] implies that all knowledge of God is only by faith. Reason is the means for formulating and developing what faith has accepted, and is the organ, not the source, of the knowledge of God.[3] The will is necessary to enable man to find God: one may look and not see. Those who do not wish to find Him do not find Him.[4] Faith, as such, depends on the will. If it were demonstrably and probably certain that its postulates were true, there would be no faith. So we may say that Mesolora distinguishes faith—that it, acceptance on authority of what is

---

[1] *Ibid.*, p. 19. But Rhôsse says: "From faith based on the authenticity of the Church's claims to authority, and using religious certitude as a means.....through practical and experimental relation with Christianity, we can obtain *scientific certainty* about it (*i. e.* the Faith), through the definition and classification of the content of the Faith, and knowledge of its inner truth, its reasonableness, and its necessity" (pp. 85-6, italics mine). "Religious certainty becomes *scientific certainty*", "by the discovery of the reason of faith, and by the resolution of the phenomena of the world. . . .into their ultimate cause in the demonstrations of the existence of God." (*ibid.*, p. 132) Religious certainty therefore is a means for achieving scientific certainty—*ibid.*

[2] Mesolora, Συμβολική, 111, p. 79.

[3] *Ibid.*, p. 81.

[4] *Ibid.*, p. 91.

revealed—from knowledge—the action of the mind in apprehending and formulating the content of what is believed. He does not attempt to grapple with the problem as to the possibility of faith being transformed into knowledge in this life.

Androutsos' two propositions (a) that dogmatic truths are founded on the Divine authenticity and are not based on human reason, and (b) that reason is the means for the formulation, appropriation, and negative vindication of them, involve his conclusion that faith and knowledge always remain two distinct and different things.[1] The theologian believes in the same way as the simple, uneducated Christian; he may know more about what he believes and may more thoroughly grasp his belief in its rational and philosophical bearings, but still the knowledge he has of it is not a sublimated faith. He is still fundamentally certain of what he holds on the same basis as the simple peasant, and the basis of his faith is the authenticity of God's own word. His reason may show him the probability of what he holds by faith, and it may justify and vindicate that faith against hostile attack,[2] but it will still be *reason* justifying *faith,* not presenting scientific demonstration of a compelling, universal, and scientific character.

Dyobouniotes, in his "Criticism" of Androutsos, work ('H Δογματική τοῦ κ. Ανδρούτσου κρινομένη) attacks this view and maintains[3] that it is inevitable that man as a rational being should have his faith lifted up into knowledge, the denial of which "change of faith to knowledge, is a denial of the rational constitution of man". This he develops at considerable length (some twelve pages) in his "Needed Answer" ('Οφειλομένη ἀπάντησις) to Androutsos' response (Δογματικαί Μελέται Α') to his criticism.[4] The Church, he says, is the divinely guided teacher who leads the individual to the knowledge of God. One

---

[1] Androutsos, *op. cit.,* pp. 12-13. So also Kephala, Χριστολογία, p. 46: "Faith is the means for the knowledge of truth;" cf. pp. 38-99, on Faith as "Illumination."

[2] Androutsos, *op. cit.,* pp. 18-20.

[3] Dyobouniotes, 'H Δογμ. 'Ανδρ. κριν., pp. 5-6.

[4] First came Androutsos' "Dogmatic," then Dyobouniotes' "Criticism" (68 pp.) followed by Androutsos' rejoinder entitled "Dogmatic Studies, 1" (148 pp.), which elicited a response of 160 pages from Dyobouniotes, to be followed by a second rejoinder of Androutsos ("Dogmatic Studies, 2").

believes on the basis of external authority, the authority of God, the Guardian of the Church. By means of her "the individual may raise his faith into knowledge—the conviction based upon external authenticity into that founded as well upon internal witness and experience."[1] He distinguishes the faith of the simple believer, whose assurance is only that of the external order, from that of the advanced theologian, whose conviction is grounded as well on certainty of an interior and personal kind. It is a difficult and baffling adventure but one well worth persisting in, and the conditions of the quest involve moral elements: "a corrupt man may become a good scientist, but a good theologian, never."[2] The change from faith to knowledge comes by the effecting of the transition from the certainty based on external authority to that based as well on internal experience. The resultant knowledge is not complete, yet it is knowledge. Faith furnishes the means for making the experiment, the result of which is knowledge. Just as we admit scientific conclusions even when the necessity of the various steps of the experiment is not demonstrable in advance, so we are scientifically justified in admitting the conclusions of religious knowledge. That these are open to question and dispute is not surprising, since many of the conclusions of science have been and still are so regarded.[3]

This whole position Androutsos vigorously combats[4] saying that reason never furnishes the content of religious knowledge. It is never the organ for the knowledge of religious truth. Faith which furnishes this content depends on reason for its assimilation. The two go on together side by side. As man develops in faith so his knowledge grows, "The element of knowledge, which is always present in faith, is developed into a further knowledge along with (the development of) faith. It is not that in this development....faith is left behind; on the contrary, the reason the simple believer and the profound theologian alike accept the truths of the faith, remains always the same—the Divine authenticity."[5] He maintains that faith

[1] 'Οφειλομένη ἀπάντησις, p. 2.
[2] *Ibid.*, p. 4.
[3] 'Οφειλομένη ἀπάντησις, Dyobouniotes, pp. 7-8.
[4] Cf. his Δογματικαὶ Μελέται, A', pp. 8-18.
[5] *Ibid.*, p. 11.

never becomes anything else and never loses its character, consequently cannot become knowledge.

Androutsos'[1] reply impugns Dyobouniotes' claim[2] that his
view is founded on Rhôsse, for Androutsos says Rhôsse does not
says what Dyobouniotes says he says. Rhôsse[3] distinguishes
immediate or religious *certainty,* based on the authority of the
Church, from mediate or scientific certainty, based on experiment and reasoned conclusions. Faith is the basis and point
or departure for knowledge.[4] From "religious certainty" we can
come to personal assurance and conviction based on practical
and vital contact with Christianity, and thus to "scientific certainty".[5] As a result of this process of appropriation and
realization of the faith in the case of the individual, religious
certainty becomes scientific certainty.[6]

The solution of these divergent views would have been facili-
tated if each or any had defined his terms. It is true, *faith* was
defined by Rhôsse,[7] as the assent of man, grounded on its divine authentication, to the truths of the Christian religion, and
knowledge, as the content of what we know about God through
faith and reason reflecting on and speculating about what this
faith tells us.[8] According to Androutsos, faith is a more or
less automatic and convulsive grasp after God which really lays
hold of Him, and it constitutes the consciousness of God's Presence in the natural and rational world.[9] "Scientific knowledge"
is of such a character, both as to method, as to the nature of
the material it deals with, and as to the kind of proof it demands, that it is utterly impossible in relation to God.[10] Consequently, we cannot say we can possibly have any "scientific
knowledge" of Him. To summarize and compare the above
theologians, it may be said that Rhôsse does not discuss the

[1] *Ibid.,* p. 17.
[2] 'Η Δογμ. 'Ανδρ. κριν., pp. 5-6.
[3] Δογματική, p. 65.
[4] Δογματική, p. 70.
[5] Rhôsse, *op. cit.,* pp. 85-86.
[6] *Ibid.,* p. 312.
[7] *Ibid.,* p. 66.
[8] *Ibid.,* p. 132.
[9] Androutsos, Δογματική, p. 37.
[10] *Ibid.,* p. 35.

problem of the relation of faith to knowledge in the sense Dyobouniotes uses these words. "Certainty" does not mean "knowledge". Rhôsse says religious "certainty" may become scientific "certainty," which means simply that, in his view, the evidence for the truth of the complex which we call the "Faith" is sufficiently complete—as a cumulative nexus of argument, faith, experience, and reason—to justify the conviction which a believer holds. Dyobouniotes means by "faith", acceptance and assent on authority; when such assent is tested and vindicated by experience, he calls the content of that which is realized by personal or religious experience, "knowledge". (It may be noted that conviction is conviction, and is the same in quality whatever be its reason, authority, or basis.) Since Androutsos means by "knowledge" a scientific, adequate, exhaustive acquaintance with all the phenomena together with a consistent theory of the whole, which has universal application and can próve itself and demand consent from all rational creations, it is obvious that such can never be said of our knowledge of God; nor does what we come to know about Him through faith, dispense with faith as a means; nor do we ever cease to *know about* Him and come to *know Him*. The four theologians really agree in these fundamental theses: that through faith man can know God; faith based on a claim which is regarded as valid and authentic generates conviction, which is deepened and developed by experience; experience does not ever dispense with faith as this necessary means of coming to know God; our knowledge is not of the same quality as that we have of mathematics, or of physics, or any other science, though our conviction of the truth of any of these may be equally strong, and identical in its nature.

(B)   ADDITIONAL NOTE ON

THE RELATION OF DOGMATIC TO THE OTHER THEOLOGICAL DISCIPLINES

Dogmatic is the center of all the theological disciplines.[1] These may be divided into two categories, theoretical and practical, each of which is in turn further subdivided.   Since the sources of *dogmatic* are the Bible and Tradition, *dogmatic* has an intimate relationship to *Bible study, exegesis, interpretation,* and *biblical theology.*   Biblical scholarship assists in ascertaining the true text and its interpretation in the light of the original meaning and content.   *Biblical theology* presents in mass the results of detailed study of the content of Holy Scripture, and is, in consequence, of the utmost importance to *dogmatic.* For Tradition, *dogmatic* uses both the *history of the Church* and the *history of dogmas.*   *Symbolic* summarizes and arranges the results of the study of Church history and the history of doctrine, codifying the decrees of the councils, the creeds, and the confessions of faith in systematic and historical order.   The relation of *dogmatic* to the practical branches of theological discipline is even more intimate.   The principle, *lex orandi, lex credendi,* establishes the close connection of *dogmatic with liturgics.*   As the content of the Faith is supernatural revelation both in relation to dogma and ethics, *ethics* draws upon *dogmatic* for its sources.[2]   The natural for *homiletics* is supplied from *dogmatic,* and all the branches of practical theology are directly dependent upon it.   The premises of *dogmatic* are demonstrated as reasonable and acceptable to man's rational nature, by *apologetic,* while *polemic* and *controversy* are concerned with wrong conceptions of the Faith and attacks upon the Orthodox doctrines.

---

[1] Androutsos, *op. cit.*, p. 20.   On this topic, cf. *ibid.*, § 6. of his Introduction; Rhôsse, *op. cit.*, pp. 23-25, note, pp. 24, 29-36, 114-124.

[2] The Orthodox Catechism is divided into two parts, "dogmatic" and "ethic", cf. *e. g.*, that of Balanos (Athens 1920).

(C) ADDITIONAL NOTE
PALMIERI ON THE ORTHODOX VIEW OF THE DEVELOPMENT OF DOCTRINE

Conspicuous, unique, and outstanding as is the historical work[1] of the Augustinian, Aurelio Palmieri, among scholars who have concerned themselves with matters Orthodox, there is no single writer to whom we are more indebted for both achieved and promised studies in Orthodox theology. His monographs on the tangled and difficult problem of the *Filioque*[2] controversy constitute perhaps the most valuable recent contributions to the subject. Few men know the Russian Church as he does, and his work on it,[3] always sympathetic, understanding, and thorough, is as Kattenbusch says *ein recht unparteiisches Bild.*[4] This text is an extraordinarily valuable contribution, frank and relentlessly honest in aim and method, profound in its intimate knowledge of the subject matter, and particularly significant at this time for the final chapter on the problem of reunion between the Slavs and the Roman See. The approbation it received in many quarters is as eloquent a testimony to its value as is the bitter opposition it elicited from certain "Panpoles",[5] who are very caustic in their criticism of it.

For our purposes, however, two other works, his Digest of Orthodox Theology,[6] of which only two volumes, of Prolegomena, have appeared, and his essay on Doctrinal Development[7] in

[1] *E. g.*, his *Dositeo, patriarca greco di Gerusalemme, contributo alla storia della teologia nel secolo* XVII, pp. 1-130, Florence, 1909.

[2] *La consustanzialità divina e la processione dello Spirito Santo*, Rome, 1900; *La missione delle divine persone e la processione dello Spirito Santo*, Rome, 1900; *L'argomento ontologico del Filioque e le obbiezioni di un teologo Russo*, Rome, 1902.

[3] *La Chiesa Russa, le sue odierne condizioni e il suo riformismo dottrinale*, Florence, 1908, pp. XV.—759.

[4] *Theologische Rundschau*, XIII. 1910, pp. 103-110.

[5] *E. g.*, Count A. Mohl, cf. criticism in *Potwarz czy nieporozumienie*, Warsaw, 1900; De Töth in *Unità Cattolica*, and *Le armonie della Fide*, IV. 1910, pp. 340-365.

[6] *Theologia Dogmatica Orthodoxa (Ecclesiae Graeco-Russicae) ad lumen Catholicae Doctrinae examinata et discussa; Prolegomena*, vol. I. Florence 1911, pp. XXV—815; vol. II. Florence 1913, pp. 1-198.

[7] *Il Progresso Dommatico nel Concetto Cattolico* (No. 1 in the *Biblioteca di Apologia Cristiana*) Florence, 1910, pp. XX—303.

Roman and Orthodox thought, are of fundamental importance. The former is undoubtedly his *magnum opus*; it has the same breadth of view, exhaustiveness of treatment, sympathy, and comprehension as his earlier works, and is animated by the best spirit of honesty and fairness, seeking always to find grounds of agreement rather than points of difference between the Orthodox and Roman teaching. It treats of the ground work of Orthodox Dogmatic, definitions, method, sources, polemic, the Roman controversy, and prospects of reunion. No other book known to the writer presents so thorough and exhaustive a bibliography, nor so full and clear an exposition of the subject matter. Of particular interest to the writer is the conception of the development of doctrine, to which Palmieri devotes the third chapter[1] of volume 1 of his *Theologia Dogmatica,* and the whole of the Italian essay on the same subject. He refutes the four types of false theories of development, presents in brief the Roman contention, and lastly the Orthodox position, with especial reference to the Roman views. It is to be noted that he works to the same conclusion as does Newman in his epoch making essay,[2] that the Roman Pontiff is the center of unity, the organ for enunciating the developed doctrine, as well as the means for guiding, checking, and directing this development. Palmieri sums up his argument in the words "development of doctrine demands for its actualization in fact a principle of visible authority," and shows to his own satisfaction, the indirect argument for this conclusion from the absence of any organ of unity and definition, infallibly functioning within its own proper scope, in Orthodoxy.[3] The three theses which embody the Roman view of the development of doctrine may be summarized as follows: (a) that development in the content of Revelation which characterized God's method of dealing with men before our Lord's Incarnation, (b) gave way to the final and complete Revelation in Him, which allows of no further development in

[1] Pp. 31-88.

[2] "On the Development of Doctrine." From the Anglican and Orthodox point of view both arguments are subject to the same strictures —cf. *e. g., The Development of English Theology in the Nineteenth Century,* V. F. Storr, Longmans, 1913, pp. VIII—486. Chapter XVI. pp. 294-316 treats of this work of Newman.

[3] *Progresso Dommatico,* pp. 127-130.

substance. (c) Nevertheless a relative development (*progressus secundum quid*) in accordance with St. Anselm's phrase: *profectus fidelis in fide potiusquam fidei in fideli,* is both possible necessary, and demonstrably a fact.[1]

Palmieri treats of various Orthodox theologians' views of the matter, and sums up his conclusions as follows:[2] "(1) Generally speaking, Orthodox Theology holds and teaches the theory of relative development of doctrine. . . . (2) This they deny in practice, while refusing to acknowledge they do so, and this denial comes about . . . . by reason of the inherent defect of Orthodoxy in . . . . lacking the authority of the supreme *magisterium.* (3) In certain individual instances hatred of Catholicism. . . .has brought out a denial of development in any sense of the word. (4) Because of the contradiction which maintains between theory and fact, which involves the denial in practice of what is acknowledged in theory, Catholic doctrine is subject to slander and misrepresentation." As indicating the appreciation of Orthodox theologians of the theory of development of doctrine, Palmieri adduces Macarius, Malinovsky, Chostin, Solovev,[3] Silvester of Kanev,[4] Sokolov,[5] the Patriarchs' letter to the Synod of Petrograd (1723)[6] and both Rhôsse and Androutsos,[7] whose views were developed in the body of Lecture 1. His conclusion is as follows: "We can certainly say that theoretically the teaching of Orthodox Greek and Russian theology is fully in line with Catholic doctrine: (a) Orthodox theology maintains that the Christian Revelation is completed and closed with the preaching of our Lord and the Apostles. (b) It contends that there are no dogmas of the Faith not contained in Holy Scripture and Tradition. (c) Since the truths of the Faith are not a buried treasure, it is necessary to concede a relative doctrinal development, (d) which

[1] *Theol. Dogm. Orth.* vol. I. pp. 37-54.
[2] *Ibid.,* p. 56.
[3] *Theol. Dogm. Orth.* vol. I. pp. 56-61, cf. also on Macarius and Malinovsky, *Prog. Dom.* pp. 81 ff.
[4] *Progresso Dom.* pp. 67-76.
[5] *Ibid.,* pp. 76-81.
[6] *Ibid.,* pp. 84-85, which, however, *esponse la dottrina ortodossa dell' immobilità dei dommi.*
[7] *Ibid.,* pp. 85-87.

progressive development is a corollary to the indefectible and
perfect life of the Church. . . . So it is evident that Catholic
and Orthodox theology are in theory in perfect accord on the
subject of doctrinal development."[1]

This theoretical agreement is of very great value, for it
means the possibility of envisaging the great issues and problems
in the same idiom of thought. The importance of this fact can
hardly be over emphasized. There is no more vital conception in modern day thinking than this idea of growth and development. It is the fundamental thesis of the historico-critical
school that human thought and the history of ideas is a kind of
unified organic whole. The rationalist would find difficulty in
postulating in the concrete the existence of the central unity
and identity of life under the various forms of Catholic thought;
he would, as Harnack does so often, see rather the episode as a
unit in itself, and apart from the whole stream of which it
forms a part, rather than as an integral element in a larger
stream of vital thought. But so far as concerns Catholic Christianity, the conception of the development of doctrine is central;
its adoption is no new thing to which modern Apologetic has
had recourse, for it has prevailed in varying degrees of explicit
and articulate formulation from St. Vincent[2] till to-day. I re-
peat, the very great value of this fact can hardly be exaggerated;
Anglo-Catholic, Roman Catholic, and Orthodox agree fundamentally in the way all three conceive of the history of Revelation, and the progress of Christian doctrine.

It is beside my point to present Palmieri's conclusions in detail. He argues on the basis of the theoretical agreement of
Roman and Orthodox theology on the matter of doctrinal development, for the need of an organ of articulation and formulation now and in these days; namely, he contends that Ortho-

[1] *Progresso Dommatico*, pp. 87-90; *Theol. Dogm. Orth.* vol. I, pp.
60-63.

[2] St. Vincent of Lerins enjoys quite as high a position among Orthodox as among Western theologians. Cf. Anthimus VII, *Encyclical*, p.
18, No. 24: σοφῶς καὶ ὀρθοδόξως χαρακτηρίζει τὴν ἀληθῆ τῆς πίστεως καὶ
τῆς Ἐκκλησίας καθολικότητα; cf. Sylvester, Filevsky, Janychev, Bieliaev,
in *Theol. Dogm. Ortho.* vol. I. pp. 81-82; and especially Chapter VII.,
"Il Canone di Vicenzo Lirinese e il progresso dommatico" in *Progresso
Dommatico*, pp. 255-274.

doxy needs the Roman Pontiff as a legitimate consequence and application of her very principles of theological thought. He attempts to prove the breaking down of the Orthodox principle in the concrete. In practice, he says, the Orthodox Church cannot do for Orthodoxy what she claims to; claiming to have as the organ of her explicit utterance the agreement of her Bishops and Councils,[1] she has conspicuously failed in using the means of expressing her mind. Contradictory decrees-and the necessity of subsequently revising and abrogating decisions of local synods[2] have made necessary the denial of any legislative or authoritative power in matters of faith to local councils.[3] So he concludes:*progressus igitur dogmaticus secundum \quid per synodos particulares non exstitit in Ecclesiis orientalibus, ac, docente experientia, neque in posterum dabitur.*[4] Equally futile, he argues, is the attempt to lodge this power of defining and promulgating the more explicitly defined teaching of the Church in the Patriarch of Constantinople, with the free agreement with him of the autocephalous Churches.[5] Hence, reasoning by a kind of method of elimination, Palmieri focuses his argument in the conclusion that the Orthodox Church needs the Roman See, according to its own principles, and according to the facts of history.[6] With his conclusions neither Orthodox nor Anglican can agree, but for his spirit, his zeal, his honesty, and the brilliance of his achievement, in clearly showing this essential unity of conception, we may all thank him and give him honor.

---

[1] Macarius, quoted in *Theol. Dogm. Orth.* vol I. pp. 63-64.

[2] *E. g.*, the Council of Moscow in 1620 decreed that Latins were to be rebaptized, and 36 and 47 years later the decision was completely reversed; cf. *op. cit.*, pp. 65-66, notes *ad. loc.* In 1660 a council at Moscow decreed that God had put His Church in the power of the Czar!

[3] Cf. Pavlov, *op. cit.*, p. 64, and A. Christodoulos, in his Δοκίμιον Ἐκκλησιαστικοῦ Δικαίου, Constantinople, 1896, p. 50:

Αἱ τοπικαὶ σύνοδοι πάντοτε ἔφερον χαρακτῆρα συμβουλευτικῶν μόνον σωματείων, αἱ ἀποφάσεις αὐτῶν, ἔχουσαι σημασίαν χειραγωγικῶν ἀρχῶν διὰ τοὺς παρευρισκομένους ἐπισκόπους δὲν ἦσαν νόμοι ἐν τῇ ἐννοίᾳ ἐκείνῃ ὁποίαν ἔλαβον αἱ ἀποφάσεις τῶν οἰκουμενικῶν συνόδων.

[4] *Op. cit.*, p. 67.

[5] *Ibid.*, p. 68.

[6] *Prog. Dom.* pp. 172 ff.

LECTURE II.
THE DOCTRINE OF GOD

LECTURE II.

THE DOCTRINE OF GOD

Contents

1. GOD AS OBJECT TO KNOWLEDGE

The subject matter of dogmatic theology is God—as He is, and as He works.[1] From the fact of His existence and His nature we go on to consider His acts in eternity and in time; so the starting point of all dogmatic theology is the Existence and Being of God. Logically we may distinguish between God's existence, *that* He is—the fact of His being—and His "Being" or "Nature", *what* He is. The words *essence, nature, character,* all belong to this second category. While we may logically distinguish "Existence" and "Being", yet the Existence of God is inseparable from His Being, "since every concrete conception of His existence is united with these or those qualities."[2] While the scholastics have claimed that His existence may be proved clearly and evidently, though the conception of God may be very incomplete, yet every such proof shows Him to be such and such, that is, it involves His qualities or characteristics. The intimate and inseparable character of these two conceptions belongs to the nature and limitation of our minds, and is inevitable because of the way in which the human mind operates.[3] In any case, the highly abstract conception of God's Existence apart from His Being, would be completely useless and inadequate for affording us any conceptions of His character. From such an abstract idea of His existence we could not derive any conception of His being and nature. It is then inevitable, if we are to have any notion of His character, that the idea of His Existence involve that of His nature.[4] The fundamental character of the belief in His unity and oneness is expressed in all the formularies of the Faith.[5] The Being of God is the abso-

---

[1] Rhôsse, *op. cit.*, pp. 23 *et al.*
[2] Androutsos, *op. cit.*, p. 32.
[3] *Ibid.*, p. 33.
[4] Rhôsse, *op. cit.*, pp. 129-130.
[5] 1st article of Creed; Gennadius, in Mesolora, *op. cit.*, I. p. 73; Metrophanes, *ibid.*, p. 280.

lute unity of His attributes and properties, in one living whole, without contradiction or actual distinction of parts. The attributes are the manifestations of His one eternal Energy or Being.[1] When we use the word "absolute" of God, it is not as a property or attribute of Him, but as constituting His Being, as revealing Him as the absolutely eternal Being, and this absolute or infinite character is involved by all the attributes we predicate of Him. "Absolute" and "infinite" are practically synonymous, and express the same idea, that He is not determined by anything other than Himself, that is, He is absolutely self-determined.[2]

Is it possible to have a really true and adequate knowledge of God? In a very true sense we cannot have any *scientific* knowledge of Him: (a) Science deals with the data of perceived phenonema. God, in His essence, is not the object of our perception, so we cannot use Him as the subject of scrutiny and investigation. (b) Science proceeds according to a fixed method of observation, analysis, and synthesis, to investigate and correlate its data, and to derive and state the nature of the forces operating under the phenomena which constitute its subject matter. If God is what He is said to be by religion and revelation, such data about Him cannot be so examined and investigated, with the result of acquiring a satisfactory and veridical conception of His character. (c) Scientific proof is the only criterion which is admissible, and we "cannot demonstrate either God's Existence or His character scientifically." Hence it is impossible to obtain this kind of scientific knowledge of God. He cannot be made the object of our scrutiny, nor are our minds capable of grasping Him.[3]

Since the subject matter of our knowledge is One whose character and essence are such as to constitute an entirely different category of data, we cannot expect to have a demonstration or proof concerning Him, of the same quality as that presented in the exact sciences.[4] If He is, He is unique. If God

[1] Rhôsse, *op. cit.*, p. 130.
[2] Rhôsse, *op. cit.*, p. 131, and cf: note 1, quotation from St. Basil *ad loc.*, *ibid.*
[3] Androutsos, *op. cit.*, p. 33.
[4] Androutsos, *op. cit.*, pp. 33-34.

exist, then knowledge of Him involves a different mode of procedure. As the subject matter of our investigation of His character is so utterly different from that of any ordinary scientific quest, we shall need to employ a different method in obtaining our data. On this hypothesis we can obtain an essentially scientific knowledge of God. It is limited, as we shall see, but so are the other sciences and their conclusions. In every scientific experiment we have an idea or conception of that which we are seeking to investigate, before we engage on the process. The innate notion of God furnishes us with a sufficient incentive and suggestion of[1] Him. With the data given us by Faith, "the foundation and point of departure for knowledge" of God,[2] we put ourselves in the way of obtaining and observing the data of religion. The objective and subjective factor of religious certainty, developed and stimulated by the Christian life, both in its corporate relation with the Church as embodying and guaranteeing the teachings of Christianity, and in its personal and intimate communion with God, generate a degree of certainty[3] which by the exercise of reason, and the scientific method, can become, as well, *scientific* certainty.[4] Scientific certainty and knowledge develop on the basis of religious knowledge and certainty. We *can* know about God, and the character of our certainty is not less scientific than that generated by any other science.

This scientific certainty is neither superfluous nor impious.[5] It is justifiable to seek and achieve it. It is especially useful and necessary in these days, when agnostic views are so prevalent. From Plotinus[6] to Schleiermacher men have denied the possibility of God's self-knowledge, and in consequence, that of man's knowledge of God. Schleiermacher holds that knowledge involves antitheses. We compare two things, and come to know them by detecting their qualities and characteristics. Self-knowledge on God's part would involve antitheses in His quali-

---

[1] On which see below pp. 63-65.
[2] Rhôsse, *op. cit.*, p. 70.
[3] *Ibid.*, pp. 72-85.
[4] *Ibid.*, pp. 85, 132.
[5] *Ibid.*, p. 133.
[6] Cf. Plotinus, *Ennead.*, 5, 1, 3; 5, 1, 6; 5, 3, 10; 6, 9, 6, etc.

ties, and our knowledge of Him would demand that He, a subject of that knowledge, be limited by the compass of our capacity for knowing. Since self-knowledge would involve antitheses in His essence, and knowledge on our part of Him would demand limitation of His character, no knowledge of God is possible, and He is only to be perceived by the feelings. But, on the contrary, knowledge does not postulate *antitheses,* but only *differences.* God as the one knowing subject and the one Object Self-known can know Himself as both Knower and Known, without any detriment to His Unity. "So man as subject knows God as object, as not altogether other than himself (since God created man, and knows Himself as Creator) but as his own Highest Cause, limited neither by our knowledge nor by our existence. Therefore God, as the Highest Cause of us and of the universe, contains us and the world as known, inasmuch as He is the cause of our existence and of the possibility of our knowledge."[1]

We derive our knowledge of God from our innate feeling and conviction of His existence, developed by our contact with the world of experience, and by the use of our rational faculty seeking to discover the reason of this innate "faith", "actuated by the desire to know the content of our Faith, and to resolve the various phenomena or energies of the world and their consequences into their Ultimate Cause."[2] The conclusions of "natural religion" are corrected, supplemented, and completed by the revelation made by God in Jesus Christ. We begin with an innate instinct about God, as St. John Damascene says: "A knowledge of the existence of God is sown in our very nature."[3] It is "the organ for the apprehension of God which He engraved in man",[4] that is, it is a means for knowing Him, a propensity, a capacity, and an impulse to know God, not a complete knowledge of Him, nor even a ready formed conception of His Nature.[5] It is a common heritage of all men,[6] as

---

[1] Rhôsse, *op. cit.,* p. 135.
[2] *Ibid.,* p. 132.
[3] Ἔκδοσις, 1, 1, 9, and 12.
[4] Androutsos, *op. cit.,* p. 34.
[5] *Ibid.,* pp. 34-5.
[6] Mesolora, *op. cit.,* III. p. 88.

we know from the history of the religious instinct in man,[1] yet as such it is only "a kind of innate feeling about God".[2] It is part of man's logical faculty, this impulse Godwards, and provokes in him a recognition of dependence upon a Higher and supernatural Power.[3] It cannot be maintained that "we have in us an instinctive conception of God which is complete and perfect".[4] We do have an innate desire and impulse to know Him, but the development of it is a moral matter. Faith and reason are both essential for its growth and development. This "innate feeling of the existence of a Higher Power"[5] leads and precedes the action of the reason: the "heart" leads the "head". The conception of God is a result of the impulse given by this instinct of man's mind and soul, and "is formed by the observation of His works, man naturally being inclined towards Him".[6] "The power by which man perceives God, revealed in general and in part (in Nature) is Faith,—the feeling by which man is led to name and acknowledge the presence of God in the natural and ethical world.... As such an attitude of accepting the unknown and mysterious, it is a necessary phenomenon of the natural constitution of man on its psychological side, and not a peculiarity of Christianity.... In Christianity this faith, purged and made living by divine Grace, both gains certainty about its divine authenticity, and develops its vital character, becoming the living power of the religious and ethical life."[7] Faith, as moral and not completely rational, is a matter of the will. Consequently the innate instinct for God may be denied its place in man's moral life, and may never become a dynamic force as means of approach to God.[8] It cannot then be the one means leading inevitably to a certain and full conception of His character, as the existence of atheism shows.

"Man must then have an idea of God in himself if Nature

---

[1] Cf. Mesolora, *op. cit.*, III, p. 88-89. n. 2, the evidence from all ancient authors from Cicero on, and cf. the "historical argument" below.

[2] Rhôsse, *op. cit.*, p. 132.

[3] Androutsos, *op. cit.*, p. 35.

[4] Dyobouniotes, Ἡ Δογματ. Ἀνδρούτσου κρινομένη, pp. 11-12.

[5] Mesolora, *op. cit.*, III. p. 90.

[6] Androutsos, p. 42.

[7] Androutsos, *op. cit.*, p. 37.

[8] Androutsos, *op. cit.*, p. 35.

is to speak through it of God. Nature is a book made only of elements in accord (συμφώνων), and we must offer that which we bear in us of these accords in order to be able to read this book. Nature both hides and reveals God. She is a veil, but it is diaphanous. But we must wish to seek God in order to find Him. Those who do not desire to seek Him, do not find Him in Nature. As all things give testimony of God to those who love and seek Him, so all things hide Him from those who do not wish to know Him."[1] We know God only through His revelation of Himself in Nature, and through our Lord. "Christian knowledge of God is based on these two factors, the natural apprehension of Him in Nature, and the certainty which the authenticity of Revelation affords."[2] By reason, we search back of the visible things of Nature to the unseen Cause behind them.[3] Nature is a mirror which reflects the greatness of God, for she reveals the might and glory of Him who created her.[4] To His revelation in Nature we owe the knowledge of His attributes and properties, as Almighty, All-present, Transcendent, and the like. Revelation changes the motive of man's religious desires so that they are not only feelings based on a conviction of creature-hood, and on gratitude for existence, but "natural religion is elevated into spiritual and ethical devotion, as God reveals Himself to man, His creature, as Love....and man is drawn to Him under the impulse of reverence and filial devotion."[5] By the Divine Revelation we are told nothing of the Divine attributes, but Revelation serves to purge our conceptions of error, and to complete the knowledge of God gained from external nature.[6] In summary, we may say that we derive our knowledge of God from the observation of nature, supplemented by Revelation, and that this process is initiated by the innate instinct of man[7]

[1] Mesolora, op. cit., III. p. 91.
[2] Androutsos, op. cit., p. 37.
[3] St. Greg. Naz., Discourse 28, 16.
[4] St. John Damascene, Ἔκδοσις, I, quoted by Androutsos, p. 36.
[5] Androutsos, op. cit., p. 36.
[6] Androutsos, Δογματική, pp. 42-43.
[7] Rhôsse, op. cit., pp. 125-6, cf. pp. 126-129, for Patristic evidence for this view. "The innate feeling about God is. . . the psychological principle and basis of our natural knowledge, which man acquires through the examination of the world" (p. 128).

reaching Godwards, and in a vague way feeling the conviction of His existence. Faith furnishes the means for the experiment, and through it only are the data made available.

Since our knowledge of God is based on His relations with the world, recognizing them we postulate certain qualities of Him, saying that He is Almighty, Eternal, All-Wise, Everywhere Present. Consequently our knowledge of Him will necessarily be imperfect. "Since the infinite God....cannot be the (direct) object of our scrutiny, but is manifested only in Revelation, the conceptions which we form of Him cannot present Him as He is, but only imperfectly and by analogy with the perfections of the finite world."[1] On the basis of the works of His creation our knowledge is imperfect, incomplete,[2] "relative and limited both in form and content." It is limited in form, for human knowledge is not absolute, since man cannot probe the depths of the nature of God on this earth.[3] It is limited in content, since his finite mind cannot compass the absolute and infinite essence and knowledge of God.[4] "We do not know clearly what He is according to His Nature, since it surpasses our comprehension."[5] We only see in part, as "through a glass, darkly".[6] His Revelation of Himself was conditioned and gauged by the capacity of man to receive it,[7] and consequently it is only a partial manifestation of Himself.[8] We may not know God, we can only know about Him; so we can speak more easily of what He is not, than of what He is.[9] "What God is in His Nature, cannot be known by any creature."[10] The silences of Revelation are as significant as its statements, since they leave the vast questions of His essence outside the bounds of the possibility of human knowledge.[11]

[1] Androutsos, *op. cit.*, p. 40.
[2] Androutsos, Δογματική, pp. 52, 45-6.
[3] Cf. 1 Cor. 2, 10.
[4] Rhôsse, *op. cit.*, p. 136.
[5] *Orth. Cat.* (Bal.) p. 10.
[6] 1. Cor. 13, 9, 12.
[7] St. John Damascene, Ἔκδοσις, 1, 1, 12.
[8] Mesolora, *op. cit.*, III. p. 98.
[9] St. Athanasius, *Epis.* V. *ad Monachos*, 2., and cf. St. Augustine *facilius dicimus quid non sit, quam quid sit* (on Psalm 8, 5).
[10] Mogila, in Mesolora, *op. cit.*, I. p. 379.
[11] Androutsos, *op. cit.*, p. 41.

Nevertheless our knowledge of God is a true knowledge, of a growing and developing character, and this progress only suggests the impossibility of an adequate and exhaustive knowledge on man's part.[1] We have no perfect and actual knowledge of Him as He is,[2] for this is one of the errors the Church condemned in Eunomius. At the same time we must admit that we can have an adequate and sufficient knowledge about Him, in contradiction to the error of Arius who said that we can have no knowledge of Him.[3] While our knowledge cannot be exhaustive, from the point of view of God as its object, still it is essential for us and of the greatest value to us. Our knowledge of Him as expressed by the attributes and properties we predicate of God, cannot be said to constitute actual and adequate representations of the Divine attributes, for it is expressed in statements which are only valid by analogy. They are only incomplete statements, representing actual relations of God with His universe, and by no means adequately and exhaustively sum up the actual properties of God viewed from the point of His Nature in itself. They are adequate for us, but not exhaustive and complete in their content or in their form.[4]

In our knowledge of the revelation of God as presented in Nature, our minds develop certain statements of the attributes of God as shown in His relations with the universe, by the three following methods of reasoning. We distinguish them by our attitude toward and reaction from the phenomena of Nature. If we postulate that God is infinitely removed from the imperfections of this world, we likewise affirm of Him all the perfections that are suggested by all that is best in Nature. This latter attitude presupposes Him as the Cause of all, for He is thought of "as the Cause which has within it perfectly, whatever is shown as result and effect in the world". Thus may be distinguished the three methods of the knowledge of God developed by the scholastics, and by them called *via negationis, via eminentiae,* and the *via affirmationis* (*causalitatis*). Pseudo-

---

[1] Rhôsse, *op. cit.*, pp. 136-137, Androutsos, p. 41.

[2] Cf. Dyobouniotes, Ἡ Δογμ. Ἀνδρούτσου κρινομένη, p. 14.

[3] Rhôsse, *op. cit.*, p. 137, Androutsos, Δογματική, p. 43.

[4] Androutsos, *op. cit.*, p. 41-2.

[5] Androutsos, *ibid.*, p. 47; Mesolora, op. cit., III. p. 98; Rhôsse, *op. cit., p.* 139.

Dionysius the Areopagite says that we may come to the knowledge of the Unknown and Transcendent God from the world
which shows Him forth "by the abstraction of Him from all
things, by postulating of Him His eminence, and by regarding
Him as cause of all."[1] As was suggested, these three methods
really are reducible to two, since the *via eminentiae* is only a
correction and completion of the *via affirmations (causalitatis).*[2] So the denial of any imperfections in God is closely
linked with the affirmation of perfections, and the *via affirmationis* is intimately bound up with the *via negationis:*[3] we attribute to God in the highest degree a perfection, which may
also be regarded as a removal of an imperfection, in the
building up of our conceptions of Him.

Our conceptions of God are then subjective, inasmuch as
they are the conclusions of our reason guided by faith and inspired by the innate feeling of God. They do however correspond to true relations of God's Nature to His universe. As
statements and ideas they are only imperfect and analogous, as
is our knowledge of God in general. "They are subjective representations of actual relations of the infinite God toward His
finite world."[4] (a) One false view of the attributes of God regarded them as actual divisions of the Divine Essence. This
took for granted the hypothesis that His Essence could be known
by us immediately and directly. Against this gross conception
Eunomius reacted, and as the one attribute of the Divine Essence postulated his theory of the "unbegottenness" of God as
constituting His Essence. He was right in rejecting the lineal
demarcation of God's Essence into attributes, as if it were an
area subject to measurement and scrutiny,[5] but wrong in denying the possibility of any knowledge of God.[6] (b) A second
wrong view is that of the Nominalists, who held that the at-

[1] *De divinis nominibus,* 7, 3.

[2] Androutsos, *op. cit.,* p. 48.

[3] Rhôsse, *op. cit.,* p. 139.

[4] Androutsos Δογ. Μελ. Α', p. 43.

[5] For this destroys the fundamental notion of God's unity and
simplicity.

[6] This is an argument of those who hold that our conceptions of
the attributes are mere ideas of our own, which have no objective
reality.

tributes of God are simply figments of our own imagination, actually revealing to us nothing of the Divine Nature. They said: "The acceptance of (these conceptions as describing) actual attributes in God's Nature (1) involves the danger of importing secondary and temporal elements into the Divine Essence; (2) takes away the unity and simplicity of God, making Him into a bearer of different attributes, and (3) imperils His absoluteness, by converting God into the attribute we predicate of Him." Both Holy Scripture and the Fathers regard the attributes they ascribe to God as not mere empty words, or as synonyms, or metaphors, but as describing actual qualities in Him. If we take the attributes simply as our conceptions of Him, without the conviction that they represent actual relations on His part with His world independent of our own view of them, the conception of Revelation is destroyed, religious feeling is brought to naught, and faith is deprived of all truth. "The religious longing for some form of conceiving God cannot be driven back to and satisfied by the general, abstract, and lifeless notion of Him as the Absolute and Infinite, but is drawn toward Him as to a Father full of all ethical perfections."[1] In answer to the Nominalist arguments, (a) it may be said that nothing contingent or secondary is introduced into the conception of His attributes, as they are only statements of His Essence as functioning in His Creation and known through it. (b) They do not take away His unity, as the attributes are only the expression of His one Nature in relation to the world. (c) We do not think of God as a partaker of righteousness, but view righteousness as actually complete in Him alone, predicating it of Him not synthetically, but analytically.[2] The attributes of God are, as it were, the refraction of the rays of light of one diamond, mirrored by lesser jewels ranged round about it.[3]

The attributes then consist of actual relations of God with His world, expressed in our own terms. Our terms are incom-

---

[1] Androutsos, Δογματική, p. 43, and cf. Rhösse, op. cit., pp. 298-300. Spinoza's omnis determinatio est negatio is one instance of this type of argument (Nominalist).

[2] Androutsos, op. cit., pp. 43-44.

[3] Scheeben, Handbuch der Katholischen Dogmatik, I, p. 507, quoted by Androutsos, op. cit., p. 47.

plete, and our knowledge relative only, nevertheless such "an acknowledgement of that which is truly present to God"[1] is both sufficient, valid, and true. These terms are not adequate in relation to Him, as they do not encompass His Nature, but they are the sufficient and best means of conceiving the actual action of the Divine Essence as it penetrates through to our understanding. Though they are subjective, we must not understand them to be "an arbitrary and unsubstantiated creation of our understanding, but as reproducing faithfully the actual relation and *rapports* of God with His world."[2] We mean by "eternal" that this is the most adequate description of His relation to time; by "almighty", the expression of His actual infinite might in contrast to the limited power of the finite creation. As St. Basil says: "We know our God from His operations, but are unable to draw near to His Essence. For His operations come down to us, while His Essence remains unapproachable".[3] What we predicate of Him is true, though its form be that of our subjective conceptions. These do sufficiently represent actual and real relations of the infinite God to His world.[4]

The human mind under the prompting of its innate feeling for God, through faith and reason develops its knowledge of God into certain terms called His qualities, attributes, and the like. These represent true insight into His dealings with His world, and are sufficient descriptions of Him as He is revealed in them. We may not know Him directly, but we may know about Him, through His Revelation of Himself in Nature and in our Lord. Such knowledge is truly scientific, and is adequate for our needs.

---

[1] *St. Basil, adversus Eunomium*, 1, 13.

[2] Androutsos, *op. cit.*, p. 45.

[3] *Epist. 234 ad Amphil.*, 2.

[4] Androutsos, *op. cit.*, pp. 46-47. cf. controversy of Androutsos and Dyobouniotes: Dyobouniotes Δογ. 'Ανδ. κριν., pp. 14-15, and Androutsos, Δογμ. Μελέται, Α', pp. 43-48. St. Thomas separates the *distinctio rationis ratiocinantis* from the *distinctio rationis ratiocinatae*,—the former being purely subjective conceptions, the latter, subjective conceptions of objective realities.

2. THE ARGUMENT FOR THE EXISTENCE OF GOD AND ITS BEARING ON OUR KNOWLEDGE OF HIM

The existence of God has been treated of in philosophy and theology under several different "proofs", more properly called "arguments". We may distinguish seven of them: the cosmological, psychological, physico-teleological, ethical, ontological, and historical, in one group,[1] and the apologetic argument from miracle. As the last takes for granted the existence of God, already believed in on different grounds, it cannot be considered here as one of the arguments to show His existence and to furnish us with data as to His attributes.[2] After presenting each argument in turn, and examining its contribution to our knowledge of God's existence and the data it furnishes as to His Nature and attributes, we shall consider them as a whole, and show their intimate relation to each other.

(1) The cosmological argument, recognizing the cause and effect relation of all that is in the world, and showing each cause to have been the effect of a preceding cause, reasons back to a "Prime Mover" or "First Cause", which is God.[3] He is not only the First Cause but also the only uncaused Cause, the Cause of causes. All causes in the phenomenal world are then contingent and secondary; He only is necessary and primary.[4] The existence of this Cause is necessary to explain and order the phenomena of Nature. Reasoning from the same data the materialist may work towards a first Cause which is itself subject to the law of necessity which governs the physical universe, and may be a cause, even *the* cause, but it is not necessarily free or unlimited. The law of necessity which prevails in the physical cosmos may be conceived of as governing the initial cause as well. Hence, the attributes of the highest *power*—in relation to the powers in the physical

[1] Following Rhôsse's division, *op. cit.*, p. 137. That of Mesolora is slightly but not essentially different—cf. *op. cit.*, III. pp. 91-95; Androutsos, *ad loc.* cf. below.

[2] Rhôsse, *op. cit.*, p. 140 (§ 70).

[3] Aristotle, *Physics* 8, 5; *Metaphysics*, 12, 6.

[4] St. Augustine, *Conf.* X, 6., and Mesolora, *op. cit.*, III, p. 92: "The whole of the finite energies of the world are only secondary causes, not the first and chief Cause."

world, the greatest *life*—in relation to the living forms of the universe, and the most eminent *good*—in relation to the contingent good of visible and phenomenal nature, are all we can postulate of this cause, by the *via affirmationis, negationis, et eminentiae*. Such a development of attributes is circumscribed, as "the efficient Cause of the world, the Highest Power, and Dynamic Energy is subject to the law of necessity."[1] So this argument from the world as a result of chance and as contingent[2] is strictly limited. It reasons from motion to a Prime Mover,[3] from causes and results to the Cause,[4] postulates of this Cause the highest of those qualities which characterize the phenomena of the physical world, but is so incomplete and unsatisfactory in itself that it demands being supplemented by the subsequent arguments.[5]

(2) The psychological argument notes the fact that self-conscious thought distinguishes in man the material body from the perceiving and knowing faculty, which is not material. Man comes to recognize his resemblance physically to other organisms in the world, to compare his body with theirs, and in the realization of his relative perfection, to reason toward a cause more perfect than himself, of his thinking, willing, and perceiving faculty. As the preceding argument tended to suggest the necessity of a First Cause of physical phenomena, so the psychological development of man points him toward a Cause of his spiritual faculties. Man comes to see himself as a microcosm,[6] and to reason that since he is not self-caused, there must be a Cause both of him, material and immaterial, and of the rest of the universe, physical and spiritual. So soon as he comes to the consciousness of the existence of persons,[7] he comes as well to the realization that they were not self-caused, any more than is he. His con-

[1] Rhôsse, *op. cit.*, p. 144 (§ 82).

[2] Androutsos, Δογματική, p. 37.

[3] Aristotle, *Met.* 12.

[4] Cf. St. John Damascene, who reasons from the created (or caused) to the Creator (or Cause) in Ἔκδοσις 1, 3; in Mesolora, *op. cit.*, 92.

[5] Rhôsse, *op. cit.*, pp. 141-145.

[6] Rhôsse, note pp. 145-148; cf. p. 147.

[7] "Person" distinguishes living organisms with self-consciousness and self-direction, from living things lacking it; *ibid.*, note 2, pp. 148-149.

sciousness of his own self-determination and self-direction brings him to postulate of this Cause the like qualities which he possesses, only in an eminent degree. This rational process serves but to confirm his natural and innate tendency toward the recognition of the Cause of himself, (the innate instinct for God mentioned above) and he then postulates of that Cause all the qualities which exist in him,—of self-determination, self-direction, forethought, reason, and will.[1] Two forms of this psychological argument link it closely with the teleological argument: (a) The imperfect human spirit seeks an adequate object of its intellectual faculty in the knowledge of the highest spiritual Being, who is the Cause of the physical and psychological world, itself Mind, Thought, Will; and (b) the recognition of the psychological demand for the existence of God is so much a part of human psychology that a denial of its claim is tantamount to a denial of one's own reason. The attributes accorded to this Cause by the psychological argument, are those of reason, free will, conscious and self-directing life, and of being the highest good (together with the possession of these qualities).[2]

(3) The teleological argument, on the basis of the two preceding, develops the evidence for design and purpose in the material and immaterial world. Observation descries in the material and physical world, both inorganic and organic, an arrangement and order, working (it is true, under a law of necessity, but yet) for some object and end. The phenomena of the visible world may be arranged in orders, of which the lower in each case subserves the purpose of the higher, inorganic matter that of non-sentient living things, plants that of animals, and animals of man. Aristotle saw this relation of the parts to the whole, of the functions of this hierarchy of creation in the relation of one part to the others.[3] Back of this necessary order and inevitable sequence of cause and effect lies a purpose or aim, the presence of which demands a mind to think it. This mind is the Reason of all the physical phenomena, and as

---

[1] Rhôsse, op. cit., pp. 145-150.

[2] Rhôsse, op. cit., pp. 150-151.

[3] Aristotle, Pol. 1, 1, 19-29; Plato, Soph., 37; Phileb., 16, 23, C-E., etc.; pp. 153-4, note 1, Rhôsse.

well an attribute of the Cause initiating and overseeing them. This Reasoning and Determining Cause must be outside the world of matter and not only resident in it; man is driven to this conclusion by the observation of blind necessity, conflict, and mutual antagonism in this world. A purely mechanical explanation of the phenomena[1] does not account for all of the facts. The physical world is not perfect, though it is purposeful, and an examination of it alone will not be adequate to explain all the phenomena of the universe, unless we continue with it the evidence of purpose in the world of consciousness.[2]

The material world stands as a whole in the same relation to the world of consciousness and mental life, as its own lower orders do to the higher whose purposes they serve. It is a means and vehicle for the use of the conscious world. Man is the master of the world, as its highest developed form, and in his relations to it sees that what he realizes as highest and most essentially characteristic of his fundamental nature, the notion of the good, is not actually realized in the world. In contrast to the law of necessity ruling in the phenomenal world, he recognizes in himself the power of self-determination and free will. Since his highest good and the exercise of his will at its noblest are frustrated and nullified in this created world, and the best and most characteristic element in him lacks fulfillment and satisfaction, he is "impelled, as it were by necessity, toward some higher Good as the End of the world and man". His life of feeling, thought, and will, demands something which he does not obtain within the limits of the world of creation, and he postulates the existence of a Highest Good as the End and Purpose of all.[3]

[1] Rhôsse, note 1, pp. 156-158.
[2] Rhôsse, *op. cit.*, pp. 151-159.
[3] *Ibid.*, pp. 160-165. cf. St. John Damascene, Ἔκδοσις τ. Ὀρθ. Πίστεως, 1, 3, quoted in Mesolora, *op. cit.*, III. p. 93. The ethical argument may also be stated as follows: (Androutsos, *op. cit.*, p. 38, note) (a) There is an ethical law in the world, but an ethical act involves the existence of free will, and a law, of a Giver. Hence the Highest Good is Giver of ethical law. (b) This ethical law involves a harmony of acts (virtue) and of their consequences or results (happiness). The conflict and opposition of the world to these and its lack of ethical harmony, suggest the existence of One to effect them, outside the world.

The cosmological argument pointed to the existence of a First and Prime Cause, who was at once the Highest Being and the Greatest Power. The psychological argument tended to show this Cause as possessing the highest and best mental faculties of self-determination, self-consciousness, self-direction, and free will. The teleological argument indicated that this Highest Cause or Power, and Highest Mind or Wisdom, was also the greatest Good and Purpose, in relation to Creation. The limitations of these conceptions of the Divine energy are obvious: they outline those elements which we recognize as true in Pantheism; God is not necessarily above and beyond His creation; they do not anywhere indicate His character as Absolute, and they constitute only certain qualities of God, without suggesting the necessity and character of His Essence apart from them, as the unifying principle of them all.[1]

(4) The ontological argument shows the Highest Cause or Power, the Highest Mind or Will, and the Highest Good, to be as well the Absolute. Since we perceive everything in this world as imperfect and finite, we necessarily have some conception of the Infinite and Perfect, or Absolute, by which we measure and judge everything in this world as finite and imperfect.[2] This notion is not the result of experience, but exists of itself. It "is not a mere abstraction devoid of any reality." It exists for itself and of itself alone, and is a necessary notion. We then postulate this note of the absolute and infinite, of God "as the infinite Power and Cause not only of the world, but of Himself."[3]

The first basis of this argument is in Plato's idealogy. St. Gregory Nyssa used to show the eternity of God,[4] and St. Augustine[5] and Boethius[6] followed him. St. Anselm developed it in his *Proslogium* as follows: the idea of the existence of God is

[1] Rhôsse, *op. cit.*, pp. 166-167.

[2] *Ibid.*, p. 168, and note 2. "Indefinite" and "infinite" had a different use in Plato and Aristotle, who applied the latter in the sense of the former, to "formless matter". For our purposes "infinite" and "absolute" are synonymous. Cf. also p. 131, note 1, p. 177 (§ 109).

[3] *Ibid.*, p. 169.

[4] In his *Catechetical Discourse* (Prologue).

[5] *De libero Arbitrio* 11, 3-5.

[6] *De consolatione phil.*, 1, 111, 10.

a notion *quo majus cogitari non potest*. If it existed only in the mind, then objective existence would be *quid majus*. Hence God *does* exist. Furthermore it is certain that nothing greater can be conceived than this existence, than which anything which did have existence would be greater if that did not. Hence God *must* exist. The value of St. Anselm's theory is that it shows that the notion of God as the highest notion must involve His existence in fact. Its limitations are that it shows God's existence relatively with regard to His universe, and not absolutely. St. Anselm regards God's existence as it were a quality of God, and as something not necessarily existing in concept, but derivative[1] and by implication, and he does not show that the conception is necessary.[2]

"A perfect formulation of the ontological argument involves the demonstration of the necessity of the conception of God and of its existence."[3] Descartes showed it as necessary, by demonstrating that as it was not caused by reflection, but was innate, it could only be caused by an Infinite Cause itself. With its presence was bound up the necessity of its existence. According to Spinoza, *substantia*—or absolute conception—is *causa sui;* if it were caused by anything else, it would not be absolute. As cause of itself this absolute conception exists of necessity. When it is known, it is known as existing necessarily, and the existence of the Absolute is as necessary as its conception. Spinoza agrees with Descartes that the innate idea is not fortuitous but necessary, and goes beyond him in thinking that with this necessary conception of it, the existence of the Absolute is correspondingly inevitable and necessary.[4] Kant held the necessity of the conception or idea of the Absolute, but denied the conclusion that it must necessarily therefore have objective reality. But if this idea, which admittedly gives coherence and unity to thought, involves no contradictions, but rather is essential to right thinking, how is it possible that it has not objective reality? If we admit the possibility of a contradiction between our reasoning and our necessary concepts, we are on the way to a scepticism which cuts the ground from

[1] He corrects this in his *Monologium*.
[2] Rhôsse, *op. cit.*, pp. 170-171.
[3] Rhôsse, *op. cit.*, p. 172 (§ 102).
[4] *Ibid.*, p .173.

under any process of thought. "If, according to Kant, the logical process of thought is impossible without the idea of God, this idea as a necessary hypothesis and premise of every mental process cannot be based only on the subjective conception of the human consciousness, but being independent of every subjective view, makes thought logical and gives unity to[1] it." Kant is in error in maintaining that it does not follow that because we necessarily think it, an idea necessarily represents an objective reality. This sceptical view is opposed by subsequent German thinkers such as Fichte, Schelling, Hegel, and Schleiermacher, who sustain the principle that "whatever is necessarily thought as existing, does actually exist."

The notion of the Infinite or Absolute does not take away the notes of self-begottenness, self-determination, self-containedness, and self-consciousness, for it means *not determined by any outside agent*. So "self-determined" signifies in its true meaning what is meant negatively by "Absolute" or "Infinite", in relation to determination.[2] The former is a positive and the latter a negative term for the same idea. Furthermore, this notion of God as Absolute, indicated by the ontological argument, is no empty and abstract conception devoid of content, or out of relation with the preceding arguments. God, as First Cause, was the Cause of Himself as of all creation, and as self-caused is Absolute: the Cause of His own existence, and of that of all existing things. This same relation of the ontological argument maintains in regard to the others—God as First Cause is the Infinite and Absolute Cause; as Wisdom and Will, the Infinite and Absolute Wisdom and Will; as Good, not only the Highest, but the Absolute, Good. So the ontological argument harmonizes, summarizes, and unifies all the preceding, which serve to lead up to it and to prepare the material and method of its contention.[3] In general, the other arguments deal only with the attributes of God in relation to this world, while the ontological arguments postulate their several conclusions of God's Essence in an absolute and infinite degree.[4] In

---

[1] Rhôsse, *op. cit.*, p. 176 (§ 107).
[2] Rhôsse, *op. cit.*, p. 297, p. 177.
[3] *Ibid.*, pp. 177-179.
[4] Rhôsse, *op. cit.*, pp. 180-181, and note.

relation to His Creation "the absolute attributes of God take on the character of relative attributes, inasmuch as through them God comes into contact with the world."[1]

The conception of God as Infinite or Absolute is negative only in form, not in content, for a negative conception states what a thing is by defining what it is not: for example, "immortality" expresses a positive conception of eternal life, "incorruptibility", an affirmation of eternal integrity of character subject to no corruption.[2] Man has of necessity to have recourse to conceptions thus negative in *form* to express an affirmation of content, because of the limited experience, power, and capacity of the finite mind. The *content* of the absolute perfections of God is not supplied by the ontological argument, but by the others preceding it.[3] The relations of the Infinite to the Finite have been regarded in three ways: as antagonistic, as identical, or as causal and interrelated. If the relation of Infinite to Finite be thought of as antagonistic, a dualistic principle is developed. When Finite and Infinite are regarded as identical then a pantheistic system results. The theistic system views the Finite as caused by the Infinite,[4] who stands as Creator in an intimate and constant relation toward it as His creature.[5]

(5) The "historical" argument, showing the consensus of opinion of mankind in favor of the existence of God,[6] with the common conviction of the great thinkers and philosophers on this point, is really not a demonstration—far less, a proof. So far as it bears witness to the innate notion or feeling of God's existence, its evidence was taken into consideration above. The existence of this conviction, deeply ingrained in human nature,[7] is only a proof of the prevalence of the notion, not a demonstration of its validity. Its universality is dubious, as no one can

[1] P. 184.
[2] Cf. St. Gregory Naz., *Discourse* 37, 9; *de Anima et Resurr.*, p. 194.
[3] Rhôsse, *op. cit.*, p. 186.
[4] Rhôsse, *op. cit.*, pp. 186-187.
[5] "Deism stands midway between dualism and theism, as regards the only and sole relation of the Infinite to the Finite as having been that of First Cause. For the rest, the relationship is neither necessary nor a matter of concern." *ibid.*
[6] Mesolora, *op. cit.*, III, p. 94, and note 2.
[7] Rhôsse, *op. cit.*, pp. 137-8.

say that there may not be a people discovered who have no notion of God, and no religion.[1]

In the above analysis of the arguments for the existence and nature of God we reduced the original number (six) to five, as the physico-teleological and ethical arguments really generate only one contention. They may further be reduced to the four main arguments, as the so-called "historical" argument is without force or connection with the rest. These four in turn really constitute one single argument or proof, of which each contributes one part. They are not four proofs, but one cumulative argument "constituting a proof of the existence of God, which in reference to His one Essence according to His different attributes, is a sufficient and true proof."[2] Each in turn is refutable. Kant assailed the cosmological argument by saying it was only another form of the ontological argument, for the conception of a Highest Cause is not derived from experience but only developed from the mind. He also criticised the teleological argument as containing the same sort of logical "jump" from the knowledge of a part of the world, to a general conclusion of a purposeful principle underlying the universe. The same objection may be brought to bear with great force against the psychologico-ethical argument. The ontological argument may be criticised as a "sophism or simple juggling of words"—particularly in its Anselmic form. On the whole, however, the general conclusion developed by these four arguments though it is "not a scientific demonstration, yet justifies faith in God, and presents the aspects in which the world is not knowable without the Absolute. The cosmological demonstration shows the religious conviction ingrained in the human conscience, of God as Cause of all; the teleological, God as the All-governing Mind; and the ontological argument says that the relation of man to God presupposes the relation of God to man."[3] "All created things and our reflections upon them may serve as guides to show us the way beyond them to Him who is above Nature, God. We say 'guides' only, because all

[1] *Ibid.*, 140. For evidence cf. Cicero, *Quaest. Tuscul.* 1, 13; Clem. Alex. *Strom.* V, 14; Lactantius, *Divin. Instit.*, 1, 2. cf. Androutsos *op. cit.*, note, p. 39.

[2] Rhôsse, *op. cit.*, p. 138, 180.

[3] Androutsos, *op. cit.*, pp. 37-39, note 2. (following Nitzsch).

the proofs of the existence of God are only indirect, not direct demonstrations. But to him who wishes to believe, these indirect proofs are sufficient."[1] So they come to substantiate and vindicate the faith which a man holds on other grounds, and to show it as logically defensible, as *argumenta ad hominem*. They are useful in suggesting the only right relation of man to the universe, yet are not necessary to practising Christians, who come by their faith through a different channel. They subserve a useful purpose in reëstablishing faith when one has difficulties and doubts. Properly speaking they do not belong to Dogmatic, since they beg the question: dogmatic concerns the exposition of the Church's Faith, which it takes for granted.[2]

3. CONTENT OF OUR KNOWLEDGE OF GOD

From our knowledge of God as partly revealed in Nature and perfectly in Jesus Christ, we make certain statements about Him, saying that He is good, just, mighty, and the like. Such qualities of God we call *attributes* in distinction to the *properties* of the three Persons of the Godhead, and to the *predicates,* by which we characterize Him as the subject of various acts—Creator, Judge, Redeemer, and the like. The Fathers called the attributes by various names: idioms, dignities, representations, virtues, prerogatives,[3] but the above division will be found simplest. By attributes we mean subjective conceptions of actual relations of the Infinite God to the finite world.[4] Various methods of arranging the attributes have been followed by different theologians, which may be resolved into two: (a) an arrangement of all the attributes about some central idea, such as love, personality, absolute character, or spirit; and (b) the empirical arrangement of the attributes under some principle of distinction, for example, the division

---

[1] Mesolora, *op. cit.*, III. p. 92.

[2] Androutsos, *op. cit.*, pp. 37-40. Cf. Dyobouniotes, Δογμ. 'Ανδρ. κρινομένη, pp. 14-16, and Androutsos, Δογμ. Μελέται, p. 49: "These proofs of the existence of God looked at logically, do not demonstrate God's existence as necessary and received by all". Androutsos distinguishes between proofs and *argumenta ad hominem*, as belonging to which class alone he regards the above arguments.

[3] Androutsos, Δογματική, p. 42.

[4] *Ibid.*, p. 44; 46; Δογματικαὶ Μελέται Α', p. 42, etc.

into "absolute" and "relative" attributes. The first method is unsatisfactory, except as an exigency of arrangement, "since every quality of God shows His Being in relation to the world; from the point of view of the subject matter we cannot relate these qualities as 'higher' or 'lower'."[1] As a matter of fact this method simply implies that the writer considers this or that attribute as central. An arrangement of all the attributes about "Love" as central is far from satisfactory: (a) it does not distinguish God from man, except the note of fore-knowledge be added to this conception; (b) it takes personality for granted; (c) it is parallel to the other attributes of God, and they cannot be developed from Love. So "Personality" as a central point of the arrangement of the attributes is not explicable of itself, and is useless as a source from which to derive the others, as it is of itself as much of an abstraction, as is the conception of the "Absolute". The latter cannot be used as a central point for the presentations of the other attributes as it is of itself barren of content, and is no real attribute but a characteristic of the Divine Essence and of every one of its attributes.[2] The arrangement of the Russian theologians who take "Spirit" as the focus of the attributes is subject to the same criticism.[3]

Various empirical divisions have been made: (1) "positive" and "negative" attributes: as this is only a formal distinction, and not one of content, it is not valid. The negative attributes affirm a perfection of God by denying an imperfection, and *vice versa;* (2) "absolute and relative", "eternal and temporal", "quiescent and active",—all distinguish the attributes on the basis of the relation of the Divine Being to the world. "But there are no absolute attributes belonging to the Divine Essence without any relation to the world, nor can the absolute attributes be thought of as not revealed in the relation of God to the world, nor the relative attributes as not founded on the abso-

[1] Androutsos, Δογματική, p. 49, cf. Rhôsse, *op. cit.*, p. 302. Rhôsse regards this ordering of the attributes as only possible in relation to the "absolute" attributes from which we derive the "relative" attributes, in which case we can speak of the latter as "lower".

[2] Androutsos, *op. cit.*, p. 51.

[3] *E. g.*, Antonius and Macarius, cf. note 3, *op. cit.*, p. 48 (Androutsos).

lute attributes."[1] We cannot speak of "relative" in the sense of "secondary", and apply it to the Being or attributes of God, any more than we can divide His attributes into "active" and "quiescent", as this distinction is based only on phenomenal life, and cannot be applied to Him who is *actus purus, semper agens et semper quietus.*

Any distinction is purely the result of the action of our minds in so ordering the material as to make it most intelligible to us. We cannot distinguish in God between His nature and His mind or His Will, hence in the following arrangement of attributes it must be kept in mind that the attributes of one class are really those of the other as well. We distinguish the attributes of God into physical: omnipresence, eternity, omnipotence; logical: omniscience, wisdom; and ethical: holiness, justice, love.[2]

(b) The Attributes of God

On the basis of the cumulative argument for the Existence of God, as well as by the ordinary threefold process of the *viae negationis, affirmationis vel causalitatis, et eminentiae,* we predicate of God and ascribe to Him certain qualities, the acme of the development of which is the notion of the Absolute. This argument with its content and conclusions is sustained, verified, and validated by the evidence of Revelation. We have come to know God as the Greatest Cause, and Might; as the Greatest Reason, Intellect, Will, and Purpose; as the Greatest Life, the Greatest Justice, and the Highest Good. All of these qualities are heightened to the degree of "Absolute", which conception affirms their infinite character and also unifies them as the sev-

---

[1] Androutsos, *op. cit.,* p. 51; and Rhôsse, *op. cit.,* p. 297.

[2] *Ibid.,* p. 52; and Rhôsse, *op. cit.,* p. 305. This is the division of Androutsos, which seems to commend itself more than that of Rhôsse, who postpones the discussion of the attributes and properties of God until after his treatment of the Doctrine of the Trinity (*op. cit.,* pp. 305 ff). He then treats of the absolute attributes (aseity, independence, self-determination, self-sufficiency, blessedness, life, harmony, good, knowledge and wisdom, will, holiness, righteousness, spacelessness, eternity, unchangeability, immateriality, simplicity, unity —pp. 305-310) and then of these attributes in relation to the world (pp. 311-329). On his view of the attributes cf. pp. 297 ff.

eral aspects of a single Absolute or Infinite Essence or Nature. While in a sense this Infinite character is an idiom of God, it is more properly applied to His Essence, and predicated of the quality of His attributes.[1] They in turn serve to give the conception of the Absolute content and specific meaning. In one sense we come to ascribe this absolute character to His Essence and to the attributes in their self-directed mutual relation alone, conceiving of the various qualities of God in relation to the world as manifestations of these attributes, and as energies of the Divine Essence directed toward the finite universe, and in consequence, in this sense speak of them as "relative".[2] But if we come to any knowledge of His attributes, and hence in some degree of His Essence, we do so from our knowledge of His world and His relations with it; hence if we predicate this Absolute Character of His Nature and attributes we cannot, save by reverent theological speculation, postulate it of any other than the Nature of God and His Attributes, as we have come to know them.[3]

"Absolute" or "Infinite" does not mean "indefinite" or "undetermined". There are determinations in God, but they are self-determinations. God is not in Himself undetermined, undefined, and indefinite.[4] He has in His Infinite Unity, physical, logical, and ethical determinations, self-created and self-recognized.[5] There can only be one such Infinite or Absolute. He has a unique, peculiar, and sole character. The existence of the world, which is contingent and finite, does not affect His Absolute Character, for it was caused by Him and owes its preservation to Him.[6] His self-determinations are neither limitations nor negations, but affirmations and self-imposed distinc-

[1] Rhôsse, op. cit., pp. 302-3.

[2] Ibid., p. 304.

[3] "There are no attributes belonging to the Divine Essence without relation to the world". . ."We cannot omit a single attribute of Him and consider that we have rightly conceived of His Essence, in which all things are determined in relation to each other and mutually dependent, so there is nothing fortuitous or capable of being omitted." cf. Dorner, in Nitzsch, Lehrbuch der Evangelischen Dogmatik, p. 387, in Androutsos, op. cit., pp. 51-52.

[4] Rhôsse, op. cit., pp. 305, 131, 177, 180-1.

[5] Ibid., p. 306.

[6] Ibid., p. 310.

tions in His Essence. These attributes are infinite, but are known to us in their relations with the world. "When God as absolutely Good, and having Absolute Might, Knowledge, Wisdom, did not will to be alone good in Himself, nor alone to be Almighty, All-knowing, All-Wise . . . . by Himself, but as Good, willed to share Himself with some other entity, ... having the knowledge, wisdom, and power to effect this Will, ... He freely with this motive of Infinite Benignity brought it about and realized it in Creation."[1]

A. The Physical Attributes

The basis of the physical attributes—Omnipresence, Eternity, and Omnipotence—is the Absolute Character of God.[2] Our source of knowledge is His revelation of His presence, His eternity, and His might in creation, and in relation to the finite.[3] The two limitations of finite creation are space and time. Because God is Absolute He is spaceless and timeless.[4] We predicate these three attributes of Him as Absolute, in His relations with His world, and as determining all things. *Omnipresence* may be conceived negatively as meaning "unlimited by space", or "incomprehensible" in the theological sense, and positively as meaning "everywhere present".[5] "Spacelessness may be conceived of as an absolute idiom, of which omnipresence is regarded as the relative idiom", according to Rhôsse.[6] "Since space is the limitation of beings having a parallel existence, and matter, a composition or synthesis and division of space",[7] God cannot be included under these categories. Hence we derive His immateriality, simplicity, and incorporeality.[8] He is spaceless and placeless,[9] without body

---

[1] *Ibid.*, pp. 311, 312.

[2] Androutsos, *op. cit.*, p. 61-2. Mesolora, *op. cit.*, III. p. 102. St. John Chrys. Ἔκδοσις 1, 15; Gennadius, in Mesolora, I, p. 73.

[3] *Ibid.*, p. 52; Rhôsse, *op. cit.*, pp. 182-186.

[4] Rhôsse, *op. cit.*, p. 308.

[5] Androutsos, *op. cit.*, p. 53.

[6] Rhôsse, *op. cit.*, p. 313.

[7] Androutsos, *op. cit.*, p. 53.

[8] Androutsos, *op. cit.*, p. 53.

[9] Isaiah, 66, 1; 1 Kings, 8, 27.

and having no material constitution however attenuated,[1]—
Pure Spirit.[2] His simplicty is that of Simple Being, having
Infinite Self-identity. It is not "an abstract simplicity; an
absence of all distinction . . . whether of hypostasis or qualities . . . but negatively, the absence of every synthesis, division, and antithesis . . . and positively, the absolutely
harmonious unity of all the self-determined distinctions of
hypostases and attributes in His Essence."[3] —

As "everywhere present" we do not say of God that He has
a potentiality of making His presence known in space, as it
were *actio in distans,* which would simply be an energy of God,
but we mean an actual essential quality.[4] Not only is He "not
far away from every one of us"[5] but He has continual and constant present intercourse with His world. "Spacelessness signifies
the essential difference of God in relation to the world as su-
pramundane Being, and His attribute of being everywhere
present constitutes His relation with His world, as God in the
world (ἐγκόσμιον Ὄν) without being confused with any of the
things in the world."[6] Through His transcendent character as
incomprehensible the Pantheistic conception is avoided; by that
of His Presence everywhere, dualistic and deistic conceptions
are removed. "As spaceless and incomprehensible, God is
transcendent Being, and through His presence everywhere He is
also immanent Being."[7] "As both incomprehensible and everywhere present, He is neither circumscribed and enclosed in any
one of the things of the world, nor is His Presence precluded
from any other. Present in each, not in part but whole, and
filling all, there is a difference . . . in the manner of His
Presence in each case contingent upon the capacity of each
thing in which He is present; so He is present in one way in

[1] As the *Clementine Homilies* and *Recognitions,* and Tertullian conceived Him. He is spaceless, but fills all space; cf. Psalm, 139, 8-10;
and St. John Chrysostom *ad loc.*
[2] St. John 4, 24; cf. Theophilus, *Ad Autolycum,* 11, 1; Clem. Alex.
Strom. 11, 2.
[3] Rhôsse, *op. cit.,* p. 309.
[4] Androutsos, *op. cit.,* p. 54.
[5] Acts, 17, 27.
[6] Rhôsse, *op. cit.,* p. 313.
[7] *ibid.,* p. 314.

heaven, in another on earth; one way in spiritual creatures, another in material and soulless creation; one way in the souls of the righteous and virtuous, another in those of sinners and the impious . . . His presence can be revealed in all sorts of different ways. Preëminently and in a unique fashion was God present in Jesus Christ."[1] Hence the scholastics distinguish three different modes of the Divine Presence: (a) *"localiter vel circumscriptive,* or potential presence, but not as if the portions of the occupied space corresponded to divisions of the Divine Essence as being identical with them;" (b) "definite", by way of indwelling—God's presence in the saints and sinners, and, as was said above, preëminently in our Lord, and particularly in the Blessed Sacrament; "as the soul in the body is limited by it, and yet everywhere present in each part, so God's Presence is everywhere entire within those limits;" and (c) "repletive", or hypostatically, the Presence *modo divino,* unbounded by space. Neither the first nor the second mode exhausts God's presence, and neither is the same as the third mode, which alone is that of God as "everywhere present".[2] Some have tried to conceive of God's presence as *substantially* and essentially in Heaven, and only *energetically* on earth.[3] But "every theory putting God outside the cosmos and accepting only a potential or dynamic presence in it orders Him in space and takes away His Absolute Character."[4] Of the mystery of the Presence of God everywhere it can best be said in summary: "God is found everywhere and always, and we can never escape His Presence."[5]

The *Eternity*[6] of God means, negatively, that He is above the limitations of time, and, positively, that He "fills it with His Presence at every instant, without succession or periods".

---

[1] *Ibid.* p. 314.

[2] Androutsos, Δογματική, pp. 54-55.

[3] As, *e. g.,* the Socinians viewed it, in order to render it intelligible to the mind of man. Such attempts are fruitless, and refutable.

[4] Cf. Androutsos, *op. cit.,* p. 55.

[5] Nitzsch, *Lehrbuch der Evangelischen Dogmatik,* p. 393, quoted by Androutsos, *op. cit.,* p. 55.

[6] Rhôsse uses the term ἀΐδιος, which is, as Androutsos admits, more correct than αἰώνιος, which the latter employs. Αἰωνιότης implies of the past "indefinite", "countless succession", but of the future as unending and involving permanence". Cf. "eternal" and "everlasting". Androutsos, note I. p. 56.

Since time is "the law of the constant motion of beings having beginning and end, and changing at every instant," the Absolute God is necessarily not limited by it. He has neither beginning nor end, nor is there any period of succession, and no alternation in Him. As the Holy Scriptures bear witness[1] to this, our reason and its conclusions are reinforced in the truth of the principle that He who is Absolute is above the limitation of time.[2] "As the Absolute and Infinite, we predicate of God aseity and self-existence . . . . for He has in Himself the reason or cause of His own being, and the End or Purpose of His existence. . . . As such He is lacking in nothing, self-contained, independent, and self-sufficient[3] . . . As Absolute, He is . . . . absolutely timeless, for neither His Essence nor His energy is limited by time . . . . As timeless He is absolutely eternal, without beginning, without end . . . for only things in time have a beginning and end of their existence, and undergo gradual development, with a transition from potential to actual, and with change or alteration and decay."[4] "Time in relation to eternity is an instant in which there is no transition from present to past, or future to present."[5] In God's sight a long period of time or the briefest moment, is alike nothing.[6] Eternity is a permanent quality of God; in Him is no change or alternation. He is therefore immutable, unswerving, and unchanging.[7] St. Augustine uses the figure of a tree on the edge of a running brook to illustrate the relation of God's unchanging and eternal character, independent of the ebb and flow of things in time.[8]

God is as well the Master and Creator of Time. "As He being beyond all space is yet everywhere present, yet not locally, so the eternal God outside time is yet present in every instant of it."[9] Yet this presence of God in time does not subject Him

[1] Psalm, 90, 2-4; Rev. 1, 8; 10, 6; 15, 7; 1 Tim. 6, 16.
[2] Androutsos, op. cit., p. 56.
[3] Rhôsse, op. cit., p. 306.
[4] Rhôsse, op. cit., pp. 308-9.
[5] Androutsos, op. cit., p. 56.
[6] 2 Peter 3, 8, and cf. Psalm 90, 4.
[7] Rhôsse, op. cit., p. 309.
[8] De Vera Religione, 49, and Conf. XI. 16.
[9] Androutsos, op. cit., p. 57; cf. Rev. 1, 4.

to the conditions of time, as if the time relations were defined in Him, but He includes time without being part of it. As there is no alternation or succession in Him, He is immutable, unchanging, and ever the same.[1] The converse is equally true—since time is the measure of change, if there be no change in God, He must be eternal. In His dealings with men He does submit to "esoteric" changes, as for example, in the Divine Economy.[2] He may seem to man to change and alter His attitude. This is only our way of viewing His unalterable and unswerving character, as compared to our changing relations with Him. When we say, "God repented Him of the evil" it is a "human expression of the relation of God to man, correlative (as) in the case of a plan or deed, to what we do when we ascribe (in the Holy Scriptures) to the Unseen, hands, feet, or eyes."[3] He is the same, and His purpose remains unchanging though He appear to one mind benignant and kindly, and to another harsh and angry. As St. Augustine says: *Quem ad modum sol oculos puros, sanos, vegetos, fortes habenti tranquillus apparet, in oculos autem lippos quasi tela aspera jaculatur; intuentem illum vegetat, hunc excruciat, non mutatus, sed mutatum: sic cum coeperis esse perversus, et tibi Deus perversus videbitur; tu mutatus es, non ille. .Erit . . . tibi poena, quod bonis gaudium*[4].

His energy is as eternal as His Essence,[5] for His Essence as timeless, is eternal.[6] As His Eternity involves not only His being above the limitations of time, but as well His immediate presence in every instant of it, His energy may be considered to alter its objective flow with the development and change in mankind. His eternal presence operates in each individual case according to a different fashion and is in a sense conditioned by the capacity and responsiveness of the individual, in the ebb

---

[1] Cf. St. James, 1, 17; Psalm 102, 26-27. Androutsos, *op. cit.,* p. 57.

[2] Mesolora, *op. cit.,* III. p. 102; Gennadius, in Mesolora, I. p. 73; St. John Damascene, Ἔκδοσις 1, 15.

[3] Androutsos, *op. cit.,* pp. 58-59.

[4] *Enarr.,* in Psalm 72, 7. Cf. Dyobouniotes Δογ. Ἀνδρ. κρινομ., p. 16 and Androutsos Δογμ. Μελέται, Α', pp. 50-52; St. John Damascene, *Dial. contra Manichaeos,* 79.

[5] Rhôsse, *op. cit.,* p. 314.

[6] *Ibid.,* p. 309.

and flow of human history. Hence it is not possible for God to regard all times as a present, but He must preserve the same relation to the past, present, and future, as prevails in the affairs of finite man. Else were "history a mere phantasy and appearance, not a reality and actuality."[1] St. Augustine held that to God all times were an eternal present. According to Rhôsse,[2] if God deals with the world in its necessary limitations of time, these must be known to Him in their real-character of past, present, and future. The distinctions of time are then real to God in His dealings with the world. According to Androutsos, God is not subject to the conditions of time in the sense that "certain events are distinguished by Him as past, others as present, and others as future,"[3] for "He knows future events, seeing them as present."[4] Each of these positions is tenable, for there is no dogmatic decree about the matter.[5]

The *Omnipotence* of God is shown in the Creation of the world from nothing, in God's preservation of it, and sustaining it in being, in God's wonders of Revelation and Miracle, and in His governance, administration, and oversight of the Universe. Consequently His omnipotence is regarded as creative, preservative, and governing.[6] The sphere of the functioning of His Almighty Power is the all, or everything.[7] The theological doctrine of the Omnipotence of God is embodied in the statement: "God can do all that He can will."[8] This takes for granted the truth of the commonly accepted theological formula that "there is no distinction between the power and will of God."[9] For

[1] *Ibid.*, pp. 314-315.
[2] *Op. cit.*, p. 57. Dyobouniotes says: "God knows the future as future, the present as present and past as past, . . otherwise there could be no right administration of the world . . . God will see the sinner who is going to repent as good, while the good man who is to fall into sin, as evil" (p. 18, Δογμ. 'Ανδρ. κριν.). Androutsos answers this, p. 55 of his pamphlet (Δογμ. Μελέται, Α'). He objects that this view involves the theory of time as not real but only apparent, and the deduction that all things are Eternal.
[3] Androutsos, Δογματική, p. 57.
[4] Androutsos, *ibid.*, p. 66; Δογματικαὶ Μελέται, Α', pp. 54-55.
[5] Cf. below on the Knowledge and Wisdom of God, pp. 93 ff.
[6] Rhôsse, *op. cit.*, pp. 312-313, Androutsos, *op. cit.*, p. 59.
[7] *ibid.*
[8] Androutsos, Δογματικαὶ Μελ., Α', p. 53.
[9] Simar, *Lehrbuch der Dogmatik*, I, p. 138, quoted *ibid.*

the purposes of human thought, however, it is useful to distinguish *will* and *power* in God, so we may resolve the above
statement into the two propositions: (a) God does whatever He
wills, and (b) He wills what is consistent with His Nature.
The first conception of the Will of God is called the "actual"
or "pragmatic" will (πραγματικὴ θέλησις) and the second conception is termed that of the "absolute power of His will"
(ἀπόλυτος δύναμις τῆς θελέσεως). We distinguish the actual will
of God in fact from the possible content of what He could have
willed.[1]   The limits of His power to Will are the self-determined limits of His Nature.[2]

(a) When we say that God does whatever He wills, we mean
that the compass of His Power to realize and make a fact what
He wills is commensurate with the content of that Will.   Just
as power involves will, so will involves personality.   We cannot
conceive of His omnipotent power being exercised apart from
His directing will, nor this will as the result of anything less
than the action of His whole Personality.   Any more precise
or any less wide conception of His Power reduces it to a mechanical and blind force, which is utterly repugnant to the
notion of the absolute Perfection of God.   In Him, furthermore, we may not apply the distinction (based on finite human
experience) between will and power, as if they in Him could
ever be in contrast or antithesis.[3]   Whatever He wills He can do.

(b) "God wills whatever He is able to will."   The limitations of His will are those of His own Essence.   Because He is
Himself, He necessarily wills what He wills.   His will is not
arbitrary; it is no whim whereby He sets out to perform the
impossible in the natural, rational, or ethical spheres.   As St.
John Damascene says, "God can do whatever He wills, but
does not will all He can do."[4]   He could, for example, destroy
the world, but does not will to do so.   "His power extends not
only to the extent of His pragmatic Will, but to everything—
even to those things which He neither wills actually, nor would
be able to will."[5]   *"Multa potest Deus et non vult; nihil autem*

---

[1] Androutsos, Δογματική, p. 59.
[2] Androutsos, Δογματική, pp. 59-60.
[3] *Ibid.*, cf. Δογμ. Μελέται, Α´, pp. 52-54.
[4] St. John Damascene, Ἔκδοσις, 1, 13.
[5] Androutsos, *op. cit.*, p. 60.

vult quod non potest."[1] "The might of God underlies His actual Will, and the one bound which it may not exceed is that of the physically, logically, or morally impossible."[2] "God cannot do what is repugnant to His Nature,"[3] and this impossibility, a seeming limitation of His Omnipotence, is not an instance of weakness but a testimony to His might.[4] "God cannot do other than what He wills" is another statement of the complete identity of will and power in the Divine Nature.[5] A view of the Divine omnipotence which sees it only in the world of Creation, governed and regulated by God,[6] takes away from the absolute quality of God's omnipotence, for it regards it as exhausted in the achievement of the universe, and consequently precludes the possibility of miracle.[7] The world is not of necessity, but of God's Free Will.[8]

B. The Logical Attributes of God

For the attributes of God now to be considered, we take personality for granted. In fact, as we have seen, the notion of personality is really essential to the conception of God's omnipotence, as well as to that of the other attributes. The logical, rational, or intellectual attributes of God even more definitely involve this notion, for "only one who has self-consciousness and the power of free self-determination can be holy, just, or wise."[9] There are those who claim that the note of personality as applied to God, "limits Him and reduces Him to the level of finite things," for the notion of personality involves

[1] St. Augustine, *Enchiridion*, 95.
[2] "For this he could neither will nor accomplish", Androutsos, *op. cit.*, pp. 60-61.
[3] Rhôsse, *op. cit.*, p. 313.
[4] Cf. Theodoret, Ἐρανιστ. διαλ. 3, and cf. Augustine, *De Civitate Dei*, V. 10. note 1, Rhôsse, *op. cit.*, p. 313.
[5] Abelard, in Androutsos, *op. cit.*, p. 61.
[6] Schleiermacher, in Androutsos, *ibid.*
[7] Cf. note on miracle, Androutsos, *op. cit.*, pp. 119-120.
[8] As versus Pantheism and Deism,—God knows Himself as *of necessity*, for the Divine Essence and Attributes are necessary. His knowledge of the world, since the world was not necessary, is a *free* knowledge. The Creation was a free act of God. Rhôsse, *op. cit.*, p. 302; Androutsos, *op. cit.*, p. 64.
[9] Androutsos, *op. cit.*, pp. 61-62.

as a necessary premise the existence of other personalities in contrast to which alone may self-consciousness be developed, and in contrast to the acts of whom the consciousness of the freedom of one's own acts may be realized. This conception, they say, is incompatible with the Absolute Character of God. In answer to this it may be said that the Absolute can not be other than He is; by His Absolute Knowledge of Himself He can be said "to know absolutely His own necessary Existence, or His Essence seen by God existing necessarily . . . It is a knowledge . . . of His one Absolute Essence in its absolute Necessity, Rationality, and Freedom. . . ."[1] But if He is necessarily what He is, and necessarily knows Himself as such, He must know Himself as necessarily *free* as well. His Reason or Wisdom, as absolute, is both the power and the energy of knowing and recognizing. Hence nothing can prevent the exercise of this Absolute Reason to know whether within or without God, whatever can be known. The former knowledge, in contrast to that of the world, is called "necessary", and the knowledge of the world, viewed as a relative attribute, is termed "free".[2]

Every category that we can make in regard to God brings Him into the realm of the finite, without which process we could have no conception of Him which would have any content. The negations we employ of Him, based on our reasoning from the finite, seem, as it were, limitations which we impose on the character of God, as we must distinguish Him from the world. If God escapes all categories then our conception of the Absolute would be barren, sterile, and empty of all content for us. The view which rejects all such categorization of God, leads to the rejection of any notion of Him.[3] If we conceive of Him at all, we must conceive Him in the only way we can conceive of anything. The basis of our consciousness of personality is obviously the recognition of the non-ego. As such it is not ultimately necessary, but only empirical and pragmatic. The recognition of personality in ourselves is the culmination of a process of observation, comparison, and contrast, which is-

---

[1] Rhôsse, *op. cit.*, p. 307.
[2] Rhôsse, *op. cit.*, p. 316.
[3] Androutsos, *op. cit.*, p. 62.

sues in self-consciousness. In Him in whom is no change, no process of knowledge, no beginning, no end, who is self-existent, self-contained, and independent, recognition of His Personality and His Freedom is an eternal, necessary, and immediate fact. It is not based upon contrast with other personalities, nor is the consciousness of God's Freewill founded on experience with other wills. Hence, philosophically, the conception of God as a Person is not impossible. It is fundamental and necessary, theologically. Religiously, the conception of a Deity who does not care about the events in the world, but who only "wound it up and started it going", or the conception of the helpless God involved by necessity in the finite world, is absolutely inadequate to meet the needs of men. Man, as having self-consciousness and free will, cannot be satisfied either with Deism or Pantheism: God must needs be at least a Person. His Reason and Will are recognized without reference to man and the finite world. "Everything constituting the imperfections and defects of our will and nature is irreconcilable with the simplicity, immutability, and Absolute Perfection of God."[1]

The course of the speculation about the necessity of the Will of God willing Himself, and His will's freedom in willing the Universe, it is not necessary to touch upon. It is a mystery inaccessible to our reason. We must distinguish between the will of God willing Himself and that willing the Universe, but cannot investigate more closely the relation of the two aspects of the Absolute Will.[2]

God is *All Knowing* in that He knows all, and this Omniscience is absolute both in form and content; in *form,* because "He knows all—timelessly, perfectly and immediately, not as a transition from past to present, and in sequence, but in one instant of immediate insight (*intuitio*) ; in *content,* as He, comprehending all, both Himself and the Universe, knows the actual and real possibilities and impossibilities of past, present, and

---

[1] Androutsos, *op. cit.,* p. 63.

[2] On this point cf. Androutsos, *op. cit.,* p. 64, quoting Strauss and Simar, and Rhôsse, *op. cit.,* pp. 287-304, *et al.* Rhôsse is more explicit on the necessary character of God's self-knowledge than is Androutsos, whom I have followed above.

future.”[1] The Absolute Reason or knowledge of God includes, as we have seen, both the power and the energy of knowing, and is an attribute of His Essence. He recognizes in Himself “His One Absolute Essence in its Absolute Necessity, Reason, and Freedom, together with all the fulness of its powers as ordered in one . . . harmonious unity. In Him are all the Eternal Truths and Eternal Laws of Nature, Reason, and Ethic, . . . decreed by His Absolute Reason and Free Will, . . . and these He knows and recognizes by His Absolute Knowledge and Reason.”[2] His knowledge of the world is as immediate and complete as that of Himself, but it is different, in that it is not gained from the latter.[3] It is not absolute in this sense, and the idea of the world in the mind of God is different from that idea realized and actualized in Creation. Hence His Knowledge of the world is different in quality from that of Himself, as He knows “about the world as it is in itself, about its causes and effects, the energies in the world and their results in fact. . . The object of His knowledge of the world is not only that which results by the action of the law of necessity in the physical sphere ordained by Himself, but as well . . . . the results issuing from the free causes He has created” . . . (Their freedom is not absolute, but only relative and created, hence it is dependent upon Him.) “He knows, through the knowledge of His Own energy which brought into being the free causes of the Universe, their existence, capacities, and limitations, but not . . . . the actual content of their deeds.”[4] If He did, these acts would only proceed from Him as source, their relative liberty would be destroyed, and He would be author of resulting evils. He does know all the acts of man nevertheless, and their consequences, even as free.[5] This knowledge may be called the *relative,* in distinction to the *absolute,* knowledge of God. He does not, however, know them by sensation, as the subject of knowing, as if He had a “certain characteristic of passively receiving sensations”, but by immediate intuition regarding man-

[1] Androutsos, *op. cit.,* pp. 64-65.

[2] Rhôsse, *op. cit.,* pp. 307-308.

[3] Rhôsse, *op., cit.,* p. 316.

[4] *Ibid.,* p. 317.

[5] “Free”, that is relatively and createdly, not “absolutely”, cf. Rhôsse, *op. cit.,* p. 319.

kind.[1] "Nothing can happen by the free action of independent agents in the world . . . without God having knowledge of it as possible and capable of occurring, through His ever-present Might and Will in the world."[2]

We distinguish then two, possibly three, objects of Divine Knowledge: (a) that which necessarily exists—God, and the possibilities existing in the idea of the Divine Nature, the knowledge of which is called "natural" knowledge;[3] (b) that which exists of God's Free Will—the created world, and its possibilities, the knowledge of which is called "free"; and a possible third (c) category, relating to that which is hypothetical and conditional, "including that possible on the basis of the occurrence of certain conditions," to which contingent type the name "middle" knowledge is applied (scientia media, scientia conditionata, scientia conditionata futurorum).[4] According to Androutsos, "the introduction of this kind of knowledge is superfluous. Since God knows what happens at any point in time. . . and also all possible things not to be realized in the event, the facts thus conditioned relegated to this category of scientia media already belong to the possible, not to be realized in fact." Hence it is unnecessary to make this category. Rhôsse, however, seems to accept it.[5]

God as Omniscient knows all things. He knows Himself, His creation as under the law of necessity, and as well what He has created with the capacity of free choice and self-direction. His knowledge is eternal in quality; hence He knows in advance, humanly speaking, what is going to happen. As we saw above, the problem of the relation of time to Eternity is for us insoluble. The problem of the relation of the prescience or fore-

[1] Ibid., pp. 316, 318.

[2] Ibid., p. 319.

[3] Also called "necessary" knowledge, according to Rhôsse, pp. 307-308, 316, note 1.

[4] Androutsos, op. cit., pp. 65; Rhôsse, op. cit., pp. 320-321 (§ 188). The authors of this theory were the Jesuits Fonseca and Molina, and the classical text illustrating the basis of this notion is St. Matt. 11, 21. "Woe unto you Chorazin! .. and Bethsaida! for if the mighty works, which were done in you, had been done in Tyre and Sidon, they would have repented long ago" . . . . cf. Dyobouniotes, Δογμ. 'Ανδρ. κριν., p. 15, and Androutsos, Δογ. Μελ. Α', p. 54.

[5] Ibid., op. cit., p. 324.

knowledge of God to events in His world is one of the aspects of that problem. If God knows all that is going to happen, how can any free agents exist beside Himself? His foreknowledge in relation to the material universe presents no difficulty. As God knows all causes, their possible effects, and the relation of all causes to their certain effects, He, as the Source of all Natural Law, knows beforehand the inevitable sequences of cause and effect. There is nothing fortuitous or accidental in the natural world, and if we cannot predict the results and consequences subsequent to the action of a nexus of causes, it is only because of our limited knowledge. The material world acts mechanically, and God's foreknowledge of its operations and their results belongs to Him as Creator, Ordainer of its laws, and Determiner of its End, as well as to Him as the Omniscient.[1]

It is otherwise with the relation of foreknowledge to the actions of free agents, whom God has created with free will and the power of self-determination. Their freedom is not absolute, but still it is real though relative; they are not self-caused, but creatures brought into existence by God. Hence "this relative and created freedom remains in a sense always dependent upon God. . . The free agents of the world at every moment receive from the ever-present and continuous energy of the Power of God the power for the exercise of their own free energy."[2] So "the Foreknowledge of God and the freedom of men's acts seem contradictory and mutually exclusive"[3] for if God knows all that man not only can, but will do, "free acts become impossible."[4] If his freedom is destroyed, his responsibility ceases as well. Of the solutions of this difficulty one type limits the foreknowledge of God, saying that God does not know the free acts of man, and another sacrifices the freedom of man, by saying that it is only apparent not real, and that man alike with the natural creation, functions under a law of necessity.[5]

A form of the first type of solution is developed in the state-

---

[1] Rhôsse, *op. cit.*, p. 322 (§ 190).
[2] *Ibid.*, pp. 317, 318-319.
[3] *Ibid.*, p. 322 (§ 190).
[4] Androutsos, *op. cit.*, p. 65.
[5] *Ibid.*, and Rhôsse, *op. cit.*, p. 323; Weisse, *Philosophische Dogmatik*, 1, § 509, follows the second view.

ment that God knows human acts only as possible, not as actual. That is, when God willed to create men as free agents, for the sake of that freedom He deliberately restricted His own fore-knowledge.[1] This view rests on a deistic basis, that knowledge of the world as part of the manifestation of the power of an omnipresent, immanent, and transcendent God, would be a re-striction of man, and that to secure man's free exercise of the power wherewith God has endowed him, God must cease to in-fluence, interfere, or concern Himself with human acts. It also rests on a false conception of human freedom as being absolute in its nature. "Only in the case of the freedom of created agents being regarded as absolute, and in consequence the estab-lishment of a principle of absolute independence of God, and of existence outside of and apart from Him, can it be maintained that God could not know the actual acts of free agents."[2]

The second type of solution suggested above denies the reality of human freedom by a wrong conception of God's Foreknowl-edge as Absolute.[3] "If the acts of free agents were initiated according to Absolute Foreordination, the Omniscience of God would include all future acts of man by an act of Divine Will exercising the Divine Reason . . . toward that outside God. But the Divine Reason and Foreknowledge do not concur with the action of the Divine Will: God knows evil as possible . . . but does not will it as actual in the world."[4] Hence the necessary distinction between God's Absolute Omniscience as knowing all things absolutely, whereby He *necessarily* knows Himself, and the direction of that knowledge outwardly toward Creation, whereby He *freely* knows all things concerning it. If God's knowledge knew the content of human acts by knowing Himself, then God would be the source of all those acts, since His Self-knowledge is a result of His Will necessarily and freely acting with His Power, and with all the other attributes of His Nature.[5] So there would be no freedom in man's acts, but they

[1] Rhôsse, *op. cit.*, p. 323.

[2] *Ibid.*, p. 324.

[3] His knowledge, as absolute, relates to the possibilities and cap-acities of free agents, not to the content of their acts, according to Rhôsse.

[4] Rhôsse, *op. cit.*, p. 323.

[5] *Ibid.*, pp. 317-318.

would be the result of necessity, following out the laws of their own being, and these laws would be only the decrees of the Divine Being.   God would then be the Cause and Creator of evil, and man would be no more responsible than is inorganic matter under natural law.   Another aspect of this same argument is that God necessarily knows not only all we *can* do, since He is the Source, Cause, and Creator of our being and knows its laws, but also knows what we *will* do, as Omniscient.   We believe that we act freely, and we do act as if we were conscious of choosing freely, but our actions and our choice are determined by our education, environment, heredity, and character.   As our choice is determined by our character, we choose consciously but not freely.   It is our ignorance on which is based the conviction we have of our freedom; God, as knowing all things, knows the causes of our actions, both as a whole and in detail, and can predict infallibly our course of action.   He does not cause it, nor does His Foreknowledge as such compel us to choose what we do choose; nevertheless our choice is determined by other things than our will.   His knowledge is exact and inerrant as to our choice, but this does not determine it.   Our choice is not a consequence of His knowledge, but neither is it free.   Fundamentally this is not essentially different from the preceding aspect of the same argument.

We must then distinguish between the Foreordaining knowledge of God as Absolute—that is, as an active coöperation of all the attributes of His Essence functioning together, in relation to human acts—and His Foreknowledge as in a sense passive and not determining the content of those acts.   It is along this line that the Orthodox presentation of the solution of the problem lies. Rhôsse denies any possibility of a passive character in God's Knowledge, as if it were subject to impressions, in other words disavows the human method of knowing as the method of God's Knowing.[1]   To him the distinction of Absolute and Relative is the means of the solution of the problems arising from the relation of the Infinite God to His finite world.   God's Omniscience is both Absolute and relative.   As Absolute, it is necessary, and its subject matter includes all that has its source in

[1] Rhôsse, *op. cit.*, p. 318.

Him. As Absolute, it concerns the world of necessity and law, and the world of possibility. As relative, it has contact with the world actually as it is, realized in fact, and the scope of this Omniscience of God as relative is not only the possible but the actual—whether past, present, or future—in the world of Creation. "As the Power of God, essentially of itself Absolute . . . has a certain relative character as the Highest Power in the world . . . so the Reason or Wisdom of God, and His Power, rightly termed Absolute in relation to His Essence, . . . receive a certain relative character as the Highest Wisdom and Power of God in the world. . . Essentially it is one and the same Power and Wisdom viewed in two aspects: in relation to the essential Nature of God, and in relation to something other than Himself."[1] Rhôsse's solution of the problem of the relation of the Foreknowledge of God to the free acts of men, is to deny the Absolute character of both the freedom of man and the knowledge of God in relation to the actual content of human acts.

Androutsos bases his solution on a distinction in the character of God's knowledge, essentially the same as that of Rhôsse. Following St. John Damascene, he holds that "the Foreknowledge of God . . . is not the cause of everything that may happen. But He knows that we are going to do this or that. . . As a physician is not the cause of the disease, if he knows in advance that some one is to fall ill, but the disease is the result of some other cause, and the foreknowledge of the physician (is) his skill in recognizing this cause, so God is not the cause or reason of the acts done by us, but our own will acting freely in determining them."[2] "God knows what is going to happen, seeing all events as present without His knowledge exercising any influence upon them."[3] So God sees all things, but His knowledge of the results of necessary or free causes does not cause these results. They come about as if they had not been seen in advance. This knowledge is not "creative" but as it were "passive or receptive", is limited by the events possible in themselves, and "the events are known by God because they ex-

[1] Rhôsse, op. cit., p. 319.
[2] Contra Manichaeos dialogus, 79.
[3] Androutsos, op. cit., p. 66.

ist, and do not exist because He knows them".[1] In a sense He is, as it were, a spectator of the acts of man. This limitation of the Knowledge of God concerning the free acts of man does not derogate from His Absolute Character, for He created man, knows all his possibilities and capacities and "orders all things so that human free will may not foil the purpose of the world. Otherwise the existence of evil cannot be explained . . . than that God knows it as a consequence of man and free will, and not as a subject of His Own Knowledge, for it would then be necessary, and have God as its Creator."[2] Essentially these two solutions do not differ. They both ascribe a different character to God's Knowledge of all matters concerning free will and its consequences, in the concrete, than they do to God's self-knowledge, and His Knowledge of the possible. They are both designed to secure: (a) omniscience on God's part and (b) free will on man's without postulating (c) the absolute character of either in relation to the other.

God is *All Wise* in that "He knows the best means for the best ends." The element of knowledge is essential to the definition, since the Wisdom of God as shown in nature,[3] in mankind, and especially in Christ, is a result not only of His Wisdom as a noetic faculty, but of His Will and Power as well. It is not enough to define it as the sublime skill or art of adapting means to ends,[4] for it is a logical prerequisite of Divine Omnipotence.[5] It is closely allied to the Divine Will and the Divine Reason, willing and determining the end of Creation, for by it all things are ordered each severally to its own end, and each to subserve as well a greater End. Foreseeing evil as a

---

[1] For otherwise they would be caused by Him necessarily, and there would be no free will, *ibid.*; Dyobouniotes ('Η Δογμ. 'Ανδρούτσου κρινομ., p. 18) objects to this distinction as "removing the Absolute Character of God, and the possibility of His governing the world, if God does not know what is going to happen;" for Androutsos' answer, cf. Δογματικαὶ Μελέται, Α', p. 56 (his reply to Dyobouniotes).

[2] Androutsos, *op. cit.*, pp. 66-67, and on his discussion of the problem of evil, cf. pp. 117-119.

[3] Prov. 3, 19, 8. (esp. 22-30); Ps. 104, 24.

[4] Cf. Macaire, *Théologie Dogmatique Orthodoxe*, Paris, 1860, vol. 1. p. 157.

[5] They are coupled together in Job 9, 4; 12, 13; Jer. 10, 12; Dan. 2, 20.

consequence of the wrong use by man of his freedom, the Divine Wisdom planned in advance the means of the removal of evil from the world—through the Redemption of man. Divine Wisdom in its prevision has provided as well that nothing human or creaturely shall mar the plan of God for His world.[1] Divine Wisdom, says Rhôsse, as an Absolute Attribute is predicated of the Divine Essence, and as relative is such because of the content of its energy and not by reason of the manner nor of the end for which it operates.[2]

C. The Ethical Attributes

Holiness, Justice, and *Love* are the three ethical attributes of God. As in the natural world the Almighty Power of God is manifested, and in the rational order, His Wisdom, so in the ethical attributes of Holiness and Justice or Righteousness, each of these attributes is lifted to its Highest Personal Perfection. Love is the characteristic of all the aspects of God's Activity and Being. "Holiness" may be termed the "full accord of the Divine Will for God;" Righteousness, "the stabilizing factor of the ethical order in its administration," and Love, "the attribute according to which God shares His good things with His creatures, and Himself with mankind."

Holiness. As one aspect of Holiness means separation from the world and from every earthly thing and imperfection (thus in the Old Testament) so the ethical aspect includes this same note of separation, inasmuch as things earthly are contaminated and unclean. Hence Holiness may be defined as "that property according to which the Divine Will is perfectly identified with the Good which it seeks; in relation to man, this object is moral cleanness, and the carrying out of the ethical law implanted in man's conscience." This good with which the Divine Will is equivalent may not be understood as something outside[3] the Divine Nature, as if the Will of God were to be conformed to some higher Good external to It, for this would take away the Absolute Character of His Will, but this Good is "the expres-

[1] Androutsos, *op. cit.,* p. 67.
[2] Rhôsse, *op. cit.,* p. 319.
[3] See below, pp. 105-106 on this phrase "outside God" in relation to the Divine Essence.

sion of the internal identity of the Divine Nature with it."[1]
The scholastic question as to "whether good is good, hence God
wills it", or "because He does will it, it is good," creates an unnecessary distinction. God can only by His Nature will what
is good, and what He wills, as proceeding from His Nature must
be only what He is, that is, good.

Righteousness. As having implanted in us His ideal of
Goodness, God is known also as Guardian and Administrator of
the Ethical Law. The Divine Will is known as Righteous when
God, judging and administering according to the Eternal Law
of Righteousness and Justice, recompenses the obedient, and
punishes the transgressor.[2] In His Eternal Essence are the
eternal truths and the Eternal Laws of Nature, Reason, and
Ethic, eternally self-originated, and self-determined in the Divine Essence. These are the object of the Divine Knowledge
and Reason,[3] and are the basis of the relations of God as Holy
and Just, to His Creation. "God as the Absolute Good hates
evil and is absolutely Holy. As He accords to each of His
powers or determinations and properties—physical, logical, and
ethical—what is fitting and proper to it in His Absolute Life
and Energy, and maintains all in Absolute balance, proportion,
and harmony, He is viewed in relation to His Eternal Self, as
absolutely Just or Righteous. . . .[4] As God wills not only
Himself and His Own Absolute Essence, but also something
other than Himself, . . . through His wisdom and Might
He realizes this Will outside Himself in the world. . . His
Will in relation to the world desires Good, not as it exists in God
seen by Himself, but as it exists and is manifest in His world,
as its highest Good. So He is the Cause of this sharing of all
Good with Creation, and also (is) its highest End, to which all
goods in the world tend—physical and material as well as spiritual. . . . As He hates and turns away from all evil in the
world, and is promoting all good in it, He is Holy. . . The
Righteousness of God as directed to this world in each of its
several units . . . . accords what is fitting to the nature and

---

[1] Androutsos, *op. cit.*, p. 68.
[2] *Ibid.*, p. 69.
[3] Rhôsse, *op. cit.*, pp. 307-308 (§ 177).
[4] Rhôsse, *op. cit.*, p. 308 (§ 177).

scope of its being, and both recompenses good and punishes evil."[1]

The relation between His Holiness and Righteousness is that between God as Creator and Originator of the ethical order, and God as "impartial Administrator of it . . . . ordering all things to their Highest End." Righteousness is not an element of Holiness, related as *species* to *genus,* as the Alexandrines thought, nor a mere objective property of it, as Marcion thought. The former mistaken view "exercised a disastrous influence on the question of Eternal Punishment, and the dogma of the Atonement", while the latter gave rise to the Marcionite doctrine of the double Principle, in the relations of God and His world. As by His Holiness God promulgates His eternal Laws (*justitia legislativa*) so by His Righteousness He actively upholds and administers this Law.[2]

In the conception of the Righteousness or Justice of God preed above it was said that God as Righteous recompenses good and punishes evil. It may be objected[3] that it is not the function of the Divine Administrator of His own Law to reward anyone for his attempts to observe it. It does not, it is said, come within the province of judicial function to reward or recompense anyone for obedience to law. Man really cannot claim any reward for obedience to God with any show of right on his side. This objection is really not valid. It is a wrong conception of God as Just to conceive of Him as a human magistrate exercising his office in the punishment of crime and law breaking.[4] God's sphere as the Righteous and Just Administrator of His Ethical Order is much wider than man's. in his capacity of judge and magistrate. Man can claim no reward as by his right. God concedes rewards and recompense of His bounty. As being self-caused and self-sufficient, lacking nothing, eternally independent, God possesses absolute Beatitude.[5] But this Beatitude or Blessedness God wills to share with man. His own Happiness as a Divine Attribute

[1] *Ibid.,* pp. 324-325.
[2] Androutsos, *op. cit.,* pp. 69-70.
[3] *E. g.,* Dyobouniotes, 'Η Δογμ. 'Ανδρούτσου κριν., p. 18.
[4] Androutsos, Δογμ. Μελ.,Α', p. 57.
[5] Rhôsse, *op. cit.,* p. 306 (§ 175).

is the source of His Will to have men come to know and share it.[1] He desires men's happiness, to secure which He freely rewards righteous men who seek the good, "ordering things according to His Holiness together with His Blessedness." Furthermore, inasmuch as the bad are punished because of the bad use of their free will, the good should be rewarded for their right use of it. Any attempt to be more precise in the analysis of the relation of the different rewards and punishments received by men here—for the evil ofttimes seems to prevail, and virtue seems to go unrewarded on this earth—cannot be satisfactory. Disease and misfortune, and the gnawings of conscience are external and internal punishments respectively. In general, "while to the impious, sufferings may serve as punishment for sin, for the righteous they may be means of testing, purification, and perfecting in the ethical life."[2]

Love. "The property by which God shares His own good things with the world and mankind, constituting created things sharers of His own Blessedness, is Love."[3] God as Eternally Perfect and Absolute did not will to remain alone in the enjoyment of His Perfections "but as Good, willed to share Himself with something other than Himself".[4] All that was Himself He recognizes as Necessarily Existing, but the "other-than-Himself" He knew as non-being and non-existing of itself. Hence the reason and cause of the existence of the other-than-Self, that is, the world, existed in the goodness and love of God, together with His Reason, Wisdom, and Might. His Love or Goodness in this aspect is, then, the "quality of imparting and giving, directed to that without Him".[5] It is the opposite and antithesis of selfishness or egoism. As self-love is always turned in upon itself and regards other entities only as contributing to self, so love, focusing its desires not on self, but impelled to go without, seeks the other than self,

[1] *Ibid.*, pp. 311-312.
[2] Androutsos, Δογματική, p. 70. Evil and suffering may by God's grace be diverted to serve a good end, cf. Rom. 8, 28. This is the practical solution of the problem of evil.
[3] Androutsos, *op. cit.*, p. 71.
[4] Rhôsse, *op. cit.*, p. 311.
[5] *Ibid.*, p. 326.

to share with it what it has, and of course, takes for granted the existence of that toward which interest is directed. Self-love focuses all things on itself; love's interest converges in other-than-self.[1] So the love of God issues in a continuous and eternal Energy between the Persons of the Blessed Trinity, and His Love to creatures issues in all His relations with His world—from His eternal plan of Creation, through the Redemption, and now in the life of His Church.[2]

In His Eternal Being God knows and recognizes not only Himself, but also the conception of other-than-self. This He first knew as non-being, then as the "whole of the ideas and conceptions of the possible and actual outside Himself", with relation to His Will, Might, and His Nature in general.[3] As this idea of the world may be conceived of as being antecedent to its realization actually, we may say that this idea of the cosmos existed in the mind of God from before time.[4] As God knew each of His Attributes as being something that the others were not, so He knew the conception of "non-being" in relation to His own necessary Being.[5] This idea of "non-being" in relation to His Absolute and Infinite Being, included both the notions of *free,* as contrasted with necessary, and *finite* and *contingent,* in relation to His Infinity. "Since God is Absolute Good . . . He wills to endow non-being with existence according to the prototype in His Nature, in order to constitute it capable of sharing His Goodness". So He regarded non-being as not completely non-being, that is, in contrast to actual Being, Himself, but as other-than-Being. The potential being, then, of the world was made actual by His Will coöperating with His Wisdom and Almighty Power, since it was capable of becoming, and was not non-being in the sense of "impossible", according to His eternal, natural, ra-

[1] Androutsos, *op. cit.,* p. 71.
[2] *Ibid.,* and Rhôsse, *op. cit.,* p. 326.
[3] Rhôsse, *op. cit.,* p. 327 (§ 193).
[4] That is, it is not eternal, in the sense that God's Self-knowledge is, nor is it in time, since the Creation made actual the content of the idea. "The conception of 'before time' lies between . . that of eternity and . . . time" (Rhôsse, *op. cit.,* p. 327, note 2; cf. p. 86, note 6, and p. 152, note 2, following).
[5] *Ibid.,* p. 327.

tional, and ethical laws.[1] "The idea of the world, having
noetic existence in the mind of God, received, through His
creative Power, relative self-existence and self-containedness."[2]
This is what we mean by existing "outside God", that is,
relative self-existence and self-containedness; not as by opposition and contrast to real Being, but as consisting in other than
that Being. This phrase requires to be supplemented by the
statement that the world is as well, "in God",[3] which signifies
its union and fellowship with Him who caused it, sustains it,
works in it, and orders it to His own End. It was His Love
which lay back of the idea of the world generated before time,
together with the plan of the Creation of man, the Incarnation, the Redemption of man, and the consummation of all
in the sharing by man of the Beatific Vision.[4] "Since Love
is the attribute by which God imparts His own Goods, the
joy arising from this sharing of them, and especially that
proceeding from the contemplation of their own Divine Perfection, constitutes the Blessedness of God."[5]

This attribute of God is a peculiarly Christian contribution to the knowledge of God. It is the climax of all perfections, and the bond uniting all the attributes of God into one.[6]
The Will of God as desiring the sharing of God's Blessedness
with man is actuated by Love. The Wisdom of God as dis-
cerning the means of knowing this End, is directed by Love.
The Power of God as making actual what was potential in the
Mind of God, in Creation, Redemption, Sanctification, is guided
by Love.[7] In its relation to Creation we may distinguish different methods of the operation of Divine Love: (a) in relation to creatures,—giving them existence, guiding, and governing all with *benevolence;* (b) toward mankind in general—
by causing them to exist, supplying them with necessities,
and with the equipment of physical, rational, and ethical faculties, as *philanthrophy* and kindliness; (1) toward sinners—

---

[1] *Ibid.,* p. 328.

[2] *Ibid.,* note 1, pp. 328-329.

[3] Cf. Acts 17, 28.

[4] Rhôsse, *op. cit.,* pp. 328-329.

[5] Androutsos, *op. cit.,* p. 72; cf. Rhôsse, p. 306 (§ 175) and Acts
17, 25; Tim. 6, 15, *et al.*

[6] Androutsos, *op. cit.,* p. 72.

[7] Rhôsse, *op. cit.,* 311-312, 327, 328.

by giving them Grace, whereby God is shown as merciful, and forgiving; by helping the unfortunate and sinful, He is shown as compassionate and of great pity; toward the obdurate, God is revealed as patient, and long-suffering;[1] (2) toward Christians,—by giving them Himself in His Son, and through Him, all of the spiritual Goods of Christianity.[2] The Revelation *par excellence* of the Nature of God, is in His attribute of Love[3] toward His Creation.[4]

4. THE HOLY TRINITY

"The dogma of the Holy Trinity is the most important of the mysteries and dogmas of the Christian religion, not only that because of it we are distinguished from the Heathen, from Jews, and Mohammedans, but because it constitutes the fundamental divine verity on which is based the true Knowledge of God, and through which we come to know the relation of God to the world. Through this mystery we perceive how God is One, and operates as Creator and Saviour. In consequence it is of the utmost necessity for Salvation, since as St. Gregory of Nyssa says:[5] 'A Christian is characterized by his faith in the Father, Son, and Holy Ghost' ".[6] "According to the Faith of the Orthodox Church, God, One in Essence, is Three in Hypostasis—Father, Son, and Holy Ghost— which three Persons are neither aspects nor manifestations of the One Divine Essence. . . .nor do they form three gods instead of One, as if they were self-existent centers or forms of Revelation in which the whole Divine Essence were partitioned off and expressed without distinction in each of them, but they are modes of the Eternal Existence of the One God, by which the Godhead is at once distinguished or divided and

[1] *Ibid.*, p. 325.

[2] Androutsos, *op. cit.*, p. 71.

[3] 1 St. John, 4, 8.

[4] "The Fathers . . distinguished an antecedent and a consequent aspect of the Will of God. The former is the Good and the Salvation of rational creatures. The latter is the spiritual death of the unrepentant. The former is founded on the Goodness of God, the latter on His Justice" (Rhôsse, *op. cit.*, pp. 325-326).

[5] *De Spiritu Sancto*, 8, 11; cf. St. John Damascene Ἔκδοσις, 1, 8.

[6] Mesolora, *op. cit.*, III. pp. 103-104.

also united together".[1] Each of the Persons is God entire,
and all of the Divine attributes in God the Father are as well
in God the Word and God the Holy Spirit. Yet neither are
there three gods, nor are the Persons intermingled or blurred
into each other. The Father is distinguished from the other
Persons as eternally begetting from His Nature God the Son,
and as breathing forth the Spirit; the Son is distinguished as
being eternally begotten of the Father; and the Holy Spirit,
as eternally proceeding from the Father. The Three Persons of the Godhead are joined with each other as being contained in each other and subsisting in each other, without
being confused—so the Father is in the Son and in the Holy
Spirit, the Son in the Father and in the Holy Spirit, and
the Holy Spirit is in the Father and in the Son.[2]

(1) Sources of the Doctrine in Holy Scripture

The sources of the doctrine of the Holy Trinity are in
God's supernatural Revelation of Himself in Holy Writ. In
the Old Testament we find the teaching about the Triune
God suggested "enigmatically and briefly" only, since "the
Divine Revelation of supernatural truths is progressive and
gradual, according to the spiritual and moral development
of those who are receiving it." Furthermore "since the Jews
were already too prone to fall into the seductions of polythe-
ism, not being able to understand the tri-personality of the
Godhead, they might easily slip into error."[3] These "dark
hints and suggestions" in the Old Testament are not a few in
number. The Fathers alluded to Gen. 1,26; 3,22, and 11,7
where the Godhead is expressed in the plural, and to Isaiah
6,3 where the three-fold *Sanctus* suggests a three-fold Personality in the Godhead.[4] God is called "Father", with reference
to all men (Mal. 2,10), especially to Israel (Deut. 32,6;
Jer. 31,9; Mal. 1,6), and eminently in relation to the devout
in Israel (2 Sam. 7,14; Wisd. 2,18), and Father of the Messiah
in Psalm 2,7. On the passage "It is I....who blot out thy
transgressions for my own sake"[5] Rhôsse says that God is

---

[1] Androutsos, *op. cit.*, pp. 72-73.
[2] Androutsos, *op. cit.*, p. 73.
[3] Mesolora, *op. cit.*, III. p. 104, and cf. *ibid.*, note 2.
[4] Androutsos, *op. cit.*, p. 73.
[5] Isaiah 43, 25.

here "distinguished as efficient and as final cause".[1] The "Spirit" of God is referred to in Gen. 1,3; Ps. 51, 13-14; and as in the world, in Ps. 104, 29-30; Job 27,3; 33,14; Ezek. 36,27; 39,29. The three conceptions in the Old Testament of the "Word", "Angel", and "Wisdom" of God, are much more clear suggestions of the truth of the Triune God, and "certain indications of the doctrine of the Trinity adumbrated in the Old Testament."[2] The "Word" is the means of God's work in Creation, (Gen. 1,1): "by the word of the Lord were the heavens made, and all the host of them by the breath (πνεῦμὰ) of his mouth" (Ps. 33,6). In commenting on Exodus 3, vs. 2, 4, 6, 14, Rhôsse[3] says: "This angel cannot be conceived as something created, though 'angels' usually means created beings."[4] The phrase "face to face"[5] means that God revealed Himself as a Person, under the guise of an angel. On the basis of the notion of "Wisdom" in the Old Testament[6] and that of the "Word", Philo conceived of the latter as almost a hypostatic intermediate between God and man.[7]

The teaching in the New Testament of the doctrine of the Holy Trinity is both explicit and implied. Such passages as St. Matt. 3,13-17; St. Mark 1,9-11; St. Luke 3,21-22; St. John 1,32, imply the doctrine of the three Persons of the Godhead—("my beloved Son in whom I am well pleased.... the Spirit of God descending like a dove"). So too, does the account of the Transfiguration.[8] The explicit command of Our Lord to baptize in the name of the Father, Son, and Holy Ghost,[9] is a clear and unmistakable declaration of the doctrine of the Blessed Trinity, "in which the Son and the Spirit are put parallel to the Father, in relation to whom they are deemed

[1] *Op. cit.*, p. 188.
[2] Androutsos, *op. cit.*, p. 74.
[3] *Op. cit.*, p. 189.
[4] Cf. Gen. 18, 20, 26.
[5] Gen. 24, 40; Exodus 33, 11; Num. 12, 8; Deut. 34, 10; Judges, 6, 12-14.
[6] Cf. Prov. 1, 24-26; Ben Sir. 1.
[7] Rhôsse, *op. cit.*, p. 189-190.
[8] St. Matt. 17, 1-8; St. Mk. 9, 2-7; St. Luke 9, 28-36; 2 St. Peter 1, 16-18; cf. also St. John 12, 20-32.
[9] St. Matt. 28, 19.

equal." There is no possible suggestion of subordination to the Father, and the formula itself involves Divine worship of the Son and Holy Spirit along with the Father.[1] The interpretation of this text in a Sabellian sense—that is, that these words do not mean to express the work of salvation as done by three Persons, but only a triple work of one Person—is impossible. The text does not deal with the unity of the three works, but concerns itself with the one act of Baptism which is referred to all three Persons, equal to each other. Further, the words "Son" and "Father" express a relation between Persons in the Godhead, not of that Godhead to Creation; the "Father" is Father of the "Son". This means to ascribe equality of rank to each of the three Persons of the One God.

St. John in many places teaches the doctrine of the Trinity (3,3-18; 16,14; and the like), but the great text (St. John 15, 26) expresses it most completely: "When the Comforter is come, whom I will send you (having received him) from the Father, the Spirit of Truth, which proceedeth from the Father, he shall testify of me." (It is necessary to insert the bracketed words to make the meaning clear[2]). This explicitly teaches the mission of the Holy Spirit in time by the Son, who had received Him from the Father from whom the Spirit eternally proceeds. In 2 Cor. 13, 13, the Father, Son, and Spirit are explicitly joined together as equal, and One. It is not as man that Jesus is thus made of equal rank with the Father, hence the Sabellian interpretation of this text is futile. "The word *God* alone signifies the hypostasis of the Father, for from Him is begotten the Son who was sent into the world, and from Him proceeds the Spirit sent into the world."[3] The words in the Prologue of St. John's Gospel

[1] Even the Ebionites used this formula. The same contention given above applies equally to the baptism "in the name of Jesus Christ" (Acts 2, 32, 33, 35-38, and Romans 6, 3. Cf. Rhôsse, *op. cit.*, pp. 190-191.)

[2] Rhôsse, *op. cit.*, p. 192. Cf. the discussion below on the Procession of the Holy Spirit (pp. 126, ff.).

[3] *Ibid.*, p. 193. Such passages refer to the "economic" Trinity, *i. e.*, "as appearing in history, but the basis of it is the eternal distinction of Persons", *i. e.*, the "transcendental" Trinity. Cf. Androutsos, *op. cit.*, p. 74, 84; Δογμ. Μελέται, Α', pp. 57-58; Dyobouniotes, 'Οφειλ. ἀπάντ., pp. 53-54.

"the Word was with God" mean. . . . "with the Father", and
cannot be taken in an Arianizing sense, since "the Word was
God". In verse 18 the Father is called "God", and often in
the New Testament "more clearly to reveal the First Hypostasis . . . the word 'Father' follows the word 'God' ".[1] Since
we received the adoption of Sons, God is our Father (St. James
1, 27; Eph. 4, 6) but more preëminently the Father of Jesus
Christ, whom He is eternally begetting. Hence the phrase,
"God and Father of Jesus Christ" (1 Cor. 15,24; 2 Cor. 1,3;
11, 31; Eph. 1, 3; 5, 20; Col. 1, 3; 3, 17; Rev. 1, 6). The
Prologue of St. John forbids not only the Arian, but also the
Sabellian construction, since the verse "the Word was with
God" shows conclusively that the "Word" was "no mere property or act of revelation of God, but a Hypostasis distinguished from the Father's, and subsisting in an eternal relation with Him. Verse 18 says that the same Eternal Only-
begotten Son has declared what God is. Hence these words
show the relation of God to Himself, seen in and by Himself."[2]

The differentiation of function in 1 Cor. 12, 4-6, involves
the distinction of God the Father as Creator and Master of
the "operations", the Son as "Lord" of the "administrations",
and the "Spirit" as Sanctifier of the "gifts". The text, however, does not deal with the distinction of the Persons in
themselves, but with the revelations of God in the world or in
His Church, which are referred to the three Hypostases in the
One Being of God.[3] "Of Him, through Him, and to Him",
in Rom. 11, 36, shows a distinction of beginning, means, and
end, which is referable to the three Hypostases in God as
seen by Himself. In 1 Cor. 8, 6, "One God, the Father",
means the Father as Origin and Principle of everything; "One
Lord Jesus Christ", the Son as Mediating Principle; and "we
unto Him" implies the Holy Spirit as Final Principle or End.[4]

[1] Rhôsse, op. cit., p. 193. Cf. Gal. 1, 1, 3; Eph. 3, 14; 6, 23; Phil.
2, 11; 1 Thes. 1, 1; 2 Tim. 1, 2; Tit. 1, 4; St. James, 3, 9, etc.
[2] Rhôsse, op. cit., p. 194.
[3] Ibid., p. 194.
[4] Ibid., p. 195; Rhôsse (ibid.) refuses to attempt to found the
Trinitarian teaching on 1 St. John 5, 7, as "its genuineness has been
called into question"; so also Androutsos, op. cit., p. 75. Mesolora
(op. cit., III. p. 105, and note 1, incorrectly printed) quotes it—one
of the two texts given in full.

In many places the New Testament ascribes to each of the
Three Persons properties which postulate the Triune God.[1]
In connection with the second Person of the Blessed Trinity
it is said that He may have had an existence prior to Creation, but this was only a pre-existence in the mind of God,
and not an eternal hypostatic existence. St. John 8, 56 refutes this notion of a merely noetic pre-existence of the Word.
It has been objected that "Son" was applied to Our Lord only
after the Incarnation, and that it expresses not an eternal
but a temporal relation. St. Athanasius and St. Gregory of
Nyssa (*Catech. Discourse* 2) refute this view, on the basis
of Eph. 3,14: human relations are only analogous to the eternal
Divine relations, but the Divine are not analogous to our
own relations of father and son in time. The same type of argument is used to show (on the basis of 1 Cor. 1,4,9 and Heb.
11,26) that the name "Christ" was referred back to the Divine Nature from the Human, which, at His Baptism, was
anointed by the Divine Nature as Son of God. So, too, it
is said that the name "Word" was applied to His Divine Nature, reasoning back from His revelation of Himself in history
(Rev. 19,13). "But as He who was the eternal Son of God..
. . took human shape in Christ Jesus born of the Virgin Mary,
so He who was the Eternal Word in God as viewed by Himself,
as His Son was revealed in Christ Jesus, the Incarnate Word."[2]
The Hypostasis of the Son did not come into being with or
because of the appearance of Christ in the world. From Gal.
4,4, it is clear that the Son existed before His Mission into
the world, and before His Incarnation and Redemptive work.
Since it was He by whom Creation was wrought (Heb. 1-3; Col.
1, 13-20), He had a distinct hypostatic existence previous to
Creation. The distinction of the Hypostases, Father and Son, is
then eternal and not temporal. The latter text ascribes to Him
properties by which His eternal existence is manifested distinctly: "Image of the invisible God, the first-born of every
creature; by Him were all things created.....He is before all

---

[1] St. John 1, 1-3; 8, 56-59; 17, 5; 3, 13; 6, 33-46; 1 Cor. 1, 4-9; Gal.
4, 4; Heb. 1, 1; 4, 12; Col. 1, 13-20; 1 St. John, 1, 1, ff.; Rev. 9, 13;
22, 16. None of these are capable of an Arian or Sabellian construction,
according to Rhôsse (p. 195).

[2] Rhôsse, *op. cit.*, pp. 205-207.

things, and by Him all things consist." The word "Son" expressed the actual pre-existence of the hypostatis of the Godhead[1] which appeared in Jesus Christ. That Christ is God is evident from Heb. 1,1-3; Tit.2,13; and Rom. 9,5. The evidence of the New Testament on this point may be summarized in the words: "The Son is distinguished, in God viewed in Himself, from the Father, and both constitute in Essence one God".[2]

In 1 Cor. 2, 10-14, St. Paul tells us explicitly that only the Spirit of God knows the things of God. According to these words God knows Himself through His Spirit, who knows "the deep things of God". The revelation of the Spirit in the world has as premise His Existence in God. The distinction between Son and Spirit has been denied on the basis of 1 Cor. 3, 17, but it is clear that in St. Matt. 28, 19; 2 Cor. 13,13; Gal. 3,6; St. John 15,26; 16,7, there is a real distinction. Though God is called "Spirit" (St. John 4,24) yet the use of this word with special reference to the third hypostasis of the One Essence is not thereby precluded. Furthermore, where the word seems to mean "emanation", "power" or any other thing less than personal, it is to be construed with the third Person as Source. " "Paraclete" is certainly not an impersonal notion (Rom. 8, 16; Eph. 4, 30; 1 Cor. 12, 11), but may stand for "the self-determined," being applied to God as Holy Spirit."[3]

The evidence of the Holy Scripture for the dogma of the Holy Trinity may be summarized under the following heads: (1) "Each Person is the Bearer of the Divine Nature and Power and is God entire," since the attributes of the Godhead are ascribed to the Father, at other times to the Son, and equally to the Holy Spirit;[4] (2) "this unity of Essence forbids any subordination of Persons in time or in rank,[5] and is shown in the simplicity of the common energy of the three

[1] *Ibid.*, p. 197.
[2] *Ibid.*, p. 198.
[3] Rhôsse, *op. cit.*, pp. 199-200.
[4] Androutsos, *op. cit.*, p. 75.
[5] Cf. Dyobouniotes 'Η Δογμ. 'Ανδρ. κρινομένη, p. 19; and Androutsos, Δογμ. Μελ. Α', pp. 58-59; Dyobouniotes, 'Οφειλομένη ἀπάντησις, pp. 50-51.

Persons operating toward that without;"[1] (3) "if this one energy proceeding from the one Will is common to all three Persons, still certain properties and special functions are ascribed to each of the Persons: the Father is the Creator of all; . . . the Son, He by whom all things were made, and through whom Redemption was wrought; the Holy Spirit, being the life-giving and sanctifying principle, completes the action of the energies alike of Father and Son, was the Factor preparing the way for Redemption by speaking through the Prophets, . . . fulfils the work of Salvation by bringing home to the individual the appropriation of the fruits of the Passion, and sanctifies men in union with the Father and the Son. . . This same energy of the Persons is not to be conceived of abstractly, as if each operated apart from the others, for *opera ad extra sunt communia indivisa* . . . and they are the multiple effects of the one Divine Will."[2]

(2) Definition of the Doctrine of the Holy Trinity.

The development and formulation of this doctrine by the Church was a process extending over several centuries. The Fathers loved to meditate and ponder over the great mystery of the Holy Trinity, to expound it philosophically and theologically, in which work "they used not only biblical illustrations and figures, but in order to give the faithful a clearer conception of it, and to refute the . . . contention that the dogma was entirely comprehensible to our limited minds"[3] they employed certain other non-biblical figures and analogies. Such figures always contained groups of three—as for example: "Sun, ray, light"; "Root, branch, fruit"; "three lamps making one single light"; "Spring, brook, river"; "Fire, glow, heat"; "Mind, reason, will"; "Consciousness, knowledge, desire"; "Loving, Beloved, Love".[4] The occasion of the formulation, as distinct from the cause (which is the mind of the Church exercising itself on the content of the Faith), was the rise and development of heretical teaching. When part of

---

[1] Androutsos, Δογματική, p. 76.

[2] Androutsos, Δογματική, pp. 76-77; cf. Δογμ. Μελέται, Α', pp. 59-60; 'Οφειλ. ἀπάντησις, pp. 51-52.

[3] Mesolora, *op. cit.*, III. p. 105.

[4] Cf. Mesolora, *op. cit.*, III. note 4, pp. 105-106.

her heritage of revealed Truth was impugned, the Church immediately developed a formulation of the portion of the Truth under attack, which would distinguish explicitly, clearly, and without possibility of misunderstanding, and would affirm and define her faith in such terms as would exclude the unorthodox interpretation. The theological controversies, first with the Gnostics, then more definitely with the Sabellians, Arians, and Macedonians, served as occasions to formulate the doctrine of the Holy Trinity as defined above, while the controversy about the *Filioque* clause is chiefly negative, in denying the truth of this addition to the originally formulated dogma. Gnosticism attacked the Christian doctrines of God in general, and in so doing had a bearing on the definition of the dogma of the Holy Trinity. Sabellianism, Arianism, Macedonianism, and the Western heresy of the double procession were each aimed against certain definite aspects of the Orthodox teaching. The course of development and formulation of the dogmas began in the simple baptismal creed, the expansion of St. Matt. 28,19, and "the teaching therein proclaimed . . . . was developed, consolidated, and affirmed by the Fathers, the great champions of the Faith."[1]

While Greek philosophy—Stoic, Platonic, and then the Aristotelian,—did exercise a great influence on the form and terminology of the dogma of the Trinity, the latter, as we have seen, was founded on biblical doctrine. The great struggle of nascent Christianity was between the ideas of the abstract monotheism of Judaism, and the polytheistic conceptions of paganism, which had their logical outcome in pantheism. In the second century arose Gnosticism, in its two forms—Judaic and Hellenic. The former type exalted and magnified the conception of a God of Righteousness, who was immeasurably above and beyond the world. The latter type, revolting against this sterile and inhumane conception of a purely transcendent Deity, proclaimed His presence in the world. Of this second type, with its origins in Greek philosophy or heathen speculation, Marcion developed a kind of dualism, taking away the absolute nature of God, teaching the opposition of love to justice, and of spirit to matter. So his con-

[1] Androutsos, Δογματική, p. 77.

ception of God was of Love, but justice was not ascribed to Him. Basilides and Valentinus developed the immanent principle of their notion of God into a monism or pantheism,— whether by the theory of 'emanations', or by that of the syzygies evolving from the abyss, that is, God. In opposition to the exaggerated notions of a sterile, abstract, and transcendent Monotheism, having only the quality of righteousness and justice, the Fathers of the early Church emphasized the love and omnipresence of God. In contra-distinction to the dualistic or pantheistic notions of Greek Gnosticism, they taught God's changelessness, His transcendence, and His righteousness. Through Christ man receives the fellowship of God, transcendent and immanent, loving and righteous, in and yet not identical with the world. It was the work of St. Irenaeus, Clement of Alexandria, Hippolytus, Tertullian, and others to roll back the tide of Gnostic speculation, and state in a unified system the separate truths in which each type of Gnostic heresy had some share.[1]

As Gnosticism served to clear the mind of the Church as to the doctrine of God, so Sabellianism, essentially Greek in origin, and Arianism, of a more Judaistic character, elicited the further statement of the doctrine of the Holy Trinity. In about 220, Sabellianism, based on the earlier doctrines of Praxeas and Noetus, became defined as a fully developed system. Basing his thought on Stoic speculation,[2] Sabellius described God as an abstract Monad, without utterance and without energy. This Monad had, however, the property of separation or disintegration, of expansion, and then of re-integration. As expanded, the Monad acquires utterance, self-expression, and energy. Consequently we know it as the "Father" in the Old Testament, as the "Son" in the work of Redemption, and as the "Holy Spirit" in the Church. These three phases are not distinctions in God as He knows Himself, but only our conceptions of Him as He comes into contact with the world. As rays of light converge in their source, so do the energies of God unite and focus in the one Monad. This process of disintegration and expansion is only a phase

---

[1] Rhôsse, *op. cit.*, pp. 200-204.
[2] So St. Athanasius says, *adv. Arianos orat.*, 4, 13.

and a period in the eternal changelessness of the Monad, and will be followed by re-integration into its normal character as silent and energyless.[1] His revelation of Himself in the world is only a temporary and passing phase of His character, and not of His real Essence as the abstract Monad.[2] "Sabellianism, regarding the Persons of the Blessed Trinity as the several manifestations of God in the world's history, and only as it were masks[3] by which the Godhead, in itself impersonal, is revealed to the world as personal, perverts the Christian conception of God in two ways: by stripping the work of the world's salvation from the essential vital principle of Divine Love, and . . . by denying the transcendent majesty of God apart from His world, since it holds that in God Himself there is neither life nor energy, and confounds, like heathen pantheism, God in His world."[4]

St. Athanasius demonstrated the impossibility of reconciling Sabellianism either with reason or with the words of Holy Scripture. The "Monad" must have been capable of becoming something which it was not before;—if it were the Father alone, then He must have become Son and Spirit; if it were not the Father alone, then the Monad was really Triad.[5] If the Monad is essentially "without utterance" it could not have achieved creation. If it acquired speech, it must have received the Word from without, or else have had the Word in it always. If the Word was in God before it was begotten, afterwards it must have been outside of Him, which contradicts the text: "I am in the Father and the Father in me."[6] If God as the silent Monad were without energy and incapable of creating, then He must be less than we who often in silence still possess energy.[7] What is the reason, he

[1] Rhôsse, *op. cit.*, p. 206.
[2] Rhôsse, *op. cit.*, pp. 205-207.
[3] πρόσωπον: used first by Hippolytus, then by Tertullian, then misused by the Sabellians (cf. Rhôsse, *op. cit.*, p. 243 § 144).
[4] Androutsos, *op. cit.*, p. 78; Marcellus of Ancyra attempted to avoid this pantheistic conclusion, and said that the expansion was not of the Essence of God, but only of His Mind and Energy. His system results, however, in Deism; cf. Rhôsse, *op. cit.*, note 1, pp. 207-208.
[5] St. Athanasius, *Adversus Arian. orat.*, 4, 13.
[6] *Ibid.*
[7] *Ibid.*, 4, 14.

asks, for the manifestation of the Monad as we know it, as Triad, if the Monad could have done all it has without the necessity of this development into three? If the Triad evolved from the Monad by reason of Creation and its relation to it, then when it ceases to be manifested as Triad, the world should cease to be as well.[1]

While Sabellianism followed Gentile Pantheism, Arianism was based on a Jewish conception of God. According to it, God, not having as Cause either Himself or something other than Himself, is the Highest Uncaused Cause of the world. The one attribute of God is then "unbegottenness", and God knows Himself as cause of all—Creator of the Son, and of the Universe—but not as self-caused or self-determined. The "Son" is an intermediary between other creatures and God, and other creatures were formed through Him, their Prototype.[2] (In so far as Arianism held tó the strict abstract monotheism of this type it had a Jewish origin, but in encouraging worship of the Son, it followed a heathen model).[3] The Son, then, according to Arian teaching, was a creature who had his beginning in time: "God was not always 'Father', but became such afterwards, nor was the Son Eternal, for He was not before He was begotten. . . . . He is not the same in essence as the Father, for He is a creature, . . . and not truly God". . .[4] God called Him "Son" whom He had made, who was "Son" only in Name, but not in nature,[5] for God only is "unbegotten", and the Son was "born".[6] He came into existence by the Will[7]

---

[1] St. Ath. *Adversus Arian. Orat.*, 4, 12; cf. Rhôsse, *op. cit.*, pp. 208-210.

[2] This is a Platonic conception—cf. *Timaeus*, 13; cf. Col. 1, 15b.

[3] Rhôsse, *op. cit.*, p. 211.

[4] St. Athanasius, *Adv. Arian. Orat.* 1, 9.

[5] "In name only was the Son the "Word", "Wisdom", "Power" of God . . There are many powers, but only that of God himself is the same and eternal. Christ is not this true Power of God, but only the acme of the powers." St. Athanasius, *ibid.*

[6] *Ibid.*, 1, 30.

[7] This was, as St. Athanasius calls it, an attempt to bind up the discussion at both ends: "If He was born by the Will of the Father, the Son was the Son of His Will; if not by His Will, then God is tyrannized over . . . How is this possible?" (cf *Adversus Arian. Orat.*, 3, 59, and St. Greg. Naz., *Orat. theol.*, 3, 6).

of the Father, and, being a creature, is like other creatures, changing and impermanent.[1] "Arianism in attempting to preserve unimpaired the majesty of God . . . and accepting the 'Word' and the 'Spirit' only in the sense of Divine powers by which God operates, itself succeeds in taking away the supernatural character of Revelation, since the Revelation th·· Jesus Christ is not that of God Himself, nor is the Holy Spirit abiding in the Church . . . God the Paraclete."[2]

The work of the great Fathers, St. Athanasius, St. Basil, St. Gregory of Nyssa and St. Gregory Nazianzen, the champions of the Orthodox Faith, rolled back all the assaults of Arianism and served as a basis for the subsequent definition and formulation of the teaching of the Church in the first two Ecumenical Councils. The fundamental distinction between the Church's doctrine and that of Arius is expressed in the two propositions: "Christ being God became man to make us Divine", and "Christ being man, afterwards became God." St. Athanasius' argument against Arianism is as follows: since in Christ is a full and perfect Revelation of God, He could not be less than God if He is to lead us to God. In God are these eternal and necessary distinctions of three Persons, in the one Godhead. The Arians say: "There was a time when the Son was not." God as eternal Father could not subsist without the Son whom He eternally begets, nor without His Word and His Wisdom, for without them He would be as a sterile and dried up spring, a barren and unproductive Deity, incapable of Creation.[3] The Son must needs be Son eternally if He is to effect our being made Divine, for He Himself would stand in need of that which we lack, and having received it, would have no more than sufficed for Him.[4] To avoid the Arian statement that the Son is only "Son", "Wisdom", "Might" figuratively,[5] and not really,

---

[1] "The Son is not unchanging as is the Father, but, like the creatures, changes by his nature", St. Ath. *Adv. Arian. Orat.*, 1, 9: for whole discussion cf. Rhôsse, *op. cit.*, pp. 211-214 (§136-137). For summary of Arian teaching cf. Mesolora, *op. cit.*, I, pp. 40-41, with references, note 1, *ibid.*

[2] Androutsos, *op cit.*, p. 78.

[3] *Adv. Arian. Orat.*, 2, 2.

[4] *De synod Arimin. et Seleuciae.*, 51.

[5] *Adv. Arian. Orat.*, 2, 37.

it is necessary to state that He is of one Essence with the Father, since otherwise He could be not a true, full, and perfect Image of Him. "Unbegotten" applies not to God in relation to the Son, but in relation to creatures. "Father" means the eternal Relation of the First Person to the Second as "Son", and not His relation to creatures.[1] The Arians attempt to force in the use of a wrong category when they speak of the "Will" of God in relation to the Eternal Begetting of the Son, for the Son is of the Father's *Nature,* not of His *Will.* This is an instance of the Arian attempt to push human analogies into the knowledge of God.[2] If the Son is then of the same Nature as the Father, He is eternally unchanging and unchangeable. As Rhôsse summarizes the argument: "The eternal Begetting of the Son is known as eternally existing in God, before the creation of the world, since God cannot know Himself as Cause of something else (the world) unless He first knows Himself as Cause of Himself, through the eternal generation of the Son".[3] The essence of the emphasis of St. Athanasius' doctrine is on the identity of the Father, Son, and Holy Spirit, and he did not attempt to distinguish from each other more clearly these Hypostases or Persons. "Person" had a bad connotation, as it had been misused by the Sabellians, and "essence" and "substance" he used as synonymous. Consequently he had to employ circumlocutions to describe the Person of the Son, as compared with that of the Father.[4]

St. Gregory Nazianzen defends the "monarchia" of God, but says that it is not of one Person. The Triad is the perfection of existence, and is the Monad energized "by reason of its richness". The eternal energy of the infinite Nature differentiates itself into three, from one Principle or Source, the Son being Begotten of, and the Holy Spirit Proceeding from, the Father. The Triune God is One—in Essence, Power, and

---

[1] *Adv. Arian. Orat.,* 1, 33.

[2] *Ibid.,* 3, 59 and 62.

[3] Rhôsse, *op. cit.,* pp. 227-228.

[4] Such as: "The Son is the Image, the Character of the Essence (or substance) of the Father." On the terms he uses cf. *De synod Arim. et Seleuciae,* 41, 53, and cf. note 1, pp. 228-229, *op. cit.,* of Rhôsse. The whole treatment of St. Athanasius' doctrine in relation to Arianism is to be found in full, pp. 214-229 (*ibid*).

Principle, as we see from the one Godhead, the one Cause, and the real and actual unity in God. "When we look to that in which the Godhead subsists, and to those eternal and equal existences coming from the First Cause, there are three that are worshipped." So the unity of Essence subsists in a Trinity of Persons.[1] St. Basil, sensible of the danger to Christian doctrine of the Trinity being construed as Tritheism, held that we call God one, not in number, but in essence.—He distinguished Father, Son, and Holy Spirit, but was loth to apply numerical sequence to the Hypostases, each of whom is a "confluence of the properties of each."[2] "The Son is in the Father, and the Father in the Son, and in Him . . . . One, so that according to the properties of each there is one and another, but according to the nature which they have in common, both are one."[3]

God is not an abstract, energyless, barren, and lifeless monad, but knows Himself as Cause and Effect—as Cause, the Father; as Effect, the Son ("nearest to Him, the Cause"), and as Effect also, the Spirit ("through the nearest-to-the-Cause").[4] Of the three Hypostases the Nature is one and the same; as in a number of individual men the human nature is one and the same, though the individuals are each different persons.[5] Yet, unlike men, the number of personal hypostases has never changed; there are eternally no more nor less than three. The name "God" tells us nothing of the Nature of God, but only serves to name and express Him whose energies are known to us in His world: it is concerned rather with His energy than with His Nature. This energy is one—the one energy of the One Essence in three Persons. Theodore of Aboukir, Bp. of Cairo, however, disagreed with this contention of St. Gregory and said that "the name of *God* is used of a certain Energy but really indicates the Nature from which that energy proceeds."[6]

As St. Athanasius emphasized the oneness of essence of the Three Persons, so St. Gregory Nazianzen drew attention to the

---

[1] Rhôsse, *op. cit.*, pp. 229-235, with authorities and sources quoted in footnotes.

[2] *Epistola*, 38, 6.

[3] *De Spiritu Sancto* 18; on him cf. Rhôsse, *op. cit.*, pp. 236-237.

[4] Quoted in Rhôsse, *op. cit.*, note 1, p. 239.

[5] *Ibid.*

[6] Rhôsse, *op. cit.*, pp. 238-243.

relations of the latter to the former. St. Basil strongly stressed the essential unity of God, and explicitly taught the theological truth that each dwells in the other Persons. St. Gregory of Nyssa went a step further in suggesting the interrelation of the three Persons in the Godhead: the "monarchia", as Cause, and the two-fold *Effect*—the Son, Begotten, and the Holy Spirit, Proceeding. Yet he was careful to distinguish the three Persons from the conception of three gods. The terminology which these Fathers employed is worthy of note. "Person", as was said, was first used by Hippolytus, and after him by Tertullian (*persona*), and since the Sabellians used it in the heretical conception, as "mask" and not to mean a real "person", its use was avoided by St. Athanasius. Since the latter used "hypostasis" as a synonym for "Essence" or "Being" (the Latin words are the same: *"essentia", "substantia"*), for lack of any adequate terminology to phrase his discussion of the Persons of the Godhead, he had to fall back on biblical terms or circumlocutions.[1] Similarly "nature" and "being" (essence) were for the Fathers practically identical in meaning, though a slight difference can be discerned.[2] The word "hypostasis" came, however, to be employed by the Greek Fathers to mean what we mean by Person, that is, "not a temporary form of the manifestation or revelation of God, but the mode of His Existence."[3] As this term might easily be confused with the word "ousia" ("Being" or "Essence"), either the discovery of some new word would be necessary, or the use of an old term with a new meaning attached to it. For this reason, the Church came to use "hypostasis" not to mean the same as "ousia", or "being", but to "express (one of) the three modes of existence of the One Divine Being." "Person" ("prosopon") came into use later; but since it means something different in modern philosophy from what the Fathers meant by it, it is more advisable to use "hypostasis" for "Person", when discussing the teaching of the Greek Fathers and the Greek Church. "Person" nowadays has come to signify "a self-conscious and self-directing being,"

---

[1] Cf. Rhôsse, *op. cit.*, p. 228.

[2] Correlative to that between "nature" and "character"; cf. note I, p. 244 (Rhôsse).

[3] Rhôsse, pp. 243-244.

but does not connote, as it did to the Fathers, a special mode
of the existence of such a being. "Person" in the Fathers
meant an "eternal mode of existence of the Divine Being".
Hence we may distinguish a difference between the meanings
of the word then and now, and "hypostasis" better expresses
the conception which the Fathers held of "Person."[1]

The "Hypostases" represent eternal and permanent relations within the Godhead,[2] as seen by God Himself and without
reference to the world. The Divine Essence and the whole of
the Divine attributes are in each of the three Hypostases, and
yet the Hypostases are not divisions or parts of that Essence.
The relation of Essence to Hypostases may not be construed as
that of the generic conception to the specific, in which case one
would be real and actual, and the other only apparent or subjective. Nor can the opposite extreme to this nominalistic
view be held, that is, a realistic conception which would make
four entities: three Persons + one Essence. We may try to
express the relation by the analogy of the genus to the individual, but must always remember that it is only a figure, and that
the great Truth is a mystery: the Nature of God is utterly
different from any of which we have knowledge; the Hypostases are in each other and in the Essence, and the latter in
and not outside them, and they are not sundered. Whenever we think of the Father, we must think also of the Son
and Holy Spirit:[3] each Hypostasis involves the others. "The
three Hypostases are different from each other, yet through
their mutual indwelling (*Circumcession, περιχώρησις*) they subsist in each other in such a way that they are not mixed
together, but, united, make one God only." This interac-

---

[1] On the discussion of the early terminology, cf. Rhôsse, *op. cit.*,
228, 244, 245; Androutsos, *op. cit.*, p. 86. There seems to be no uni-
formity in Greek Orothodox terminology of the period succeeding the
Great Schism; *e. g.* Gennadius' *Confession* speaks of three "idioms,
which we call three Hypostases, that is to say, Persons" (early 15th
century. Cf. text, Mesolora, I, *op. cit.*, pp. 73 ff.). Mesolora (III, pp.
100, 110), Rhôsse (*e. g.*, pp. 248, 297, 306), and Androutsos (pp. 42
ff) all use "attributes," "qualities", "properties", and "predicates" in
slightly different senses.

[2] Cf. St. John Damascene, Ἔκδοσις I. 2, 10; St. Epiphanius says
that Hypostases mean "the properties of the 'Persons'" (*Haer.* 73, 16).

[3] St. Athanasius, *Ad Serapionem*, 1, 4.

tion and interrelation constitutes the one Eternal Being of God, not "as an abstraction but as a concrete Unity."[1]

(3) The Properties of the Persons

The Church teaches that the hypostatic property of the First Person is Fatherhood, and Unbegottenness, and, in relation to the other Hypostases, Cause, Principle, or Source. By paternity He begets eternally the Son, and by spiration the Holy Spirit is sent forth from Him. The property of the Son is His Sonhood, and His being Begotten of the Father. The property of the Spirit in His Procession from the Father. The Father is the one Source and Cause;[2] the Son and spirit, the Effects of this Cause or Principle. The Father is called the Begetter of the Son and the Spirator of the Spirit. The Son, as Effect, is that nearest the First (that is, nearest the Father, as Cause) and the Spirit, as Effect, that through-the-nearest-the First, according to St. Gregory of Nyssa.[3] The ordering of Father, Son, and Spirit and the relation suggested above of "Cause" and "Effect" do not mean to imply any subordination in rank in the Blessed Trinity. St. Basil gives four ways by which one thing can be greater than another: (1) "by reason of cause"; (2) "because of greater might", (3) "more excellent worth", and (4) "by reason of greater weight",[4] of which the first only can be applied to the order of Persons in the Trinity. "Nor can we think of the Persons as the Father first, the Son second, and the Spirit third. . . . This order, given in Holy Scripture, . . . does not show any superiority in time or rank, since all three Persons are co-eternal and co-equal, . . . but only suggests the relation of the Father, as Cause, to Son and Spirit."[5] The Son, as Begotten, and the Spirit as Proceed-

[1] Rhôsse, *op. cit.*, p. 248, and cf. for the above discussion pp. 245-248.

[2] Cf. Androutsos: "One thing remains clear, that in the Godhead there is one and only one Cause or Principle, and it behooves us to avoid any possible expression or statement, which might lead to the recognition of two principles" (*op. cit.*, p. 79).

[3] *Ad Ablabium*, 45, 2, quoted Rhôsse, *op. cit.*, p. 239, note 1.

[4] *Adv. Eunom.* 1, 25.

[5] Androutsos, *op. cit.*, pp. 88-89; Mesolora seems to use the word *Mind* for "Principle", "Cause", or "Source" (cf. *op. cit.*, III, p. 108).

ing must not be thought of in relation to these properties as being in any sense passive, but as active and energetic. The order then is simply logical, and there is not any suggestion of subordination of any Person to the other.[1]

The Son is eternally begotten of the Father's Nature, and His origin is utterly different from that of creatures in two respects: He is being eternally begotten by the eternal energy in the Being of God, and is begotten "of the Nature of the Father, not without His Will, but according to that Absolute internal necessity in Absolute harmony with the rational knowledge and Free Will of God directed towards His eternal self-relation."[2] Creatures are not born of God's nature, but only of His Free Will. As we saw above, the Arians tried to force a dilemma on the Church: either Christ was Begotten *of* the Will of God, or He was Begotten *against* His Will. St. Athanasius answered that this category is a purely human one, and that the deductions we base on the effect, circumstances, and functioning of our wills are in no wise applicable to God. As God is Good, not because of the acceptance of and obedience to some imposed ethical standard, but because of His very Nature, His Son is begotten of His Nature, nor is there any question of willing or not willing.[3] (He used "will" in its relative sense, and did not draw the distinction between the necessary goodness of God, as an inevitable result of His Nature, and the free will of His work in creation.) Because He is what He is, and so of necessity, He begat the Son eternally, "of His Nature" or "according to His Nature"—by which St. Athanasius practically means of *His self-determined freely-defined necessity.* This is deducible from his distinction of "something which lies above the will of God" (that is, His will, as relative to Creation). He did not work out all the relations of Will and Nature in God, and as a consequence "there is a certain incompleteness in St.

[1] Rhôsse, *op. cit.*, pp. 248-249; Dyobouniotes notes that this subordination would be possible if there were only *unity* and not *identity* of Essence in the Godhead, and on this point scores against Androutsos. ('Οφειλ. ἀπάντ., pp. 51-2; Δογμ. Μελέται, Α', pp. 58-59; Ἡ Δογμ. 'Ανδρ. κρινομένη, p. 19, and Androutsos Δογματική, p. 76.)
[2] Rhôsse, *op. cit.*, p. 249 (§ 147); Mesolora, *op. cit.*, III, p. 111.
[3] *Adv. Arian. Orat.*, 3, 59.

Athanasius' teaching due to the necessities and circumstances of his day."[1]

The Procession of the Holy Spirit

The doctrine of the procession of the Holy Spirit from the Father alone is the chief dogmatic difference between the Eastern and Western Churches. It is the gravamen of Orthodox polemic against Roman Catholic theological teaching.[2] Orthodox Doctrine is summarized in the Constantinopolitan supplement made to the Nicene Creed at the 2d Ecumenical Council in 381: "The Lord and Giver of Life, who proceedeth from the Father, and together with the Father and the Son is worshipped and glorified."[3] The great "proof text" of this doctrine is that alluded to above—St. John 15, 26-27. The second Council was convened to deal with the Macedonian heresy, which maintained that the Holy Spirit was a creature, for otherwise He would be either a second Son of God, or else a grandson. St. Athanasius refuted their doctrine, showing that the Spirit was of the same essence and nature as the Son, and that in the One Godhead were three equal Persons. He confuted their anthropomorphic attempt to grapple with this Mystery, and wrote strenuously to uphold the Orthodox Doctrine.[4]

In a local synod at Toledo (589) and in that at Aix-la-Chapelle (809) the *Filioque* clause was added to the ancient creed, but as yet without the official sanction of the Bishop of Rome, and without the incorporation of this addition, which later (in 1014) came to pass, into the creed of the Western Church as a whole. All Orthodox theologians deny its validity and truth.[5] "One thing is evident—there is but one principle or source in the Godhead. . . . To this the Western addition of the *Filioque* is diametrically opposed. . . . The belief in one single principle in the Godhead is demanded by a logical conception of the Triune God."[6] "It is not only technically illegal

---

[1] Rhôsse, *op. cit.*, pp. 252-253.
[2] Cf. note at the end of this lecture, pp. 136-143, on the *Filioque*.
[3] Cf. Mesolora, *op. cit.*, I, pp. 45-53.
[4] *Ad Serap.* 4, 1-6; cf. Rhôsse, pp. 255-254 (§ § 150, 151).
[5] Mesolora, *op. cit.*, I. pp. 46-53.
[6] *Op. cit.*, pp. 78-80, and cf. p. 82: "The addition of the *Filioque* is not only irregular, but is, in fact, counterfeit and false."

and illegitimate, but essentially wrong. . . . Even as a theological opinion it is vicious and inadmissible."[1] Western theologians have confused the "Mission" of the Holy Spirit in time with His "Procession" in eternity, which has given rise to their distorted theology on the subject.[2] The passage in St. Augustine (*De Trinitate,* 15,17,29) which the Westerns appeal to, according to Mesolora, does teach Orthodox doctrine, since it distinguishes between *procedere principaliter* and simply *procedere,* showing the distinction between the Eternal Procession from the Father and the Mission in time by the Son.[3] According to Rhôsse, following Photius, the passage may be well regarded as spurious.[4] We have three distinct questions to deal with in examining Patristic evidence: (a) The Eternal Procession of the Spirit from the Father; (b) the Eternal Procession from the Father through the Son; (c) the Mission in time by the Son of the Holy Spirit into the world.[5] The distinction of Mission and Procession involves that between the "Transcendental" and "Economic" Trinity, under which categories, rather than those just mentioned, some theologians[6] prefer to deal with the subject matter.

Many of the Greek Fathers taught that the Holy Spirit proceeds from the Father *through* the Son, while none of them held that He proceeds from the Father *and* the Son. While they do not always use the word "proceeds" (from the Father through the Son) they employ almost its equivalents—"shows forth", "comes forth", "appears", and the like. Among the Fathers who so teach may be numbered St. Gregory Thaumaturgus, St. Athanasius,[7] St. Basil,[8] St. Gregory of Nyssa,[9] St. Epiphanius,[10]

---

[1] Rhôsse, *op. cit.,* pp. 254-255.
[2] *Ibid.,* p. 255; Mesolora, *op. cit.,* III, pp. 120-123.
[3] Mesolora, *op. cit.,* III. pp. 118-119.
[4] *Op. cit.,* p. 255; cf. Migne, *P.G.,* t. CII, col. 352.
[5] Clearly distinguished by the Patriarch Jeremiah Il. (in Mesolora, *op. cit.,* I. p. 196).
[6] *E. g.,* Androutsos, *op. cit.,* pp. 74, 85.
[7] *Ad Serap.* 1, 2.
[8] *Ad Gregorium fratrem,* 38, 4. and cf. *Adv. Eunomium,* 5.
[9] *Contra Eunomium* 1.
[10] *Haer.* 73, 16; 74.

St. Cyril Alex.,[1] Theodoret,[2] Maximus, and St. John Damascene.[3]
These Fathers all agree in teaching one sole Principle, Source,
or Cause alone in the Godhead, and in stating that the Father
is this Principle. Some of the passages apply as well to the
eternal relations of the Persons of the Godhead as to their relations in time and with the world, for example St. Epiphanius:
(*Haer.* 73, 16) "subsisting from the Father through the Son";
"the Spirit *takes* from the Son, and proceeds from the Father";
St. Cyril: "Since the Spirit is in nature the same as the Son,
He subsists in Him, and comes forth through Him"; St. John
Damascene: . . . "and the Spirit of the Son, not as *of* Him,
but as proceeding *through* Him from the Father. . . ."[4] In
commenting on this fact, Rhôsse notes that "certain of the
Greek Fathers . . . . added as a theological opinion the view
that the Holy Spirit proceeds . . . . through the Son from
the Father, ... which view, not being repugnant to true
teaching, ... may be regarded as a true theological opinion . . . "[5]

Androutsos finds that in only two clear instances—
Maximus, and St. John Damascene—does the phrase "through
the Son" offer any difficulty. Grammatically, the prepositions
"through" and *"from"* the Son are very nearly alike, as the latter has reference to a first or efficient cause, the former to a mediate or constitutive cause. Strictly speaking, the use of
"through" with the second Person suggests Him as secondary
Cause. Yet this construction, possible grammatically, is forbidden by the sense of the biblical texts, which in every case
insist upon one Cause alone, the Father. Therefore "through
the Son" may be construed to apply to the *Mission* of the Spirit
by the Son into the world, that is, must be referred to the economic Trinity (*cf.* St. John 15, 26), or by reason of the logical
order of the Persons (Father first, Son second, Spirit third) be
referred to the transcendental Trinity. The former interpreta-

---

[1] *Epistola ad Joann.* 39; *De adoratione in spiritu et veritate,* 1.
[2] Cf. Rhôsse, *op. cit.,* p. 261 for quotations.
[3] Έκδοσις, 1, 13; 8; 13; etc.
[4] Έκδοσις 1, 13, but cf. other quotations which have a strictly temporal significance and Rhôsse's comments, *op. cit.,* p. 263—cf. *ibid.,* pp.
256-263, for fuller quotations and discussion of the text.
[5] *Ibid.,* p. 254.

tion of "through the Son" would make it a "concise phrase expressing the eternal existence of the Spirit, and His appearance in the world accomplished through the Son". The second interpretation would construe "through the Son" to express "the middle position of the Son in reference to the Spirit in the logical order of the transcendental Trinity."[1] Strictly speaking, in this latter sense the word is wrongly applied, since it cannot be taken to have any dogmatic meaning in relation to the Procession of the Holy Spirit. Mark Eugenicus takes it to mean "with the Son", as does Macarius.[2] The contention supported by the Greeks at the Bonn Conference in 1874 is given in the *Bericht,* and discussed by Rhôsse.[3]

Photius wrote voluminously on the controversy about the *Filioque* clause. His "Discourse about the Mystery of the Holy Spirit",[4] his *Encyclical,* especially 2, 15, his letter to the Archbishop of Aquileia, and the summary of the whole controversy by Nicholas Methones[5] contain thirty-one arguments against the Procession of the Holy Spirit through the Son. The following may serve as a brief summary of them: (1) The Son cannot be an intermediary between Father and Spirit, since the Spirit is not the property of the Son. (2) The simplicity of the Godhead is destroyed if it have two Principles. (3) If things held in common by two Persons may be predicated of the Third, then the Spirit would become His own mediating Principle and Cause. (4) If the Spirit proceed from both Father and Son, His Procession from the Father alone must be either complete or incomplete; if incomplete, the Procession from the two Persons is rather more mechanical and incomplete than from the

[1] Androutsos, *op. cit.*, pp. 82-84. This view is clearly and adequately presented by Eugenius Bulgaris, quoted in Rhôsse, note 1, pp. 281-282 (*op. cit.*).

[2] *Théologie dogmatique orthodoxe*, Paris, 1860, vol. I. p. 406. On the monk Job, and the views of other Orthodox writers, cf. Androutsos, *op. cit.*, p. 86 note 1.

[3] On this, cf. Rhôsse, *op. cit.*, pp. 278-287; his reports to the Holy Synod on the Bonn Conference (1874-1876) and Reusch, *Bericht über die Unions-Conferenzen, Bonn*, 1874, 1875.

[4] In Migne, *P.G*, t. CII.; cf. note 4, p. 139 following.

[5] In Vol. I, pp. 371 ff., of the 'Εκκλησιαστικὴ βιβλιοθήκη, of A. Demetrakopoulos; for bibliography, cf. p. 87, n. 3.

One alone. (5) If not incomplete, why was it necessary for Him to proceed from the Son too? Why is the Spirit chosen for this less dignified treatment in the Divine Economy? (6) If a hypostatic property or idiom of the Father is shared by the Son, and Son and Holy Spirit become indistinguishable, the theory verges on Semi-Sabellianism. (7) The theory of a double Principle in the Godhead takes away the essential character of Christian theism, if there are two correlative principles, one of which is self-originated, and the second receives its origin from the former. (8) It would be more consistent to extend this Double Principle into a Triple Principle, in accordance with our knowledge of the Holy Trinity. (9) As the Father is "Principle" or "Cause" not because of the Divine Nature of the Godhead, but because of His hypostatic character, since that Hypostasis does not include the Son, the latter cannot be Principle or Cause. (10) The *Filioque* practically divides the Father's Hypostasis into two, or makes the Son's Hypostasis a part of the Father's. (11) On the supposition, that, if in comparing two things one can be shown to have something which is not the property of another, they are shown not to be of the same nature, the Holy Spirit (by the *Filioque* hypothesis) can be shown to be of different Nature from the Son. Furthermore, the Son's properties must be interchangeable with the Father's. (12) If the Procession of the Spirit from the Father were perfect, there could be no necessity for that from the Son as well. (13) The Spirit, according to the *Filioque,* is "twice removed" from the Father, and hence holds a much lower rank than the Son. (14) Of the three Persons, the Spirit is the only one who would have more than one Origin or Beginning (ἀρχή). (15) The Father and Son are drawn closer together by the *Filioque* hypothesis, than the Father and the Spirit, since the Son shares not only the Father's Nature but the Father's Properties. (16) The Procession of the Spirit from the Son is either (a) the same as that from the Father, in which case distinction of Persons is lost by confusion of properties, or (b) different, in which case there is an antithesis in the Holy Trinity. (17) With the principle that what is not common to all three Persons is proper to but one of the three, how may the Double Procession be reconciled? (18)

Why does not something proceed from the Spirit to balance the relation between the Persons? (19) By the *Filioque* the Father is shown to be partial to the Son. (20) The Father is either more Cause than the Son, or less: if more, it is insulting to the Son's dignity; if less, to the Father's. (21) If the Son causes the Spirit to proceed from Himself, must He not convey all His own power in thus emitting an equal Hypostasis? (22) The Latins make the Son greater than the Spirit, because of the Cause relation, and also impiously place Him closer to the Father. (23) By introducing a secondary Cause into the Holy Trinity the Latins insult the Son, in making Him a Cause Who is already caused, for as Cause He is not needed. (24) They divide the Holy Spirit into two parts—that from the Father, and that from the Son. (25) So He is made up of a Perfect and an imperfect Cause! (26) In the Blessed Trinity united in indissoluble Unity, all three Hypostases are preserved inviolate, but if to Sonship is added the Property of Spirating the Spirit, the Sonship is impaired and the hypostatic properties marred. (27) If at the Son's Begetting was given Him the power of Spirating the Holy Spirit, then how was not His very character of Son destroyed, if in being caused He became Cause of another, equal to and of the same Nature as Himself? (28) According to the *Filioque* theory it is impossible to see why the Holy Spirit may not be called "the Grandson". (29) If the Father is Cause of the Son who is secondary Cause of the Spirit, then the Father is both remote and proximate Cause of the Spirit! (30) The double Cause—Primary and Secondary—in the Godhead inevitably involves a double result, hence the Person of the Spirit must be double. (31) Since there are no time relations in the Holy Trinity, the Spirit must have been begotten along with the Son, if He proceeds from Him.[1]

The arguments of Photius have formed the basis of the dogmatic teaching and controversical writings of subsequent Orthodox theologians. At the Bonn Conferences the Six Propositions,[2] based on St. John Damascene, met with the approval

---

[1] On these, *in extenso*, cf. Rhôsse, *op. cit.*, pp. 263-276. On St. John 16, 14, Photius accuses the Latins of confusing possessive and personal pronouns: "He shall take of Mine"—"the Spirit which is of one essence with His Son", etc.

[2] Reusch, *Bericht über die Unions-Conferenzen*, Bonn, 1875, pp. 91-94.

of the Greeks, who subsequently felt them inadequate, since they did not explicitly exclude the view that in some way the Spirit may have had His origin from the Son as well, which the Old Catholics held was a tenable opinion. This was brought into the foreground in a later discussion between a Russian and an Old Catholic Committee. The failure on the part of the Old Catholics to exclude even an opinion which allowed of the possibility of there being two principles, led to the rupture of relations and the dissolution of these negotiations. The Orthodox Church held tenaciously to the position of Photius, allowing as an opinion the referring of the clause "through the Son" to the transcendental Trinity. The Orthodox Position is in brief as follows: the Father is the One Source, Principle, or Cause in the Godhead, from whom alone proceeds the Spirit. It may be said that He "shines forth", is "manifested", and the like, "through the Son"; but while it is possible for this phrase to be referred to the transcendental Trinity, it is much better applied to the work of the Spirit in relation to the world, who was for this purpose sent through or by the Son. There can be no compromise in the least, nor any receding from this position on the part of Orthodoxy.[1]

(4) Theological Theory in Regard to the Blessed Trinity

As was suggested above, in expositions of the doctrine of the Blessed Trinity there is often embodied an attempt to illustrate or expound it by the use of figures, or to speculate and try to suggest in some way the secret of the great mystery. So Gennadius, in his *Confession* (*cir.* 1450), uses the figures of Fire, Light, and Heat to explain and illustrate the doctrine of the Trinity, and also called the three Persons "Mind, Reason, and Will—one God", just as mind, reason, and will in man

[1] Cf. Rhôsse, *op. cit.*, pp. 285-287; the first section of the second "Answer" of the Patriarch Jeremiah II (1569) contains an excellent treatment of the Orthodox Doctrine of the Procession of the Holy Spirit (in Mesolora, *op. cit.*, I, pp. 195-214). He uses Photius at length in refuting the *Filioque*. Cf. Kritopoulos' *Confession* (1625) in Mesolora, *op. cit.*, I, pp. 281-295; *ibid.*, pp. 378-381 for Peter of Mogila's *Confession*.

constitute one single soul.[1] So too, Kritopoulos (1625) uses "Mind" of the Father, and "Logos" (=*Reason* and *Word*) of the Son.[2] "Such distinctions have no real analogy or likeness to the Holy Trinity", as Androutsos says,[3] "in which Father, Son, and Holy Spirit are not powers or elements of the whole conception of God, as these distinctions (mentioned above) are with us, but they are actual Persons." In full knowledge of this fact St. Gregory of Nyssa observed: "Only by way of figure and not in any sense by way of real likeness may the soul be compared to the Holy Trinity."[4] However, Rhôsse builds up a rather elaborate philosophical theory of the doctrine of the Blessed Trinity on lines similar to Dorner's, to whom he pays his respects in a note.[5] His reasoning may be summarized as follows: God knows Himself as Cause and Caused; as Cause, He is Father, and as Caused, Son and Holy Spirit. The causal relationship is one of absolute necessity in accordance with the Nature of God. The first relationship of the three Persons of the Blessed Trinity to each other is then that of the ultimately necessary Divine Nature—the Father as Cause, Begetter, and Spirator. "Since there is no passivity in God, but only Absolute Energy, that which is the effect is equally as infinite as the Cause.... When this twofold Effect is seen under the two other aspects of God—of Absolute Reason and....Absolute Free Will—it is as that which is active absolutely by Reason, and by Will. That which operates in God by Reason is His Eternal Word, and that functioning by Will is the Holy Spirit." The eternal and necessary determinations of the Being of God are not only the inevitable and infinite result of that Divine Nature, but they are as well that which the Eternal Reason contemplates; that is, God knows Himself as being such a Nature, and as being so self-constituted and self-determined, as He also knows Himself as that which the Eternal Free Will wills—that is, God wills Himself to be what He is. This theory of the Father as Cause, the Son as Reason, and the Holy Spirit as Will or

[1] Mesolora, *op. cit.*, I. pp. 73-74.
[2] *Ibid.*, p. 281.
[3] *Op. cit.*, p. 90.
[4] In Migne, *P.G.*, t. XLIV, col. 1344.
[5] *Op. cit.*, pp. 287-288.

Love, involves implicates which preclude the possibility of a tritheistic conception of the Godhead. "In these three distinctions or Hypostases in God—the natural, the rational or logical, and the ethical—there is not only Unity of Cause, but also Unity and Identity of Essence."[1]

Both the Unity of Essence subsisting in the Trinity of Persons, and the Persons—each subsisting in each other, inseparably united in the Godhead—are objective and actual. So the Unity is not a generic conception in relation to the Hypostases, as we know the relation of a generic conception to the individual, but it is the prototype of all such created relationships. So the determinations in the Godhead—the attributes, properties, qualities, and the like—are not only necessary but also known and willed. "If the determinations of the Divine Essence existed only by His Reason and Will and not by His Nature as well, they would be merely conceptual and subjective, not actual; they would be arbitrary and not necessary determinations of His Being. If they existed only as by His Nature, in the form of natural Hypostases, they would not be rational and ethical but merely natural.. determinations." "These determinations in the Father by Nature, in the Son by Reason, are also (by the Spirit) freely chosen as ethical determinations, as freely willed or as the object of His Love. Through these three forms or Hypostases God is thus self-energized, self-conscious, and self-determined or infinitely self-directed, as both Cause and at the same time Effect of Himself."[2]

As in God, One by Nature, by Reason, and by Will, His Unity is the Prototype of all Oneness, so in Him by Nature, Truth, as also such by Reason and Will, lies all Truth Absolutely. By the same method of reasoning, His Goodness by Nature is Goodness as well by Reason and Will, and in consequence the Good exists in Him absolutely and generically. So also with the conception of Justice: the idea of the Good and the Just in Him by Nature, is also in the Divine Nature as rational Good, or rational Justice, and at the same time as ethical or freely-willed Good and Justice. "Hence God as Triune

[1] *Op. cit.*, pp. 289-291.
[2] Rhôsse, *op. cit.*, pp. 292-294 (§ § 163-164).

is the Absolute Truth, Justice, Good, and the like, as such by
Nature, Reason, and Will, which severally are the Principle
and Prototype of all truth, justice, and goodness in the world."[1]
So, too, God is the source of the generic conceptions of identity
and difference:[2] the notion of *identity* is based on that of the
essential self-identity and unity of the Divine Being; that of
difference, on the distinctions of Hypostases in the Divine
Nature.[3]

This theory of the Holy Trinity, Rhôsse maintains, presents the solution of two philosophic difficulties which have
long troubled human thought: the relation of necessity to free
will, and the problem of the absolute and relative. "The harmonious unity of the archetypal Truth, Goodness, and Justice
in the Divine Nature, in accordance with both necessity and
free will in the Godhead, removes the antithesis between neces-
ity and reason or, rather, between it and freedom." If in the
Divine Nature absolute Truth and absolute Goodness and absolute Justice, exist objectively, our conceptions of these, though
subjective and relative, are still conceptions of what has actual
and objective reality, quite apart from ourselves and our thinking.[4] In short, "as the Being of God gathers in One the three
Hypostases which subsist in It, and It in them, so each of
the three Hypostases binds up in one the attributes corresponding. Hence the Hypostasis of the Father gathers into one the
physical or natural attributes of God, or the natural determinations of His Essence, that of the Son or the Word sums
up the rational or logical attributes, and that of the Spirit
the ethical attributes or determinations....Since the Hypostases subsist in each other in such a way that in each one of
them subsists the other two, . . . so all the attributes subsist in
each Hypostasis, and the Good, Justice, and Truth are not
only such by Reason, but as well by Nature and by Will."[5]

The difficulties arising from philosophic speculation in re-

---

[1] *Ibid.,* pp. 294-296 (§ 165).
[2] These exist in actuality in God, but in man only in mind or concept. Cf. St. John Damascene, Ἔκδοσις 1, 8, and Androutsos Δογμ.
Μελ., Α', p. 63.
[3] Rhôsse, *op. cit.,* p. 289, note 1.
[4] *Ibid.,* pp. 296-297 (§ 166).
[5] *Ibid.,* pp. 302-303.

gard to the relation of the One Divine Nature to the Three Hypostases, on the basis of attempts to reduce the problem to a merely rational basis, elicited and developed in ancient times a four-fold defence of the Orthodox doctrine on the part of the Fathers. They maintained the Unity of God as against Tritheism; they contended that the generic conception of Unity in Trinity was not a mental abstraction made by human reasoning, but an objective reality in the eternal identity of the One Divine Essence; they taught that the Godhead was undivided in the Trinity of Persons; and asserted that the Persons are distinguished, but not separated or divided from each other.[1] Androutsos contends that all the attempts to realize and illuminate the mystery of the Holy Trinity through illustrations and figures have been, and, by the nature of the question, must always be, futile. Whether such illustrations be taken from human psychology, or from nature, or from the study of comparative religion, or even in such an ethical division as "Lover, Beloved, and Love", they are all alike useless and futile. This last illustration he characterizes as an "explanation of the unknown by the unknown". "Such analogies carried out logically empty the mystery of the Holy Trinity of its supernatural content."[2] So we must be content with the Truths of Revelation, and never press a figure, illustration, or analogy too far. The Mystery is in its fundamental character insoluble for our minds, says Androutsos.

Additional Note on the Filioque Controversy

It is not within the scope of these lectures to attempt any detailed treatment of the difficulties connected with the *Filioque* clause as regards the relations of the Western and Eastern Churches. At this time when the urge of the desire for reunion is so strong in men's minds, it is above all necssary to think clearly and not to be swung about by any sentimental or irrational appeal, towards judgments and decisions which must needs be subject to revision in the light of subsequent

---

[1] Androutsos, *op. cit.*, pp. 87-88.
[2] *Ibid.*, pp. 89-92.

study and investigation.[1] Before abandoning the clause in use
in the Western Church for ten centuries and more, it is well
to discover what it means, why it is there, and what losses
and gains there might accrue by its excision.

In the discussion of any controversy of long standing it is
above all necessary to investigate origins with every care as to
historical accuracy. This is particularly true in all ecclesiastical matters, and preëminently the case with regard to this
vexed question of the *Filioque*. In order to come to an understanding now we must first get clear in our minds at least two
important facts which the history of the controversy indicates.
(1) While it is true, as we all shall see, that the whole question bulks very large in the minds of the Orthodox as the
fundamental cause of the separation of the East and West, the
blame for which is attributed universally to the attitude of
the Roman Church and the Pope,[2] nevertheless it is not without
significance that Ambraze can say: "The *Filioque* clause existed
for many years in certain Western Churches before the separation of the two Churches, without the Eastern Bishops concerning themselves about it or pronouncing those churches
heretical. . . . The Creed was sung in all the churches of Gaul
with the *Filioque* addition, from the end of the 8th century. .
. .But the Easterns certainly did keep on in communion with
the Gaulish and Spanish Bishops, whose churches used the
additional clause, and they were all in intercommunion, for

---

[1] Cf. G. B. Howard, *The Schism between the Oriental and Western
Churches*, London, 1892, p. 88 *et al;* on him, Hall, *The Trinity*, New
York, 1910, p. 96 note 1, and Palmieri, *Theologia Dogmatica Orthodoxa*, vol. I, pp. 346 ff. and note 3; also Overbeck, *The Filioque and
the American Church* in *The Orthodox Catholic Review* for 1867,
vol. I. pp. 246-252; Howard, *An English View of the Filioque Question, as bearing on the Reunion Movement* in *Revue Internationale
de théologie*, vol. V. 1897, p. 67.

[2] Cf. Demetracopoulos, Ἡ ἱστορία τοῦ Σχίσματος, Leipzig 1867, and
the unanimous verdict of Orthodox controversialists that the Roman
See in its insistence on the *Filioque* was the chief cause of the Schism;
Palmieri, *Theologia Dogmatica Orthodoxa*, vol. II, whole text *passim*.
This was Neale's opinion; cf. his *History of the Holy Eastern Church*,
London, 1850, vol. II. p. 1168: "Its insertion in the creed was an act
utterly unjustifiable, and throws on the Roman Church the chief guilt
in the horrible schism of 1054."

the Church was one."[1]   The fact, as Palmieri notes,[2] that some three centuries elapsed before any breach of unity occurred, is sufficient to indicate that the cause of the separation lay elsewhere than in the *Filioque* clause.   (2) A second comment that naturally formulates itself upon investigating the course of the controversy and it's theological consequences, is that the question involved is largely speculative and theoretical.   Had the doctrine involved in the *Filioque* been so radically and substantially untrue, there certainly would have emerged in the history of the last ten centuries in the Western Church, some definite evidence of falsity in theory incurring evil con-sequences in practice, whether in dogma, doctrine, or the spir-itual or moral life of Western Catholicism.   By no stretch of the wildest theological imagination has any controversialist ever been justified in attempting to magnify the *Filioque* ques-tion into the proportions of a heresy of the dimensions of Arianism or Sabellianism. Controversy has entirely warped Orthodox perspective in the matter.

No single difference between East and West has aroused so much bitterness on the part of Orthodox writers as has the matter of the *Filioque*.   It is to the fore in every con-troversial and polemic work of Eastern writers since the Schism.[3]   The Protosynkellos Chrysostom calls it "an arbitrary opinion, an heretical novelty, an impious and perverse doctrine, false, untrue, contrary to the Gospel, revealed by the Devil, the father of lies."[4]   A priest-monk, Constantius, says: "The Roman Church has committed the mortal sin of blasphemy in saying that the Holy Ghost proceeds also from the Son . . . She has fallen away from the VII Councils by this addition, separated herself from the Church, and incurred anathema."[5] "The addition of the *Filioque* is both in letter and spirit con-trary to Holy Scripture."[6]   The mere presence of the words

[1] 'Η 'Ορθόδοξος 'Εκκλησία, Athens, 1902, p. 52-53.

[2] *Op. cit.*, vol. I, pp. 338 ff.

[3] Even a cursory examination of the course of Orthodox-Roman con-troversy as given in Palmieri's second volume (*op. cit.*) would prove this abundantly.

[4] Περὶ 'Εκκλησίας, Athens, 1896, vol. II. pp. 382, 389.

[5] 'Ιερὰ Βίβλος, καλουμένη Χρηστοήθεια τῶν Χριστιανῶν, Constantinople, 1898, vol I. pp. 65, 68.

[6] Mesolora, Συμβολική, vol. I. Athens, 1883, p. 51.

in the Athanasian creed vitiate it; "the purpose of the *Filioque* and its uncanonical addition reduce largely its significance".[1] Õne writer finds the Anglican use of this Symbol a great difficulty in establishing relations between us and the Orthodox, since the Athanasian creed "was forged by Papist theologians to uphold their own false teaching as to the *Filioque*."[2] In earlier times certain Greek confessions of Faith required an explicit repudiation of the doctrine of the *Filioque*.[3] In the main, the controversy has not been illuminated by any further contributions, save in acrimony and vilification, than those of Photius,[4] beyond whom there has been no advance in theological acumen or insight. When the progress of the controversy is read in the light of history one thing is abundantly evident: Western theologians certainly do not teach what the Orthodox claim they do, as they do not hold to two *principia* ($ἀρχαί, πηγαί,$) in the Godhead.[5] Furthermore, even so partial and pro-Orthodox a scholar as Neale, after fully investigating the whole question from the Fathers on, concludes: "The indirect testimony preponderates incomparably on the Greek side; the direct testimony preponderates on the Latin side."[6]

Quite rightly Pusey[7] distinguished two distinct questions

---

[1] *Ibid.* p. 63, and cf. note 1, p. 374 of vol. I. of Palmieri, *op cit.*

[2] N. Technopoulos, writing in the "Ενωσις των 'Εκκλησιών, London, 1904, note 40, pp. 638-644, on 'Η δογματικὴ θέσις τῆς ἀγγλικῆς 'Εκκλησίας καθ' ἑαυτὴν ἐξεταζομένη. On the general position of Orthodoxy, cf. Palmieri, *op. cit.*, I. pp. 336-407.

[3] *E. g.*, Miklosich and Müller, *Acta Patriarchatus const.* (1315-1402) *e codicibus manuscriptis bibliothecae palatinae vindobonensis*, Vienna, 1872, vol. II. p. 8, and cf. vol. I. pp. 501, 506, 550; vol. II. pp. 84, 160, etc.

[4] *Liber de Spiritus Sancti Mystagogia*, in Migne, *P. G.*, t. CII, cols. 279-392; edited with critical notes, by Hergenröther, Ratisbon, 1867; *Encyclical Letter* to the Eastern Archbishops, Migne, *P. G.*, t. CII, cols. 721-742; Letter to the Archbishop of Aquileia, in Jäger, *Histoire de Photius, patriarche de Constantinople*, Paris, 1845, pp. 452-464, and Valetta, Φωτίου 'Επιστολαί, London, 1864, pp. 181-200. Cf. Rhalle and Potle, Σύνταγμα, Athens, 1854, vol. IV, pp. 407 ff.

[5] Cf. F. J. Hall, *The Trinity*, N. Y. 1910, p. 94-96; Palmieri, *op. cit.*, I. p. 342.

[6] *Op. cit.*, I. p. 1131.

[7] Cf. *On the Clause "And the Son" in regard to the Eastern Church and the Bonn Conference*, Oxford, 1876, pp. 33 ff.

as to the *Filioque*.   One is that of the legality or regularity of
the addition.   The other is in regard to the truth or falsity of
the doctrines involved.   As to the former Hall says[1] that
"modern conditions have caused (the canonical questions involved in the *Filioque controversy*) to have only an academic
interest."   As to the dogmatic truth he says: "The *Filoque* has
come to serve in the West as a practically indispensable safeguard of two leading particulars of the catholic doctrine of the
Trinity; and its abandonment, even in the interests of canonical regularity and reunion with the East, may not be permitted
until sufficient provision has been made for a continued maintenance and assertion of the truths which the clause in question
protects.   These truths are the co-equality of the Son with the
Father, obscured by modern and semi-pantheistic interpretations of the ὁμοούσιος; and the eternal relation of the Holy Spirit
to the Son, which, by reason of their controversial attitude in behalf of the Father's sole *principatus,* the Easterns are inclined to
disregard."[2]   Dr. Pusey's hope that mutual explanation might
serve to clear up misunderstanding is not yet justified: "If the
Greeks come to understand our Western terms, all difference dis-
appears."[3]   Despite Lyons, Florence, and the Bonn conferences,[4]
theological misconception still persists and maintains.   One is
tempted to quote here some rather sharp words of Palmieri:
"Contro il *Filioque* insorge unicamente l'anemica teologia greco-
russa, che dopo la scissione delle Chiese, langue affetta da senile
marasmo.   Ragionado a fil di logica, per dar ragione all'
ortodossia, noi dovremmo ammettere che una minorità infima
nel cristianesimo, una minorità la quale non personifica nè la
scienza, nè l'erudizione, nè l'onestà letteraria, in un difficilissimo
problema teologico imbrocchi la soluzione vera; dovremmo
ammettere che i grandi teologi del cattolicismo . . . per-

---

[1] *Op. cit.,* pp. 236-7.

[2] *Op. cit.,* p. 237, and cf. *ibid.,* pp. 230-237.

[3] *Op. cit.,* p. 171, and cf. pp. 106-7, and 172 ff.

[4] On the two former, cf. Palmieri, *op. cit.,* 11, pp. 87-101; Pusey,
op. cit., pp. 102-108; on the Bonn Conferences, cf. Reusch *Bericht
über die vom* 10 *bis* 16 *August* 1875 *zu Bonn gehaltenen Unionscon-
ferenzen,* Bonn., 1875, and that for the subsequent year; Reports on
the same, edited by the Rev. H. P. Liddon, 1875 and 1876, and Rhôsse's
reports to the Holy Synod of Athens, same years.

correndo gli annali della tradizione cristiana, hanno avuto le traveggole agli occhi, scoprendo in essi le prove storiche dell' antichità del *Filioque,* laddove un nucleo di retori bizantini e di monaci fanatici[1] sono gli araldi della verità, quando affermano che queste prove storiche non esistono!"[2]

In the recent pamphlet, *Terms of Intercommunion suggested between the Church of England and the Churches in Communion with Her and the Eastern Orthodox Church,*[3] Sections VII and VIII are concerned with the *Doctrines of the Holy Spirit* and *the Filoque Clause.* The latter says: "We agree in acknowledging that this addition (to the Creed) was not made 'in an ecclesiastically regular manner,' and that in assemblies of Easterns and Westerns the one Creed of the Universal Church ought to be recited without those words; but we are also agreed that, since the added words are used in an orthodox sense, it is lawful for any Church which has received the Creed as containing these words to continue so to recite it in the Services of the Church."[4] The first statement is No. II of the Preliminary Resolutions of the Bonn Conference, and is still subject to the same criticism as Pusey brought against it, that it is a truism, useless as the basis of an Eirenicon, clears up nothing, but allows the imputation that the *Filioque* clause was a wilful interpolation.[5] This suggested emendation is given in Note 1 to his Essay, which is very worthy of consideration in view of present negotions, as are all the "proposed amendments" to the Bonn Propositions.[6] In every way we must guard against parting with "what, through so many centuries, has been the

---

[1] Gerlach reported that Zygomalas, when questioned about the *Filioque,* answered: "Etsi Christus ipse de coelo descenderet, dicens Spiritum Sanctum a Patre et Filio procedere, tamen Graecos id non esse credituros," in Geisius, *Destinata inter Constantinopolitanum patriarchum Ieremiam, et theologos witembergenses conjunctio,* Wittemberg, 1705, XX.

[2] *Il Progresso Dommatico,* Florence, 1910, p. 171. For his treatment of the subject here, cf. pp. 165-172, and his monographs, cf. above p. 51.

[3] London, S. P. C. K., 1921.

[4] *Ibid.,* p. 7.

[5] Cf. *op. cit.,* pp. 33-90, and note 1, pp. 182-184; and *Terms of Intercommunion,* pp. 7 and 13-14.

[6] Pusey, *Eirenicon,* pp. 263-266.

expression of our common faith, (while) we might still reject with Anathema the heresy which, since Photius, has been imputed to it, and which the Greek Church now seems by an inveterate prejudice, to think to be involved in it. . . . We only ask to continue to use the formula, which without any act of our own, has been the expression of our faith immemorially . . If, on such terms and on such explanations of our belief as she (the Greek Church) may require and we could give, communion should be restored between us, a great step would have been gained towards the reunion of all Christendom."

In conclusion we may note that, aside from the entanglements of controversy in the past, the economic, political, racial, and social causes working for the cleavage between Eastern and Western Christendom, two outstanding comments on the *Filioque* difficulty deserve consideration: (a) The radical difference in point of view between Eastern and Western theologians in envisaging the doctrine of the Holy Trinity. The Eastern mind would conceive of the relations of the Persons in and by the Divine Life within the Godhead, while the Western idea of the relations of the Persons is, as it were, more from without. The former looks constantly towards the great theological truth of the one Source or *principium* in the Godhead; the latter sees the results of the Divine activity as springing from the One Fount and Cause.   (b) The radical difference in language.   We do not use the words to mean what the Easterns consider them to mean.   On this Dr. Pusey has an excellent comment:[1]   "Dr. Döllinger (at the Bonn Conferences) rightly insisted that the Greeks attached to the Greek expression, ἐκπορεύεσθαι, a meaning which we do not attach to our Western, 'proceed from' . . . It, in itself, only signifies 'to proceed out of'. It does not in itself signify 'to proceed out of *as the original source of Being.*' No one questions their right to ascribe to it, for *themselves,* what meaning they please. . . Nor have they any authority to blame us for not attaching that meaning to our Lord's word in Holy Scriptures, or to our own substitute for it, 'to proceed from'.   It does not lie in the word itself; nor has the Church authoritatively so limited its use.   We do not speak Greek, nor

[1] *On the Clause "and the Son", in regard to the Eastern Church and the Bonn Conference,* pp. 106-107.

require the Greeks to use our language. But we, Westerns, are the judges of what we mean by our own. In fact, as Dr. Döllinger pointed out, the case is parallel to the confusions, which there were, in the Arian period, about the word 'Hypostasis', 'Prosopon', and 'Persona'. When the misapprehension was cleared up, each went on using his own terms."

LECTURE III.
SIN AND SALVATION

LECTURE III.

SIN AND SALVATION

CONTENTS

I

SIN AND SALVATION

The Orthodox teaching concerning the Office, Person, and work of the Saviour involves the doctrines of Creation, Anthropology, the Fall, and Sin. As the logical presuppositions of Orthodox Christology, the doctrine of the Orthodox Church may be divided into these four heads, of which the exposition in summary follows.

I. CREATION, MAN, AND THE FALL

As we have seen, God, who is all good, wished to give existence to non-being, in accordance with the prototype existing in Him, in order that He might constitute other entities capable of sharing His goodness.[1] The actualization and realization of this plan of God, whether the plan be regarded as existing "eternally" or only "before time" in His mind, was effected by the Creation of the "world".[2] By bringing to bear His Almighty Power in conjunction with His Love and His Will, He brought about the existence of the world in fact, which had had existence potentially in His Mind. "The reason and cause of the existence . . . of the world lies in God Himself."[3] "The goodness of God . . . gives us the reason of Creation. Crea-

[3] Rhôsse, op. cit., p. 326.
[2] "The word 'world' ($\kappa \acute{o} \sigma \mu o s$) signifies the same as the ancient use of it would imply, i. e.—the system of heaven and earth, and all they contain" (Mesolora, $\Sigma \nu \mu \beta o \lambda \iota \kappa \acute{\eta}$, III. p. 129). The term is practically equivalent to our word "universe".
[1] Rhôsse, $\Delta o \gamma \mu \alpha \tau \iota \kappa \acute{\eta}$, p. 328.

tion is the work of great wisdom and might and proceeds forth from the hands of the Allwise and Almighty."[1] Since the world is God's work, each of the Persons in the Godhead had His own share in it: God the Father is the Primary Cause, God the Son, the Effective Cause, and God the Holy Ghost, the Perfecting Cause.[2] So "that by the will of the Father (the ministering spirits) have their existence, by the coöperation of the Son they are brought into being, and by the presence of the Holy Spirit they are perfected."[3] Creation has not only God as its Cause, but Orthodox teaching, founded on Holy Scripture[4] and the united teaching of the Fathers, claims that it was His free act, and that He created it from nothing. Such theories as hold Him to have created of necessity, or from pre-existent matter, are entirely opposed to the Orthodox doctrine, which is "in direct opposition both to the pantheistic notions (held by neo-platonic philosophy and by some of the gnostic heresies) of emanations from God, as well as to the dualistic and materialistic hypothesis."[5] "It is superfluous to show," says Androutsos,[6] "that the Christian Faith, postulating as it does the dependence of the world upon God, at the same time preserves whole and intact the conception of God as transcending matter and all 'becoming', and the conception of the world as absolutely dependent upon God; and also . . . opposes every cosmological and philosophical speculation about the origin of the world, of ancient and modern times—whether it be the Hylozoism of the ancients, according to which all things came into being from pre-existent chaotic matter, or Pantheism, which intermingles God and the world and regards the world as a natural emanation from the Divine substance as from an overfull cup, or the Plato-

[1] Kephala, Χριστολογία, p. 124.
[2] The Holy Spirit is "the informing Principle of matter;" cf. Androutsos, Δογματική, p. 93.
[3] Περὶ ἁγίου Πνεύματος, St. Basil, ch. 16; in Mesolora, Συμβολική, III. p. 325, and p. ·131. Cf. St. John Damascene, Ἔκδοσις 2, 17; Gennadius, in Mesolora, op. cit., vol. I. pp. 73-74; 1st Answer of Jeremiah II. ibid., p. 126; Metrophanes Kritopoulos, ibid., p. 297., Mogila, question 6, ibid., p. 385; Conf. of Dositheus, § 4 ibid., p. 105, etc.
[4] For a catena cf. Rhôsse, Δογματική, pp. 331-333.
[5] Ibid., p. 334.
[6] Op. cit., p. 93.

nistic dualism which, while it views God as the informing and ordering Principle, does not hold Him to be the Creative Principle."[1]

The dogma that God is the Creator of the world "both as to its substance as well as to its form, . . is a mystery of the Faith . . . God has only revealed to us what is of most importance for our needs, and what is sufficient for our salvation."[2] It is like the apprehension of the truth of God's freedom, of His Essence, or of His Will—beyond our comprehension.[3] "Though it is in a measure intelligible to us,....it still has a mysterious and incomprehensible side....and remains in a sense a miracle—the greatest, the primal, miracle."[4] Like any other truth of Revelation, it is not in all its bearings subject to our scrutiny, nor entirely within the range of our capacity to discover or ascertain by the use of unaided reason and human experience. The Orthodox doctrine of Creation may be analyzed into four subheads: (a) God created the world from nothing, by the exercise of His own free will; (b) He created it in time; (c) with both an adequate aim and end; and (d) orders and guides it according to His own Almighty Will and Wisdom.

That God created the world from nothing is clear from Holy

---

[1] Cf. Androutsos, Ἡ τοῦ Πλάτωνος θεωρία τῆς γνώσεως, Athens, 1912, p. 113.   Rhôsse points out (op. cit., pp. 336-337) that the Platonic and Aristotelian conception of the Infinite is not that of the unlimited, but that of the undetermined.   Matter without form does not exist save as an abstraction, and the conception of form as "otherness from God as pure Spirit" and as being determined, is an antithesis to the idea of God.   But the opposition, Rhôsse says, is really not between form and God as Spirit, but between Infinite spirit and finite spirit, nor logically that between spirit and matter.   God, therefore, to be Infinite must be the Creator of form, as well as of matter.   For matter is admittedly not absolute, but imperfect and subject to change, and so it could not be self-originated.   The same reasoning holds as regards form as such, for the finite is not one, but many, and so not infinite, being other-than-God.   "The finite number of the multiplicity of entities and things in the world, ordered to an end, and the world, the actualization of divers genera and species (i. e., from out of their existence in the Divine mind) constitutes an ordered and simple whole" (Rhôsse, op. cit., pp. 340-341).

[2] Mesolora, Συμβολική, III. p. 130.

[3] Androutsos, Δογματική, p. 96.

[4] Rhôsse, op. cit., p. 338.

Scripture.[1] He did not bring it into being from pre-existent matter[2]. . . . This is the teaching of both the Fathers and the Symbolic Books as well[3]. . . . "The teaching of the Church about Creation from nothing is not. . . . opposed to reason. . . . for it regards God as the sufficient reason or Highest Cause of the world's existence both as to matter and form."[4] "The principle *ex nihilo nihil fit* strengthens rather than destroys the dogma of Creation; since if by it one understands matter to be something necessary, because of God as Creator, and because of the. . . . energy. . . of natural powers in general, he then falls into the well-known blunder in logic of begging the question; if he holds that there is a cause by or from which everything has come about, then. . . . this cause must be God Himself."[5] It follows then that "there was no reason compelling God to create the world. It was not a work of necessity."[6] Since what God does as the Infinite and Almighty He does consonant with His nature as free of any external limitations, Creation could neither have been of necessity nor could it have been the result of chance, or of something fortuitous.[7] The former hypothesis, that the world was necessary and inevitable, either is based upon pantheistic premises, or logically leads to Pantheism.[8] Furthermore, if matter had existed before Creation, from which God formed the world, it would have involved an external limitation on His Eternity and Almightiness; in short, this theory would militate against His Character as Absolute and Infinite.[9] Another consequence of the denial of the truth that Creation was a free act on God's part, would be the cutting of the ground from under- the possibility of religion, which consists of a *free* relationship between God and man.[10]

[1] Cf. 2 Mac. 7, 28; Job 38, 4; Ps. 8, 3; 33, 6.
[2] Heb. 11, 3; Wisd. 11, 17.
[3] *E. g.*, St. Athanasius, *de Incarnatione Verbi*, 2; *contra gentes*, 39; Gennadius, in Mesolora, *op. cit.*, I, pp. 73-4; 1st *Answer* of Jeremiah II, *ibid.*, p. 126, etc.; cf. Rhôsse, *op. cit.*, pp. 331-335.
[4] *Ibid.*, p. 336.
[5] Androutsos, *op. cit.*, pp. 95-96.
[6] Kephala, *op. cit.*, p. 124.
[7] Mesolora, *op. cit.*, III. pp. 137-138.
[8] Androutsos, *op. cit.*, p. 96.
[9] Rhôsse, *op. cit.*, p. 339.
[10] Androutsos, *ibid.*

Linked with the above is the truth that Creation took place in or with time, and not from eternity.[1] "Since eternity is the undetermined and absolute form of God's existence and energy as viewed in relation to Himself, and time is the finite form of the energy of the finite world,....the existence of the idea of the world in the mind and will of God may not be conceived as eternal, as is God's own existence (in Himself), but as before time.... Time took its beginning with Creation."[2] · Since matter is finite it must have had a beginning, and the words "in the beginning"[3] mean, according to the Fathers, "in the beginning *of time.*"[4] Origen's difficulty,[5] according to Rhôsse,[6] lay in his not distinguishing between the relative and absolute attributes of God; according to Androutsos, in his having failed to distinguish between God's creative power in Himself, and its exercise in fact, in Creation—between His idea of the world and its realization and actualization in Creation.[7] The relation of time to eternity is suggested in the foregoing. "Since Creation is the calling forth from non-being into being, it is clear

---

[1] Cf. St. Augustine: *Mundus non in tempore sed cum tempore factus est*, and St. Thomas Acquin., *Summa*, 1, 9, 46 (§ 2).

[2] Rhôsse, *op. cit.*, pp. 342-343; he has a three-fold distinction, (a) "temporal" (τοῦ χρόνου), (b) "eternal" (ἀΐδιον), and (c) "pretemporal" (προαιώνιον). God's idea of the world was not "eternal", but only "before time". The conception of "pretemporal" is intermediate between that of time and eternity (p. 327 note 2). Time, according to him, is the "finite form of finite energy"; according to Androutsos, it is "properly the measure of the sequence of created energy and is naturally bound up with creatures" (*op. cit.*, p. 98). While Rhôsse would not call the world eternal, it may yet be described as being everlasting (αἰωνιότης="everlastingness"), and though it had a beginning in time yet may be "without end" (ἀτελεύτητος), *op. cit.*, p. 343. Androutsos does not agree with Rhôsse's three-fold distinction and says that "God's will concerning the world is clearly bound up with His eternal character" otherwise He would not be conceived as simple or unchanging (*op. cit.*, p. 101). "There is no mean between time and eternity. Besides, it introduces a former and a latter, *i. e.*, a time relation, into the Being of God", p. 102, note 2. On space and time, cf. Rhôsse, *op. cit.*, p. 344, note 1.

[3] Gen. 1, 1; St. John 1, 1; cf. also, Ps. 90, 2; Ps. 93, 2; St. John 17, 5; Eph. 1, 4.

[4] Androutsos *op. cit.*, p. 98.

[5] Cf. Περὶ ἀρχῶν 1, 2, 10.

[6] *Op. cit.*, pp. 341-342.

[7] *Op. cit.*, p. 97.

that....the creative energy of God....must needs be manifested in the temporal beginning of the world".[1] Because time
began with Creation it cannot be thought to have existed before
the world, else the world would be older than itself. But God
as eternal is "antecedent to the world not chronologically, but
logically....Yet while the world is only logically later than He
it does not follow that it is coeval with Him,"[2] for this would
impair His absolute character.[3] That His will and plan for the
world were either "eternal", according to Androutsos,
or "before time" acording to Rhôsse, does not involve the
corollary "that this will should have an eternal fulfilment,
nor that God became the Cause of the world only
when He created it."[4] There must be a sharp distinction in
our thinking between the conception of God's will for Creation
and His plan and design, which were in Him before Creation,
and the carrying out and realization of His will in the fact of
Creation. It is an essential and valid distinction, even though
the Platonic envisagement of the idea "on the part of some of
the Fathers led them into metaphysical speculations unsupported by Revelation."[5]

"The reason of the world's existence", in the words of Kephala, "is the goodness of God.....which of its own great abun-
dance imparted itself in Creation, that it might externalize its
richness, and even constitute other beings sharers in this Goodness and Blessedness."[7] This, as was said in Lecture II under
the "Ethical attributes of God",[8] is the characteristic Orthodox
interpretation of God's Love, in this aspect of that attribute.
"The world is a result of a cause beyond (and outside of) itself, a consequence of God's free knowledge and will....(It is)

[1] Androutsos, *op. cit.*, p. 100. He notes that the very conception
of a beginningless creation (ἀνάρχου δημιουργίας) is a contradiction
of predicates. (*ibid.*)
[2] *Ibid.*, pp. 98-99; Rhôsse, *op. cit.*, p. 343.
[3] Androutsos, *op. cit.*, p. 100, and Rhôsse, *op. cit.*, p. 339.
[4] Androutsos, *op. cit.*, p. 102.
[5] Androutsos, *op. cit.*, pp. 103-104.
[6] *Op. cit.*, p. 124.
[7] Cf. on this, Gennadius, in Mesolora, *op. cit.*, I. p. 74; Kritopoulos,
ibid., p. 297; Dositheus, *ibid.*, pp. 105-106; Mogila, pp. 378-379; a
summary of this doctrine in Rhôsse, *op. cit.*, p. 361.
[8] Cf. pp. 101-102.

His work, both as to matter and form,....made with ease by His Omnipotent power, and in accordance with the Divine fore-knowledge and wisdom, wisely, and in graduated and purpose-ful order."[1] As was said above, the world was freely created by God, and was not the result of either chance or accident. So it follows that He who freely created it had an object or aim in view. This end which God had in view (the *causa finalis*) con-stitutes at the same time the efficient cause (*causa impulsiva*) of Creation, since both refer to the same thing.[2] Since we may not conceive God as incomplete or lacking in anything, by rea-son of which external need He must have created the world, we may not seek the aim and purpose of the world save in His own Nature. The content of this aim and purpose of God in Creation is resolvable into the *proximate* end, the happiness of rational creatures, and the *final* end, the glory of God.[3] Furthermore, since the aim of the Redemption is the perfection of Creation, and may be defined as "the foundation of the Kingdom of God, to His Glory,[4] it is clear that the purpose of the world cannot be different from (that of) the Redemption in Christ. . . . Hence . . . . the proximate end of Creation may not be sundered from the final end, but constitutes together with it one unique and indivisible whole."[5] It is in relation to its end that the world is said to be "good", that is, 'in agreement with the plan of God concerning it.[6] God will not allow His final end to miscarry. It is, however, unjustifiable to say that it is "the best possible" world, as do the absolute optimists, or to assert that it is the "only possible" world, reasoning that God might have created or might not, but that since He did, this was the only possible effect of His will in Creation. This spec-

---

[1] Mesolora, *op. cit.*, III. pp. 134-135.

[2] *Causa finalis*: . . . *id cujus gratia aliquid fit; causa im-pulsiva vel efficiens*: *id a quo aliquid fit*. Cf. *Manual of Modern Scholas-tic Philosophy*, Card. Mercier, (Eng. transl.) 2 vols. London 1919; vol. II. p. 508.

[3] Androutsos, *op. cit.*, pp. 104-105; cf. Ps. 19, 1; Prov. 16, 4; Rom. 11, 36; Heb. 2, 10; Song of the Three Children, vs. 35; St. Luke 2, 14; Rom. 1, 19-20; Deut. 10, 21.

[4] Cf. St. John, 17, 4; Eph. 1, 5-6; Col. 1, 16.

[5] Androutsos, *op. cit.*, pp. 105-106.

[6] Mesolora, *op. cit.*, III. pp. 138-139.

ulation, Androutsos says,[1] both limits God's freedom, and transgresses the limitations of our reasoning, since the mystery of Divine free will is not subject to our scrutiny nor within the compass of our comprehension.

Of the order of Creation we know that there was a progress from the simple to the complex, from the general to the particular, from the imperfect to the more perfect, from the inorganic to the organic, and from the unrational to the rational, "with man as the link uniting visible and invisible nature, the microcosm embracing both matter and spirit."[2] The biblical account teaches us that each new species was a separate creation of God.[3] The various speculations and problems connected with Genesis, the meaning of the "six days", reconciliation of this account with the results of scientific investigation, and the like, form no part of Dogmatic, according to Androutsos,[4] though Rhôsse devotes some attention to them.[5] A right view of Holy Scripture helps to clear away misconceptions, for "Holy Scripture is not a book on natural science, but presents its content in a form and language agreeable to the ideas and comprehensions of those for whom it was written. It has in view the purpose of ascribing the genesis of the world to God."[6] It is not, says Mesolora, "either a work on nature, nor on geology, nor on geography, but a religious text, exactly fulfilling the end for which it was designed". . . . He goes on to say that "it is certainly true, furthermore, that we cannot interpret everything in it literally."[7]

Closely connected, in Orthodox theology, with the doctrine of Creation, is that concerning the Providence of God. Since the world was a result and consequence of God's overflowing goodness and bounty, it is impossible that He should have

[1] *Op. cit.*, pp. 107-109.
[2] Mesolora, *op. cit.*, III. pp. 135-136;   Androutsos, *op. cit.*, p. 109.
[3] Androutsos, *ibid.*, p. 110.
[4] *Op. cit.*, pp. 110-111.
[5] *Op. cit.*, pp. 371-382.   According to him the Darwinian hypothesis is certainly not proven, for (a) there is no evidence proving the origin of species in the Darwinian sense and according to that theory, nor (b) does man's nature allow the possibility of the origin Darwin and Haeckel postulate.   (*ibid.*)
[6] Androutsos, *op. cit.*, p. 111.
[7] *Op. cit.*, III, p. 136 and note.

abandoned it after having brought it into being.[1]   God's Providence (πρόνοια) is shown in two ways: in His oversight and
preservation of His Creation (συντήρησις), and in His governance and direction of it (κυβέρνησις).[2]   Androutsos and Rhôsse
both agree in this division.   Some theologians add a third type
of Divine Providence, "coöperation" (συνέργεια),[3] which, according to Androutsos, does not constitute a genuine third element, but only refers to the manner by which God governs and
preserves His world through the powers of Nature.[4]   God's
preservation and fostering care of His universe is His coöperation in the laws and powers with which He has endowed the
world, not as by a new creation, nor as solely by a negative protection against dissolution and destruction, but by a positive
and immediate exercise of His Will and Might in His world.[5]
God rules the whole of His universe, sustains it in being, and
oversees it in whole and in part.   So far as concerns the physical world, His oversight is "to be referred to it as a whole, and
in relation to its substance, rather than . . . to its form".[6]
This preservation and oversight may not rightly be understood
as a kind of *creatio continua,* but "as a coöperation of the omnipresent Highest Cause" of the world in its every detail.   It is
extended to each and everything in the world, and especially to
man, "the center of creation", who is the peculiar care and concern of God's oversight and preservation.[7]

As all and each are within the scope of God's oversight and
protection,[8] so His direction and governance extend throughout
His universe, ordering and guiding it to its highest end—the

[1] Kephala, *op. cit.,* p. 124.
[2] That this is the doctrine of both Holy Scriptures and the Fathers,
Rhôsse (*op cit.,* pp. 346-347) shows from texts, e. g. St. John 5, 17; St.
Matt. 6, 26; 10, 29; Col. 1, 17; Heb. 1, 3; St. Matt. 12, 28; 1 Cor. 12, 4.
The *Confession* of Dositheus asserts it clearly (in Mesolora *op. cit.,* vol.
I. p. 106, and Kimmel, *op. cit.,* II. p. 461).
[3] *E. g.,* Macarius, *op. cit.,* vol. I. p. 629.
[4] *Op. cit.,* pp. 112-113.
[5] *Ibid.,* pp. 113-114, and Rhôsse, *op. cit.,* pp. 348-349.
[6] Rhôsse, *op. cit.,* pp. 350 ff.   He explains this restriction by reference to the extinction of certain species.
[7] Androutsos, *op. cit.,* p. 116.
[8] Cf. Gen. 45, 5; 50, 20; Exod. 9, 15-16; Prov. 16, 33; Acts, 2, 23;
Rom. 9, 22-23.

salvation of man and the glory of God. The denial of God's oversight and guidance of His world issues in the denial of all religion and morality, and in a loss of faith in prayer.[1] This governing and overruling of His world may be presented as *immediate,* in revelation and miracle, and as *mediate,* in the functioning of the laws and powers of nature.[2] God, as Governor of the universe, displays His directive and governing energy in relation to man, in two ways—external and internal: the former refers to God's ordering and directing the circumstances and environing influences of man's life, and the latter, to God's part in man's thoughts, memory, and plans.[3] While He guides and manages inanimate creation to the end proposed by means of His laws and the circumstances and conditions of natural life, He assists rational beings towards their end, coöperates and strengthens them toward the good, but not towards evil, for at the most God may be said only to tolerate evil within determined limits. While man's motives and choices are free, the consequences of his acts are directly under God's providential care, oversight, and direction. He makes the consequences of evil serve His end, and overrules evil for good.[4] His Divine governing activity "does not take away the relative self-directed activity of beings in the natural order, nor the relative freedom of self-directing rational creatures of the spiritual order, but only directs them in accordance with the final end in view."[5] (The problem of the relation of God's foreknowledge and fore-ordination to man's free will has been considered in Lecture II,[6] and does not call for extended treatment. Mesolora[7] in his chapter on "Foreknowledge and Foreordination" presents the evidence of the teaching of the symbolic texts.) God's Providence extends to everything in His Creation, yet saves man's free will. Man's acts are not pre-determined, for God knows his free acts as free, and His knowledge does not affect them.

---

[1] Androutsos, *op. cit.,* pp. 116-117.
[2] Mesolora, *op. cit.,* III. p. 185, note 1; he gives patristic and symbolic sources for the whole subject, pp. 185-191, *ibid.*
[3] Rhôsse, *op. cit.,* p. 356.
[4] Androutsos, *op. cit.,* pp. 117-118.
[5] Rhôsse, *op. cit.,* p. 358.
[6] Cf. pp. 95-100.
[7] *Op. cit,* III. pp 192-199, and cf. Rhôsse, *op. cit.,* pp. 356-370.

"As concerns the way in which human acts are woven into the divine scheme of governing and directing the universe, we are not able to understand in all its bearings."[1] Moral evil, that is, evil in man's will, is an inherent possibility involved in the freedom of man's will, and physical evil is a consequence of it. Neither the dualistic nor neoplatonic systems are philosophically satisfactory, and neither is justified in practice. Evil, according to human experience, is not something merely apparent, but positive in the world, to combat and conquer which only our Redemption in Jesus Christ and the foreordination of man to glory, are effective.[2]

2. MAN

"The result of the creative and providential energy of God is the world, an ordered whole ordained to a definite end. . . . Man is the link joining the spiritual and material orders of the world, ... the capstone and end of material creation, belonging in body to the physical order, and in soul or spirit to the spiritual order."[3] Yet man is not two, but one—a unity, consisting of body and soul, between which there is no dualistic antagonism. Over-emphasis in either direction leads to a denial of the truth. "The right doctrine of man", says Androutsos,[4] "protests on the one hand against Materialism and the false hypothesis of the Darwinian theory, and as strongly, on the other hand, against the over-emphasized stress of certain 'spiritualistics'[5] theories, which maintain that the body is a kind of mere representation and prison of the soul. . . . The body does not over-shadow the soul, nor imprison the spirit, . . . but is the divinely created organ forever united with it." So

[1] Androutsos, *op. cit.*, p. 117.
[2] *Ibid.*, pp. 118-119. Here Androutsos follows with a note on miracle with reference to God's Providence, on which cf. above, Lecture 1, Sec. 3, especially note 2, p. 15 (cf. pp. 119-120 Androutsos, *ibid.*).
[3] Rhôsse, *op. cit.*, pp. 382, 398; cf. also *ibid.* p. 356; Androutsos, *op. cit.*, pp. 104-106, 116; Mesolora, *op. cit.*, III. pp. 185 ff.
[4] *Op. cit.*, p. 130.
[5] "Spiritualistic" (*spiritualism—πνευματισμός*) as applied to the philosophic speculation which would exaggerate man's non-material endowment at the expense of the natural, physical, or material. Cf. Liljenkrantz, *Spiritism*, for the distinction between *spiritualism* and *spiritism*.

there is no place for a dualism which puts spirit and matter in opposition to each other. The question as to man's nature and constitution, whether man as a whole is three-fold or two-fold,[1] is dealt with in detail by both Androutsos and Rhôsse. The latter, after examining biblical and patristic teachings, says that the word "spirit" in the biblical passages, "does not signify the higher faculties of man's "soul", nor constitute a third element in his nature, but (means) the energy and Grace of the Holy Spirit, illuminating, sanctifying, and quickening the faculties of man's soul".[2] The apparent trichotomism of the Fathers is really resolvable into dichotomism.[3] So, too, Androutsos,[4] who says that the three-fold division of man's nature is the result of counting as two elements the double aspect of the spiritual part of man—"soul" as applied to it on its natural and vital plane, and "spirit" as regards its higher and spiritual aspect. Rhôsse treats the same ideas in somewhat different guise.[5] So both regard man as a unity consisting of body and soul, the latter element being called "spirit" in its higher aspect.

The whole human race is derived from a single pair, our first parents.[6] This fact is borne out by the evidence offered by the study of psychology, history, and philology, despite the great differences in men, which may be accounted for by facts of climate, environment, food, and other such conditions. The solidarity of the race is shown not only in the fact of all men having sprung from a single stock and sharing a common origin, but as well in the fact that all men share in a common state of sinfulness and in a common need of Redemption.[7] It is also indicated in the relationships of man; in the family as the unit

[1] The trichotomistic division says that man consists of three elements,—body ($\sigma\acute{\alpha}\rho\xi$ or $\sigma\tilde{\omega}\mu\alpha$), soul ($\psi\upsilon\chi\acute{\eta}$), and spirit ($\pi\nu\epsilon\tilde{\upsilon}\mu\alpha$). The dichotomistic division makes of the two latter one single element, "soul" ($\psi\upsilon\chi\acute{\eta}$), correlative with "body", as constituting man's nature.

[2] Rhôsse, op. cit., p. 402.

[3] Rhôsse, op. cit., pp. 403-405.

[4] Op. cit., p. 132.

[5] Op. cit., p. 407. On the difference between soul and body, cf. pp. 408-413; on the objections to this view, cf. ibid., pp. 413-414; on the union of body and soul, their interrelation and effect upon each other, pp. 414-417.

[6] Rhôsse, op. cit., pp. 430-432; Androutsos, op. cit., p. 132.

[7] Mesolora, op. cit., III. pp. 180-182; Androutsos, op. cit., p. 133.

of human life, "the first form of the actualization of God's . . idea[1] concerning the individual in his relation with the idea of mankind;"[2] in the self-consciousness of the individual in his sense of corporate unity with the rest of mankind; and in his consciousness of relationship with God, an indication of the working out of God's plan realized in Creation, of an ordered whole of which the individual forms a single unit of relationship, in the family and in political and religious fellowship.[3]

The soul has its origin direct from God. This is the teaching of Holy Scripture as well as of the Church Councils.[4] The Fifth Ecumenical Council condemned the theory of the pre-existence of the soul, but did not define any particular theory of its origin as being *de fide*. Theological speculation has exercised itself upon this problem, and the resulting hypotheses may be reduced to four: (a) the theory of *pre-existence;* (b) that of *creationism;* (c) *traducianism* or *generationism;* (d) the *pantheistic theory,* which holds that the human soul is a part of the very essence of the Divine Nature. The first theory, as was said, cannot be held by any Orthodox theologian, but there seems to be no unanimity, either in the use of terminology or in agreement as to which is to be preferred of the others. As far as concerns phraseology, for example, *traducianism* or *generationism* is rendered by Androutsos,[5] μεταφύτευσις, by Mesolora,[6] μετάδοσις or μεταλαμπάδευσις, and Rhôsse[7] uses μετάδοσις, explaining it by the words ἀποσπάδες and παραφυάδες (*traduces*). As regards preference, Mesolora[8] inclines towards *creationism;* Rhôsse[9] is more favorable to the theory of *traducianism* "as it seems the most reasonable", while the other theories are too one-sided and incomplete; and Androutsos, having discussed

[1] God's idea of man, according to Rhôsse, is a *pre-temporal* idea.

[2] Rhôsse, *op. cit.*, p. 432.

[3] Rhôsse, *op. cit.*, p. 433.

[4] For quotations and references from the Bible, the Fathers, Councils, and Symbolic Books, cf. Mesolora, *op. cit.*, III. pp. 181 ff; and especially Mogila in *ibid.*, I. p. 392.

[5] *Op. cit.*, p. 134.

[6] *Op. cit.*, III. p. 183.

[7] *Op. cit.*, pp. 424 ff. He only enumerates the fourth theory, the others discuss only three.

[8] *Op. cit.*, III. pp. 183-184

[9] *Op. cit.*, pp. 427-428.

each in turn,[1] sums up as follows:[2] "The right view of the origin of the soul lies rather in a combination of the theories of creationism and traducianism, so that man would be a result of both Divine and human activity, and God's creative power be involved and exercised in the generation of each individual".

Of the immortality of the soul, "which constitutes one of the fundamental bases and premises of the edifice of Christianity",[3] Rhôsse offers four proofs in his Δογματική[4]—the historical, metaphysical, teleological, and moral. Androutsos regards such attempted "proofs" as subject to the same objections and strictures as those for the existence of God.[5] He objects that they cannot in the nature of the case achieve their object, that is— proof and demonstration of the immortality of the soul; that a grasp of this truth may be assisted by the exercise of reason, but never attained by it solely, for it belongs to the realm of faith; he says that on the other hand, reason cannot demonstrate the impossibility of the immortality of the soul, or prove it illogical, or disprove it, and finally views the whole subject as one more proper to philosophy and apologetic than to dogmatic.[6]

In the order of the creation of spiritual beings, man follows the angels, the "body-less beings", of whom some fell by disobedience, and became evil spirits.[7] Man was created "with all the physical and spiritual endowments necessary for the fulfilment of the end for which God had foreordained him."[8] This is the teaching both of the Fathers and of Holy Scripture.[9] The words "let us make man in our own image, after our likeness"[10] have always been taken to summarize man's endowment

[1] Op. cit., pp. 134-135.
[2] Ibid., p. 136.
[3] Androutsos, op. cit., p. 409.
[4] Pp. 418-424.
[5] Ibid., pp. 39 ff.
[6] Op. cit., pp. 409-410.
[7] Rhôsse, op. cit., pp. 382-390; Androutsos, op. cit., pp. 121-129; Mesolora, op. cit., III. pp. 139-150.
[8] Androutsos, op. cit., p. 136.
[9] Cf. Mesolora, III. pp. 150-161.
[10] Gen. 1, 26.

of faculties, powers, and character. According to Androutsos' "image" applies to man's spiritual endowment in so far as it is referred to God, and not solely to his rational, voluntative, and self-determinative qualities, in which interpretation Androutsos is persuaded that he is more accurate than are other Orthodox dogmaticians and the Orthodox Catechisms. Under his interpretation of "image" Androutsos would include man's rule over creaturedom, which is the teaching of the Fathers, notably St. John Chrysostom (Homily 9 on Genesis), and Theodoret, on I Cor. 11, 7. According to Mesolora, interpreting the Fathers and the Symbolic Books,[2] "image" refers to the powers with which man was endowed at Creation, and "likeness", to that perfection, potential in him, and possible through the exercise of these powers.[3] So also Rhôsse:[4] "image" applies to the endow-

[1] *Op. cit.*, p. 137. Dyobouniotes takes exception to this in his Ἡ Δογματικὴ τοῦ Χρήστου Ἀνδρούτσου κρινομένη, Athens, 1907, (p. 27) as being "completely false", for "the tendency of man Godward cannot constitute the 'image' of God in him." He constructs his criticism in syllogistic form, which Androutsos answered in his Δογματικαὶ Μελέται, Α', (Athens, 1907) pp. 79-81. Dyobouniotes reiterates his criticism, saying that Androutsos' view involves the theory of the total loss of man's reason and will in the Fall (Ὀφειλομένη ἀπάντησις, Athens, 1908, p. 74). He further accuses Androutsos of having founded his argument "on Protestant ideas." (The two theologians came into conflict on nearly every other important point in Androutsos' Dogmatic, but often the criticisms brought by Dyobouniotes seem captious, and there is in the course of their disputes, more than a mere suggestion of odium theologicum.) In this connection, however Dyobouniotes notes that Androutsos' teaching about the original state of man is not agreeable with that of the Fathers, "according to which man came from the hands of His Creator, perfect" (Ὀφειλομένη ἀπάντησις, p. 75). He had previously criticized Androutsos' conception as "lacking in clearness" (Ἡ Δογμ. Ἀνδρ. κριν., p. 29). In his Δογματ. Μελέται, Α', (p. 85) Androutsos exposes himself again to Dyobouniotes' criticism: "This idea . . . I call Protestant", since the Protestant view is that the original state of man was (purely) natural. (cf. Ὀφειλ. ἀπάντ., pp. 78 ff.) Androutsos' position on these points is then neither above suspicion nor beyond attack, from certain quarters in Greece. Cf. the brief treatment of this subject in Ambraze, Ἡ Ὀρθόδοξος Ἐκκλησία, p. 202.
[2] Cf. Kritopoulos, in Mesolora, *op. cit.*, pp. 299 ff; St. John Damascene, Ἔκδοσις, 2, 29; Jeremiah II. in Mesolora, *op. cit.*, I. p. 217; Mogila, *ibid.*, p. 387; St. Gregory Nyssa on Gen. 1, 26, etc.
[3] *Op. cit.*, III. p. 154.   [4] *Op. cit.*, pp. 433-434.

ment of man's nature with reason and free-will, both as resident faculties and as functioning energies; . . . "the words
'according to the image' as distinguished from 'according to the
likeness' indicate the mind and will as innate powers; 'according to the likeness' (express) the desire and impulse (or tendency, σπουδή) which the first man would need, rightly to
employ his innate powers to become like God and develop as
much as lay in him, actual perfection." Androutsos describes
the original state of man as one of perfect harmony in a three-
fold relationship—towards himself, towards nature, and towards God. His "righteousness" was not a complete and perfect
thing, for it was only potential; the first man could be said
posse non mori, but this potential possibility of freedom from
death depended upon his freedom from sin both in act and will.[1]
"The whole state of the first man, then . . . . was not one of
innate and complete holiness and righteousness—for virtue and
an implanted quality (ἔμφυτον) are contradictory[2]—nor was it
a mere negative and indifferent state (that is, "unmoral"), in
ethical matters, but one of goodness and innocence, as says the
Confession of Mogila."[3] The first man, "according to 1 Cor.
15, 45-47; Eph. 4, 24, had need to develop his own powers, so
that becoming established in the good, he should become spiritual."[4]

As St. Basil says,[5] if the word "image" implies potential
possession of the "likeness", which was to be the actualization of
man's end, then, Androutsos notes, the endowment of knowledge

[1] *Op. cit.*, p. 138.

[2] A virtue must be developed in order to be a virtue; "goodness"
involves the right exercise and determination of the will in the direction of the good, to become an ethical or moral quality. So Androutsos
criticises Macarius (*Théologie Dogmatique Orthodoxe*, Paris, 1860,
vol I. p. 563) who considers the first man to have been *endowed* with
a perfect purity and holiness.

[3] Androutsos, *op. cit.*, pp. 138-139; for Mogila, cf. Kimmel, *op. cit.*,
vol. I. p. 85.

[4] Androutsos, *op. cit.*, pp. 140-141; cf. St. Gregory Nyssa, *De hominis opificio* 7; St. Athanasius, *Adv. Arian. Orat.*, 2, 59; St. John
Dam. Ἔκδοσις, 11, 29; who hold that the final term of man's potential
spiritual development, frustrated by the Fall, was spiritual life in
Christ (Androutsos, *ibid*).

[5] Περὶ κατασκευῆς ἀνθρώπ., 21.

and will were "the basis and point of departure for the realization of likeness to God."[1] These qualities were not morally indifferent, but naturally disposed toward the good and the true; otherwise man could neither have been impelled in this direction, nor could he have been able to distinguish good from evil, nor his will have been free to do the good. The original state of man was one of potential, but not completed or achieved, perfection. Had man been absolutely or completely perfect, the fall would have been impossible.[2]

The Orthodox position is brought out more clearly in contrast to the Protestant and Roman views of man's primitive state.[3] According to Roman teaching, original righteousness (*justitia originalis*) consisted in a supernatural gift of God (*donum supernaturale*) which was not inherent or resident in man's nature as such, even potentially, but an addition to his endowment at Creation (an *accident* in the scholastic sense— *accidens*=συμβεβηκός).[4] The Protestant view holds equally strongly to the notion of a complete and perfect holiness and righteousness as the original state of man, but assigns it to the natural endowment of the whole man—unlike the Roman hypothesis, which ascribes it to a perfection by means of a special super-added gift of God. The Protestant view holds this primitive or original righteousness to be resident in the natural man, *qua* man, and independent of grace; the Roman theory would make it consist essentially and solely of the special super-added grace.[5] The Orthodox view—for example, that of both Androutsos and Rhôsse—is that man's original state was potentially perfect, and "original righteousness was the result of the coöperation of the Spirit of God with the natural powers implanted in the human soul in Creation," according to Rhôsse.[6] Androutsos disagrees with Rhôsse on this point,[7] saying that his meaning is not clear: "If he understands original righteous-

---

[1] Androutsos, *op. cit.*, p. 142.
[2] *Ibid.*, pp. 143-144.
[3] Full discussion in Androutsos, Συμβολική, pp. 138-153.
[4] *Catech. Rom.* 1, 2, 18; quoted in Rhôsse *op. cit.*, pp. 435-436.
[5] Rhôsse, *ibid.*, pp. 436, 437, and Androutsos *op. cit.*, pp. 143-144.
[6] Rhôsse, *op. cit.*, pp. 434, 437, 438.
[7] On which Dyobouniotes in turn attacks him as leaning toward the Protestant view, cf. 'Οφειλ. ἀπάντ., pp. 78, *et al.*

ness to mean that inhering in the seed of man . . . . it would be merely a creation of God; if he mean . . . . a fully formed and perfected righteousness, or that into which man by his spiritual development should fit himself to enter, ... how can it be regarded as existing prior to the Fall, and as having been lost through it?"[1] As against the Roman view, Androutsos agrees with Rhôsse in denouncing it as "a magical and mechanical working of the Grace of God".[2] It makes of original sin "merely a deprivation of super-added gifts," and leads inevitably to Pelagianism.[3] While Mesolora does not enter upon the question with the same detail, he agrees that the original state of man was one of potential perfection of body and soul, which could be made actual by the free coöperation of man's will with the will and grace of God, toward the realization of the end for which he was designed.[4] God's Grace and coöperation with man were contingent on man's response, and were forfeited through the Fall. So man's perfection was not realized until the coming of the Perfect Man.

3. THE FALL

"The first man did not remain in the state of original righteousness, but, transgressing the command of God, fell away from it, and with him fell the whole human race which descended from him."[5] His sin, as all sin, consisted in transgressing and disobeying the will of God.[6] The natural perfection of Adam had need of trial and testing to be transmuted into moral and ethical perfection, but by his own will he turned aside from his own true end, at the instigation of the Evil One, to serve his

---

[1] *Op. cit.*, p. 142, note 1.

[2] Rhôsse, *op. cit.*, p. 436.

[3] Androutsos, Δογματική, p. 144.

[4] *Op. cit.*, III. pp. 156-161.

[5] Androutsos, *op. cit.*, p. 145; Mesolora, *op. cit.*, III. p. 162.

[6] Androutsos, *op. cit.*, p. 145; and Mesolora, *op. cit.*, III. p. 163, for biblical, patristic, and symbolic authority cf. pp. 162-170, and cf. St. John Dam. Ἔκδοσις, 47; Kritopoulos, in Mesolora, I. p. 464; and *ibid.*, pp. 300-301; Dositheus, *ibid.*, p. 105; Mogila, *ibid.*, p. 391; Jeremiah II's 2d *Answer*, *ibid.*, pp. 215-218; Macarius, *op. cit.*, I. p. 617, etc.

own will in preference to that of his Creator.[1] Adam's sin, then, brought about a state of the soul which became in itself as sinful as was the act of sin. The "transgression of the first man created the state of sin imparted to all his descendants", and this entail was of a continuous and persisting character.[2] The truth of this fact is asserted in Holy Scripture, demonstrated by human experience, confirmed by human testimony, and proved by history. So "Adam is the source and fount of the opposite state to that of righteousness—sin, and death. . . As the One Lord transmitted to us remission of sins, so did the head of the race (*progenitor*=γενάρχης) leave to his descendents the heritage of sin."[3] The Church doctrine is further illustrated by the practice of infant Baptism,[4] which is made necessary "by the universality of original sin, and the necessity of salvation through Baptism. . . By it original sin is taken away."[5]

4. ORIGINAL SIN

Inasmuch as sin, the perverted direction of the will of man or his turning aside from the will and law of God, involved losses and penalties, the sin of the First Man may be regarded under two aspects, the formal and the material. (a) Materially, the sin of Adam may be considered negatively—the loss of original righteousness, and positively—the injury done to man's spiritual and ethical nature, the blinding and darkening of the mind, the resulting tendency of his otherwise free will towards evil, or the presence of concupiscence (*concupiscentia*, ἐπιθυμία τῆς σαρκός). But since original righteousness consisted not in the addition of some extra super-added gift, but was integrally involved in the right attitude and functioning of his spiritual and ethical state, these two aspects of the material side of original sin may not rightly be severed, nor may they be

---

[1] Androutsos, *op. cit.*, pp. 145-147.

[2] Androutsos, *op. cit.*, p. 147.

[3] *Ibid.*, pp. 149-150. cf. Rom. 5, 12, the words ἐν ᾧ πάντες Androutsos interprets as "inasmuch as all . . . have sinned", cf. also vs. 18-19.

[4] Cf. Mesolora, *op. cit.*, III, pp. 173-174.

[5] Dyobouniotes, Τὰ Μυστήρια, pp. 45-51; Mesolora, *op. cit.*, III, pp. 177-179; Androutsos, *op. cit.*, pp. 150-151. The latter here refutes the Immaculate Conception as a "dogma", since it lacks biblical and traditional support and foundation. For a fuller treatment of his Συμβολική, pp. 173 ff.

considered apart from the nature of man.[1] Of the state of man after the Fall, Kephala[2] says: "The estrangement from God so darkened his understanding as to involve a loss both of wisdom and knowledge, and he became unable to discern and practise what is good, well-pleasing, and perfect before God. Sin darkened the eyes of his soul . . . . so that he could not see to read the law of God written in his heart . . . .by his Creator."

Yet the Fall did not result in total depravity, nor was God's image destroyed in man,[3] but only "blackened",[4] or "enfeebled".[5] While his mind was dulled and blinded to spiritual things, still not every ray of divine light was extinguished in his soul, and it kept struggling upwards blindly. Nor did the Fall destroy the freedom of man's will, nor determine its direction towards evil.[6] Unregenerate man is yet capable of good thoughts and desires, as we know from Holy Scripture.[7] St. Augustine's doctrine of the *splendida vitia* of the heathen, according to Androutsos, is entirely unwarranted by Holy Scripture, involves a dualistic conception of man's nature, and is logically insupportable.[8] "Concupiscence" has a sinful character, and constitutes the other element of original sin. Sinful passion does not inhere in the nature of man, but grows up as from a ground infected and decayed by sin.[9] It has a sinful character in the case of the unbaptized and "natural" man, since the tendencies of his passionate nature resident in an unregenerate soul, would be towards evil and sin.[10] There is a considerable divergence on this point in current Orthodox teaching, since there is no

[1] Androutsos, *op. cit.*, p. 152, and Mesolora, *op. cit.*, III. pp. 167-8, and note 1.
[2] Χριστολογία, p. 135.
[3] Androutsos, *op. cit.*, p. 137: "The fact of being 'in God's image' was still the case even in the Fall, in which vestiges of man's craving for Divine things and of impulses towards good were still preserved."
[4] Dyobouniotes 'Οφειλ. ἀπάντ., p. 74.
[5] Mesolora, *op. cit.*, III. p. 168.
[6] Cf. *Confession* of Dositheus, in Mesolora, *op. cit.*, I. p. 105 or Kimmel, *op. cit.*, I. p. 447.
[7] Cf. Rom. Rom. 1, 19-20; 2, 14-15; Ex. 1, 17; Josh. 6, 24; St. Matt. 5, 46; 7, 9; 19, 17; Acts 28, 2, etc.
[8] Androutsos, *op. cit.*, pp. 153-5.
[9] Romans, 7, 15-24.
[10] Androutsos, *op. cit.*, pp. 155-156.

official pronouncement on the matter: for example, Damalas regards "concupiscence" as in itself morally indifferent, and Philaret of Moscow, as in itself actually sinful.[1]

(b) The guilt of sin, which is its formal and peculiar note, is the relation of the sinner towards God and the Divine Righteousness (or Justice—δικαιοσύνη). The sinner, by his infringement of God's law and his impairing of the divine order, is guilty before God, and stands in need of making reparation and satisfaction. Inasmuch as the act of sin (ἁμάρτημα or πρᾶξις ἁμαρτίας=peccatum actuale) proceeds from and forms part of the state of sin (κατάστασις ἁμαρτίας=peccatum habituale), "which is as well the subjective basis for all sins, ... it is clear that guilt inheres not only in the several sins individually but in our whole sinful state."[2] So original sin (προπατορικὸν ἁμάρτημα) is imputed to us not as the personal sin of Adam (immediate imputation) but as vitiositas, the state of sin of each of us (mediate imputation) . . . Original sin may be then defined as "the sinful state of our nature with which we were born."[3] It is, however, only under the aspect of mediate imputation that Orthodox dogmatic treats of the problem of original sin. Androutsos devotes two monographs to the subject, which go into the question in considerable detail.[4] He criticises the ordinary treatment of the subject by some modern writers as working out logically in a denial of the dogma.[5] The punish-

---

[1] Their views and references to their works may be found in Androutsos, op. cit., p. 155, note 3, and a longer discussion in his Συμβολική, pp. 109-151, 160. Among the losses by man in the Fall, Dyobouniotes notes that Androutsos has failed explicitly to include that of Divine Grace ('Η Δογματική 'Ανδρούτσου κρινομένη, p. 30). In spite of Androutsos' defense of his own position, Dyobouniotes attacks him more sharply in his 'Οφειλομένη ἀπάντησις, p. 84, saying that it is one more instance of the Protestant bias and protestantizing tendency of Androutsos.

[2] Androutsos, op. cit., p. 156.

[3] Mesolora, op. cit., III. p. 170.

[4] "Εν μάθημα περὶ προπατορικοῦ ἁμαρτήματος, Constantinople, 1896, Δεύτερον μάθημα . . ibid., 1896; for the older Orthodox views, cf. Mogila, Sec. 13. quest. 20, in Mesolora, op. cit., I. pp. 465 ff.; Dositheus ibid., pp. 106, 112-113; biblical texts and exposition in op. cit., III. pp. 173-175.

[5] Δογματική, p. 157.

ment of sin in the fact of having an impaired nature presupposes the existence of inherited sin and guilt.

The chief problem and "difficulty, by reason of which the dogma becomes incomprehensible to us, is the lack of the element of free will in original sin."[1] Of the possible explanations offered to elucidate this problem, three may be mentioned here: (a) "God imputed Adam's sin to the whole human race." But this would militate against our instinctive notions of God's justice, for "God cannot regard as a sinner one who is not really so, nor can He arbitrarily condemn to punishment one who is not guilty."[2] (b) "Humanity sinned in the person of Adam." This physiological view propounded and developed by St. Augustine has no support save in a wrong interpretation of Rom. 5, 12, and 2 Cor. 5, 15.[3] The Apostle states a fact, but does not explain it. This theory would imply either (1) that all men pre-existed in Adam, willing and thinking along with him, or (2) that the will of Adam was not his own personal will but that of the whole human race. The case for this view might be strengthened if it be said that the will of mankind was, as it were, implicit and potential in that of the first man, but yet it is difficult to understand how ethical relations and states could be inherited.[4] (c) "Adam sinned not as an individual, but as the representative of the whole race, just as Christ, the second Adam, acted as its Representative in His life of reconciliation, and work of Redemption." Yet the parallel is neither true and genuine, nor exact. How can it be conceived that Adam was given *carte blanche* to act as plenipotentiary for the whole race of men? Why was the fate of all bound up in that one? The dilemma which emerges involves the alternative of considering that God ordained man to sin. Androutsos' conclusion is that "it would seem better to accept the dogma in faith, and to regard it as a mystery, rather than to attempt such explanations as only darken rather than illuminate the dogma of original sin."[5]

---

[1] Androutsos, Δογματική, p. 157.   [2] *Ibid*, p. 158.

[3] *Ibid.*, p. 149, for his exegesis of Rom. 5, 12; and p. 159.

[4] *Ibid.*, pp. 159-160.

[5] *Ibid.*, pp. 161-162. Cf. St. Augustine: *si potes, intellige; si non potes, crede;* and St. Bernard, *justum sed occultum Dei judicium* (Androutsos, *ibid.*).

Transgression of the Divine Law and Will involve in some manner consequences which will be both punishment for the sin involved, vindication of the righteousness of God's law, and satisfaction or reparation for impairing and infringing His command and will. There is then inevitable punishment for sin, original and actual, which may be regarded under two aspects—natural and positive. The former includes the inevitable consequence of transgression, in the natural order; the latter belongs to the ethical and moral plane, in which God's immediate justificatory and punitive attitude is made known in a positive way. Both types are really aspects of one relation of the One God, to whom both natural and ethical orders are referred as to Source, Ordainer, and Governor. Original sin itself as an inheritance, is a punishment of Adam's sin.[1] Other punitive consequences of sin are the misery and torture of the conscience, labouring under the conviction of sin, with the torment of self-conviction and of the sense of guilt, as well as all the various ills and evils in the world. The greatest of these last is death, "the wages (ὀψώνια) of sin" as St. Paul calls it, in its three degrees—natural or physical (*corporalis*), spiritual (*spiritualis*), and eternal (*aeterna*). The second, "spiritual" death, is the severing and sundering of the bond between the soul and God, and the resultant moral misery, which both bears witness to the estrangement from fellowship with God, and constitutes as well the *matter* of sin, rather than its consequences. The third, "eternal" death, means the eternal separation of God and man, as both a punishment for sin and as the inevitable result of it.[2] "Temporal", "natural", or "physical", death is, according to Gen. 2, 17; 3, 17, the consequence of and punishment for, sin.[3] Exemption from this now inevitable termination of our life on earth would have been by a special act of God, as a consequence of obedience to His Will. So we can say that *posse non mori* belonged to man's original endowment in his primitive state, and would have been his especial prerogative. The first man forfeited this, however, in the Fall, not only for himself but for all his de-

---

[1] Cf. St. Augustine, *Opus imperfectum*, 1, 47.
[2] Rom. 6, 16; 5, 16, 18; 1 Cor. 15, 22.
[3] Cf. also, Rom. 5, 12.

scendants, and death became the penalty for sin, as a relation of effect to cause, as is apparent from Rom. 5,12. "Yet it is clear", says Androutsos in summing up his treatment of the subject, "that the penalties and consequences of original sin are relieved of their penal character or lose it completely, through the Redemption wrought in Christ. Sufferings of whatever kind, and the other resultant miseries of human life emanating from Adam, serve the sons of God as opportunities for discipline, confirm and strengthen them in the good, and are means for the manifestation of God's glory. Eternal death is taken away through Jesus Christ, and physical death, when man is cleansed from sin and guilt in Him, loses its dominant, terrifying, and minatory aspect, and becomes the means of passing from the earthly and temporal, into the eternal kingdom of God."[1]

II. SALVATION AND THE SAVIOUR

1. The Causes and Purpose of the Incarnation

Christian thought has variously conceived the work and office of Christ in the world. From early times, and even in the pages of the New Testament itself, different writers have emphasized various aspects of the work of our Lord. Not only is there a difference of emphasis and accent in the teaching about His office and work, but there is as well a difference in the views of Christian writers regarding the cause and aim of the Incarnation. Of these different views two came into sharp contrast in the Scotist-Thomist positions, with the clearer distinctions brought about in the course of centuries of Christian thinking. In the earlier days there were only divergent emphases—Christ was regarded either as a Bringer of the Great Revelation of what God was, or as the One who by making propitiation for man, brought again into union man and God. As Revealer, our Lord showed us God; becoming Incarnate, He portrayed in a living person the full perfection of human nature in its completed whole and full destiny of union with God. As Redeemer and Saviour He came to make salvation possible, to bridge over the gulf between man and God, and be Himself the Atonement for sin, and the means of Salvation.

[1] *Op. cit.*, p. 164, and cf. pp. 161-164 for whole discussion.

In the main these views of the life and work of Christ issued in the speculations concerning the cause of the Incarnation, of which the Scotist and Thomist theories respectively are typical examples. According to the former theory, the second Person of the Blessed Trinity would in any case have become Incarnate, even if man had not sinned. The Scotist holds that the Incarnation was but the complement and necessary sequence of Creation,[1] and as man was made in God's image, this fact suggests a further participation in His nature[2] than man could have attained at any stage of God's dealings with him, short of the Incarnation. Furthermore, the benefits of the Incarnation transcend mere salvation from sin and its consequences: to share in the nature of One united with us on the human side, and being in Himself God, is a glory far exceeding that lost by the Fall. The Scotist would admit, however, that the Incarnation, coming to pass after the Fall, was attended by suffering and humiliation, which would not have accompanied it had not man sinned. The Thomist reasons that the purpose of the Incarnation was salvation from sin and death,[3] and explains the texts referred to by the Scotist to mean that as the Fall was foreseen by God, so too the Incarnation and Passion were foreseen from the beginning, in view of sin foreseen, and not as the necessary sequence of Creation.[4] Both views take full cognizance of all the facts, but each results in a difference of interpretation and emphasis in what is after all a speculative theological question and not a matter of faith. Each holds to a different cause for and purpose of, the Incarnation.

From what has already been quoted from Rhôsse, it is clear that his definitions of Christianity as a "mutual relationship or fellowship between God and man, the result of Divine energy and as well of human receptivity and co-operation,"[5] and of Christian dogma,[6] as "the teachings of the

[1] Cf. Eph. 1, 9-12; Col. 1, 19.
[2] Cf. 2 St. Pet. 1, 4.
[3] 1 St. John 3, 5.
[4] St. Thomas Aquinas, *Summa* III, 1-3.
[5] *Op. cit.*, p. 21.
[6] Cf. Lecture I, pp. 5-6; on this definition Palmieri makes an interesting criticism, in his *Theol. Dog. Orth.* vol. I. pp. 18-20.

Christian Faith concerning the operations of God", as well as his whole treatment of the subject of Revelation, would suggest his alignment on the Scotist side in the questions concerning the Incarnation. "The possibility and necessity of the Incarnation of the Word of God", he says, "lies both in the right concept of God held in general by Theism, according to which God is not only the transcendent Being, but as well the immanent Being, possessing both absolute and relative attributes, and also lies in the nature and aim (σκοπός) of man, created according to the image of God, that in mutual fellowship with Him man might become like Him and finally achieve entire perfection. This perfection of man is bound up with the perfecting of religion, and the necessity of perfecting religion involves necessarily the Incarnation of the Word of God in that Person in which there would be not only a perfect imparting of divine truth, power, and life, but also a perfect human vehicle to receive this imparted (divine truth, power, and life)....Hence the Incarnation of the Word would have been necessary for the perfection of man even without (man's) sin. Still more did it become necessary because of the fact of sin, since man did slip into sin by the wrong use of his reason and free will. So because of this sin of the human race Divine Revelation in religion (that is, the Incarnation) attains its destined end, the perfection of man, not directly, but by the redemption of man from sin. Hence the Divine Revelation, before leading man on to perfection, has first to redeem him from sin by means of the Incarnation of the Word by whom the world and man were created, and by whom man's perfection is achieved. Hence the idea of the God-man and its actualization in the historic person of Jesus Christ is at once the Miracle and the loftiest miracle. But it is not in opposition to the human mind in its healthy state, but is rather demanded by it as necessary for man's perfection".[1] By this Rhôsse means that the Incarnation would have taken place in

---

[1] Rhôsse, op. cit., pp. 465-466, and see Lecture I, pp. 9-16. It will be seen that this passage is bound up with Rhôsse's whole contention as to the subject of Revelation, of which it is the conclusion. It is in line with one phase of St. Irenaeus' thought, his doctrine of the ἀνακεφαλαίωσις. Cf. Rhôsse, op. cit., p. 464 where he employs the chief text for this doctrine (Eph. 1, 10).

any case, but the fact of sin determined some of the conditions by which its purpose would be achieved. Man in his "healthy state" still required the completion of his nature and capacities by the Incarnation; far more in his state of sin did he require it.

Kephala leans rather to the Scotist side in his interpretation of the Incarnation, though not in such a complete and thorough way as does Rhôsse. "The coming of a Saviour and Redeemer was the common expectation of all peoples", Jews as well as Gentiles.[1] His coming "appears absolutely necessary . . . to stabilize the shaken hopes of people, to inspire religious reverence, to fill the void in men's hearts, to satisfy the longings of the spirit, to quicken political and moral life, and to reform and regenerate man corrupted by sin."[2] Kephala is not absolutely Scotist in his treatment of the causes and purpose of the Incarnation, as is seen in the quotation above, yet his emphasis on the work of our Lord as completing and fulfilling human needs,[3] his list of the characteristic notes of the Saviour's character and work,[4] his enumeration of the objects and purposes of the Incarnation,[5] are all consistent with a Scotist point of view. Revelation "is necessary . . . . because of the conditions into which the human race had fallen, with man's spiritual faculties darkened and his highest destiny forgotten. Through Revelation God leads the race into the way of truth and lifts it from its prostrate condition."[6] Our Lord's work was "to give eternal life to those who believed in Him, and to teach them to know and worship in spirit and in truth the one true God, and Jesus Christ whom He had sent."[7] Since "man without knowledge of God is an incomprehensible mystery, without fellowship

---

[1] Kephala, Χριστολογία, pp. 10, 11-17; revelation to and expectation by the Gentiles, pp. 17-21.

[2] Ibid., p. 23.

[3] "Since the desire of eternal life is innate, it is true", ibid., p. 29, and in Jesus this desire had its satisfaction and fulfilment (ibid., pp. 32-34.)

[4] E. g., His divine character, words, deeds, fulfilment of prophesies, miracles; submission to Him of angels, men, and nature; His Church, the results of Faith, etc. (ibid., pp. 34-37).

[5] He came "to save man from ignorance, doubt, despair, hatred," etc. (ibid., p. 37).

[6] Ibid., p. 129.

[7] Ibid., p. 175.

with Him something inexplicable[1] . . . (for God made man for the purpose of constituting him a sharer in His own Goodness and blessedness),[2] . . . He sent His Son to turn man from the folly of his way, to lead him to his heavenly Father, and teach him his destiny on earth."[3] He sums up our Lord's purpose in the words: "The mission of the Saviour was the glory of God—by making known the true God, whom mankind because of sin had forgotten, and by turning man from the folly of his way."[4] Kephala seems then to waver between the Scotist and Thomist theories, but his greatest emphasis seems to be on our Lord as the complement and fulfilment of man's needs and aspirations, and as the complete Revelation supplanting and fulfilling that which had gone before. He does not deal directly with the question whether or not God the Son would have become Incarnate had not man sinned, but the implication drawn from the general tenor of his thought, is that Kephala is more Scotist than Thomist.

Mesolora is more explicitly Thomist in his treatment of the subject.[5] "Man, as a rational creature endowed with free-will, has been and is under a special providence of God[6] who does not desire the death of a sinner—for the first parents did not fall of their own proper volition nor with full consciousness (of their act). Consequently . . man did not lose completely the image of God, but there remained in him traces of good. For this reason his salvation and rehabilitation were possible. . . The way and means of reconciliation of man with

[1] *Ibid.*, p. 176.
[2] *Ibid.*, p. 177.
[3] *Ibid.*
[4] *Ibid.*, p. 179.
[5] He devotes pp. 199-242 of vol. III. of his Συμβολική, to the Incarnation. His definitions (p. 204, note 1) are most valuable: the subject of Our Lord and His work may be termed "divine economy", for from it we learn that God in a divine and mysterious way arranged (ᾠκονόμησε) the salvation of man; "His redemptive work may also be called "the Incarnate economy" (ἔνσαρκον οἰκονομίαν); Redemption "(ἀπολύτρωσις)" "in its wider meaning, signifies all the means which God uses to effect the removal of sin", and "Christology" . . treats of Christ the Saviour.
[6] This passage links up with his treatment of "the Divine Providence and Governance of the world" (pp. 185-191) and "Foreknowledge and Foreordination" (pp. 192-199) immediately preceding.

God were found through the mediatorship of the Son and Word of God."[1] The appearance of the Incarnate God "was the greatest evidence of God's special providence for the salvation of man."[2] "The Old Testament describes the causes of the sin and fall of man, teaching that man could not by his own powers (alone) achieve redemption and deliverance from evil, for the recognition of which fact alone were the Law and the Prophets given, (and) to serve to prepare the way for salvation . . It was necessary that the Eternal Word of God by whom the world was created, should take flesh in order to save the lost sheep."[3] According to Mesolora, sin was the cause of the Incarnation, the purpose of which was to save sinful mankind.

This same doctrine is clearly and definitely taught by Androutsos. "Man having fallen under the power of sin and the Devil, was unable to be saved and to have fellowship with God, but was under condemnation to destruction and eternal death. This destruction of the human race the Creator would not allow, and in His mercy, His love for men, and His kindness[4] (or by what other name His love for sinful man may be called) formed the means of deliverance from evil, and planned to send His Son into the world for the salvation of men. This plan of God was conceived before the foundation of the world, eternally. . . Hence it is called 'foreknowledge', 'foreordination', 'purpose', 'the mystery of His Will,'[5] and the like. The conception of God as unchanging and above time demands that this will of God be eternal—in His determining the redemption of the world in Christ Jesus in His eternal aspect in relation to Creation. This will the Son and Word of God carried out, becoming Incarnate 'in the fulness of time' "[6] . . . Androutsos goes on to say: "The cause of the Incarnation of Jesus Christ is . . . the restoration (ἀνάστασις="resurrection") of fallen man, to which Holy Scripture bears witness in many places,[7]

[1] *Op. cit.*, III. p. 199.
[2] *Op. cit.*, III. p. 200.
[3] *Ibid.*, p. 204.
[4] Cf. Eph. 2, 4; Tit. 3, 5.
[5] Eph. 1, 9, 11; 3, 9, 11; Rom. 16, 25; Col. 1, 26.
[6] (Gal. 4, 4.) Androutsos, Δογματική, pp. 165-166.
[7] *E. g.*, St. John 3, 16; 12, 47; 2 Cor. 5, 19; 1 Tim. 1, 15; St. Luke 19, 10.

. . and which the Church describes in the words 'who for us men and for our salvation came down from Heaven'."[1] Androutsos states the Scotist contention and says of it: "This theory has no foundation in Scripture, but has the explicit statements of weighty Fathers against it. The antithesis between the second Adam and the first in the New Testament does not show that the coming of the Saviour was necessary to complete the works of creation. The words in Eph. 1, 10 take for granted the disruption of the unity of the world through sin, and in 1 Cor. 15, 43 Christ is termed 'the heavenly' (Adam) because of the Resurrection and not because of His Incarnation. Of the Fathers, St. Irenaeus[2] says: 'The Word would not have been Incarnate had it not been for the salvation of flesh'; St. Ambrose said that the *causa incarnationis* was *ut caro quae peccaverat, per se redimeretur.*[3] Rightly Augustine observed: *si homo non periisset, filius hominus non venisset.*"[4]

The preparation for the Incarnation, whether it was for a completion and fulfilment of human needs, desires, nature, and aspiration, or for the reconciliation of man with God, his deliverance from sin, and his restoration and rehabilitation, was a work of divine love acting in many ways and in all peoples. It may be considered under two aspects,—in relation to the Gentile world and in relation to the Jews. The former were prepared by nature and by the results of their thinking and reflection. Ethical consciousness demanded a standard of truth and right, and human experience brought about the conviction of failure and helplessness in attaining the ideal and norm set by the moral consciousness of man. Ignorance, doubts, difficulties, the consciousness of moral impotence, all served as a negative preparation[5] of Gentile humanity for the coming of Him who would satisfy the cravings of the ethical nature of man, stabilize his shattered hopes, strengthen his

---

[1] *Op. cit.*, p. 168.

[2] *Adv. Haer.*, V, 14, 1.

[3] *De incarnationis dominicae sacramento*, 6, 56.

[4] *Serm.* 174, 2, 2, and cf. *ibid.*, 175, 1. Androutsos, *op. cit.*, pp. 168-169 and notes.

[5] Kephala, *op. cit.*, pp. 12-21, 23, 37, 38-90, etc.; Mesolora, *op. cit.*, p. 200.

convictions as to right and truth, and illuminate and enlighten
the darkness of his natural understanding.[1] The presence of
the moral and ethical nature and the resulting consciousness
by man of the good and true, combined with the conviction of
his own helplessness and futility as regards the attainment of
the ideal he knew vaguely, served to make ready the road for
the coming of one who was both the final Revelation, the Perfect Character, and the Saviour of all men.[2] The Jews were "a
specially chosen section of humanity, as it were a leaven,"[3]
whom God prepared in many ways for the Incarnation: there
were, first of all, the prophecies in the Old Testament, beginning
with Gen. 3, 15 and occurring throughout the whole book; the
revelation of the Law, and its whole system as a means both of
effecting the conviction of sin and guilt, and of arousing the
desire and need for redemption; the sacrificial system, itself a
prophecy of divine help and a witness to its necessity, its symbolism a type of God's grace conveyed by fellowship with Christ,
on which Androutsos observes that "only through faith in the
coming Redeemer could one be saved".[4] The Law acted as
pedagogue,[5] and the prophecies and messianic expectations led
the Jewish folk still further toward Him who was Messiah,
High Priest, and Law Giver, the Supreme Antitype and Fulfilment of all the types in the Old Testament.[6]

Of the place of the Christological teaching in Orthodox
dogmatic, Androutsos says: "Religious doctrines about God and
man are nothing else than the premises of Redemption in Christ,
and the knowledge that God is full of love for man fallen from
his first destiny through sin, constitutes the means of access to
the mystery of the Incarnation. . . All the truths and facts in

[1] Androutsos, *op. cit.*, p. 166.
[2] Cf. St. Justin, *Apologia* I, 63-64; Tertullian, *Apologeticus*, 47; Theophilus, *ad Autolycum*, 11, 37; Clem. Alex *Strom.* I, 15, 22; V. 4,
etc., cf. St. John 1, 9; Heb. 11, 3. Mesolora notes the place of the
Greek language, philosophy, literature, the LXX, etc., and the Roman
government, in the divine scheme of preparation, *op. cit.*, III, pp. 201-2.
[3] Mesolora, *op. cit.*, III, pp. 200-201.
[4] *Op. cit.*, p. 167.
[5] Gal. 3, 24.
[6] Mesolora, *op. cit.*, III. pp. 201-2, and cf. Mogila, *ibid.*, I. p. 390;
Kritopoulos *ibid.*, I, pp. 302-304; St. John Dam., Ἔκδοσις 3, 4,
8; Kephala, *op. cit.*, pp. 34-37, 165-166, 177-179.

the life of Our Lord have dogmatic and religious value, for example, the truths of His sinlessness and of His Resurrection, . . . which are necessary bases for His work of saving the world. Only as Sinless could the Saviour reconcile God and man, and had He not risen from the dead His death would not have had atoning power and significance."[1] Since all subsequent exposition depends upon the work of the Saviour and His Person, and the doctrine of His work is based upon that of His Person, the Greek theologians agree in aligning their material in the following order: I. The doctrine of the Person of Jesus Christ, with its implications, and II. The doctrine of his work and offices, with a consideration of the Descent into Hell, the Resurrection, and the like.[2] All Revelation led up to Him, the Revelation *par excellence;* all miracles pointed to Him, the Great Miracle; all prophets pointed to Him, the Great Prophet; all priesthood looked forward to Him, the Great High Priest; all religion looked forward to completion by Him; all needs of humanity were satisfied in Him, and sinfulness done away by Him.[3] So the doctrine about Christ is the central point of Orthodox teaching.

2. THE DOCTRINE OF OUR LORD'S PERSON

A. The Person of Christ

"Both Holy Scripture and the Church teach that Jesus Christ is God-Man ($\Theta\epsilon\acute{a}\nu\theta\rho\omega\pi\sigma$) or true God assuming human nature and becoming like the human race in every respect save sin."[4] "It was necessary in order to accomplish the work of sal-

---

[1] *Op. cit.*, pp. 169-170. As was said in Lecture I, his *Dogmatic* is divided into two parts, "The Premises of Redemption in Christ" (pp. 32-164) and "The Redemption in Christ" (pp. 165-448). The center and heart of Orthodox dogmatic is, as this division illustrates, the doctrine of the God-Man.

[2] So Androutsos, *op.* cit., pp. 170-217; Mesolora, III, pp. 205-242.

[3] Rhôsse, *op. cit.*, pp. 453-466; Kephala, *op. cit.*, pp. 11-38, 129-179. Androutsos, *op. cit.*, pp. 196-207, 168-169; Mesolora, *op. cit.*, III. pp. 228-238, *et al.*

[4] Androutsos, *op. cit.*, p. 170. Dyobouniotes criticises this phraseology, saying ('Η Δογμ. 'Ανδρ. κριν., p. 33): "Christ did not assume human nature in general but a definite human nature (in particular) be-

vation that the Saviour be perfect God, Son of God, and perfect Man, Son of Man, ... becoming obedient even to the death of the cross, in order to satisfy (ἱκανοποιήσῃ) the divine righteousness rightly requiring the punishment of sinful man, and also to conciliate (συμβιβάσῃ) the divine mercy which did not desire the death of its creature."[1] While the synoptic Gospels emphasize His human nature, the Gospel of St. John "exalts His divine nature, without passing over in silence the human factor[2] in our Lord. The other expressions about Our Lord used by the Apostles are referable either to His human side (μέρος), as man . . . suffering, hungering, thirsting, . . or to His divine (side), His pre-existence and His Greatness . . . as Son of God. So the names applied to the Saviour in the New Testament are referred to His double Nature—'son of man' (Dan. 7, 13), . . . and 'Son of God or simply 'Son', or 'Only Begotten'."[3] "In Christ were united unchanged and unconfused, two Natures, human and divine, in one hypostatic union, that is, in one Person, of

coming like us men, not like the race . . . ," to which Androutsos answers in his Δογμ. Μελ., Α', (pp. 90-91), giving St. John Dam., Ἔκδοσις, III, 3, as the authority for his language. Cf. Dyobouniotes' Ὀφειλομ. ἁπάντ., pp. 87-89.

[1] Mesolora, op. cit., III. p. 205.

[2] Dyobouniotes criticizes the use of this word very sharply ('Η Δογμ. 'Ανδρ. κριν., p. 33) as "not being a theological term". As an illustration of the amenities of such theological disputes, the discussion may be summarized here: Androutsos defends himself by saying that it is in common use in scientific theology, together with other phrases of which "it is not strange that his critic (Dyobouniotes) is ignorant." But in any case the term ("factor", παράγων) does not introduce anything novel into Orthodox theology, and means just what St. John Dam. (Ἔκδοσις, III. 4) means by describing the "natures" as "parts" (μέρη, Androutsos, in Δογμ. Μελ., Α', p. 92, note). Dyobouniotes says ironically (in his Ὀφειλ. ἁπάντ., p. 90): "It would be ridiculous for us, who have our terms already fixed by the ecumenical councils, to say instead of: 'in Christ there are two natures'—'in Christ there are two factors'." His concluding sentence verges on the personal when he writes: "That I do not know the term factor must be regarded as one of those jokes with which Mr. Androutsos fills up the void in the arguments of his Dogmatic Studies, and arouses the risibilities of his reader."

[3] Androutsos, Δογματική, p. 170-171. He gives in his notes full references to scripture passages on the subject.

one Essence with the Father according to His Divinity as begotten of God."[1] "The Church affirms His miraculous Birth of
the Virgin Mary, teaching that His conception and birth were
not according to the natural order, for His conception took place
through the Holy Spirit, and His Birth did not impair the
virginity of the Mother of God, who after the Nativity remained
ever Virgin."[2] "As there are in Christ two natures unconfused,
thus there are in Him two wills and two natural operations
(ἐνεργείαι), divine and human, united unconfusedly, inseparably,
unchangeably, of which the latter follows and is subject to the
former. . . "[3] It follows that "all who dispute or impugn the
truth and fulness of either the human or divine nature, take
away the truth of the Incarnation and Redemption." Christ's
divine Nature is perfect and complete, of one essence with the
Father. His human nature, "formed of the Virgin Mary mi-
raculously, was in all respects like our own save for sin alone.
It was subject to all the bodily and spiritual suffering of human
flesh which . . . have not a sinful character or presuppose
sin—suffering, thirsting, grieving, rejoicing, dying, and being
buried. But He was delivered from all sin, original or personal;
by His supernatural birth He was delivered from the former, because original sin is inherited through physical generation, and
by the hypostatic union of His two Natures He was delivered
from the latter."[4]

The great problem, which challenged the theological speculation of the early Church and provoked the rise of heresies,
is, as Androutsos notes, "how the divine and human natures
which constitute the Person of Jesus Christ could be so
united that after the union the character of each should be

[1] Mesolora, *op. cit.*, III. p. 205.

[2] Androutsos, *op. cit.*, pp. 171-2, and cf. note on the perpetual virginity
of the Blessed Virgin Mary. While it "is not contained in Holy
Scripture yet the great bulk of patristic evidence supports it unanimously." He refutes the ordinary objections, quoting texts and authorities. Cf. also Mesolora, *op. cit.*, III. p. 215, note 2.

[3] Mesolora, *ibid.*

[4] Androutsos, *op. cit.*, p. 173. It is unnecessary in so brief a summary as this to go into detail on teaching based entirely on the Ecumenical Councils, and on which all branches of the Catholic Church are
in accord. For a brief summary, cf. Mesolora, *op. cit.*, III. pp. 213-
224, which gives biblical and symbolical authorities.

preserved unimpaired?"[1] The answer of the Church to this
most difficult problem was the result of her action in combat-
ing the heresies which arose in the early days impugning now
the human, now the divine nature, falsely reasoning on the
basis of human experience, or carrying logic into the realms
of faith.[2] On the basis of the Ephesine, Chalcedonian, and
Constantinopolitan decrees, the Church withstood and contra-
dicted the errors of Nestorians, Monthelites, and Monophysites, so that we understand that "God the Word took to
Himself not human nature in general, but one nature in particular, yet not in the sense of acquiring thereby a person,
since the personal principle of the assumed human nature was
that of God the Word.[3] So there was in Christ but one Person, that of the Word of God, in the two natures, . . . human
and divine."[4] This two-fold union of the natures, or intimate
indwelling (ἐνδοτάτην ἐνοίκησιν), St. John Damascene calls
περιχώρησις ("circumcession," "mutual inherence"). It is
not a consequence of the hypostatic union, but another aspect
of it, expressing the duality of the natures and the uniting
principle, God the Word.[5] "If I say that God the Word assumed human flesh into His Person (ὑπόστασις) or that the
two natures as (being) of the one unity of Person are united
within, I say one and the same thing under different aspects."[6]
The doctrine of the *perichoresis* in the case of the doctrine of
Christ serves the same purpose as it does in regard to the
Blessed Trinity—as a touchstone for the opposing heresies,
denying both Nestorian and Monophysite views of Our Lord's
Person. "As God, the Redeemer joins to His perfect Redemp-

[1] Androutsos, *op. cit.*, pp. 173-174.

[2] On the heresies concerning the Person of Christ, cf. Sect. 22 of
Mesolora, *op. cit.*, III. pp. 208-213, where he reviews briefly the rise
of the various Christological heresies of the Cerinthians, Ebionites,
Philonists, Docetists, Platonists, Gnostics, Sabellians, Arians, Apollinarians, Nestorians, Monophysites, Monothelites, Socinians, and Rationalists.

[3] Cf. St. John Dam., Ἔκδοσις, III. 11, and Dyobouniotes' monograph
on St. John Dam., pp. 78 ff.

[4] Androutsos, *op. cit.*, pp. 174-175.

[5] Androutsos, Δογματική, p. 175.

[6] Androutsos, Δογμ. Μελ., Α΄, p. 93; cf. Dyobouniotes, Ἡ Δογμ. Ἀνδρ.
κριν., p. 34 and Ὀφειλ. ἀπάντ., pp. 87-88.

tion absolute power and worth; as Man,[1] representing the human race He presents the Redemption as a work of Mankind. At the same time the union of the Divine and human natures in Christ is the type of our moral union with God: that His human will was in perfect accord with His divine will, serves as the aim and destiny of man, that he be united by the Grace of the Holy Spirit with the will of God. . . .and continue to abide in that union."[2] The human nature alone can be said to be "perfected" by the hypostatic union, for no change could take place in the Divine Nature, nor would it be possible to conceive of it as capable of being perfected. Both natures are Our Lord's for eternity, and, in His ascended glory, He has our nature eternally with Him in Heaven. Nor did His death sever the bond uniting His two natures, even for an instant, as St. John Damascene shows.[3]

[1] Cf. Kephala: "By the term "Son' of Man" Our Lord would show that He is a member of our race, one of us, and also that He is above all humanity, being at the same time the legitimate and final Son, the true Scion of mankind, Man *par excellence*, towards whom all history tended, in whom humanity finds its own unity, . . . towards whom all previous history turned as to its term, and from whom all subsequent history has its rise. He is the epitome and summary of humanity and the purpose of its history. . . His Person . . . has in it a universal quality. . . Each people has its heroes . . in whom it sees itself, as it were, embodied, but none of these heroes sums up in himself the fulness of history . . Jesus only is the perfect and utterly complete representative of the whole human race" (Χριστολογία, pp. 165-166).

[2] Androutsos, Δογματική, p. 175.

[3] Androutsos, *op. cit.*, p. 177. The two chief objections brought against Chalcedonian terminology by certain moderns are: (a) it assigns reason and will but not personality to human nature, whereas reason and will constitute the essence of personality; (b) while the fulness of human nature is ascribed to Christ, yet in fact it takes it away, for it conceives of human nature as impersonal. But, Androutsos says, "person" in the usage of the Fathers, did not mean what it does in this modern sense as involving mind and will, but they call: " 'person', the 'hypostasis' of the logical or spiritual essence or nature. 'Person' is what 'hypostasis' is: the self-subsisting essence constituting a complete whole. If 'person' be distinguished from 'hypostasis', the latter is applied to the spiritual nature of the 'person'. To know and to will are notes not directly of the 'person' but of the nature (of man) and through it, of the 'person'. A 'nature' does not exist of itself, but in a certain 'hypostasis', yet many natures may

B. Corollaries and Implications

As corollaries of the hypostatic union the doctrine of the *communicatio idiomatum*[1] is first in order. From the unity of His Person we may ascribe to His divine nature the properties of His human nature, since the Person is the bearer of both natures. So when He is called "God" we may yet predicate human properties of Him, and when He is called "Man" we may predicate divine properties. This doctrine is founded on Holy Scripture,[2] the teaching of the Fathers, and the implications involved in the Ephesine decrees. "To the Person (hypostasis) whether we call Him as of both or of one only of His Parts (that is, *natures*), we ascribe the properties of both natures. For Christ as both is called God and Man; created and uncreated; passible and impassible. When from one of the two Parts He is called 'Son of God' or 'God', He receives the properties of the other consubsisting nature.... God is said to suffer, and the Lord of Glory is said to be crucified—not as God but as man. When He is called 'man' and 'Son of Man' He receives the properties of His divine nature: . . . a child, who is before time, a man without beginning—not as child and man however, but as God, is He before time, having become a child late in time. This is the manner of the communion (ἀντίδοσις) or the sharing (of the proper-

have but one 'hypostasis' . . . . Human nature of itself without hypostasis, yet possessing reason and will, subsisted in the hypostasis of Jesus Christ". Dyobouniotes said of Androutsos that "he has not formed a clear idea as concerns the person of Jesus Christ... On page 187 he identifies 'person' in the ancient usage with 'person' of modern philosophy, regarding it as residing in the ego." He says that Androutsos' treatment is "superficial," and claims that he uses the word in several senses. Cf. Ἡ Δογμ. ᾽Ανδρ. κριν., pp. 32-33; ᾽Οφειλ. ἀπάντησις, pp. 87-29. Androutsos' answer (note to p. 92 of his Δογμ. Μελ. Α᾽), is that the Church Fathers used the word "person" in two senses, as that known as subsisting in itself, and as that constituting a unified whole (the *continuum* of the Scholastics?).

[1] ᾽Αντίδοσις or κοινοποίησις τῶν ἰδιωμάτων (Androutsos); κοινωνία τ. ι. (Mesolora); ἰδιοποίησις (Cyril Alex.); τρόπος ἀντιδόσεως St. John Dam.); cf. Androutsos, *op. cit.*, p. 178; Mesolora, *op. cit.*, III, pp. 206, 222 and note 2; Theodoret (*Epist.* 127) uses κοινὰ ποιεῖ.

[2] Cf. Acts. 20, 28; Rom. 6, 10; 1 Cor. 15, 47; 2 Cor. 13' 4; St. John 3, 13, *et al.*

ties) of each nature with the other through the union of the Person.... So we can say of Christ: 'this one, our God, appeared on earth and held converse with men', and, 'this man is uncreated, impassible, incomprehensible'."[1] The basis of the *communicatio idiomatum* is the theory of the union of the natures in one Person,[2] hence the criterion is: "God is man and man is God" but not: "Divinity is Humanity and Humanity is Divinity." That is, the natures are viewed in the hypostatic union not as abstract but as concrete, and the concrete terms and names imply the Person; the natures are united unconfusedly in Christ. It is not a mere sharing of names and titles, but an actual possession and communication of properties.[3] Each nature partakes of the properties of the other,[4] for God the Word appropriates the properties and states of the human nature, and shares with it His own. We speak of the activities and operations (ἐνέργειαι) of the Incarnate as *theandric,* since in Him were two wills and operations proceeding from the two natures, yet the Bearer of the two natures was the one Person, who was the One who willed and acted. "He did not do human acts in a human way (only), for He was not only man but God; nor did He perform divine acts divinely, for He was not only God, but man."[5] "But it is to be noted that in this mutuality of sharing.... the divine nature energizes and imparts, the human nature receives, so that we may not say that God suffered *through* the flesh, but *in* the flesh; the same Person suffered in His human nature, without these sufferings being felt in His other nature, —the divine (nature)."[6]

[1] St. John Dam. Ἔκδοσις, III. 4, and cf. also *ibid.*, III. 50, 51, 52.

[2] Cf. Mesolora's discussion of the natures and wills in Christ, *op. cit.*, III. pp. 218-224.

[3] Androutsos, *op. cit.*, p. 179.

[4] Mesolora, *op. cit.*, III, p. 206. What Mesolora says on this page is hardly reconcilable with what has just been given in the text above taken from Androutsos; *e. g.*, "*Divinity* (ἡ θεότης) shared with the flesh"; "All that *Divinity* had He gave"; "*Divinity* assumed the humiliation" etc. On the symbolic evidence for the *communicatio idiomatum*, cf. Mesolora, *op. cit.*, vol. I,—Metrophanes, p. 304; Mogila, p. 384; Dositheus, p. 411; *ibid.*, also II., pp. 106-107.

[5] St. John Dam., Ἔκδοσις, III, 15; cf. also *ibid.*, III, p. 7, 19, 51.

[6] Androutsos, *op. cit.*, p. 180. On which cf. Dyobouniotes, Ἡ Δογμ. Ἀνδρ. κριν., p. 34: "So one can say that the divine nature of Christ

"The human nature hypostatically united with God receives gifts, which, however, did not destroy its finite character but elevated it to its greatest possible height. . . . They are properly referred. . . . to the knowledge and will of the human nature.   The human knowledge of Christ was preserved from error but yet not transformed into omniscience, which is a divine attribute.   What ·was the relation of the two knowledges in the one subject is beyond our ken.   Certainly His human knowledge developed in the same way as it does with other men, ... by advancing and making progress.   So we are to understand St. Luke 2, 52. . . . not as a manifestation of the undeveloped wisdom of Christ,[1] but as an actual increase of empirical knowledge[2]. . . . How   the   human   knowledge   (of Christ) functions in its own sphere within the circle of omniscience. . . . is incomprehensible to man.   The will (that is, the human will) which has as its Bearer the Person of the Godman, being guided by Him in all its operations and enriched through grace and virtue, was closed to sin, both personal and original, since the Saviour, conceived by the Holy Ghost, had no share in it."[3]

is mortal, and His human nature immortal!" and p. 35. Androutsos Δογμ. Μελ., A', pp. 90-94 answers the criticism, but Dyobouniotes goes on further to censure Androutsos' entire presentation of the subject, in his 'Οφειλ. ἀπάντ. (pp. 86-87) saying that "in Mr. Androutsos' teaching about the *communicatio* we encounter these three ideas: 1. the ἀντίδοσις takes place mutually between the natures on account of the hypostatic union; 2. it is given from both natures to the Person; 3. it takes · place only from the divine to the human and not from the human to the divine." He claims the three are "contradictory", and says that Androutsos' denial of the fact is "characterized by the kind of dogmatic flippancy of those who think they know everything." (!)

[1] As *e. g.*, St. Athanasius in *adv. Arianos Orat.*, 4; St. John Dam., Ἔκδοσις, III. 22.

[2] So St. Augustine, *De Incarnatione*, VIII. 71. On the patristic interpretations of such texts as St. Mark 13, 32, cf. Androutsos, *op. cit.*, p. 181-182 and notes *ad loc:*

[3] Androutsos, *op. cit.*, p. 181-182. Dyobouniotes argued that if there were an actual increase of empirical knowledge on Our Lord's part, His knowledge could not have been even perfect and ripe human knowledge, since He died before reaching maturity. (Η 'Δογμ. 'Ανδρ., κρινομ., pp. 35-36). Androutsos shows from St. John Dam. (*op. cit.*, III. 18, 14.) that Our Lord had two knowledges, human and divine, and

The second great corollary and consequence of the doctrine of the *communicatio idiomatum* is the statement that the Blessed Virgin Mary is truly the Mother of God, Θεοτόκος. She is not only the Mother of Jesus, as the Nestorians held, but the Mother of God. The Nestorian statement is opposed both to Holy Scripture (cf. St. Luke 1, 35, 43 ; Rom. 1, 3 ; 9,5 ; Gal. 4,4.) and to the teaching of the Fathers and Tradition. The Councils of Ephesus, Chalcedon, and Constantinople II defined the dogma[1] that the Blessed Virgin is Θεοτόκος.

"It appears clearly in Holy Scripture and Tradition (and it is also intrinsically reasonable) that worship is due Jesus Christ even in His human nature, since the divine nature is not sundered from the human nature, and he who does divide them must accept two persons."[2] This worship is accorded Christ "as God-Man, not as God alone," as St. Athanasius says.[3]

Not only was Our Lord sinless, according to Greek Orthodoxy, but He was impeccable, incapable of sin. The patristic teaching, founded on Holy Scripture,[4] is that not only *did* Our Lord not sin, but He *could* not. It is the difference between the German words *Unsündigkeit* and *Unsündlichkeit*. His impeccability is a consequence of the hypostatic union and not of His Conception by the Holy Spirit, which is not the general reason or cause of His sinlessness. The doctrine of His utter sinlessness appears also in polemic against the heresies which denied it directly or by implication. This is the case in rela-

that to deny the validity of the argument for the growth of His human knowledge is tantamount to denying His human nature, and is counter to the Ecumenical Councils, the unanimous consent of the Fathers, and Holy Scripture (Δογμ. Μελέται, Α', pp. 95-99, and cf. Dyobouniotes, 'Οφειλ. ἀπάντ., pp. 90-93). On the Lutheran doctrine of the omnipresence of the Body of Christ, cf. Androutsos, Δογματική, pp. 182-183 (note) and his Συμβολική, pp. 181 ff; Mesolora, *op. cit.*, pp. 222-223 (note 2).

[1] Androutsos, Δογματική, pp. 183-184, with authorities given in the notes.

[2] *Ibid.*, p. 184; biblical references in notes; cf. St. Athanasius, *Epistola ad Adelphium*, 3; St. John Dam., Ἔκδοσις, III, 7 in Migne, *P. G.* t. xciv, 1013.

[3] Mesolora, *op. cit.*, III. p. 224, gives St. Athanasius, St. Cyril Alex. and St. John Dam. *ad loc.*

[4] Cf. St. John 8, 46; 14, 30; 1 St. John, 3, 5; 1 St. Peter 2, 22; Hebrews 4, 15.

tion to the Arians, Theodore of Mopsuestia and the Nestorians, and the Apollinarians and the Monothelites.[1] "The hypostatic union demands that all the acts of the Lord be directed and effected by the divine nature in Him, which constitutes the personal hypostasis of the Saviour, as in a way all the external actions of His bodily members are also under the dominion of His will. Otherwise there would be a *communicatio* in name only, and it would be supposed that there were two personal principles, two *egos* in Christ, which is counter to the teaching of the Church: the human nature was not assumed as person (al) into the hypostasis of God the Word, who Himself was the personal Bearer . . . of both natures. God the Word *could* not sin; the opinion that His human nature could sin would indicate that God the Word could, since under His inspiration all the operations of His human will were brought into play. Hence it is clear that the hypostatic union demands the perfect sinlessness of Our Lord." The matter may be put in another way: since we know that sin is the assertion of self-will in preference to God's will (for sin is essentially self-love and self-assertion) inasmuch as His human nature had no *ego* or self and did not love self as it loved God, it is lacking in the fundamental form and basis of sin, self-love. . . . "The notion, then, that Jesus Christ could sin implies that He could have fallen as did Adam, and the Redemption through Him might have been brought to naught; but the fall of the God-Man is not only nowhere suggested in Holy Scripture, but the very idea of it is blasphemous to those who hold to the incarnate economy",[2] that is, the Redemption.

[1] Against whom the Fathers—*e. g.* Dionysius Alex., St. Athanasius, St. Cyril Alex., and the conciliar decrees brought out the doctrine of Our Lord's sinlessness. Cf. Can. XII of the 8th Ecumenical Council; St. Augustine *Enchiridion*, c. 40, etc.

[2] Androutsos, Δογματική, pp. 187-189. In answer to Dyobouniotes' strictures ('Η Δογμ. 'Ανδρ. κριν., p. 36-37), he says further: "There could be no doubt that human nature of itself can sin, since this is a property of human nature . . . " but in the hypostatic union this was impossible (Δογμ. Μελ., Α', p. 101, and cf. pp. ff). Dyobouniotes ('Οφειλ. ἀπάντ., pp. 94-96) says that this theory involves an utter change in the human nature assumed by Our Lord as a consequence of the union—a view which is contrary to the teaching of the Fathers. Cf. Mesolora, *op. cit.*, III, p. 215.

In view of what has been said, how shall we understand the
Temptations of our Lord? The Fathers agree that He was subjected to every temptation. "That is, either from His interior
nature sin could in some way torment Him, or else His human
will could be externally subject to the irritation of temptation,
so as to be tossed about or driven in some manner by it. Yet
every such temptation was external,[1] and every one was immediately repulsed so soon as it presented itself." Adam stood in
need of trial and testing, but not so the Lord, who as Incarnate
God had come to save men. The first Adam had need of moral
and ethical probation before he be allowed to share God's blessedness, but the second Adam could not be touched by sin nor as
God-Man be liable to fall.[2] He is our example and Prototype[3]
in that He is the ideal of divine perfection in our nature, and
as well the example of the loftiest humility. While we may not
discern the relationship between His human free-will and His
sinlessness, yet we may understand sufficiently His Person and
His life as a whole. Though He could not sin, yet His choice
of the death of the Cross was a free choice. It is useless to con-
struct the scholastic dilemma: 'if our Lord necessarily underwent the death of the Cross He could not have been free, or else
if He were free He might not have done so, and so was not necessarily sinless, since He might have refused to follow the will
of God.' "But if one reason that the possibility of sin does not
lie in the essence of the human nature and that by the hypostatic
union the human will was not a choice between good and evil
but, on the contrary, illuminated and led without coercion or
necessity, was wholly directed towards God and united with the
divine will, it is possible then that some rays of light may shine
upon the matter of the self-direction and freedom of His human
will and on the perfect harmony of the two wills in Christ."[4]

[1] Cf. Gregory the Great, *Hom.*, I, 16, 1 (on St. Matthew): *omnis
diabolica illa tentatio foris, non intus fuit,* and St. Leo *Epist.* 35, 3.
[2] Cf. St. Augustine, *De Trinitate*, I, 13, 18; St. Cyril Alex., on
St. John 7, 39 (Migne, *P. G.* t. LXXIII, 756.); *ibid., adv. Nestorium,*
III, (in Migne, *P. G.* t. LXXVI, 164).
[3] Cf. 1 St. Peter, 2, 21.
[4] Androutsos, *op. cit.*, pp. 189-191. With this teaching agree most
of the Greek theologians—e. g., Macarius, *op. cit.*, II, 87; Eugenius
Bulgaris, *Theologikon*, pp. 442, 544; Damalas' Catechism, p. 62;—but

3. THE DOCTRINE OF OUR LORD'S WORK

A. The Three Offices of Christ

As we have seen in the exposition given above of original sin
and the ills consequent upon the Fall, humanity incurred the
guilt and punishment of sin, the darkening of the mind and
judgment, and as well a weakening of the will, so that there is
an inclination towards evil and a turning towards earthly things.
As there is a three-fold loss by sin, so there is a three-fold restoration in the Redemption. The divine Justice and Righteousness, affronted and flouted by the disobedience of sin, are
vindicated and satisfied by the atoning and propitiatory work
of the Saviour. The mind of man, darkened and confused by
sin, is illuminated and enlightened by the revelatory and prophetic work of Our Lord. As the will of man was weakened
and became prone to evil, through His royal achievement as con-
queror of the powers of evil He uplifts and empowers the human
will by the Grace which comes from Him, to fight and conquer
evil and turn completely towards God and the good. Hence
His work is divided into the three functions, priestly, prophetic,
and kingly.[1] From another viewpoint the Saviour completed
His work of salvation of man through coming down from
Heaven, humbling Himself, and being glorified—"becoming
man, being crucified, and rising again. There was a triple function of Our Lord in the world, and it is described in the name
'Christ', . . . given to prophets, priests, and kings . ."[2]

This three-fold office of Our Lord is suggested in Holy Scrip-

---

not the famous Professor of Christian Ethics at the Seminary at Chalki,
Basil Antoniades. Androutsos quotes him as follows, from the work
'Η Χριστιανικὴ 'Ηθική, section 73: "To sin as a man was a possibility
which might have taken place in Christ Jesus without being precluded
by His divine nature. And in this fact exactly lies the moral lofti-
ness and grandeur of the Saviour, that while a fall even in His case
was possible, yet He did *not* fall but remained sinless, not because
He was not able to sin, but because He was able not to sin." (In Androutsos' Δογματική, end of note, pp. 191-193.)

[1] Androutsos, *op. cit.*, p. 194.

[2] Mesolora, *op. cit.*, III. pp. 224-225.

ture,[1] and "whatever in the Old Testament is as it were a symbol and prophecy, becomes fact (lit. *truth*) and realization in the New. The public life of Our Lord is the fulfilment of His three-fold office: up to His death He exercised His prophetic office, in His passion and death His priestly work is manifested, and in the foundation and ordering of His Kingdom. . . He exercised His royal office."[2] The Fathers saw in part the implications of Holy Scripture, but "the scientific working out of His three-fold office belongs to later times." We must not think, however, that there was an actual division or separation in the work of Our Lord Himself. We only distinguish the three offices as a help to our own reasoning and thinking. Yet it is true that "the center of His three-fold office was Our Lord's priestly work by which He reconciled man and God. The other two serve as means for this end—the prophetic, by preparing the spirit of man to receive His teaching, and the kingly work, by bestowing the grace of Redemption and perfecting the believer in the Kingdom of God."[3]

(a) Our Lord as High Priest

"The Saviour as the Great High Priest offered Himself as a spotless sacrifice to God the Father, a sacrifice of propitiation, being Himself both Priest and Victim, and both appeased (ἐξιλάσατο) and satisfied the righteousness of God offended by the sin of man in his transgression of the divine law. He took on Himself, as the sinless Representative of the human race, the punishment for sin . . . to which sinful man was liable, and poured out on the Cross His precious and saving Blood, establishing the New Covenant which He made with the Father, through which everyone who believes in Him is saved, confessing the propitiation of His death on the Cross."[4] His priestly work

---

[1] Old Testament: *e. g.*, Deut. 18, 15; Is. 42, 1-4; Ps. 110-4; Ezek. 40, ff. Ps. 2, 71; 110; Mic. 2 ,13; 5, 2; Zach. 6, 9 ff. New Testament: *e. g.* St. Luke 13, 33; St. Matt. 13, 57; Acts 3, 22; 7, 37—St. John 17, 19; St. Matt. 20, 28; Heb. 4, 14; 5, 1-5;—St. Matt. 25, 31-4; St. Luke 19, 12 ff.

[2] Androutsos, *op. cit.*, p. 195.
[3] Androutsos, *op. cit.*, p. 196.
[4] Kephala, *op. cit.*, p. 188.

includes all the sufferings[1] which our Lord underwent for us, from Bethlehem to Calvary. Though man by sin is under sentence of death by the righteous and holy decree of God, yet God's mercy demanded that man be saved from destruction and that he be restored to fellowship with God after his guilt and condemnation had been removed. Since man was incapable of accomplishing this for himself and achieving his own salvation, God found the means to accomplish it, in the Incarnation. Our Lord taking our nature, compensates for the guilt and punishment of sin by suffering for us, and His death counter-balances the eternal death to which our race was doomed. His work then as *priest* is unique and sole, once for all and final, as the words of Ps. 110, 4 (cf. Heb. 6,20) signify. He offered a true sacrifice as the true Priest, His Body and His Life, not only as an act of obedience but as well as an evidence of His Love. He "became a curse for us" to redeem the world from the curse of the law.[2] So His work is described as propitiatory.[3] The idea of sacrifice, symbolized in the Old Testament, was realized in the fact of His Sacrifice whereby He made atonement for us with God.[4] "His death on the Cross was the Propitiation *par excellence,* and the Great Sacrifice of Redemption. From it flowed, as from a source, the merit of Christ, conveying forgiveness of sins through Him the great High Priest, the Mediator between God and man." It was absolutely necessary for the salvation of man, and His death was in behalf of, and for, man.[5] "His Sacrifice is the cleansing bath of humanity, purifying and washing away every taint of sin from the race, and sanctifying those who believe in Him." His priesthood is as different from

[1] So Androutsos (*op. cit.*, p. 196), Macarius (*op. cit.*, II, pp. 152-186), and Mesolora (*op. cit.*, III, p. 235) who *loc. cit.*, gives other references.

[2] Gal. 3, 13; Heb. 5, 1; 8, 3; Phil. 2, 8; Rom. 5, 19; Gal. 1, 4; 2, 20; 1 Cor. 15, 3, 5, 7; Rom. 3, 25; 2 Cor. 5, 21; 1 St. Pet. 2, 20-24; 1 St. John 2, 2.

[3] On the seven titles of the Saviour in the New Testament, cf. Kephala, *op. cit.*, pp. 189-190; references, *ibid.*

[4] Androutsos, *op. cit.*, pp. 197-198.

[5] Mesolora, *op. cit.*, III. pp. 230-231; for the evidence of the Symbolic Books, cf. in vol. I. *ibid.*, Mogila, pp. 309-401; Kritopoulos, pp. 305-306; Gennadius, p. 76; vol II. Dositheus, p. 107. Platon's Catech. sect. 23; Macarius, *op. cit.*, II. pp. 152-187.

that of Aaron "as a body is from the shadow which accompanies it," for the Aaronic priesthood was only a type, a foreshadowing, and a promise, of what was to come.[1]

Scriptural teaching as to the Atonement was naturally subject to development and more extended exposition with the progress of Christian thought. The early Fathers, notably Origen, St. Gregory of Nyssa, St. Ambrose, and St. Gregory the Great, expounding the notion of Our Lord's death from the side of love, not of justice, interpreted it as redemption from the power of Satan. Yet St. Irenaeus[2] and St. Athanasius both brought out the other aspect of the death of Christ on Calvary, as a representative sacrifice removing the guilt of sin. "He offered a sacrifice for all," St. Athansius says, "in behalf of all giving over the temple of Himself unto death."[3] The moral necessity of the death of the Cross, St. Anselm developed in his theory founded on the idea of guilt and satisfaction, as did Nicholas of Methone independently of St. Anselm. The theory of Nicholas[4] may be summarized as follows: "Men as sinful are subject to death and to its originator, the devil. Deliverance . . . can be achieved through the death not of a man—for he as himself guilty, could only make expiation for himself and for none other—but of some sinless being. God foresaw this contingency and His love decreed that His Son should, by becoming man, offer Himself for men to deliver them from slavery to Satan and sin. This Redeemer must needs be God-Man—God, that His sacrifice could be efficacious, and man, that He should be able to suffer, and serve men as the prototype in the struggle for the conquest over evil."

"While Nicholas sees the death of the Lord as necessary . . in order to do away with the power of Satan, St. Anselm relates it to the divine Holiness. Sin is, for him, an injury to the honor of God, in that the sinner refuses to offer God the honor due Him by not submitting his will to God. . . The only attitude God

---

[1] Kephala, op. cit., p. 189.

[2] Adv. haer., III. 18, 1.

[3] De Incarnatione verbi Dei, 20, and Adv. Arianos Orat., 1, 60, in Migne, P.G. t. XXVI, 139.

[4] Anecd. 1, 25, quoted by Androutsos (op. cit., pp. 199-200) from Hagenbach's Dogmengeschichte (5th Ed., pp. 417 ff.).

may adopt towards such conduct on the part of His creature (to preserve both His honor and the harmony and order of His universe) is either (to demand) satisfaction for or punishment of, sin. That is, to compensate for His outraged dignity He demands one of two things: either that man should freely make satisfaction to God by yielding over what is God's due, or else that God should punish man by depriving him of the blessedness and of the other good things that would have been his had he not sinned. Of the two ways God, in His mercy, chose the way of satisfaction. . . But man could not in any way make satisfaction to God, since all that he is and has to offer, he is already obliged to offer to God. So God's charge against man is so great that it cannot be compensated for by the whole world, or by anything and everything outside God, but only by something still greater, that is by God Himself. . . Hence since God cannot Himself make satisfaction (nor can man) for what man owes, only one who combines divinity and manhood, or, God as man, can satisfy the divine righteousness. This satisfaction by the God-Man must not be merely submission of the God-Man to God, since every rational being owes this to God in any case . . but the death of the Cross which the Lord was not bound to offer, either naturally or morally. . . So the death to which the Saviour submitted is the perfect satisfaction of God. As dying is the greatest loss of man, and life the greatest good, it is obvious that the oblation of His life on the part of the God-Man possessed propitiatory and satisfying power, compensating and even more than compensating, for all the sins of the world. . . Since Christ as God offered what was not His bounden duty, the recompense He made is transferred to (the credit of) all His brethren after the flesh who were bound to make it."[1] "It is apparent", says Androutsos commenting upon this theory, "that this latter theory of the *merit* of Christ is entirely superfluous. Since the satisfaction of God is the deliverance of man from punishment, and the punishment consisted in being deprived of the good things for which man was created, *satisfaction* restores man to his first state and achieves just what Christ's *merit* achieves. The Anselmic theory differs from previous conceptions of Christ's death in the Church . . . by making use of

[1] In Androutsos, *op. cit.*, pp. 199-201.

elements either entirely other than those in the Church's theory or rather by being developed under the influence of alien factors —such as the conception of sin in this acceptance of the term, as a detraction of God's honor. . . . The notion, however, of Christ's death as reconciling . . . God's holiness or His righteousness with His love, and as substitutionary in assuming the punishment of men, is the basis upon which in Holy Scripture the death of Christ is founded, the height from which the Fathers also view it."[1]

Protestant theories of the Atonement have attempted to grapple with a very real difficulty involved in the dogma: how it is possible for the death of one to make satisfaction for others as their representative, and how an innocent man may suffer or be punished for the guilty. So Protestant theology sees in the Atonement only the manifestation of the greatness of the love of God, of the appalling enormity of sin, and of the gulf between man and God created by sin. Such a conception of the Cross deprives the death of Christ of its fundamental character, making of it something secondary and unnecessary.[2]

The Sacrifice of the Cross is of the greatest value and worth, in that not only did human nature suffer, the *principium quo,* but that also He who offered that Sacrifice and was Himself sacrificed, the *principium quod,* was God Himself. The magnitude of the oblation is also apparent from the greatness of the self-abnegation of Our Lord in giving Himself to His Passion and Death. Hence "both the power and fruits of it extend. . . . to all men of all times and to nature groaning and waiting for freedom from the bondage of corruption."[3] "The power of the atoning death of Christ", says Mesolora, "together with its consequences, extends over all men, . . . avails for all sins, . . . and operates through all time, from the beginning of the Fall of man until the consummation of the world."[4] The death of the Cross also availed to obtain a glory "which is not only a natural consequence of the hypostatic union but at

---

[1] *Ibid.,* p. 201.

[2] Androutsos, Δογματική, pp. 201-202; for more extended treatment, cf. Συμβολική, pp. 182-190.

[3] Δογματική, p. 202; cf. Rom. 8, 21; 2 St. Pet. 3, 13.

[4] *Op. cit.,* III. p. 236; cf. 1 St. John 2, 2; 1 St. John 1, 7; Heb. 1, 14.

the same time a positive reward which the Saviour obtained
for the human race, having accomplished His saving work
and undergone (the death of) the Cross."[1]

The Sacrifice of the Cross is entire, complete, and plenary,
and there is no ground for the Roman doctrine of "superabundant satisfaction" even in such texts as St. John 2, 2,
Heb. 10, 14, and Rom. 5, 15.[2] According to the Roman notion,
the Grace of Christ abounds and exceeds the sin of men; if
the two were put into a balance-scale, His Grace would immeasurably outweigh our sin. This sort of deduction is entirely foreign to the Apostle's thought, for he simply says that
if transgression brought death upon men, it is the more certain
that the Grace of Christ brings salvation. So too in the
Fathers, the comparison is only to indicate the greatness of
the Redemption in Christ as against the sin of man and its
consequences. "But this notion of the superabounding satisfaction of Our Lord is a matter without any practical significance, since whether the satisfaction be sufficient or more than
sufficient, it amounts to the same thing: in His death....all
the sins of man are atoned for." Its only practical connection
is with the development of the theory of the treasury of merits
and indulgences, which will be noticed later.[3]

"The Sacrifice of the Cross once for all consummated,
takes place, so to speak, both in heaven and on earth. So in
the Sacrifice of the Eucharist (which is an actual Sacrifice
in which Our Lord, as we shall see, offers Himself through
the priest for the personal application of the fruits of Golgotha), (and) in heaven, "He maketh intercession for us",[4]
through which Intercession He makes the benefits of the Cross
available to men....It is an actual prayer like that which He
made upon earth for us", as the above text implies.

Finally, the doctrine of the Church is firmly opposed to

[1] Androutsos, op. cit., p. 203 and cf. notes; see also Dyobouniotes'
'Η Δογμ. 'Ανδρ. κριν., p. 38 and Androutsos' Δογμ. Μελ., Α', pp. 102-103.

[2] Macarius (op. cit., II. p. 176) and Antonius (op. cit., p. 258)
both follow Roman teaching on this point, on which cf. Androutsos,
Δογματική, p. 203-4, note 6, and Mesolora's discussion, op. cit., III.
pp. 237-239.

[3] Androutsos, op. cit., pp. 204-205. On the Roman doctrine of works
of supererogation and indulgences, cf. pp. 367-370 following.

[4] Heb. 5, 25 and cf. 9, 24; 1 St. John 2, 1; Rom. 8, 34.

any notion of the Sacrifice of the Cross based upon dualistic principles, such as Manichaeism or Gnosticism, as well as against the Pelagian and pantheistic notions. According to Manichaeism, the Sacrifice was only the deliverance of the soul from the evil of the physical body. Pelagianism held it as superfluous, since the Saviour came "not to make atonement but to teach and stimulate men by His example." According to the pantheistic hypothesis, evil is only a stage in the evolution of man, and is outgrown in the course of his development. "The Church (in opposition to these theories) teaches..that sin does not proceed....from matter but from the free will of man; that Redemption is not only a deliverance from a hostile principle but also friendship with God....; that sin proceeds from human freedom, which has involved man in a depth of corruption from which only the Sacrifice of the Cross could save us;....that Redemption is a real and actual thing—we have in Christ Jesus not simply the consciousness of Redemption but atonement from our sins in very fact."[1]

(b) Our Lord as Prophet[2]

As Prophet, Our Lord taught in word and deed the eternal truth of which He was the embodiment incarnate. He "is the Way, the Truth, and the Life."[3] He came to deliver man from the evil of his perverse way, and to restore to him the possibility of knowing the truth for which he was created,[4] both in the sphere of religious truth and in that of moral or ethical truth. He only could lead man to this fulness of knowledge; He only "satisfied the mind and filled the void of men's hearts and appeased....the longing desires of the human soul."[5] Our Lord announced the eternal plan and will of God, the full truths of the Faith, and the true principles of worship. He was more than a prophet, for His wisdom was the boundless wisdom of God. His teaching was not only in

[1] Androutsos, *op. cit.*, pp. 205-207.
[2] This arrangement of the material is that of Androutsos, not of Mesolora and Kephala, who put the priestly office second.
[3] Cf. Kephala, *op. cit.*, pp. 7-9.
[4] *Ibid.*, p. 177-179.
[5] *Ibid.*, pp. 181-182.

word, but in deed, evidencing His mission by miracles, signs, and wonders.[1] In Him prophecy was complete, who was the highest and greatest teacher of mankind.[2] The truths He revealed were those about God—His Nature, Persons, Properties, and Attributes; about Himself as the Only Begotten, sent into the world, to suffer, die, and rise again; about the Holy Spirit; about man—his fall, need of regeneration, immortality, the brotherhood of all men, and the like.[3] As prophet He foretold the fall of Jerusalem and the future of His Church.[4] As His miracles exceeded in power, in character, and in their source, those of the prophets before Him, so did His teaching.[5] There is a threefold difference between Our Lord and the prophets of the Old Testament: they were inspired by the Word—He *was* the Word in whom inhered all wisdom and might; they taught about Him, the Word, and He proclaimed and lived what they taught in prophecy; the prophets spake once, or according to the term of their natural lives, but He "as the Eternal Prophet speaks eternally in His Church.."[6] Both the Mosaic law, the ritual and ceremonial ordinances which looked forward to Him by promise, and the moral law, had fulfilment and completion in Him, who delivered them from the meticulous and literal observance which they had at the hands of the Pharisees and other Jewish teachers. This same office Our Lord exercises in His Church, illuminating its teachings by the light of His Holy Spirit and guiding and directing it in the understanding and interpretation of His Word.[7]

(c) Our Lord as King

As the Old Testament accorded to the expected Messiah the powers of royalty,[8] so in His fulfilment of these prophecies did our Lord show forth His office as King. He "bore the

[1] *Ibid.*, p. 182; cf. St. John 10, 38.
[2] Androutsos, *op. cit.*, p. 207.
[3] Kephala, *op. cit.*, pp. 183-184, with full references.
[4] Kephala, *ibid.*, pp. 185-186.
[5] Androutsos, *ibid.*, pp. 207-208.
[6] Kephala, *op. cit.*, p. 187.
[7] Androutsos, *op. cit.*, pp. 208-209, and cf. Mesolora, III. p. 225.
[8] Cf. Ps. 2, 71; Isaiah, 9, 6-7; Jer. 23, 5-6; Zech. 9, 9-10.

kingly crown, whether as glorified by God and named His
Beloved Son, or as founding His Church and Kingdom, or as
performing miracles, being shown thereby as Lord of heaven
and earth, of things visible and invisible. His royal glory
was completed in the Ascension and Session at the right hand
of the Father, whence through His Spirit He administers
His Church and judges the world, being at the same time
Judge and merciful King, having all power in heaven and
earth."[1] The Jews expected a King, but awaited one who
was to be a worldly ruler and prince. The Kingdom of our
Lord, however, is of a nature consistent with the divine plan
of redemption, a spiritual and moral, not an earthly, kingdom.[2]
"Having purchased back mankind from the bondage of death
and sin at the price of His death on the cross, He founded His
spiritual Kingdom.... In it He achieves His work of
salvation, teaching men through the Holy Spirit the word of
God, and communicates His Grace through the sacraments. . . .
Thus His kingly office is inextricably bound up with His
priestly and prophetic offices."[3] "As King..He is to judge
the quick and the dead and reward each according to his
works."[4] His royal office Our Lord exercised only in part on
earth, in working miracles, establishing the laws of His Kingdom, and the like, but His royal power is chiefly seen in
His descent into hell, His Ascension, and His heavenly work.[5]

Our Lord's triumphant entry into the domain of death
has always been part of the Christian Faith. The evidence
of Holy Scripture is more explicitly expounded by the Fathers,
the summary of which is, that the Lord after His death on
the Cross descended with His soul into Hell.[6] According to
Mesolora, the purpose of Our Lord's descent was "to preach

[1] Mesolora op. cit., III. p. 226.
[2] Cf. St. Luke 1, 33; 1 Tim. 6, 15; St. Matt. 28, 18; cf. also Kephala, op. cit., p. 191.
[3] Androutsos, op. cit., p. 210.
[4] Kephala, op. cit., p. 191.
[5] Androutsos, op. cit., p. 211, cf. St. Matt. 10, 914; 1; St. Luke
10, 16.
[6] Cf. Acts, 2, 27; Eph. 4, 9, and 1 St. Peter 3, 18; 4, 6; patristic
evidence, p. 212 of Androutsos, op. cit., note 1; symbolic evidence, Mesolora, 1. op. cit., Mogila, p. 402; Kritopoulos, p. 306; St. John Dam.,
Ἔκδοσις, III. 70, 76, et al.

salvation and forgiveness to the captives, and to extend to those who had gone before, His Redemptive work"[1] and its benefits. The vast range of speculation and supposition about the significance of the descent into Hell has developed many questions: Was it only an extension of His Prophetic work? Was it simply as extending His redemption to those not on earth? Did He descend directly after His death or after His Resurrection? What is "hell"—the place of condemnation, or the *limbus patrum,* as the Western Church holds? In default of explicit revelation on the subject, Androutsos[2] says that we should keep free from speculation where it has no warrant, and confine ourselves to the definite teaching of the Church. This may be summarized in the three statements: (a) "The descent into hell took place before the Resurrection, as the Fathers held and as the mention of the fact in the Apostles' Creed, between the burial and the Resurrection, indicates; (b) it is both a confirmation of the death of Our Lord and of the existence in Him of a human soul, as well as the actual triumphant manifestation of Our Lord entering and despoiling the power of death. . . . ;(c) it exercised a salutary effect on the state of the dead. But what this was and to whom it was extended cannot be determined. . . . The opinion of many Fathers seems to commend itself as more probable that the deliverance of the righteous men of the Old Testament was the saving operation of Our Lord in descending into hell."[3]

"Our Lord's Resurrection is the seal and validation of that truth of our Faith which constitutes the center of the evangelical message, and is at the same time the guarantee and earnest of the Resurrection of all. The Ascension and Session at the right hand..show forth the glory, the might, and the authority which Our Lord had, even in His human nature, over all that is in heaven, on earth, and under the earth. The final act and manifestation of the kingly might of our Lord is the last judgment of the world in time, in which He will judge the quick and the dead, and make a

[1] Mesolora *op. cit.,* III. p. 240.

[2] *Op. cit.,* p. 213.

[3] *Op. cit.,* p. 214, and cf. the whole discussion in **Mesolora,** *op. cit.,* III. pp. 239-242.

new heaven and earth in which He will rule with the elect of His Kingdom forever."[1]

B. Redemption, Atonement, and Salvation

The work of Our Lord in making atonement for man, in achieving his redemption, and propitiating the Divine Justice has, as has been shown above, a universal, complete, and final character. The Greek theologians distinguish two meanings of Redemption: objectively, it is the deliverance of fallen man from sin, and subjectively, the personal appropriation of this great achievement by the individual, through the Holy Spirit.[2] "Redemption", says Mesolora, "in its widest meaning includes the whole Revelation of God, His Providence and His particular activity directed towards the salvation of man. In general, all the works of God to the end of removing sin, from the Fall of man on, are called 'redemption', which is, negatively, the deliverance from sin, and positively, the sanctification of man. Redemption includes three things—(a) the doctrine of Our Lord as Redeemer of the world; (b) the doctrine of His redemptive work applied to men by Grace and adoption; and (c) the doctrine of the continuity, preservation, and functioning of the Church founded by Him."[3] In another connection he says: "The Atonement, through the death of our Lord on the Cross, did not render sin non-existent, nor does it take away the consequences and burden of it, for this is in entire opposition to the ethical order of the universe and to the Holiness of God. Atonement and Redemption removed only the middle wall of partition separating man from God, and procured eternal life. The merit of Christ lies for us in the forgiveness of sins and union with God. This was attained objectively through the Sacrifice of the Cross; it is accomplished subjectively in each of us by

[1] Androutsos, *op. cit.*, pp. 214-215. He has a note at the end of the chapter (pp. 215-217) on the question of the two states of Our Lord—*humiliation* and *exaltation*. This two-fold division is often used as the scheme for presenting Christology in Orthodox dogmatic. For eschatological doctrine, cf. pp. 416-422 following.

[2] Cf. Androutsos, *op. cit.*, p. 167; Mesolora, *op. cit.*, III, p. 204, note 1.

[3] *Op. cit.*, III. p. 229, note I.

his own appropriation of the Grace flowing from the Cross, and the life of faith. . . . As Christ died to sin to make satisfaction to the divine righteousness, so each man must die to sin, having the life and suffering of the Saviour as his example. Only one who strives and conquers in this struggle,—through the life-giving Grace of God revealed completely in the death on the Cross of the Only Begotten Son of God, and through the exercise of his own free will coöperating with it,—is redeemed, justified, sanctified, and saved. . . ."[1] In Androutsos' words: "The death of the Cross established fellowship between God and man in the sense that there was no obstacle on God's side for the rehabilitation of man, and the way of salvation and eternal life was opened up to man. But in order for man to lay hold of and make these good things his own it is necessary that God should extend to him a helping hand; man having fallen into the depth of destruction through sin cannot raise himself up. . . . He stands in need of divine assistance throughout. . . . The whole doctrine of Grace, the Church, and the Sacraments. . is concerned with the appropriation of the redemptive work"[2] of our Lord.

[1] *Op. cit.*, pp. 231-232, note I.
[2] Androutsos, *op. cit.*, p. 218.

LECTURE IV.

IV.—DOCTRINE OF GRACE AND OF THE CHURCH

LECTURE IV.

THE DOCTRINE OF GRACE AND OF THE CHURCH

CONTENTS

DOCTRINE OF GRACE AND OF THE CHURCH

Introduction: The Sources of Modern Orthodox Teaching

The subject matter of the present lecture is distinguished from that of the preceding lectures in several respects. In the first place the development of the theology of Grace, so far as concerns the Eastern Church, is in the largest degree a modern achievement. For practically all the explicit teaching we are dependent upon the work of synods and councils subsequent to the Ecumenical Councils for the basis of the material of this and the following lectures. This brings up the question, Of what weight are the dogmatic formulations of Orthodoxy since the time of the Ecumenical Councils? As we saw in Lecture I,[1] the full tradition of the Church includes more than the decrees of the Ecumenical Councils, since important doctrines of the Church—the Sacraments, Justification, and the like—were not enunciated until after the Schism.[2] Rhôsse holds that the decrees and definitions of the Councils and Synods of the 16th century and on, have binding force upon every true member of the Orthodox Church;[3] Mesolora says that they have not the obligatory character of the Creed and of the Seven Ecumenical Councils, but are only of illustrative and secondary value;[4] Androutsos calls them "secondary authorities."[5] The decisions of local synods and councils, particularly those since the Schism, are valid insofar as they "add nothing new, but simply expound by way of defense or by way of refuting errors, those dogmatic....truths for-

[1] Pp. 27-30.
[2] Rhôsse, *op. cit.*, pp. 59-60 and note.
[3] *Ibid.*
[4] *Op. cit.*, I. pp. 12-13.
[5] Δογματική, p. 20.

mulated or simply touched upon in the Ecumenical Councils."[1] In other words, such councils subsequent to the Schism as confirm, expound, and more explicitly state the content of the Faith—consonant with the decrees of the Ecumenical Councils, the Fathers, and the Creed—have binding force upon all Orthodox. In this sense only are they "secondary", and not on a par with the Ecumenical Councils. "Local synods have always had the character of consultative" (that is, rather than legislative) "bodies. Their rulings have the weight of directive principles because of the Bishops who were present, but they are not laws in the sense in which the rulings of the Ecumenical Councils are so described."[2] The rulings of such councils were subject to revision, ratification, and re-affirmation on the part of subsequent gatherings. The seal of acceptance by the mind of the Church in later synods served to consolidate and make immutable, decrees passed in local gatherings. For instance, the rulings of the Synod of 1667 were subsequently ratified in 1682, and this latter synod said: "We pronounce that all other acts done by the Holy Synod stand unchanged and immutable (ἀμετακίνητα καὶ ἀμετάτρεπτα) as having been done rightly and lawfully."[3] It is apparent then, that the subsequent ratification of the acts of a local synod by other assemblies or councils accords to such acts a real, definite, and *binding* authority, and that the reason prompting such ratification and validation, in the case of dogmatic pronouncements, is their consistency in doctrine and its formulation with what had been defined[4] before by the chief authorities of the Orthodox Church—the Bible, and Sacred Tradition, that is, the Ecumenical Councils and the teaching of the Fathers. There is then a genuine and actual development of doctrine in the Orthodox Church, and an adequate organ for its formulation, Palmieri to the contrary

---

[1] Mesolora, Πρακτικὴ Θεολογία, p. 29, note 1; cf. his definitions of Orthodoxy, and his discussion of Dogmatic, pp. 17-18, 28-31 *ibid.*

[2] Δοκίμιον Ἐκκλησιαστικοῦ Δικαίου, by the Archimandrite Apostolos Christodoulos, Constantinople, 1896, p. 50; cf. pp. 255-259 following.

[3] Πατριαρχικὰ Ἔγγραφα, Dilikanis, vol. III. Constantinople, 1905, pp. 199-200.

[4] Cf. Sakellaropoulos, Ἐκκλησιαστικὸν δίκαιον τῆς ἀνατολικῆς ὀρθοδόξου Ἐκκλησίας, Athens, 1898, p. 37.

notwithstanding.[1] The Orthodox Church claims that she "has never added to nor changed what had been decreed by the Ecumenical Councils....Her dogmas are those of the early Church....Her teaching is primitive Christianity.... She holds unaltered and immutable the primitive and genuine Christianity of the first eight centuries, which was first preached by the Apostles in the Greek countries and in the Greek language."[2] The Vincentian canon, according to Rhôsse, is "in harmony with the local and sectional (μερικαί) councils of the Eastern Church and with them only"—that is, in contrast to Roman development—"for they have neither added to, nor taken away from the dogmas of the ancient Catholic Church of the time before the Schism, but remain faithful to them, thus by their unanimity of teaching and true orthodoxy forming the continuation, truly and canonically, of the ancient Catholic Church."[3] What is taught then by the synods of the 16th century and on, being only the amplification and formulation in explicit language of the teaching of the Catholic Church, has for all practical purposes the authority of dogma for the Orthodox Church.

The explicit formulation of the doctrines of Grace, Justification, the Church,[4] and the Sacraments, is due chiefly to the local synods and councils subsequent to the Reformation. We have come to discern in the history of dogma a shifting of interest and emphasis in the presentation of the content of the Christian Truth in the various ages of the Church. As the earliest years of the Church's life were devoted to the statement of its doctrine of God against the attacks of heresies, and the first four Ecumenical Councils were given over to the problems of Christology under the stimulus of heretical teaching, so the implications of the third clause of

---

[1] Cf. *Theologia Dogm. Orth.*, vol. I. Ch. 3, particularly pp. 63 ff.

[2] Ἀντιπαπικά, Diomede Kyriakos, Athens, 1893, pp. 28, 46; cf. the Ἐγκύκλιος τῆς μιᾶς, ἁγίας, καθολικῆς καὶ ἀποστολικῆς Ἐκκλησίας Ἐπιστολὴ πρὸς τοὺς ἀπανταχοῦ ὀρθοδόξους, Constantinople, 1863; *Epistola Dogmatica Synoda Constantinopolitanae*, 1723-3, in Mansi, etc.

[3] Δογματική, pp. 103-104.

[4] "The doctrine of the Church, from the (time of the) Reformation, became particularly the 'sign spoken against,' about which all other dogmatic differences center." Androutsos, Συμβολική, p. 56.

the Creed were left to the work of the Church in the times subsequent to the Ecumenical Councils for explicit statement and formulation. As the great problems which agitated the Church of the first eight centuries were settled once for all by the Ecumenical Councils, the questions brought up answered, and the discussion closed, so, also, in regard to the matters which engaged the attention of the Church of the sixteenth and following centuries. The discussion has been closed "in a sense" only, for as the formulation of the Christological doctrine of the Church served to determine the course of subsequent theological thought, so the decrees of the synods and councils subsequent to the Schism, and particularly those of the last three centuries, have defined in advance the direction in which Orthodox thought was to move. They have determined its course but not sterilized its development. In other words, no Orthodox theologian has called into question any of the doctrines embodied in authoritative decrees of the synods from the 17th century on, in the matters of which this lecture is to treat: for an Orthodox dogmatician these questions have been decided, and for him these decrees have the force of dogma.[1]

---

[1] But cf. Diomede Kyriakos, writing in the *Jahrbücher für protestantische Theologie*, vol. XVI. 1890, p. 153:   *Die theologische Wissenschaft bewegt sich freier bei uns als in der päpstlichen Kirche. Der Katechismus von Mogilas, und die Bestimmungen einigen kleinen Synoden des XVII. Jahrhunderts haben bei uns keine absolute Geltung.* Kyriakos was writing clearly for Protestant consumption, and his words here must be taken in connection with those quoted from him above. He would not, for example, question the dogmas about the Seven Sacraments or about the Church, yet their formulation was the work of the "small synods of the 17th century." The Orthodox theologian does not ground his conviction of the truth of these doctrines on the basis of the local synods of the 17th century, save in so far as they expressed the mind of the Church as previously declared in the Ecumenical Councils and found in the Holy Scriptures. Palmieri, after mentioning the *Confessions* of Metrophanes Kritopoulos, Dositheus, the Catechisms of Mogila and Philaret, etc., states: *"nullum igitur ex praecitatis monumentis fidei orthodoxae charactere symbolico oecomenico instruitur"* (*op. cit.,* vol. I. p. 650; cf. his whole section, *de auctoritate librorum symbolicorum Ecclesiarum orthodoxarum,* pp. 649-660, *ibid.* His argument is that which is developed in his *Il Progresso Dommatico,* that the Orthodox theory breaks down in practice, and hence that Orthodoxy needs the Pope as a center of unity

The effect of the Reformation on the Orthodox Church is seen in the work of the 17th century synods. It is not my purpose here to discuss the history of the times in which the various "Symbolic Books" and *Confessions* had their origin, nor to enter upon the various questions as to authorship, sources, causes, and occasions which provoked them. Our

and as the organ for the infallible definition of dogma. This fact must be kept in mind in reading his work.) In short, no Orthodox questions the validity and truth of the accepted declarations of the Councils, though the degree in which he accords formal authority to a specific council differs with the writer. As Ambraze says: "The *Confessions* are considered by all as sources of Orthodox teaching, though they do not have that obligatory character which belongs to the Creed and the decrees of the Ecumenical Councils. These *Confessions* have validity insofar as their content is agreeable to the dogmatic definitions of the Ecumenical Councils, or rather, all the aforesaid Confessions derive their dogmatic teaching from the Creed and are based upon it. But they develop and interpret more fully certain truths as circumstances and necessity give rise for the Church to counter and wage war on wrong teachings of heretical Christian Churches" ('Η 'Ορθόδοξος 'Εκκλησία περιέχων τὰς μεταξὺ τῶν χριστιανικῶν 'Εκκλησιῶν διαφοράς, . . .Athens, 1903, p. 73). In other words, Ecumenical Councils, says Androutsos, are valid in and of themselves, *jure divino et ipso jure,* and "their decrees infallible of themselves and not because of the consent to them and acceptance of them by the Church", "whose acceptance nevertheless constitutes the eternal criterion of ecumenicity" (Δογματική, p. 290). "Decrees of local synods have no immediate authenticity, but are infallible on the basis of their being received by the Church" (Δογμ. Μελ., Α', pp. 129-130 and cf. p. 11, Δογματική). In the words of the Archimandrite Chrysostom Papadopoulos, these *Confessions* "have not absolute and infallible weight, but (do possess) relative theological and historical worth . . . since they are neither decrees of Ecumenical Councils, nor 'Symbols of the Faith' " (Δοσίθεος, πατριάρχης 'Ιεροσολύμων in Νέα Σίων, vol. V. 1907, p. 127, cf. Αἱ Σύνοδοι καὶ αἱ ὁμολογίαι τοῦ ιζ' αἰῶνος, *ibid.,* vol. VII. 1908, p. 724). Against the Roman arguments in this connection, which Palmieri presents so effectively, cf. Σύντομος ἀπάντησις πρὸς τὸ λοιδωρὸν φυλλάδιον τοῦ δυτικοῦ ἀρχιεπισκόπου 'Ιουλιανοῦ Μαρία 'Ιλλερώ, Athens, 1884. In answer to Palmieri's three conclusions (*op. cit.,* pp. 654-655) it may be answered that Orthodoxy neither claims nor understands Infallibility in the sense in which the Roman Church uses it. The Orthodox answer (cf. Papadoupoulos above) is very much like the Anglican contention in regard to Roman claims. The lines upon which the so-called "Branch Theory" is developed are entirely consistent with the method in which Orthodoxy has acted, even though there is no explicit acceptance of the theory by the Orthodox Church.

interest in them is solely because they are sources for the
dogmatic teaching of the Orthodox Church. With the exception of the *Confession of Gennadius Scholarius,*[1] written
sometime between 1453 and 1468, all the remaining Symbolic
Books were the result entirely of the Reformation, directly or
indirectly. These texts include: (a) the *Answers* of the Patriarch Jeremiah II to the Tübingen theologians, of the years
1576, 1579, and 1581, which while they were written against
the Lutherans, yet have little polemic coloring, and do not
show a controversial spirit.[2] They deal practically with the

[1] Introduction and text in Mesolora *op. cit.*, I. pp. 66-67; on him
cf. Palmieri *op. cit.*, pp. 434-441; Greek-Turkish text, pp. 442-452, *ibid.*,
bibliography on Gennadius pp. 435-436 (note 2) *ibid.;* Papaioannes in
'Εκκλησιαστ. 'Αλήθεια, Constantinople, vol. XVIII. 1898, pp. 430-434;
vol. XIX. 1899, pp. 24-28. Androutsos disparages its value as a dogmatic text, "since it only deals with Christian doctrine in general
and does not concern itself with the differences in teaching in the
various Christian churches" (Συμβολική, p. 32).

[2] During the reign of Joasaph II. Patriarch of Constantinople
(1555-1565), relations between the Orthodox and the Lutherans were
initiated, which developed in 1573 in a mission of the Lutherans to
Constantinople. David Ungnad, Stephen Gerlach, Martin Crusius,
and Jacob Andreas were the prime movers in this negotiation, which as
Crucius testified was undertaken: *"ut ipsos ad nos perducere conati
sumus."* He naively writes: *"si aeternae animarum saluti consultum
isti cupiant, necesse est eos ad nos accedere, nostramque amplecti doc-
trinam aut in aeternum perire"* (*Prooemium* to *Acta et scripta theologorum wirtembergensium et Patriarchae Constantinopolitani. . . .*
Würtemberg, 1584; reprinted in 1758 at Leipzig by Gedeon Cyprius
(Latin and Greek)). The deputation brought a copy of the *Confession
of Augsburg* translated into Greek, together with letters from Crusius and Andreas. In the year 1576 Jeremiah II (Tranos, Patriarch
1572-1579, 1580-1584, 1588-1595), whom Meletios calls "a man endowed
with every virtue" ('Εκκλησιαστική 'Ιστορία, vol. III, pp. 401-404) wrote
his first *Answer*, discussing the Confession of Augsburg. (text in
Mesolora, I. pp. 124-194, preceded by historical notes and introduction,
pp. 78-123 *ibid.*). To this Crusius, Andreas, and Osiander wrote a response in 1578, which elicited Jeremiah's *Second Answer* the year following (text, Mesolora, *op. cit.*, I, pp. 195-247). The Lutherans wrote
again justifying their position, and Jeremiah's *Third Answer* (1581),
after discussing Free Will, the Sacraments, and the Invocation of
Saints, ends the discussion asking them to "go their own way and
not to write again on dogmatic matters, and if they do write, to do so
only on the score of friendship" (Mesolora, I, p. 264, whole text,
pp. 248-264 *ibid*). Palmieri says of the *Answers* that they expound

whole range of the Orthodox Faith, with special emphasis on matters of difference between Orthodoxy and Lutheranism. (b) The *Confession* of Metrophanes Kritopoulos, Patriarch of Alexandria, written at Helmstadt in 1625 at the request of Lutheran friends. It is so sympathetic with Protestant thought and so conversant with Protestant terminology as to lend color to the accusation of being heretical and not truly Orthodox.[1] (c) The *Orthodox Confession* of Peter Mogila, Met-

Orthodox doctrine by appealing to tradition, are without either the style or color of polemic, and are rightly included among the Symbolic Books (*op cit.*, p. 458, and cf. pp. 461-463 for the amusing outcome of Sokolov's book on the *Answers*).

[1] Born in 1599, Kritopoulos became a monk of Mt. Athos and was singled out for distinction by Cyril Lucar, who sent him to England, in 1616, where he studied at Oxford. He went to the Continent in 1623, traveled extensively, and in 1625 wrote his *Confession* ('Ομολογία τῆς ἀνατολικῆς 'Εκκλησίας). The autographed copy of the work is preserved in the library at Wolfenbüttel, of which the genuineness has been impugned by some Greek writers e. g., Sathas in his Νεοελληνικὴ φιλολογία, p. 298, and as strongly demonstrated by others (e. g., Andronicus Demetracopoulos, Δοκίμιον περὶ τοῦ βίου καὶ συγγραμμάτων Μητροφάνους τοῦ Κριτοπούλου, Leipzig, 1870, pp. 40-41; and in the 'Εκκλησιαστ. 'Αλήθεια, vol. III. 1882, pp. 634-636). It was published in Greek and Latin at Helmstadt in 1661, and the text (pp. 279-361), with an introduction (pp. 265-278) is given in Mesolora, Συμβολική, vol. I. It treats of the whole compass of the Orthodox Faith, and is distinguished by certain peculiarities: (a) his definition of the Church (Mesolora, *op. cit.*, I. p. 316) with which cf. the *Augsburg Confession*, part I. article VII; (b) the number of the Sacraments (Mesolora, *op. cit.*, I. p. 312-313); (c) his enumerations of the books of Holy Scripture (*ibid.*, pp. 318-319); (d) while he calls the effect of the consecration in the Mass a "change" (μεταβολή,) he says: "The manner of this charge is unknown to us and inexplicable . . It may only be apprehended through faith" (*ibid.*, pp. 327-328). It is to be noticed that he does not use the term *transubstantiation*. Though it be only a private and personal profession of faith, it rightly holds its place among the Symbolic Books of Orthodoxy, according to Mesolora, (*ibid.*, pp. 277-278) who regards it as entirely Orthodox. Mazarakis declares it clear and free from every taint of Protestantism (Μητροφάνης Κριτόπℓυλος, Πατ. 'Αλεξ...., Cairo, 1884, p. 45). Androutsos says that those who fasten on such details as these, miss the whole point of the *Confession*, and wrongly impute Protestant opinions to Kritopoulos (Συμβολική, p. 37). Palmieri (*op. cit.*, pp. 573-576) says: *Constat sententias lutheranas haud semel in Confessionem Metrophanis irrepsisse, eisque adstipulari disertis verbis Metrophanem declarasse. Ergo neque characterem privatae Confessionis ei vindicandum ducimus.*

ropolitan of Kiev (b. 1596, d. 1646), which appeared in Greek for the first time in its present form probably about 1667.[1] There are two works of Mogila—the *Confession* and an Orthodox *Catechism*—and they are often confused, since both are written in the catechetical style. There is a difference in teaching between them, and the mystery of the relationship between the two has not yet been solved. A synod in 1640 at Kiev, having examined a catechism submitted to it by Mogila, amplified it and then endorsed it. Mogila then submitted it to the Patriarch (Nectarius) of Constantinople, who turned it over to the council of Jassy (1642) where it was subject to revision, and then finally (1643?) endorsed by a synod at Constantinople. The *Catechism* was published

[1] Following Legrand, *Bibliographie hellénique* (XVII. *siècle*) vol. IV. Paris, 1896, and vol. II. *ibid.*, p. 204; cf. Mesolora's introduction, *op. cit.*, I. pp. 362-369. Mogila had two practical difficulties with which to deal: (a) the Roman Church, with its strong hold on Poland, the policy of the Uniat movement, and the presence of Jesuits; and (b) Protestantism, which had no inconsiderable influence at this juncture on Orthodoxy, disrupted by the defection of Cyril Lucar, and unable to cope with Western scholarship and learning. The first sentence of the *Confession* comes into sharp conflict with Protestantism on the subject of faith and works, (cf. Mesolora, *op. cit.*, I. p. 376), while the treatment of the *Filioque* (*ibid.*, pp. 412-413) leaves no room for the suspicion of a pro-Roman tendency. Its final endorsement by Nectarius of Constantinople, Joannicius of Alexandria, Macarius of Antioch, Paisius of Jerusalem, nine metropolitans, and others, in 1662, set the seal of Orthodox official approval on the *Confession*. (Cf. Parthenius' Encyclical and the list of signatories, *op. cit.*, pp. 370-375.) Its value has been variously estimated by Orthodox writers. Damalas (Περὶ ἀρχῶν, Leipzig, 1863, p. 9.) considers it to be "an Orthodox Catechism which neither from its writer nor from the synod which endorsed it . . . has any claim to ecumenical character or weight." "It is a full and perfect symbolic text, woven together and worked with the greatest skill and subtlety, and at the same time a perfect talisman for dogma and morals, both in faith and practice, for the Orthodox Christian" (The Protosynkellos Chrysostom, in Περὶ Ἐκκλησίας, vol. I. p. 6). Androutsos says of it: "While the distinction of *substance* and his divisions and subdivisions are not all useful, and certain chapters, especially those on the Sacraments and the seven deadly sins, are obviously strongly under the influence of scholastic theology, yet the work of Mogila on the whole breathes the spirit of the Orthodox Eastern Church in all its pristine character, . . . and remains permanently a most precious monument of Orthodoxy and a wholesome aid in the study of Symbolic" (Συμβολική, p. 35). Balanos, on the

first in 1621, and the *Confession,* possibly soon after its endorsement in 1643-5, the great edition being the aforementioned one of 1667. The *Confession* is divided into three sections, on *Faith, Hope,* and *Love,* and in a popular and brief style treats of the fundamentals of Orthodoxy. (d) The *Acts*[1] of the Synods of Constantinople (1638), Jassy (1641-1642), Jerusalem (1672),[2] and Constantinople (1672). Of these

other hand, depreciates its value since "it is a Catechism, and must be regarded as such. No catechism can ever be more than a production of its own time, and do more than follow the spiritual condition contemporaneous with it" (Εἶναι ἡ ὀρθόδοξος Ἑλληνικὴ Ἐκκλησία μόνον κοινωνία λατρείας; Athens, 1904, p. 9). For complete text of the *Confession,* cf. Mesolora, *op. cit.,* I. pp. 376-487; and on Mogila, the critical problems connected with the text, chronology, bibliography, and Russian opinion, cf. Palmieri, *op. cit.,* I, pp. 537-563. English editions of the text are in *The Doctrine of the Russian Church, translated from the Slavano-Russian Original,* W. Blackmore, Aberdeen, 1845; *The Orthodox Confession of the Catholic and Apostolic Eastern Church,* from the Version of Peter Mogila, translated into English, with preface by J. J. Overbeck, and introductory notice by J. N. Robertson, London, 1898; cf. also *The Teaching of the Russian Church,* by A. C. Headlam, London, 1897, and *History, Authority,* and *Theology,* by the same, Milwaukee, 1910, especially chapters, V, VI, and VII.

[1] These *Acts* are all in Mesolora, *op. cit.,* vol. II. On pp. 7-24 he gives a history of Cyril Lucar leading up to an introduction to the Synod of Constantinople (pp. 24-28), acts of the same (pp. 28-32); introduction to the Synod of Jassy (pp. 32-37), the two *Epistles,* (pp. 37-42); introduction to the Council of Jerusalem (pp. 43-54), and text of the *Acts* (pp. 55-87).

[2] The alleged *Confession* of Cyril Lucar (b. 1572, d. 1638), published in Geneva in 1629, was the occasion of all of these synods, the basis of their decrees, and in large measure the cause which called them together. It is published in English by J. N. Robertson, *The Acts and Decrees of the Synod of Jerusalem . . . with an Appendix containing the Confession published with the name of Cyril Lucar, condemned by the Synod.* London, 1899. Like Metrophanes Kritopoulos, of whom we spoke above, Cyril Lucar is of interest to Anglican Churchmen, for he gave the celebrated uncial Manuscript, *Codex Alexandrinus,* to Sir Thomas Roe, King Charles I's Ambassador to Turkey, from whom it came into the possession of the British Museum where it is at present. He is a most interesting personage, was very much in contact with all of the movements of his time, and his effect on his Church during and after his life-time was far-reaching. In 1601 he was raised to the throne of the Patriarchate of Alexandria. As an illustration of the extraordinary character of the times, and of the relation between the Sublime Porte and the Phanar, it may be said in passing that after

Synods, by far the most significant is that of Jerusalem. All of them dealt with practical problems arising out of the *Confession* of Cyril Lucar, which was strongly Calvinistic in tone. The difficulties of the Orthodox Church were many—pressure

his first election to the Patriarchate of Constantinople (1612) he held the position of Patriarch six times, with intervals between his reigns (1620-1623; 1623-1630; 1630-1633; 1633-1634; 1634-1635; 1637-1638). The publication of the *Confession* which purported to be by him, in 1629, was followed by a Greek edition in 1633. It aroused a great storm among the Orthodox, and was greeted with acclamation by the Continental Protestants. Theophanus II. of Jerusalem, repudiated in Cyril's name his authorship of the *Confession*. After Cyril Lucar's execution in 1638, a Cyril Contarene succeeded to the throne for the third time, who immediately called a Synod which met in Constantinople that same year, and condemned both Cyril Lucar and his doctrines (text, in Mesolora, II, pp. 28-32). All the Calvinistic doctrines which had been enunciated under Lucar's name in the *Confession* were strongly repudiated in this ψῆφος ("Vote"). Jerusalem and Alexandria, together with twenty-one bishops and twenty-three prelates and clergy, signed the decree. Of the results Mesolora says: "The Acts of this synod rightly formulate the teaching of the Orthodox Church . . . Cyril Contarene showed then and now . . . that the Eastern Orthodox Church does not tolerate any Protestant innovations" (*ibid.*, p. 25). The *Acts* of the Synod of Jassy (the capital of the then principality of Moldavia, now part of Roumania) consist only of two Synodical Epistles: (a) to the Synod in Jassy from Parthenius I. Patriarch of Constantinople (successor of Cyril Contarene—1639-1644); (b) to the Duke of Moldavia from the Synod itself. Forty-five prelates attended, among whom was Peter Mogila. The significance of this Synod lies chiefly in the fact that "at it were assembled both Greeks and Russians, who showed the Jesuits and the Protestants that the Orthodox Church was alive, that she preserved her dogmas unshaken, . . . and rejected all Western innovations" (Mesolora, *op. cit.*, II, p. 36). The first Epistle emanated, as was said above, from Constantinople, and dealt in turn with each of the propositions of the *Confession* attributed to Lucar, save that on Christology. It is significant, however, that these articles were condemned without including the person of Cyril Lucar, showing that Parthenius was unwilling to fasten their authorship on him. As a matter of fact, the "Synod" of Jassy was merely an extension of that of Constantinople, and practically met only to confirm the condemnation of the propositions of the alleged Lucarian *Confession*. The Synod of Jerusalem (1672) is by all comparison the most important. As its Acts declare, it was assembled to bear witness to the Orthodox Faith and to repudiate Lutheran and Calvinistic doctrines of whatever sort. The occasion of the convocation of this Synod was the dedication of the renovated sanctuary of the Nativity at Bethlehem, which served Dositheus the Patriarch of Jeru-

from Continental Protestantism, from Roman proselytism under French protection, and the normal difficulties of the Church under Turkish domination. *The Confession of Faith* of Dositheus, appended to the *Acts* of the Synod of Jerusalem, con-

salem as a proper season, time, and place, to obtain an explicit ratification of the Orthodox Faith at the hands of a large concourse of prelates and clergy. The *Acts* survive in two documents—"the Shield of the Orthodox Faith" and the "Confession of Faith," (text, Mesolora, II. pp. 55-86, and pp. 103-129). Both are probably due to Dositheus. The purpose of the former was two-fold: (a) to inveigh against Protestantism, and (b) to clear the name of Lucar from the imputation of having written the *Confession* published ostensibly as his work. Mesolora sets a very high value indeed on these Acts, saying that they show how the Orthodox Church has faithfully adhered to her Saviour's teaching, has kept the middle way between two extremes of error, and displays "the spirit of the ancient Church in opposition . . . to the opinions of both the Romans and the Protestants . . . " (*op. cit.*, II, pp. 48-49). *The Confession of Faith* is a document of very great value. It is alluded to in the sixth chapter of the "Shield", and is an integral part of the *Acts* of the Synod. It is arranged in the decrees, which Mesolora (*op. cit.*, pp. 91-99) has compared with corresponding passages in the *Confession* attributed to Lucar. It is a closely knit, carefully worked out summary of theological doctrine, in its phraseology very strongly impregnated with scholastic terminology, and in the exactness of its language and dialectical distinctions refreshingly clear and lucid. It employs the term *transubstantiation* (Mesolora, II. p. 117); explicitly states the necessity of both faith and works (*ibid.*, p. 112); teaches a state of purgation after death, without calling it purgatory (*ibid.*, pp. 119-120); and the *questions* at the end deal with certain practical matters in a manner utterly repugnant to Protestantism. In his *Enchiridion* (1690) he retracted somewhat from his teaching as to the state of the dead, but reaffirmed very strongly his eucharistic doctrine. With slight changes the *Confession* of Faith of Dositheus was embodied in the *Answer* of the Patriarchs of Constantinople, Antioch, and Jerusalem, to the Non-Jurors in 1723. The same *Confession* was translated into Russian in 1728, and a century later was published in a form showing considerable revision —*e. g.*, Dositheus teaches the indelible character of Baptism as well as Holy Order (Mesolora, II. p. 116); Philaret of Moscow expunged this, as he did the section on the Deutero-Canonical books of the Old Testament, the denial of the permission for all to read the Bible, etc. Palmieri says: *Confessio Dosithei praecipuum tenet locum inter symbolica graecae Ecclesiae documenta* (*op. cit.*, I, p. 503). Mesolora sets the highest value on it (*op. cit.*, II. pp. 89, 91), though by his silence Androutsos seems to regard it as do other Orthodox writers, disparagingly (*e. g.*, Macarius, Sylvester, and many of the Russians, on whom cf. Palmieri, *ibid.*, pp. 504-505). So Chrysostom Papadopou-

tains matter of fundamental value for the student of modern Orthodox theology. The last Synod (Constantinople, 1672)[1] did little of import. Its acts are mostly of a practical character, and concern discipline and practice rather than dogma and theology.

los would minimize its Latin cast of thought (Νέα Σιών, 1907, vol. V. pp. 104-108) saying that "the influence of Latin theology was entirely external and ought not be overemphasized. This superficial similarity of expression in its teaching ought not be regarded as identity in thought" (with Latin theology) (in Δοσίθεος, Πατριάρχης Ἱεροσολύμων, Jerusalem, 1907, p. 32).

The question as to the authenticity of Lucar's *Confession*, which document provoked all of the synods discussed above, is too vast to be entered upon here. (A very full bibliography is given in Palmieri, *op. cit.*, pp. 464-468, notes; and pp. 506-507, notes.) Mesolora states that "Cyril did not write the *Confession* attributed to him, but some other person, possibly a Latin, in order to slander him with the imputation of Calvinism" (*op. cit.*, II, p. 18). Sathas (in Νεοελληνικὴ φιλολογία, p. 244) denies his authorship of it and attributes it to Protestants. Chrysostom Papadopoulos repudiates the imputation that Lucar wrote the *Confession* ('Απολογία Κυρίλλου τοῦ Λουκάρεως, in Νέα Σιών, vol. II. 1905, pp. 17-35; ibid., vol. V. 1907, pp. 525-533; *ibid.*, Κύριλλος Λούκαρις, Tergesti, 1907, etc.), as does Ezechiel Velandiotes, ('Ο 'Εθνόμαρτυς Κύριλλος Λούκαρις, Athens, 1906). On the other hand, Renieris (Κύριλλος Λούκαρις, ὁ οἰκουμενικὸς Πατριάρχης, Athens, 1889, pp. 54-55), Demetrius Balanos ('Η 'Ομολογία Κυρίλλου τοῦ Λουκάρεως, Athens, 1906, p. 5), and Androutsos (Συμβολική p., 33) are convinced that he did, whether from purely religious motives and by conviction (Balanos), or under the pressure of circumstances (Androutsos). The *Confession* is certainly not a document of the Orthodox Church. Palmieri's discussion is in *op. cit.*, pp. 464-537, (vol. I.).

[1] It was convened by Dionysius IV, five times Patriarch of Constantinople (1671-1673; 1676-1679; 1683-1684; 1686-1687; 1693-1694), as an answer to difficulties propounded to the Orthodox Church, many of which reflect Protestant stimulation. The *Acts* deal with the Sacraments, the Eucharist (as a "transmutation" of the elements) infant baptism, the arch-episcopate, the marriage of clergy, the Church, ikons, fasting, and the canon of Holy Scripture. Introduction in Mesolora, vol. II. pp. 130-139, text, pp. 139-145. He also adds the account of another small synod in 1691 at Constantinople (pp. 147-150) the chief work of which was the confirmation of the acts of the Synod of Jerusalem, and a reiteration of the doctrine of *transubstantiation*, which Mesolora says "constitutes the one important act of the Synod" (p. 149 *ibid.*). He does not give the texts of the *Acts*. The strong justification and vindication of the term by this Synod is not without great theological interest. Text in Mansi-Petit, vol. XXXVII, and the passage in question, in column 465.

Despite the fact that Orthodoxy and Protestantism have in common as essential characteristics a strongly anti-Roman and anti-Papal bias, despite the fact also that they both appeal to primitive Christianity, the upshot of all the negotiations between Continental Protestantism and the Orthodox Church was the discovery that there really was nothing fundamental in theology or spirit upon the basis of which Orthodox and Protestantism could unite. It is significant that with the exception of the abortive attempt of the Non-Jurors, no Anglican advances have yet met Orthodox repudiation. All of the later synods direct their fulminations against Calvinistic and Lutheran doctrines. It is also significant that in the main the development of Greek theology has paralleled that of the Western Church. The doctrine of Grace, the Church, and the Sacraments is indigenous, legitimate, and inevitable in both East and West. In both East and West the formulation of doctrine has taken place subsequent to the Schism between the Eastern and Western Churches.

I. THE DOCTRINE OF GRACE

1. The Nature of Grace

During the sixteenth and seventeeth centuries the minds of men in the West were occupied with questions concerning the doctrine of grace, faith, free-will, predestination, and the efficacy of the sacraments. To this movement of thought in the West, with its parallel effect in Orthodox circles, we are indebted for the explicit definition of Orthodox teaching on these matters. The doctrine of Grace has a very wide range of contact in any Christian dogmatic system. In Orthodox doctrine this is particularly true. (a) It is bound up with the doctrine of God, since God who is preëminently good, and acts freely in all He does, freely created man of His own goodness and benevolence. So it is of His nature as Christians know it, that He give to man, beyond man's deserts and without the consideration of expediency or of a covenant obligation, what is so essential to man's needs. In this sense Rhôsse speaks of the Grace of the Holy Spirit of God coöperating with man's natural endowment, the coöperation of man with it constituting his pristine state of righteousness and innocence.[1] (b) The doctrine of Grace is closely knit up with the teaching about man, who being created by God with relative free-will, endowed by Him with all he needed to lead a life of happiness in obedience to God, was yet to be sustained by God's constant protection and empowering oversight. Still more did man after his Fall stand in need of that without which he could never hope for recovery, the gift of which is so entirely consistent with God's Nature and Essence. (c) The doctrine of Grace is intimately connected with the problem of man's free-will and God's Providence, His Foreknowledge, and Foreordination. (d) Preëminently is the doctrine of Grace involved in the dogma of Redemption, for by Grace only can man appropriate the fruits of the redemptive and atoning work of the Saviour and make them effective in his own individual life. As Christian dogma forms a unified whole, so the whole nexus of doctrine, especially in its practical religious and moral bearings, is permeated with the teaching about Grace. It is obvious also that this doctrine constitutes the starting point and basis for all of the rest of Orthodox dogmatic. Androutsos' definition of Grace involves its relation to the doctrine of the Church and of the Sacraments.

"Grace is", he says,[2] "the divine power by which we appropriate the redemptive work of Our Lord. Since it works the justification and salvation of man it depends upon certain subjective conditions in him. It is stored up in the Church, and administered through the Sacraments....In general, it is the manifestation of the love and benevolence of God towards man; in particular, it means the saving power of God by which. He brings home to each individual the Redemption consummated for all by Our Lord, regenerating and cultivating the life in Christ and preparing (man) for eternal life." "By the death of our Lord on the Cross, who was the Mediator between God and Man, mankind was reconciled with its God and Father, thereby was reëstablished the re-

---

[1] Rhôsse, Δογματική, p. 434.

[2] Androutsos, Δογματική, pp. 218-219. He takes occasion to note the various distinctions and definitions, such as "prevenient and concomitant", "external and internal", etc. of scholastic terminology, but says that they are "without actual content or significance" (ibid.).

lation of fellowship with God, sundered because of original sin, and God's saving Grace made known to man. This Grace we need to lay hold of through faith in Christ generated by love, by which we become God's children.... The redeeming work of the Saviour is called divine Grace because by it salvation is bestowed from God on us . . . The continuous operation and energy of the Holy Spirit is also (called) divine Grace . . . In this sense, then, it may be defined as that supernatural power of the Holy Spirit by which the appropriation of the redeeming work of the Saviour is achieved."[1] In the divine economy the ministry of Grace is the work of the Holy Spirit, while our Lord is the cause of our receiving it. This is testified in Holy Scripture, and is the reason for calling the Holy Ghost, "the Spirit of Christ."[2] The term is applied not to natural helps towards righteousness, nor to the example of Our Lord's life, nor to God's law or will, but to that "power which regenerates and nourishes the spiritual life, given freely by God and not by reason of our merit."[3]

We may distinguish three characteristic notes of Grace, all of which are essential to the true conception of it. It is (a) absolutely necessary, (b) it is free, and (c) it is universal. It is absolutely *necessary* "since man cannot be justified and saved by his own works, nor could he even believe unless Christ first draw him, and unless . . . his will be aroused by some higher energy."[4] Man could not attain communion with God by his own efforts, nor secure the necessary nourishment for his own spiritual life.[5] He could not secure deliverance from sin, actual or original, by anything he can do of himself. Grace is, in short, as necessary as was Redemption: if the work of Christ was an unnecessary work on God's part, then so is Grace unnecessary, as the Pelagians held.[6]

---

[1] Mesolora, *op. cit.*, III. pp. 243-244.

[2] Rom. 8, 9; Gal. 4, 6; Acts 1, 8; St. John 6, 44; Acts 2, 33; 10, 44; Eph. 3, 5; Róm. 5, 5.

[3] Androutsos, *ibid.*

[4] Mesolora, *ibid.*, p. 247, and cf. St. John 3, 5.

[5] St. John 6, 44.

[6] Androutsos, *op. cit.*, p. 221, and cf. Mesolora, *op. cit.*, p. 246. The Pelagians were condemned by the Council of Carthage, cf. Canons 113 (124).

Grace is, secondly, *free,* as the very word implies. This means that it is based upon no human covenant, whereby it is given by God as the fulfilment of a promise or an obligation. It is not a return for human merit or deserving, but a free gift of God's love.[1] No righteous action of man can be presumed upon as the cause of God's Grace being given to him. Even in the case of Cornelius (Acts 10, 35) it was not "natural powers which made the bridge by which the natural man enters into the domain of grace", for the chasm between grace and nature is impassable by man. "The word *grace* does not mean 'something given in return' (ἀποδιδόμενον) but a 'gift freely given', bestowed purely out of the divine Love."[2] "It is of God to give Grace—of man, to receive it."[3]

Thirdly, grace is *universal,* but not *irresistible.* "The Grace of Redemption is offered to all men, calling them to salvation and assisting them to every good work. If some accept the call, many on the other hand approach . . . but fall away from it, which phenomenon is to be attributed to the free will of man who may accept or reject the call and fall from Grace. Since all that happens in time and in the world is constituted by the eternal will and design of God, and the Redemption in a very special sense is, as we have seen, the carrying out of God's eternal Will, it is clear that the election of some to life in Christ and the rejection of others are things determined and decreed before the world by God. Before the foundation of the world He chose them, foreordaining some to eternal life, and others to eternal condemnation."[4] This third aspect of the doctrine of Grace involves the problem of free-will and predestination, which has already been considered in part in Lecture II.[5]

God's foreknowledge belongs to His character as omnis-

[1] Rom. 9, 11, 18; 11, 6; 2 Tim. 1, 9; Tit. 3, 5.

[2] Androutsos, *op. cit.,* pp. 222-223.

[3] Mesolora, *op. cit.,* III, p. 248, and cf. p. 247; cf. St. Augustine, *De peccato originali,* 24; *non enim gratia gratia erit ullo modo, nisi gratuita fuerit omni modo.* Cf. Jeremiah II, in Mesolora, *op. cit.,* I, pp. 170-173; 215-218; 260-263; Mogila *ibid.,* p. 391; Dositheus, II. pp. 103-104; Kritopoulos, I. p. 310 and Macarius, *op. cit.,* II. pp. 338-341.

[4] Androutsos, *loc. cit.*

[5] Pp. 93-100.

cient; He knows all the future as well as the present and the past.   According to Rhôsse, God knows the acts of His free creatures only in general, not as to their actual content.   If He knows not only all that man can do, but in detail what He will do, then (a) He becomes partaker in this sense in what man does, whether for good or evil, and (b) man's free will is lost.   Hence God must know man's acts relatively not absolutely, and in general not in particular.[1]   Androutsos says that God does know what is going to happen in every possible instance, but that His knowledge exercises no influence on such acts.   "The events are known by God because they exist, and do not exist because He knows them."   His foreknowledge does not determine events but merely foresees them.[2]   This foreknowledge on God's part does not make Him a cause of, or sharer in, the acts which are contrary to His will for good: His Providence overrules all such acts and brings good out of evil.   His final end and ultimate purpose in Creation He will not suffer to miscarry.   God's foreknowledge, according to Mesolora, is that divine power by which God foresees all things that are to happen, whether the works and thoughts of man or whatever is dependent upon man as a rational creature endowed with free will.   "But it does not follow that because God foresees all things, that He is the cause of them all; consequently, He does not *foresee* everything in the absolute sense of *foreordination*, but according to His foreknowing will and power He foreordains those things which are not in man's province . . . such as Creation, the salvation of mankind," and the like.[3]   St. John Damascene writes: "It is well to know how it is that God foresees everything, yet does not foreordain everything.   He foresees even the things which have to do with us, but does not foreordain them, since He neither wishes evil to happen nor is constrained by virtue so that the work of His foreseeing will should be foreordination.   He foreordains what does not concern us according to His foreknowledge, according to which also God judges all things in advance according to His goodness and

---

[1] *Op. cit.*, pp. 316-324.
[2] *Op. cit.*, pp. 66-67; 118-119.
[3] *Op. cit.*, III, p. 192.

righteousness."[1] "This foreknowledge", says Mesolora, "does not abrogate either man's reason or his free-will, because it depends upon us whether we remain in virtue or renounce it. . . Nor does it contravene either the goodness or righteousness of God, who wills that all be saved and all come to the knowledge of the truth. . . .The foreordination which St. Paul speaks of (in Rom. 8, 29-30) is founded upon the foreknowledge of God, which takes for granted the existence of the rational use by man of his natural light, or the innate law of God in him. . . . .together with his free will. God knows in advance those who are to be worthy of His Grace, which prevents, helps, and calls all men, of whom some by the right use of their reason, will, and knowledge of the good, lay hold of it and are thereby justified, and others, making no use of these faculties,. . . .stand apart from God, and are thus self-ordained to condemnation; while God foresaw what they would do. . . .He did not foreordain them to it, inasmuch as He simply knew in advance what would happen. . . . So these as *foreknown,* God *foreordains.* . . .and as foreordained, He calls them through the Holy Spirit, whom receiving as working with them to receive His Grace, He justifies. . . . .So the cause of the merit of the elect and of their righteousness is not the foreknowledge of God. . . . . . Our Church teaches that God foresees all things but does not foreordain all things: He foreordains the things which are not in our province, according to His foreknowledge. . . .'By grace we are saved', ...for Grace goes before, and the will of man follows after, and accepts it."[2] "We believe that God knows in advance through His omniscience those who are 'to be conformed to the image of His Son,'[3] in life and deed, by the coöperation of con-

---

[1] Ἔκδοσις, II. 47, and cf. 46.

[2] Mesolora, *op. cit.,* III. pp. 193-195. This is a summary of the teaching of the Symbolic Books, of which cf. Kritopoulos on Rom. 8, 29-30, in Mesolora, I, p. 308; Mogila, *ibid.,* pp. 390-391, 393; Synods of Jassy and Jerusalem, vol. II. pp. 29, 38, 64-65; Dositheus, *ibid.,* p. 105; Gennadius' *De divina providentia et praedestinatione tractatus;* Eugenius Bulgaris, *Theologikon,* c. 28 (Greek ed., pp. 175-210); Jeremiah's II's first and second *Answers,* Mesolora, *op. cit.,* I. pp. 170, 215, etc.

[3] Rom. 8, 29.

comitant and prevenient Grace.[1] These also He foreordained, according to His righteousness and goodness, to enjoy eternal life and divine glory."[2] According to Androutsos, "this fore-ordination of some men to destruction and of others to salvation is not arbitrary and absolute, but relative. . . . It is based upon the foreknowledge of God, but without prejudice to the free-will of man. Hence the foreordination of man is dependent upon human conditions, and no one. ... .can be sure whether he will remain in Grace, or. . . .absolutely sure that he is predestined to life or that he will be saved. Both these truths, the universality of Grace and of the call (to salvation), and the foreordination of man, relative because of his free-will, are clearly taught by the Church[3] and the Bible[4] . . . The many references in Holy Scripture to conversion,. . . .and the other promises and threats,[5] have no meaning if Grace operates necessarily. . . . Man becomes subject to Grace voluntarily, and it never coerces him. This freedom constitutes his ethical worth and his merit."[6] Mesolora brings out strongly the two-fold character of the doctrine of Grace. "The energy of the Holy Spirit (in Grace). . . .does not take away man's free-will, which remains always unharmed, nor does (Grace) compel it, for then

---

[1] This differentiation of the kinds of grace into "illuminating" or "prevenient" ($\phi\omega\tau\iota\sigma\tau\iota\kappa\acute{\eta}$, $\pi\rho\omega\kappa\alpha\tau\alpha\rho\kappa\tau\iota\kappa\acute{\eta}$,) and "concomitant", "personal", "coöperating", and "enabling" ($\sigma\upsilon\nu\epsilon\rho\gamma\omega\widehat{\upsilon}\sigma\alpha$, $\iota\delta\iota\kappa\acute{\eta}$ [$\epsilon\iota\delta\iota\kappa\acute{\eta}$], $\epsilon\nu\delta\upsilon\nu\alpha\mu\omega\widehat{\upsilon}\sigma\alpha$,) is due to Dositheus *Confession*, article 3 (cf. for text Mesolora, *op. cit.*, II, p. 104), on which Mesolora says: "Although we distinguish the divine Grace in the redeeming work of the Saviour from that which coöperates with man's free will in appropriating the former, yet the unity of Grace as one whole is not taken away by this distinction" (*op. cit.*, III, p. 224, note 2).

[2] Mesolora, *op. cit.*, III., p. 199.

[3] Thus clearly in Dositheus' *Confession*, in Mesolora, *op. cit.*, II. pp. 64-65, 104-105.

[4] Cf. 1 Tim. 2, 4, 6; 2 Cor. 5, 15; 1 St. John 2, 2; St. Mt. 20, 16 (in *textus receptus*, 16b has "many be called, but few chosen—" MSS. *Aleph*. B. L. etc., have this; cf. St. Matt. 22, 14.) Rev. 3, 20; Acts. 7, 51.

[5] Cf. Prov. 1, 24-25; Isaiah. 5, 4; 65, 2; St. Matt. 11, 21; Ezek. 18, 23; St. Matt. 3, 8; Acts 2, 38; 2 Cor. 6, 17; 1 Thess. 5, 19; 2 St. Pet. 3, 9; Rev. 3, 19, 20, etc.

[6] Androutsos, $\Delta o\gamma\mu\alpha\tau\iota\kappa\acute{\eta}$, pp. 224-225; cf. St. John Chrysostom, Theodoret, etc. note 8, pp. 225-226 *ibid*.

his regeneration. . . .would have no moral value.. ..Redemption was wrought because of the wrong use of man's free-will. Without this free-will divine Grace could neither uplift, illuminate, nor save man. . . . The Orthodox Church" (in contrast to the over-emphasis of the West on the importance of Grace as against Pelagianism, and on works as against Protestantism)[1] "has kept a middle road, teaching that man's salvation is achieved first through Grace. . . .and secondly_through the free acceptance of it by man. . . . The Saviour proclaimed this truth, saying 'whosoever will to come after me'.[2] The free will of man is the determining factor and the basis for the operation of divine Grace.'"[3] "Man needs to appropriate, or to make his own, the merit of Christ, first through divine Grace, that is, through the operation and help of the Holy Spirit of God, and secondly, through his own effort and choice by the power of his free will."[4] These two factors theoretically involve contradictory and irreconcilable notions. "If in theory we are unable to understand how the circle of human freedom operates in God without violating His Absolute character, yet in practice we may not dispose of the human factor, which cutting the Gordian knot of the theoretical difficulties, offers a solution which satisfies human instinct. The omnipotence of God respects human freedom, which is the basis of the existence of the moral world. Otherwise, sacrificing human freedom and regarding Grace as absolute, we fall into the errors of absolute predestination."[5]

[1] Cf. *op. cit.*, III, pp. 245-246.
[2] Cf. St. Matt. 16, 24; St. Mark 8, 34; St. Luke 9, 23; Rev. 22, 7.
[3] Mesolora, *op. cit.*, III. pp. 245-247.
[4] *Ibid.*, p. 252, which is his summary of the teaching of the Symbolic Books given *ad loc.*
[5] Androutsos, *op. cit.*, 227. The doctrine of absolute predestination is founded on such texts as Rom. 8, 29-30; Eph. 1, 4-11; Phil. 2, 13; 1 Cor. 4, 7, and the whole 9th Chapter of Romans. Androutsos says: "The Apostle does not here deal with the subjective factor of God's energy, that is, man's free will, but neither does he rule it out . . . In many other places he speaks of this human factor (*e. g.*, 2 Cor. 6, 1; 1 Thes. 1, 6; 1 Cor. 1, 21; Rom. 1, 16; Phil. 2, 12; Rom. 8, 32; 11, 32; 1 Tim. 2, 4; Tit. 2, 11, etc.) as a condition of salvation...and as often as he talks about foreordination to salvation he everywhere presupposes an analogous disposition on the

2. THE OPERATION OF GRACE

The operation of Grace in the concrete is regarded properly as a process—a progress and development of the individual in the Christian life, beginning with conversion and regeneration and ending in the glory to which man is called. Six states of this progress have been enumerated by different Orthodox theologians: the *call, conversion, regeneration, justification sanctification,* and *mystical union.* Thus Antonius[1] and Mesolora.[2] Androutsos does not see the necessity of this division and on the basis of Rom. 8, 29-30 distinguishes: (a) "the *call,* or *conversion* or *preparation for justification,* (b) *justification* or *sanctification,* and (c) *glory,*—in which *justification* holds the middle place following the *call* and preceding *glory.*"[3] These three stages only he regards as necessary.[4] (a) The *call* is comprised of two elements—the external, the preaching of the word, and the internal, the receptive attitude of man by which he through Grace accepts the invitation of God. This action of Grace on the inner man creates the *fidem informem,* by which he is disposed to accept God's revelation, and directly affects his whole spiritual nature, bringing into him the graces of faith, hope, and love.[5] "This preparation is the *sine qua non*

part of man, which . . . constitutes the reason explaining God's condemnation or His approval . . . Protestantism naturally and necessarily holds to the notion of absolute predestination; naturally, since it regards the natural man as spiritually and morally dead (*i. e.,* totally depraved) and hence God's Grace must be the sole factor in salvation, and as such cannot be lost or escaped; and necessarily, since it is inevitable that the doctrine of absolute predestination and of irresistible Grace result from these premises" (*op. cit.,* pp. 226-228) ; cf. his Συμβολική for a more extended treatment of the subject, pp. 198-204 ff.; *Confession* of Dositheus, in Mesolora, *op. cit.,* II, pp. 104-105, and Mesolora, III. pp. 252-254.

[1] *Op. cit.,* pp. 275 ff.
[2] *Op. cit.,* III. pp. 254-269.
[3] *Op. cit.,* pp. 229-230.
[4] "Most of these (above six) distinctions are, on examination,... seen to be only different expressions or aspects of the same thing" (p. 229 *ibid.*). This view is subject to Dyobouniotes' censure in his Ἡ Δογμ. ᾽Ανδρ. κριν., p. 41, and his ᾽Οφειλομένη ἀπάντ., pp. 99-101, who maintains that they are valid and real distinctions, marking different steps and grades in the way of salvation.
[5] Cf. Dositheus in Mesolora, *op. cit.,* II, p. 104.

and condition of justification....not the efficient cause of it."
Man cannot merit the gift of justifying Grace in the sense that
God is bound to give it to him in return for his meritorious
acts.

(b) "Justification as an actual change in man is both the
doing away with sin and guilt, and the implanting of a new
life;....negatively, the remission of sins, and positively, sanctification. So justification and salvation are often used interchangeably, and it may be said either that man is *justified* or
that he is *saved,* by faith and works. If men died immediately
after justification they are saved, just as much as, if they live
thence forward without falling from Grace, they are potentially
inheritors of eternal life which is dependent on justification.
The two elements, forgiveness of sins and sanctification, are
not separate from each other in time as if sanctification followed
upon cleansing from sin, but they are two aspects of one and
the same thing.... This remission of sins is no mere imputation of freedom from sin....but an actual effacement of it....
The judge in pronouncing an accused man innocent does not
make him so, but only publicly proclaims him what he already
is. But God in judging a sinner does not regard him as righteous while he is a sinner, but makes him actually righteous....
The state of sin is removed entirely by God's power in the act
of justification. We say 'entirely' because while the impulse
to sin yet remains in the justified, it is not accounted to him
as sin, since his will does not follow the tendency of this impulse
to sin.... The principle and basis of sin, the perversion of the
will, is entirely removed and the regenerate will is borne Godward.... The assertion that the energies of sin, however they
may be defined, cannot be removed, cannot be explained in any
other way than on the hypothesis either (a) that God cannot
do this—in which case sin would be regarded as being of too
great power for even the Almighty to break....or (b) that
God does not wish to do away with sin—which violates the idea
of God as merciful, and is in opposition to the whole economy
of Redemption."[1] Androutsos rejects every theory of there being two justifications—one in which a sinner is pronounced
righteous and one in which he has actually attained righteous-

[1] Δογματική, pp. 231-233.

ness.[1] Consequently God does not call a man righteous in whom there is only "righteousness in germ", "potential righteousness", but makes him actually what he pronounces him to be. In opposing this theory Androutsos asks: "From whence does this state of 'potential righteousness' proceed? From man, or from God? If you answer, 'from man', then this is Pelagianism.... if you say 'from God', then you hold to the Roman doctrine of infused Grace....and regard the justification coming through Baptism as being only such 'in germ'!"

Justification is then "the principle (and beginning) of a new life developed gradually through the free will of the justified,"[2] and in this sense, with emphasis on the progressive and developing character of the process, Mesolora understands it. After quoting Rom. 3, 24, he defines justification as "the proclaiming of a man as righteous (just) by God, and regarding him as such before Him, for the sake of the objective Justification wrought by Jesus by His death on the Cross.[3] This justification is only potentially that final and complete justification which is developed gradually on the part of the subject, and, by the coöperation of man through faith working by love, has as its consequence sanctification and salvation[4]....It is not only the external imputation of righteousness to man by the death of the Lord, but the appropriation in the case of each individual ....of the redeeming work of Christ, by which we achieve sanctification—the predestined end, and the *terminus ad quem* of the true Christian[5]....Justification is the work both of divine power—by which we are not only pronounced just though we are sinners, but are also raised up to receive the Grace which first justified us in the death of the Lord,—and as well the work of man—in accepting and receiving, in constant faith....by his own act of will the continuous operation of divine Grace, and showing it through a living faith by which he is constituted and is, actually righteous[6] .... The divine Grace not only pro-

---

[1] Dyobouniotes expounds this view, p. 43 of his Δογμ. 'Ανδρ. κριν., and pp. 103-104 of his 'Οφειλ. ἀπάντησις.

[2] Androutsos, Δογμ. Μελ. Α', p. 110.

[3] *Op. cit.*, III. p. 260.

[4] *Ibid.*

[5] *Ibid.*, p. 263.

[6] *Ibid.*, p. 265.

nounces, but makes us righteous, in Justification."[1] This teaching that justification is more than simply the pronouncement of God on man's new relation towards Him, is supported by Holy Scripture. It is clear that many passages[2] taken by themselves may be interpreted in a forensic sense, but others' "indicate much more than the mere not imputing of sins. The Apostle's freedom in linking together 'righteousness' and 'holiness', 'justification' and 'sanctification'[4]....shows that the connection of justification and sanctification is much more intimate than the Protestants imagine....Sanctification, or moral conversion, is consummated after justification,....but this new life in Christ may not be separated from justification, but is originally bound up with it....The 'renewal of the inner man' is presented in Holy Scripture as the immediate gift of Baptism, or of Redemption in Christ, or of the Holy Spirit,[5] as well as the end towards which man should endeavor to go[6]....In Church teaching[7]....the conception of Justification and that of a just God demand that justification be taken in the sense of an actual renewal of the inner man. In Holy Scripture justification and righteousness are opposed to unrighteousness and....sin. Hence the state of righteousness.... must be considered as opposite to that of sin[8]....As sin which came from Adam is a very real thing, so the righteousness from Christ must be equally as real. Thus a man to be considered as righteous by God must either be so or be made so—otherwise

[1] *Ibid.*, p. 267.

[2] E. g., Gal. 3, 11; Rom. 3, 20; 4, 7; 5, 9, 10; Eph. 1, 7; Col. 1, 14; Heb. 9, 22; Col. 2, 13; Heb. 10, 17; 2 Cor. 5, 19.

[3] E. g., Rom. 8, 11; 6, 4; 1 Cor. 6, 11; Gal. 3, 21; Col. 1, 13; Eph. 2, 6; Rom. 8, 20; 2 Cor. 4, 16; Tit. 3, 5; Rom. 8; 16; 6, 6 etc.

[3] E. g., 1 Cor. 6, 11; 2 Thes. 2, 13.

[5] Tit. 3, 5; Eph. 2, 10; 2 Cor. 3, 18.

[6] 1 St. John 3, 3.

[7] On the effects of Baptism, cf. Tertullian: *remissio delictorum, absolutio mortis, regeneratio hominis, consecutio Spiritus sancti* (*Adv. Marc.* 1, 28.) ; St. Basil, *de Spiritu Sancto*, 15, 15, 35; St. Greg. Naz. *Oratio* 40, 3; St. Augustine, *In Joan.* tr. 26, 1; *Opus imperf.*, 11, 168; Dositheus, in Mesolora, II, p. 116.

[8] Cf. Rom. 5, 19.

230 IV.—DOCTRINE OF GRACE AND OF THE CHURCH

God judges falsely in pronouncing an unrighteous man righteous[1]...."

The doctrine of *sanctification,* like that of justification, is
indebted largely to Protestant contentions and the need of
defining Orthodox teaching against them, for the particular
character of its formulation. According to Mesolora, "by sanctification we understand that perfect religious and moral state
of the Christian, achieved first by the operation of the Holy
Spirit, preserving, increasing, and perfecting his life in Christ,
and secondly by the coöperation of man, manifesting the perfect religious and moral life of a Christian in good works.
Sanctification is then a further development and progress of
justification, by which man is advanced and perfected in virtue.... By it we are perfectly united with Jesus, as the branch
in the Vine, bring forth fruit, and are made members of the
one Body, Jesus Christ[2] . ." According to Androutsos it is
"the good disposition, the holy purpose, formed in us by the
indwelling Grace of God, and strengthening faith and love in
man, shown forth in joy for the good and in the irresistible
desire to carry it out....by good works....Inasmuch as sanctification constitutes....the essence of justification, it is obvious that justification, according to both Orthodox and Roman
teaching, is different in individual believers, and capable of
greater development and progress."[3] If justification is not a
forensic act and consequently not the same in every case, then
sanctification has its degrees and grades as has glory,[4] and is
not the same in every one of the faithful. It also follows that
since the gift of justification is neither irresistible nor ina-
missible, Grace may be lost through sin, and even those once
justified may fall grievously. That "there is a sin unto death",[5]
and that we ask forgiveness of our sins[6] in the Lord's Prayer,
implies that justification does not necessarily involve sancti-

---

[1] Androutsos, Δογματική, pp. 233-237; on δικαιοῦν in the New Testament cf. note 2, p. 236.

[2] Mesolora, *op. cit.,* III, p. 266.

[3] Δογματική, pp. 237-238.

[4] Cf. 1 Cor. 15, 41.

[5] St. John 5, 16, 17; and cf. St. Jas. 3, 2; St. Augustine *de dono
perseverentiae,* 2, 4.

[6] On the distinction of sins cf. Androutsos' Συμβολική, pp. 240 ff.

fication and salvation. We may fall from Grace any time: "he that thinketh he standeth must take heed lest he fall."[1] Consequently "no one may be sure of his own salvation nor may he predict with certainty that he will be able to keep himself from grievous sins in the future and remain in (the state of) justification."[2]

3. FAITH AND GOOD WORKS

The one and only way by which we may appropriate the merit of our Saviour and come to apprehend it by sanctification, is *faith,* which means obedience to the voice of God. "Faith is not a mere acceptance of the truths of the Faith, but a cleaving to the Saviour and an adherence to His work bound up with acceptance of Gospel Truth. It is not only a work of the intellect, but is above all moral, . . . since giving up this world and cleaving to the Saviour means to love Him, which love takes for granted the action of the will." Justifying Faith is essentially a moral matter and is inevitably bound up with love. "Since love for God and love for one's neighbor constitute the essence of good works, it is apparent that good works also, the inevitable expression and manifestation of love, are involved in justification and salvation in Christ."[3] "Love is the essence and soul of good works, as they are the natural embodiment of love."[4] "Good works are the touchstone", says Dyobouniotes, "of developed love: where such exist, unless they proceed from other motives, there is love in its perfect form; where they are absent, unless this absence be due to causes beyond the control of the person's will, there love is absent—at least, that love which is able to justify."[5] It is obvious that where there is no occasion to prompt good works or material means available for carrying them out, love is not without its virtuous character, and has the same ethical

[1] 1 Cor. 10, 12, and cf. Rom. 11, 20; 1 Cor. 9, 27; Rev. 3, 11; St. Jas. 1, 14-15; 1 Cor. 6, 9-10; 2 St. Pet. 2, 20-21.

[2] Androutsos, Δογματική, p. 241 and cf. pp. 238-240.

[3] Androutsos, Δογματική, pp. 241-242.

[4] *Ibid.*, Δογμ. Μελ., Α', p. 106.

[5] 'Οφειλ. ἀπάντ., pp. 102-103.

value as if it could have been manifested in good works.[1]
"Whether one say that faith or love or good works or the carrying out of God's commandments justify and save, it is all one,
because of the intimate connection between faith and love. . . .
The full statement. . . . which includes both the theoretical and
practical element. . . . is the proposition that man is justified
through faith that worketh by love."[2]

The great problem of the relationship between faith and
good works is presented by the seemingly contradictory teachings of St. Paul's and St. James' epistles. Dyobouniotes on
this basis distinguishes two justifications, of St. Paul and St.
James; one, a potential justification, or "justification in germ",
in which God pronounces a man just for the sake of that which
he may become, and the other, the actual attainment of righteousness by faith and good works, related as the beginning
and the development of the life in Christ. "The Eastern
Church cannot regard justification as does the Protestant
Church, simply as a forensic act of pronouncing a man righteous, but as an internal change. Yet this. . . . does not preclude
the distinction of beginning and end in justification, nor prevent one from calling this beginning, the first, and the end,
the second, justification. . . . The first is the proclaiming of a
man as just by God, . . . inasmuch . . . as the internal change,
even if it has not yet become a state, yet exists in germ, and the
second as the actual realization of this state. . . .'To justify'
is taken in Holy Scripture in two senses. . . . So justification
as a forensic act may be regarded as proceeding from faith,
and salvation as of faith and works."[3]   Other Orthodox writers
have effected a reconciliation of St. Paul's and St. James'
thought by this doctrine of two justifications—one in this
present life through faith, and the other at the second coming,
through faith with good works.   So teach Damalas,[4] Antonius

---

[1] Androutsos, Δογματική, p. 242.

[2] *Ibid.;* cf. Gal. 5, 6, and Dositheus in Mesolora, *op. cit.*, II, p. 112;
Dyobouniotes takes exception to this passage in 'Η Δογμ. 'Ανδρ. κριν.,
p. 42 and 'Οφειλ. ἀπάντ., p. 101.   St. Paul used ἐνεργουμένη, not ἐνερ-
γούσης (Androutsos).   Cf. Androutsos, Δογμ. Μελ. Α', p. 106-108.

[3] Dyobouniotes, 'Η Δογμ. 'Ανδρ. κριν., pp. 43 ff; 'Οφειλ. ἀπάντ., pp.
103-109.

[4] Περὶ ἀρχῶν, p. 132.

(in commenting on Gal. 2, 16),[1] Macarius,[2] and Balanos, whose monograph[3] is designed to substantiate this teaching. Androutsos distinguishes in the biblical passages *ad loc.*, two aspects of justification: the active, as the energy of God by which is effected the transition from unrighteousness to justification, and the passive, the state of righteousness, the right relation of man to God.[4] . . . . He says further: "No one can rightly speak of two justifications according to Holy Scripture, for justification is one, distinguished from salvation as the reason is from its result and consequence. .,. . According to this relationship one may say one of two things: either that justification and salvation depend upon faith. . . . or that they depend upon faith and works[5]. . . . So when the above mentioned dogmaticians distinguish two justifications, ... they do not actually distinguish them in fact from each other, ... since faith working through love may not be separated from faith and good works. . . . According to Orthodox teaching, faith, in order to justify, must be animated by love involving the whole man, evolving from a merely noetic into an ethical work. . . . . . Hence the terms by which they distinguish two justifications, which are really in essence only one, cannot be employed as distinguishing features[6]. . . . "

Androutsos, while admitting two senses of the word in St. Paul's and St. James' usage, does not regard them as necessarily different and mutually exclusive, and so does not solve the problem of justification by this method. "Both[7] are talking about different aspects of the one process. St. James, consistently with his practical aim, ranges works over against faith, as something standing by itself and establishing a proper equilibrium, but elsewhere[8] frequently postulates the organic union of both, discussing faith as the foundation of works and works

---

[1] Δογματικὴ Θεολογία . . . translated by Theodore Ballianos, Athens, 1858, p. 240.

[2] *Op. cit.*, II. p. 361-363.

[3] ‘Η περὶ δικαιώσεως διδασκαλία τῆς ’Ορθ. ’Ελληνικῆς ’Εκκλησ., pp. 39 ff.

[4] Δογματική, p. 255.

[5] Androutsos, Δογματική, p. 256.

[6] *Ibid.*, pp. 256-258 and cf. his Δογμ. Μελ., Α’, pp. 106-113.

[7] Cf. St. Jas. 2, 24; Gal. 5, 6.

[8] *E. g.*, 1, 3, 4; 2, 17, 18, 20, 24-26.

as the complement of faith.... St. Paul lays down the terms
of justification according to their internal organic connection.
....When he contrasts faith and works he does not mean faith
as separated from love, nor does what he says stand in opposition to St. James. . . In 1 Cor. 13, 2, he speaks of faith apart
from love as vain.... From Heb. 11, 6, we see....that faith
is not a mere acceptance by the intellect of the truths of the
Gospel, but a good intention and disposition of the soul turned
toward the Saviour, out of which good works naturally flow.
It is apparent that the faith of St. James which the demons
have is not the justifying faith of St. Paul.... Furthermore
'the works of the Law' in St. Paul do not mean 'good works'"[1]
..but the Apostle is inveighing against the attitude of claiming justification as something due from God in return for
performing works, while "he who is justified through
the merits of the Saviour receives his justification freely as
a gift of God's Grace."[2]   This is the way in which the Fathers
have understood justification by faith,[3] of whom some follow[4]
St. James with a practical purpose in view, not intending to
expound the inner unity of works from faith through love
"Like St. James, they also regard good works as the fruit and
manifestation of faith, and as the standard and witness of the
existence of faith and of its vital power."[5]

The Protestant objection to the doctrine of faith and works
as taught by the Orthodox Church, is that "works" bring about
a certain sense of merit and pride in the believer, and hence
the view that they are essential may not be accepted. As Mesolora says: "The Christian may not boast about his good works
nor believe that he can be justified through them alone, for

---

[1] Cf. Mesolora, *op. cit.*, III, p. 247; the Apostle "means works of the
Mosaic Law . . . which was only a schoolmaster leading the way to
Christ."

[2] Cf. Rom. 4, 4; 3, 24; Eph. 2, 8;   Androutsos' Δογματική, p. 244-
245.

[3] *E. g.*, St. Justin Martyr, *Dialogus cum Tryph.*, 47; *Shepherd of
Hermas*, 1, 3, 8; Clem. Alex. *Strom.*, VI. 9; St. Irenaeus *Adv. Haer.*
IV, 27, 2; Tertullian, *adv. Marc.*, V, 3, etc.

[4] St. Irenaeus, *Adv. Haer.* IV. 13;   St. Cyril Jerus., *Cat.*, VI. 2;
St. Basil *De Fide;* St. John Dam., Ἔκδοσις, IV. 10·

[5] Androutsos, *ibid.*, pp. 246-247, cf. note 1.

......our justification depends in the first place upon divine
Grace and the merits of the Saviour from whom we have our
faith as a free gift.... Our Church teaches that faith only
cannot justify or sanctify a man, nor can good works of themselves perfectly fulfill the divine will, since they are not sufficient for salvation without faith, . . . but are well pleasing to
God and necessary to salvation . . as demonstrating the life and
power of God's Grace in us, and our appropriation of the redeeming work of Christ."[1] Protestantism is wrong in refusing
any merit to good works. "The merit of Christian works
is not absolute but relative, for the former can only be had
between equals, when each gives in turn what is the other's
due."[2] We have no absolute merit before God, as St. Luke
17, 10 shows, yet Holy Scripture teaches us[3] that "Christian
works become meritorious, or that by them we may become
worthy of the Kingdom of Heaven. But it is to be noticed
that good or meritorious works are only those achieved by the
power of Christ, with which our will coöperates and concurs,
and that those done by the natural man, still in sin, or those
external works which are devoid of any good intention animating them, such as love of God and one's neighbor, are deprived
of any meritorious character.... Furthermore....the merit
of our works may not exceed the measure of our duty"[4]....
Consequently the Roman doctrine of "works of supererogation"
and "the treasury of merits" is a "teaching which is both
unjustified and unreasonable."[5] The distinction between counsel and precept may be objectively valid, but subjectively it is
without force. Our Lord's words to the young man in St. Matt.
19, 21, do not mean that "one can do more than is required

[1] *Op. cit.*, III. pp. 275, 279; for the evidence of the Symbolic Books cf.
in Mesolora, *op. cit.*, Jeremiah II's *Answer* I. pp. 185-186; second *Answer*, *ibid.*, pp. 220-221, 224; Kritopoulos, *ibid.*, p. 316; against
the Roman doctrine of supererogation, *ibid.*, p. 348; Mogila, *ibid.*,
pp. 376-378; pp. 460, 461-463; Dositheus, *ibid.*, II. pp. 107-108; Jeremiah, II. in *ibid.*, 1, p. 174.
[2] Androutsos, Δογματική, p. 247.
[3] St. Luke 12, 33; Rom. 2, 6; Tim. 4, 8; 1 Cor. 3, 8, 14; Heb.
10, 35; Col. 3, 24, etc.
[4] Androutsos, *ibid.*, p. 249.
[5] For a full discussion of the Roman doctrine and of the Orthodox
position against it, cf. Androutsos' Συμβολική, pp. 235 ff.

for the attainment of eternal life, but were said to show how imperfect and incomplete was his fulfilment of the Law."[1] The Roman doctrine of the superabundant merits of the Saints, which may be applied to those yet in debt, has no foundation in Holy Scripture, for "the Saints may be helped by the prayers of the faithful."[2]   In general, Roman and Orthodox teaching agree[3] as to the conditions and terms of justification, against the Protestant theory of justification by faith only. "While Orthodox teaching regards justifying faith as naturally manifesting itself in good works, the Protestants regard it as a passive and receptive organ only and think that God justifies a man as he believes (that is, 'accepts'), not as he loves, thus forcibly sundering faith and works; they are worlds apart from the teaching of Orthodoxy."[4]

---

[1] Androutsos, *op. cit.*, pp. 249-250.

[2] *Ibid.*

[3] Androutsos, *op. cit.*, p. 251.   With this statement many Orthodox theologians disagree, *e. g.*, Mesolora, *op. cit.*, II. p. 263; Damalas, Περὶ ἀρχῶν, p. 151;   Balanos, *op. cit.*, pp. 41, 58, and Dyobouniotes, Ἡ Δογμ. Ἀνδρ. κριν., p. 39, Ὀφειλ. ἀπάντησις, pp. 96-99.   The latter says: "There is no possibility of doubt that the basis of the doctrine of justification is the teaching about the original state of man, and the doctrine of the Fall.   Since Roman and Orthodox doctrine differ widely on this point, it follows that their doctrine of justification must be different . . . Not only do they differ as to infused Grace but also as to the merit of good works, . . . as Philaret of Moscow observes, even if the distinction be a delicate one" (pp. 97-98, Ὀφειλ. ἀπάντ.). Androutsos denies that this deduction follows from the premises (Δογμ. Μελέται. Α΄, p. 105). "Justification, both according to our own and the Roman teaching, is not only the removal of sin but an actual change and renewal of the inner man, as teach Damalas (*op. cit.*, p. 147) and Mesolora (*op. cit.*, III, pp. 263-266). . . . The Roman phrase, *virtus infusa*, . . . is a technical term . . . to mean the steadfast turning of the man towards God . . . which is a common doctrine of all who hold justification to be a moral matter." "If there be any difference between us and the Latins as to the terms of justification, these are in respect to practice not theory," and to the deductions made by Rome from legitimate doctrine.   (Androutsos, Δογματική, pp. 251-252, note, and his Συμβολική, pp. 215 ff.)

[4] Androutsos, Δογματική, p. 251-252.

2. THE DOCTRINE OF THE CHURCH

1. Conception and Mission of the Church

The word "church" in its early general meaning signified an assembly of men for any purpose, then became limited to gatherings for a religious purpose, and afterwards was applied to the place in which such meetings were held.[1] In the Christian sense it was loosely applied to the local Christian congregation, or to the whole totality of such local assemblies, or to the constituent officers of the organization. Specifically under the Fathers and the theologians the word came to denote all those who constitute the people of God,[2] whether living on earth or triumphant in heaven. Hence the distinction between the "Church Militant" and the "Church Triumphant."[3] In the Orthodox sense, according to Androutsos,[4] it means "only the totality of all the Orthodox of all times." In the New Testament and the Fathers, various partial aspects of the Church's mission and character are indicated, without the specific definition of the word in exact and concrete forms.[5] This gave rise in early days to incomplete conceptions and definitions against which the Orthodox have always reacted. The Protestant conception of the Church as essentially "invisible" is legitimately in line of succession from Montanism, Donatism, and Novatianism. The Roman conception of the Church, as Mesolora puts it, is that, "the Pope is the Church",[6] and is a reaction in entirely the opposite direction.

[1] Androutsos, Δογματική, p. 259; Mesolora, op. cit., IV. p. 6, note 1; cf. Acts 19, 32, 39; 7, 38; Heb. 2, 12.

[2] Androutsos, ibid., cf. St. Augustine Enchiridon, 56, and on Ps. 92, and cf. Eph. 1, 22.

[3] Androutsos, ibid., p. 260, and Mesolora, ibid., p. 7.

[4] Ibid., and cf. below, on the "notes" of the Church pp. 243-246 following.

[5] Cf. 1 Tim. 3, 15; 1 Cor. 3, 16; Eph. 1, 23; 5, 23; Rev. 19, 7; Gal. 4, 26; St. John 15, 1; 10, 1-7, etc.; St. Ignatius exalted the Church's episcopal organization; St. Cyprian and Tertullian, its priestly function; St. John Chrysostom presents it as "a fellowship of the Faithful", as does St. Epiphanius, etc.; cf. Androutsos, op. cit., p. 260.

[6] Op. cit., p. 11; cf. Androutsos, note 2, pp. 261-262 on the Protestant conception.

The Church is both visible and invisible, divine and human, and may be defined as "that holy foundation made by
the Incarnate Word of God for the salvation and sanctification
of men, bearing His own authority and authentication, constituted of men having one faith and sharing the same sacraments, who are divided into lay and clergy. . . . and the latter,
who rule the Church, trace their beginning through unbroken
succession to the Apostles and through them to our Lord."[1]
To which definition Mesolora would add: "This divine and . . .
spiritual foundation, having its inception in the will and plan
of God before the foundation of the world, was effected on
earth through Jesus Christ and the descent of the Holy Spirit
at Pentecost . . . and has as its Head, Jesus Christ, and as its
Guide, the Holy Spirit."[2] This definition involves the Church's
object and mission—the salvation of men,[3] which may be conceived of as the extension and continuation of the work of
our Lord's three-fold office, as Prophet, Priest, and King.[4] It
also states the two-fold character of the Church: "As a foundation with definite aim on earth it is visible, and employs a
visible organism . . . The Church is an organic body, a peculiar
community with visible and sensible signs. . . . But at the same
time it is a spiritual, invisible, and eternal Foundation. . . .
The Church is invisible, since to God only is known who are its
true members . . . united with Him invisibly, since external
union with it frequently happens to be false, as is external
worship in many cases."[5] It is also to be noted that the
Orthodox definition involves unity of Faith, for "Our Lord
founded the Church on faith in Him. . . . A distinguishing
mark of the genuineness of the Church has been, and is, unity
of faith, external and internal, and the guardianship of the
Holy Spirit in the bond of peace."[6] The above definition
leads to the exposition of its three constituent elements: (a)
the divine establishment and foundation of the Church, with

[1] Androutsos, *op. cit.*, p. 262, and cf. Dyobouniotes' criticism, in
'Η Δογμ. 'Ανδρ. κριν., p. 45.
[2] Mesolora, *op. cit.*, IV. p. 6, (and Kephala, *op. cit.*, p. 192).
[3] *Ibid.*, p. 7.
[4] Androutsos, *op. cit.*, pp. 264, 282.
[5] Mesolora, *op. cit.*, p. 10.
[6] Mesolora, *op. cit.*, p. 9.

the corollaries involved; (b) the essential character and nature of the Church; (c) the organization and constitution of the Church.[1]

2. The Church Divinely Founded and Established

The Messiah was to found a universal and permanent kingdom on earth, as the Old Testament shows, and our Lord fulfilled this prophecy in His Church, against which the gates of hell could not prevail, and for which He shed His Blood.[3] On Pentecost, the birthday of the Church, He gave it actual form and shape, and straightway His Apostles went forth to propagate faith in Him and to carry out their commission of extending the Church He founded. While the Church grew up under the wings of the Synagogue, it speedily emancipated itself and became an independent entity. Our Lord founded His Church as "the center and organ of His redeeming Work,....and the Church is nothing less than the continuation and extension of His prophetic, priestly, and kingly power....The means and the authority for the carrying out of her mission, the Church received from her Founder, ...who endowed the Apostles and their successors with His own authority and authenticity.. So the Church and her Founder are inextricably bound together: . . . the Church is Christ with us....She always teaches His truth with certainty and transmits His Grace. In her (the believer) acquires an unshaken conviction as to the trustworthiness of what he believes. . . . "[4] Since the Church is guided by the Holy Spirit, it follows that she cannot fall away from the truth,[5] and is infallible.[6] "This infallibility is not ascribed to the members

[1] Following Androutsos, op. cit., p. 282.

[2] Isaiah 2, 2; 54, 1; Dan. 2, 44, etc.; in this connection cf. the general treatment by Kephala, Χριστολογία, pp. 192 ff.

[3] St. Matt. 16, 18; Acts. 20, 28.

[4] Cor. 4, 1; 3, 8; Acts 4, 19, 20; St. Luke 10, 16; St. Matt. 18, 18; Acts. 4, 12; Androutsos, op. cit., pp. 262-265.

[5] Mesolora, op. cit., IV. pp. 17 ff; Dositheus in Mesolora II. pp. 111-112; Acts of Synod of Jassy, ibid., pp. 38-39.

[6] Cf. St. Athanasius on Ps. 88, 38; St. John Chrysostom, Oratio de Eutrop., in Migne P. G., 52, 402; St. Ambrose Hexaem, IV. 2, 7. Mesolora's "notes" of infallibility are: (1) agreement and unanimity of teach-

of the Church as such, either in part or as a whole, but to the
Saviour, who as Founder necessarily dwells in His Church,
and to the Holy Spirit,....both of whom are the efficient
cause of infallibility."[1] As the Church possesses her title to
infallibility from her Founder's commission, which gave her
His authority in the work of salvation, both Holy Scripture[2]
and the Fathers[3] testify to the truth of the doctrine that the
Church is the one way of salvation.

Extra Ecclesiam nulla salus.[4]

The truth embodied in the phrase "outside the Church
there is no salvation" must not lead to spiritual and moral
inertia, as if membership in the Church assured salvation. This
is an erroneous conception with which the Church has to cope,
and she constantly teaches that not *every* member of the
Church is saved but only every *true* member. Androutsos
would interpret the principle above in its affirmative and positive content, to mean that "the normal and regularly constituted
conveyor of the terms of salvation is the Church, in which
the Saviour deposited the means of salvation, and that heresy,
schism, or any other religious body have no claim to be 'labora-
tories (ἐργαστήρια) of salvation'," since they only hold out
illusions of salvation to their adherents. This position, he
maintains, is the objective aspect of the principle. Subjectively the problem resolves itself into the question, "can anyone be saved outside the Church?" No Orthodox can maintain that all outside the Church are damned. As a personal
problem, the answer of the question must be left in the hands
of Him "who desireth not the death of a sinner" but wills
"that all men be saved" (1 Tim. 2, 4). In the individual instance it is both logically and theologically possible for a man

ing; (2) acceptance and consent to this teaching without addition or
subtraction; (3) faithful adherence to the 'faith once delivered';—
op. cit., IV, p. 19, and cf. Kritopoulos, I, pp. 318-319.

[1] Mesolora, *ibid.*, p. 21.
[2] Cf. St. Luke 10, 16; St. Matt. 18, 18, 17; Tit. 3, 10; 1 St. John
2, 18 ff.
[3] St. Irenaeus *adv. Haer.*, III, 24, 1; St. Cyprian, *de cath. eccl. unitate*, 4.
[4] Origen, *In Jesu Nave hom.*, 3, 5; St. Cyprian, Epist. 73, 21.

to be saved outside the Church: (a) sincerity coupled with invincible ignorance may inhibit a man from accepting the formulations of the Faith presented to him; (b) he may have no opportunity to come to the knowledge of the truth; (c) the formularies of his own profession of belief "may serve as a basis for supernatural life and fellowship with the Light", inasmuch as they contain portions and aspects of revealed truth; (d) we may not contend that God, who is free, restricts Himself to the use of the one means of Grace He has appointed. "Other extraordinary acts of Grace are not precluded" by maintaining the conviction that "every true member of the Church certainly shares in salvation."[1]

3. The Nature of the Church

The Church has, as we have seen, two aspects—she is both invisible and visible. As invisible, she is the bearer of divine gifts and powers, and is engaged in transforming mankind into the Kingdom of God. As visible, she is constituted of men professing a common faith, observing common customs, and using visible means of Grace. The latter is the external aspect of her mission; the former, the unseen aim and purpose of her Founder. The Church is visible, because her Founder was incarnate and lived among men, because she ministers Grace under tangible signs and symbols, because she outwardly professes one Faith, because she has a visible organization and government by succession from the Apostles, and because her membership is constituted of visible men. Her two aspects are inextricably united; as the two Natures are in our Lord's Person, so "the Church is a holy bond uniting two elements, divine and human, of which the former is the life-giving and abiding principle, and the visible the external manifestation of the divine and the necessary organ for the operation of salvation." The higher principle is not subject to human scrutiny, but is discerned by the eye of faith only. "That inward union with our Lord is the object towards which

[1] Androutsos, Δογματική, p. 267; cf. Ἡ Δογμ. Ἀνδρ. κριν. by Dyobouniotes, p. 46 and Ὀφειλ. ἀπάντησις, ibid., p. 112; Androutsos, Δογμ. Μελ., Α', p. 128, and Αἱ βάσεις τῆς ἑνώσεως τῶν Ἐκκλησιῶν, pp. 50-53; note 2, pp. 267-269 of his Δογματική.

the Church aims, is true, yet this mystical union can take place only on the basis of the Church, and is only promoted through her"....The early writers emphasized the ecclesiastical character of Christianity again and again. The visible Church is the sole guardian and teacher of the Faith, and the one means by which the divine Grace is transmitted—"the Pillar and Ground of the truth", the Ark of Salvation. As the soul is to the body, so is the spirit of Christ to His Church.[1]

Consequently every notion of the Church which would exalt or over-emphasize her invisible character to the exclusion of her visible aspect, is to be condemned and rejected. The notion of an invisible and ideal church, of which the various bodies of Christians formed into distinct organizations and calling themselves "Churches", are partial and incomplete embodiments, is utterly foreign to Orthodox teaching and to historical and biblical authority. The Church is an actual, tangible, visible entity, not an unrealized and unrealizable ideal.[2] Even as a means of realizing the ideal Church of Protestant thought, the visible Church would be an absolute necessity.[3] This conception deprives Revelation of its final and absolute character; if each portion of organized Christianity is each to hold one aspect only of the truth, who is to act as arbiter and definer of the content of the whole of Revelation?[4] The Protestant conception of the ideal Church whose members are known only to God, violates the teaching that the members of the Church are not perfected saints, but sinners. This rests upon the Protestant conception of justification, which is entirely opposite to that of Orthodoxy and Holy Scripture.[5] The function of the Church, as is evident even from the Protestant

[1] Androutsos, Δογματική, pp. 268-273; cf. St. John 16, 13; 1 Tim. 3, 15; Eph. 1, 25; 5, 25; Rev. 19, 7; Mesolora, op. cit., IV. p. 14 Note 1. "The Church is the perpetual extension of Christ, and her aim the sanctification of men and their exaltation into religious and moral life". Androutsos, op. cit., p. 293.
[2] Cf. Androutsos, Αἱ βάσεις . . . τῆς ἑνώσεως, p. 7-10.
[3] Ibid., p. 12.
[4] Ibid., pp. 14-18, and on the whole question, Δογματική, pp. 261-262, note 2.
[5] E. g., St. Matt. 13, 24; 3, 12; 13, 47; 22, 11.

definition of it,[1] is to save sinners. "If the Church is an assembly of saints, then the second part of the Augsburg definition (*in qua evangelium recte docetur et recte administrantur sacramenta*) is superfluous,....since preaching and the sacraments would be unnecessary if all were holy, righteous, and devout."[2] The mission of "the Church is to promote the repentance and reformation of sinners, and from her are excluded only the heretics, schismatics, and excommunicate."[3] "The Fathers condemned unanimously every exaggerated view.... of those who held the Church to be a fellowship of perfected saints."[4]

The Church according to the Creed is "One, Holy, Catholic, and Apostolic," which four terms are called the "notes" of the Church. By ascribing *unity* to the Church we mean that she is one in origin, one in Faith and discipline, and one in essence. All her members constitute one body, are animated by the one Holy Spirit, and profess alike one single Faith,[5] the bond uniting them to each other and to their Lord. Our Lord founded only one Church,[6] and His foundation has a unique and sole character. The necessity of oneness in faith was strongly emphasized by St. Paul,[7] and is shown in the Church's unity of teaching, of which unity in worship is a manifestation. The necessity of unity in discipline and order of government is apparent from the New Testament; "thus the Church conscious of herself as the guardian of unity has never recognized heresy or schism as constituting parallel organizations dealing with salvation, but has cut them off from the healthy body, in order to induce repentance and return to it ...."[8] Such excommunications have always been deemed delivery over to the power of Satan. This teaching about unity

---

[1] Cf. note 2, p. 12, Mesolora, *op. cit.*, IV.

[2] *Ibid.*, p. 13.

[3] Androutsos, Δογματική, p. 270; cf. Dositheus, in Mesolora, *op. cit.*, II. p. 111.

[4] *Ibid.*, p. 279.

[5] Mesolora, *op. cit.*, IV. p. 14.

[6] St. John 10, 16; 21, 15; Heb. 3, 6; 10, 21; Eph. 5, 27; Rom. 12, 5. Cf. Αἱ βάσεις . . . τῆς ἑνώσεως, pp. 1-6.

[7] Cf. Eph. 4, 3-15; 1 Cor. 1, 10; Gal. 1, 6-8; Tit. 3, 10.

[8] Cf. 1 Cor. 10-13; Gal. 5, 20. Androutsos, Δογματική, p. 274.

is that of the Fathers.[1] Unity of doctrine is not impaired even
if all members of the Church do not have the same mind about
the articles of the Faith, as long as they maintain the principle
of the Church's authority.[2] Schisms from the body are points
of departure for heterodoxy in teaching, and so schismatics
are often considered heretics as well.[3]

Our modern conception of unity would make it consist
"in agreement as to the fundamentals of the Faith," maintaining that "while external unity is desirable, it is not indispensable for the preservation of church unity." But separated
bodies are such because they have been cut off from unity
with the Church, which hopes thereby to bring them to a sense
of their guilt. They stand then in a permanently anomalous
relationship to the Church. Furthermore there is no possible
authority in antiquity for the distinction into central or fundamental doctrine, and secondary or non-essential teaching. "It
is both historically and logically indefensible".... "Christian
teaching in theory constitutes a unified and organic whole,
one doctrine presupposing another, and the denial of certain
doctrines....leads as a consequence into the denial of the
basis and hypotheses of all." In practice there can be no distinction between any of the doctrines having the Church's
authority: heterodoxy leads inevitably to heresy. Furthermore,
what would be the criterion by which to judge between what
is essential and what is not? This distinction would involve the
denial of the infallibility of the Church.[4]

The Church is "Holy" because her Founder is Holy and
her function is to make her members holy. The early Church
used the words "saints" of the members of the Body, for they
are sanctified by Baptism and fellowship with God, and sepa-

---

[2] E. g., St. Irenaeus, adv. Haer. I, 10, 2; St. Ignatius ad. Phil., 3;
St. Justin, cum Tryph., 63; St. Basil, Epist., 92; St. John Chrysostom
on Eph. 11; St. Clem. Rom., I, 37; St. Cyprian, de unitate, etc.

[2] Androutsos op. cit., p. 275.

[3] Ibid., p. 276; Can. 6 of 2nd Council.

[4] Androutsos, Δογματική, pp. 276-278; Αἱ βάσεις . . . τῆς ἑνώσεως,
pp. 15-18, 45, 49. Dyobouniotes subjects this position of Androutsos to
criticism in his Ἡ Δογμ. Ἀνδρ. κριν.,p. 47, and Ὀφειλ. ἀπάντησις, pp. 114
ff.; for Androutsos' answer, cf. his Δογμ. Μελ. Α', p. 129. Dyobouniotes
does not seem to have substantiated his contention that Androutsos
admits in practice the very distinction ·he denies and inveighs against.

rated from the profane world without. As is our Lord, so His means of Grace, His teaching, and the aim He proposes for His Church are *holy,* and she is sanctified by Him. As an actual fact the Church begets saints—the heroes of the Faith who demonstrate her capacity for the sanctification of humanity. The fact that there are sinners, hypocrites, and false members in the Church does not militate against her character as holy, for her task is always to inspire and stimulate all that leads to holiness among her children,[1] though she retain unworthy members, hoping for their amendment.

The word "Catholic" means etymologically "what concerns the whole," that is, it means "universal"; but figuratively, as applied to the Church, it indicates the fact of her claiming adherents everywhere in the known world. As "universal" in this sense, it was employed by St. Cyril of Jerusalem and St. Athanasius.[2] It must not be thought that the word rightly means actual universality in a numerical sense, for that would forbid the early Church having any claim to the title.[3] The Apostles went forth armed with the commission to proclaim everywhere the one Gospel for all.[4] As the word of salvation was for all, and the means of Grace, conveying the Redemption wrought by our Lord for all, were universal in their scope, so the Church which was the agent of these ministrations was said to be "Catholic". The word has another meaning in relation to doctrine, since the universality of the preaching of a doctrine established its "Catholic" character,[5] and the word was thus used in relation to the organic life of the Church as distinguished from the sects and divisions of heresies. The Vincentian canon has always been the standard of "Catholicity". So the word in the Creed means "the one simple and unique whole in teaching and discipline uniting the many separate

---

[1] Acts. 9, 32; Rom. 1, 7, 12, 13; Eph. 1, 1; Eph. 4, 11-12; 5, 25-27; cf. St. Ignatius *Proemium, ad. Smyrn;* St. Iren. *adv. Haer.,* 3, 24; St. Cyprian, *de unitate Ecclesiae,* 6; St. Augustine, *Sermo* 214. Androutsos, Δογματική, pp. 278-279; Dositheus in Mesolora II, p. 111; *ibid.,* IV. pp. 14-15.

[2] Cf. Androutsos, *op. cit.,* p. 280, note 1, for references.

[3] Αἱ βάσεις . . . τῆς ἐνώσεως, pp. 27-28 and ff.

[4] St. Mark 16, 20.

[5] In this sense, *Catholic=Orthodox.*

local churches." This is the sense in which it is used by St. Cyril of Jerusalem, St. Ignatius, and others.[1]

The Church is called "Apostolic" as having been "built upon the foundation of the apostles....Jesus Christ Himself being the chief corner-stone."[2] It is shown as *apostolic* in the profession of the Faith of the Apostles and in "the discipline of the early Church—that is, in the succession of bishops, the successors of the Apostles." The doctrine of the Church is the basis of her fellowship with the Apostles, as "apostolic succession is the external witness and evidence that the Church is true in agreement with the primitive Church in teaching and discipline....The Fathers, in reprehending doctrine not in accord with apostolic teaching (for example, St. Irenaeus (*adv. Haer.* III, 3) and St. Jerome (*Epist.* 84)) confounded the heretics by showing their departures from this doctrine, and regarded apostolic succession as both the means for the transmission of Apostolic teaching as well as the distinguishing mark of the true Church, separating it from the false."[3]

4.   The Constitution and Organization of the Church

"The Saviour founded His Church . . . for the salvation of men, and in so doing gave it everything useful and necessary for its visible maintenance. . ."[4] "As a visible fellowship it has need of its own proper administrative system in order to exercise our Lord's three-fold office—to preach the word of God, to administer His priestly office through the sacraments, and to govern the Faithful." Our Lord first chose the twelve and the seventy to whom He gave His own authority and power, and endowed them with the power of the Holy Spirit. "The Apostles not only exercised this office committed to them but communicated the priestly authority to others, separating out by the Holy Spirit deacons and presbyters, and constituting

---

[1] *Cat.* XVIII. 11; *Ad Smyr*, 8, 2; 16, 2; Eusebius *H. E.* 5, 16; Tertullian, *de Praescript.*, 26, 20; Clem. Alex., *Strom.* VII. 17; Androutsos, Δογματική, pp. 279-281. cf. Kritopoulos in Mesolora, I. pp. 316-317, and Mogila, *ibid.*, pp. 416-419.

[2] Eph. 2, 20.

[3] Δογματική, pp. 281-282.

[4] Mesolora, *op. cit.*, IV. p. 45.

their own successors. Thus the Church is divided into two orders, clerical and lay, the whole flock in the wide meaning of the word being called 'priests'."[1] This, however, does not imply the absence in the Christian Church of a special order distinct from the laity, any more than it did among the Jews. The clerical office is "a special order founded by our Lord, the individuals being consecrated thereto by a proper service of the Church called ordination."[2] The Fathers witness to the fact and origin of the Church's hierarchy.[3]

This hierarchy includes the three grades—deacons, priests, and bishops—bound together, yet distinguished one from the other. "The bishop . . . is the center of spiritual authority and the head of the local Church; the indispensable condition of the existence of the Church, as distinct from priests and deacons. The latter serve the pastors in their third rank, and the presbyters, receiving their spiritual authority over their flocks from the Bishop,[4] rule the Church and perform every function of the Bishop (save ordination and the consecration of the myrrh), and are called 'priests' because they offer a real sacrifice, the Eucharist."[5] "These three grades of the hierarchy, distinguished from each other, existed in the Church from the beginning, and were defined by our Lord and His Apostles, as all Church tradition witnesses."[6] While the names "bishop" and "presbyter" were originally of the same force and were used interchangeably,[7] yet the functions soon came to be distinguished clearly, as is evident from the Fathers and Tradition.[8] The bishops differed from the Apostles in name only.[9]

---

[1] 1 St. Peter 2, 9; Androutsos, Δογματική, pp. 282-283.

[2] Mesolora, *ibid.*, p. 57.

[3] St. Augustine, *de Civitate Dei*, XX. 10 St. Clem. Rom. 1 Cor. 43-44; St. Ignatius *ad Trall.*, 3; Διδαχή, 15; St. Cyprian, *Epist* 66.

[4] To this phrase Dyobouniotes takes exception, pp. 117-118 'Οφειλ. ἀπάντ.; Androutsos' justification of it, Δογμ. Μελ., Α', p. 134.

[5] Δογματική, pp. 284-285; Mesolora, Πρακτικὴ Θεολογία, pp. 45-47, 54-58.

[6] Mesolora, Συμβολική, IV, pp. 59-60.

[7] *E. g.*, Phil. 1; Acts. 20, 28.

[8] Theodoret on 1 Tim, 3, 1; St. John Chrysostom *In Phil homiliae*, 1; 1, St. Ignatius, *ad Trall.*, 3; *ad Phil.*, 1, 1; 2, 1; *ad Eph.*, 3; Eusebius on Ps. 9, 14; the "angels" of the Apocalypse were Bishops (Androutsos).

[9] Androutsos, Δογματική, p. 286.

The bishops *jure divino* are all equal, but *jure ecclesiastico* certain bishops of important cities or dioceses were distinguished from the others as "Metropolitans" and "Patriarchs". Since the Schism there have been four patriarchates—Constantinople. Alexandria, Antioch, and Jerusalem.[1] The administrative unit in every autocephalous Church is the synod. Despite St. Jerome's theory of the origin of the episcopate as having evolved upward from the presbyterate, the Church maintains the divine origin of that order, which St. Jerome elsewhere himself recognizes. For had the highest order developed upward from the second order, according to the Roman theory, there would have been a breach in Church discipline of which some record would certainly remain. "The Episcopate is the highest grade of the ministry (ἱερωσύνη) created by our Lord through the Apostles, and the Bishop is the chief shepherd over the local Church to whose spiritual authority both cleric and lay pay obedience."[2]

"As the Bishop is the highest bearer of ecclesiastical jurisdiction, it is clear that the highest authority of the Church in a place is the synod of bishops, and of all the Orthodox Churches, the whole of the bishops." Hence the bishops constitute the organ by which is expressed the infallibility wherewith the Church is endowed. This is the unanimous teaching of Church tradition[3] founded on the texts of Scripture which teach the Church's infallibility. The Councils themselves bear witness to it,[4] as do the Fathers. Thus St. Athanasius,[5] St. Basil,[6] St. Gregory Nazianzen,[7] and St. Cyril.[8] "Mere numbers do not constitute the note of an Ecumenical Council. . . As an external crite-

---

[1] *Ibid.*, and Mesolora, *op. cit.*, IV. p. 60, pp. 76-81. Since the Russian Revolution the Patriarchate of Moscow has been added to the number to take the place of Rome, lost to the Church by heresy and schism.

[2] Androutsos, *op. cit.*, p. 287.

[3] Dositheus, in Mesolora, II. p. 111.

[4] In Mansi, VI. 672; Nicea, 1.

[5] *Ad Afros*, 2.

[6] *Epistolae*, 114, 162.

[7] *Orat.*, 21, 4.

[8] *Epist.* 39. The cases of St. Gregory (in *Epistola* 130) and St. Augustine (*de Baptismo contra Donat.*, II, 3) have no connection with disproving the statements above, cf. Androutsos, Δογματική, p. 289.

rion of ecumenicity we have the acceptance of the decrees of a council by the whole Church. Yet since the Holy Spirit is the principle of Ecumenical Councils and the pontiffs deliberating freely act in their own right, their decrees are of themselves infallible, and not so from the consent of the Church, . . . which is only an evidence and external criterion of ecumenicity. . . . The bishops assemble in council not as representing their dioceses nor as mandatories, but act in their own right; . . . the presence of the Holy Spirit does not mean the inspiration and revelation of new doctrines, but only His guiding and overseeing presence to illuminate them and to guard them from error. . . The bishops were not actuated mechanically by the Holy Spirit, but worked entirely in a normal human fashion,[1] disputing, investigating, and deliberating. . . The scope of infallible pronouncements is the range of the Church's mission: whatever has to do with salvation,—that is, faith and morals,—constitutes the subject matter on which is exercised the infallible action of the Councils and synods."[2]

5. The Orthodox Church

On the basis of what has been presented above of the present-day doctrine of Greek Orthodox theologians, it may be asked what is its application, in view of the practical and actual situation of Christianity to-day? Has Orthodoxy a theory of the Church which will apply not only to the Catholic Church in ideal, but to the present condition of Christendom? What position does the Orthodox Church claim for herself? How does she stand in regard to the question of Ecumenical Councils? to that of the Infallibility of the Church? to the rival theories of the Roman Church? to the "Branch Theory" of

[1] Cf. Acts 15, 17.

[2] Androutsos, *op. cit.*, pp. 290-292. For a refutation of the counter-arguments of Protestants and of the Papal claim to infallibility, in connection with the conciliar action of the Church, cf. his Συμβολική, pp. 79-87, ff. and Mesolora, *op. cit.*, IV. pp. 44-56, "on the Primacy of the Pope." He rejects the Papal claims on the following grounds: (1) a visible head of the Church is not needed, (2) is unscriptural, (3) St. Peter did not claim it, (4) Tradition and (5) reason and logic are against it (p. 54, ibid.). Cf. also Timothy Anastasius' Ἐπιστολή, pp. 16-30, etc.

Anglicanism?—I have reserved some of the detailed discussions concerning the Church until this point, in order the better to present a unified whole of Orthodox teaching and opinion with a view to answering concretely and definitely some of the above questions.

. All Orthodox formularies and pronouncements claim clearly and distinctly that the Orthodox Church has kept the Faith immaculate and intact, without addition or subtraction, without alteration or omission, as taught by Holy Scripture and Sacred Tradition.[1] Inasmuch as the holding to the Faith "as once delivered to the Saints" constitutes one of the fundamental and essential notes of the Church, deviation from true teaching involves loss of continuity with the life of the Church. It was apparent in the exposition above that this emphasis on oneness of faith is very strongly brought out in Orthodox teaching. So much is unity of the Faith necessary that deviation from or repudiation of any of the elements of the Church's faith brings about separation from the Church, and in consequence, loss of fellowship with the Holy Spirit. "It is a doctrine of the Orthodox Church, (as of every other Church which claims to be the true Church) . . . that the Church constitutes one body of the Faithful inseparably united with the Saviour, presenting the Word . . made flesh as ever . . in a present relation with men. As the Lord is the one Saviour of mankind . . . thus His Bride, the Church, is the one bearer of Grace, the one steward of the mysteries, and the one ark of salvation. So every theoretical deviation from the teaching of the Church is heresy, and every act of insubordination against her constitutional principles is schism. Both constitute a state of opposition to the divine authority of the Church and, according to the unanimous decision of the Fathers, (heretics and schismatics) are cut off from the Church and consequently from the fellowship of the Holy Spirit."[2] Thus wrong doctrine and heretical teach-

[1] *E. g., Epist. Dogm. Synod Const. ad orthodoxos Antiochenos,* 1722, in Mansi, XXXVII, cols. 128, 205; Ἔκδοσις Πίστεως of Const. 1723, *ibid.,* col. 897; Anthimus VI *Encyclical,* p. 36; Jeremiah II in Mesolora I. pp. 124 ff; Kritopoulos, *ibid.,* pp. 316-321; Mogila, *ibid.,* pp. 416-423; Dositheus, *ibid.,* II. pp. 111-112; cf. Ἀντιπαπικά, D. Kyriakos, Athens, 1893, pp. 28, 46; etc.

[2] Androutsos, Αἱ βάσεις . . . τῆς ἑνώσεως, pp. 32-33.

ing *ipso facto* both cut off from the unity of the Church. On this basis we may understand Rhôsse's conclusions. "The Christian Faith", he says in a footnote to his definition of dogma, "we may not simply define as the teachings about the operations of God . . . as formulated in the . . synods of the *Catholic* Church, . . . or of the 'Christian Church', . . . since the Church of Rome under the Pope calls itself the Catholic Church, though since the schism of the 9th century it is certainly not truly so,—and since other Christian bodies split off from it call themselves 'Catholic' or 'Christian' churches in some general or indefinite or elastic sense of these words: because the only true and genuine Catholic Church is the Orthodox Eastern Church, and to distinguish herself from the non-genuine 'Catholic' Church she is called the 'true Catholic and Orthodox Church of Christ'."[1]

In his section "on the true conception of the Orthodox Catholic Church as having authentic validity" he says: "The Orthodox and genuine Catholic Church is that fellowship of men founded and established by Christ and His Apostles, bound to Him and to each other by the right Faith, hope and love, by right dogmas, and by the true worship, and governed by bishops who are true and genuine successors of the Apostles." This general definition he goes on to explain, saying that up until the 9th century the Church consisted of two parts, Eastern and Western, holding the Orthodox faith, preserving the genuine tradition, the same dogmas and basis of worship, and the same organization and constitutional administration. "Since the 9th century, when the Western Church of Rome under the Pope was split off from the true Catholic and Orthodox Church of the first eight centuries, through (her) arrogant claims, innovations in dogma, worship, and discipline....and at divers other times different sections..split off in turn from the Church of Rome...., the Orthodox and genuine Catholic Church includes only the separate local Churches of the East, agreeing in the Faith (ὁμοδόξους) and Orthodox, and these constitute the Orthodox Apostolic Church, the continuation truly and canonically of the ancient Catholic Church of before the Schism." This

[1] *Op. cit.*, pp. 23-24, note.

252 IV.—DOCTRINE OF GRACE AND OF THE CHURCH

Church, he goes on to say, constitutes an organic whole, and is the only one which has preserved, intact and unalloyed, the genuine oral and written teaching of our Lord and the Apostles, the true dogmas of the Faith, right worship, and the genuine discipline of the Church.[1] Later on he expounds the Vincentian canon, saying that the conditions it lays down can "only be held to apply to the local and sectional Churches of the East and West up to the 9th century. . . . Thereafter the Churches of the West were sundered from the ancient Catholic Church by reason of innovation in doctrine, discipline, and worship. . . . and the words of St. Vincent apply only to the . . . . Churches of the East, which have neither added nor taken away, but have remained faithful in their teaching to the ancient Church of before the Schism. Hence the Orthodox. . . . are the true and canonical succession of the ancient Catholic Church."[2]

Since heresy forfeits membership in and communion with the Catholic Church and involves the loss of the Holy Spirit, Orthodox writers claim that the Orthodox Church is the only true Church. They are certainly convinced that the Roman Church is not a part of the Catholic Church, as their vast polemic and controversial literature shows. Invective, abuse, bitterness, recrimination, and violence of language characterize most of the products of this controversy, but even irenic and peaceful works do not retract from the position presented above.[3] In the year 1902 appeared a synodical letter from Constantinople, a treatise "on the Relations of the Autocephalous Orthodox Churches, and on other General Questions," emanating from the Patriarch, together with the answers thereto of the autocephalous Churches (Jerusalem, Greece, Russian, Serbia, Roumania, Montenegro), and the Patriarch's final

---

[1] Rhôsse, op. cit., pp. 56-57, and cf. his Αἱ θεμελιώδεις δογματικαὶ ἀρχαὶ τῆς ὀρθοδόξου ἀνατολικῆς Ἐκκλησίας, pp. 10, 28-30, etc.

[2] Op. cit., pp. 100-104.

[3] E. g., Ambraze, Ἡ Ὀρθόδοξος Ἐκκλησία. . . Athens, 1902 cf. pp. 1 57, et al.; Timothy Anastasius' Ἐπιστολὴ περὶ ἐνώσεως τ. ἐκκλησιῶν, to Prince Max of Saxony, Athens, 1910. In Palmieri (op. cit. vols. I. II.) may be found the history of the controversy, particularly, vol. I. pp. 661-698, 763-805.

response.[1] The cause of the issuing of this *encyclical* was un-doubtedly the whole question of reunion. With the authority of all the Orthodox Churches which endorse it, it contains official and definite teaching on matters which might otherwise be moot points.

"The central idea of these documents", says Androutsos in his tractate on "the Bases of the Unity of the Churches according to the Recent Pronouncements of the Orthodox Churches" (Αἱ τῆς ἑνώσεως τῶν ἐκκλησιῶν βάσεις κατὰ τὰ ἀρτιφανῆ τῶν ὀρθοδόξων Ἐκκλησιῶν Γράμματα, Constantinople, 1905, pp. 1-87) "is that the Eastern Church is the true Church of Christ—the One Holy Catholic and Apostolic Church of the Creed."[2] "Since the Schism the Orthodox Church is the only true and natural continuation of the undivided Church, bearing the promise and the validity of her invisible Head."[3] Macarius says: "It is an obvious truth that this Church (the Orthodox Church) is now the only Church which remains faithful to the ancient Ecumenical Councils, and in consequence she alone represents the true Catholic Church of Christ, which is infallible."[4] This is the mind of the *Encyclical* of the year 1848,[5] the synod of 1872 (Constantinople) expelling the Bulgarians from "the one Catholic and Apostolic Church,"[6] and of the *Encyclical* of 1896, which says: "The Orthodox Churches of the East and North (Russia) alone constitute to-day the only One Holy Catholic and Apostolic Church of Christ, the pillar and ground of the truth."[7] In the official *Encyclical* of 1902 referred to above, are the words: "Our Church only, the Orthodox Eastern

[1] Ἡ περὶ τῶν σχεσέων τῶν αὐτοκεφάλων ὀρθοδόξων Ἐκκλησιῶν καὶ περὶ ἄλλων γενικῶν ζητημάτων πατριαρχικὴ καὶ συνοδικὴ ἐγκύκλιος τοῦ 1902, αἱ εἰς αὐτὴν ἀπαντήσεις, κ. τ. λ.

[2] *Op. cit.*, p. 2.

[3] Androutsos, Αἱ βάσεις, p. 20. He quotes Platon of Moscow in his Catechism as saying: "The Orthodox Church is not only the true Church but the only Church" (*ibid.*, p. 21).

[4] Εἰσαγωγὴ εἰς τὴν ὀρθοδ. θεολογίαν, p. 955.

[5] P. 39 (Greek text); on it cf. Palmieri, *op. cit.*, I, p. 635.

[6] Cf. Papadopoulos, Ἡ σύγχρονος ἱεραρχία τῆς ὀρθοδόξου ἀνατολικῆς Ἐκκλησίας, Athens, 1895, p. 664.

[7] Ἐγκύκλιος πατριαρχικὴ κ. συνοδικὴ ἐπιστολή, Constantinople, 1895, p. 1, on which cf. Palmieri *op. cit.*, I. pp. 637 ff.

Church, having preserved incorruptedly the whole deposit of Christ, is at the present day the Universal (οἰκουμενική) Church."[1]

It is thus clear that the Orthodox Church claims not only to be the Catholic Church, but to be the whole and only Church. The next question is then in order: does the Orthodox Church maintain the doctrine of the Infallibility of the Church with distinct reference to her present situation? The Council of Constantinople (1672) defined: "About the Catholic Orthodox Church we say, that she is certain and unwavering, since she is led by Christ, her Head; that she is of herself true, and taught by the Spirit of truth. It is impossible for her to err."[2] That there is only one Head of the Church and that He is Christ, is taught clearly by all Orthodox authorities. On the basis of Eph. 5, 23, and 1 Cor. 3, 11, Mesolora says: "The Church proclaims Christ to be her only Head visible and invisible, for from Him she takes her origin, as a building established of God, and continues to be bound to Him as with her Founder and Highest Ruler, . . . the only source of her life."[3] As the Church under the leadership and headship of our Lord, having preserved inviolate all the dogmas of the Faith, "which the Saviour taught and His Apostles developed, and the Fathers formulated with one voice and without essential change, in the definitions and canons . . . of the ecumenical and local councils . . . the Eastern Church is the one true and Orthodox Church, which has her beginning from our Lord and the Apostles, which maintains unity with the ancient Church, is governed according to the canons, . . . and rejects innovations and everything leading to worldly and tyrannical power . . . Our Church only is infallible. . ."[4] "She only bears the marks of the religious fellowship founded by Jesus . . . She only bears the stamp of antiquity and unanimity in doctrine, discipline, and worship, and she only begets

---

[1] Pp. 33-34.

[2] Mesolora, *op. cit.*, II. p. 143.

[3] Cf. 1 St. Peter, 5, 4; 1 Cor. 12, 27; Mesolora, *op. cit.*, IV, p. 40, and cf. his whole treatment of the subject pp. 39-44; Eugenius Bulgaris, Θεολογικόν, pp. 49, 591-2; Kritopoulos, in Mesolora, *op. cit.*, I. pp. 359-360; Mogila, *ibid.*, pp. 417-418; Dositheus, *ibid.*, II. pp. 108, 112.

[4] Mesolora, *op. cit.*, IV. pp. 38-39.

the true spirit . . . and type of the Christian Faith."[1] "Our Church being an organic and visible body with a soul, whose Head is Christ and whose soul is the Holy Spirit, ever lives on, and without interruption ever operates under the guidance of the Holy Spirit abiding in her, 'leading her into all truth,' having the authority not only to counsel as to the right and the true, but also to call those who have strayed away, back to submission, possessing infallibility in her utterances concerning the Faith, and hence being able to settle any ecclesiastical question. She is constituted the Supreme judge of all ecclesiastical questions and affairs."[2]

The Orthodox Church, then, does lay claim to infallibility. In what sphere and by what means is it exercised? As was said above, the sphere of this infallibility is whatever concerns faith and morals[3]—"the true and genuine . . . knowledge of the whole Christian teaching."[4] Inasmuch as the content of the Faith was not fully realized at the first, nor is entirely perceived at any given stage of the Church's life, development and formulation of that Faith is necessary, as was seen in Lecture I. "The incomplete formulation of a dogma . . . is not an imperfection in the Faith, nor may it be ascribed to the Church as if by reason of this she is fallible . . . but it is only incompleteness in the knowledge of the Faith which, along with the growth of the Body, is gradually formulated little by little."[5] The organ for the formulation of doctrine is the Episcopate which when representing the whole Church, functions *ipso jure* infallibly.[6] The Ecumenical Councils represent such infallible action on the part of the Church, and are "Councils consisting of the whole Church or of all bishops or their delegated representatives convened for the purpose . . . of deliberating and expressing the mind (of the Church), of which the spirit and essence is in either the Holy Scripture or the ancient and genuine Tradition, written and unwritten, pre-

---

[1] *Ibid.*, p. 26.
[2] *Ibid.*, pp. 27-28.
[3] Cf. Androutsos, Δογματική, p. 291.
[4] Mesolora, *op. cit.*, IV. p. 21.
[5] Mesolora, *op. cit.*, IV. pp. 20-21.
[6] Androutsos, *ibid.*, p. 290.

served in the Church as a whole."[1]   Consequently whatever the
Episcopate teaches is infallible, "whether as in part in local
dioceses, or assembling as a whole in Ecumenical Councils."[2]

The Orthodox Church holds that infallibility belongs not
only to the Ecumenical Councils and their decrees, but as well
"to the local synods ratified by them and particularly to those
. . . from the 16th century on, which did nothing else than
formulate and define what was either universally accepted and
acknowledged by the conscience of the Faithful, or preserved in
the practice and customs of the Faithful, or had not yet been
defined in definite terms and enactments previous to the meeting of the synod, in opposition to false or heterodox doctrine
which up till then had not made its appearance."[3]   "Local
synods have not the obligatory, final, and divine authority
which belongs to the first Councils . . . but are recognized
by the Church as rightly developing and formulating its teaching. . . They did nothing else than formulate without change
the Orthodox spirit of the Church up till that time undeveloped
and unproclaimed publicly, because no error or contradiction
had made its appearance,"[4] necessitating such formulation.
Hence not only the definitions and decrees of the Ecumenical
Councils, but as well those of such synods as the above-men-
tioned, form part of Orthodox teaching, and "together with
Holy Scripture constitute the genuine and infallible rule of
Faith. . .   These synods of the Eastern Church . . . are
thus distinguished from other synods, Roman and Protestant,
. . . and in this possess infallibility, define and set down the
Orthodox Christian spirit, and constitute the continuation of
the true Catholic Tradition."[5]   The difference, then, between
Ecumenical Councils and local synods is this: the bishops as-

---

[1] Mesolora, ibid., p. 29.
[2] Androutsos, ibid.; pp. 287-288.
[3] Mesolora, op. cit., IV. p. 31.
[4] Mesolora, op. cit., IV. pp. 35-36. Chrysostom Papadopoulos, in
Δοσίθεος, Πατρ. Ἱεροσολ., in Νέα Σιών, vol. V. 1907, pp. 127, 128; Αἱ σύνοδοι
καὶ αἱ ὁμολογίαι τοῦ ιξ᾽ αἰῶνος, Νέα Σιών, vol. VII, 1908, p. 747; ibid.,
1909, vol. VIII. p. 358, discusses the formal character of these synods
in themselves.
[5] Ibid., pp. 36-37; cf. Eugenius Bulgaris, Θεολογικόν, pp. 61-63, and
pp. 48-59; Jeremiah II, in Mesolora, I, p. 124, pp. 236, 247, 264.

sembled in council, representing the whole Church, and engaged on matters within the province of infallibility, in their own right and by virtue of their office and position, constitute the organ for the infallible formulation of the Church's Faith. Their decisions are irreformable and of themselves infallible, and not from the acceptance of these enactments by the Church. This consent and acceptance is only the external criterion of ecumenicity and infallibility.[1] The decrees of a local synod are not thus immediately infallible, but only so by the consent of the Church, whether through ratification by an Ecumenical Council, or by acceptance on the part of the Church as a whole, in its several parts.[2] To the definitions and pronouncements of local synods subsequently ratified and accepted, is attached the infallible character with which our Lord endowed His Church.

This is in flat contradiction to the contentions of Palmieri, who in the chapter devoted to dogmatic development, attempts to show that "there has been . . . no relative development (*progressus dogmaticus secundum quid*) in the local synods of the Orthodox Church, nor, judging from past experience, can there be such in the future."[3] It is perfectly true that there is no *magisterium* in the Roman sense in the Orthodox Church. But his statement that there is "no authoritative *magisterium* in the Orthodox Churches . . . in matters of faith"[4] is entirely in opposition to the teaching and practice of Orthodoxy, as the exposition above shows. The unanimous mind of Orthodoxy on the subjects of Grace, the seven sacraments, the authority and nature of the Church, and the like, so far as the form of these doctrines goes, is entirely the result of the synods subsequent to the Schism of the two Churches. Variations as to disciplinary regulations, variety and contrariety of opinions as to the matters of excommunication, the expediency of the use of οἰκονομία in relation to Roman Catholics desiring to become Orthodox and the question of their rebap-

[1] Androutsos Δογματική, pp. 288-291.
[2] Androutsos, *ibid.*, and p. 11; Δογμ. Μελέται, A', pp. 129-130; cf. Dyobouniotes, 'Η Δογμ. 'Ανδρ. κριν., p. 49 and 'Οφειλ. ἀπάντ., p. 119; Androutsos, Δογμ. Μελ. A', pp. 142-143.
[3] *Op. cit.*, I. p. 67.
[4] *Ibid.*, p. 627, clearly phrased in three propositions, pp. 654-655.

tism, the divergence of opinion between Constantinople and Russia on the Bulgarian question—none of these proves Palmieri's case, according to the Orthodox mind. All of these apparent difficulties can be reconciled with the Orthodox theory of the infallibility of their Church, since all have to do with discipline and not with dogma.

As to the question, whether or not the Orthodox Church could convene an Ecumenical Council, Androutsos is quite clear. He devotes the central portion[1] of his tractate on Unity to the refutation of Dr. Neale's five contentions.[2] Dr. Neale argued for the "Branch Theory" and believed that it was entirely consistent with Orthodox teaching, since: (1) the Orthodox Church nowhere officially claims to be the one and only true Church; (2) she uses the titles "Eastern" and "Orthodox" in preference to "Catholic"; (3) she has relatively few adherents; (4) she recognizes as valid, sacraments not administered in her own Communion; (5) she does not proselyte among Roman Catholics and Protestants.[3] Androutsos rightly notes that the fact that the Orthodox Church, since the Schism of the 9th century, has never attempted to convene an Ecumenical Council, has given rise to the theory that she has not done so because she was not conscious of herself as constituting the whole Church, and in consequence, could not call an Ecumenical Council. This he says may be the opinion of a few so-called Orthodox writers,[4] but it certainly is contrary to the mind of Orthodoxy.[5] In the first place, there has not arisen a need sufficient to demand an Ecumenical Council. In the second place, difficulties of a practical nature have always been a factor, which is the case even in the present day as the *Encyclical* of 1902 shows.[6] That the convening of an Ecumenical Council is neither impossible nor improbable, is evident from the fact

---

[1] Pp. 19-58.

[2] *A History of the Holy Eastern Church*, vol. II, of *Introduction*, pp. 1199-1200.

[3] Androutsos, p. 19.

[4] Palmieri quotes but two such, both Russians, pp. 653-654, *op. cit.*, vol. I.

[5] On those who thus deviate from recognized Orthodoxy, cf. Androutsos, *op. cit.*, p. 20, and Συμβολική, p. 8.

[6] P. 25, quoted on p. 22 of Androutsos (Αἱ βάσεις . . . τῆς ἑνώσεως).

that the advisability of convening an Ecumenical Council was debated at the time of the Synod of 1872 (on the Bulgarian question), and more recently in Russia. In both cases the suggestion was disputed and finally rejected, but never was there "heard the slightest suggestion that the convening of a Council was in principle impossible because of the separation of the Eastern and Western Churches."[1] The Eastern Church furthermore does claim to be the one Catholic Church "to which all the notes of the true Church of Christ apply. . . . As the voice of the Church expressing itself in an Ecumenical Council is infallible . . . so the unanimous mind of the hierarchy of the Church everywhere (consensus ecclesiae dispersae), is not less the indication and authentic expression of the mind of the whole Church."[2]

It follows that if the Orthodox Church claim to be the Catholic Church and herself alone to possess infallibility, she can recognize no "branches" or "sections" of the Church. The Orthodox doctrine is both explicit and clear, according to Androutsos. There can be only one Church founded by our Lord, and in that Church there can be but one single Faith. This one Church is the Orthodox Church; the one Faith is the whole of Orthodox doctrine. There is no possible place for the theory that the unity of the Church was broken in the 9th and then in the 16th centuries. (a) There are not three "divisions" of the Church—Roman, Protestant, and Orthodox—as the Protestants hold; nor (b) three "Branches" of the Church—Roman, Anglican, and Orthodox—as the Anglicans believe. Either Rome or Orthodoxy must be right, as each claims to be the whole Catholic Church. Since Rome cannot substantiate her claim, Orthodoxy proves to be the true and only Church.[3] (a) The Protestant theory has already been disposed of, in the arguments adduced in the earlier portion of this lecture. (b) What of the "Branch Theory?"

According to Androutsos, the "Branch Theory" rests on a double fallacy: (1) that there is a unity of faith possible to communions which possess "essential" dogmas in common, and

---

[1] *Ibid.*, pp. 22-23, and cf. Ἐκκλησιαστ. Ἀλήθεια, 1889, no. 9.
[2] *Ibid.*, p. 24. This refutes Palmieri, *op. cit.*, I, pp. 653-655.
[3] *Ibid.*, pp. 2-6.

(2) a unity of organization and discipline in those which maintain a valid Apostolic Succession.[1] As was shown above, the distinction between "essential"and "secondary" dogmas is, according to Orthodox opinion, entirely illegitimate. It is not primitive, is historically unjustifiable, and was unknown until the Reformation in the 16th century.[2] If it were true, it would yet be necessary to discover some authority to expound the limits of fundamental as against secondary, dogmas. It can only be held on the principle that the Church has lost her infallibility, which Orthodoxy denies, and that the Catholic Church is sundered, which is impossible. "If our Lord founded His Church on earth . . . with which He abides being united with it forever . . . it is beyond dispute that it must be a unified and unique organic whole."[3] As the Orthodox Church is this one and only Church and is thereby infallible, whatever she teaches and all she teaches, is "of faith", and there can be no picking and choosing, no arbitrary selection among her doctrines, no division into "fundamental" and "secondary". In the words of the *Encyclical* of 1902: "We must guard in its integrity the divine jewel, the dogmas of the Orthodox Faith, which we have preserved intact for all the centuries past. We must preserve every liturgical custom of whatever sort which clearly symbolizes the essence of these dogmas. . . We must preserve entire the whole external life of Orthodoxy."[4] "The Ecumenical Councils did not formulate", says Androutsos in his tractate, "all the dogmas of the Orthodox Church, but many are enunciated in the local synods of the 17th century."[5] It is impossible, then, to limit the doctrines of the Church to those of the first five centuries, for example.[6] As Church teaching forms an organic whole[7] there is no choice but to ac-

---

[1] Δογματική, p. 262, note.
[2] Αἱ βάσεις . . . τῆς ἐνώσεως, pp. 15-18; Δογματική, pp. 276-277; but Ambraze's popular work ('Η 'Ορθόδοξος 'Εκκλησία...), which is primarily irenic and not dogmatic, employs this distinction; especially pp. 157 ff.
[3] Αἱ βάσεις . . . τῆς ἐνώσεως, p. 9, and cf. p. 13.
[4] P. 58, and cf. p. 61.
[5] Αἱ βάσεις . . . τῆς ἐνώσεως, p. 9, and cf. p. 40.
[6] *Ibid.*, p. 60.
[7] Δογματική, p. 277.

cept or reject it all. Negotiations towards reunion between the
Orthodox and the Old Catholics fell through because the latter,
believing that the Church's infallibility had disappeared with
the Schism in the 8th century, would not admit the binding
force of any dogmas formulated since the Ecumenical Councils.[1]
As Androutsos says: "The teaching of the Eastern Church, if
examined as to its essential character, shows itself to be the
same after as before the Schism, and is only different in definition and external form."[2] So in answer to the contention of
those who attempt to claim identity in fundamental teaching
as constituting dogmatic unity, Androutsos would say that there
is no differentiation of dogmas into fundamental and secondary;
all are on a par and all must be accepted. Agreement on the
basis of certain chosen doctrines does not constitute dogmatic
unity.

(2) In answer to the second contention, that episcopal ordination, and the preservation of a valid hierarchy constitutes
of itself the evidence of membership in the One Body, in spite
of external divisions and the absence of inter-communion, Androutsos says that the Catholic Church can recognize no body
but herself as belonging to the Church. Both the Protestant
theory of the "invisible Church" and the modern "Branch Theory" were unheard of in early times.[3] The Orthodox Church,
which claims to be the one Church, does call itself Catholic—
the preference for the term "Orthodox" not in the least proving Dr. Neale's point.[4] As to Dr. Neale's fourth contention,
that the Orthodox Church acknowledges as valid sacraments

[1] Cf. Mesolora, op. cit., IV, p. 30; Jeremiah II, in ibid., I, pp. 124,
193, 247, 264; Rhôsse, op. cit., pp. 59 ff. note; pp. 489-491; ibid.,
'Ορθοδοξίας καὶ Παλαιοκαθολικισμοῦ ἀντιθέσεις, pp. 16-28; Ὁ Παλαιοκαθολικισ-
μὸς ἐν σχέσει πρὸς τὴν γνησίαν καθολικότητα καὶ ὀρθοδοξίαν τ. 'Ανατ. 'Εκκλ.,
Athens, 1896; Palmieri, op. cit., I. p. 82 note, and II. pp. 188-189;
Androutsos, Αἱ βάσεις . . . τῆς ἐνώσεως, pp. 59-69.
[2] Αἱ βάσεις . . . τῆς ἐνώσεως, p. 65.
[3] Ibid., p. 49.
[4] Cf. ibid., pp. 25-32. The terms "Eastern" and "Orthodox" came
into use to distinguish the Church of the East from the Roman or
Western Church, and the title "Catholic", used officially by the Orthodox Church, has the same connotation of "Roman" in the East as in
the West.

administered outside her own Church,[1] Androutsos points out that the Eastern Church is quite consistent in her theory, but her practice, upon which Dr. Neale fastens, is open to misinterpretation. Since heretics and schismatics are not of the Church and are *ipso facto* sundered from the Body of Christ and the fellowship of the Holy Spirit, Orthodoxy acknowledges no sacraments as valid save those of the one true Church, that is, herself. To do so would be to acknowledge the parity and equality of heretics and schismatics with the Catholic Church, which, as will be seen, she may not do. But in cases where the Orthodox Church has deemed it for the good and need of souls, she may as "the sovereign over the sacraments. . . according to circumstances change invalid rites into valid sacraments." This she does by "economy" ($\kappa\alpha\tau$' $oi\kappa o\nu o\mu i\alpha\nu$) when she deviates from her normal and strict ($\kappa\alpha\tau$' $\dot{\alpha}\kappa\rho i\beta\epsilon\iota\alpha\nu$) manner of administration. It is impossible to discover the principle governing the use of "economy" in this matter, nor is there a *rationale* to determine the exercise of "economy" in any given case. Yet the Church exercises this right as mistress of the Grace of God, and has allowed as valid the baptism of heretics, which normally and regularly she pronounces entirely invalid. It is not a question of the due matter and form, or of the proper intention: a body even with formally valid orders outside the Church has lost the fellowship of the Holy Spirit by whose agency only the Sacraments become realities. This is clearly shown by the *Acts* of the synod which condemned the Bulgarian Church, in which it was said that the excommunicated bishops "played with what ought not be played with, since they had fallen from the Grace of Orders, and profess to transmit to others the Grace of Orders, from which they had fallen. Who is able to give, as says the synod of Carthage, what he has not, or how may the Holy Spirit, having cast them forth (through them), work spiritual effects?"[2] So the exercise of "economy"[3] does not mean that the Orthodox Church recognizes, either in theory or practice, the

---

[1] *Ibid.*, p. 19.

[2] *Acts* of the Synod of 1872, p. 57 quoted by Androutsos, p. 36. His whole discussion epitomized above, is on pp. 32-53 *op. cit.*

[3] On this whole subject cf. Lecture V. on *The Sacraments*, and J. A. Douglas, *The Relations of the Anglican Churches with the Eastern-Orthodox*, London, 1921, on this question of "economy".

existence of any other body than herself as having valid orders, and so having this much claim to be part of the Church. She recognizes no Church but herself.[1]

In summary we may state, (a) that the Orthodox Church claims to be the whole and only Catholic Church; (b) that as such she claims infallibility; (c) that she can recognize no unity of doctrine save on the basis of the acceptance of the whole of her teaching; (d) that she cannot admit the existence of any "members" or "branches" of the Church, since it is constituted of herself alone, nor the validity of any sacraments save her own. Consequently her ideal of unity is not that of gathering up and uniting the divided portions of the Church, but a return of all heretical or schismatical bodies to the one Church. "As the Orthodox Church constitutes the true Church of Christ, any 'Church' outside her cannot be a true or equal member of the true Church, and if reunion should take place between Orthodoxy and these Churches, it would not constitute a reëstablishment of the broken and destroyed unity of the Church, but only a return to the true form of Christianity."[2] . . . "Our desire", says the *Encyclical* of 1902, "is that all heterodox shall come into the bosom of the Orthodox Church of Christ, which only is able to give them salvation."[3]

Additional Note on the Rebaptism of Latins

The theory of the Orthodox Church as to the validity of sacraments has been given above: no sacraments are valid outside the Church, in which only the Holy Spirit is present as the agent in all sacraments. It is much more consistent, according to Androutsos, than the Roman theory inherited from St. Augustine. According to this theory, Baptism may be validly administered by anyone whatsoever who uses the proper matter and form with the proper intention. In the case of a heretic or infidel baptising a person, he does not act *qua* here-

---

[1] *Ibid.*, pp. 25-26, cf. note below on the question of the rebaptism of Latins.

[2] Androutsos, p. 4 (Αἱ βάσεις . . . τῆς ἑνώσεως).

[3] P. 48. The Orthodox theory, as herein presented, is thus perfectly lucid, consistent, and utterly inelastic. It is significant that there is no room in it for the "Branch Theory" of the Anglican Church. (Cf. Androutsos, *op. cit.*, pp. 84-85.

tic but, for the time being, as a member of the Church. In all cases it is our Lord's command which is being obeyed, and His efficient Word brings to pass what He has enjoined, despite the unworthiness or the anomalous position of the officiant. So far as validity is concerned, sacraments may then be administered validly outside the Church.[1] The Orthodox objections brought against this view are weighty: (a) it is not the primitive conception, for the distinction of "regularity" and "validity" was unknown to the early Church;[2] (b) if those who act in good faith, being outside the Church but carefully satisfying all the required conditions for the validity of sacraments, are truly recipients of Grace, are made regenerate in Baptism, and receive the grace of the Eucharist, then both theoretically and practically the dogma of the unity of the one true Church is made of no effect: theoretically, the acceptance of validity of sacraments outside the Church extends the Church beyond the bounds of the visible Church and makes it equivalent to the "invisible Church" of the Protestants; practically, such an admission is tantamount to the acknowledgment of a certain status of other religious bodies as possessing in some degree membership in the Catholic Church, and thus violating the essential principle of the actual and objective unity of the Church.[3] (c) It involves an utterly mechanical and magical conception of the Sacraments, which the early Church neither recognized nor accepted.[4]

If the difficulties and inconsistencies in the Roman theory are apparent, the difficulties of the Orthodox theory, large as they may bulk in the eyes of outsiders, are all resolvable by the theory of "economy". The Orthodox Church recognizes no sacraments outside herself as valid, yet may in practice relax the stringency of her theory and accept them as valid under certain circumstances in the case of outsiders coming into the

[1] Androutsos, Αἱ βάσεις . . . τῆς ἐνώσεως, pp. 36-38.

[2] *Ibid*, p. 34. The Eastern Fathers did not recognize baptism by heretics, *e. g.*, St. Basil, St. Athanasius, St. Gregory Nazianzen, St. Cyril of Jerusalem, St. Cyprian, St. Firmilian, the local synods in Africa and Asia Minor, etc.

[3] Androutsos, *ibid.*, pp. 40-45.

[4] Dyobouniotes, Τὰ Μυστήρια, pp. 30-31, and cf. p. 65, Androutsos, Δογματική, pp. 300-301, *et al.*

Church. This she does because the Church is the guardian, administrator, and sovereign of the sacraments. While we may not predict the circumstances and occasions in which she may so exercise discretion and condescension in her practice, nevertheless, granted the principle, she is entirely consistent in theory. If she allows Baptism by any other than a priest (who is the regular minister of that sacrament) she does so by the use of "economy".[1] All of the occasions in which her practice seems inconsistent, illogical, and without a fixed principle determining her course of action, may be accounted for on the basis of "economy".[2]

In the Orthodox Church there has been a great diversity of rulings on the part of local synods and councils, on the question of rebaptism of Roman Catholics, and the recognition of Roman, Nestorian, or Armenian orders as valid. This diversity has laid her open to the charge of having no principle at all in such matters.[3] Palmieri points out that the synod of Moscow in 1620 held the baptism of Latins invalid, but those of 1656 and 1666-1667 reversed this judgment. The attitude of the Greeks was equally inconsistent. Macarius of Antioch (1648-72) regarded Roman Baptism as valid, but subsequent synods, under the Patriarchs Cyril V (1748-1751; 1752-1757) and Paisius II (1751-1752), reversed this decision, saying "we regard them as unbaptized and as needing to be baptized."[4] Again, the synod of Constantinople in 1875 writing to the Holy Synod of Athens, said that this ruling had been "necessary in view of the circumstances of Orthodoxy",[5] and reversed it. Three years later it sanctioned the practice of admitting "Romans and Armenians by Holy Baptism according to the regulations of our Orthodox Church, and not by anoint-

[1] *Ibid.*, note 2 pp. 30-31.

[2] Cf. Theotokas, Νομολογία τοῦ Οἰκουμενικοῦ Πατριαρχείου, Constantinople, 1896, pp. 367 ff; on the difficulties in attempting to discern the principle guiding the exercise of "economy" cf. Androutsos *op. cit.*

[3] E. g., Palmieri, *Le rebaptisation des latins chez les Grecs*, in *Révue de l'Orient chrétien*, vol. VII, 1902, pp. 618-646; VIII, 1903, pp. 111-143; *Un document inédit sur la rebaptisation des latins chez les Grecs*, in *Révue Bénédictine*, 1906, pp. 215-231.

[4] In Gedeon, Κανονικαί διατάξεις, vol. I. p. 254—cf. Palmieri, *Theol. Dog. Orth.*, I. pp. 623-625, 617-618, and cf. pp. 8-9.

[5] In Thotokas, *op. cit.*, p. 369.

ing with Holy Chrism alone.'"[1] In 1879 it "allowed . . . three Protestants and Roman Catholics to be received into the Orthodox Church by anointing with Holy Chrism'"[2] alone. Palmieri makes much of these variations in practice, as he does of the repudiation by the Russian Church of the excommunication of the Bulgarians pronounced by Constantinople in 1872.[3] On the Roman theory all such deviations would be utterly anomalous. On the Orthodox theory they are certainly not. If the Orthodox premises are true and the Church can administer the sacraments as she deems wise—in this case relaxing her strictness, in that observing it—there is nothing at all wrong in principle in all these varieties in practice. Whether or not occasions of the exercise of "economy" can become a precedent for other cases in which the circumstances may be adjudged similar, is an entirely different question.[4]

"The Greek Church", says Androutsos, "from the time of the Schism generally accepted the Baptism of Roman Catholics, consonant with the synod of 1484 which met at Constantinople. From 1756 in accordance with a decision given in synod under Cyril V, it baptized Latins and Protestants over again, though instances are not lacking of their reception without rebaptism, for example, the case of Princess Sophia the consort of the Heir Apparent.[5] On the contrary, the Russian Church and with it the other autocephalous Churches, formerly rebaptized them, which practice the synod of Moscow under Philaret confirmed, but since that held in Moscow in 1667 they

[1] *Ibid.*, p. 370.
[2] *Ibid.*
[3] Cf. his *Theol. Dog. Orth.*, I, pp. 9-10 *et al.*
[4] Ambraze ('Η 'Ορθόδοξος 'Εκκλησία) gives on pp. 161 ff. a list of such instances of the exercise of "economy", using them as possible precedents for indicating the course of the Orthodox Church in the problem of Reunion. It is questionable whether such instances may be quoted as precedents. On the subject cf. J. A. Douglas, *op. cit.*, Androutsos on *The Validity of English Ordinations from an Orthodox-Catholic Point of View*, London, 1909, and in the lectures following pp. 282-286, 292-303, 377-378.
[5] On the service for her admission, and a brief history of the occasion, cf. Ambraze, 'Η 'Ορθόδοξος 'Εκκλησία, pp. 168-170. She is the wife of Constantine, and is the present Queen of Greece. She was baptized in the German Evangelical Church.

have been receiving Latins by document,[1] or by anointing,[2] if they have not been anointed (=confirmed), and Protestants by anointing, according to the decision of 1718. This difference can be explained on historical grounds, since it is to be attributed to the scandalous proselyting efforts of the Papists at different times in Turkey and Russia. From the dogmatic standpoint, however, we can gain nothing from this explanation, for as Baptism is a sacrament and possesses dogmatic significance, recognition of it or the reverse may not be considered as the work of the Church in her disciplinary capacity, altering its decision as it does with places and seasons. The reason adduced by some Orthodox writers—the lack of the trine immersion, considered formerly as essential except only in the cases of clinical Baptism under urgent necessity—cannot explain both practices, but only one of the two. For either trine immersion is necessary, and for lack of it Romans and Protestants are unbaptized, or else it is relatively necessary, and Roman and Protestants, as baptized by clinical Baptism, need not be baptized again, for he who rebaptizes them incurs the severe interdict for sin of this nature. The difficulty lies deeper, in the acceptance of the theory that there may be Grace outside the Church. It is certainly the case that in the Eastern Church the validity of sacraments after the Schism was not properly regarded from the standpoint of the Church as the one steward of Grace and salvation. The sacraments of the Latins and Protestants were rejected rather because of the violation of the ritual parts—the trine immersion. But if one take the Armenians into consideration, who although baptized by immersion yet oftentimes on coming into Orthodoxy were rebaptized by us,[3] he will recognize that the ancient theory that outside the Church Grace does not operate and consequently sacraments are *ab initio* invalid, even though it were not studied out in theory, underlies the practice of the Church at all times and is everywhere presupposed."[4]

[1] *I. e.*, a recantation of heretical beliefs, and a profession of Orthodoxy.

[2] διὰ μύρου—oil of the catechumens. It is not the Chrism (of Confirmation).

[3] Cf. Theotokas Νομολογία, p. 366.

[4] Androutsos, Δογματική, pp. 332-333, note, and cf. Dyobouniotes, Τὰ Μυστήρια, pp. 64-65, note 1.

LECTURE V.

V.—THE DOCTRINE OF THE SACRAMENTS

LECTURE V.

THE DOCTRINE OF THE SACRAMENTS

CONTENTS

I. THE SACRAMENTS IN GENERAL

1. The Notion and Purpose of Sacraments

The Orthodox Church uses the term "mystery" for what in the Western Church is called "sacrament". The word "mystery" (μυστήριον) is derived from the verb μύειν, to initiate, originally signifying "to close the means of communication"—the eyes, ears, and lips. So it was used by the "mystery religions", and in the Orphic and Eleusinian "Mysteries".[1] "The initiates (μεμνημένοι) had not the right to look upon the rites and speak of the teachings in public, but had to preserve them secretly (μυστικῶς) and reverence them in silence. Hence the word μύειν came to mean to teach sacred and mysterious things."[2] By extension of this meaning the word "mystery" came to denote anything hidden or incomprehensible,—in English, a "mystery"or "secret".[3] Thus it was applied to what we call "mysteries" of the Faith,—the Cross, the works of Redemption, the doctrine of the Holy Trinity, and the like. Finally it came to have a special application, by reason of its double connotation of "religious", and "secret" or "mysterious", to certain definite means of Grace in the Church, to which in its technical meaning it is exclusively referred.[4] The word "sacrament" from *sacrare,* to "dedicate" or "make holy", came to be used to mean "oath". Tertullian applied it to the Christian's oath of Baptism, by which he becomes a soldier of the Church militant. Its subsequent development was somewhat analogous to that of the term "mystery", and it finally came to be applied exclusively to the seven definite means of Grace

---

[1] Dyobouniotes, Τὰ Μυστήρια, p. 8 note.
[2] Mesolora, *op. cit.,* IV. p. 138, note 2.
[3] *E g.,* Tim. 3, 16; Eph. 1, 9; 3, 9; 5, 32; Col. 1, 27; St. Matt. 13, 11, etc. Dyobouniotes *ibid.*
[4] Androutsos, Δογματική, p. 294 and note.

of the Catholic Church.[1] Mesolora claims that the word "mystery" is the more exact, and is to be preferred to "sacrament" in that "it expresses more deeply and amply the mysterious character of the power and concurrence of divine Grace in the believer."[2] In these lectures the English word "sacrament" will be used for the Greek μυστήριον.

"Regenerating, justifying, and sanctifying Grace is brought to the faithful in the Christian Church by means of the sacraments",[3] which are external and tangible means and acts. "As such, the sacraments are founded on the close connection of spirit and matter, of the supernatural and the material, which pervades the whole of Christianity. That which is perceptible is neither unclean nor naturally evil....but is elevated by Christianity in its wholesome form, into a symbol and bearer of spiritual and supernatural power:....that saving power which flows from the death of Christ."[4] There can be no dualism or manicheism in genuine Christianity. The two-fold character of the means of Grace is demanded by and involved in the two-fold character of the Church,—visible and invisible,—for the Church as visible must use visible means to convey her invisible Grace in accordance with the aim of her Founder.[5] This is the teaching of the Fathers.[6] The sacraments are "the various manifestations of our Lord's saving power, and the means by which Christ is present and works in His Church....As the Church is the perpetual extension of Christ,....so the sacraments are the power by which the Church sanctifies men, and the seven pillars which uphold the religious and moral life of the Faithful."[7] The sacraments

[1] Dyobouniotes, *ibid.*, and p. 9, note.

[2] *Ibid.*, p. 149. For the Latin word, cf. Tertullian, *adv. Marc.* 2, 27; *de praescrip. haer.*, 40; St. Cyprian, *Epistola*, 73, 22; St. Augustine on St. John 80, on Ps. 73; St. Hugo of St. Victor's *de Sacramentis Christianae Fidei.*

[3] Dyobouniotes, *op. cit.*, p. 3.

[4] Androutsos, *op. cit.*, pp. 292-293.

[5] Mesolora, *op. cit.*, IV, pp. 139-140, and cf. (in Mesolora, I,) Jeremiah II's *First Answer*, p. 141; *Second Answer*, p. 229; Kritopoulos, *ibid.*, p. 312.

[6] Cf. St. John 1, 17; St. John Chrysostom, in 1 *Epist. ad Cor. hom.* 7; St. Augustine, *Sermo* 272; Dositheus in Mesolora, II, p. 114, *et al.*

[7] Androutsos, *op. cit.*, p. 293.

may then be defined as "the divine rites instituted by Christ and His Apostles, which through visible signs convey hiddenly the Grace of God."[1] The word μυστήριον in its technical meaning is distinguished from the wider meaning in regard both to the thing concerned, the sanctification of man, and the manner of accomplishing this end,—not by symbolizing, but by actually communicating, sanctifying Grace. The sacraments are then "the divinely instituted rites manifesting and communicating invisible Grace."[2] The aim and object of the sacraments is thus apparent from the definition. They are "the abundant springs of divine Grace by which the Saviour satisfies all the spiritual needs of the members of the Church". Their purpose, Mesolora says, is four-fold: "(a) the communication and guarantee of divine Grace; (b) the distinctive notes of the true Church; (c) the bond of love and incentive for the exercise of virtues,.. and (d) the memorial of the great and wondrous deeds wrought by our God and Saviour for us men."[3]

(a) The distinctive and constituent notes of the sacraments involved in the definitions above are three: (a) divine institution, (b) outward sign, and (c) inward Grace given. All Orthodox teaching unites in asserting that our Lord instituted and established all seven sacraments. All that the Apostles did was done in His name,[4] and while we have the explicit record of our Lord's institution of the sacraments of Baptism and the Eucharist, but no scriptural record of His having established the other five, still "inasmuch as Holy Scripture does not show the contrary, . . . what is true of Baptism and the Eucharist is taken by analogy as true of the other sacraments as well."[5] On the basis of the definite witness of our Lord's having established the two sacraments of Baptism and the Eucharist, Dyobouniotes says: "We may presume with great certainty that the others, like Baptism and the Euchar-

---

[1] Dyobouniotes, *op. cit.*, pp. 8-9.

[2] Androutsos, *op. cit.*, pp. 294-295. Mesolora's definition (*op. cit.*, IV, p. 143) is substantially the same, but less concise.

[3] Mesolora, *op. cit.*, IV. pp. 140-141; cf. Mogila in Mesolora, I., pp. 423-424.

[4] Cf. 1 Cor. 4, 1; St. Matt. 28, 19; St. John 20, 21-23; Heb. 2; 10; 10, 7; Gal. 4, 4; 2 Cor. 5, 19, etc.

[5] Androutsos, *op. cit.*, p. 295.

ist, were instituted by our Lord."[1] "It is necessary", says Mesolora, "that they have their beginning, institution, and warrant, either from our Lord and God, as Founder of the Christian religion, as "Captain of our Salvation" and Source of Grace, or from the Apostles who founded the Church on Christ the Cornerstone, from Whom directly or indirectly they received the command regarding the hallowing of certain fixed rites, the sacraments."[2] The first explicit mention of this doctrine is found in Ps. Ambrose, in the words: *quis est auctor sacramentorum nisi Dominus Jesus? De coelo sacramenta venerunt.*[3] While it is not legitimate to ascribe the establishment of the other five sacraments to the Church, it is consistent with Orthodox thought to hold that they were instituted not directly by our Lord, but indirectly through the Apostles, which "opinion does not detract from their divine institution, in that it holds that they were founded by our Lord's command through His Apostles,"[4] nor "does it diminish in the least their divine validity. . . . Whether mediately or immediately, the institution of these mysteries is ascribed to our Lord, and the fact is essentially the same either way." It is also allowable to consider that our Lord did not prescribe or order these five sacraments in detail, but left the determination of their outward signs to the Apostles.[5] Both of these theories, however, are only theological opinions and not dogma.

(b) Inasmuch as the Church is both visible and invisible, and man, to whom our Lord ministers through her, is composed of body and soul, every sacrament must have an outward and visible sign. The Church thereby refutes every dualistic

---

[1] *Op. cit.*, p. 10.

[2] *Op. cit.*, IV. p. 163; cf. Jeremiah II. in Mesolora I. pp. 229, 140-141, 263; Dositheus, *ibid.*, II. pp. 113-114; Kritopoulos, I. pp. 339, 320.

[3] *De Sacr.* 4, 4, 13.

[4] Dyobouniotes, *op. cit.*, p. 11; for the general principle cf. the words of Kritopoulos: "The Apostles would not have dared to do something not enjoined upon them (by our Lord)" (in Mesolora, I, p. 337).

[5] Androutsos, *op. cit.*, pp. 296-297. Dyobouniotes seems to prefer the theory that the outward signs were also ordained by our Lord for the other five sacraments, since: (a) they are so early, (b) so universal, and (c) without diversity of custom or (d) ascription of any human origin (*op. cit.*, p. 13).

theory, as was mentioned above, and this principle is clearly taught form the earliest times.[1] By "outward signs" the Church means the external acts and words, the physical and tangible part as a whole, in contrast to the Grace given,—the invisible and spiritual part of the sacraments. The "rites and words which are absolutely essential to the consummation of the sacrament and the conveying of its Grace" constitutes the "outward sign."[2] Orthodox theologians with a few excep. tions[3] eschew the refinements of scholastic dialectical distinctions, both as involving the whole scholastic theological outlook, and as unnecessary.[4]

(c) The outward signs in the sacraments convey and transmit Grace not of themselves but by the presence of the Holy Spirit,[5] and this Grace is not the same in every sacrament, but is in each case different and ordered for its own particular end. So in Baptism and Chrism one is justified, in the Eucharist he is fed and quickened, and the like.[6] The Grace is not merely symbolized or promised, but actually conveyed to the believer; and the true conception of sacrament necessarily involves this.[7] The Protestant conception of the sacraments as merely "signs" or "symbols" is utterly contrary to the teaching of Holy Scripture and the Church.[8] What the relation is between the outward sign and the Grace given by it has been a subject of theological speculation for centuries. The outward sign serves to "externalize the invisible and hidden Grace of God" which it conveys,[9] but does the Grace accompany the sign or is it enshrined within it? Origen and his disciples seemed to hold the former theory, and St. Cyril

---

[1] Cf. St. John Chrysostom, on St. Matt. 84, 2.

[2] Dyobouniotes, op. cit., pp. 13-14.

[3] E. g., Jeremiah II, 1st Answer, in Mesolora, op. cit., I, p. 140, uses the distinction of matter and form.

[4] Cf. Androutsos, op. cit., pp. 297-298; Dyobouniotes, pp. 11-15, and Mesolora, IV. p. 164 (with references).

[5] Dyobouniotes, op. cit., p. 15.

[6] Androutsos, op. cit., p. 298.

[7] Ibid., p. 299; Dyobouniotes op. cit., pp. 16-17.

[8] Ibid., and Mesolora, op. cit., IV. pp. 144-5, 147, 165; and cf. Androutsos, Συμβολική, pp. 251 ff.

[9] Mesolora, loc cit., p. 164.

of Alexandria the latter.[1] Gabriel of Philadelphia[2] and the *Confession* of Mogila[3] both regard the Grace as being within the sign (ἐγκεκαλυμμένην; ἀποκάτω εἰς εἶδος). Dyobouniotes says that as the Fathers professed ignorance of the manner whereby Grace is conveyed in the sacraments, neither Gabriel nor Mogila may be taken as rightly representing the mind of the Church.[4] Androutsos says that the question is in any case without importance for dogmatic.[5]

Inasmuch as our Lord instituted the sacraments, "the Grace conveyed by them is absolutely necessary to salvation."[6] This is true not only because of the divine institution but also because the Grace conveyed by the sacraments, "guaranteeing and sealing our salvation,"[7] is indispensible for us.[8] Hence the lack of them means the lack of salvation. This does not mean that everyone must make use of all the sacraments, but that each must use those necessary for him. We may not say, in the absence of any revelation on the subject, that one may not be saved without them, provided the failure to receive them has not been due to contempt of them or unpardonable negligence on our part.[9] If failure to use them is due to these causes then one is deprived of salvation. "But God is certainly able to save....otherwise than through the sacraments....Nevertheless he who despises or is indifferent to the divinely instituted means of Grace is surely not to be excused."[10]

---

[1] St. Cyril in Migne, *P. G.* t. LXXIII, 245.

[2] *De Sacramentis* 4, quoted by Androutsos, p. 298, note 2.

[3] In Mesolora, *op. cit.*, I, p. 423.

[4] *Op. cit.*, p. 18.

[5] *Op. cit.*, p. 299.

[6] Dyobouniotes, p. 23.

[7] Mesolora, IV. p. 141.

[8] Androutsos, p. 299.

[9] Cf. St. Augustine: *non defectus sed contemptus sacramenti damnat.*

[10] Androutsos, *op. cit.*, pp. 299-300, and Dyobouniotes (*op. cit.*, pp. 23-24) comes to almost the same conclusion.

2. The Number and Classification of the Sacraments

The seven sacraments of the Orthodox Church are: Baptism, Chrism,[1] Eucharist, Penance, Orders (ἱερωσύνη="priesthood"), Marriage, and ,Unction. · "Each of these seven sacraments is founded upon express words of Holy Scripture and the New Testament, of which the conception was interpreted and defined from early times by sacred Tradition and the voice of the Church as a whole."[2] Accordingly, *Baptism* is referred to St. Matt. 28, 19-20; *Chrism* to Acts 8, 14-17; 19, 2-7, (Heb. 6,2) ; the *Euchdrist* to St. Matt. 26, 26-28; St. Mark 14, 22-25; St. Luke 22, 19-20; 1 Cor. 11, 23-25; *Penance* to St. John 20, 21-23 (St. Matt. 16, 19; 18, 17, 18; Acts 19, 18) ; *Orders* to 1 Tim. 4, 14; 2 Tim. 1, 6; Acts. 6, 6; 8, 17; (13, 3) ; *Marriage* to Eph. 5, 22-32; 1 Cor. 7, 14, 39; (St. Matt. 19, 6), and *Unc-tion* to St. Jas. 5, 13-15.[3] There have been different explanations of the number—the satisfaction of the sevenfold needs of man's spiritual and moral life by corresponding provisions of Grace, the seven gifts of Grace as in a way parallel to the seven gifts of the Holy Spirit, and the like. All such, says Androutsos, "are not logical proofs that there ought to be seven sacraments . . . but conjectures *ex post facto* to show that the divinely instituted sacraments are fitted to the nature and needs of man."[4] While the seven sacraments were known from the earliest times, yet the definition that there were seven came much later.[5] The fact of Grace being communicated by these seven means was early recognized, but "not only in Tradition is the distinct and specific numbering of them as seven lacking, but the sacraments are mentioned along with other holy acts and deeds—the monastic life, services for the dead, the sign of the cross, and the like. To explain this phenomenon one must consider that Revelation does not present dogmas systematically, and that the Church defines them officially only when they are

[1] Dositheus calls it βεβαίωσις (Confirmation), in Mesolora, *op. cit.,* II. p. 113.
[2] Mesolora, *op. cit.,* IV, p. 160 and cf. Kephala, Χριστολογία, pp. 197-198.
[3] Mesolora *ibid.,* and p. 161; Dyobouniotes, *op. cit.,* p. 19.
[4] *Op. cit.,* pp. 312-313.
[5] Dyobouniotes, *op. cit.,* p. 20 and note 1.

brought into question."[1] So we do not find the full enumeration in the Fathers—some of them mentioning two only,[2] others three,[3] and others four.[4] "But if the general notion of the sacraments and their enumeration only came about later, yet the faith in the seven sacraments as divinely instituted means of Grace has always existed in the Church."[5] The first mention in the East of all seven sacraments is by the monk Job in 1270,[6] who, however, counts the monastic state as one of the seven, omitting Penance, and also by Michael Paleologus at the synod of Lyons in 1274.[7] The first appearance of the explicit enumeration of the seven in the West is by Peter Lombard[8] and Alexander III.[9]

Both West and East are officially committed to the doctrine of the seven sacraments. The evidence of the Symbolic Books is most explicit. Dositheus says in his *Confession* (article 15): "We believe that there are gospel sacraments in the Church and these are seven , . . no more and no less."[10] So too, Jeremiah II,[11] Kritopoulos,[12] the Synod of Constantinople,[13] and Mogila.[14] Despite the absence of explicit testimony from early times, the evidence for the seven sacraments is very strong indeed, and may be summarized as follows: (a) both East and West, Rome and Orthodoxy, agree in the number and names of the seven sacraments, which teaching is official and *de fide* in both Communions; (b) the Nestorians and Monophysites (5th cent.) both teach seven sacraments, and it is impossible

[1] Androutsos, *op. cit.*, p. 315.

[2] *E. g.*, St. Justin Martyr, *Apologia*, I; St. Augustine on Ps. 108; St. John Damascene ("Εκδοσις, IV. 9 and 13), St. John Chrysostom, etc.

[3] St. Cyril of Jerusalem, *Cat.*, 1-3; 1-4; St. John Damascene, *op. cit.*, IV, 4, 13; St. Ambrose, *de Sacramentis*, 3 and 4.

[4] St. Augustine, *de bapt.* 5, 20.

[5] Androutsos, *ibid.*, p. 316.

[6] *Ibid.*, pp. 314-316 and Dyobouniotes, *op. cit.*, p. 20.

[7] On which cf. Palmieri, *op. cit.*, p. 89.

[8] *Sent.*, 4, 13; not by Hugo of St. Victor, to whom the authorship of *de caeremoniis* was wrongly attributed.

[9] Androutsos and Dyobouniotes, *loc. cit.*

[10] In Mesolora, II, p. 113 and p. 114.

[11] Mesolora, I, pp. 141, 229, 263, *et al.*

[12] *Ibid.*, pp. 320-339.

[13] II. p. 30.

[14] I, pp. 423 ff.

that they should have received this doctrine from without, since the hostility between them and the Orthodox would have made it impossible; (c) while there was, it is true, no explicit enumeration of all seven in the early Church, yet the teaching as to each of them finds support in the Fathers and in Tradition.[1]

Various classifications of the seven sacraments are found in Orthodox writers. The fact that the institution of Baptism and the Eucharist by our Lord is explicitly given in the New Testament accords them a preëminent position. "Of the sacraments," says Androutsos, "Baptism and the Eucharist hold a special place as the chief."[2] As regards the Anglican doctrine of the "two Sacraments generally necessary to salvation" and the restriction of the use of the term to those "ordained of Christ in the Gospel . . . with a visible sign or ceremony ordained of God",[3] both Mesolora[4] and Androutsos,[5] on the basis of the Bishop of Salisbury's exposition of the Anglican belief,[6] seem to find it acceptable. Ambraze, with earnest zeal for reunion, presents effectively this diversity of usage in Orthodoxy with special reference to the Anglican formularies.[7] In his book on "the Orthodox Church in relation to all other Christian bodies" he says:[8] "The *Orthodox Confession* (that is, that of Mogila), regards the 'sacrament of the Eucharist as above all the others, and more than the others necessary for our salvation."[9] The Patriarch Jeremiah II regards 'Baptism and the Eucharist as the chiefest of the sacraments' "[10] . . . Metrophanes Kritopoulos says of these two

---

[1] Dyobouniotes, *op. cit.*, pp. 20-21 and notes; Androutsos, *op. cit.*, pp. 316-317; Mesolora, *op. cit.*, IV. p. 155.

[2] *Op. cit.*, p. 313.

[3] Cf. Art. XXXV. of B. C. P.

[4] *Op. cit.*, IV. pp. 146-148 and notes.

[5] *Op. cit.*, p. 317.

[6] Θέματα τῆς διδασκαλίας τῆς ᾽Εκκλησίας τῆς ᾽Αγγλίας πρὸς πληροφορίαν τῶν ᾽Ορθοδόξων ἐκδοθέντα, by John, Lord Bishop of Salisbury.

[7] Cf. his Δοκίμιον περὶ ἐνώσεως τῶν ᾽Αγγλικῶν ᾽Επισκοπιανῶν μετὰ τῆς ᾽Ορθοδόξου ᾽Ανατολικῆς ᾽Εκκλ., Athens, 1891, pp. 73-79.

[8] ῾Η ᾽Ορθόδοξος ᾽Εκκλησία . . . Athens, 1902, *ibid.*, p. 85, ff.

[9] Mesolora, I, p. 427.

[10] Mesolora, I, p. 228.

that they are "called sacraments . . . (as) consisting of visible matter and the Holy Spirit. . ." With Penance they constitute "the three sacraments necessary for salvation. . . Besides which necessary sacraments are other mystical rites also called sacraments by the Church."[1] Ambraze also quotes the Protopresbyter Constantine as saying in his Catechism that "there are two chief and preëminent sacraments of the New Testament, Baptism and the Eucharist," and Platon of Moscow to the same purpose.[2] Nevertheless, as we have seen, there are seven sacraments according to Orthodox teaching, which are sufficient to satisfy all the religious needs of man, the Grace given through which being absolutely necessary for salvation,[3] all seven must be accepted "as being necessary for the salvation of the faithful."[4] "According to the spirit of Orthodoxy", says Mesolora, "all the seven sacraments are divinely instituted, and of equal rank."[5]

Besides regarding the sacraments as only "signs" and "symbols",[6] Protestantism rejects the five sacraments of which the institution is not explicitly recorded in Holy Scripture, accepting only two, Baptism and the Eucharist. This refusal to accept five of the sacraments of the Church proceeds from the Protestant rejection of Tradition "as of equal weight with Holy Scripture, as a source"[7] of divine teaching; it is consistent with the Protestant notion of the Church as being essentially invisible and with an erroneous conception of justification.[8] Still, as Dyobouniotes observes, "certainly Holy Scripture never declares explicitly that there are seven sacraments; yet this may be well explained from the character of Holy Scripture, which does not profess to be a dogmatic treatise. Accordingly the contention of Protestants that (the doctrine of) the seven

[1] *Ibid.*, pp. 313-314.
[2] *Op. cit.*, p. 86.
[3] Dyobouniotes, *op. cit.*, p. 23, and Mesolora, IV. p. 156.
[4] Mesolora, *op. cit.*, p. 152, quoting the *Acts* of the synod of Constantinople (1672); text referred to, in vol. II. p. 140.
[5] *Op. cit.*, IV, p. 153.   H
[6] Cf. Androutsos, Συμβολική, pp. 258 ff; and Mesolora, *op. cit.*, IV, pp. 144-149.
[7] Androutsos, Δογματική, p. 317.
[8] Mesolora, *op. cit.*, IV. p. 159.

sacraments cannot be accepted, since Holy Scripture never explicitly defines that there are seven, is neither correct nor logical—the more so as in this case the acceptance of even two sacraments by Protestants would be equally groundless, for there is no explicit reference in Holy Scripture to the fact that there are two sacraments."[1]

There are other divisions of the sacraments besides those mentioned. Mesolora distinguishes them according to the purpose of each severally and their personal application to individual needs, into those of (a) "general obligation" (ὑποχρεωτικά), of which two, Baptism and the Eucharist, are "chief and preëminent", and the other three are Chrism, Penance, and Unction, which five are of "general" application to all the Faithful; and those (b) of a voluntary and individual character, Holy Order and Marriage (προαιρετικά).[2] In his treatment of the subject he discusses Baptism, Chrism, Penance, and the Eucharist in the first category and the other three in the second.[3] This is the more usual classification of the sacraments, yet neither Androutsos nor Dyobouniotes employs it. The latter says: "The customary distinction of the sacraments into those 'of general obligation' and 'those which have a voluntary character', into 'necessary' and those which are not so, is not correct, since all the sacraments are of obligation according to the circumstances of this or that need of the believer. That this distinction is erroneous is clear from the fact that in the Church Baptism has from early times been joined with Chrism, and the Eucharist with Penance, and also from the fact that there is no agreement among theologians as to which of the sacraments are of obligation and which are not."[4]

Another classification of the sacraments is "into those which may be had again and those which may not. To the second category belong Baptism, Chrism, and Orders; the

---

[1] *Op. cit.*, pp. 19-20.
[2] *Op. cit.*, IV. p. 152.
[3] Cf. pp. 180-320 for the first category; pp. 321-367 for the second. He departs from his first classification, as will be noticed above, in putting Unction under the second division, in the body of his work.
[4] *Op. cit.*, pp. 23-24, note 3.

others may be repeated."[1] By "being repeated" or "iterated" is meant that they may be given again to the same person. Those which may not be given again to one who has once received them duly and regularly, are the above three; the sacrament of Marriage may be had three times in all.[2] This distinction gave rise to the Scholastic theory of the *indelible character* of these three sacraments. This theory, based on Optatus of Milevis, and St. Augustine,[3] was expressly taught at the councils of Florence[4] and Trent,[5] at which latter council it was solemnly defined.[6] According to the Roman theory, each of these three sacraments, besides conveying its own Grace, gives a "character" which is ineffaceable. To illustrate what is meant by *character* Scotus uses the figure of the badges distinctive of three grades of civil society—the royal household, the army, and the official members of the latter. It has been a "question whether the faculty in which the character inheres as its subject be the will (Scotists) or the practical reason (Thomists)";[7] yet the doctrine of the "imprinting of a character on the soul, which is a certain spiritual and ineffaceable mark (*signum*), whence these sacraments cannot be iterated"[8] is part of Latin theological teaching, *de fide* since Trent. "This seal or sign is indelible, so that even if the divine Grace given through the sacrament be lost, the seal remains. Thus is explained the fact witnessed to by the history of the early Church, that the return into the Church of those who had lost the Grace of the sacraments was made not through the repetition of the sacraments but simply through a service . . restoring the lost Grace."[9] The *Confession* of Dositheus expressly teaches this doctrine: "Baptism conveys an indelible

---

[1] Androutsos, *op. cit.*, pp. 313-314.

[2] Mesolora, *op. cit.*, p. 154. cf. the teaching on *Marriage* below.

[3] *Contra Parmen. Don.*, V, 3-7, *et passim; Epistola* 98, 5; *Contra Epist. Parmen.*, 2, 13, 29.

[4] *Sess. ult.; Decret. Eugenii* IV, 5.

[5] *Sess.* VII. *can* IX, and XXIII, *cap.* IV, and *can.* IV.

[6] *Sess. ult. can.* VII.

[7] M. J. Ryan, *s. v.*, in *Catholic Encycl.*, III. pp. 586-588.

[8] *Concil. Trid. Sess. ult. can.* VII: *imprimi characterem in anima... unde ea* (sacramenta) *iterari non possunt.* St. Thomas Aquinas, *Summa*, III. 9. lxiii.

[9] Dyobouniotes, *op. cit.*, pp. 24-26.

character just as does Holy Order",[1] which fact has subjected this formulary to hostile animadversion on the part of some Orthodox writers.[2]

Inasmuch as the theory of *indelible character* is an attempt to explain the fact that certain sacraments are not to be iterated, it is only to be judged from the standpoint of a theory and cannot be considered a dogma, since "it lacks the very character of dogma, as it is not based upon either Holy Scripture or Sacred Tradition."[3] The texts used in support of it, for example, Eph. 1, 13; 2 Cor. 1, 21-22, and the quotations from the Fathers,[4] prove nothing, for they cannot at all be applied to justify the theory, according to both Androutsos and Dyobouniotes. Furthermore it is impossible, they maintain, to discern either, what is the nature of the *character* which is impressed, or the part of the soul into which it is stamped, or the reason why certain sacraments should be set apart from others as imparting this *character*. For all these reasons and because of the weighty difficulties involved in the theory the modern writers all agree in abandoning it. "If we examine this Latin theory", says Christodoulos, "we find it first to be without foundation, and secondly to be pernicious in its consequences. The idea of an indelible character which is supposed to be imprinted in ordination, cannot be supported by any clear evidence of any sort from our Canons. There is nothing said about it in the Canons, and the expression itself does not once occur in them."[5] Androutsos[6] and Dyobouniotes[7] both reject it for the reasons given above.

A better explanation, Dyobouniotes asserts, can be found for the facts than that offered by the theory of *indelible char-*

[1] In Mesolora, *op. cit.*, II. p. 116.

[2] Cf. Palmieri, *Dositeo, Patriarca di Gerusalemme*, Florence, 1909; Chrysostom Papadopoulos devotes considerable effort to minimize and depreciate the Latin cast of Dositheus' *Confession*; cf. Δοσίθεος, Πατριάρχης Ἱεροσολύμων, Jerusalem, 1907, p. 32 *et al.*; and in Νέα Σιών, 1907, vol V. pp. 104-108.

[3] Androutsos, *op. cit.*, p. 314, note 1.

[4] Cf. *ibid.*, p. 315, and Dyobouniotes, p. 26, note 1.

[5] Δοκίμιον ἐκκλησιαστικοῦ δικαίου, Constantinople, 1896, p. 205.

[6] *Op. cit.*, pp. 314-315.

[7] *Op. cit.*, pp. 26-27.

acter.[1] That is, in brief, that all sacraments are in a sense indelible. "There is no doubt", says he, "that the effects of the sacraments are in themselves perfect and complete, and need no completion nor fulfilling." If a good confession is made, the penitent receives absolution and stands in no need of further grace of forgiveness. So with all the other sacraments. "In this sense then all the sacraments, so far as concerns their effect, are not repeated nor ought be repeated, for such iteration would be an act of disbelief and tempting God. . . . When in practice certain sacraments are iterated it is because of the general difference in their energies and operations". . . A penitent who is shriven, after confession may fall into other sins, and in consequence stand again in need of absolution. He receives it again, not as a fulfilment, as it were, of an imperfect or incomplete gift of Grace, but because of new conditions in his soul. Hence "the iteration of certain sacraments proceeds from and depends upon their operation and energy. . . This theory does not accept differences of energies in the sacraments in the sense that some imprint *character* and others do not", but on the basis of differences in the need of the recipient and in the nature of the Grace given.[2] Two difficulties in regard to this theory result from the fact that it would seem to conflict with Orthodox practice in regard to the remarriage of two people who have been divorced from each other,[3] and in regard to the practice of anointing again a sick person, even if no change has occurred in his condition of illness. As to the first, Dyobouniotes says that current theological opinion inclines to support his theory and condemn the practice; especially is this the case in Russia. As to the second, he claims that

---

[1] As the word is a convenient term, it may find its way occasionally into Orthodox writings, but yet, says Androutsos, "by using it... we do not mean to explain the fact of the noniteration of sacraments according to the Roman theory, but taking the word objectively we mean to say this only, that certain sacraments performed in the Orthodox Church are not done again, even though those who receive them fall away or lapse into heresy or schism, and return again to Orthodoxy" (Δογματική, pp. 339-340, note 3. Full discussion in his Συμβολική, pp. 282 ff.).

[2] *Op. cit.,* pp. 27-28.

[3] Cf. Christodoulos, *op. cit.,* p. 407.

there has been no official pronouncement of Orthodoxy on the matter, and feels that the Roman ruling is in main correct, in spite of the differences in principle between the Roman and Orthodox doctrine of Unction.[1] So, too, Androutsos holds that the practice of not iterating the three sacraments "may be accounted for in another way. As one is only born once ($ἅπαξ$) naturally, so spiritually he is born once only through Baptism and Chrism joined with it. As Ordination is the entrance into the priestly service, it has no reason even to be iterated."[2] Modern Greek opinion, then, strongly repudiates the notion of *indelible character* in the sacraments of Baptism, Chrism, and Holy Order, and accounts for the fact that these sacraments may not be iterated on the basis of the character and kind of their operation and energy. In all the sacraments the Grace bestowed is impressed in the soul so that that Grace may not be repeated.[3]

3. The Administration of the Sacraments

"That the administration of a sacrament should effect on the catechumens or the Faithful its saving energy, three conditions must be satisfied: (a) the administration must be done through the use of the outward sign and the words and acts prescribed by the Church, (b) by the proper minister,—a bishop or a priest, (c) and the individual must be prepared and receptive for the Grace to come."[4] These three terms or conditions must be complied with in every case, for the sacrament to be "valid" in itself (to borrow western terminology), and "efficacious" for the individual. It is to be observed that Orthodox theology does not sunder the treatment of these two subjects, validity and efficacy. It is also worth noticing that even modern Orthodox theology manages to discuss the

[1] *Op. cit.*, pp. 29-30, and notes 1 and 2.
[2] *Op. cit.*, p. 315, in note. The question of indelibility of character is related to that of reordination and rebaptism of those who are outside the fold of Orthodoxy. cf. additional note to Lecture IV. and *infra* pp. 292 ff.
[3] Cf. Dyobouniotes, *op. cit.*, p. 159.
[4] Androutsos, *op. cit.*, pp. 300, 301, 310-311.

question of the administration of the sacraments without employing the categories of "regular" and "valid or invalid".[1] Keeping in mind these two facts we may go on to consider the terms or conditions for the administration or consummation of the sacraments.

(a) The first condition involves the fulfilment of the necessary rites and ceremonies, the use of the proper matter, words, and acts, laid down by the Church. Some of these are a development and extension of the original simple service and are not of rigid necessity since the omission of them would not invalidate the sacrament. So the "outward sign" of Baptism includes what is necessary for the consummation of the sacrament, the fulfilment of one of the conditions making the sacrament a possible means of Grace. The "outward signs" of this sacrament are the trine immersion and emersion, together with the words of the priest: "The servant of God is baptized in the name of the Father and of the Son and of the Holy Ghost", "without which the sacrament cannot be con-

[1] With the possible exception of Mesolora, whose work (Συμβολική) aims to expound but not to correlate the various elements of Orthodox teaching. Thus he mentions, but does not discuss, *indelible character* (*op. cit.*, IV. p. 154). In his treatment of Baptism he does use the words "irregular" and "valid" in connection with Anglican Baptism. He says: "The Baptism of the Anglicans may be considered *valid*, as having been done with water and in the name of the Holy Trinity, and as conveying divine Grace,...but still it is not regarded as *licit* and *regular*, since it is not performed according to the order prevailing in the Church from early times" (p. 203). The introduction of this category, which is essentially alien to Orthodox thought, leads Mesolora into quite obvious difficulties and inconsistencies; for he says, even granted the fulfilment of all prescribed conditions, only on the basis of *urgent necessity* may such sacraments, performed by non-Orthodox, be adjudged valid, in the absence of which absolute necessity they may not be so reckoned, and "in consequence must be iterated, or rather, be performed *regularly* (κανονικῶς)". The reason he adduces for the Orthodox Church not ordinarily recognizing the Baptism of those not of its fold who desire to come into Orthodoxy, is that she "does not regard their Baptism as valid and regular" (p. 204). This anticipates a little what will be discussed farther on in this lecture (cf. pp. 292 ff.) but in conclusion it may be suggested that Mesolora uses "necessity" to cover the cases of the exercise of "economy", which may serve to reconcile his inchoate theory with the facts and with other Orthodox teaching.

summated."[1]   According to Dyobouniotes' definition of "outward signs", as: "those services and words instituted by Christ and the Apostles, which are absolutely necessary for the accomplishment of the sacrament and for the communication through it of divine Grace", the Church service, that is, the prescribed rites and ceremonies, as Androutsos also observes,[2] includes elements which are not essential. "Yet it does not follow that the rites of the sacraments which are prescribed by the Church are voluntary, as if the priest had the right to omit or change anything in them at his own discretion. It is only the Church, as history shows, which can change, curtail, or add rites which do not constitute the 'outward signs', in the performance of the sacraments."[3]   Kritopoulos says: "The Church, moved by the Holy Spirit, prescribes the manner (of the administration of the sacraments), collecting all the elements from Holy Scripture."[4]   The rites, ceremonies, and prescribed additions not essential to the consummation of the sacrament, are "the logical presentation and expression of the faith of the Church through which she gives and professes to give the special Grace of the sacraments."   So the form of the rites of non-Orthodox bodies has a bearing on the question as to whether "economy" may be exercised in a given case: there can be no such exercise of economy when the rite of a sacrament and the teaching and practice of the religious communion using it are utterly divergent.[5]

The external part in the administration of the sacrament, including the "outward signs", may not be thought of as magic, as if in and of itself the due performance of these external rites and words with the proper visible elements, worked mechanically to produce Grace.[6]   As Saint Basil

[1] Dyobouniotes, *op. cit.*, p. 14, note 1.
[2] *Op. cit.*, p. 300.
[3] Dyobouniotes, *op. cit.*, pp. 13-14 and note 1; cf. Mesolora, *op. cit.*, IV. pp. 167-168, who arranges the essentials for the proper and effectual administration of the sacraments in a different order, as he discusses these along with the three essential characteristics of a sacrament, pp. 163 ff.
[4] Mesolora, *op. cit.*, I. pp. 319-320.
[5] Androutsos, *op. cit.*, p. 300.
[6] *Ibid.*, and p. 311.

observes: "Whatever Grace there be in the water (of Baptism) is not there of the nature of the water, but of the presence of the Holy Spirit."[1]   The Grace is that flowing from the work of our Lord in Redemption.[2] The view that Jews and heathen can "baptize validly, really amounts to the acceptance of the external act as something working mechanically by means of sound, syllables, and actions, and (thereby) conveying Grace."[3]

(b) The proper minister or officiant in the administration of the sacraments is a bishop or a priest,[4] canonically ordained,[5] with proper jurisdiction and authority given him from the Church.[6] Orthodox writers emphasize again in this connection that neither of these two conditions—the fulfilment of the proper form of words and acts, by the proper person— may be understood in any magical or mechanical sense. "By the acceptance of the validity of sacraments . . . performed by the laity," says Dyobouniotes, "a kind of magical power is attributed to the outward signs of the sacraments, through which the sacrament is magically consummated along with the pronouncing of the words in connection with the outward signs. But this magical power and mechanical communication of divine Grace the ancient Church never acknowledged nor accepted."[7] "He, who accomplishes the sacraments," says Androutsos, "is not the priest, but the Founder of the sacraments, Jesus Christ, who abides continually in His mystical Body, the Church, exactly administering His saving power. The priest is the indispensable organ by which the unseen divine power accomplishes the sacrament."[8] The priest consummates the sacrament by the use of the proper outward signs in the form of rite prescribed by the Church, by "virtue of the power of the Holy Spirit."[9]

[1] *De Spiritu Sancto*, 15, and cf. St. Jerome on Isaiah 4, 4.

[2] Cf. St. Ireneaus: *Si non vere passus esset* (Christus), *nulla gratia ei cum nulla fuerit passio* (*Adv. Haer.* III, 18, 6).

[3] Androutsos, *op. cit.*, p. 300.

[4] *Ibid.*, and Jeremiah II. in Mesolora, *op. cit.*, I. p. 162.

[5] Dyobouniotes, *op. cit.*, p. 30 and note I; Mogila in Mesolora, I. pp. 424, 429-430.

[6] Mesolora, *op. cit.*, IV. pp. 165-166.

[7] *Op. cit.*, pp. 30-31.

[8] *Op. cit.*, p. 301.

[9] Mogila in Mesolora, *op. cit.*, I. p. 424.

The accomplishment of the sacraments does not depend on the faith or moral perfection of the officiating priest, since he is simply the organ and means by which Christ gives His Grace. Hence the popular contention that the priest "cannot give what he has not", is without foundation, since "it is based on the erroneous idea that he who administers the sacrament is the one who imparts Grace as from himself. If the consummation of the sacrament did depend on the faith and moral perfection of the priest, then salvation would be something uncertain as well in the individual as in the Church, and the existence of the latter as a visible communion would be brought into question . . . Accordingly the faith and moral perfection of the priest are not essential."[1] "Grace may operate and be given through unworthy ministers . . . for the sacraments are not given by reason of our worthiness but of that of the Saviour."[2] So the priest acts as the organ of Christ and as the representative of His Church. Just as the mind of the Church is reflected and manifested in her rites and ceremonies, on the principle *lex orandi, lex credendi,* so the acts of the priest are those not of himself personally but of the Church of which he stands as representative.

What is required of the officiant is that he "have the intention to do what the Church does."[3] He consummates the sacrament by the use of the proper rite and the necessary outward signs "with a will (γνώμη) determined to consecrate."[4] This *intention* or disposition of the priest "is shown externally, and involves the will to administer the sacrament not in play nor for teaching purposes, but soberly in accordance with the prescribed forms of the Church. A sacrament as an act presupposes the general elements of every human act—consciousness and free will. . . It is sufficient that the priest act freely and

---

[1] Dyobouniotes, *op. cit.,* pp. 31-32 and note 2; Androutsos, *op. cit.,* p. 301. Cf. St. Cyril Jerus., *Cat.* 17, 35; St. Athanasius, *de Trinitate,* 40; St. John Chrysostom, Homily 14, 3, on Acts, and 50, 3 on St. Mt.

[2] Mesolora, *op. cit.,* pp. 170, 169; Jeremiah II in *ibid.,* pp. 144 ff; Dositheus, *ibid.,* II. pp. 114, 118, 119. Exposition and refutation of Protestant view in Mesolora, IV, pp. 171-174.

[3] Dyobouniotes, *op. cit.,* pp. 32-33.

[4] Mogila, in Mesolora, *op. cit.,* I. p. 424. He uses γνώμη ἀποφασισμένη for the theological terms πρόθεσις or θέλησις.

with full consciousness of what he is doing, and that he conform externally to the order the Church enjoins." This is all that is required to determine *intention,* and Orthodoxy rejects the subtle and unnecessary distinctions of scholastic theologians in their whole treatment of the subject.[1]

A natural consequence of the theory that the validity of sacraments depends on the religious and moral state of the officiating priest, Androutsos notes, is the denial of the dogma of the unity of the Church, and of that of the Church as a visible organism. Another consequence is "the opinion that sacraments administered by heretics are valid if they are rightly performed."[2] Since the officiant acts not only in his own name or by his own power but independently of his merits or vices, purely as the representative of the Church which is functioning by him, "the Orthodox Church, holding the view that the Grace of the Holy Spirit does not function outside the Church, has always rejected sacraments performed outside herself—not only those which were not rightly celebrated but even those in which the outward part had been carefully preserved intact."[3] The sacrament depends not on the minister, as a Protestant view would have it, but quite the contrary, on the Church. Since the Orthodox theory demands a priest or bishop as the officiant in all sacraments, "the validity of the Baptism of heretics depends, from long usage in the Church, not only on the canonical fulfilment of Baptism but on the recognition of the validity of priesthood among the heretics and chiefly on the idea of the Church as the guardian of divine Grace. Hence it comes about that the question of the validity . . . of heretical Baptism can be properly settled (only) if the question of the validity . . . of the priesthood (=Orders) of heretics be first examined and answered."[4]

---

[1] Androutsos, *op. cit.,* pp. 309-310; Mesolora, *op. cit.,* IV. pp. 168-169; Macarius, *op. cit.,* II. p. 611.

[2] *Op. cit.,* pp. 301, 302.

[3] *Ibid.,* p. 303, and Δογματικαὶ Μελέται, Α', pp. 135-136; Dyobouniotes, Ἡ Δογμ. Ἀνδρ. κριν., p. 51, and Ὀφειλ. ἀπάντ., pp. 126-128.

[4] Dyobouniotes, Τὰ Μυστήρια, p. 65.

The Doctrine of Economy[1]

It seems well at this point, at the risk of repeating what has already been considered in part and of anticipating what properly belongs in another connection, to discuss as succinctly as possible the Orthodox theory of *"economy"* with reference to the validity of sacraments outside the Orthodox Church. Impinging upon this question and intimately related to it is the matter of the non-iteration of the three sacraments of Baptism, Chrism, and Orders. As we have seen, the practice of the non-iteration of these sacraments once validly performed, prevails and has prevailed in both East and West. The theory of the West, that these sacraments, besides their own proper Grace, convey an *indelible character,* modern Orthodox opinion on the whole strongly rejects. The theory which Orthodox writers feel accounts for all the facts without involving the objections and inconveniences of the Latin doctrine of *indelible character,* explains the non-iteration of these sacraments on the basis of the nature of the Grace conferred by them and the peculiar character of its operation. Properly speaking, the question of *character* does not come into the province of *economy,* since the employment of *economy* is only in relation to sacraments performed outside the Orthodox Church. Dyobouniotes, however, would extend it in another direction to cover cases of sacraments performed by Orthodox, yet not entirely according to the full measure of the rites prescribed by the current use of the Church.[2] It covers, too, by common consent, the Baptism

---

[1] The most illuminating discussion of this subject known to the writer is to be found in the Rev. J. A. Douglas' *The Relations of the Anglican Churches with the Eastern-Orthodox* (London, 1921), pp. 55-69, *et al.*

[2] There is a difference of opinion between Dyobouniotes and Androutsos on the necessity of all the elements of the "service" or rite of administration of a sacrament according to the use of the Church, beyond those of the "outward signs". The latter holds that the Church has extended and amplified the simpler essential "external signs" (=all the parts of the sacrament save the "Grace conferred") beyond the minimum necessary for validity (*op. cit.,* p. 300). The former holds that "the Church in prescribing the rites of the sacraments.. makes all of obligation for the performance of the sacraments, agreeable to her own definition, since the Church only has power

"of necessity", performed by an Orthodox layman or laywoman when it is impossible to obtain a priest.[1]

The Orthodox estimate of sacraments performed outside the Church is, as we have seen, that they are all invalid. "This view is based on the idea that Grace is confined exclusively to the Church, outside of which there is no Grace, and so the sacraments cannot be administered."[2] This is the teaching of the Fathers. St. Irenaeus says: *ubi Ecclesia, ibi et Spiritus Sanctus,* and St. Augustine agrees with this view in his distinction between the Holy Spirit's assisting Grace *indwelling* and *not-yet-indwelling.*[3] "St. Athanasius,[4] St. Cyril of Jerusalem,[5] St. Basil,[6] St. Gregory Nazianzen[7] and others[8] denied in principle heretical Baptism, agreeing with the view of St. Cyprian, Firmilian, and the synods held in Africa and Asia Minor. The holy canons do not know the later exact distinction between *invalid* and *irregular* ordination, . . . pronouncing both the Baptism and Orders of heretics invalid and regarding 'those baptized or ordained by heretics as neither of the company of the faithful nor in the ranks of the clergy',[9] like St. Basil."[10] The latter says that those who split off from the Church "had not the Grace of the Holy Spirit with them . . . For the first who withdrew from the Fathers had Orders,

to make this or that change"...The omission of any such prescribed additions to the essential "external signs" renders the sacrament incapable of being pronounced valid save by the exercise of *economy.* He maintains that it is within the Church's province to determine the rite thus necessary for validity ('Η Δογμ. 'Ανδρ. κριν., p. 51, and 'Οφειλ. ἀπάντησις, pp. 124-126; Androutsos, Δογμ. Μελ., Α', p. 140).

[1] Dyobouniotes, *ibid.,* and Τὰ Μυστήρια, p. 30; Androutsos, *ibid.,* and Δογματική, pp. 324, 323-324, etc.

[2] Dyobouniotes, Τὰ Μυστήρια, p. 161.

[3] *Spiritus sanctus aliter adjuvat nondum inhabitans, aliter inhabitans; nam nondum inhabitans, ut sint fideles, inhabitans adjuvat jam fideles;* in *Epist.* 194, 4, 18.

[4] Viewed Arian Baptism as invalid even if performed properly.

[5] Προκατήχησις, 7.

[6] In *Epist.* 199, he rejects Marcionite Baptism, even if performed in the name of the Holy Trinity.

[7] Cf. *Orat.* 40, 26, in Migne, *P. G.,* t. XXXVI, 396.

[8] *E. g.,* St. Gregory of Nyssa, in Migne, *P. G.,* t. XLV, 881.

[9] *Apostolic canons,* 67.

[10] Androutsos, Δογματική, pp. 304-306.

and through the laying on of hands had the spiritual charisma. But when they tore themselves away they became laymen and had not the authority either to baptize or ordain, since they were unable to impart to others that Grace of the Holy Spirit from which they themselves had fallen away."[1]

In the early Church a practical question arose in the case of many of these heresies. While their sacraments were not recognized as valid,[2] what should be the course of the Church's action in regard to individuals who wished to come from heresy and schism into union with the Church? The case of those baptized or ordained in the Catholic Church, who afterwards lapsed into heresy or schism and then recanted, desiring re-admission into the Church, was clear enough: after doing penance they were reconciled without rebaptism or reordination, since those sacraments once validly administered (Baptism, Chrism, and Orders), might not be iterated.[3] In the case of those coming from heresy and schism with Baptism or ordination from heretics or schismatics, the action of the Early Church differed in different cases; sometimes their Baptism and Orders were validated by the Church, and at other times such persons were again baptized and ordained.[4] "Such persons desiring to come into the Church," says St. Basil, "having been baptized as it were by laymen, they (that is, the Fathers in Synod), ordered to be cleansed again by the true Baptism, that is, that of the Church;" but, he adds, for the sake "οἰκονομίας τῶν πολλῶν", the Baptism of the Cathari might be accepted.[5] The Orthodox use of "economy", then, dates back

---

[1] *Epist.* 188, and cf. 204, 3.

[2] "The Early Church," says Dyobouniotes, "regarded as invalid the Orders of the Montanists, Paulitians, Arians, Nestorians, Macedonians, Sabbatians, Novatians, Tetradites, Apollinarians and all other heretics like them" (*op. cit.*, p. 161, note 3 with references).

[3] Dyobouniotes, *op. cit.*, p. 160.

[4] Androutsos, *op. cit.*, pp. 306-307. "The ordination of such schismatics and heretics must not be regarded as reordination, which is forbidden by the Church, but as the first ordination, since that ordination had in schism or heresy was not actually such" (Dyobouniotes *op. cit.*, p. 161, note 2). Neither the Early Church nor the Orthodox Church has ever known the use of *hypothetical* or *conditional Baptism* (Androutsos, *ibid.*, p. 301, note 1).

[5] *Epist.* 188.

to St. Basil and the practice of the Early Church. The early synods, it may be noted, declared the Baptism of many of the heresies void and invalid, "even though it is certain historically that they observed scrupulously the outward form and acts, as did the Montanists, Manicheans, and Paulitians, according to St. Athanasius."[1] Yet there was even in early times a great variety of practice, since the Church recognized some sacraments as valid when those who had had them in heresy or schism came into the Church,[2] and refused to recognize others.

"The recognition by *economy* of the sacraments of heretics may be explained in two ways:—either (a) that the sacraments of schismatics and heretics coming into the Church were as it were revivified and quickened by reason of entrance into the Church,[3] or (b) that the Church, as a steward of Grace and dispenser of the sacraments, has the power to change the validity of sacraments, making those that are invalid valid, and *vice versa.* The former view prevails in the Western Church, which distinguishes *character* and *Grace* in (certain of) the sacraments, and holds that *character* may be impressed by the canonical accomplishment of the sacraments even among schismatics and heretics. This view cannot be accepted, since it is contrary to the practice of the Church which regards many of the sacraments of heretics as invalid and according to circumstances (pronounces) them valid and invalid. The practice of the Church can only be explained by the second view, which is the more acceptable, in that it is based on the idea that outside the Church the Grace of God does not exist, and precludes the distinction in the sacraments of *character* and *Grace,* which distinction cannot be founded either on Holy Scripture or Tradition."[4] The Latin view is rejected by all Orthodox theologians on the grounds suggested above: (a) it violates the principle of the one true and visible Church; (b)

[1] *Adv. Arian. orat.*, 2, 43, in Migne, *P. G.* t. XXVI, 237. Androutsos, *op. cit.*, pp. 306-307.
[2] *E. g.*, the Cathari, Donatists, Encratites, and Massalians were recognized; cf. Dyobouniotes, *op. cit.*, p. 163 note 1.
[3] "This view" says Androutsos, "is untenable, since it presupposes that there are heretics who have valid sacraments, which the Orthodox Church does not accept" (*op. cit.*, p. 308).
[4] Dyobouniotes, *op. cit.*, pp. 162-163. note 1.

it makes of the sacraments magical and mechanical rites auto-
matically effecting supernatural results, without proper regard
to the truths involved in the doctrine of the sacraments, (that
our Lord is Himself the celebrant, and the Holy Spirit the
agent accomplishing the sacraments); (c) that it involves
the distinction of *character* and *Grace,* and the doctrine of *indelible character,* which is totally unsupported by Holy Scripture and Tradition, imports needless distinctions among the
sacraments, and in any case is incapable of being exactly defined; (d) it involves the recognition in theory and practice of
heretics and schismatics as quasi-members of the Church, and
of their communions as in some sense sections or portions of
the Body of Christ.[1]

The whole theory and practice of the use of *economy* rests
on the Orthodox doctrine of the Church expounded in Lecture
IV, and on the deduction that the Church is the guardian and
administrator of Grace, the dispenser and steward of the sacraments, and the center of the operations and energies of the
Holy Spirit.[2]   In her modern life she appeals back to the practice of the Early Church and to the principle of St. Basil. "If
the Church is the dispenser of Grace . . . she may recognize
. . . the sacraments of heretics coming into her for the sake
of the resulting good in order to avoid worse evil, by *economy,*
condescendingly or by accommodation, or by whatever other
terms may be described her deviation in many instances . . .
from the exact and strict way of her principles."[3]   "By *economy"* (κατ' οἰκονομίαν) is contrasted with "by strictness"
(κατ' ἀκρίβειαν).   Some meanings of the word *economy* correspond closely to what we mean by "indulgence", and "dispensation:" the dispensation from the Friday fast, permission
to marry a cousin, a dispensation to lay aside the priestly garb
—these are all exercises of "economy."   Again, it means the
carrying out of the spirit rather than the exact and rigid letter of a law, which would be described as being κατ' ἀκρίβειαν.

---

[1] Cf. *ibid.,* and p. 166, note 3; Androutsos, *op. cit.,* pp. 302-304, note;
pp. 390 ff; his Αἱ βάσεις τῆς ἐνώσεως, pp. 36-43; Τὸ κῦρος τῶν 'Αγγλικανικῶν χειροτονιῶν, pp. 15, *et al.;* the additional note to the previous
lecture, pp. 263-267, above.

[2] Androutsos, *op. cit.,* p. 306, and Αἱ βάσεις τῆς 'Ενώσεως, p. 38.

[3] Androutsos, Δογματική, p. 307.

It may never be a contravention of the spirit of any prescription, canonical or legal,[1] but is as it were a mean between ἀσέβεια and ἀκρίβεια. The writer had the word explained to him once by a prominent Orthodox ecclesiastic under the figure of a ship in a storm being lightened of valuable cargo for the purpose of saving human life. Exercises of *economy* are always in view of some emergency or contingency not contemplated in the general terms of prescriptive law, custom, usage, or dogmatic teaching. They may serve as precedent only when conditions, circumstances, and needs are demonstrably the same.[2]

The motive animating the Church in the exercise of economy is the good of souls. "The Church, as a self-directing fellowship, gauges the exercise of *strictness* or *economy* and in general her whole attitude concerning the sacraments, according to what commends itself to her, having in view the salvation of all and taking into consideration both her own children and her members who have fallen away from her. . . Though it has not yet been officially formulated, nor the question thoroughly investigated from the theological standpoint to determine the scope of the exercise of *economy*, yet this notion of it is founded on the practice of the Church, in which the same sacrament in different circumstances has been pronounced at one time valid and at another invalid."[3] This lack of consistency has brought it about "that there is a discrepancy between theory and practice, and that the Church seems to be teaching one thing and doing another."[4] There has been no official investigation of the principle guiding the exercise of *economy*, says Androutsos, nor any authoritative explanation of her seemingly inconsistent course of action.[5] "While in the

[1] On the canonical aspects of the question, cf. A. Christodoulos, Δοκίμιον ἐκκλησιαστικοῦ δικαίου, pp. 407 ff.

[2] There is also the technical use of the word, common to theology, in the phrases "the *economy* of Redemption", *e. g.*, in Gennadius, 7 (Mesolora, *op. cit.*, I, p. 5); Jeremiah II., 1st *Answer* (*ibid.*, p. 155) etc; the meaning "administration" (of the sacraments, *e. g.*) in Mesolora, *op. cit.*, IV. p. 302; the meaning "economy" in the sense of order, dispensation, scheme,— cf. Jeremiah, in Mesolora, I. p. 184.

[3] Androutsos, *op. cit.*, p. 308.

[4] *Ibid.*, p. 306.

[5] *Ibid.*, pp. 308-309.

concrete it is possible for terms and conditions to be laid down (in a given case), on the basis of which the Church accepts heretics by *economy* without rebaptism, yet in general the principle dictating the use of *strictness* and *economy* is inscrutable, nor can any theory be formulated to explain her course of action and supply the reason which actuates the Church in one case to accept, and in another to reject, the sacraments of heretics."[1]

Dyobouniotes, in his treatment of the sacrament of Orders, goes into the question with some fulness. He holds that there are certain principles on which in the concrete the Church may act in the matter of recognizing heretical or schismatic ordination. "The Church as the administrator and steward of divine Grace can recognize by *economy* the orders and sacraments of schismatics and heretics.[2] In the exercise of this *economy* the Church takes into consideration not only in a general way the faith of those heretics and schismatics coming to her, and particularly their view of the sacraments both of Orders and Baptism, and the fact as to the canonicity of the ministration of these sacraments, but also the unbroken succession of the episcopal authority from the times of the Apostles. Accordingly this is the explanation of the general action of the Church in declaring invalid the orders and sacraments of those heretics and schismatics in whom either the episcopal succession from apostolic times was broken or the Faith perverted, especially in the case of the doctrine of the sacraments, or the regularity of the administration of the sacraments destroyed, and at the same time the Church's recognition as valid of the orders of schismatics and heretics whose line of episcopal succession from the Apostles was not impaired, nor their Faith, especially in regard to the sacraments, perverted, nor the regularity of the administration of the sacraments questioned. Yet it must be understood that the Church, as the dispenser of

[1] Αἱ βάσεις τῆς ἑνώσεως, p. 39; Τὸ κῦρος τ. ᾿Αγγλικ χειροτον., pp. 11-13; the charge of expediency, as the sole principle in the course of Orthodox procedure, is intimated by Palmieri in commenting on the synod of Constantinople (of 1875), cf. *op. cit.*, I. p. 624. Text of *Acts* in Theotokas, Νομολογία τ. οἰκουμεν. πατρ., Constantinople, 1897, pp. 367 ff; on which cf. note 2 on pp. 307-308 of Androutsos' Δογματική.

[2] On the differences in practice in the early Church, cf. Androutsos, Δογματική, pp. 393-395, note.

divine Grace, *can* recognize the orders and the sacraments in general of schismatics and heretics even if they have not been performed canonically and even if the Apostolic Succession be broken; and for reasons which seem to her good and necessary the Church *may reject* the Orders and the sacraments in general of heretics and schismatics who do preserve the canonical order in the administration of the sacraments and possess unimpaired the Apostolic Succession. This is the explanation of the inconstancy of the Church's action . . . at one time pronouncing invalid the sacraments . . . of heretics and schismatics, though they be canonically performed, . . . and at another pronouncing valid the sacraments of heretics and schismatics, . . . although they have not been canonically performed."[1]

In early days as well as in later times there has been a wide divergence of practice in the Orthodox Church.[2] There has also been a wide divergence of opinion among Orthodox writers. It would be impossible to go into the question historically, or treat of it in these lectures in any detail. One example may suffice as an illustration. In 1872 a synod at Constantinople solemnly excommunicated the Bulgarians because of "phyletism", and "rationalism". There was not the slightest question as to Orthodoxy of belief, nor validity of orders, nor unbroken Apostolic Succession. The sentence of the synod pronounced them "alien to the One, Holy Catholic, and Apostolic Church, and for this reason, schismatics."[3] It anathematized all their clerics, all who held fellowship with them, and said: all who "regard their orders and priestly acts as valid, both clerics and laymen, we pronounce schismatics and strangers, outside the fold of the Orthodox Church of Christ."[4] Their sacraments could not be regarded as valid, since their prelates had fallen from the Grace of Orders, and could not therefore communicate to others what they had lost.[5] This synod,

---

[1] Dyobouniotes, Τὰ Μυστήρια, pp. 162-165.

[2] On which cf. Ambraze's arguments in 'Η 'Ορθόδοξος 'Εκκλησία, pp. 161-177.

[3] In Papadopoulos, 'Η σύγχρονος ἱεραρχία τῆς 'Ορθοδόξου ἀνατολικῆς 'Εκκλησίας, Athens, 1895, p. 664.

[4] *Ibid.*

[5] P. 57 of the Acts, quoted by Androutsos, pp. 35-36, of his Aἰ

under Anthimus VI (1871-1873, his third time of being Patriarch), was attended by representatives from Alexandria and Antioch, and by many metropolitans, bishops, and prelates of the Greek Church. Jerusalem did not subscribe to the anathema against the Bulgarians nor did he attend the synod. He lost his throne for this reason.[1] The Russian Church did not at all concur in this condemnation of the Bulgarians. A few years later (1878-1879), the question came up regarding the treatment of excommunicated Bulgarians desiring to return to the Orthodox Church, and the general question as to the validity of orders received from heretics and schismatics. "The committee appointed by the Ecumenical Patriarch for the investigation and solution of the question regarding the validity . . . of orders received from excommunicated or schismatic bishops, reported (July 21, 1879) that 'such . . . can be received into communion, each in his own clerical rank and dignity, according . . . to the 8th Canon of the 1st Ecumenical Council.' The Synod accepted this judgment, except the Church of Greece, which voiced scruples about it, inclining rather to reordination, but yet finally accepted the view of the synod of Constantinople."[2]

Just what is the status and sacramental capacity, so to speak, of validly ordained clergy who have fallen into heresy or schism, it is difficult to discern. In one place Dyobouniotes wrote: "A priest falling into heresy from Orthodoxy still retains his priesthood, for it has indelible character, but loses its Grace so that he cannot communicate such (Grace) through the sacraments."[3] By implication Dyobouniotes would maintain that on returning to the Church he would recover this lost Grace.[4]

βάσεις τῆς ἑνώσεως. On the synod, cf. M. Gedeon, Ἔγγραφα πατριαρχικὰ κ. συνοδικὰ περὶ τ. βουλγαρικοῦ ζητήματος (1852-1873), Constantinople, 1908; bibliography of the Russian view of the synod and its action, in Palmieri, op. cit., I, p. 619, note 1, and cf. his Un documenta prezioso sul decadimento dell' ortodossia, Rome, 1900.

[1] According to Palmieri, op. cit., I. p. 619, note 2, on the basis of Ἡ Ἐκκλησία Ἱεροσολύμων κατὰ τοὺς τεσσάρας τελεταίους αἰώνας, Athens, 1900, pp. 104-105.

[2] Dyobouniotes, op. cit., pp. 164-165 note 2, and Androutsos, Δογματική, p. 395 note.

[3] Ἡ Δογμ. Ἀνδρ. κριν., p. 51.

[4] Ὀφειλ. ἀπάντησις, p. 129.

Androutsos criticizes this statement as combining two mutually exclusive theories, the Orthodox and the Latin, and rejects it completely;[1] such a person, . . he says, on his return to Orthodoxy, can be recognized as a priest only by the Church exercising *economy*. Basil, the Metropolitan of Smyrna, in his work on the validity of heretical orders, says: "By deposition the Grace (Χάρισμα) of the priesthood is neither removed nor destroyed— for the efficient cause (of the priesthood) is the Holy Spirit, —but its energy and operation are circumscribed and impeded."[2] He claims that there is no definite precedent in the action of early synods and the Councils to deal with these cases, "since they never say explicitly whether to determine and allow, or to forbid, the acceptance as valid of the orders of those ordained solely by excommunicated bishops."[3] Rhôsse, in his study of Old Catholicism to which he devoted much time and attention, finally came to the conclusion that Old Catholic orders were invalid.[4] "A bishop who falls away from the true Ecumenical Church of the first eight centuries, and perverts his Faith by the acceptance of novel doctrines, can not give to others either the true episcopal office or the true priesthood."[5] Rhôsse envisages the whole problem in terms of doctrinal teaching: heresy forfeits Grace; Orthodoxy has as its chief claim to Catholicity the preservation unimpaired of the true doctrines of Christianity. Mesolora in his section "on the Grace of Orders and the validity of heretical ordination"[6] says that when the Grace of Orders is once given, canonically and rightly, it may not be done again,[7] and that the Church may, by the exercise of *economy*, receive those heretically ordained, by the lay-

---

[1] Δογμ. Μελέται, Α', pp. 118-119. It is to be noticed that Dyobouniotes in his later works abandons the theory of *indelible* character, as we saw above.

[2] Περὶ τοῦ κύρους τῆς χειροτονίας κληρικῶν ὑπὸ ἐπισκόπων καθηρημένων καὶ σχισματικῶν χειροτονηθέντων, Smyrna, 1887, p. 18.

[3] *Ibid.*, p. 7.

[4] Cf. his Δογματική, pp. 60-61, note 286-287; 489-491; and his Ἔκθεσις πρὸς τὴν ἱερὸν Σύνοδον, of 1874, pp. 22-23. On the literature of the subject and the history of the relations of Old Catholics and Orthodox, cf. Palmieri, *op. cit.*, II. p. 189.

[5] Ὀρθοδοξίας καὶ Παλαιοκαθολικισμοῦ ἀντίθεσις, Athens, 1876, p. 51.

[6] *Op. cit.*, IV. pp. 331-336.

[7] He here seems to hold the theory of *indelible character*.

ing on of hands (not ordination), and prayer, upon a repudiation by them of their heresy and an expression of penitence.[1]
"We are of the opinion," he says, "that the Church may receive
those clerics ordained by excommunicated or schismatic bishops, without reordination, . . . but those ordained by heretical bishops by reordination, since . . . they have perverted
the true Faith by heresies and novel doctrines . . . and in
so doing have fallen from the true . . . Church and from the
bond of priestly succession bound up with it. Such cannot impart genuine episcopal orders nor the true priesthood. . .
Hence Romans and Protestants ought to be reordained."[2]

The question of Anglican orders may be briefly touched
upon here, as this is the obvious place for reference to it. An-
droustsos' monograph on the subject[3] has been translated into
English,[4] and is a most valuable contribution to the subject.
Taking as proven the historical fact of Parker's consecration,
he says: "The Orthodox Church may by *economy* recognize
the priesthood of Anglicans coming into Orthodoxy . . . on
the condition that the Anglican Church declare herself in an
Orthodox manner on certain doctrines."[5] Rhôsse[6] and Mesolora[7] both say that the Orthodox Church cannot recognize the
validity of Anglican Orders. "The Anglican Church, although
she preserves the three grades of the Ministry, . . . nevertheless rejects the sacrament of Orders as conveying a special

[1] *Ibid.*

[2] *Ibid.*, pp. 335-336.

[3] Τὸ κῦρος τῶν 'Αγγλικανικῶν χειροτονιῶν, Constantinople, 1903.

[4] *The Validity of English Ordinations from an Orthodox-Catholic point of view*, translated by F. W. Grove Campbell, LL.D., London, 1909.

[5] Pp. 82-83, *ibid.*, these are: the doctrine of the seven sacraments, confession, the Eucharist as a real sacrifice and the doctrine of the Real Presence, the authority of the Ecumenical Councils; cf. his Δογματική, p. 392, note; cf. also Androutsos' note Αἱ ἀγγλικανικαὶ χειροτονίαι, in 'Ιερὸς Σύνδεσμος, Athens, Feb. 16-March 1, 1922, pp. 102-103. This brief recapitulation of the subject is characterized by no little acerbity, and considerable ignorance of the facts about the Eng-lish Church. It is a standing example of the futility of obtaining facts second hand; Mr. Androutsos' information is derived from Ger-man sources. But compare the pronouncement of His Holiness, Mele-tios IV, given in full in *The Christian East*, October, 1922.

[6] Δογματική, p. 286, note 1.

[7] *Op. cit.*, IV. pp. 331-336.

Grace. . . . Hence it follows that it has not the dogmatic character which our Church ascribes to it, and so their service of the Laying on of Hands cannot be recognized as valid. As to the historical question, it has not yet been shown clearly that the consecration of their first bishop, Parker, was done canonically and that their Orders have an unbroken and genuine Apostolic Succession."[1] Ambraze is distinctly in favor of their validity.[2] Dyobouniotes says that the "solution of the question of the validity of Anglican Orders depends on the proof (a) of the canonical character of the consecration of the first bishop of the Anglican Church since the Reformation, Abp. Parker, and (b) on the correctness of the teaching of the Anglican Church about Orders and the sacraments in general, and its agreement with the teaching of the Eastern Church. Of these two problems the first may be solved by historical research, ... but the second can only be settled satisfactorily and certainly when the Episcopal Church shall define officially and authoritatively her teaching about Holy Orders and the sacraments in general, the inconsistency and indefiniteness of which (now) does not allow (the forming of) certain conclusions based on sure and unquestioned teaching."[3] The most recent discussion of the subject is in a brochure of Prof. Komnenos of the Chalki Theological Seminary. He says: "The reserved attitude of our Church towards Anglican Orders is altogether unreasonable. . . We are of unhesitating opinion that the same rule (as applies to Roman Catholics), ought to be applied to the Anglican Clergy, inasmuch as they also are demonstrated by the relative *notabilia* to have received not the semblance of ordination but one which is real and is based upon . . . historic Succession from the Apostles, upon its canonical transmission, and upon an essentially and fundamentally right conception of it."[4]

[1] *Ibid.*, p. 336, and note 2.
[2] Op. cit., pp. 66-90, and his Δοκίμιον περὶ ἑνώσεως τῶν ᾿Αγγλικανῶν ᾿Επισκοπιανῶν μετὰ τῆς ᾿Ορθοδόξου ᾿Ανατολικῆς ᾿Εκκλησίας, Athens, 1891. For bibliography on the subject cf. Palmieri, *op. cit.*, II. p. 188, notes.
[3] Τὰ Μυστήρια, p. 164 note 1.
[4] From his Συμβολαὶ εἰς τὰς προσπαθείας πρὸς ἕνωσιν, Constantinople, 1921, p. 9; translation of the Rev. J. A. Douglas in *The Church Times* of July 15, 1921; cf. also pp. 18, ff. of the Rev. J. A. Douglas, *The*

(c) The third condition or term of the administration of
the sacraments is concerned with their relation to the individual
recipient. It is entirely a subjective condition, and without it
the sacrament may fail of its effect. While "the sacraments are
accomplished by divine command, or directly upon the fulfilment of the prescribed ecclesiastical act by the officiant, . . .
yet in order that they be effective to work saving power on
those who receive them, these must be prepared for the reception of divine Grace. This distinction between the actual content of the sacraments performed by divine command and their
saving energy, appears in 1 Cor. 11, 29." Other passages in
Holy Scripture[1] testify to the sacraments as objective means of
justifying and sanctifying Grace, and the Fathers[2] clearly hold
to the objective character of this Grace irrespective either of
the officiant or the recipient.[3] "As the sun lightens all, as the
echo strikes the ears of all, healthy and deaf, so the sacraments
offer to all, the believing and the virtuous as well as those who
are not so, the Grace of God. But as the light and the sound
operate where there are healthy sense organs (to receive them),
thus the Grace proffered by the sacraments operates and brings
about its proper effects only where there is such receptivity."[4]
"If the power of the sacraments comes forth from God for Jesus
Christ's sake, yet for its proper reception and personal value
it is necessary that there be a preparation of those who receive
the sacrament." This consists in faith, the conviction of sin,
in the desire and craving for the help of God, with special reference to the Grace of each sacrament. "If we wish to express
this subjective preparation in a single phrase, including the
case of infants, it is clear that 'passive receptivity'[5] would be

*Relations of the Anglican Churches with the Eastern-Orthodox, es-
pecially in regard to Anglican Orders*, Faith Press, London, 1921, and
F. Gavin, *The Greek Church and the Anglican Question*, in the *A.
C. M.* May, 1921, pp. 206-224.

[1] *E. g.*, Rom. 3, 20; Tit. 3, 5; Acts 8, 17; 19, 8.

[2] St. Augustine, *contra Cresconium Don.*, 4, 16, *et passim*.

[3] Androutsos, Δογματική, p. 310.

[4] Dyobouniotes, Τὰ Μυστήρια, p. 34, and Mesolora, *op. cit.*, IV. pp.
177-178.

[5] Dyobouniotes takes exception to this phrase of Androutsos in his
'Η Δογμ. 'Ανδρ., κριν., p. 52, and 'Οφειλ. ἀπάντ., pp. 120-130; cf. An-

the expression in a succinct form of the fundamental characteristic of the personal factors in the appropriation of the saving Grace of the sacraments." This Androutsos finds to be the
essential attitude of all recipients of the sacraments, both of
infants at their Baptism as well as of those of riper years who
"become conscious of the chasm of sin separating them from
God, and ardently long for His help."[1]

Just as the sacraments do not depend for their accomplishment and fulfilment on the person or state of the officiating
priest, so they are likewise independent of the state of the recipient. The change in the Eucharist, for example, of the
bread and wine into the Body and Blood of Christ, takes place
irrespective of the faith or ethical state of celebrant or people.
Hence is derived the doctrine that the sacraments are achieved
and consummated *ex opere operato,* independently of the personal qualities of officiant or recipient, provided that they be
canonically and rightly celebrated by the proper person with
the necessary intention.[2]

Besides the sacraments, the Church employs certain sacramental services, or *sacramentals.* They may be defined as "those
services instituted by the Church by means of which the influence of evil spirits is averted, the course of man's life is
hallowed, and the material objects connected with it made holy."[3]
The sacramentals do not work *ex opere operato* nor may they
claim divine institution and authority. They include exorcisms,
benedictions, dedications, the sign of the Cross, special blessings,
and the like. "These services, depending on the receptivity and
faith of those who take part, do not operate of necessity as do the
sacraments, nor yet are they merely empty symbols of divine
truths or simply definite methods of prayer to God."[4]

droutsos' reply to the criticism, justifying his use of these words, pp.
130-131 of his Δογματικαὶ Μελέται, Α'.

[1] Androutsos, Δογματική, p. 311.

[2] *Ibid.,* and p. 312; Dyobouniotes, Τὰ Μυστήρια, pp. 33-36. Mesolora
seems to have misconceived the theological implications of this doctrine and to reject it; cf. *op. cit.,* IV, pp. 175-179.

[3] Dyobouniotes, Τὰ Μυστήρια, p. 35, note 1.

[4] Androutsos, *op. cit.,* pp. 317, note.

II. THE SACRAMENTS IN PARTICULAR

I. Baptism

"Baptism is the sacrament in which he who is thrice immersed in water in the Name of the Father and of the Son and of the Holy Ghost, is cleansed from all sin and regenerated spiritually."[1] It is the door into the Church,[2] the spiritual and mystical grafting of the wild olive into the good olive,[3] the entrance into the participation of the other sacraments.[4] The institution of the sacrament[5] came after our Lord's Resurrection and before His Ascension into Heaven,[6] since the discourse with Nicodemus[7] was a prophecy of the establishment of Baptism. Of the testimony of the Fathers to the institution, purpose, and scope of the sacrament it is not necessary to give examples.[8]

The institution of Baptism was foreshadowed and prefigured both in prophecy and in typical institutions, of which Dyobouniotes[9] names "as chief": circumcision, the levitical ablutions and purifications of the Old Testament, the saving of Noah by the waters of the Flood, the passing of the children of Israel through

[1] Dyobouniotes, Τὰ Μυστήρια, p. 38. He finds the definition given by Androutsos (Δογματική, p. 318: "the divinely instituted service by which one immersed in water is regenerated spiritually") incomplete and consequently "erroneous, since it ought to include the essential elements" ('Η Δογμ. 'Ανδρ. κριν., p. 53, cf. 'Οφειλ. ἀπάντησις, pp. 130-132). Androutsos responds to this criticism (pp. 114, 117 of his Δογμ. Μελ., Α'.) by showing that the general definition given involves the essentials further expounded in the text. For Mesolora's diffuse definition cf. op. cit., IV. pp. 180-181.

[2] Androutsos, Δογματική, p. 318.

[3] Kephala, Χριστολογία, p. 197.

[4] Androutsos, ibid.; for the other terms to denote Baptism, in early usage both of East and West, cf. Mesolora, IV. p. 182; Dyobouniotes, op. cit., p. 38.

[5] Dyobouniotes and Androutsos ibid., and p. 319 (Androutsos op. cit.).

[6] For refutation of contrary theory cf. note 1. p. 39, Dyobouniotes.

[7] Dyobouniotes, ibid., and Mesolora, IV. pp. 184-185.

[8] Cf. Androutsos, p. 319; Dyobouniotes, p. 39; Mesolora IV, p. 183; Mogila, in Mesolora, I. p. 424; Dositheus, ibid., II. p. 104; Dyobouniotes, p. 43.

[9] Op. cit., pp. 39-42.

the Red Sea, the custom of baptizing proselytes to Judaism, the Baptism of John the Baptist, and that done by the Apostles previous to the day of Pentecost. Our Lord's Baptism by St. John was "not only in order to fulfil all righteousness, but in order that He might become the Door and the Way into Life, and might hallow the nature of water . . . so as to give to those baptized in His Baptism the Grace of the Holy Spirit."[1]

The administration of the sacrament must, under all normal conditions, be at the hands of a bishop or a priest. As we know from Holy Scripture, the Apostles and disciples communicated their authority to baptize to others, and the Church has restricted this function to the priesthood exclusively.[2] It was very rarely allowed to a Deacon (according to the example of Philip in Acts 8, 12), and then only when no priest or bishop was available; only in cases of dire necessity may baptism be performed by a lay person. "Such baptism must be validated . . . afterwards by the Church."[3] Mogila says in his *Orthodox Confession*:" Baptism may not be administered by any other save a regular (lawful, canonical), priest, but in time of urgent necessity a lay person, either man or woman, may perform this sacrament," which person, Dositheus adds, must be Orthodox.[4] This exceptional case, which is lawful according to ancient precedent, is only so in the event of absolute and urgent necessity.[5]

The "external signs" in Baptism are threefold: (a) water, (b) trine immersion and emersion, and (c) the use of the

---

[1] Mesolora, *op. cit.*, IV. p. 183.

[2] Androutsos, *op. cit.*, p. 333 and notes.

[3] Dyobouniotes, *op. cit.*, p. 45; cf. Mesolora, *op. cit.*, pp. 218-219: "The canons prescribe that the priest must complete the...rite in the case of a child so baptized," and cf. note 1, *ibid.*

[4] In Mesolora, *op. cit.*, I, p. 425, and II, p. 115.

[5] Mesolora, IV. p. 201. On the testimony of the Fathers, cf. Dyobouniotes, *op. cit.*, p. 45, and Androutsos, p. 334. Both observe that the objection of St. Epiphanius, Irenaeus, and Tertullian to the practice of Baptism in certain of the sects of their day, by women, was based on the fact that such Baptism was "solemnly, regularly, and publicly" performed by women; this is an utterly different matter from Baptism in the case of urgent necessity by a lay woman (*loc. cit.*).

proper formula. In general, "the outward act must include
all that which from Apostolic times has been regarded as necessary for the canonical administration of the sacrament."[1] The
irreducible minimum of these necessary conditions is the invocation of the Holy Trinity and trine immersion in water.[2]
The use of water is testified by Holy Scripture, the early
Church, the Fathers, and the universal practice of the Church.
Water, "as the natural means of physical cleansing, is the most
appropriate symbol of spiritual cleansing from sin."[3] No other
matter is allowed or accepted by the Orthodox Church.[4]
The word "baptism" itself means "dipping" or "immersion",
and this was universally the primitive practice. This is testified by the Fathers,[5] even of the West,[6] by the existence in the
baptistries of older churches of fonts built for immersion, and
by the terminology employed in regard to the sacrament of
Baptism.[7] This immersion "means the submersion of the whole
body of the baptizand in the water."[8] There must be three

[1] Androutsos, *op. cit.*, p. 329.
[2] *Ibid.*, and cf. Mesolora, *op. cit.*, IV. pp. 196-197. The only cases
in which the Orthodox Church has shown herself "accommodating in
practice, while in principle she denies the validity of alien Baptism
entirely, is when such.....has been had by trine immersion, affusion,
or aspersion, and in the name of the Holy Trinity...This *economy* is
not absolute, but is limited by certain conditions; in the present case,
the invocation of the Holy Trinity is the *sine qua non*" (Androutsos,
op. cit., pp. 332-333).
[3] Dyobouniotes, *op. cit.*, p. 51.
[4] *Ibid.*, Androutsos, *op. cit.*, p. 329 and note 1; cf. Kritopoulos, in
Mesolora, I. p. 320; Mogila *ibid.*, p. 425. Mesolora seems to differ
from this absolute prohibition, in cases of extreme necessity allowing
the use of the sign of the Cross only with the proper formula (*op. cit.*,
IV, p. 194, note 3), or the use of other material substances than water
(p. 210 *ibid.*, and note 2). The cases of *clinical baptism* by aspersion
(*ibid.*, p. 200) are "the exception which proves the rule" in Orthodox
practice. People so baptized are not capable of taking Orders (Mesolora, *ibid.*, p. 200, note 1, and Androutsos, *op. cit.*, p. 331).
[5] Cf. Dyobouniotes, *op. cit.*, p. 53; Androutsos, pp. 330-331, and notes.
[6] *E. g.*, St. Thomas Aquinas calls it *communior, laudabilior, tutior*.
[7] Dyobouniotes, *op. cit.*, p. 54; λουτρόν, *lavacrum, balneum*. On the
evidence of the Symbolic Books, cf. in Mesolora,—Jeremiah II. I. p.
226; Mogila, *ibid.*, p. 425; Kritopoulos, *ibid.*, p. 320; Dositheus, II.
p. 115, etc.
[8] Mesolora, *op. cit.*, IV. p. 198.

immersions and emersions, according to Orthodox teaching. This was undoubtedly the primitive practice,[1] but some latitude of usage came in later, for example, in Spain, where one immersion became the custom as a profession of faith in the Unity of Essence in the Godhead.[2] Trine immersion meant profession of faith in the three Persons of the Godhead, and also "symbolized the three-day burial of our Lord and His Resurrection."[3] No case can be made out for the practice of "affusion" or "aspersion". It is contrary to primitive custom, against the very significance of the word "Baptism", foreign to all of the terminology and phraseology employed, and does violence to the divine institution.[4] It is a perversion and a false usage, and cannot in the least find support in the recognition of clinical Baptism in early times. Quoting examples of the use of *economy* proves nothing.[5]

The use of the formula, "the servant of God, *N.,* is baptized in the Name of the Father and of the Son and of the Holy Ghost," is necessary for a valid Baptism, though the Latin formula actually amounts to the same thing. The difference is only one of phraseology. "The officiating priest in the Orthodox Church is lost to sight, so to speak, under the sacraments which he performs, and their operation is ascribed directly to God[6]. . . In the Latin form the priest appears as achieving and administering divine Grace . . . , in which the sharp separation of clergy from laity is apparent."[7] "The difference between the two forms lies generally in the . . . fact that the

[1] *Ibid.,* p. 196, and Dyobouniotes, *op. cit.,* p. 54, where patristic references are given.

[2] Dyobouniotes, *ibid.* "The invalidity of the Baptism of the Eunomians performed with only one immersion...was not on account of this fact, but because of the anti-Trinitarian teaching of the sect." Cf. also, Androutsos, *op. cit.,* note 3, p. 330.

[3] Androutsos, *op. cit.,* p. 330, and Dyobouniotes, *ibid.*

[4] Mesolora, *op. cit.,* IV. pp. 200 and ff.

[5] Androutsos, *op. cit.,* pp. 330-331, and Dyobouniotes, *op. cit.,* p. 54, note.

[6] Dyobouniotes sharply criticizes this aspect of the distinction which Androutsos draws, cf. Ἡ Δογμ. Ἀνδρ. κριν., p. 54, and Ὀφειλ. ἀπάντ., pp. 133 and 383, and Androutsos' Δογμ. Μελ., Α', p. 126.

[7] Androutsos, *op. cit.,* pp. 334-335.

Latin Church emphasizes the priest's part"[1] in consummating the sacrament. What is essential and a *sine qua non* in the formula is the invocation of the Holy Trinity.[2] The mention in the New Testament of Baptism "in the name of the Lord"[3] does not preclude Baptism in the name of the Holy Trinity, but according to St. John Damascene[4] meant that "those who believed in Him were to be baptized," or "meant that Baptism instituted by our Lord and performed according to His command or in His power", according to other Fathers.[5] Baptism performed any other way than in the name of the Holy Trinity is absolutely void.[6] In the administration of Baptism,[7] the Orthodox rite employs the oil of the catechumens,[8] and "the renunciations of Satan and the exorcisms, which were from early times associated with Baptism, but which do not constitute its 'outward signs' . . . according to the general acceptance of the word."[9]

The inward Grace conveyed in the sacrament of Baptism is two-fold, effecting (a) the forgiveness of all sins, original and actual or personal, and (b) regenerating and justifying the soul, by adoption making the Christian an heir of salvation.[10] "The energy of Baptism", says Androutsos, "is that of justification, just as the organ by which we receive justifying Grace is Baptism." The forgiveness of all sins—not only the removal of guilt and punishment, but the doing away with the whole body of sin—is the negative, while the life-giving, regenerating power of Grace implanting faith, hope, and love . . .

---

[1] "But not as himself *proffering* the Grace, as some wrongly hold,"—Dyobouniotes, *op. cit.*, p. 55, note 1, and cf. Mesolora, *op. cit.*, IV. pp. 206-207.

[2] Androutsos, *ibid.*

[3] *E. g.*, Acts 2, 38; 8, 12, 16; 10, 48; 19, 5.

[4] Ἔκδοσις, IV. 9, quoted by Dyobouniotes, *op. cit.*, p. 56.

[5] Quoted by Androutsos, *op. cit.*, pp. 329-330, references *ad loc.*

[6] Dyobouniotes, *op. cit.*, p. 56; cf. St. John Dam., *loc. cit.*, Mesolora, *op. cit.*, IV. pp. 197-199; Androutsos, *op. cit.*, pp. 332-333.

[7] Discussed in detail by Mesolora, *op. cit.*, pp. 211-215.

[8] *Ibid.*, pp. 194-195, and cf. Kritopoulos, in Mesolora, I. p. 320.

[9] Dyobouniotes, *op. cit.*, p. 57.

[10] Cf. St. John 3, 6; Tit. 3, 5; Gal. 3, 26-28; I Cor. 12, 15; St. Mark 16, 16; 1 St. Pet. 3, 21.

is the positive aspect of the Grace of Baptism.[1] These two effects of Baptism the Fathers and Doctors emphasize and teach.[2] "They are so intimately bound together that no one can say where one leaves off and the other begins,"[3] for "they together constitute one indivisible whole."[4] It has been the particular genius of the Greek Fathers to lay special stress on the positive effects of the Grace of Baptism—as *regeneration* (Tit. 3, 5), and *illumination* (cf. Heb. 6, 4; 10, 32),—while the West has tended more to emphasize the negative side of baptismal Grace.[5] Yet the Orthodox Church has not been deficient in her doctrine of the remission of sins by Baptism, but teaches that it is an utter extirpation and effacement of sin in the Christian: *all* sin is done away, as Dositheus says.[6] While this is true, the *lust of the flesh* still remains in the baptized, undestroyed. This impulse, however, is not in itself sinful, but only may lead to sin, if the will coöperates with it. The sinful character which it possesses in the natural man[7] is completely done away by Baptism. *Concupiscentia* remains along with other difficulties in the baptized—suffering, pain, and death—but all lose their fearful and absolute character by reason of the life in Grace. As pain and suffering serve the Christian as occasions for the development of virtues, so *concupiscence*—the spark which may enkindle the evil passion, the instinct or desire which if not conquered may become sin if the will surrender—can be the means of strength and spiritual development if the Christian cleaves closely to God's Grace.[8]

---

[1] Androutsos, *op. cit.*, p. 320; cf. on this passage Dyobouniotes' comments in 'Η Δογμ. 'Ανδρ. κριν., p. 54 and 'Οφειλ. ἀπάντ., p. 132, and Androutsos in Δογμ. Μελ., Α', p. 117; Kritopoulos, in Mesolora, *op. cit.*, I. pp. 321-322, and Mesolara, *op. cit.*, IV. pp. 207-8.

[2] Cf. note 1, p. 58 of Dyobouniotes, *op. cit.*, and pp. 320-321 of Androutsos, *op. cit.*

[3] Dyobouniotes, *op. cit.*, p. 58.

[4] Androutsos, p. 320.

[5] *Ibid.*, p. 321 and cf. notes for references.

[6] Cf. Mesolora, *op. cit.*, II, p. 115.

[7] Cf. Rom. 7.

[8] So explicitly in Androutsos, *op. cit.*, pp. 322-324; Mesolora is more guarded, avoids committing himself to the use of the term, which is used in Protestant formularies which he discredits (*op. cit.*, IV. p. 209), but accepts the idea, *e. g*: "We may not deny that there remain

From the nature of the Grace of Baptism, it is obvious that it is universally necessary for salvation.[1] "He who receives not the seal of the water (of Baptism) . . . cannot enter into the Kingdom of Heaven."[2] That it is the indispensable means for all men to receive salvation is apparent from Holy Scripture and the Fathers.[3] Without it man cannot be saved,[4] and on the basis of St. Matt. 26, 25, 30, and 5, 16, "the Church has regarded as baptized those who have witnessed to the Faith" by martyrdom, deeming them to have the *Baptism of blood.*[5] "Another extraordinary means to serve in lieu of Baptism by water, which we Orthodox disallow," says Androutsos, "but the Western Church recognizes—is the so-called *Baptism of desire.*" There is no authority for it in Holy Scripture or Tradition.[6]

Since the Grace of Baptism is absolutely necessary for all, the sacrament is to be denied to no one, not even infants.[7] It is for everyone, irrespective of sex or age, and Infant Baptism became normal in the Church just so soon as circumstances allowed it. As original sin is universal and the need for release from it universal, the Church wisely and justly allows infants to receive the Grace which cleanses them from its stain

over after Baptism. . . certain traces, the desire of the flesh, even when original sin be entirely done away. . . an inclination toward evil," etc. (*ibid.*, pp. 210-211); Dyobouniotes does not endorse the doctrine, but gives it without comment as Western teaching (*op. cit.*, p. 59). The passage from the synod of Jassy referred to by Mesolora (*ibid.*) forms a rather dubious authority for the doctrine (*q. v.*, vol II. Mesolora, p. 40).

[1] *E. g.*, Dositheus in Mesolora II. p. 115; Jeremiah II. *ibid.*, I. p. 140; Mesolora, *op. cit.*, IV. pp. 187-188; St. John 3, 5.

[2] St. Cyril Jer., *Cat.* III, 2.

[3] Androutsos, *op. cit.*, p. 324; cf. St. Mark 16, 15, 16; Acts 2, 28, 22, 16; Eph. 5, 16, and refs. *ibid.* (Androutsos).

[4] Dyobouniotes, *op. cit.*, pp. 60-61.

[5] *Ibid.*, and cf. Androutsos, *op. cit.*, pp. 326-327, for early references to the recognition of it by the Church. "The Feast of the Infants slaughtered by Herod, kept by the Church on Dec. 29, is one indication of the belief of the Church in the *Baptism of blood*," *ibid.*, and cf. Dyobouniotes, pp. 62-63.

[6] Androutsos, *op. cit.*, pp. 327-328; Dyobouniotes (*op. cit.*, p. 63) gives the Latin doctrine without comment and simply presents it objectively.

[7] Dyobouniotes, *op. cit.*, p. 45.

and gives them, in their innocency, the equipment to fight victoriously against sin.[1] Christ received little children; the Old Testament prescribed circumcision, the prototype of Baptism, for male infants on the eighth day of their life, and we know that whole households were baptized by the Apostles.[2] Not only the legitimacy but the necessity of Infant Baptism is attested by the Fathers[3] and the Symbolic Books.[4] "The little ones have need of the regeneration of Baptism, since they have original sin.... They are capable of receiving the Grace of Christ since they are unable to offer it any personal obstacle, in the general way of free-will in its relation to Grace, which when there is no opposition, can bring about its effects unhindered."[5] Consequently the objections to Infant Baptism cannot have great weight. These may be reduced to two: (a) infants have neither consciousness nor faith, and so cannot be fit recipients of Baptism; (b) Infant Baptism violates the free will and deliberately disregards the possible choice of the children, and hence is reprehensible. Against these it may be urged that according to Orthodox doctrine the sacraments act in every case *ex opere operato* and the Protestants' objection proceeds from the falsely reasoned premises of their doctrine of the sacraments.[6] According to Mesolora, "the faith of the officiant..parents..and sponsors makes up for the lack of it in the infant."[7] They know the child's needs, and oversee its spiritual progress. So far as the second objection goes, it is equally groundless. Just as parents provide the necessary physical cleansings of the child, supply it with food, guide it and educate it without regard to the will of the child, so, having in view interests far higher, they provide for its spiritual regen-

[1] *Ibid.*, p. 45.

[2] Cf. St. Matt. 19, 14; 1 Cor. 1, 16; Acts 10, 16, 18; Mesolora *op. cit.*, IV. p. 189.

[3] For the Fathers, cf. Dyobouniotes, *op. cit.*, p. 47; Androutsos, *op. cit.*, p. 325 and notes.

[4] Symbolic Books, in Mesolora, *op. cit.*, Jeremiah II. in 1. p. 147; Kritopoulos, *ibid.*, p. 34; Mogila, *ibid.*, p. 425; Dositheus, II. p. 115.

[5] Androutsos, *op. cit.*, p. 326, substantially repeated by Dyobouniotes, *op. cit.*, p. 50.

[6] Dyobouniotes, *ibid.*, pp. 47-49.

[7] *Op. cit.*, IV. p. 191.

eration, and oversee its spiritual needs.[1] As to the state of unbaptized infants the Orthodox Church has made no official pronouncement, yet inclines to the view that "they may not inherit the Heavenly Kingdom, though they undergo no punishment."[2]

"For a worthy reception of Baptism is demanded, . . . in the case of adults, a two-fold preparation,—Faith in the Saviour and in Christian Truth, and Repentance and the conviction of sin."[3] In the early Church preparation for Baptism involved a course of instructions and a period of testing,—the Catechumenate. This custom has left its trace in the "prayers for the catechumens"; thereupon follow the exorcisms, renunciations, and recitation of the Creed.[4] This moral and intellectual preparation is compensated for, in the case of infants, by their state of personal sinlessness, their receptivity, and their inability to offer any obstacles to the working of Grace, since "where there is no will, or where Grace finds no personal impediment, it can operate absolutely."[5] "As without their will they share by nature in the sin of the author of the race, so much more[6] can they without will become partakers in the redeeming Grace of the Saviour."[7] Androutsos holds that there is no necessary internal bond between the Grace of Baptism and the faith of the godparents,[8] for the latter are to fulfil the lack of it on the child's part "in time". Infants are not baptized in the faith of their sponsors and parents, but they

[1] Dyobouniotes, ibid., p. 49-50; Androutsos, op. cit., pp. 325-326. On the institution of sponsors, cf. Dyobouniotes, note 2. p. 49; Mesolora, ibid., p. 191, pp. 211-212.

[2] Cf. St. Gregory Nazianzen, Orat., 40, 23; Response of Cyril of Constantinople in 1815 (Androutsos, op. cit., p. 328, note 3); Constantine Economos, Κατήχησις ἢ ὀρθόδοξος διδασκαλία τῆς πίστεως, Vienna, 1813, c. 15, on which most of the theological opinions are based. Cf. Androutsos, loc. cit., Dyobouniotes, op. cit., note 1. pp. 61-62, and Mesolora, op. cit., IV. note 6, pp. 187-188, and note 1. pp. 219-220.

[3] Androutsos, op. cit., p. 335.

[4] Mesolora, op. cit., IV. pp. 211-212; Dyobouniotes, op. cit., p. 60.

[5] Androutsos, Δογμ. Μελ., Α', p. 136.

[6] On this phrase cf. Dyobouniotes' criticism, Ἡ Δογμ. Ἀνδρ. κριν., p. 55, and Ὀφειλ. ἀπάντ., p. 135.

[7] Androutsos, Δογματική, p. 335.

[8] As against Mesolora, quoted above; Macarius, op. cit., II, p. 409, and Economos' Catechism, p. 64 (op. cit.).

are constituted sharers in Baptism looking forward to the personal acquisition on their own part, of such faith.[1] In the case of both infants and adults, the Grace of Baptism is like all sacramental Grace, objective, and its "energy operates independently of the faith and moral condition of the recipient."[2] But this bestowed regeneration has to be appropriated by the person receiving it, in order that it may become his own personal possession, and be capable of development. "The apprehension and development of this Grace does depend on the faith and moral character of the baptized. Baptism bestows regeneration, but as it were in germ, and it has need of development depending on the soil into which it falls, that is, the religious and moral condition of the person."[3]

Inasmuch as Baptism is by nature something like physical birth, which may only occur once, so as spiritual regeneration it can only take place once.[4] Baptism canonically performed may not be iterated.[5] This is the teaching of the Fathers, for example, Tertullian: *denuo ablui non licet,*[6] St. John Chrysostom: "Just as it is not now possible for Christ to be crucified again, so it is impossible to be baptized a second time"[7]; Theodore,[8] St. John Damascene,[9] and others. "Like the priesthood", says Dositheus, "which may not be received twice, so one who is once rightly baptized may not be baptized again, no matter how many sins he may fall into.... If he wish to return unto the Lord he receives again the adoption which he lost, by the sacrament of Penance."[10] Anyone who has been baptized twice, even through ignorance,

---

[1] Androutsos, Δογματική, pp. 335-336.

[2] Dyobouniotes, Τὰ Μυστήρια, p. 59.

[3] *Ibid.,* p. 60.

[4] *Ibid.,* p. 63-64.

[5] Mesolora, *op. cit.,* IV. p. 204.

[6] *De poenitentia,* 1.

[7] *Homily* 9, 3, on the Epistle to the Hebrews.

[8] "As Christ suffered once for all, so we may not share in His sufferings but once only; through Baptism we are buried and rise with Him. We have no need to receive Baptism a second time" (on Heb. 6, 6).

[9] ῎Εκδοσις, IV. 9; St. Cyril Jer. Προω. εἰς κατήχη. 16; Tertullian, *de Baptismo,* 15.

[10] In Mesolora, II, pp. 116-117.

can not receive Holy Orders.[1] So questions of "rebaptism" are not properly so called, for they only describe instances in which the Church has properly baptized a person who has not received the sacrament at all.[2] But the mere fulfilment of the necessary outward signs by one in Orders is not sufficient to make a Baptism valid, if not performed inside the Orthodox Church. The question of the recognition of Baptism outside the Church, is, as we have seen, bound up with that of the validity of the priesthood, and "chiefly with the idea of the Church as the steward of divine Grace."[3]

2. The Sacrament of Chrism

The sacrament of Chrism[4] is "that divinely instituted rite by which the bodily members of the baptized person are anointed, and his incipient spiritual life strengthened and perfected"[5] by the bestowal of the gifts of the Holy Spirit.[6] It is actually the completion and perfection of the sacrament of Baptism, the "indispensable and necessary complement"[7] of that sacrament, "a royal seal validating as well as confirming Holy Baptism, just as the *Amen* validates and confirms the creed."[8] "Baptism, the birth and entrance of the Christian into the spiritual life in Christ, is completed by the bestowal of all the gifts necessary for that life" and by the firm establishment of the steps of the life opened up by Baptism, looking forward to "the long course of spiritual con-

---

[1] Dyobouniotes, *op. cit.*, p. 65.

[2] Mesolora, *op. cit.*, IV. p. 204.

[3] Dyobouniotes, *ibid.*, cf. additional note to preceding lecture and the section on Economy in this present, pp. 292 ff.

[4] Or "Myrrh" (μύρον), Mesolora, *op. cit.*, IV, p. 219, or "Confirmation" (βεβαίωσις), Dositheus in Mesolora, II. p. 113; other names used for this sacrament, in Dyobouniotes, *op. cit.*, p. 66; Mesolora, IV. pp. 222-223.

[5] Androutsos, Δογματική, p. 336.

[6] Dyobouniotes, Τὰ Μυστήρια, p. 66; Mesolora, *op. cit.*, IV, p. 219; cf. Mogila (in Mesolora, I. pp. 425-426): "When the priest anoints the baptized with the Holy Myrrh, the gifts of the Holy Spirit are poured out upon him...By this unction...he is sealed and strengthened in the gifts of the Holy Ghost."

[7] Mesolora, IV. p. 221.

[8] Kritopoulos, in Mesolora, *op. cit.*, I. p. 321.

flicts in the Christian warfare into which it leads him."[1] As
the complement of Baptism, the rite of Chrism is always
immediately connected with the administration of Baptism,[2]
to which practice Jeremiah II.[3], Mogila,[4] and the other Symbolic Books bear witness.

The evidence in Holy Scripture for the sacrament is found
chiefly in Acts 8, 14-17 and 19, 2-6.[5] In two other passages,
2 Cor. 1, 21,22 and 1 St. John 2, 20,27, occur the words
"unction", "anointing", and "sealed", which some Orthodox
writers quote as the authority for the use of anointing. These
texts furnish rather flimsy support, as Dybouniotes admits, who
says in the body of his text: "It appears that the inward bestowal of the gifts of the Holy Spirit is made by means of
outward anointing", but in the note: "One cannot be sure
that....these texts refer to an external anointing with
oil, . . . as the words in Old and New Testament usage often
mean simply the inward anointing without the outward."[6]
"These passages", says Androutsos, "are concerned with the
inward anointing in a metaphorical sense, but the words 'confirmation' and 'unction' seem to imply an outward anointing
by which the Grace of the Holy Spirit is bestowed."[7] The
evidence in Holy Scripture for anointing with Chrism can

[1] Androutsos, op. cit., p. 339. His definition of the Grace given
in Chrism, which "increases and strengthens the spiritual life of the
neophyte" (ibid.), Dyobouniotes subjects to criticism ('Η Δογμ. 'Ανδρ.
κρ., 55), saying that this is not correct, but the Grace given is the
Holy Spirit in His seven gifts. He says that Androutsos is entirely
under the influence of the Roman notion of Confirmation ('Οφειλ.
ἀπάντ., p. 136). Androutsos answers that he is defining the operation rather than the nature of the Grace bestowed, which he takes
for granted as being the gifts of the Holy Spirit (Δογμ. Μελ. Α', pp.
141, 143).
[2] Dyobouniotes, Τὰ Μυστήρια, pp. 82-83.
[3] In Mesolora, I, p. 426, and cf. pp. 226, 228-229.
[4] Ibid., I p. 321. "According to the practice of the Orthodox Church,"
says Androutsos (op. cit., p. 343), "Chrism is inseparably united with
Baptism...This truth is far from being repugnant to Holy Scripture,
is confirmed by it, and witnessed to clearly by Tradition." For historical evidence cf. loc. cit., notes, and p. 344.
[5] Androutsos, op. cit., p. 337.
[6] Op. cit., p. 71.
[7] Op. cit., p. 336.

be based only on these two texts. That Orthodox writers
have felt the difficulty, is apparent from the words of Jeremiah II: "The sacrament of Holy Myrrh is not brought out
(ἐμφέρεται) in Holy Scripture, but is handed down by the disciples of the Word."[1] According to an Orthodox Tradition
the institution of the sacrament by our Lord took place on
Maundy Thursday night after the Foot Washing and before
the Institution of the Last Supper,[2] hence the custom of the
consecration of the oil on this day.[3] This view, according to
Dyobouniotes, is "improbable", and we have no definite information about the time of the institution from Holy Scripture.[4]

The promises of the gift of the Holy Spirit[5] were fulfilled
at Pentecost, and "the Apostles having received the Holy Ghost
bestowed Him on the faithful by the laying on of hands."[6]
The texts from Acts referred to above give us authentic information of the fact that "the Apostles laid their hands
on the baptized in order to convey to them gifts different from
those bestowed in Baptism."[7] "This laying on of hands and
the communication of the gifts of the Holy Spirit is not
something of a passing nature, but something permanent, the
more so as it would be incomprehensible for the bestowal of
the regular gifts of the Holy Spirit by the laying on of hands
to have then been necessary in the Apostles' time but not
afterwards."[8] The Apostles in so doing must have been carrying out a command of our Lord, and the manner of the act
alone would indicate that "these outward acts were effectual
means of Grace."[9] The evidence, then, for the bestowal of
Grace by the laying on of hands is perfectly clear, and the
indirect evidence for our Lord's having instituted this means
is equally certain: the Apostles were not observing a personal

---

[1] In Mesolora, I, p. 142.
[2] Mesolora, op. cit., IV. pp. 225-226, note 3.
[3] Ibid., pp. 332-333, note 3.
[4] Op. cit., p. 70, note 1.
[5] E. g., St. John 13, 14, 15; St. Luke 24, 49; Acts 1, 8.
[6] Acts 2; Dyobouniotes, op. cit., pp. 66-67.
[7] Ibid., p. 68.
[8] Ibid., p. 69.
[9] Androutsos, op. cit., p. 337.

and individual ruling made by themselves for "nothing essential in the Christian religion was commanded by them save by our Lord's injunction."[1] The question then arises, granted the evidence for the bestowal of Grace by means of the laying on of the hands of the Apostles, (a) is this the same thing as the sacrament of Chrism, or (b) merely the conveyance of extraordinary gifts in an extraordinary manner? As to the second, it is clear from Holy Scripture[2] that this does not refer to "the special gifts given only to certain people . . . . but to the regular gifts of the Holy Spirit indispensable for every true Christian."[3] As to the first, it is abundantly apparent from the evidence of the Fathers, who "refer the sacrament to the afore-mentioned passages from Acts, ascribe the saving energy of the Holy Spirit to Chrism, and do not distinguish it from the laying on of hands",[4] that this laying on of hands by the Apostles is the sacrament of Chrism.

The evidence from the Fathers is all but unanimous[5] in speaking of the sacrament as that of anointing with Chrism.[6] So too the evidence of the early Councils, and the fact that the schismatic bodies which split off from the Church from early times until the 4th or 5th centuries, have the sacrament of Chrism as it is observed by the Orthodox. "From what has been said above," continues Dyobouniotes, "it becomes clear that both Holy Scripture and Tradition recognize Chrism as a sacrament."[7] Since there are two usages in question, the laying on of hands and anointing with Chrism, the question naturally arises, what is the relation of the two "outward signs"? Both cannot be such, for in "that case we should

---

[1] Dyobouniotes, *op. cit.*, p. 70.

[2] *E. g.*, 1 Cor. 12, 29; St. John 7, 33-40.

[3] Dyobouniotes, *ibid.*, pp. 68-69.

[4] Androutsos, *op. cit.*, pp. 337-338, *q. v.*, for patristic references.

[5] "Only Tertullian (*De Baptismo*, 8), Cyprian (*Epistle*, 73), and Augustine (in Migne, *P. L.* 21, 777) mention the laying on of hands as a constituent element of the sacrament" (Androutsos, *op. cit.*, p. 338).

[6] Dyobouniotes, *op. cit.*, p. 73. *q. v.*, for patristic evidence. He quotes Pope Melchisedek († 314) on the close connection of Baptism and Chrism, by implication indicating "Chrism" rather than the Western "Confirmation" by a Bishop (p. 83, note 3, *ibid*).

[7] Dyobouniotes, *op. cit.*, p. 74, references in notes.

have the unique and singular phenomenon of two essential outward signs in one and the same sacrament! . . . Of the two, ...one must constitute the essential outward sign....Which of the two it is not easy to discover from Holy Scripture, which refers to both,[1] or from Tradition which is (equally) indefinite and uncertain, now emphasizing one, and now the other, and sometimes both."[2] "This phenomenon", says Androutsos, "may be explained in three ways,[3] either (a) the sacrament was originally administered by the laying on of hands, but later, whether by definition or by the growth of the custom in the Church, the anointing came to be the usage; or (b) Chrism was used from early times along with the laying on of hands; or (c) the Apostles themselves, having at the first performed the sacrament by the laying on of hands, afterwards substituted for it the use of Chrism."[4] He finds the first improbable because the Church does not change an apostolic ordinance, and there is no evidence of the introduction of the change anywhere in early Church history. The second is equally inacceptable, for the lack of evidence and because of general improbability. "The third hypothesis is the only probable one, that the sacrament, administered by the Apostles by the laying on of hands in the early Church with its small numbers, afterwards, when Christianity began to grow, came to be administered through Chrism by any priest....If certain Churches of the West preserved the laying on of hands,[5] the custom appeared to them the more nec-

[1] Dyobouniotes says that "the sacrament was administered in the same apostolic time by the laying on of hands of the Apostles *and by* Chrism" (*op. cit.*, p. 71), which seems rather an unwarranted assumption, on the basis of his own words quoted above.

[2] *Op. cit.*, pp. 71-72.

[3] Dyobouniotes discusses *four* possible ways of explaining the relation of the two: (a) the laying on of hands is essential and anointing not so, (b) anointing essential, and the laying on of hands not essential, (c) both are essential, and (d) either may be used canonically (p. 72, note 1).

[4] Androutsos, *op. cit.*, p. 338.

[5] Not only in the West, but elsewhere as well, *e. g.*, Eulogius the Patriarch of Alexandria († 608) writing to Photius, testifies that the "gift of the Holy Spirit is had by the laying on of hands"; Simeon of Thessalonica refers to the use of both laying on of hands and Chrism.—cf. Dyobouniotes, *op. cit.*, p. 75 note 2.

essary in that Chrism was performed by bishops."[1] Dyobouniotes holds much the same theory, that the sacrament, originally administered by the Apostles by the laying on of hands,
was from later apostolic times administered by Chrism. "Why
this substiution was effected we do not know.. The opinion
that with the growth of the Church and the increase of her
membership, the Apostles, so few in number, were unable to
cope with the work of bestowing the gifts of the Holy Spirit
by the laying on of hands....as there were so many baptized
· scattered about over many places....and (consequently) ruled
that the sacrament should be administered by presbyters by
means of oil blessed by the Apostles, seems not improbable."[2]

The outward signs of this sacrament are "the signing of the
neophyte with the Cross, with oil blessed by the Church mixed
with other oleaginous substances to symbolize the manifold
gifts of the Holy Spirit, and at the same time the pronouncing of
the words: 'The seal of the gift of the Holy Spirit, Amen'."[3]
The use of the "myrrh" or "chrism'", now made of some forty
sweet-smelling ingredients,[4] is a substitute for the laying on
of hands, and consequently the latter . . . "is not necessary
in the administration of the sacrament."[5] Mesolora would not
say that the laying on of hands is abolished,[6] but that its substitute is the myrrh, "made by the laying on of hands of the
bishop who blessed and hallowed it." According to Kritopoulos, the myrrh must be prepared by the bishops, who distribute
it to the churches in their jurisdiction,[7] and to Mogila, it must

---

[1] St. Cyprian testifies to "Chrism" administered by the Bishop
with the laying on of hands (*Epist.* 73, 9); Androutsos, *op. cit.*, pp.
338-339.

[2] *Op. cit.*, p. 72. This same explanation is given by Mesolora, *op. cit.*,
IV. p. 225. On the basis of 1 St. John 7, 26-27, and 2 Cor. 1, 21, he
concludes that Chrism was used by the Apostles (*ibid.*).

[3] Androutsos, *op. cit.*, p. 341.

[4] Dyobouniotes, *op. cit.*, p. 77; Mesolora, *op. cit.*, IV. pp. 232-233.

[5] Dyobouniotes, *ibid.*, p. 75.

[6] *Op. cit.*, IV. p. 234. But it does not constitute the outward sign
of the sacrament, according to Dyobouniotes: "The Grace of the Holy
Spirit is bestowed by the myrrh and not by the laying on of hands"
(*op. cit.*, p. 6 and note 2).

[7] In Mesolora, *op. cit.*, 1, p. 321.

be had from the highest bishop.[1] This is an early usage, as
the ruling of the synod of Carthage (318), the testimony of
the Fathers, and of the early heresies shows.[2] "The consecration of the myrrh belongs from ancient customs to the bishop;
its administration to the priest."[3] If certain Fathers witness
that the bishops on occasion used to administer the sacrament,
this was only as St. Jerome says: *ad honorem potius sacerdotii
quam ad legis necessitatem.*[4] "Each autocephalous Church can
bless its own myrrh. The Church of Greece receives it from
the Ecumenical Patriarch as a token of respect to him and
a memorial of its former union with the Patriarchate,"[5] which
Church, says Mesolora, "we call Mother."[6] The right to administer this sacrament is inherent in the priesthood and is
bestowed with ordination.[7] In the administration of the sacrament the priest anoints the various members of the body of
the baptized with myrrh episcopally consecrated, at the same
time using the formula given above. The anointing, done
with the sign of the Cross on the different parts of the body,
has most ancient authority, hence the Roman custom of anointing the forehead alone is contrary to Tradition.[8] The words
of the formula come from Holy Scripture and are of very
early origin.[9]

The gifts of the Holy Spirit, which constitute the Grace
conveyed by the sacrament, are enumerated either according
to Isaiah 11, 2, 3, or Gal. 5, 22.[10] These are manifested in the
recognition on the part of the recipient of Christian verities,
in his progress in the spiritual life, and in his growth in Chris-

---

[1] *Ibid.*, p. 426.

[2] Androutsos, *op. cit.*, p. 342, with copious references.

[3] Dyobouniotes, *op. cit.*, pp. 78-79.

[4] Androutsos, *ibid.*, St. Jerome, *adv. Lucifer*, 9. The present practice of the Roman Church, both writers claim, is anomalous and without justification; cf. *loc. cit.*

[5] Dyobouniotes, *ibid.*, p. 81.

[6] *Op. cit.*, IV. pp. 232-233, note 3.

[7] Dyobouniotes, *op. cit.*, p. 80 note 1.

[8] *Ibid.*, pp. 77-78; cf. notes and *ad loc.*

[9] *Ibid.*, and Androutsos, *op. cit.*, p. 341.

[10] Dyobouniotes, *op. cit.*, p. 81.

tian character.[1] They provide against the contingencies and difficulties that beset the Christian in the course of his warfare against sin, strengthen him, and equip him for this struggle.[2] It is the complement and fulfilment of the Grace of Baptism, the further potential development of the Christian life thereby initiated.[3] As the connection with Baptism is so intimate and the nature of the sacraments so similar, two conclusions follow: (a) the sundering of the administration of the two sacraments in the West is totally unjustifiable. It is not only not primitive[4] and contrary to Tradition,[5] but illogical as well. If it be argued that Confirmation should be had when the child has come to an age to understand, why does not this argument apply as well to Baptism? Yet Infant Baptism is as universal in the Roman as in the Orthodox Church.[6] Furthermore, both Churches regard the sacraments as functioning *ex opere operato*.[7] (b) The sacrament may not be iterated, anymore than may Baptism.[8] Only those who return from heresy having once been anointed in the Orthodox Church, are to be anointed again. This is the principle involved in the case of Orthodox who had lapsed into the Paulitian heresy and on their return were anointed again.[9]

"But this second anointing," says Dyobouniotes, "neither is, nor may be regarded as, a repetition of the sacrament of Chrism."[10] It is like the reception of ex-Arians by the laying on of hands in the Western Church, which Pope Gregory I. distinguished carefully from Confirmation.[11] "Since Chrism is the confirmation and as it were the complement (lit. "roofing

---

[1] *Ibid.*, p. 82, provided of course he coöperate in will, and act with the Grace bestowed.

[2] Androutsos, *op. cit.*, p. 339.

[3] *Ibid.*, and Dyobouniotes, *loc. cit.*

[4] "As it only arose in the 13th century, as an innovation," Androutsos, *op. cit.*, p. 344.

[5] For evidence, cf. *ibid.*, p. 343.

[6] Dyobouniotes, *op. cit.*, pp. 83-84.

[7] *Ibid.*, and Androutsos, *op. cit.*, p. 344.

[8] Dyobouniotes, p. 84; cf. Mogila, in Mesolora, *op. cit.*, I. p. 426.

[9] Cf. Rhalle and Potle, Σύνταγμα τῶν θείων καὶ ἱερῶν κανόνων, Athens, vols. I. and II. 1852; (vol. II. p. 169).

[10] *Op. cit.*, p. 84.

[11] *Epist.* 11, 67.

in"=ἐπιστέγασμα), of Baptism, its . . . Grace is only bestowed once. . . . In the cases of a second administration of
Chrism to those coming in from heresy or returning from it
to Orthodoxy, . . . there is no iteration of the sacrament,
properly speaking. Those who come from heresy are anointed
for the first time, for even if they had previously been anointed,
according to Orthodox principle, sacraments administered outside the Church are invalid. For those returning to Orthodoxy
the Chrism is the service of readmission of penitents into the
bosom of the Church."[1] He compares the anointing of Churches
and ikons in the service of consecration, to this use of Chrism
in the case of the returning Orthodox who had lapsed into
heresy or schism, and adds: "This intinction with myrrh has
never been considered as an iteration of the sacrament, but is
as it were the rededication of the new life of those returning
to Orthodoxy, by the prayers and blessings of the Church and
the invocation of the Holy Spirit."[2] The anointing of a king
is also utterly different from the sacrament of Chrism, as it is
analogous to that in the Old Testament and bestows the Grace
necessary for a ruler to fulfil his office and duties.[3]

3. The Holy Eucharist: (a) Definition and Institution

The Holy Eucharist, "which excells all the other sacraments
and is more than all of them necessary for our salvation"[4] is
that sacrament "in which he who receives the Bread and Wine,
consecrated and changed by the priest into the Body and Blood
of the Lord, receives this very Body and Blood of Christ for
the forgiveness of sins and eternal life."[5] Mesolora's definition[6]
mentions explicitly the "transubstantiated Bread and Wine",
while Androutsos speaks of the Real Presence of our Lord

[1] Androutsos, op. cit., p. 340.

[2] Ibid., p. 341, and cf. note 3, p. 339.

[3] Cf. Mesolora, op. cit., IV. p. 231, note 4, quoting Macarius; Dyobouniotes op. cit. p. 84.

[4] Mogila, in Mesolora, op. cit., I. p. 427.

[5] So Dyobouniotes, Τὰ Μυστήρια, p. 86. The last phrase ("for the
forgiveness of sins and eternal life") is part of the sentence of administration in the Liturgy,—cf. Ἐγκόλπιον λειτουργικόν, Odessa, 1911,
p. 91.

[6] Op. cit., IV. p. 244.

"under the forms of bread and wine."[1] As the Great Sacrament of the Christian Religion, it was prefigured and foreshadowed in the Old Testament. Of these prophecies and antitypes the chief are: (a) the Passover, the commemoration by the Jews of the passing-over of the Angel to slaughter the First-born of the Egyptians, and to deliver the children of Israel from bondage, and the passage of the Red Sea. "The celebration of Passover", says Dyobouniotes, "was first of all a propitiatory sacrifice, by which the Jewish folk, conscious of sin . . . sought remission of sins, and also a sacrifice of Thanksgiving, by which the people gave thanks to God for their deliverance and miraculous salvation." The fulfilment and term of the Passover is found in the Passover of the New Covenant, as the paschal lamb was the foreshadowing of the true Paschal Lamb, Christ. (b) The Manna, the heavenly food, is a type of Christ who gives Himself in the Eucharist as the true Food of the soul. (c) The general prophecies in the Old Testament concerning the true sacrifice found their fulfilment in that of the Eucharist. (d) "The sacrifice of Melchisedek is regarded by the writer of the Epistle to the Hebrews . . . as the foreshadowing of the true Sacrifice, the Holy Eucharist."[2]

The Divine Institution of the Eucharist was proclaimed in advance and promised by our Lord Himself, in His discourses in St. John 6,[3] of which vs. 32-51 may be taken as a "discourse about the food of the soul, the divine teaching made available through faith, and the latter part (vs. 51-63), as a discourse about the Holy Eucharist as the Body and Blood of Christ."[4] Thus may be explained the absence of the account of the Institution in St. John, for his Gospel supplements what was already set down in the first three gospels, and he presents here the summary of the doctrine of the Eucharist, to be taken not allegorically nor generally, but literally and specifically.[5] The account of the Institution we have explicitly in four places

---

[1] *Op. cit.*, p. 344, subjected to a very sharp criticism by Dyobouniotes, which will be discussed later.

[2] Tὰ Μυστήρια, pp. 94-95.

[3] Mesolora, IV. p. 254.

[4] Dyobouniotes, *op. cit.*, p. 90, note 1.

[5] *Ibid.*, pp. 89-90, and cf. Androutsos, *op. cit.*, p. 346.

in the New Testament—St. Mark 14, 22-24; St. Matt. 26, 26-28; St. Luke 22, 19-20; and 1 Cor. 11, 23-25.[1] It is not necessary here to summarize the well-known words,[2] but to call attention first to what they do not mean and then to what they do.

The words, "this is my body . . . . this is my blood", may not be taken metaphorically, as if the word *is* meant "shows", "stands for", "represents", or the words *my body . . my blood* meant "the likeness of" *my body.............of my blood,* or as if the demonstrative, *this,* meant *"this bread* understood in a spiritual and symbolic sense". "These metaphorical interpretations are alike arbitrary and erroneous."[3] As against these conceptions it may be urged: while the copula *is* may sometimes bear an allegorical significance, as obviously it does in Gen. 41, 26 ff., or Gal. 4, 24, yet "the reasons involving the acceptance of an allegorical sense do not prevail here; . . .hence the literal meaning is the natural and unforced one." Especially must it be interpreted literally in this case, as it is the sense in which the Apostles and the Church have always taken it. To impugn their understanding of our Lord's meaning would be to shake the very basis of faith in Him, as if our Lord in the Institution of the Eucharist spoke so enigmatically and figuratively that His very Apostles misunderstood Him.[4] Besides it is difficult to see how the same small word could in the same passage serve both as a copula and as implying the meaning "represents" or "stands for".[5] The notion that *my body* meant the "likeness" or "figure" of *my body,* is also impossible: there is no symbolic resemblance between bread and the human body,[6] nor do the words *body* and *blood* in Greek ever mean "figure" or "representation" of the body and blood.[7]

---

[1] The Narrative of the Institution in the Liturgy presents an interesting conflated text based on all four accounts, together with some few additions not there found; cf. Ἐγκόλπιον, pp. 78-79 (St. John Chrysostom).

[2] Cf. Dyobouniotes, pp. 87-89.

[3] *Ibid.,* p. 92.

[4] Androutsos, *op. cit.,* p. 348.

[5] Dyobouniotes, *op. cit.,* p. 82.

[6] Androutsos, *ibid.,* p. 349.

[7] Dyobouniotes, *ibid.,* p. 93.

As a symbol, the Passover would have been far better and more comprehensible.[1] Furthermore, "in the institution of the greatest sacrament of the New Testament . . . our Lord would have taken care that the terms He used in founding and establishing this sacrament should be clear and free of possible misinterpretation, since at that time He was 'speaking plainly and not in proverbs'.[2] Besides, what would the words *take, eat,* . . . *drink ye all of it,* mean, if the bread and wine of the Eucharist were simply 'signs and likenesses' of His Body and Blood? How could the Eucharist, if bestowing no more than the Passover, be the fulfilment of it? Finally such passages as 1 Cor. 10, 3 ff., and 11, 27, show plainly that the Words of the Institution must be taken in their obvious and usual sense."[3] It is clear from the circumstances and purpose that our Lord was not speaking figuratively or symbolically, and the overwhelming unanimity of evidence demands the literal and proper sense of these words.[4] This is clear also from a consideration of the discourse in St. John 6, which prophetic message confirms the strict and simple interpretation of the words of the Institution.[5] The words, *eat my flesh,* have, it is true, another meaning in the Old Testament, namely, "to slander",[6] but this is obviously inapplicable here. It is quite certain that the words must be taken as the people of Capernaum understood them, in their obvious and clear meaning with prophetic application to the Eucharist, the promise of which they convey. This is the sense in which the Fathers have always taken the passage.[7]

The interpretation the Church has always put on the New Testament text is that born out and testified to by Tradition: it was our Lord who instituted the Eucharist, and His words

---

[1] Androutsos, *op. cit.*, p. 349.

[2] *E. g.*, St. John 16, 29.

[3] Dyobouniotes, *ibid.*, p. 93.

[4] Androutsos, *op. cit.*, p. 349.

[5] Dyobouniotes, *op. cit.*, pp. 89-90, *e. g.*, vs. 55: "My flesh is *truly* food and my blood *truly* drink" (A. V. translates ἀληθῶς, *indeed;* W. H. has ἀληθής,—adj. instead of adv.).

[6] *E. g.*, Ps. 27, 2 (LXX 26, 2); Mic. 3, 3; Ezek. 59, 17, 18; St. Jas. 5, 3.

[7] Androutsos, *op. cit.*, pp. 346-347.

mean that the bread and wine are changed into His Body and
Blood. This is the simple and obvious interpretation of the
passages in the New Testament, and is the clear teaching of
the Church from the earliest times. The bread and wine
could not be considered ordinary bread and wine, "but the very
Body and Blood of the Lord".[2] This belief is shown in the reverence paid to the Consecrated Species, in the preference, by
Christians, of death to the betrayal of them to the heathen.[3] St.
Ignatius is quite clear in teaching that the Eucharist is the
Body of the Saviour: "the Medicine of immortality, the Pre-
ventative ('Antidote') of death."[3] So too, St. Justin Martyr,[4]
St. Irenaeus,[5] and St. Cyril of Jerusalem, who say: "That
which seems bread is not bread, even if it is so perceived by the
taste, but is the Body of Christ."[6] This was taught by St.
Gregory of Nyssa, and by the Ecumenical Councils.[7] All the
early liturgies give the same testimony, even those of the
early heretics and schismatics.[8] This teaching may be summed
up as: *the belief in the Real Presence of our Lord and in the
Change* (Conversion) *of the elements into His Body and Blood.*[9]

(b) The Doctrine of the Change (Conversion), or Transubstantiation

The early teaching of the Fathers and the Church regarding the Change (Conversion), or their doctrine of the *Real
Presence,* was neither explicit nor fully developed. If certain
passages culled out of their context seem to imply doctrine not
in accord with what came to be explicitly defined by the Church

[1] Dyobouniotes, *op. cit.,* p. 96.
[2] *Ibid.*
[3] *Ad Smyrnos* 7; *ad Ephes.* 20; *ad Philad.* 4; cf. Androutsos, *op.
cit.,* p. 350, note 2.
[4] *Apol.* 1, 66.
[5] *Adv. Haer.,* IV, 18; V, 2.
[6] *Cat.* 22-3, 6, 9.
[7] Cf. Dyobouniotes, *op. cit.*
[8] *Ibid.*
[9] Androutsos uses the former more frequently, while Dyobouniotes uses the latter, cf. *op. cit., passim.* Mesolora adheres strictly to the
word *transubstantiation.*

—such as Tertullian's use of *repraesentare, figura corporis*,[1] and St. Augustine's, of *signum, figura corporis et sanguinis, sacramentum memoriae*[2]—"such phrases," says Dyobouniotes, "do not represent the teaching of these very Fathers . . . as the investigation of their teaching as a whole plainly shows." Tertullian elsewhere "emphasizes and teaches the Change",[3] as does St. Augustine explicitly in other passages.[4] "If the Fathers spoke . . . about the Eucharist without clearness and definiteness, such passages may not be taken to mean . . . . that the Real Presence was not universally taught . . . but that it had not yet been subject to question, and that theological definitions which were exact and definitely formulated had not been formed".[5] The same remarks made above in regard to Tertullian and St. Augustine apply as well to the teaching of the Alexandrian School, for Origen and St. Clement, in spite of a phrase here and there cut out of its context, did teach the doctrine of the Change.[6] The early terminology, says Dyobouniotes, clearly demonstrates the conviction of the Fathers as to the fact of the Change, for example, the words: "become" (St. Athanasius) "to become other" (ἑτέραν γίγνεσθαι in Theodoret), "to be re-formed" (μεταποιεῖσθαι, St. Gregory of Nyssa), "to be converted", "transelemented" (μεταστοιχειοῦσθαι), "transfigured", and the like.[7] All such words take the Change for granted, and the various terms are simply phrases of equal force and significance, to mean the Change (μεταβολή), but do not show the manner of its accomplishment.[8] "As to

---

[1] *Adv. Marc.* 1, 14, *et* 3, 9; 4, 14; on which Androutsos says: "If these words do not apply to the elements before consecration, they are said in the symbolic use peculiar to the Fathers, according to which a symbol did not stand for something not there but...manifested something actually existing in the symbol" (*op. cit.*, pp. 350-351).

[2] On Ps. 3; *contra Adimantum*, 12, 3; *contra Faustum*, 10, 21; *Epist.* 23.

[3] *E. g., de pud.* 9; *de idol.* 7; *de orat.* 6, etc.

[4] *De Civitate Dei*, 21, 20, *et al.; Enarr.* in Ps. 33; *contra adv. leg. et proph.*, 2, 33; *contra Cresc.*, 1, 5; cf. Dyobouniotes, *op. cit.*, p. 98.

[5] Androutsos *op. cit.*, p. 98.

[6] Dyobouniotes, *op. cit.*, pp. 98-99.

[7] *Ibid.;* for the fuller list, cf. Androutsos, *op. cit.*, p. 353, and Mesolora, *op. cit.*, IV. p. 271, note 2 (and p. 272).

[8] Dyobouniotes, *op. cit.*, p. 99.

the manner in which the Presence of the Lord is effected in
the Eucharist", says Mesolora, "the primitive Church never
defined,"[1] as Dyobouniotes also states emphatically. The various attempts made in the early Church "to illuminate the
doctrine of the Change and make it accessible to human reason"
were futile and doomed to failure.[2] Thus St. Irenaeus, and St.
Cyril's attempts were unhappy,[3] as the method and manner of
the Change are not within the power of our minds to apprehend.

Orthodox thought has always held strongly to this position, saying with St. John Damascene: "If now you ask, how
the bread becomes the Body of Christ and the wine and water
His Blood? I say, the Holy Spirit descends and achieves it,—
(an accomplishment), above reason and comprehension. . .
The bread and wine are not 'types' of His Body and Blood. .
. but His Body and Blood in very fact . . ."[4] "The bread
and wine . . . are by the invocation and descent of the Holy
Spirit converted into the Body and Blood of Christ."[5] "But
the manner of this Change is unknown to us and inscrutable:
the solution and explanation are reserved for the elect in the
Kingdom of Heaven."[6] This reverent agnosticism is the characteristic of Orthodox writers generally, from St. John Damascene,[7] who says that the manner of the Change cannot be
searched out, to the present day Orthodox theologians, who reiterate this view.[8] But this attitude of reserve has not hindered
a growth in explicitness and definiteness in regard to the doctrine of the Change.

In a rather sweeping indictment of Androutsos' definition
of the Eucharist (that it is "that divinely instituted sacrament
in which Jesus Christ is present actually and really *under the
forms* of bread and wine",[9]), Dyobouniotes says: "This expres-

---

[1] *Op. cit.*, IV. p. 269, and cf. Dyobouniotes, *ibid.*, and p. 101.
[2] Androutsos, *op. cit.*, pp. 353-354.
[3] Dyobouniotes, *op. cit.*, pp. 99-100.
[4] Ἔκδοσις, IV. 14.
[5] Jeremiah 11, in Mesolora, *op. cit.*, I. p. 228.
[6] Kritopoulos, *ibid.*, p. 327.
[7] Ἔκδοσις, IV. 13.
[8] On which all lay emphasis,—Androutsos, *op. cit.*, p. 354; Mesolora,
op. cit., IV. pp. 269 ff., but especially Dyobouniotes, *op. cit.*, pp. 99,
101 ff.
[9] Androutsos, *op. cit.*, p. 344.

sion, . . . used frequently by the writer, . . . is based on the Roman doctrine . . . of transubstantiation, and cannot be accepted in the Eastern Church, whose Fathers teach that the bread and wine are changed (converted), into the Body and Blood of Christ . . . (Our Lord) said: "Take eat, *this* is my body,' not *'under this* is my body' . . . If we repudiate in every way the Protestant attempt to interpret these words to mean *this* 'represents, stands for' . . . how much less may we dare to substitute *under this* for His word, "this?"[1] . . . Dyobouniotes expounds his views at length in his 'Οφειλομένη ἀπάντησις, and as they represent his individual teaching they may be summarized here. He says that the conviction of the Change was accepted and known in the early Church;[2] that in the 4th century new terms came into use, yet without any attempt to search deeper into the manner of the Change, but only further to express the fact.[3] In the Western Church, from the 11th century on, there began to be developed the theory of *transubstantiation* as an attempt to explain the Change. This is, in brief, that the *substance* of the bread and wine is changed into that of the Body and Blood of Christ, while the *accidents* (color, taste, etc.) remain. In the 15th century the Eastern Church took over the term without the theory, and used it as synonymous with the term "Change" (Conversion) (μεταβολή).[4] "The Eastern Church," he says, "does not recognize that the *substance* of the bread and wine is changed into the Body and Blood of Christ while the *accidents* remain, under which the Body and Blood of Christ exist, but simply says that the bread and wine are changed into the Body and Blood of Christ by the descent of the Holy Spirit, through whom these things surpassing reason and understanding are achieved."[5] He quotes Dositheus' *Confession*[6] as showing that the manner of the Change is incomprehensible to us, and denies that the Orthodox Church holds that the substance of the

---

[1] 'Η Δογματική τοῦ κ. 'Ανδρούτσου κρινομένη, p. 58.
[2] P. 142.
[3] P. 143.
[4] Pp. 143-144.
[5] P. 144, quoting St. John Damascene,"Εκδοσις, IV. 14.
[6] In Mesolora, *op. cit.*, I. p. 119.

elements is changed, but asserts that she teaches that "the elements as a whole are changed into the Body and Blood of Christ, without searching into the manner of the Change."[1] Hence the phrase *under the forms of bread and wine* is erroneous and wrong. The theory of *transubstantiation,* he says further, is "contrary not only to the teaching of Holy Scripture and Tradition, but to the natural sciences and the universal experience of man." He goes on to criticize the distinction of *substance* and *accidents* as "a false and incomprehensible theory of the nature of bodies."[2] This same position he develops at length in his treatment of the Eucharist, where he calls the Roman doctrine of *transubstantiation,* taken over from Hildebert of Tours, the "attempt to explain the manner of the Change," on the basis of an ancient philosophy which distinguished *substance* and *accidents.*[3] "The Western Church uses the word . . . to present its own peculiar theory of the *manner* of the Change of the bread and wine into the Body and Blood of Christ, . . . while the Eastern Church uses it as equivalent to the term 'Change', and still continues to believe as did the primitive Church, that the manner of the Change is incomprehensible to the human mind."[4] He quotes the same passage of Dositheus' *Confession,* in which the latter states that the term *transubstantiation* (μετουσίωσις) does not explain the manner of the Change, and refers to Kritopoulos,[5] Macarius,[6] Chrysostom Papadopoulos,[7] and the Synod of 1691 (Constantinople).[8] The word, according to him, means the same as "Change," does not explain the *manner* of the Change, and may not be used to imply the distinction of *substance* and *accidents* and the Change of the substance of the elements

---

[1] *Op. cit.,* p. 145.

[2] Pp. 145-146.

[3] Τὰ Μυστήρια, pp. 100-101.

[4] *Ibid.,* p. 101.

[5] Quoted above p. 330 from Mesolora, *op. cit.,* I, p. 327.

[6] "The word *transubstantiation* does not explain the manner....of the Change,...for no one can understand it save God...The word means that the Bread and Wine are changed (converted) by the Consecration into the Body and Blood of Christ" (*op. cit.,* II. pp. 405 ff.).

[7] Δοσίθεος, Πατριάρχης Ἱεροσολύμων, Jerusalem, 1907, pp. 27-28, who is much of Dyobouniotes' mind, judging from the passage quoted.

[8] On which, cf. Mansi-Petit (*Concil.*) vol. XXXVII, cols. 465 ff.

while the accidents remain.[1] "All of the bread and wine is changed," says he, "into the Body and Blood of Christ, and not only a part of them."[2] He inveighs again against the scholastic theory, quotes St. John Damascene again, and the part of Dositheus' *Confession* twice referred to.[3]

In all the above it is exceedingly difficult to acquit Dyobouniotes of misrepresenting the facts. For one thing, he quotes frequently one passage from Dositheus' *Confession,* and entirely omits to mention the following: —"(In the Eucharist) the Lord Jesus Christ is present not typically, nor symbolically, nor figuratively . . . nor contingently . . . but truly and really, so that after the consecration of the bread and wine, they are converted, transubstantiated, transformed, changed—the bread into the very same true Body of Christ, which was born in Bethlehem of Mary ever-Virgin, which was baptized in Jordan, suffered, was buried, rose again, etc.— the wine is converted and transubstantiated into the very true Blood of Christ which, when He was crucified, was poured out for the life of the world. Yet after the consecration of the bread and wine, the *substance* of the bread and wine no longer remains, but the Body and Blood of Christ, in the form and type of the bread and of the wine, that is to say, under the *accidents* of the bread. . . The Body and Blood of Christ are cut and divided by hands and teeth *accidently,* or according to the *accidents* of bread and wine, in which they are confessed to be visible and tangible, but in themselves to remain undivided and inseparable."[4] "The word *transubstantiation* means . . . not that an *accident* of the bread and wine is transformed into an *accident* of the Body and Blood of Christ, but that truly, actually, and *substantially* the bread becomes His Body and the wine His blood."[5] Androutsos' definition, including the phrase *under the forms of bread and wine,* is justified by reference to Mogila who uses the words: "under

---

[1] *Op. cit.,* pp. 102-103.

[2] *Ibid.,* p. 105.

[3] *Ibid.,* pp. 105-106.

[4] Section 17 of the *Confession,* in Mesolora, *op. cit.,* II. p. 117.

[5] This is the immediate sequence of the passage quoted by Dyobouniotes, in fact the latter half of the same sentence of which he quotes only the first part (p. 119, *ibid.*).

the appearance (θεωρίαν) of bread and wine",[1] and "under
the covering (lit. vestment, garment—ἔνδυμα), of bread and
wine."[2] In his rejoinder to Dyobouniotes' criticism Androutsos quotes Macarius, Antonius, and Rhôsse, as being in agreement with his position,[3] as was Dyobouniotes himself at an
earlier period.[4]

The doctrine of *transubstantiation,* that is, "that the elements are changed into the Body and Blood of the Lord, and
only their outward forms remain", is held in common by
both the Eastern and Western Churches.[5] It is based fundamentally on the words of the Institution. "The words *this
is my body . . . this is my blood,* literally . . . taken do
not mean: '*in* the bread exists my body' and '*in* the wine my
blood' . . . but: 'that which is given you *is in its substance
(κατ' οὐσίαν) my body',* or (which is the same thing), 'that
which appears to you to be bread, *is my Body*' etc."[6] The
Lutheran doctrine is without force and absolutely unjustifiable: the elements cannot *contain* the Body and Blood of
Christ, for there is no suggestion that our Lord intimated
that this would be the case, nor is there any natural conformity in the nature of bread, that it should be understood to contain a human body. *This is* cannot by any stretch of logic
be referred to an unseen and supernatural content of the bread.
It is clear on exegetical grounds that the words of our Lord
signify a Change, and not consubstantiation.[7] The term *transubstantiation,* originating probably with Hildebert of Tours,
in 1134, speedily became part of Western terminology.[8] It
seems first to have been used in the East by Michael Paleologus (†1282) in writing to Pope Gregory X. Gennadius Scholarius (†1460), in his homily on the Body of our Lord, uses
the word, saying that it was identical with the Western theory

[1] In Mesolora, I. p. 426.
[2] *Ibid.,* p. 428.
[3] Δογματικαὶ Μελέται, Α', pp. 122-123.
[4] Cf. Dyobouniotes, 'Ιοάννης ὁ Δαμασκηνός, p. 152.
[5] Androutsos, Δογματική, pp. 351-352.
[6] *Ibid.,* p. 352.
[7] Androutsos, Δογματική, pp. 351-352.
[8] Note 1, *ibid.*

. . . "the change of *substance* into *Substance* occurring in an instant (by the words of Consecration), while the *accidents* remain unchanged."[1] As we have seen, it appears explicitly with the distinct and characteristic meaning attached to it, in Dositheus' *Confession,* and in the 17th century its use became widespread, as the only possible word to deny Protestant heresy and at the same time affirm the Orthodox belief. Mogila says: "Immediately upon the words (of Consecration), *transubstantiation* takes place, and the bread changes into the true Body of Christ, and the wine into His true Blood. There remain only the forms by which they appear, and this is according to the divine economy . . . that we may believe, though we may not see how these words (are true) : *'this is my Body'.*"[2] Before Dositheus, many Greek writers had used the term— George Coresius, the Protosynkellos Dionysius, Gabriel of Philadelphia,[3] and also Maximus of Cytheraea, Meletius Pigas, Patriarch of Alexandria, and Nectarius of Jerusalem. The latter are quoted by the Synod of Constantinople in 1691, which strongly vindicated the use of the term, as not being a novelty, and having good Orthodox authority for its use, saying: "This term the Church employs constantly from one end to the other, nor has anyone protested against its use by the Church save heretics."[4] Mesolora constantly uses it, and says: "We believe and maintain . . . that after the consecration . . . the bread and wine (even though after their external *form* . . . and taste they still seem to be such), in their *essence* are the Body and Blood of the Lord, who is present truly and really in the Holy Eucharist. This Change or conversion is generally called *transubstantiation* . . ."[5] "The Orthodox and the Westerns accept the Real Presence of the Body and Blood of Christ, transubstantiated by the coming down of the Holy Spirit. . . . We hold that after the consecration (there is) the *transubstantiation* of the Holy Gifts . . . into the

[1] Dyobouniotes, *op. cit.,* p. 101, note 1.
[2] In Mesolora, *op. cit.,* p. 427.
[3] Palmieri, *op. cit.,* I, p. 500 quoting Simon, *Fides ecclesiae Orientalis,* p. 119.
[4] In Mansi-Petit, XXXVII, col. 465.
[5] *Op. cit.,* IV. p. 271.

Body and Blood of Christ under the *accidents* of bread and wine."[1] Everywhere he speaks of the *transubstantiation* of the elements, for example, in his definition of the sacrament,[2] and elsewhere, in preference to using "Real Presence" or "Change".[3]

Essentially there then is no distinction in Orthodox teaching between the Orthodox doctrine of transubstantiation and the Roman doctrine,[4] the only difference on this point between West and East being one of temperament: the Orthodox disavows any attempt to explain the manner of the Change, but uses the term and maintains the theory of *transubstantiation*. Such evidence as that of the Symbolic Books—some implicitly, others (Mogila and Dositheus), explicitly—of many ecclesiastical writers, and all modern theologians (except Dyobouniotes), to the fact that the doctrine of *transubstantiation* is part of the official teaching of the Orthodox Church,[5] tends to discredit the contentions advanced by Dyobouniotes. In short, the teaching of the Orthodox Church as to the Real Presence is indistinguishable from that of the Roman Church as defined in the Council of Trent. Putting the matter in another way, both Roman and Orthodox Churches agree distinctly and explicitly in their doctrine of the Holy Eucharist, and define it in the term and by the theory involved, as *transubstantiation*.

(c) The Eucharist as Sacrament

The Eucharist is distinguished from the other sacraments not only by reason of its preëminent and unique character, in that our Lord's presence is vouchsafed "not in the way of superabounding Grace as in the other sacraments . . . but

[1] P. 288.
[2] *Ibid.*, p. 244.
[3] *E. g.*, p. 263, p. 266, p. 286, etc.
[4] Δογματικαὶ Μελέται, Α', p. 122; Δογματική, pp. 351-352; Mesolora, *loc. cit.*
[5] Even Kritopoulos, in his section on the Eucharist (under the title, "The Lord's Supper"), cannot be regarded as teaching anything less than this doctrine, despite the obviously irenic form in which his *Confession* is cast and its predominantly apologetic aim, as distinguished from the purely objective, dogmatic, polemic, and didatic

truly and really",[1] whereby He gives Himself "as spiritual food for the faithful, quickening the soul and leading man into immediate fellowship with Him",[2] but in the peculiar and distinctive difference which characterizes the Eucharist as both a sacrament and a sacrifice. The eucharistic nomenclature clearly manifests this two-fold aspect: as sacrament is it called in accordance with its various aspects, *Eucharist* or *Blessing* (εὐλογία), . . . the *Lord's Supper,* with reference to the time of the Institution, the *Body of Christ* and the *Holy Cup,* by reason of the Real Presence of our Lord's Body and Blood, *Communion* and *Viaticum,* because of its action and results; as sacrifice, it is termed, the *Sacrifice, the Oblation,* with various adjectives qualifying these nouns, for example, *holy, reasonable, mystic, unbloody,* and the like.[3] In it is revealed both the superabounding love of God for man, as well as His wisdom",[4] which correspond in general to the two aspects of the Eucharist.

As a sacrament the Eucharist possesses the three constituent features of sacraments in general—the outward signs, the minister, and the Grace bestowed. The outward signs or the "matter"[5] of the sacrament include the proper elements, bread and wine, and the prayer of consecration. Following our Lord's example we may be certain that bread and wine must be used, and the Church in early times forbade the use of any other matter than this.[6] The bread for the Eucharist must be leavened, may not be unleavened,[7] and must be wheaten. The evidence for the use of leavened bread may be sum-

character of other *Confessions;* cf. in Mesolora, *op. cit.,* I, pp. 322-330. It was as a scientific *theological term* that *transubstantiation* was formally adopted into the official formulations of Orthodoxy; cf. Papadoupolos, *op. cit.,* p. 30.

[1] Dositheus, in Mesolora, *op. cit.,* II, p. 117.
[2] Kephala, Χριστολογία, p. 197.
[3] Androutsos, Δογματική, pp. 344-345.
[4] Mesolora *op. cit.,* IV. p. 244.
[5] So *ibid.,* p. 255.
[6] Dyobouniotes, *op. cit.,* p. 108.
[7] Kritopoulos devotes several pages to proving that leavened bread is the only proper element for the Eucharist (in Mesolora, I. pp. 322-326) and specifies that it must be in one loaf, "as Christ is one ...His Body one...and we are one in Him" (p. 326 *ibid.*).

marized as follows: it was leavened bread which our Lord used, as the Institution took place on Thursday the 13th of Nisan and the use of unleavened bread began the next night, the eve of the Passover (on the Sabbath);[1] the symbolism of the Eucharist would be both more effective and more appropriate if, in the sacrament which was to be universal in scope and for all times, the bread used were that common to all men, and not that peculiarly associated with the distinctive rite of a certain people at one particular season;[2] the use of our Lord and of the early Church[3] must be maintained, and there is no reason justifying the innovation made by the West in the 11th century;[4] not only does the universal practice of the early Church, the rubrics in the early liturgies, and the practice of Orthodoxy show an unvarying use of leavened bread, but the liturgies and usages of the early heresies also prove the same.[5] Even up to the 11th century the Western Church used leavened bread.[6]

The wine of the Eucharist must be grape wine, pure, and red in color.[7] As our Lord used a "mixed chalice" the practice of the Church has followed His example, on the basis also of St. John 19, 34.[8] This was enjoined by several early councils.[9]

The prayer which constitutes the other part of the outward sign of this sacrament is that which is the essential element in the liturgy. "For the sanctification of the Precious

[1] Cf. St. John 18, 28.
[2] Androutsos, *op. cit.*, p. 363.
[3] Dyobouniotes claims that the Apostles and the primitive Church used leavened bread only,—*op. cit.*, p. 109.
[4] "The use of unleavened bread was introduced in a later time among the Latins in opposition to and as a distinction from, the Orthodox Church from which they had split off" (Dyobouniotes, *op. cit.*, note 1. p. 110).
[5] *Ibid.*, p. 110.
[6] Mesolora, *op. cit.*, IV. p. 256, and cf. his whole discussion, pp 255-259.
[7] Dyobouniotes, *op. cit.*, p. 111.
[8] Androutsos, *op. cit.*, p. 363.
[9] *E. g.*, Carthage 397, and that "in Trullo" (Σύνοδος Πενθέκτη,) 692; cf. note 3, Androutsos, *ibid.;* cf. also Mesolora, *op. cit.*, IV, pp. 259-261.

Gifts," says Dyobouniotes, "it is certainly necessary that the whole liturgy be read, especially the secret prayer, but chiefly (necessary is) the prayer to God for the Change of the bread and wine into the Body and Blood of Christ by the operation of the Holy Spirit, by which the Sanctification and Change of the elements is effected."[1] While the whole liturgy constitutes the rite or the service of the Holy Eucharist,[2] the part which follows the Liturgy of the Catechumens, properly beginning with the *sursum corda*, is the central section of it and essential part of it.[3] According to Mesolora, the narrative of the Institution and the Consecration "constitute one and the same indivisable act, the consummation of the sacrament of the Holy Eucharist in which the bread and wine are *transubstantiated* into the Body and Blood of Christ."[4] "After the historical account of the Institution . . . the celebrant prays and supplicates God to send His Holy Spirit on him that he may be fit to offer the reasonable and bloodless Sacrifice, and over the gifts . . . which he blesses, he says 'and make this bread the Precious Body of thy Christ . . . and that in this cup the Precious Blood of thy Christ', and blessing both the forms, says 'changing them by thy Holy Spirit'.[5] At this . . . instant, through the prayer and blessing of the officiant, the bread is transubstantiated into the Body, and the wine into the Blood of our Lord, God, and Saviour, by the coming down of the Holy Spirit and by His power and operation."[6] The whole liturgy is a preparation and fulfilment directed toward the consecration of the Holy Gifts,[7] which is effected at that instant when the officiant prays God to send the Holy Spirit . . . to change them into the Body and Blood of Christ.[8] The words of Institution form only the introduction, and the prayer for the Holy Spirit "constitutes the essential part of

[1] *Op. cit.*, p. 115.
[2] Mesolora, *op. cit.*, IV. p. 261.
[3] *Ibid.*, p. 262.
[4] *Ibid.*, p. 263.
[5] Cf. 'Εγκόλπιον, pp. 80-81.
[6] *Ibid.*, p. 264.
[7] Cf. Jeremiah, 11, in Mesolora, I, p. 157.
[8] Mesolora, IV. pp. 265, 266.

the Liturgy."[1]   The *epiklesis* is contained in practically all the early Liturgies, which unite with the testimony of the Fathers, the early Church, and even the heretical Liturgies, in affirming that the Consecration is effected by it and not by the words of Institution.[2]   "So all the *Confessions* of our Church", says Mesolora, "teach with one accord that the bread and wine are transubstantiated into the Body and Blood of Christ, through the operation of the Holy Spirit whom the officiant invokes. . .   After these words the *transubstantiation* is effected immediately."[3]   Consequently the Orthodox Church rejects the novel teaching and practice of the Roman Church in ascribing the Consecration to the words of Institution, "which do not constitute the outward sign of the sacrament."[4]

From what has been said certain doctrinal and practical conclusions follow.   (a) After the consecration the bread and wine "have been supernaturally changed into the Body and Blood of Christ, and they are not two, but one and the same."[5] "The bread is not only changed into the Body but also into the Blood of our Lord, and the wine not only into His Blood but into His Body as well."   This is shown by the practice in extraordinary circumstances of communicating the sick under one species alone.[6]   (b) "Not only is Christ present whole and entire under both kinds, but in every particle of the bread and the wine."[7]   The subdivided Elements are not so many parts of His Body and Blood but each is "our Lord entire, perfect God and perfect Man."[8]   (c) Therefore "one and the same Body and Blood of the one Christ exist everywhere in all the Churches . . . where the Eucharist is celebrated."[9]   (d) His Pres-

---

[1] Androutsos, *op. cit.*, pp. 363-364.

[2] For patristic quotations, the evidence of early liturgies, etc. cf. Androutsos, *ibid.*, and notes, Dyobouniotes, *op. cit.*, pp. 114-116, and notes.

[3] *Op. cit.*, IV. p. 268; cf. Mogila, in Mesolora, I. p. 427; Jeremiah II. *ibid.*, pp. 156-157, 228, 229; Dositheus, *ibid.*, I1. pp. 117-119, etc.

[4] Dyobouniotes, *op. cit.*, p. 116; cf. Mesolora, *op. cit.*, IV. pp. 267-268, and notes.

[5] Jeremiah II. in Mesolora, *op. cit.*, I. p. 228.

[6] Dyobouniotes, *op. cit.*, p. 112.

[7] Androutsos, *op. cit.*, pp. 354-355.

[8] Dositheus, in Mesolora, II. p. 118.

[9] Androutsos, *ibid.*, p. 355, and cf. Dositheus, *loc. cit.*

ence does not cease with the end of the Liturgy, as is wrongly imagined by heretics, but "just as a piece of cloth once dyed remains of the same fixed color which may not be washed out, so the Consecration in this sacrament abides always ineffaceable." "The Reserved Sacrament does not lose its consecration which it received once for all", but this remains indelible.[1] The practice of Reservation is a definite indication of the faith of the Church in this regard, for "after the Consecration the Body of the Lord remains the same, before being used, in being used, and after it."[2] (e) The Real Presence of our Lord is not dependent upon Communion, for "our Lord in giving the Bread and Wine . . . was present in them before the Apostles communicated."[3] At the Institution our Lord gave His disciples His very Body and Blood, and the Eucharist of the Church to-day is essentially and fundamentally identical with the First.[4] As then, so it is now: He is present before and independently of, the communion of the faithful.[5] (f) The belief of the Church is further manifested "in the reverence and worship of the Eucharist as such, independently of Communion."[6] The faithful pay worship to the Holy Gifts after they have been consecrated, and the Church, by virtue of the Presence of our Lord, "abiding under the form of bread and wine", is not a meeting place, but the house of God. "This worship belongs to the Consecrated Elements," . . . says Androutsos, "not abstractly but concretely, in their union with the Person of the Word of God.[7] As the human nature of our

---

[1] Kritopoulos, in Mesolora, I. p. 329.

[2] Dositheus, ibid., II. pp. 118, 119; Dyobouniotes, op. cit., p. 128; Androutsos, op. cit., p. 355. The Mass of the Presanctified is another proof of the Church's doctrine on the subject, cf. Androutsos, loc. cit., and Mesolora, op. cit., IV. pp. 226-227, note 1, and Dyobouniotes, loc. cit.

[3] Androutsos, op. cit., p. 355.

[4] Dyobouniotes, op. cit., p. 91 note 1.

[5] Ibid., p. 127.

[6] Ibid.

[7] Against this expression and its context Dyobouniotes brings to bear two charges: (a) Androutsos seems to speak of the union of our Lord with the elements, and (b) consequently teaches the theory of a spiritual Presence and Communion, as against the Orthodox view of the Change of the elements into His Body and Blood, which does not

Lord is an object of worship not as regarded in itself, abstractly, but by virtue of the hypostatic union, . . . so the Holy Gifts are worshipped,[1] not as viewed of themselves, but by reference to the Person of the God-man to whom they belong. . . His Presence with soul and Divinity . . . in every particle of the Consecrated Elements . . . is implied in the Church's doctrine of His Eucharistic Presence. . . But the Bread is not converted into His Soul but into His Body, . . . and neither element . . . into His Divinity. Neither before the Institution nor after the Resurrection were His Body and Blood separated . . The Risen Christ, into whose Body and Blood the Elements are transmuted, never dies, having a spiritual and glorified Body undivided from His Blood. In the Eucharist He is present with all His constituent elements, His soul and His Divinity, . . . Body and Blood undivided; . . . division and multiplicity belong to the forms of bread and wine. . . So the fraction of the Host or the division of the Reserved Particles is not regarded as a new break or division of the supernatural Food, but a Communion of the Christ entire."[2]

With regard to the question here involved, whether the Presence of our Lord in each particle of the Bread and Wine occurs before or after the Fraction and Division of the Elements,[3] Androutsos seems to hold the former view. Those arguing for the latter, use as an illustration the breaking of

exist "in" or "under" them, but involves the statement that "each particle of Bread and Wine is Christ" ('Η Δογμ. 'Ανδρ. κριν., p. 56). Androutsos' rejoinder is that this distorted and twisted perversion of his meaning would be impossible if one take into account his further statements: that our Lord's Presence is without bodily extension, but nevertheless real and actual, and not merely "spiritual" (in the Calvinistic sense which Dyobouniotes imputes to him,—'Οφειλ. ἀπάντησις, pp. 120-122). Dyobouniotes' reiteration, elaborated, will be found on pp. 136-141 of his 'Οφειλ. ἀπάντησις,

[1] "The Body and Blood of our Lord in the sacrament of the Eucharist must be reverenced exceedingly and adored with worship (λατρευτικῶς), for the same reverence is due the Holy Trinity and the Body and Blood of our Lord" (Dositheus, in Mesolora, II, p. 118).

[2] Androutsos, Δογματική, pp. 356-368.

[3] Dyobouniotes presents both views in a foot-note, without espousing either (op. cit., pp. 112-113, note 2).

a mirror which when whole reflects one single image, and after being broken, each fragment completely reflects the whole image. Those who defend the former, hold that the Presence of our Lord is like that of the soul in the body, nowhere localized but yet everywhere present; so in the Eucharist our Lord is everywhere present in the Elements after consecration. The view that He becomes present in each particle after the fraction would seem to imply a second Change of the Elements. In any case, says Androutsos, "the apprehension of the sacrament of the Eucharist is impossible for our understanding." Our Lord is not circumscribed by the elements, nor is He present with physical extension. The analogies and illustrations used in the attempts to reason out this mystery, such as a "second creation", "natural change" (the figure drawn from nourishment by food), "spiritual regeneration", are all alike futile. "In the Eucharist one substance, losing its own being, is converted into another which previously exists. . ." Consequently the examples and likenesses adduced have no resemblance or essential similarity. We may come to the knowledge of this Mystery only through faith.[1]

Certain practical consequences result from the doctrines given in summary above. No liturgical recognition follows upon the recitation of the words of Institution, but after the *epiklesis* the celebrant and congregation all worship and adore our Lord under the forms of bread and wine.[2] The Holy Communion is given to all the baptized who are prepared to receive It, in both kinds. Infant Communion is based upon St. John 6, 53, and is vouched for by the primitive practice of the Church.[3] As it is absolutely necessary for salvation, every baptized person has the right to receive, and there is no reason why infants should be denied that privilege. "It is the primitive and devout practice of the Church."[4] The words of St. Paul in 1 Cor. 11, 29, cannot be applied to forbid the Eucharist being administered to children, "since from their age they

---

[1] *Op. cit.*, 358-360.
[2] Not prescribed by rubric *ad loc.*, but an almost universal custom.
[3] Androutsos, *op. cit.*, p. 365 and cf. evidence in Dyobouniotes,
[4] Mesolora, *op. cit.*, IV. p. 291.
op. cit., p. 127.

are unable to distinguish the Body and Blood of our Lord (from ordinary food), and in consequence are incapable of making unworthy Communions."[1] The arguments against it, based on the lack of faith on the part of infants, cannot be held to apply, since the Sacraments do not depend upon the faith of the recipient but work *ex opere operato*.[2] The same arguments both for and against, apply equally to Infant Baptism and Chrismation. "If infants are capable of receiving Baptism . . . they ought to be entirely fit to receive the Eucharist."[3] Consequently Orthodoxy repudiates as a novelty and perversity the innovation in Church custom introduced by the Latin Church, of restricting Communion to those of more advanced age.[4] Withholding the cup from the laity is again a modern innovation of the Roman Church, unjustified by necessity or expediency, and lacking precedent and authority in ancient usage. The Roman innovation is both arbitrary and irreverent.[5] The Orthodox custom is loyal to our Lord's injunction[6] ("Drink ye *all*"), and faithful to the witness of the early Church and Fathers, for the practice of Communion in one Kind was unknown save in very exceptional circumstances.[7] The Roman custom—to borrow the words of Pope Leo I —is a "sacrilege",[8] and is strongly condemned by all Orthodox writers.[9] The theory of concomitance ought not be brought in to justify the Roman practice, for its true reason is not based on this but is simply the desire to exalt the clerical order. "Since Christ commanded Communion under both forms, every attempt to correct His ordinance for a dogmatic or prac-

---

[1] Androutsos, *op. cit.*, pp. 365-366.

[2] *Ibid.*, and Dyobouniotes, *op. cit.*, p. 126; cf. Kritopoulos, in Mesolora, I. p. 327.

[3] Dyobouniotes, *ibid.*, p. 127.

[4] *Loc. cit.*, and Mesolora, IV. pp. 290-291.

[5] Mesolora, *ibid.*, IV. p. 278.

[6] Both Species are administered together, that of Bread being "impregnated" with that of Wine, and given into the recipient's mouth by the spoon, the *labis;* cf. Dyobouniotes, *op. cit.*, p. 112 note 1.

[7] Androútsos, *op. cit.*, p. 366.

[8] Dyobouniotes, *op. cit.*, p. 113.

[9] Cf. Kritopoulos, in Mesolora, I, p. 327; Mogila, *ibid.*, p. 428, etc.; cf. Mesolora's discussion, *op. cit.*, IV. pp. 277-283.

tical reason, is both sacrilege as well as insolence and arbitrariness unheard of in the history of the Church."[1]

Bishops and priests only have the right of celebrating the Holy Eucharist. Deacons may in emergency communicate the faithful, and in absolute necessity it is possible for laymen to administer the Sacrament, but, of course, it is not possible for them to consecrate It. Women cannot administer It in any case.[2]

The Grace bestowed in the sacrament of the Holy Eucharist is suggested by the definition: he who receives the sacrament receives the Body and Blood of Christ. "By the Eucharist, in the communion of His Body and Blood, we are united with our Lord and made partakers in the divine virtue. . . We are fed, quickened, endued with power, and perfected spiritually by the gift of divine Grace."[3] All that He did for us on the Cross is made available to us in the Eucharist. Our spiritual life is strengthened and developed, and we are united with Him and as well with each other in the "sacrament of unity".[4] "The Holy Eucharist, developing and strengthening the spiritual life, bestows everything that makes for devotion and a holy life, developes love, and opens up the view into the blessed kingdom beyond death into which after the Resurrection the faithful are to enter."[5] "This union on our part with our Lord, which is had through the Eucharist, brings remission of sins and life eternal. . . So the Eucharist is the earnest of our resurrection through union with our Risen Lord."[6] The words of administration "for remission of sins and eternal life" might seem to indicate that the Eucharist is the means of forgiving sins, but "this cannot mean the forgiveness of mortal

---

[1] Androutsos, op. cit., p. 367; Dyobouniotes, op. cit., pp. 113-114 note 1 (pp. 114-115,) gives a summary of Roman arguments.

[2] Cf. Dyobouniotes, op. cit., p. 125 where references are given, and Androutsos, op. cit., pp. 364-365.

[3] Mesolora, op. cit., IV. pp. 283-284. St. John Damascene in his Ἔκδοσις (IV. 13) distinguishes "Communion" (κοινωνία) and "Reception" (μετάληψις).

[4] Dyobouniotes, op. cit., pp. 117-118, which cf. for patristic references.

[5] Androutsos, op. cit., p. 361.

[6] Dyobouniotes, op. cit., p. 118.

sins, since they are absolved in the sacrament of Penance. . . .
The word 'remission' is here used only in a general sense."[1]
"The chief energy or operation of the sacrament . . . is not
remission of sins, but union with our Lord. Remission of sins
and eternal life are secondary effects and consequences of the
chief operation of the sacrament."[2] The gift of this Grace
is independent of the state of the recipient, but its appropriation by him is conditioned by his preparation for the sacrament, if he be an adult. He "must prepare himself by repentance and obtain absolution by confession", lest the threat
of the Apostle be fulfilled in him.[3] Wilful indifference to
Communion or carelessness in regard to it precludes the possibility of blessedness. Everyone of the faithful must receive the
Eucharist after careful preparation, as its Grace is absolutely
necessary to salvation,[4] and this preparation includes both confession and fasting, in accordance with the early custom of the
Church.[5]

---

[1] Androutsos, *ibid.*, note 1.

[2] Dyobouniotes, *op. cit.*, p. 119. He adds a note on frequent Communion, saying that "not only may the faithful communicate frequently, but they ought to do so". The ordinarily devout Orthodox
receives the Eucharist after the quarterly fasts,—at Christmas, Easter,
the Feast of the Apostles (SS. Peter & Paul), and the Falling Asleep
of the Mother of God (Aug. 15); cf. note 1. p. 286 of Mesolora, *op. cit.*,
IV.

[3] 1 Cor. 11, 29; Androutsos, *op. cit.*, p. 365.

[4] *Ibid.*, and cf. Mesolora, *op. cit*, IV. pp. 283-287; Mogila in *ibid.*,
I. pp. 428-429; Kritopoulos, *ibid.* I. p. 328; Jeremiah, I. p. 228, etc.

[5] On which, in some detail, cf. Dyobouniotes, *op. cit.*, pp. 125-126.
Dyobouniotes seems to have changed his views of the fruits of the
Holy Eucharist since he wrote his criticism of Androutsos' *Dogmatic.*
The latter says that the sentence of administration (εἰς ἄφεσιν ἁμαρτιῶν
καὶ εἰς ζωὴν αἰώνιον) may not be understood to refer to the remission
of mortal sins, (for Penance does this) but "remission of sins is
here said in a general sense" (Δογματική, p. 361 and note 1). Dyobouniotes ('Η Δογμ. 'Ανδρ. κριν., p. 59) finds fault with this and Androutsos'
general treatment of the fruits of the Holy Eucharist, saying that
"he departs from...and in part denies...the Orthodox doctrine on
the subject, holding that the Eucharist does not confer the remission
of sins and eternal life, but simply the hope of immortality and the
preservation from mortal sins" Androutsos answers: "If he thought
that Penance is an indispensable means for (receiving) the Holy Communion, and is the remission of all sins, he would then understand

(d) The Eucharist as Sacrifice

The Eucharist is not only a sacrament but "the one propitiatory sacrifice offered to God for the quick and the dead."[1] "As sacrifice, it is the continuation and application of the sacrifice of Golgotha, inasmuch as the Saviour as Priest and Victim offers the Father His Body and Blood under the forms of bread and wine."[2] The very words and method of the Institution clearly show this. The use of bread and wine manifest the separation of the Body and Blood of our Lord,[3] the terms our Lord used, "my Body *given*[4] . . . *broken*[5] for you", "my Blood . . . *shed* for many[6] for the remission of sins",[7] "the New Testament in my Blood . . . *shed* for you", indicate surely that the Eucharist is itself a propitiatory sacrifice, and may not primarily be referred to Calvary. So also the words . . . "my flesh, which I will give for the life of the world"[8] characterize the Eucharist as a sacrifice.[9] St. Paul clearly implies that the Eucharist is a sacrifice, when he contrasts "the table of the Lord" and "the table of devils", when in the previous verse he had spoken of the Gentiles sacrificing to devils,

that the Eucharist is not the remission of sins, since they were absolved in the sacrament of Penance which preceded the Eucharist...This he implies is Orthodox doctrine. As to his account of the fruits of the Eucharist he refers his critic to Macarius, whose enumeration is the same as his (Androutsos')" (Δογμ. Μελέται, A' pp. 143-144). In Dyobouniotes' rejoinder to this work ('Οφειλ. ἀπάντησις) he maintains his former view of Androutsos (pp. 148-149) quoting Timothy Anastasius' 'Η θεία Εὐχαριστία, p. 100, that "through the Holy Eucharist remission of sins is sought and obtained" (p. 150 *ibid.*). This general contention he seems to have abandoned by the time of writing his Τὰ Μυστήρια, the teaching of which on this subject substantially agrees with Androutsos' (*op. cit.*, pp. 118 and 119).

[1] Mesolora, *op. cit.*, IV. p. 244.
[2] Androutsos, *op. cit.*, p. 367.
[3] "The mystical sundering of body from blood indicates the sacrificial character of the Eucharist" *ibid.*
[4] St. Luke 22, 19, 20.
[5] 1 Cor. 11, 24, 25.
[6] St. Mark 14, 24.
[7] St. Matt. 26, 28.
[8] St. John 6, 51.
[9] Androutsos, *ibid.*

not to God.[1] The references in Hebrews 10 are to the sacrifices
of the Old Testament, to which Calvary[2] and the Eucharist are
compared as fulfilment and antitype to prefigured type. This
is clear from the terminology: "altar, . . . eat, . . . meats,
 . . . serve the Tabernacle."[3] The foreshadowings of the
Eucharist in the Passover, the sacrifice of Melchisedek, and
the prophecy in Mal. 1, 10, 11, surely indicate the sacrificial
character of the Eucharist.[4] "It follows then that the Eucharist offered on the Lord's table is a Sacrifice, . . . to which
fact Sacred Tradition with a single and unbroken witness
testifies." The writings of the early Fathers, the *Didache,* the
early Liturgies and the early synods, all unanimously proclaim
this great fact.[5] "The altars which the early churches used,
as shown in the symbolic representation in the catacombs, . . .
all the figures and illustrative representations of the eucharistic sacrifice, and above all, the Liturgies, present the Eucharist
as a sacrifice prepared for in the oblation ($\pi\rho o\sigma\kappa o\mu\iota\delta\dot{\eta}$), and
consummated in the Change, and manifest . . . the unceas-
ing faith of the Church in the Eucharist as a sacrifice."[6]

The essence of the sacrificial character of the Eucharist
may be discerned by discovering the relation between the Eucharist and the sacrifice of the Cross. The Eucharist as a memorial of the death on the Cross is a re-presentation and commemoration of the sacrifice of Calvary.[7] "But it is not merely
a representation of the death of our Lord, but an actual and
real sacrifice, in which the Offerer and the Victim are one
and the same, our Lord, even if the sacrifice be offered by the
priest;"[8] it is "not simply a reminder or commemoration of the
historical fact of Golgotha, but an actual and objective sacri-

---

[1] Cor. 10, 20, 21; Androutsos, *ibid.,* p. 368, and Dyobouniotes,
op. cit., pp. 120-121.
[2] Cf. note 1, p. 121, Dyobouniotes, *op. cit.*
[3] Heb. 13, 9-10 etc.; cf. Androutsos and Dyobouniotes, *loc. cit.*
[4] Androutsos, *op. cit.,* p. 369 and Dyobouniotes, p. 121.
[5] Androutsos, *ibid.*
[6] *Ibid.,* p. 370. For the Symbolic Books, cf. Mesolora, *op. cit.,* Mogila, I, pp. 426-429; Jeremiah II, *ibid.,* 162-163, 228; Dositheus
II. p. 117.
[7] Androutsos, *op. cit.,* p. 370; cf. 1 Cor. 11, 26.
[8] Dyobouniotes, *op. cit.,* p. 122.

fice, inasmuch as our Lord in His high priestly office is really present."¹ The bond between the sacrifice of the Eucharist and that of Calvary is so intimate and necessary that one might say that "they coincide, inasmuch as both have the same Offerer and the same Thing Offered, the same Sacrificer and the same Victim—our Lord Jesus Christ."² The first historical evidence we have that this doctrine was questioned, is the case of Soterichos Panteugonos in the 12th century, who in his recantation was made to profess his faith in the "one and the same sacrifice" of Calvary and the Eucharist.³ In the negotiations with the Old Catholics the words "representation and presence" of the one Oblation, as used by the latter, could be taken in an Orthodox sense, as Rhôsse says, "if by these words . . . is not meant (merely) a tangible and apparent re-presentation, but if the internal bond of union between the sacrifice in the Eucharist and that in heaven be thereby professed."⁴ "In the Eucharist the same sacrifice is consummated as that on the Cross."⁵

What then are the differences and likenesses between the sacrifice of the Eucharist and that of the Cross? The resemblance consists in the identity of Victim, Offerer, and Act. The differences are in the form, purpose, and circumstances of the Eucharist as distinguished from Calvary. The death of Christ occurred once for all, and may not be repeated.⁶ "By the death of the Cross our Lord wrought the Redemption of mankind in general, reconciling man with God; the aim of the sacrifice of the Eucharist is the personal appropriation and reception of the benefits of the Cross. . . On Golgotha our Lord offered His bodily life in a bloody sacrifice; in the Eucharist He sacrifices Himself by the priest in a bloodless and mystical way." The bond between the two sacrifices is brought

¹ Androutsos, *ibid.*
² *Ibid.*, and p. 371.
³ Given in the *Tübinger Quartalschrift* for 1833, note 1, p. 173.
⁴ In his Ἔκδοσις πρὸς τὴν Ἱερὰν Σύνοδον τῆς Ἑλλάδος, Athens, 1874, p. 25.
⁵ Dyobouniotes, *ibid.*
⁶ *Ibid.*

out clearly in the Liturgies.[1] Androutsos says elsewhere:[2] "The Eucharist is not a new act of immolation of Jesus Christ different from that of Golgotha as to its content and its power, but a new representation before God of that sacrifice made once for all, and a new mystical (sacramental) reiteration of it. The sacrifice of the Eucharist is both a re-presentation of the sacrifice of the Cross, and also itself an actual sacrifice. It is a representation, in that by the consecration of the bread and wine it presents or symbolizes the bloody sacrifice, the actual separation of Body and Blood . . . on the Cross. It is an actual sacrifice, in that Jesus Christ, the Great High Priest, really present in the Eucharist, consummates on earth what He does in Heaven. . . As such it must be a reiteration of the death of the Cross, the manner of its accomplishment—whether through blood, or sacramentally, and whether with a more restricted scope than that of Golgotha—not being significant. . . It must be in a sense a new oblation and offering of Christ. . . If He who was sacrificed on Calvary is sacrificed (in the Eucharist), without blood . . . then we have in the Eucharist an actual sacrifice or a mystic (sacramental) reiteration of the death of the Cross[3]. . . In the Eucharist, our Lord, actuated by the same love and obedience from which the sacrifice of Golgotha proceeded, presents anew the sacrifice consummated on Golgotha, for the personal acceptance and application of its benefits."[4] "It is not a new act

---

[1] Androutsos, *op. cit.*, p. 371; cf. Dyobouniotes, *op. cit.*, pp. 122-123. Macarius brings out the resemblances and differences very clearly: "On the Cross the Saviour offered visibly His most holy Body and Blood;...in the Eucharist He offers the same under the forms of bread and wine...By the Sacrifice of the Cross was accomplished the Redemption of all mankind, and the divine righteousness was satisfied for the sins of all the world. The Bloodless Sacrifice makes propitiation for the sins of those only for whom it is offered, conveying the fruits of the Sacrifice of the Cross to them only;" *op. cit.*, II. p. 429, and cf. Mesolora, *op. cit.*, IV. pp. 247-249.

[2] In his Δογμ. Μελ. Α', in answer to Dyobouniotes' criticism that Androutsos would "diminish the boundless efficacy of the death of Christ on the Cross" ('Η Δογμ. 'Ανδρ. κριν., pp. 58-59) ; cf. also the 'Οφειλ. ἀπάντησις, pp. 146-148.

[3] Δογμ. Μελ., Α', pp. 124-126 and cf. Δογματική, pp. 372-373.

[4] Δογματική, p. 374.

of immolation of Christ, but a new presentation of the sole and final sacrifice.[1]

In answer to the question, in what does the sacrificial aspect of the Eucharist consist? various theories have been propounded. The meaning of the word "sacrifice" involves three things—a priest, a victim, and the act of sacrificing—either immolation or destruction of the victim by death or burning, or its change (*immutatio*).[2] One theory would make the essential sacrificial element of the Eucharist to consist in the "Consecration, the essential act of the sacrifice, whereby the Body and Blood of Christ are present on the altar, sundered from each other, under the form of bread and wine, and a symbolic representation is made of the actual separation of the two (the "destruction" or "immolation" of the Victim), which took place in the death on the Cross. . . This symbolic representation is only satisfactory . . . in the case in which a sacrifice is relative (as in the Eucharist), and not absolute (as on the Cross)." Others regard the Consecration as only pointing to the death of Christ, in which the Body and Blood were sundered, and which constitutes the fundamental immolative note of the Eucharist. The Consecration, however, may only be referred to the glorified Body and Blood, in regard to which there can be no question of sundering or separating. Others view the Consecration as the epitome of our Lord's humility in descending to become our Food, and thereby being the act of sacrifice. But, Androutsos says, the latter is certainly impossible, since Communion presupposes the sacrifice, and the sacrifice could not be constituted by the Change of the elements since our Lord suffers no change, but the Change takes place only in the bread and wine.[3] This view is inacceptable, for the essential element of sacrifice is absent,[4] and there is no obvious connection between the sacrifice of the Eucharist and that of Calvary. "The act of the sacrifice must then be found

---

[1] *Ibid.*

[2] *Ibid.*, p. 371.

[3] This view Dyobouniotes also rejects,—Τὰ Μυστήρια, pp. 120-121, note 1.

[4] Dyobouniotes, *ibid*: "This is much less acceptable."

in the Consecration."[1] "The sacrifice of the Eucharist is relative, being predetermined by the sacrifice of the Cross in regard to its content and its merit or worth, and the act of immolation of Christ's manhood is that surrender of His life
made on the Cross which our Lord offers anew to God as the
sacrifice once for all made in behalf of the world."[2]

The sacrificial character of the Eucharist has a three-fold
aspect. The Eucharist is an expiatory and propitiatory sacrifice, a sacrifice of "Praise and Thanksgiving", and an impetratory and intercessory sacrifice. These constitute the essential
character of the Eucharist as a sacrifice, as well as the fruits of
that sacrifice.[3] Inasmuch as the sacrifice of the Cross had as
end and purpose the reconciliation of man with God, the atonement for the sins of man and their expiation, and the Redemption of man by its means, so the sacrifice of the Eucharist has
this same character,[4] differing only in the application of this
end, as we have seen: whereas the sacrifice of Calvary was made
generally for all, the Eucharist is offered for specific people, in
order that application of the general benefits of the death of the
Cross may be made for those for whom the Eucharist is celebrated. "The fruits of the Eucharist", says Mogila, "are . . .
the commemoration of the sinless Passion and Death of Christ,
the benefits accruing to us of propitiation . . . for our sins,
both for the living and the dead. . ."[5] "It is a true and expiatory sacrifice", says Dositheus, "offered for all the devout,
living and dead, and in behalf of the needs of all men."[6] "By it
we propitiate and appease God."[7] As a Sacrifice of Thanksgiving, Worship, and Praise, we offer God thanks and praise for
His goodness and loving kindness "which (praise) the congregation, joined with the priest, sends up on high because of

[1] "According to the most probable and generally prevailing opinion,
the conception of the eucharistic sacrifice lies in the separation of the
bread and wine, the Body and Blood of Christ, which thus symbolically
and mystically presents again the slaughtered and sacrificed Lord"
(ibid.).

[2] Androutsos, Δογματική, pp. 372-374.

[3] Ibid., p. 374.

[4] Ibid.

[5] In Mesolora, op. cit., I. pp. 428-429.

[6] Ibid., II. p. 118.

[7] Dyoboūniotes, op. cit., p. 123.

THE SACRAMENTS IN PARTICULAR

God's infinite beneficence, offering Him Jesus Christ as a worthy expression of gratitude."[1] "As a sacrifice of supplication and intercession is it the request not only for spiritual, but even for material goods, as these may serve for spiritual ends."[2] This three-fold character of the eucharistic sacrifice the Holy Scriptures, the Fathers, and the Liturgies all teach with one voice.[3] Its impetratory and efficacious power is not dependent on us or our failings, but on the intrinsic worth and merits of Him who is offered. It is only as Holy Communion that personal conditions enter into the question as determining the effects and fruits of this great Sacrifice. As a sacrifice of intercession it is predetermined in its scope by the will of the all-wise and all-loving God alone.[4]

[1] Androutsos, *op. cit., p.* 374.

[2] *Ibid.*, and p. 375.

[3] For copious references and quotations, cf. *loc. cit.*, in Androutsos and Dyobouniotes, also Mesolora, *op. cit.*, IV. pp. 244-249, 283-293.

[4] Androutsos, *op. cit.*, pp. 375-376; cf. Dyobouniotes, *op. cit.*, pp. 125-126.

LECTURE VI.

THE DOCTRINE OF THE SACRAMENTS
(Concluded) AND OF THE LAST THINGS

LECTURE VI.

THE DOCTRINE OF THE SACRAMENTS (concluded) AND OF THE LAST THINGS

CONTENTS

THE DOCTRINE OF THE SACRAMENTS (concluded) AND OF THE LAST THINGS

4. Penance

Of the seven means of saving Grace founded by our Lord, the Orthodox Church reckons the sacrament of Penance (μετάνοια) as the fourth. It is defined as that "sacrament in which the forgiveness of sins committed after Baptism is bestowed by God through a priest on a person who confesses his sins and sincerely repents of them."[1] According to Kritopoulos it is one of the three sacraments universally "necessary for salvation", and he finds in the triad of Baptism, the Eucharist, and Penance a type of the Holy Trinity: Baptism is the sacrament of our adoption as sons by the Father, the Eucharist is that of union with the Son, and Penance is "a witness of the abiding presence of the Holy Spirit in the soul, piercing the heart whenever one sins" . . . By Penance, whatever injury be done to divine Grace by sinning voluntarily . . . "may be repaired and recovered".[2] Mesolora says that "Penance or Confession of Sins with the absolution by the priest, is that sacrament ordained of God whereby through the merit of Christ is given by means of priestly absolution the forgiveness of sins for reconciliation with God, to one who has sinned after Baptism and has repented seriously and sorrowfully."[3] Since one who is baptized may fall into grievous sin, the Saviour established this particular sacrament to cleanse from sin and to bind up again the sinner with God. "Since the personal conditions in this sacrament are indispensable—not only for the saving energy of it, as in the other sacraments, but for

[1] Dyobouniotes, Τὰ Μυστήρια, p. 129.
[2] In Mesolora, op. cit., I, pp. 313-314.
[3] Op. cit., IV. p. 296 note. His name for it is Confession (ἐξομολόγησις, cf. ibid., p. 293 et al.).

its very constitution—it is clear that these must be examined along with the essence of the sacrament of which they form the chief part."[1]

Our Lord instituted this sacrament after His Resurrection, in the fulfilment of the promise of power and authority to absolve given in St. Matt. 16, 19, and 18, 17-18, in the words (St. John 20, 22-23): "Receive ye the Holy Ghost: whose soever sins ye remit, they are remitted unto them; and whose soever sins ye retain, they are retained."[2] "From these texts it is clear that Christ gave His Apostles and their successors the power and authority to forgive sins. . . This absolution of sins, as we learn from Tradition, takes place by means of a certain rite, which, being founded by our Lord and conveying Grace, constitutes it a sacrament."[3] The general authority committed to the Church is exercised in a concrete and outward act, "which is in harmony with the nature of the Church as a visible foundation, associating with visible things the bestowal of divine Grace which she conveys through them."[4] Tradition of the earliest date[5] testifies to the exercise of the power of absolution by the Church, so it becomes apparent that the Church from the earliest times received and recognized the sacrament of Penance. This is confirmed by the practice of the early heresies as well.[6]

As to the province and scope of this absolution and remission of sins, the study of ancient Church history and the Fathers confirms the present doctrine of the Church: all sins may be forgiven, and no limit is set to the exercise of the forgiving Grace of God. No restriction is made in either Holy Scripture or Tradition. "The blasphemy against the Holy Spirit"[7] and the sins "unto death"[8] are explained in part by Heb. 6,4-10:

[1] Androutsos, Δογματική, pp. 376-377.
[2] Dyobouniotes, op. cit., pp. 129-130.
[3] Ibid., pp. 130-131.
[4] Androutsos, op. cit., p. 377.
[5] E. g., Hermas, St. Irenaeus, St. Barnabas, St. Clement of Rome, Tertullian, etc.; Dyobouniotes, op. cit., pp. 131-132 (references ad loc.) and Androutsos, op. cit., pp. 378-379.
[6] Dyobouniotes, ibid., p. 133.
[7] St. Matt. 12, 31-32.
[8] 1 St. John 5, 16.

certain grievous "sins are unforgivable, not as from the pow-
erlessness of God or the Church, but because by their nature
they make those committing them unrepentant and callous, so
that in such cases divine Grace cannot operate."[1]   Absolution
is extended to all sorts of sins even the most grievous,[2] if there
is any contrition and penitence on the part of the sinner.[3]   This
doctrine is confirmed by the practice of the Church in condemning the early "disciplinary" heresies, such as those of the
Novatians, Donatists, Montanists, and the like, who would have
set bounds to the exercise of forgiveness.[4]   The ruling of the
VII Ecumenical Council settled this question finally.[5]   The action of the early Church in excommunicating certain persons
and barring them from Church fellowship did not mean that
their sins were not forgivable, but that the conditions of forgiveness were not fulfilled in such given cases.   "The general
rule and practice of the Church has always been in accord with
what she teaches, that every sin may be forgiven, if the necessary personal conditions be present."[6]

These personal conditions form part of the outward signs
of this sacrament, and are three: (a) confession proceeding
from penitence, (b) the laying on of the hands of the officiant
on the penitent, and (c) the prayer of absolution.[7]   Confession
as a part of the outward sign of the sacrament is necessary in
order that the priest may know the sins of the penitent and his
interior dispositions, and may absolve his sins with the necessary exhortations and counsel.[8]   Confession must proceed from
penitence.   Mesolora counts five factors in penitence, the first
part of the sacrament: (a) the sense of sin and the knowledge of it; (b) contrition; (c) firm resolve for amendment,
and faith in the saving power of Christ alone; and (e) reconciliation with one's neighbor against whom one has sinned.
All these constitute the first element from which confession

---

[1] Androutsos, *op. cit.*, p. 379.
[2] Dyobouniotes, *op. cit.*, p. 142.
[3] Androutsos, *ibid.*
[4] *Ibid.*, and p. 380.
[5] Dyobouniotes, *op. cit.*, pp. 143-144, quotes canon 5.
[6] Androutsos, *op. cit.*, p. 380.
[7] Following Dyobouniotes, *op. cit.*, p. 133.
[8] *Ibid.*

naturally and inevitably follows.[1] Androutsos regards penitence as necessarily first, and true penitence of itself issues
in confession. "Penitence is that interior sorrow and contrition of soul for sins committed, flowing from faith and love,
together with the firm determination to amend." It may not
proceed from fear, for fear may not be regarded as a proper
condition for justification.[2] Dyobouniotes names two constituent elements in repentance: (a) contrition and compunction
of heart because of sins, and (b) a steadfast determination of
amendment.[3] "True penitence," he says, "is the more necessary for the operation of the sacrament inasmuch as sacramental
Grace never coerces man, but operates where there is no
opposition. In a person who has not sincerely turned away from
sin, who has not resolved upon correction of himself, in whom,
in short, there is no true penitence, the subjective factor absolutely indispensable for the operation of the sacrament is absent.
. . . So true penitence is absolutely necessary for the remission of sins."[4] "It is the condition which makes remission of
sins possible, since it is the beginning and point of departure of
the moral life, when . . . it begets a fixed resolve of conversion."[5]

"Where there is a true internal penitence there is also the
desire for confession. So much is this true that one may say
that where there is no desire for confession it is a result and
manifestation of the absence of true penitence."[6] "Verbal confession of all sins one by one ought to follow upon contrition of
heart",[7] says Mogila. The necessity of confession may be shown
in several ways: it is a necessary test and proof of penitence and
the desire of amendment;[8] as we have seen above, it is necessary
in order that the priest may know the sins of the penitent,[9] and

[1] *Op. cit.,* IV. p. 302.
[2] Androutsos, *op. cit.,* p. 381.
[3] *Op. cit.,* note 3, pp. 136-137.
[4] *Ibid.,* p. 137.
[5] Androutsos, *op. cit.,* p. 381.
[6] Dyobouniotes, *ibid.,* p. 133.
[7] In Mesolora, *op. cit.,* I, p. 431.
[8] Mesolora, *op. cit.,* IV. p. 303.
[9] *Ibid.,* and Dyobouniotes, *op. cit.,* p. 133; Mogila, in Mesolora,
I. p. 431.

give due counsel, and "prescribe remedies for the wounds appropriate to the nature of the sins."[1] It is necessary also from the nature and manner of the divine institution of the sacrament. He who has the power to bind and loose must first know the sins committed before he can exercise that power. "Hence the stipulation of confession of sins is involved in the very power of binding and loosing with which the Church is endowed by our Lord."[2] This power implies and presupposes confession of sins, without which its exercise would be both arbitrary and pointless. "Confession of sins was deemed necessary for receiving absolution in the early Church",[3] as the evidence of the early Fathers shows. It is likewise necessary on the basis of man's nature. "In human nature lies the necessity for expressing externally one's inner feelings and especially those which are vital."[4] "That confession is psychologically an indispensable manifestation of perfect love and true penitence, is obvious", says Androutsos. "As every mental process must find external expression, as every thought finds its natural fulfilment and complement in the spoken word, so penitence, when it is true and real, issues in confession of sins by the law of psychological necessity, and souls weighted down by sins find peace and repose in the confessional."[5]

Confession must be sincere, and must involve evidence of sorrow for sin.[6] It must be by word of mouth, full, complete, and explicit.[7] It involves the statement and acknowledgment of concrete sins,[8] "humbly, devoutly, truly, sincerely, categori-

---

[1] Jeremiah, in Mesolora, I, p. 184, "for a physician could not heal a disease except he first know of what nature it is" (Kritopoulos, in Mesolora, I. p. 331).

[2] Androutsos, op. cit., p. 381.

[3] Dyobouniotes, op. cit., pp. 134-135, q. v. for references from Tertullian, St. Irenaeus, St. Cyprian, St. Gregory of Nyssa, the early Councils, the primitive terminology, etc.; cf. also Androutsos, ibid., though the latter says that there is no definite indication of the manner of such confession. "Later on public confession gave way to private confession" (ibid., p. 382).

[4] Dyobouniotes, op. cit., p. 133.

[5] Op. cit., p. 382, and cf. Mesolora, IV. p. 294.

[6] Ibid., p 381.

[7] Dyobouniotes, op. cit., p. 135.

[8] Mesolora, op. cit., IV. p. 302.

cally."[1] Irrelevant matter must be kept out of confession, "for the priest wants only a general notion of the sins of the penitent"[2]. So Kritopoulos says it is not necessary for the priest to inquire about the persons, the manner, and the time of the commission of sins,[3] and Jeremiah says: "Such things as are not explicitly acknowledged because of grief or shame . . . leave to the mercy of God for forgiveness."[4] In this sense Mesolora says that the Orthodox Church does not absolutely demand a detailed confession.[5] Yet as Dyobouniotes observes: "It must be understood that where there is true penitence there is also such a consciousness of the necessity for confession that a sense of shame is easily distinguished from egoism. Otherwise it would be both paradoxical and absurd that a man who was shameless enough to commit a certain sin, would be too ashamed to express his penitence for having committed it."[6] "Both interior penitence and confession are indispensable conditions and terms for the forgiveness of sins bestowed through a priest."[7] From what has been said of the necessity of penitence "it does not follow that it of itself entails forgiveness of sins, as certain Western theologians think."[8] There is no authority in Holy Scripture or in Tradition for this view. Logically, the notion that a sincerely penitent person, desirous of making his confession to a priest and yet unable to do so for any good and sufficient reason, by reason of his penitence thereby secures remission of sins, is both futile and pointless, since we have no revelation on the subject in Holy Scripture.[9] Furthermore it makes of priestly absolution only what it is held to be by Protestants: a declaration and pronouncement of the fact of forgiven sins, rather than a mediation of such

---

[1] Jeremiah, II. in Mesolora, I. p. 184.
[2] Dyobouniotes, op. cit., p. 136.
[3] In Mesolora, op. cit., I, p. 321.
[4] Ibid., p. 148.
[5] In note 1, (op. cit., IV, p. 303); cf. Jeremiah, op. cit., I, pp. 184 and 148.
[6] Dyobouniotes, op. cit., note 2, p. 136.
[7] Androutsos, op. cit., p. 387.
[8] Dyobouniotes, ibid., p. 137.
[9] Androutsos, ibid., p. 388.

forgiveness.[1] The notion that one may secure forgiveness immediately from God without confession to a priest, is regarded by the Orthodox as impious and silly.[2] Penitence and confession to a priest are therefore absolutely necessary for receiving absolution from sin.[3]

The second outward sign of the sacrament is the laying on of hands by which the absolution is conveyed,—which was the primitive custom. "Absolution of sins", says Dyobouniotes, "according to the explicit testimony of ancient tradition was conveyed by the laying on of hands."[4]

The third outward sign is the prayer of absolution, which is pronounced by the priest while laying his hands upon the penitent. The formula for absolution is precatory, not declarative: . . . "What thou hast said to me . . . and what thou hast not succeeded in saying whether from ignorance or forgetfulness, may God forgive thee now and for the future."[5] "From a comparison of the two forms", says Dyobouniotes, "it becomes clear that in the Eastern Church the priest prays God to forgive the penitent, and in the Western Church he appears to forgive the penitent himself. The precatory form of the Eastern Church is more ancient and more in accord with the conception of the sacrament than is that of the Western Church, which up to the twelfth century usually employed the precatory form."[6] "The difference between Orthodox and Latins lies in the despotic spirit of the latter, reaching out in their form of this sacrament not only to a sovereignty over souls and consciences, but to an exaltation of the officiant's office, as if he were reckoned as God; yet we too acknowledge

---

[1] *Ibid.*, and Dyobouniotes, p. 138, who quotes (note 1) Kritopoulos: "God willed tó administer forgiveness of sins through man." (Cf. Mesolora, *op. cit.*, I. p. 331.)

[2] Androutsos, *ibid.*, p. 387.

[3] Dyobouniotes (*loc. cit.*) implies the possibility of holding that God may forgive sin directly in the case of a genuinely penitent person who cannot get to a priest. Androutsos says "no one can say with certainty" (p. 387, *ibid.*).

[4] Cf. *op. cit.*, p. 138, and Mesolora, *loc. cit.*

[5] Cf. Εὐχολόγιον τὸ μεγά, pp. 234-235, for full formula, and other prayers used at the administration of this sacrament.

[6] *Op. cit.*, p. 139; cf. references, St. Cyprian, *Epist.* 55, 28; St. Ambrose, *de Spiritu Sancto*, 3, 28; St. Leo, *Epist.* 108, 2, and 268, 2, etc.

that 'the sins are forgiven that very instant by God through the priest'."[1] Androutsos observes that "the only difference between the two forms is that the precatory form is consonant with the nature of the sacrament, with historical usage, and with the general spirit of the Orthodox Church , . . for it is our Lord who consummates the sacrament, and the priest acts only as His representative and organ; . . up to the 12th century it prevailed universally in the Church .. . . and the request for pardon of sins in the sacrament . . . is more in accord with the spirit of the Orthodox Church, which never exalts the clerical order above the laity, but, as it were, hides the officiant under the sacraments, the Grace of which is con-- veyed through a form of words (phrases) in the passive voice, or by the invocation of the Holy Spirit."[2] Nevertheless between the two forms there is no essential difference; "whether one say, as do the Orthodox, that God or the divine Grace pardons sins through the priest, or, as do the Westerns, that the priest absolves the penitent through the power with which he is invested by our Lord, the case is in essence the same either way, for he who is truly penitent is in fact forgiven by God through the priest."[3] So, too, Dyobouniotes denies that there is any substantial difference, as some Protestants seem to think, "for the two forms concur and coincide."[4]

The minister of the sacrament must be either a bishop or a priest. The power of binding and loosing given to the Apostles was passed on to their successors, as all Church Tradition shows clearly.[5] It is not allowed to a deacon or lay- person to absolve.[6] The Roman view that in case of necessity confession should be made to a layman, thereafter to be repeated to a priest, is not admissible. "In necessity confession should better be made to God than to a layman," says Dyobouniotes.[7]

---

[1] Mesolora, op. cit., IV, pp. 318-319. He quotes Mogila,—op. cit., I, p. 431.

[2] Op. cit., pp. 383-384.

[3] Ibid.

[4] Op. cit., p. 139.

[5] Dyobouniotes, op. cit., p. 139, and p. 140 for references and quotations.

[6] Ibid., and Androutsos, op. cit., p. 384.

[7] Op. cit., p. 141, note 2.

The Protestant view that in early times confession was made to God alone and not before a priest, is not correct,[1] as the true explanation of the several proof texts shows. The priest receives at his ordination the *power* to absolve but he must receive a *faculty* or *authorization* from the bishop, in order to be a confessor. This permission or authority from the chief shepherd of the flock gives him the right to exercise the power committed to him with his priesthood, and may be either temporary or indefinite in its character.[2] The priest as confessor acts as judge and representative of God,[3] "having been given the authority, agreeable to the law of God and the state of the sinner, either to release him or not to release him from the bonds of sin. The one difference between him and the worldly judge is that while the latter not only acquits but also pronounces guilty, the priest pronounces judgment only of acquittal and not condemnation, since not to absolve from sin is something negative."[4]

In the administration of the sacrament the priest asks any necessary questions, weighs the case, and, as a good physician, gives counsel and prescribes the appropriate remedies. "God, ever-loving and ever-benevolent in His care for man, knows the weakness of our nature and its tendency to fall, and . . . provided in advanced the medicine of Penance."[5] "It is necessary for those who believe in the economy of the sacraments to confess their sins. . . The priest applies the medicines for the wound opposite to the nature of the sins committed."[6] The priest is to assign certain penances[7] in the nature of remedial and salutary devotions, imposing them "upon those whom he absolves, for the healing of their spiritual ailments, to establish them in their state of pardon, and to guard them from new occasions of falling, . . . and upon those whom he does

---

[1] *Ibid.*, p. 140.
[2] *Ibid.*, and note 2, pp. 140-141, but not so in Russia,—cf. Mesolora, *op. cit.*, IV. p. 331, note 4.
[3] Mesolora, *op. cit.*, IV. p. 318.
[4] Androutsos, *op. cit.*, pp. 382-383.
[5] Kritopoulos, in Mesolora, *op. cit.*, I. p. 330.
[6] *Ibid.*, p. 184.
[7] Mogila, *ibid.*, pp. 431-432. cf. St. James 5, 16.

not absolve, to elicit in them true penitence."[1] These penalties he imposes as a good physician,[2] with a view not to punishment but to healing. Such are, for example, frequent prayer, spiritual reading, almsgiving, pilgrimage to shrines, fasting, exclusion from Communion for a time, and the like.[3] "These penances are not vindictive punishments by which satisfaction is made for sin committed, but they are remedial, as a safeguard for the preservation of convalescence and a protection"[4] against relapse. The authority for the imposition of such penances is found both in Holy Scripture[5] and in Tradition.[6] The relation of penances to absolution will be seen after the exposition of the Orthodox doctrine of absolution, especially in contrast to that of the Roman Church.

The absolution is a full, complete, and entire forgiveness and remission of all sins and a restoration and return to the state of Grace.[7] It covers all sins committed after Baptism, and involves the deliverance from external penalties of sin, the recovery of the hope of eternal salvation and of peace with God.[8] As the fruits of absolution Mogila enumerates: the regaining and reacquisition of the state of baptismal innocence lost by sin, of the gift of Grace forfeited by sin, of the gift of freedom from the power of the Devil, and of the gift of peace and confidence, instead of fear.[9] Furthermore, the absolution is so complete and full as to demand no further supplementing.[10] So penances may not be conceived of as the fulfilment

[1] Dyobouniotes, op. cit., p. 144, and note 4, and Androutsos, op. cit., p. 384.

[2] Mesolora, op. cit., IV. p. 306. Such are assigned "not for money or as in barter but as remedies for each sin" by the priest as physician (Jeremiah in Mesolora, op. cit., I, p. 150).

[3] Cf. Androutsos, ibid., Dyobouniotes, op. cit., for references, e. g., St.

[4] Androutsos, ibid.

[5] Cf. note 3, p. 144 of Dyobouniotes, op. cit., for references, e. g., St. Matt. 18, 18; 1 Cor. 5, 1-5. On the canonical aspect of penances, cf. Rhalli and Potli, op. cit., pp. 59 ff.

[6] Cf. e. g., 1 Ecumenical Council, Canons 11 and 12; Tertullian de Poenitentia; St. Cyprian, Epist. 6, 52; Apostolic Const. 11, 16, 18, 41; St. Irenaeus, adv. Haer. 1, 13, V. 3, 4.

[7] Androutsos, op. cit., p. 382.

[8] Dyobouniotes, op. cit., pp. 141-142.

[9] In Mesolora, op. cit., I, p. 432 (question 114).

[10] Dyobouniotes, ibid., p. 144.

and completion of something left undone in either the confession or the absolution. They may not be thought of as supplementing either the work of penitence or the operation of Grace; they are not demanded by God as a reparation and satisfaction for sins committed, nor to placate His wrath, but are solely remedial and medicinal, and not vindictive or punitive. The magnitude and vastness of our Lord's merit precludes any "satisfaction" on our part, and "according to the fundamental teachings of Christianity 'the Blood of Jesus . . . cleanses us from all sin"[1] . . . nor is 'there (any) condemnation to them which are in Christ Jesus',[2] that is, those justified through the sacrament of Penance. . . To demand therefore any other satisfaction from man, cannot but mean that the Blood of the Lord has not the needed expiatory power always and for all sins, and that God in pardoning sin still reserves to Himself a spark, as it were, of wrath which must be extinguished by expiatory work on man's part . . . propitiating the divine justice."[3] When the Apostle imposed a penance on the incestuous Corinthian he did so "that the spirit may be saved"[4] and not as a satisfaction of divine righteousness.[5]

On this point Orthodoxy comes into sharp conflict with Roman teaching. According to the latter, there are two sorts of penalties due to sin—eternal and temporal. Baptism remits both, but Penance only the former. Hence there remains in the case of sin forgiven in Penance a certain temporal penalty due to that sin, which must be worked off, as it were, by the penitent. These temporal penalties and consequences due to sin are normally discharged in Purgatory, since the span of natural life does not suffice for the task, but they may be remitted by the Church drawing upon the treasury of merits, due to the superabounding Grace emanating from our Lord's Passion and the works of supererogation done by the Saints. Hence the doctrine of indulgences. "All of this teaching", says Androutsos, "falls to the ground if the theory of temporal penalties and supererogatory works be impugned,

---

[1] 1 St. John 1, 7.
[2] Rom. 8, 1.
[3] Androutsos, *op. cit.*, pp. 385-386.
[4] 1 Cor. 5, 5.
[5] Dyobouniotes, *op. cit.*, pp. 145-146.

of which they are the necessary consequents."[1] Neither of these two doctrines may be held by Orthodoxy, as we saw above, for the doctrine of works of supererogation does violence to the spirit and nature of Christianity, is without authority, and is in itself vicious and false. The theory of "purgatorial fire" is likewise impossible of acceptance. "The fallacious notion of penances", according to Dyobouniotes, "among other things takes away the absolute worth and power of our Lord's redeeming work . . . conceiving of it as imperfect and as standing in need of completion." "The use of indulgences in the Western Church is erroneous not only because it is based on erroneous premises (the idea of the necessity of propitiating the divine righteousness by means of penalty), but because it involves the false doctrine of superabounding merits. . . Neither upon Holy Scripture nor upon Tradition may the Western Church base the doctrine of indulgences. . . In the early Church they were often given, it is true, ... but not on the basis of the merits of the martyr . . . but on that of the Penance to which the confessors and martyrs witnessed."[2] This radical divergence in teaching and practice constitutes one of the greatest differences between Orthodoxy and Roman Catholicism. It is the subject of denunciation and refutation in all Orthodox writings devoted either to the exposition of theological teaching,[1] polemic[2] and controversy, or irenic.[3]

Penances are not of the *esse* of the sacrament of Penance, as all Orthodox theologians teach. Such "satisfactions" . . . "may not be conceived of generally as an indispensable part of the sacrament, since they are not always imposed", as Meso-

---

[1] Androutsos, *ibid.*, note 1, p. 386.

[2] Dyobouniotes *op. cit.*, pp. 146-147, *q. v.*, for references and quotations. For a more complete treatment of the subject, cf. Androutsos, Συμβολική, pp. 320, ff.

[3] *Vide supra.*

[4] Cf. works of Gabriel Severus, metropolitan of Philadelphia (*e. g.*, his Ἔκθεσις, p. 5; Maximus Peloponnesiacus Ἐγχειρίδιον; Macarius of Patmos' Ἔλεγχοι; Tantalides' Παπιστικοὶ ἔλεγχοι; the Πηδάλιον; Timothy Anastasius' Ἐπιστολὴ περὶ ἑνώσεως...pp. 10-13, *et al.*; on which cf. Palmieri, *op. cit.*, I. pp. 763-805, and vol. II.

[5] *E. g.*, Ambraze, Ἡ Ὀρθόδοξος Ἐκκλησία, pp. 54-56, *et al.*; cf. Mesolora, *op. cit.*, IV. pp. 306-313, 316.

lora says.[1] So also Androutsos, who says that "the imposition
of penances cannot be considered as universally necessary since
. . . the thief, the prostitute, the Ninevites, and others were
forgiven without having to undergo any temporal punishment,
as Holy Scripture testifies."[2] They are neither an essential
part of the sacrament, as they come after repentance and confession, nor a complementary part of it. They are not integrally connected with the sacrament at all, for the benefits
of the sacrament are bestowed not on the basis of penances to
be performed, but on that of repentance and confession. In
the early Church they were not considered as conditions of
receiving absolution, but as preparation for righteousness, and
help for eliciting sincerity of intention and disposing to true
penitence. "The assignment of works of penitence after the
absolution looks to the moral betterment of the penitent, to
the preservation of his present state of healing just attained,
and to guarding him in advance from new occasions of falling
into sin."[3] Thus the essential conditions for absolution are
penitence and confession only, and these are absolutely indispensable for receiving remission of sins, which is conveyed
only by the priest. He may assign penances, but they are
beneficial and remedial, and may never be considered as conditions of absolution, or as its completion.

5. Holy Order

The usual word now current to designate this sacrament is
ἱεροσύνη, literally, "priesthood". Among other terms, two—
χειροτονία and χειροθεσία (χειροεπιθεσία),—were anciently employed to denote the sacrament of Holy Order. The former
means "extension of the hands" and the latter, "laying on of
hands". Later there came about a distinction by which
χειροτονία was especially and properly applied to ordination,
and χειροθεσία, to any other rite or service of the laying on of

---

[1] *Op. cit.*, IV. p. 305.
[2] *Op. cit.*, p. 387.
[3] *Ibid.*, pp. 388-389; they "are useful but not necessary", Mesolora,
op. cit., IV. p. 316.

hands—as, for example, the sacrament of Chrism.[1] It may not be without interest to note that there have been substantial contributions to the literature on this sacrament on the part of Greek Orthodox writers[2] in recent days, such as, for example, the works of Basil of Smyrna,[3] Eutaxia,[4] Petrakakos,[5] and Androutsos.[6] Holy Order is "that sacrament in which, through the laying on of hands of a bishop, with prayer, the Grace of the Holy Spirit comes down upon the ordinand, sanctifying him, and constituting him a worthy minister (λειτουργός) of the Church,"[7] and "ordaining the candidate to one of three orders of the ministry."[8]

"Our Lord in founding His Church established the means of salvation and assigned their administration to certain persons, the Apostles, whom He sent to preach the Word, . . . to administer the sacraments, . . . and to govern the Church." As this office and ministry was to endure permanently, it must needs be transferable and communicable. This necessity is apparent from the facts recorded in the New Testament. "Ordination was had by the laying on of hands, by which . . . divine Grace was conveyed, . . . and this laying on of hands and bestowal of Grace . . . was not (instituted) according to a personal ruling of the Apostles . . . but in obedience

---

[1] Cf. Dyobouniotes, op. cit., p. 148 note 1; Mesolora, op. cit., IV. pp. 322-324, note 5: "Χειροθεσία means laying on of hands in general, allowed to priests in the sacrament of Penance," while χειροτονία means specifically ordination. Gabriel of Philadelphia in Περὶ τῶν θείων μυστηρίων says: "Ἱεροσύνη is derived from ἵημι, to send, for the priests 'send up' sacrifices to God; or else from ἱερεύω, to sacrifice" (ch. 2, p. 91).

[2] Few such monographs or treatises on the particular sacraments have appeared.

[3] Πραγματεία περὶ τοῦ κύρους τῆς χειροτονίας τῶν ὑπὸ ἐπισκόπου καθῃρημένου καὶ σχισματικοῦ χειροτονηθέντων, Smyrna, 1887.

[4] Τοῦ κανονικοῦ δικαίου τῆς ὀρθοδόξου ἀνατολικῆς Ἐκκλησίας τὰ περὶ ἱερατικῆς ἐξουσίας, Athens, 1872.

[5] Τινὰ περὶ τοῦ κύρους τῶν χειροτονιῶν in Ἐκκλησιαστικῇ Ἀληθείᾳ, vol. 30, (1910) pp. 134-408.

[6] Op. cit., on Anglican Orders (Τὸ κῦρος τῶν Ἀγγλικῶν χειροτονιῶν); cf. also Comnenos, Συμβολαὶ ...πρὸς ἕνωσιν, Constantinople, 1921.

[7] Dyobouniotes, op. cit., p. 148, q. v. for other names used for the sacrament; cf. also Mesolora, op. cit., IV. p. 321.

[8] Androutsos, Δογματική, p. 389.

to an express injunction of our Lord."[1] By ordination Timothy was advanced to the episcopal order. The passage 2 Tim. 1, 6, is especially remarkable, in that the Grace given by the laying on of hands, "is not simply . . . the Grace of an office, but . . . a power inherent in him, sanctifying him, and leading him into all virtue."[2] It is "as a sacrament, founded by our Lord and bestowing Grace through outward signs, that Holy Sripture regards Holy Order."[3] This is amply witnessed to by the Fathers, and by Tradition, as the writings of St. John Chrysostom, St. Basil, St. Gregory of Nyssa, and St. Ambrose testify.[4] The same evidence is afforded by the heretical bodies of the fourth and fifth centuries.[5] It is consequently more than a mere setting apart of certain official representatives to conduct Church worship:[6] as a sacrament, Holy Order is not only useful but necessary to the life of the Church.[7] "In general", observes Androutsos,[8] "the significance of Holy Order is brought out strongly in Sacred Tradition, inasmuch as without it no authoritative or infallible teaching of the Word,[9] no celebration of the Holy Eucharist and of the other sacraments, and no administration of the Christian community in the Holy Spirit, is possible."

The outward signs of the sacrament of Holy Order are two—the laying on of the hands of the bishop, and the prayer.

[1] Dyobouniotes, *op. cit.*, pp. 149-150, *q. v.* for copious references.

[2] Androutsos, *op. cit.*, pp. 389-390.

[3] Dyobouniotes, *op. cit.*, p. 151. Androutsos observes (*loc. cit.*) that while no express mention is made in the New Testament of the outward sign of the sacrament as being of divine institution, still the apostolic practice must be referred back to our Lord "according to whose injunction and institution the Apostles acted in all matters relating to the Kingdom of God."

[4] Cf. Androutsos, *ibid.*, and Dyobouniotes, *op. cit.*, pp. 151-152, for references and quotations.

[5] Dyobouniotes, p. 152.

[6] Mesolora, *op. cit.*, IV. p. 322.

[7] Dyobouniotes, *ibid.*

[8] *Op. cit.*, p. 390.

[9] In answer to Dyobouniotes' criticism of this phrase, Androutsos explains it as meaning that "the hierarchy is the authentic interpreter and teacher of the divine writings" (Δογμ. Μελέται, Α.' p. 137). For Dyobouniotes *ad loc.*, cf. 'Η Δογμ. 'Ανδρ. κριν., p. 60, and 'Οφειλ. ἀπάντ., pp. 150-151.

Both are essential, and both are of the earliest authority.[1] The consent of the laity expressed formally in the present service of ordination of the Orthodox Church by the cry of "he is worthy" (ἄξιος), does not constitute one of the outward signs of the sacrament.[2] As Eutaxia observes: "The right of choice in regard to bishops as well as other clerics has belonged from early days to the clergy and people, but it does not follow that these have also the authority to ordain. By their choice is designated only the person felt to be worthy for ordination, but the actual ordination is an act absoutely distinct from this choice or election."[3] Both the imposition of hands and the prayer of ordination are referred to apostolic practice.[4] Mesolora regards the prayer as the *form* of ordination, but after recounting the various steps in the rite of ordination says: "All these things as well as the whole service combined with the holy Liturgy, without which ordination is not performed, constitute the outward signs and form of it."[5] The formula of ordination as given in the prayer is, in accordance with Orthodox custom, impersonal: "The divine Grace, everywhere healing weaknesses and fulfilling all that is lacking, ordains *N.* to the grade of deacon (priest, or bishop). Let us therefore pray for him that the Grace of the All-Holy Spirit may come down upon him."

The minister of the sacrament must be a bishop, according to Holy Scripture, the Fathers, and the laws and custom of the Church. St. John Chrysostom, St. Epiphanius, Theodoret, St. Jerome, and St. Athanasius[6] "all regard (the power of) ordination as (constituting) the essential superiority of the

---

[1] Dyobouniotes, Τὰ Μυστήρια, pp. 153-154, *q. v.* for quotations and authorities.

[2] *Ibid.*

[3] *Op. cit.*, p. 161.

[4] Mesolora, *op. cit.*, IV. pp. 327-328. "The Orthodox regard as the outward sign and form of this sacrament, the laying on of the hands of the bishop with the accompanying prayer and supplication" (p. 337).

[5] *Ibid.*, pp. 328-329; cf. his Λειτουργική, pp. 206-212. Kritopoulos specifies the two essentials, the laying on of hands and the prayer, in his *Confession*, Chapter II. in Mesolora, *op. cit.*, I. p. 332, and cf. Mogila, *ibid.*, p. 429. (The latter counts Holy Order as the fourth, and Penance as the fifth sacrament.)

[6] References in notes 2-6, p. 395 of Androutsos, *op. cit.*

episcopal order as above the priest."[1]   It is the distinguishing
and peculiar prerogative of the bishop, who only may ordain.[2]
The words of St. Paul: "the gift in thee—given by prophecy,
with the laying on of the hands of the presbytery",[3] may not
be taken to mean that priests may ordain. St. Paul the
Apostle ordained St. Timothy himself,[4] and the latter part of
the passage refers "to the consent and recognition on the part
of the presbytery of the election, without, however, (conveying)
the gift of Grace which the Apostle, the celebrant of the sacrament, bestowed."[5]   In the case of the ordination of any
cleric save a bishop, one bishop suffices to administer the sacrament.[6] For the consecration of a bishop it is necessary that
at least two,[7] preferably three,[8] bishops officiate, with atten-
dant priests and deacons. Commenting on the fourth Canon
of the First Council (which embodies this prescription),
Eutaxia says: "The reason why one bishop may not alone perform canonically the consecration of an (other) bishop, even if
he should have the consent thereto of the others concerned, is
that by this act . . . is proclaimed the fact that no one
bishop has the authority to ordain a shepherd for (a part of)
the Church not consigned to his jurisdiction, and that only in
conjunction with others may he rightly do anything outside
his own jurisdiction without impairing the rights of others
and transgressing the bounds of his own authority laid down
by the canons."[9]

[1] *Ibid*, text.
[2] Dyobouniotes, *op. cit.*, p. 154.
[3] 1 Tim. 4, 11.
[4] 2 Tim. 1, 6.
[5] Dyobouniotes, *op. cit.*, note 1, pp. 154-155 and cf. St. John Chrysostom, *Homily* 13, 1, on 1 Tim.
[6] Dyobouniotes, and Androutsos, *op. cit.*, *ibid.*
[7] Thus the moderns.
[8] The 4th Canon of 1 Nicaea allows three only as the minimum, so
also Kritopoulos: "(Bishops) are ordained by three bishops at least"
(in Mesolora, *op. cit.*, I, p. 333). Mesolora says: "At the consecration
of a bishop three or at least two, bishops concelebrate." He gives the
place in the Liturgy where each order is ordained and comments in-
terestingly on the significance of the differences (*op. cit.*, IV, note 3,
and text, p. 329).
[9] *Op. cit.*, p. 202, and cf. pp. 203-266. *The Apostolic Constitutions*
allow two bishops as a minimum; cf. Dyobouniotes, *op. cit.*, p. 156, for

As we have seen, there are but three orders of the ministry—bishops, priests, and deacons.[1] In addition to these are certain dignities—such as those of metropolitans, archbishops, patriarchs, and the like[2]—and a series of so-called "minor orders". On the latter Mogila says: "The priesthood includes in it all the grades . . . with all appertaining to each of them: reader, singer, lamp lighter (λαμπαδάριος), subdeacon, and deacon."[3] According to Kritopoulos, "the orders of the ministry (ἱεροσύνη) are . . . seven, of which the first and highest is that of bishops . . . then of priests, third of deacons, after which that of subdeacons, fifth of readers, sixth of exorcists, seventh of door keepers."[4] But the modern Greek theologians seem to be unanimous in maintaining the three-fold order of the ministry, and in stating that it consists of those three orders only—bishops, priests, and deacons. "The Orthodox Church accepts three grades of the ministry."[5] "The lower grades . . . (of which our Church recognizes three)", says Dyobouniotes, "do not constitute a part of the sacrament of Holy Order, since the rite was not instituted by our Lord, nor does it convey any special Grace as do the sacraments. . . They are not part of the sacrament of Holy Order . . . but are only *sacramentals*."[6]

Candidates for Holy Orders must be persons who are fit by reason of good moral character, knowledge, and training, and are physically whole.[7] They must be baptized males, en-

patristic and conciliar references. Dositheus says: "The episcopal office is so necessary in the Church that without it there could be neither Church nor Christian. The bishop is not ordained by a priest, but by two or three bishops" (in Mesolora, *op. cit.*, II, p. 108-109).

[1] Cf. Lect. IV. "On the Constitution and Organization of the Church" (11, § 4. pp. 246-248). "The divinely instituted hierachy embraces three orders, deacons, priests, and bishops, bound together but yet distinguished from each other" (Androutsos, *op. cit.*, p. 384).

[2] On which cf. Mesolora, *op. cit.*, IV. note 4, pp. 329-330, pp. 60, 70-81; Gabriel of Philadelphia, Περὶ τῶν μυστηρίων, pp. 96-97.

[3] In Mesolora, *op. cit.*, I, p. 430.

[4] *Ibid.*, p. 332. He gives a summary of the duties of each office, *ibid.*, and p. 333.

[5] Mesolora, *op. cit.*, IV. p. 336; cf. Androutsos, *op. cit.*, pp. 284 ff.

[6] *Op. cit.*, note 1, p. 157.

[7] Mogila, in Mesolora, *op. cit.*, I, p. 430. For the qualifications of a candidate according to Kritopoulos, cf. *ibid.*, p 334.

dowed with the necessary equipment of faith, piety, and knowledge, with which qualifications Canon Law deals.[1] All the prescriptions regarding ordinands are regulated by early and later canonical definitions, as for example, those of the Apostolic Constitutions, the Ecumenical Councils, and the like. Dyobouniotes summarizes these necessary qualifications and conditions as follows: (a) that the ordinands be Orthodox Christians, not recently converted, of irreproachable faith and moral character; (b) that they be learned in Holy Scripture and Canon Law; (c) that they be healthy in body and without any physical impairment which would prevent the fulfillment of the duties of their ministry duly and canonically; (d) that the candidate for the diaconate be 25 years old, and for the priesthood and episcopate 30 years; (e) that he be unmarried or already married if he be a candidate for the diaconate or priesthood, and unmarried or else living apart from his wife, if he be a candidate for the episcopal office—since no one may marry after ordination,[2] and bishops must be celibate.

The Grace of the sacrament is the spiritual authority to fulfil all that which pertains to the office, together with which, in the case of one worthily receiving the sacrament, the particular assistance of God enabling him to fulfil all his duties worthily and in a manner pleasing to God, and to live a virtuous life in conformity with his calling.[3] This Grace, constituting the ordained a worthy and fit minister of the Church, is distinctly spoken of in Holy Scripture, and expressly taught by Tradition.[4] It is one, and is bestowed on the ordinands in varying measure for the grade to which they are being ordained, and the service to which they are thereby[5] designated. There are not different graces, so to speak, imparted in each ordination, but "one only, apportioned in gradations—to the deacon receiving it, for his elevation to the higher order, and to the priest, for his advancement to the highest office. Thus the bishop is the preacher of truth *par excellence,* the administrator of the sacraments, and the shepherd over the flock of

[1] Androutsos, *op. cit.,* pp. 385-38.
[2] *Op. cit.,* pp. 167-168, notes and references; cf. also Androutsos, *ibid.*
[3] Androutsos, *op. cit.,* pp. 390-391.
[4] Dyobouniotes, *op. cit.,* p. 156, *q. v.* for references.
[5] Mesolora, *op. cit.,* IV. p. 333.

the Church; the priest preaches the word of God and performs all sacraments save ordination and the consecration of the myrrh, ruling his church in obedience to the bishop; the deacon assists the bishop and priest in the services, but has not the right to teach, perform the sacraments, or shepherd the Church. All three orders . . . constitute one sacrament, of which the Grace and the effects are bestowed in part and in degree. The three-fold character of the Holy Order does not abrogate the unity of the sacrament . . . nor does the unity of the sacrament take away the three-fold mystic act, since ordination must be regarded as the ordination not only of a priest but as well of a bishop and a deacon."[1] The phrase "stewards of the mysteries of God"[2] Mogila quotes as the summary of sacerdotal duties, saying: "Two things are involved in this stewardship: first, the power and authority to forgive . . . sins . . . and second, the power and authority to teach," under which he includes pastoral work and the administration of the other sacraments.[3] Kritopoulos epitomizes the work of a priest as "the ministry of the Word and the celebration of the sacraments."[4]

"As in the other sacraments, so also in that of Orders, the Grace bestowed is so stamped into the soul of the ordained that it cannot be lost at all."[5] Since in a sense all sacraments imprint an indelible seal, so especially in Orders and Baptism is the Grace once bestowed a permanent and inalienable possession. "Baptism and Orders occupy a parallel position,"[6] in

[1] Dyobouniotes, op. cit., pp. 157-159.
[2] 1 Cor. 4, 1.
[3] In Mesolora, op. cit., I, p. 430.
[4] Ibid., p. 335. cf. Kephala: "The priesthood as a sacrament designates the priest as the organ of divine Grace, as the minister of the holy sacraments, as the teacher of piety and the acceptable mediator between God and man, that, like God's angel, he may offer up the prayers and supplications of the faithful to God and bring down from heaven divine gifts...Holy Order is that sacrament by which a man from among men stands for men in relation to God" (op. cit., pp. 187-198).
[5] Dyobouniotes, op. cit., p. 159, and Mesolora, op. cit., IV. pp. 333 ff.; cf. the discussion of indelible character in Lecture V, pp. 283-286, and Dyobouniotes' theory ibid.
[6] Androutsos, op. cit., p. 393.

that the character of the Grace bestowed is such that by its nature it is non-iterable. One may be baptized, chrismated, and ordained only once, since the effect achieved by the Grace of these sacraments is of a once-for-all character. The other sacraments are never, properly speaking, repeated, since the condition of the recipient creates anew the need for a further access of the Grace which they mediate. But no such possible contingency can occur in relation to Baptism or Holy Order. One who is baptized is born again, and cannot be "un-born". One who is ordained is once for all set apart into the ranks of the hierarchy. Consequently Holy Order may neither be iterated, nor may its Grace be repudiated and thereby be excised or deleted from the soul which has once received it.[1] As we have seen, the teaching and practice of the Orthodox Church in relation to heretical orders may be reconciled on the basis of the principle of *economy*. Similarly she accepts the Orders and Baptism of Orthodox who have lapsed into heresy or schism, because of the original validity of these sacraments and by reason of their non-iterable character. The recent action of the Church of Russia in allowing the return to lay life of clerics, acceding to their express request, cannot be justified. "The renunciation of the clerical office and its abdication is not allowed by the canons under any condition. . . . The ruling recently made in Russia by which permission is given (to clerics to) ask release from their spiritual order and rank, and to return to the ranks of the laity, is destitute of any canonical basis",[2] and "is contrary to the canons of the Church."[3]

6. Matrimony

In the sacrament of Marriage or Holy Matrimony, the Grace of the Holy Spirit is bestowed to sanctify the union of man and wife, and to enable them to attain the end which marriage has in view: the preservation and increase of the human race, particularly of members of the Church, the pro-

---

[1] Dyobouniotes, *op. cit.*, p. 159, and Androutsos, *op. cit.*, p. 391.

[2] Androutsos, *ibid.*, note 3.

[3] Dyobouniotes, *op. cit.*, note 3, pp. 159-160. Both refer to Milas, *Kirchenrecht*, pp. 392 ff. (translation of M. Apostolopoulos).

motion of mutual helpfulness, the restraint of the passions and their submission to the moral law, and the Christian nurture and upbringing of children.[1] It is "an holy act of divine origin, in which the Grace of the Holy Spirit is imparted by the priest to two people freely and willingly coming together, to sanctify and uplift the otherwise natural bond of their union."[2] Kritopoulos specifies the procreation of children in his definition of the sacrament,[3] as does Jeremiah II.[4] Mogila emphasizes the confirmation and ratification by the priest of the bond freely and publicly entered upon.[5] Mesolora enumerates the objects of marriage as the lawful relation of man and wife and their cohabitation in purity, the procreation of children and their upbringing as Christians, and the mutual partnership and succour in sickness and times of difficulty.[6]

All Orthodox *Confessions* count Marriage as a sacrament, which implies that it must have a divine foundation and must through outward signs convey Grace. The divine foundation or establishment of the sacrament is nowhere explicitly alluded to in the New Testament. That our Lord elevated and exalted the bond of union between man and wife, which was a natural law with its origin in God's decree and which had God's blessing,[7] is apparent from Holy Scripture. "But yet we have no clear and definite statement in the New Testament witnessing to this elevation of marriage into a sacrament by our Lord."[8] Yet our Lord accepted and uplifted the existing institution of marriage, made a wedding the occasion of His first miracle, and gave laws concerning marriage.[9] But the significant passage "upon which both in early times and to-

---

[1] Dyobouniotes, *op. cit.*, pp. 169-170, *q. v.* for references.

[2] Androutsos, *op. cit.*, p. 396.

[3] In Mesolora, *op. cit.*, I, pp. 141, 224.

[4] *Ibid.*, p. 335.

[5] P. 433; for Dositheus' definition cf. *ibid.*, II. p. 114.

[6] *Op. cit.*, IV. p. 340.

[7] Cf. Mesolora, *ibid.*, p. 342, where he gives an account of the origin of marriage. In view of this aspect, cf. Kephala's definition of Marriage as "the sacrament...in which the Church consecrates the blessing given to the human race in Paradise" (Gen. 1, 28), in his Χριστολογία, p. 198.

[8] Androutsos, *op. cit.*, pp. 396-397.

[9] *E. g.*, in St. Matt. 19, 4-6.

day the doctrine of the sacrament of Marriage is based"[1] is
Eph. 5, 22-33. Here the Apostle speaks of the relation of husband and wife as like that of Christ and His Church, and uses
the words: "This is a great mystery"[2] (μυστήριον). The phrase
may not be understood to imply directly that marriage is a
sacrament, but "nevertheless from the context it is clear that
it is conceived by the Apostle as something conveying divine
Grace or at least based upon it and presupposing it."[3] "The
elevation by our Lord of the natural bond", says Androutsos,
"into spiritual union, in accordance with the prototype of the
union of Christ with the Church, must needs be manifested
in mutual love, and is impossible of being constituted without
the blessing of the Saviour and the influence of divine Grace."[4]
This exegesis is entirely consistent with the mind of the Apostle as expressed elsewhere.[5] Nevertheless, there is a gap between the conception of marriage as under the influence of
divine Grace . . . and as a sacrament, "an effectual means of
grace" in the Church's sense of the word.[6] This lacuna between
Marriage "as founded upon and presupposing divine Grace"[7]
and developed sacramental doctrine is filled in by the evidence
presented by Sacred Tradition.

Tradition teaches "that Holy Scripture holds that Grace
is given through the service (rite) of Marriage, which rite was
established by our Lord or His Apostles, . . . and, consequently, views Marriage as a sacrament."[8] According to

[1] Androutsos, ibid.
[2] vs. 32.
[3] Dyobouniotes, op. cit., p. 171.
[4] Androutsos, op. cit., p. 397.
[5] As e. g., in Tim. 2, 15; Col. ff.; 1 Cor. 7, 14, 39, etc.
[6] Androutsos, ibid., p. 397-398.
[7] Dyobouniotes ibid., p. 172. Christ did not found the institution
of marriage, but exalted and uplifted it into a sacrament (Androutsos,
op. cit., pp. 396-398). When did He establish the sacrament of Marriage? One opinion is that He did so at the Marriage of Cana (St.
John 2, 1); another, on the occasion of His conflict with the Pharisees
(St. Matt. 19, 4-6). "But," says Dyobouniotes, "there is nothing said
in Holy Scripture about the Institution of the sacrament...by our
Lord, or about the circumstances. ...The most probable view is that
its Institution occurred...in the time between the Resurrection and
Ascension" (op. cit., pp. 173-174).
[8] Ibid., p. 173.

Mesolora: "All the Fathers of the Church, in view of the words of Holy Writ about it, taught and wrote that Marriage is a sacrament divinely established, constituting the natural bond and law a holy union, through prayers, through appropriate signs, and through the blessing of the Church's ministers."[1] This evidence for the sacramental character of Holy Matrimony is gathered from the Fathers,[2] the early office books, the continuous and constant teaching of the Church, and is even proved by the teaching and practice of the early heretics, such as the Copts, Armenians, Maronites, Abyssinians, and Nestorians, all of whom regard Marriage as a sacrament.[3] Dyobouniotes says in summary: "Both Holy Scripture and Sacred Tradition regard and recognize Marriage as a sacrament."[4]

The outward signs in the sacrament of Marriage, Mesolora reckons as four: the profession publicly before the Church, of willing and free consent by both parties; the rings exchanged in the ceremony; the crowns used;[5] and the various prayers and blessings,— . . . the *form* properly being the actual words of marriage, that is, the prayer to God to stretch forth His Hand upon the two persons, and the formulae: "*N.* the servant (handmaid) of God is espoused" . . . "*N.* the servant

---

[1] *Op. cit.*, IV. p. 343.

[2] For references and quotations, cf. Dyobouniotes, *op. cit.*, pp. 174-175, and notes; Androutsos *op. cit.*, p. 398.

[3] Cf. *ibid.*, and Mesolora, *op. cit.*, IV, pp. 343-344.

[4] *Op. cit.*, p. 176.

[5] "The *rings* are a symbol of the earnest, the betrothal,....which takes place before the wedding." Formerly the man's ring was of gold ...and the woman's of silver, which symbolized the sun and moon respectively. The betrothal now ordinarily takes place privately, but may be made part of the service in which the two people are married. "The crowns are the sign of the bond between the newly married, and of the glory and honor which crowns them in the sacrament." In Russia the crowns are replicas of the Royal Crown and are kept among the Church vessels. In the Greek Church they are of flowers or evergreen. Wine is taken as a remembrance of the Marriage in Cana where our Lord performed His first miracle. "It denotes the mutual sharing in the sorrow and trials of life." The rite of crowning is of such significance that Marriage is usually known as στέψις, στεφάνωμα,—cf. Mesolora, *op. cit.*, IV. p. 346, and notes; *ibid.*, Λειτουργική, pp. 212-218; on the canonical aspects of the relation of the Betrothal to the Marriage, cf. Ἐκκλησιαστικὸν δίκαιον, by Christodoulos, pp. 436-440 and ff.

(handmaid) of God is crowned."[1] Both Dyobouniotes and Androutsos, however, reduce the outward signs to two only: the declaration publicly of free consent and agreement on the part of the two parties, and the blessing of the priest. The consent of each of the two persons is demanded by the priest, and is an integral part of the sacrament. "As . . . in the sacrament of Penance", writes Dyobouniotes, "confession is absolutely necessary for the operation of the sacrament, so in the sacrament of Marriage the willing and free consent of both persons is absolutely necessary for the operation of the sacrament of Marriage."[2]

The blessing of the priest is likewise essential for the consummation of the sacrament. Early testimony to the necessity of the priestly blessing is found in the writings of such Fathers as St. Ignatius, St. Basil, St. Clement Alex., Tertullian, St. John Chrysostom, and St. Ambrose.[3] It is true that there are instances of the acceptance by the Church of marriages not blessed by a priest, as valid, but this does not indicate that the Church ordinarily gave such recognition. The similar case of the recognition of the validity of the marriages of heterodox, heretics, or schismatics, comes under the same principle: the use of *economy*.[4] The Church does not recognize any sacraments not performed by herself, and prescribes that the officiant be a priest in every case.[5] In all the sacraments, as we saw above, the priest is the minister of the Grace bestowed, and Marriage is no exception to this rule. The Roman view that the ministers of the sacrament are the two parties who are to be made man and wife, is both wrong and vicious. It is wrong because it is contrary to Tradition, to the practice of the Church, and to the sacramental principle just referred to. It is vicious, in that it regards the religious service not as

---

[1] *Op. cit.*, IV. pp. 347-348.
[2] Dyobouniotes, *op. cit.*, p. 176, and cf. Androutsos, *op. cit.*, p. 398.
[3] Cf. Dyobouniotes, *op. cit.*, p. 177 and note 1, for references.
[4] *Ibid.*, note 5 (pp. 177-178), and Androutsos, *op. cit.*, p. 399 note. ..
[5] The one possible case of clinical Baptism, or Baptism in any pressing necessity, by a layman, only allowable and "validatable", so to speak, by the exercise of *economy*, may not be appealed to (as the Roman theologians do in this instance) as it has no bearing on the question whatever (cf. Androutsos, *loc. cit.*).

conveying the necessary Grace, but only as "laudable" and "edifying", and consequently does not view it as essential.[1] As a result of this view, marriage and the sacrament of Marriage would coincide.[2] The Roman "view leads directly to civil marriage, and makes the logical basis on which Roman theologians found their opposition to it absolutely untenable."[3] "The Church has declared her mind on the subject of the ministers (of the sacrament) of marriage, not only in the penalties she imposes on those who have been joined together as man and wife without the use of the prescribed ceremony, but also in her practice and her decrees, (where) she makes the completion of the sacrament dependent . . . upon the Church's blessing."[4]

It is presupposed that the two people to be married are Christians, for the Church forbids marriage with a non-Christian.[5] Formerly she prohibited any marriage with heretics or schismatics as well. At the beginning of the 19th century she began to allow the marriage of an Orthodox with a Roman, Protestant, or Schismatic.[6] In such a case the Church prescribes that an orthodox priest perform the sacrament and that a promise shall have been made to bring up the children in the Orthodox Faith.[7] Such "mixed marriages" are strongly discouraged. There must, of course, be no impediment in the case of either party. They must be of proper age, physically capable of being married, not already married, and there must be no impediment by reason of consanguinity, affinity by marriage, or spiritual relationship.[8]

"The inward Grace bestowed by the sacrament sanctifies

[1] Cf. Mesolora, op. cit., IV. pp. 350-351, q. v. for references.

[2] Dyobouniotes, op. cit., p. 177.

[3] Ibid.

[4] Androutsos, op. cit., note 4, pp. 398-399.

[5] Androutsos, op. cit., p. 401; Dyobouniotes, op. cit., p. 178; cf. Can. 14 of the IV Ecum. Council, and 72 of that in Trullo.

[6] Mesolora, op. cit., p. 353, and note 1.

[7] Op. cit.; for a treatise on the subject from the standpoint of Canon Law, cf. M. J. Theotoka, Τὰ κρατοῦντα περὶ μικτῶν γάμων ἐν τῇ ὀρθοδόξῳ ἀνατολικῇ Ἐκκλησίᾳ, Constantinople, 1899; and ibid., Νομολογία, pp. 354 ff.

[8] Mesolora, op. cit., p. 345, and note 2, q. v. for references to Canon Law on the subject.

the natural bond and uplifts it to become the center of moral perfection and mutual love."[1] This effect of Grace is given that "marriage be honorable in all, and the bed undefiled."[2] It assists, makes attainable, and promotes the end for which Marriage is designed, and involves two things—monogamy and the indissolubility of the bond,[3] which are both presupposed and demanded by Christian Marriage. "When by reason of the Fall the permanent and indissoluble character of Marriage had been perverted through polygamy and easy divorce—not only among the heathen but also among the Jews as well—our Lord came and restored Marriage to its first and rightful place, exalting its permanent and indissoluble character."[4] "Polygamy is opposed to the teaching of Holy Scripture and Sacred Tradition, defeats the moral aims of Marriage, since it oppresses and degrades woman, subverts the well-being of the household . . . and is detrimental to the nurture of children."[5]

"Both Holy Scripture and Tradition emphasize the indissoluble character of Marriage, recognizing but one sole cause for the dissolution of the marriage tie—'fornication'." This does not mean that in case of such sin divorce is absolutely necessary or obligatory, for upon reconciliation and by agreement the bond of marriage may still be preserved intact.[6] But inasmuch as the express words of our Lord allow dissolubility of marriage on this ground, it is erroneous to say, as do the Romans, that marriage is *absolutely* indissoluble,[7] or to conceive this exception as not being a real one or as not actually dissolving the bond.[8] According to Androutsos, the natural solvent of the bond of marriage is death, after which the surviving partner may contract a second, or by special dispensation, even a third marriage.[9] The indissolubility of marriage is subject to one limitation, since divorce is allowed in the

[1] Androutsos, *op. cit.*, pp. 398-399.
[2] Heb. 13, 4; and cf. 1 Thess. 4, 3-4; Eph. 5, 22-33.
[3] Dyobouniotes, *op. cit.*, p. 178.
[4] Androutsos, *op. cit.*, p. 399; cf. Dyobouniotes, *ibid.*, and p. 179.
[5] Dyobouniotes, *op. cit.*, p. 179.
[6] *Ibid.*, and note 4.
[7] *Ibid.*, p. 181.
[8] As Dyobouniotes seems to think that Androutsos holds. Cf. his Ἡ Δογμ. Ἀνδρ. κριν., p. 60; Ὀφειλ. ἀπάντ., pp. 151-152.
[9] *Op. cit.*, pp 399-400; cf. Kritopoulos, in Mesolora, *op. cit.*, I. p. 336.

case of "fornication" according to the words of our Lord. In case of a separation *a mensa et toro* the innocent party should, according to the text, have the right of remarriage, which the Roman Church will not admit, as it holds to the absolute indissolubility of the bond in defiance of Holy Scripture. "Our Lord in giving the right to dissolve the bond does not preclude the right to remarry, nor is there the least reason why the innocent party should be deprived of the right to form a new marriage."[1] The Roman theory and practice are both unjustifiable according to the Orthodox view. "By the interpretation of St. Matt. 5, 32, and 19, 9 . . . and, in connection with it, of St. Luke 16, 18, and St. Mk. 10, 2-12, . . . dissolution of marriage is allowed by reason of 'Fornication'." The Roman exegesis which would make the last word mean "an illicit union", in order to maintain the absolute indissolubility of marriage, is forced and inacceptable, as it does violence to the meaning of the words. The words "her that is put away" may not be taken in a general, but in a specific sense, and in connection with the passage from St. Matthew. They mean: (St. Luke 16, 18), "he who marrieth her that is put away from her husband for any other reason *and not because of fornication* committeth adultery". . . "Yet even if the passage is of general application, it would still mean that the marriage of the member put away is forbidden, but not that of the innocent party". . . "The separation *a toro et mensa* of the Roman Church was utterly unknown in the early Church". . . The patristic basis of the Roman argument is not found in the general teaching of the primitive Church as a whole, but solely in certain Fathers who were interested in forbidding second marriages (which they felt were wrong), if necessary, "conceiving them as evidence of incontinence and as only a seemly form of adultery."[2] It is true that second and third marriages are not looked upon with favor by the Church, but yet they are al-

---

[1] *Op. cit.*, p. 400. In the case of the reunion of divorced people, they are not remarried, "since the sacrament is not repeated, for there it is not a question of a new relationship but of the same one" (Dyobouniotes, *op. cit.*, pp. 182-183; cf. N. Demetracopoulos, in 'Ελληνογαλλικῇ Νομολογία [1906-1907], vol. XXVI. 'Ανασύστασις λυθέντος γάμου, pp. 271 ff.).

[2] Dyobouniotes, *op. cit.*, pp. 180-181 note 2.

lowed. A fourth marriage is absolutely prohibited.[1] Though
neither Androutsos nor Dyobouniotes treat of the matter, Mesolora asserts definitely that "the Orthodox allow divorce generally for the cause of adultery and also for other grave causes
which make married life impossible, giving permission for a
second and third marriage."[2] Among these 'other causes' for
which divorce is granted are: a plot against the life of one or
the other by the husband or wife; adultery; causes leading or
related to adultery; procuring or inducing abortion or mis-
carriage; assuming the office of God-parent of the same child
at a Baptism; physical impotence; insanity; the monastic
state. "But the reason for divorce is generally adultery, . . .
as well as anything related to it when it is officially certified
and proven."[3]

Inasmuch as the Orthodox Church rates the state of virginity as higher than that of matrimony in the scale of moral
perfection, following the Bible and Tradition,[4] she demands
that the bishops be celibate, and that monks who have taken the
tonsure or have received ordination remain unmarried. In
the case of bishops, her ruling has in view not only this idea
but also the "work of the episcopal office, which with its many
cares and duties could not be adequately attended to . . . in
the married state with the domestic duties it involves, nor
could the bishop show that self-denial and self-sacrifice which
his office demands and presupposes."[5]

7. Unction

The seventh sacrament is that of Holy Unction, which is
a divinely instituted sacrament in which a sick person is anointed
with oil, and divine Grace heals both his bodily and his

---

[1] *Ibid.*, p 182 and cf notes for references *ad rem.*

[2] *Op. cit.*, IV. p. 351.

[3] *Ibid.*, note 6, pp. 349-350; for legal and canonical aspect of
divorce and the proper measures in instituting proceedings, cf. Sakellaropoulos, Ἐκκλ. δίκαιον, pp. 538-550; Christodoulos, *op. cit.*, pp.
443-448.

[4] Cf. 1 Cor 7, 38, 40; St. Matt 19, 11; St. Augustine, *de bon. conj.*,
8, 8; St. Cyprian, *de hab. virg.*, 3; St. Jerome, *adv. Jov.* 1, 21; etc.

[5] Dyobouniotes, *op. cit.*, p. 183, and note 2, *ibid.;* cf. also Mesolora, *op. cit.*, IV. p. 352 and note 1, and 2.

spiritual ills.[1] The name now applied to the sacrament
(εὐχέλαιον), is probably due to the monk Job, who formed the
term by a combination of two words expressing the outward
signs of the sacrament—"prayer" (εὐχή) and "oil" (ἔλαιον).[2]
The passage in the New Testament which refers to this sacrament is St. James 5, 14-15. A careful examination of the
text will yield the following conclusions: (a) "When St.
James enjoins this practice he is not establishing something
new,"[3] nor could it be "something unknown to the Christians,
. . . but it had been a well known institution before that
time, since the Apostles preached nothing of themselves but
only what the Lord had commissioned them to do."[4] In the
words of Kritopoulos written in this connection: "The Apostles would not have dared do what they had not been commanded
to do."[5] In this passage, says Androutsos, "we have an outward action—the anointing with oil—to which is joined a
supernatural operation: in other words (we have) the constituent elements of a sacrament. Certainly . . . there is
no mention of the other essential note, . . establishment
by our Lord. But if we reason that St. James could not of
himself have enjoined a practice of such consequence, then the
certainty and conviction with which he pronounces in regard
to the effects, cannot be otherwise accounted for, save on the
basis that the Apostle knew that the Church's practice of
anointing with oil was an institution established by our Lord;
so we do have in this passage a witness to the divine origin
of this sacrament."[6] (b) Secondly, we do not have here merely
a reference to "a well-known and customary means of healing. . . . Oil was used by almost all peoples . . . for this
purpose, it is true, . . yet this cannot be the topic here under
discussion, since this anointing . . . is said to heal all dis-

[1] Androutsos, op. cit., p. 401.
[2] Dyobouniotes, op. cit., note 1, p. 184, and note 1, Mesolora, op.
cit., IV. p. 363. Job also thought Unction was to be limited to those
in articulo mortis; cf. Περὶ τῶν θείων μυστηρ. of Gabriel of Philadelphia,
pp. 136-141, for the other titles and terms applied to the sacrament;
cf. text ibid., and p. 185.; Mesolora, op. cit., IV. p. 355
[3] Mesolora, ibid., p. 357.
[4] Dyobouniotes, op. cit., p. 185.
[5] In Mesolora, op. cit., I, p. 337; cf. Gal. 1, 11-12.
[6] Op. cit., p. 402.

eases, and to confer remission of sins, while the healing power
of medicinal anointing has only a limited scope, being employed
for certain specified diseases only, . . . and never confers
the remission of sins.   Besides, it is emphasized that this anointing must be performed by priests of the Church with prayer,
which would certainly not have been necessary in the case of
ordinary medicinal anointing which anyone could do."[1]   "Furthermore, St. James makes the healing dependent not simply
on the anointing but on the *prayer of faith.*"   In the case of
medicinal unction anyone could perform it for the sick without having to call in priests.[2]   Thirdly, (c) "it is not spoken
of as a 'gift of healing,'[3] . . . which was a general charisma,
not, as here, something expressly restricted to priests, and
which did not impart the forgiveness of sins but only the healing of bodily ills."[4]   Fourthly, (d) "this sacrament is not called
the *last anointing* or *extreme unction* (*extrema unctio, unctio
in extremis, sacramentum exeuntium*)" says Kritopoulos, "but
'prayer-oil' (εὐχέλαιον).   For we do not wait till the last and
then have recourse to it, but use the sacrament while there is
yet good hope of recovery. . .   So it is to be used not once
in a lifetime but often, . . . just as we use medical remedies as often as we are sick."[5]   "St. James says simply: 'is
any sick among you?' that is, 'whenever anyone is sick;' he is
not dealing with grievous illnesses in which the sick person
is drawing his last breath."[6]   In practice the Orthodox Church
"differs essentially" from the Roman Church, which withholds

---

[1] Dyobouniotes, *op. cit.*, p. 186.

[2] Androutsos, *op. cit.*, p. 402.

[3] Cf. St. Mark 6, 13, and 1 Cor. 12, 9. "The view...that (St. Mk.
6, 13) refers to Unction is incorrect,...and the opinion that the institution of the sacrament is based upon this passage is erroneous"
(Dyobouniotes, *op. cit.*, note 3, p. 186).   The latter thinks that the
institution of this sacrament "like that of Baptism and Penance,
took place...in the time between the Resurrection and Ascension"
(note 4, *ibid.*, and p. 187).

[4] Dyobouniotes, *ibid.*, p. 186, and cf. Androutsos, *loc. cit.*

[5] In Mesolora, *op. cit.*, I, p. 339.   But Dyobouniotes seems to recognize a proper use of the expression *extrema unctio* (ἐσχάτη χρῖσις)
as meaning "the last of the anointings", in which sense it is legitimate
(note 1, p. 185, *op. cit.*).

[6] Mesolora, *op. cit.*, IV. note I. p. 356.

the sacrament from the ordinarily sick and restricts it to those nearing death. The Roman practice violates both spirit and letter of the text, and is contrary to the universal custom of the Church up until the twelfth century.[1] Fifthly, (e) "the notion . . . that it is the 'prayer of faith *of the sick*' which saves him is erroneous, since . . . the context shows that this prayer means that said *by the priest* over the sick, which together with the anointing (the other outward sign), conveys divine Grace."[2] On the basis of the evidence afforded by this passage we may conclude "that before the occasion of the writing of this Epistle, the practice of anointing the sick with oil . . . existed in the Church and was a true sacrament, founded by our Lord, having outward signs, and conveying Grace."[3]

"The evidence given by Sacred Tradition, if not as abundant as that for the other sacraments (since Unction was . . . often joined with Penance, of which it was regarded as the complement), is yet not altogether lacking."[4] Such references as those in Origen, St. John Chrysostom, and St. Cyril of Alexandria, speak only of Unction in connection with Penance.[5] Victor of Antioch, Pope Innocent I, and Caesarius (†542), all refer to it as a sacrament.[6] The antiquity of the rite is shown by its preservation in the Coptic and Jacobite Churches.[7] The evidence, from the seventh century on, is full and definite. All the Orthodox *Confessions* teach that Unction is the seventh sacrament.[8]

The outward signs of the sacrament are three: the oils, the

---

[1] *Ibid.*, pp. 355-356; cf. Dyobouniotes, *op. cit.*, note 1, p. 185; Androutsos, *op. cit.*, p. 406.

[2] Dyobouniotes, *op. cit.*, note 1, p. 187.

[3] *Ibid.*, pp. 186-187.

[4] Androutsos, *op. cit.*, p. 403, and Dyobouniotes, *op. cit.*, p. 187.

[5] *Ibid.*, and note.

[6] Dyobouniotes, *ibid.*, p. 188.

[7] *Ibid.;* "The Syrians and Maronites call it the 'sacrament of the lamps' from their custom of using the oil from the lamps in the church and especially that of the everburning lamp inside the Iconostasis for the sacrament" (*ibid.*, p. 185).

[8] Cf. in Mesolora, *op. cit.*, Kritopoulos, I, pp. 37 ff: Jeremiah, II, I, p. 141; Mogila I, pp. 433-434: Synod of Constantinople *ibid.*, II, p. 140.

anointing therewith of the bodily members of the sick person, and the prayer.[1] The oil must be pure and unmixed with any other matter.[2] In the early Church, the practice varied in regard to the parts of the body anointed: the breast, the part affected by the sickness, the head, the forehead, cheeks, hands, feet, were each severally anointed, by the one anointing used in the service, at various times in the history of the Church. According to present use the priests in succession anoint the forehead, nostrils, cheeks, lips, breast, and hands of the sick person.[3] The prayer used is: "Holy Father, Physician of soul and body, who didst send thine only-begotten Son our Lord Jesus Christ, the Healer of every ill and the Redeemer from death, heal this thy servant N. of his present bodily and spiritual weakness and quicken him by the Grace of thy Christ."[4]

The ministers of the sacrament are normally seven priests,[5] though one may suffice in case of necessity.[6] The oil is blessed by the priests and not by the bishop. The custom of restricting this office to the bishop is contrary to the text of Holy Scripture and primitive practice.[7] "The sacrament is administered, according to the words of institution and the most ancient tradition of the Church, to all sick persons irrespec-

[1] Mogila, in Mesolora, op. cit., I. p. 433; Dyobouniotes, op. cit., pp. 188-189.

[2] Among others, Mogila (in Mesolora, op. cit., I. p. 338) prescribes oil and wine, with reference to the Parable of the Good Samaritan. This is the custom in the Russian Church (cf. Mesolora, op cit., IV. note 2, p. 359), but not in the Greek (Dyobouniotes, ibid.).

[3] Dyobouniotes, op. cit., pp. 189-190.

[4] Cf. the Εὐχολόγιον τὸ μεγά (p. 270). It is almost the same as that given by Kritopoulos (Mesolora, I. p. 338); on it cf. Symeon of Thessalonica, Ἡ τελετὴ τοῦ εὐχελαίου, chapter 2. Mesolora gives the following cases in which the use of the sacrament is forbidden: (a) sick persons who have lost consciousness, (b) infants, (c) those who are well but are in imminent danger of death, as e. g., soldiers going into battle, condemned criminals, etc. (op. cit., IV, note 2, pp. 360-361). For the canonical aspects of the administration of the sacrament, cf. Christodoulos, op. cit., pp. 418 ff. Full text of the prayer in Dyobouniotes, loc. cit., and in Androutsos, op. cit., note 3, p. 403.

[5] As the rubrics direct, and as the various references in the Symbolic Books indicate; cf. Dyobouniotes, op. cit., p. 191.

[6] Cf. Kritopoulos, loc. cit.; Androutsos, op. cit., p. 405.

[7] Mesolora, op. cit., IV. p. 356, loc. cit., and Dyobouniotes, op. cit., p. 190.

tive of the gravity of their sickness or of the lightness of the attack."[1] "All sick people may be anointed, not only those in serious danger" . . . The sacrament is not only a *viaticum* but is to be used in any case of sickness. Restricting its use to the last moments perverts the object for which it was instituted and frustrates one of the two effects of the Grace given.[2] "The incorrectness of this view of the sacrament," says Dyobouniotes, "is made clear by reference to the words used by St. James": *sick* and *ill* (ἀσθενεῖν, κάμνειν), neither in the New Testament nor in Greek generally mean exclusively and only those 'grievously sick' or 'at the point of death'."[3]

In the sacrament of Unction "the Church by her prayers heals the sick in body and soul, raises him from his bed of sickness, and manifests him whole and healthy in both respects."[4] The *Acts* of the Synod of Constantinople specify two effects of this sacrament, "one applied to the healing of the soul, the other, to that of the body."[5] The teaching of the passage in St. James,[6] of the early Church, and of the Symbolic Books,[7] is that the Grace "conveyed in the sacrament of Unction serves for the healing of the body and for the forgiveness of sin."[8] The chief fruit of the sacrament is the former,[9] as is evident from the text of St. James. "Those who belonged to Him our Lord did not wish to leave in their weaknesses," says Androutsos, "so it pleased Him to institute a sacrament

---

[1] Dyobouniotes, *op. cit.*, p. 191.

[2] Androutsos, *op. cit.*, p. 406. Macarius (*op. cit.*, II. pp. 267-268) seems, on the contrary, to hold that it should be reserved for those seriously sick, with whom Dyobouniotes (*op. cit.*, p. 91, cf. note 4) and Androutsos (*loc. cit.*,) disagree.

[3] *Op. cit.*, p. 191.

[4] Kephala, *op. cit.*, p. 198.

[5] In Mesolora, *op. cit.*, II, p. 140.

[6] The text may not be interpreted figuratively, to mean only the remission of sins, since this latter effect "is added as a new operation (of the Grace) of the sacrament, which the writer contrasts with the preceding one, which must consequently be different from the remission of sins" (Dyobouniotes, *op. cit.*, note 1, p. 192).

[7] Cf. *ibid.*, and references above in the symbolic texts.

[8] Androutsos, *op. cit.*, p. 403.

[9] So Macarius, *op. cit.*, II, p. 561; Athanasius of Paros, Ἐπιτομὴ τῶν Θείων δογμάτων, p. 383; Androutsos, *op. cit.*, p. 404; Dyobouniotes, *op. cit.*, p. 193.

of particular help and blessing. If the Grace conveyed by it does not always work the healing of the body, this must not generally be attributed to the weakness of the faith of the recipient, but in general is consistent with the intention of the Founder, who in establishing this sacrament did not mean to deliver His followers . . . from *all* bodily illness."[1] That healing of body is the chief object of the sacrament is true and certain, yet in the cases where such restoration to health does not ensue upon the use of Unction, we may not attribute it to lack of faith entirely, says Dyobouniotes,[2] for "God knows which is better in a given case, the healing of sickness and restoration to life or the reverse. We must not forget that this sacrament was not given to men by God for our earthly immortality."[3]

Mogila observes that while often the healing of the body may not occur, yet the forgiveness of sins always ensues upon penitence,[4] in the use of this sacrament. Restoration to health follows upon the will of the Lord in any given instance.[5] The forgiveness of sins imparted by this sacrament does not supply or supplant the effects of Penance, nor does it diminish the value of the latter sacrament. "Unction completes the operation of Penance, but not in the sense that Penance is deficient

---

[1] *Op. cit.*, p. 404. But Dyobouniotes (in his 'Η Δογμ. 'Ανδρ. κριν., p. 61) objects, that this violates the terms of the foundation of the sacrament: "is *any* sick among you?", in which it is said generally that "*any* sick person among you" is promised the healing of *all* his ills, not only of certain ones, by unction with oil and the prayer of faith. "We must accept these words literally", says he, and "believe it, even if we cannot understand it completely" ('Οφειλομένη ἀπάντησις, pp. 152-153). Androutsos rejoins that if this were so no Christian would die, and it would follow that if any Christian die, he must have been without faith. Hence we are driven back to the statement that "Christ does not always work the recovery of those who are suffering from physical ills by the sacrament of Unction, as our experience testifies. The reason is not always lack of faith... but the will of the Founder of the sacrament..." (cf. Δογματικαὶ Μελέται, Α', pp. 138-139).

[2] In his treatise, Τὰ Μυστήρια, which seems to be at variance with his former position as presented in the preceding note.

[3] *Op. cit.*, p. 194.

[4] In Mesolora, *op. cit.*, I, p. 434.

[5] Mesolora, *op. cit.*, IV. pp. 361, 354-355.

and needs fulfilling, but because of its conditions (of which confession of sins is one), which often cannot be satisfied on account of illness. So in Unction is bestowed forgiveness of sins in general, and chiefly of those which the sick man is unable, because of his condition, to confess."[1] "The prayer of faith is always heard", says Androutsos, "for forgiveness of sins is conveyed by the sacrament to the sincerely penitent, since bodily infirmities are often the result of sin. With this in view the Orthodox Church joins Unction with Penance . . . as also with Holy Communion. Thus the second fruit of the Grace bestowed in the sacrament of Unction is the remission of our spiritual sickness, sin, the more so because sin is often the cause of our bodily sickness."[2] By the Grace of this sacrament the soul is strengthened to withstand the powers of evil and to fight against the repetition of sins which may have become besetting sins from the frequency of their occurrence. In Orthodox practice the usual order followed is Penance, Unction, and the Holy Communion.[3]

The sacrament of Unction is then not a preparation for death, as the Roman Church teaches[4] (for which the early Church used the Eucharist[5]), but its purpose is the healing of a sick person in body and soul. Consequently any baptized person may rightly have recourse to this sacrament, and may use it as often as is necessary.[6] The Roman view of it distorts its purpose,[7] depreciates its chief object, and promotes to the first place, the secondary end of the sacrament.[8]

---

[1] Dyobouniotes, *op. cit.*, p. 193.

[2] *Op. cit.*, p. 405; cf. Kritopoulos, in Mesolora, *op. cit.*, I. p. 337.

[3] Dyobouniotes, *op. cit.*, p 194.

[4] Dyobouniotes, *op. cit.*, p. 195.

[5] Cf. 13 Can. of 1st Ecumenical Council, and St. Gregory Nyssa, *Epist. ad Letaeon*, 5.

[6] Dyobouniotes, *op. cit.*, pp. 195-196.

[7] *Ibid.*, cf. note 2.

[8] Androutsos, *op. cit.*, p. 406; Mesolora, *op. cit.*, IV. pp. 362-363, 365.

II. THE DOCTRINE OF THE LAST THINGS

The seven sacraments are the channels and means of the Grace flowing from the redemptive work of our Lord, of which the Church is the steward and administrator. As we said above, according to St. Paul's own division[1] there are three stages or steps in the process of the operation of Grace: the *preparation,* including the "call", "conversion", and the like; *justification,* and *sanctification,* including "regeneration"; and the third term, *glory*—the consummation and fulfilment of the working of Grace.[2] This life is the sphere of Grace. The life beyond is its term and completion. "At death men pass on out of the process of development and progress here into a state incapable of change, the final term of their whole life here. The whole world also is to be renewed and perfected in correspondence with man's perfection and glory, since it had both a beginning and a cause, and an end and purpose to which it was ordered, namely, this very perfection and renewal."[3] The last section of dogmatic is concerned with this mysterious verity and is called "eschatology" (since it concerns the *last things*), or "consummation", or "glory".[4] All religious truths have a practical value, and this is especially true of those concerned with the hereafter: the life beyond the grave, as one of happiness and blessedness, is the incentive for man to work for good here, and as a possible state of horror and terror, acts as a deterrent from evil in the life of this world.[5] The content of Orthodox doctrine on these subjects will be presented under the two topics *the Particular Judgment* and *the General Judgment.*

[1] Rom. 8, 30.
[2] Cf. Androutsos, *op. cit.,* pp. 338 ff.
[3] *Ibid.,* p. 407.
[4] Note 1, *ibid.*
[5] *Ibid.,* p. 408.

1. The Particular Judgment

Physical death, the separation of soul and body, is both a punishment and result of sin, and is universal.[1] Nevertheless it loses its fearful aspect for those who are redeemed in Christ,[2] who believe with conviction in the fundamental truth of the immortality of the soul.[3] According to the teaching of the Orthodox Church, death ends man's probation, and immediately after death he is judged. His fate in eternity is determined by his whole moral state at the moment of death.[4] This "whole moral state" on which his future lot depends is not each of his works but the whole result of the deeds and thoughts of his life, that is, his relation and attitude to the Redemption wrought by Christ: whether he accepted it and made it his own; whether he rejected the Grace offered him; or whether, having once accepted it, he fell away from it. In the "particular" or "individual" judgment men are divided into the justified or saved, and the sinners or damned. The ensuing bliss or pangs are relative and proportional, differing each case with the moral state of each individual,[5] and though all the dead are thus judged, they do not receive the full measure either of reward or punishment until the general judgment, at which soul and body are reunited for eternity. This state of the dead, from the time of departure from the world until the General Judgment, is called the "intermediate state". During this time the soul is apart from the body, but has consciousness and exercises its own energies, for the word "sleep"[6] applies only to the body.[7] This doctrine is declared in the *Confession* of Dositheus (and so embodied in the *Acts* of the Synod of Constantinople, 1672), as follows: "We believe that the souls of the departed are in either repose or torment as each one wrought, for immediately after the separation from the body they are pronounced either for bliss or for suffering and sorrow, yet we confess that neither the joy nor the

[1] Cf. Lecture III, pp. 170-171.
[2] Androutsos, *op. cit.*, p. 164.
[3] Cf. p. 161 of these Lectures, and Androutsos, *op. cit.*, pp. 408-409.
[4] Androutsos, *ibid.*, p. 409.
[5] Androutsos, *op. cit.*, p. 410.
[6] *E. g.*, 1 Cor. 15, 51.
[7] Androutsos, *ibid.*, p. 411.

condemnation are as yet complete. After the general resurrection, when the soul is united to the body, each one will receive the full measure of joy or condemnation due to him for the way in which he conducted himself, whether well or ill."[1]

The doctrine of the Particular Judgment is based upon Holy Scripture and Sacred Tradition, as are all the dogmas of the Faith. Holy Writ distinguishes two states of the soul: that after death, and that after the General Judgment. Some of the Apostles and early Christians overlooked the intermediate state in their expectation of the immediate Coming of our Lord. "This mistake is attributable to the fact that our Lord revealed His Coming to no one."[2] So they confused the two, regarding the judgment after the resurrection as taking place in general after death. 2 Cor. 5, 10, explicitly teaches a general judgment by Christ, in which each man is rewarded according to his deeds in the body, and in St. Matt. 16, 27; 25, 37, this is associated with our Lord's Second Coming. Heb. 9, 27, refers not to the Particular but to the General Judgment, without specifying the time, except to state that it is after death. From the context we understand that this Judgment is connected with the Second Coming.[3] By a logical inference from the words of Holy Scripture we are compelled to acknowledge the truth of the Particular Judgment. "If souls passing out from the world are not judged by God, then they do one of two things: await impassively the general Judgment, or perfect themselves in the development of their own individual spiritual states. . . According to the first theory, the intermediate interval is a time either of rest or slumber, or of uneasy expectation—sorrowful alike for both righteous and sinful souls. According to the second, . . . it is a continuation of the present (condition) and there is no difference between the state of the soul there and here . . . except the absence of the body. Both these hypotheses are contrary to the teaching of Holy Scripture." The parable of the Rich Man and Lazarus teaches definitely that "of the souls passing from this

[1] In Mesolora, op. cit., II, p. 119.
[2] Androutsos, op. cit., p. 411; cf. St. Mark 13, 32; Act 1, 6, 7; and Androutsos, ibid., pp. 437-438.
[3] Androutsos, op. cit., p. 412.

world, the righteous go to the presence of God,' and the sinners to a place of torment." This is implied also in Phil. 1, 21, 23, and in the Church's conviction that "the Saints are glorified and blessed in Heaven."[1] That this world is different from the world to come in being the sphere (lit. "arena") of Grace, on which depends the state of the future life, and that the lot of man after death is fixed and permanent, is clear from Holy Scripture.[2] Death is the term limiting the moral energy of man, and the present life is the probation and testing on which depends the eternal destiny of the individual.

The Fathers, with a few exceptions,[3] taught a distinction between the condition of the righteous and the sinners—in fact, "that a special judgment of each individual takes place immediately after death."[4] This is implicit, for example, in St. Cyril's doctrine of the evil spirits.[5] In condemning the Universalism of Origen, the Church was governed by the premise that the state of the soul at the end of the life here is fixed and unalterable.[6] Not only did the Church condemn the notion of a development or progress after death, but also the theory of the "sleep of the soul".[7] These speculations—and others like them on the problem of the state of the unbaptized heathen, of unbaptized infants, of those cut off before having the opportu-

---

[1] *Ibid.*, pp. 412-413. In note 2 he says that the mention of the Saints' names in the Liturgies "is not made by the Church for expiation of their sins, as if they were not justified or already in bliss, but the Church gives thanks to the Saviour for His Grace in the saints... and in making memorial of them beseeches the Lord to hearken to their prayers for all men, both the quick and the dead...As St. Cyril of Jerusalem explains it:..."that God by their prayers and intercessions may receive our prayer" (*Catechet. Mystagog.* V. 9; cf. St. John Chrysostom, on Acts, *Homily* 21, 4) and St. Augustine; *cum martyres recitantur ad altare Dei, non pro ipsis oratur; injuria est enim pro martyre orare, cujus nos debemus orationibus commendari* (*Sermo* 159)."

[2] For references, cf. notes 1 and 2, p. 414 *op. cit.*

[3] As *e. g.*, St. Justin, Tertullian, and Origen.

[4] Androutsos, *op. cit.*, p. 414.

[5] Cf. his περὶ ἐξόδου ψυχῆς.

[6] Androutsos, *ibid.*, p. 415.

[7] This developed chiefly in Semitic-Christian circles; cf. Eusebius H E VI. 37, and *The Sleep of the Soul in the early Syriac Church*, F. Gavin, JAOS, April 1920, pp. 103-120.

nity to develop and grow spiritually in this life—are, to say the least, hazardous. Every such theological theory, says Androutsos, "must be based on clear and unmistakable passages of Holy Writ, must be self-consistent, and neither in itself nor in its corollaries may it in any degree run counter to the formulated dogmas of the Church. The hypotheses and attempts . . . by which certain theologians force the meaning of scriptural texts by trying to penetrate into the province of the unknown or to render the mysterious and hidden accessible to our minds, and in satisfying human curiosity and the thirst for the knowledge of the occult and secret, must not find their way into Orthodox dogmatic, which holds firmly to the positive and defined field of Revelation."[1]

The two-fold state as fixed by the Particular Judgment, whether for weal or woe, is an anticipation of the verdict of the General Judgment. But the cases of any two individual souls could not be exactly alike, since each life has been ordered differently from every other. Inasmuch as justification and sanctification are neither mechanical processes nor forensic pronouncements, the state of each person, as in life so after death, is different from that of every other. Hence "the Orthodox conception of justification demands various grades in the intermediate state . . . and the state after death is without doubt analogous to the moral state of each individual."[2] Holy Scripture is neither detailed nor definite as to the form of the bliss or pangs of the intermediate stage, or as to the distinction between the Particular and the General Judgment. The various figurative and symbolic terms used[3] do not give us definite information. From them "at the most we ascertain that the blessedness of the righteous and the misery of the sinners is not only something inward—a peace or remorse of conscience—but is also determined by external goods or torments."[4]

From the standpoint of our present limitations we are naturally unable to distinguish between the state of the soul at the Particular Judgment and at the General, except by char-

---

[1] Androutsos, *op. cit.*, p. 416.
[2] *Ibid.*, p. 417.
[3] For references cf. Androutsos, *ad. loc.*
[4] *Ibid.*, p. 418.

acterizing one as incomplete and the other as complete. Two
extremes are to be avoided—one, of exalting the General Judgment at the expense of the Particular Judgment, and the reverse. As an instance of a too great emphasis on the Particular Judgment to be the detriment of the truth of the General
Judgment, may be taken the teaching and practice of the Roman Church, which really makes the General Judgment superfluous.[1] It is contrary to patristic teaching, which did not regard the Saints as having fully attained their reward, and held
that this would only be consummated at the Last Judgment.[2]
Various hyperbolic expressions of certain Fathers in oratorical
and eulogistic style, with much said, as it were, proleptically,
cannot in this matter be construed to mean that the Saints
are now in complete enjoyment of their reward. In dogmatic
treatises by these same Fathers may be found explicitly the
doctrine that "the righteous enjoy eternal joys in advance,
but for the full enjoyment of them must await the General
Resurrection."[3] This is clearly illustrated in the cases of St.
Gregory Nazianzen and St. Photius, both of whom in oratorical and panegyric discourses spoke in ways which allow of an
interpretation forbidden by their dogmatic teaching.[4]

According to the teaching of the Orthodox Church, death
does not dissolve the bond of union between the members of the
Church.[5] The Church is conceived of as of two great sections,
the Church Militant and the Church Triumphant, but in a
sense also includes a third division, the Church of Repentance.[6]
Death serves but to establish a "mutual relation of the living
with the members of the Church Triumphant, the Saints, that
is, all who having departed in faith and love . . . enjoy the

---

[1] Cf. Androutsos, Συμβολική, pp. 339 ff. The whole Roman system
is contrary to Orthodox teaching, as is clear from what was said above
on the doctrine of works of supererogation, the superabundant merits
of the Saints, etc.

[2] Androutsos, Δογματική, p. 419.

[3] *Ibid.*, p. 420, and cf. notes.

[4] *Ibid.*, pp. 420, 421, and notes *ad loc.*

[5] *Ibid.*, p. 421.

[6] As Androutsos' treatment of the subject matter would seem to
imply. § 69 is on "the Relation of the Church Militant to the Church
Triumphant" and § 70 on "the Relation of the Church Militant to the
Sinners" (pp. 421-426, 426-437, *ibid.*).

glory of God and taste in advance eternal blessedness."[1] With
the Saints are included the Angels, who likewise possess the enjoyment of the Lord. Both Angels and Saints intercede for
the living, by so doing showing their concern for and fellowship with them, and the living in turn hold communion with
them by asking their prayers and "venerating them as models
of the perfect Christian life and virtue." This doctrine is
not explicitly taught by Holy Scripture. Yet we are told that
the Angels intercede for the living before God, and "if they,
how much more the Saints, who are so much nearer us by
reason of their oneness with our nature?" If our prayers for
each other are both reasonable and useful, why should death
bring about an intermittance of the interest, care, and concern
of the best of our race in relation to the rest of us? In 2 Macc.
15, 12, Judas Maccabaeus saw in a dream Onias and Jeremiah
interceding for the people.[2] "The Saints then do intercede
not only for the whole Church, but for individual persons."
If the Angels of God "rejoice over one sinner that repenteth"
how much more do the Saints? If a finite Angel know of
the individual case in a way which is not comprehensible to us,
there is nothing which would suggest that the Saints, though
they be human beings, should be precluded from having this
same intimate knowledge of our needs and circumstances.
There is no question, in the case of the intercessions of the
Saints, of any impairment to, or diminution of, the Intercessory Office or Merit of Christ. Since prayer for others by living people is both reasonable and right, and is always considered useful and beneficial, without any detriment to the
Intercession of the Great High Priest, there is certainly nothing derogatory to His Office as the One Mediator, in the doctrine of the Communion and Intercession of the Saints.[3]

Kritopoulos uses as an illustration the growth in means of
knowledge among men, whereby they had come to know "what
is going on in America and in Ethiopia,"[4] and says: "The
Saints must have some means of knowing what is happening at

---

[1] *Ibid.*, p. 422.
[2] *Ibid.*, p. 422.
[3] Androutsos, *op. cit.*, p. 423.
[4] In Mesolora, *op. cit.*, I, p. 344.

a distance, otherwise they would be less than us in that respect, . . . and this is . . . the revelation by the All-holy
Spirit, everywhere present and ignorant of nothing . . .
who makes known as He wills, what the needs of men are". .

"We do not say to a saint, "Saint *N.*, save, or redeem, or see
that I obtain such and such goods' . . . but 'Saint *N.*, pray
for us' . . . Nor do we call the Saints 'Mediators,' for there
is only one Mediator between God and man, . . . Jesus
Christ, who only is able to mediate between the Father and
us. . . Not as mediators do we call upon the Saints, but
as intercessors . . . before God for us, who are our brethren. . . . "[1] "The Holy Spirit makes known to them the needs
of those who invoke them . . . and they intercede saying,
'not in our own deeds or merits—for we have nothing worthy in
Thy sight—but in the deeds and merits of thy Only-Begotten
Son, . . . do we pray to Thy Majesty, O Thou Most High God'
. . . Whence the Church asks nothing more from the Saints
than that they intercede to God for us and beseech Him for all
things needful to us."[3]

"The Church Triumphant, which cannot be insensible to
the needs and sufferings of the Church Militant on earth, . . .
as if immersed in sleep, drugged by a narcotic,"[4] is related to
the Church on earth in "this bond of love which never may be
severed and which those who are perfected preserve for those
who are left on earth as they did in life."[5] This relationship
the Church on earth expresses in three ways—by the invocation of the Saints, the veneration of holy ikons, and of the
relics of the Saints.[6] Inasmuch as the intercession of the
Saints does not violate the Mediatorship of Christ, "it follows
that we are justified in invoking their intercession, as being
both reasonable and useful."[7] The Church bears witness to
the practice in the writings of the Fathers and in the Litur-

---

[1] *Ibid.*, p. 345.
[e] *Ibid.*, p. 344.
[3] *Ibid.*, p. 346.
[4] *Ibid.*, p. 344.
[5] Mesolora, *op. cit.*, IV. p. 411.
[6] Kritopoulos, in Mesolora, *op. cit.*, I. p. 340.
[7] Androutsos, *op. cit.*, p. 423.

gies,[1] and condemned the opposite view of the Eustathians in the synod of Gangra.[2] Of the Saints, the Church particularly asks the prayers of the Mother of God addressed "to Him whom she bore", and honors her above others, "since she was marked out by God for this great and distinguished function."[3] Yet, as Kritopoulos says, she was not without original sin,[4] though "she received the special gift from God enabling her to have lived without the commission of any actual sin. God bestowed upon her the great and wonderful gift of being sinless."[5] Mesolora says of the Invocation of Saints: "There is in mankind a sense and reverence for moral greatness" (which finds expression in the veneration of the Saints). ". . . If the Saints are before God in glory, and live in Him, having attained honor from Him, how ought not we, who are less than they, give them honor and reverence, and invoke their help and intercession before God, who rejoice in His glory and in the Vision of Him?"[6] Jeremiah points out that the memorial of the Saints strengthens our faith, and that our invocation of them, though relative and different from our prayer to God, is both useful and valuable.[7] Dositheus is even more explicit in the phrasing of this doctrine, since, says he, the Saints in their enjoyment of the Beatific Vision see our needs the more clearly, and are in a position the better to help us by their intercession, as in glory and honor before God.[8] "The benefit accruing to the believer from honoring and invoking the Saints", concludes Mesolora, "is the greatest: he is brought into the circle of the Elect of God, and is made greater than

---

[1] Cf. *ibid.*, note 2, pp. 413-414.

[2] *Ibid.*, p. 424, note 1. Canon 20 of the acts of Gangra anathematizes those who refuse to assist at the *synaxes* of the Martyrs, their memorials, etc.; cf. St. Jerome's *contra Vigilantium*. The latter maintained that the Saints before the General Resurrection were not in Heaven, and consequently could not know of the requests of men to them for their intercession.

[3] Mesolora, *op. cit.*, IV. p. 412.

[4] He refutes at some length the Roman doctrine of the Immaculate Conception, cf. Mesolora, *op. cit.*, I. pp. 346-347.

[5] *Ibid.*, p. 347.

[6] *Op. cit.*, IV. p. 414.

[7] Cf. Mesolora, *op. cit.*, I, p. 181.

[8] *Ibid.*, II. p. 107.

himself through his converse with them; he is strengthened and invigorated in the accomplishment of good works; his faith toward God is made strong, in Him as the one who crowns those who do the good; finally, his desire is aroused for union with the Saints, that the Church Triumphant in Heaven may be increased."[1]

The honor and reverence paid to the Saints, as persons eminent in the struggle for faith and in virtue, who have been deemed worthy of glory and blessedness, is distinguished from that given only to God. The ecclesiastical terms, however, προσκύνησις and λατρεία ("worship"), are not always restricted in actual usage to their legitimate reference to God alone, but are sometimes used of the "veneration" and "reverence" given to the Saints. Nevertheless the distinction between "worship" and "veneration" remains clearly marked. It is shown in the keeping of the Feasts of the Saints, in the veneration of ikons and of the holy relics, as well as in the Invocation of Saints.[2]   Of the Feast-days of the Saints, Mesolora says that they "were kept of old by the Church, not only to excite the faithful to emulate their lives and works, but also to express the intimate bond between the Church Militant and Triumphant.   In these Feasts . . . is manifested the true and dynamic power of the Christian Faith which through the Saints conquered the world."[3] "We keep their Feast-days", says Jeremiah II, in his first *Answer,* "honoring them as the friends of God."[4]   Yet the Church never confuses the veneration of the Saints with the worship due to God alone, for "distinguishing these carefully, she still accords to the Saints great honor, as her martyrologies, the inscriptions in the Catacombs, the Liturgies, and the doctrine of the Fathers, show."[5]   Furthermore, no passage in Holy Writ can be adduced against the veneration of ikons and relics.[6] The Church very early placed relics in the altars[7] and gave

[1] Mesolora, *op. cit.,* IV. pp. 414-415.

[2] Androutsos, *op. cit.,* p. 424.

[3] *Op. cit.,* IV. pp. 432-433, *q. v.* (pp. ff.) for an extended treatment of the subject; cf. also Dositheus, *ibid.,* II. p. 122.

[4] In Mesolora, *op. cit.,* I, p. 168.

[5] Androutsos, *op. cit.,* p. 425.

[6] Cf. notes, *ibid.*

[7] *Ibid.,* for references.

them great honor. Many Fathers spoke of the miracles wrought by the relics of the Saints.[1] Neither practice may be stigmatized as idolatry, as St. Augustine and the VII Council prove. "The veneration of ikons and relics is relative only, and is referred not to the things in themselves but in relation to the persons to whom the reverence is being offered. . . Thus faith is elicited, and the desire for the imitation of these examples of the Christian life is stimulated."[2]

The Church Militant has a further relation to "those who have departed from this world with the stains of sin, yet in the Faith and Communion of the Church."[3] The exact bounds of this relationship, and the conception of the state of such persons and of their condition before the General Judgment do not seem to be very clear from current Orthodox teaching. The determining factors in defining the conformation of such doctrine have been a dislike of Roman teaching and a reluctance to be precise where there is no explicit revelation. In the main, it may be stated that the vagueness of teaching of the early Church developed into fairly definite form in the Symbolic Books. The teaching not fully expounded in these sources subsequent theologians have preferred either to leave more or less undeveloped and uncorrelated, as, for example, Androutsos, or have engaged to elucidate, by expounding the implications and developing them through reverent theological speculation, as, for example, Macarius and Dybouniotes. Before examining the evidence of the Symbolic Books, certain of the chief aspects of the problem may well be presented.

Holy Scripture nowhere explicitly enjoins prayers for the dead.[4] In 2 Mac. 12, 43 Judas made "a sin offering for the

---

[1] *Ibid.*

[2] Androutsos, *ibid.*, p. 426. Mogila (Mesolora, *op. cit.*, I. pp. 340-343) devotes two chapters to the subject; Mesolora (*op. cit.*, IV. pp. 418-428) two whole sections *q. v.* for fuller treatment and references. Dositheus is also most explicit and detailed. cf. in Mesolora, *op. cit.*, II. p. 107, and pp. 128-129.

[3] Androutsos, *op. cit.*, p. 427.

[4] Though Macarius, *op. cit.*, II. pp. 710, ff. attempts to base the practice on the precarious foundation of such texts as St. Jas. 5, 16; 1 Tim. 2, 1; 1 St. John 5, 16, etc. For a refutation of these views cf. Androutsos, *ibid.*, note 1, pp. 427-428.

dead", "which is the first very early witness to such memorials."[1] Yet all the Liturgies, the practice of the early Church, and the writings of the Fathers demonstrate clearly the belief that "through charitable works, the prayers of the Church, and the Holy Eucharist, help and comfort are afforded to those who have died in the Faith."[2] Such good works and prayers however, are of no avail to the entirely evil or to the incorrigible. It is manifestly difficult to discern the principle guiding such devotional practices and regulating the relation of the assistance and help thereby afforded the souls of the departed, to the truth of the Particular Judgment. If by the good offices of the Church on earth comfort and help are given to such souls, it may not be understood to imply a change in their state, for this would violate the verdict already passed on the soul in the Particular Judgment. To reconcile the two—the benefit given the souls by the Church's prayers, and the final and irrevocable character of the Particular Judgment—two views are advanced: (a) the souls are punished only for a time for their deeds in this life, or (b) the souls are perfected in the exercise of moral qualities which, as it were, lay dormant and in germ in their life on earth. According to the first theory the Church's efforts result in a diminution or removal of punishment; according to the second, the souls are capable of Grace and satisfy the conditions necessary for the saving work of prayer and the offering of the Holy Sacrifice.[3] Both speculations, according to Androutsos, are inacceptable. The first leads to the Roman teaching about Purgatory, and involves the two ancillary doctrines of the superabounding merits of the Saints and of works of supererogation. As was shown above, this is all quite impossible in Orthodox theology. The Roman teaching further implies the doctrine of penances as satisfactions rather than as medicines, for sin. It impugns the doctrine of the Grace of Penance as sufficient and complete.[4] The second theory is likewise "inacceptable, . . . as inexorably in-

---

[1] Androutsos, *ibid.*, p. 427.

[2] *Ibid.*, p. 428.

[3] Androutsos, *op. cit.*, p. 429.

[4] Cf. *ibid.*, p. 430; pp. 385 ff., and his Συμβολική, pp. 320 ff.

volving a violation of the doctrine of the Particular Judgment."[1]

The theory that there is a place for the moral and spiritual
development of those who have died in the faith of the Church
but still with the stain of sin upon them, presents certain real
difficulties, says Androutsos. In the first place, it is hard to
see why this development should be restricted to those souls
only which had a certain moral endowment here, and should not
be extended to all sinners alike. It is an arbitrary limitation,
he says, since the soul is not inactive after death but may develop
and perfect itself (according to this theory). It involves the
notion that the gate of penitence is open even after death, and
that the possibility of conversion is still offered to the soul. "If
we confine this development to the repentant only," says Androutsos, "then we do not take repentance in the same sense as
they, and this theory contradicts the dogma of the Particular
Judgment . . . For if, according to Orthodox teaching, the
departing soul truly and really repents . . . (and makes confession), this repentance (μετάνοια) is a full and complete remission of sins . . . which justifies and saves the person. If
the person did not succeed in repenting, he then naturally does
not belong to those for whom the Church's prayers are offered."[2]
What this theory really comes to, says Androutsos, is this, that
"besides the unrepentant and hardened sinners there are other
souls distinguished from them, who are stained with sin and
may not enter either into the Kingdom of Heaven or into everlasting punishment." But according to Orthodox teaching, penitence and confession secure a full and perfect remission of sins
and a restoration of the baptismal state of innocence. In this
state one is justified and saved without the performance or satisfaction of any additional remaining penances or penalties,
"for there is no room in the Orthodox system for expiatory punishments."[3] This theory then is contrary to the dogma of the
Particular Judgment and the involved truth that there is no
place for repentance beyond the grave. "The acceptance of this
theory of perfection depreciates the moral value of the life here,

---

[1] Δογματική, p. 431.
[2] Ibid., p. 431.
[3] Op. cit., p. 432.

fosters the adjournment of reformation and amendment to the life beyond the grave, and destroys the view of Heaven and Hell . . . on which Christians rest their belief."[1]

Before examining further the interpretation of the practice of the Orthodox Church of praying for the dead, it may be well to indicate the teaching on this subject of the Symbolic Books. Jeremiah II speaks of almsgiving and the offering of the Holy Sacrifice for the dead, as being "useful to them", "affording them needed help", "as giving them assistance", and "as being a benefit and gain to them".[2] Chapter 20 of Kritopoulos' *Confession* is devoted to this topic. He refers to the teaching of the Fathers on the subject[3] and then says: "Two things are especially to be noticed: . . . one, that certain persons immediately after death attain converse with Christ; . . . the other, that others do not attain to the operation of salvation immediately after death except potentially, and receive it in hope. But it is in a sure and certain hope—for having first experienced the fatherly correction of God they are then made worthy in time of actually laying hold of salvation. The Church, knowing this, . . . discovered the way to show them kindness, which is to offer up prayers and intercessions to God for them that one of two things may occur—either that they may speedily find relief from the miseries which encompass them, or that rest and consolation from God may be given them in their prison." Kritopoulos is quite explicit in denying that these agonies and pangs are physical or material, and says that they are "afflictions and sorrows of conscience, the torment of remorse" for sins committed in life.[4] As to the term of confinement or the time of release, nothing may be defined. There is no "purgatorial fire" but only the torment of conscience—yet not without hope—which will endure so long as God wills it to.[5]

Mogila expounds the doctrine of the Particular Judgment clearly and definitely, saying that each knows his lot immedi-

[1] *Ibid.*, p. 433.
[2] In Mesolora, *op. cit.*, I, pp. 154-155; cf. also pp. 166-167, *ibid.*
[3] *Ibid.*, pp. 352-353.
[4] *Ibid.*, pp. 353-354.
[5] *Ibid.*, p. 354.

ately after death—the righteous, the bliss in store, and the sinner, his torment to come. "But neither righteous nor sinners receive their full reward before the Last Judgment, nor are they sent to the same place. Yet the Particular Judgment must needs be", in order that this separation may take place.[1] He proceeds to state the fact of the different steps or degrees in blessedness or punishment.[2] In answer to the questions[3] about the state of men who die and yet are neither of the saved or lost, he says: "There are none of such a sort. Yet certainly many of the sinners are delivered from the bonds of hell, yet not by their own penitence or confession . . . but by the good works of the living, the prayers of the Church, and the Bloodless Sacrifice which the Church offers daily for all, both quick and dead—since Christ died for all. They are not freed by their own efforts, as Theophylact says on St. Luke 6,[4] commenting on the words of Christ (where He says "that the Son of man hath power on earth to forgive sins") : 'Notice, it is *on earth* that sins are forgiven. So long as we are on earth we can blot out our sins; after we have departed from the earth we are no longer able to blot them out by confession, for the door is shut'. And on St. Matthew 21,[5] interpreting the words 'Bind him hand and foot' to mean the practical powers of the soul, he says: 'In this world it is possible to do and practise, but in the world to come, all the practical powers of the soul are bound, and it is not possible to do anything as reparation for sin'. From which words it is apparent that after death the soul cannot be freed, nor can it repent, nor can it do any work to redeem itself from the bondage of hell; the Holy Liturgy only, and the prayers and alms deeds which are done for it by the living, these help it very greatly, and free it from the bonds of hell."[6] In answering the next question[7] he quotes Theophylact again, on St. Luke 12, 5, who distinguishes be-

[1] *Ibid.*, p. 407.
[2] *Ibid.*, p. 408.
[3] (No. 63).
[4] This should be 5. The citation is from St. Luke 5, 24.
[5] Vs. 13.
[6] *Ibid.*, pp. 408-409.
[7] "What should we think about alms deeds and good works done in behalf of the dead?" (no. 65.)

tween "the *power* to cast into hell" and the *excercise* of that power. God who has the power to condemn has the power to forgive. "This I say of the oblations and offerings made for the dead, that they help, not a little, even those who have died in grievous sin. For He does not call all into hell whom He has slain, though He has the power to do so." By good offices wrought for the dead we can propitiate Him to stay the exercise of this power, and forgive them. We can do these for the dead, giving them a very real help, and thereby do for them what they are incapable of doing for themselves.[1] The theory of the fire of Purgatory is not mentioned in Holy Scripture, nor any temporal punishment purifying the soul after death.[2] Since the soul can receive no sacraments, the Church offers for it the Bloodless Sacrifice and prayers, asking forgiveness of its sins. It cannot of itself repent or secure forgiveness.[3]

Dositheus is even more explicit. After a brief statement of the doctrine of the Particular and the General Judgments,[4] he discusses the condition of those who had committed mortal sins for which they had repented, yet had not had space to show forth the fruit of repentance in this life. "Such souls go to hell for a time and remain there to work off the punishment due for these sins. They are conscious of coming deliverance from that condition, and are freed by the Sublime Goodness because of the prayers of the priests and the good works which their relatives perform for them. Of the greatest efficacy is the offering of the Bloodless Sacrifice which the . . . Church . . . makes daily. We may not know the time of their deliverance: that they are freed from these afflictions we know and believe, but as to when this takes place, we are ignorant."[5]

In one sense, suggested in the above texts, the good deeds done for the departed are done as it were by himself, since before death he may leave instructions for the performance of certain good works, the giving of certain alms, and the like.[6]

[1] *Ibid.*, p. 409.
[2] *Ibid.*, question 66.
[3] *Ibid.*, p. 410.
[4] *Ibid.*, II. p. 119.
[5] *Ibid.*, p. 120.
[6] Cf. Jeremiah II, above, in Mesolora, *op. cit.*, I, p. 155 *et al.*

These good works include primarily the memorial of the dead by name in the Oblation of the Holy Sacrifice, memorials on the various days connected with the departed,[1] almsdeeds in memory of the dead, and the offering of the *collybes*. This custom of offering roasted grain in connection with the memorials of the departed has a double significance. It is a reminder of the miracle wrought by the Martyr St. Theodore under Julian the Apostate (362), when the Christians ate grain for a whole day because the meats vended in the markets were polluted by the blood of the idol sacrifices, and also a representation and foreshadowing of the Resurrection of the Dead, according to the parable of St. John 12, 24. Such grain offered at this time is "one form of charity toward the poor, for the pardon of the souls of the departed."[2] The general practice of the Church takes varied forms and is very interesting from the historical point of view.[3] Mesolora[4] thus summarizes the doctrines involved: "We do these things believing that God will forgive the sins of the departed, 'not in our own righteousness' nor by reason of any return payment of Grace nor by offering money, but by the righteousness, the Grace, and loving-kindness of Him, these prayers and Liturgies become acceptable and well pleasing to the Glory of God and (avail) for the benefit of the soul, for the 'prayer of a righteous man availeth much in its working,' among the faithful and those worthy of Divine Grace."[5]

From the above quotations the evidence offered by the Symbolic Books may be thus summarized: Jeremiah states that the prayers of the Church and the good works done by her in behalf of the dead, help and benefit the departed, and implies the possible interpretation that such good deeds are, by a kind of extension, done by the person himself by deputy. He does not

---

[1] Cf. Kritopoulos, *ibid.*, p. 353 for a list of such days.

[2] Mesolora, *op. cit.*, IV. note 2, p. 397.

[3] On the subject, historically and doctrinally, Nectarius Kephala, Metropolitan of Pentapolis, wrote an interesting work: Μελέτη περὶ ἀθανασίας τῆς ψυχῆς καὶ περὶ τῶν ἱερῶν μνημοσύνων, Athens, 1901, especially pp. 104-158.

[4] Cf. his whole section devoted to the subject, *op. cit.*, IV, p. 395-399.

[5] *Ibid.*, p. 399.

attempt to explain how they are thus helped. Kritopoulos divides those who depart in the Faith (excluding from further mention those certainly damned), into the classes of the already perfected and those potentially saved, which latter are greatly helped by the Church's good offices. He specifies that the torments and afflictions of the latter are subjective and are of the nature of remorse of conscience and regret. Mogila holds fast to the doctrine of the probationary character of the life here and of the final and irrevocable fixing of the state of the soul by death. Yet he admits that certain souls are released from hell by the good works and prayers of the Church, which stay the hand of God from condemning the soul of the sinner, and by means of the merits of Christ interpose to redeem from the pangs of hell a soul which would otherwise be damned. The souls of the departed are themselves helpless and incapable of any effort to assist themselves. The Church may do for them what they cannot do for themselves. Dositheus seems clearly to imply a doctrine of Purgatory, which is apparently otherwise not met with in Orthodox thought. He seems to consider punishment for a time as in the nature of expiation and satisfaction for sins committed in the flesh. Such punishment is only temporary and is in some way alleviated by the work of the Church. All the Symbolic Books unite in teaching the doctrine of the Particular and of the General Judgment. All of them hold clearly the Orthodox doctrine that no self-initiated repentance is possible after death, and that death closes the door to a voluntary change of attitude towards God. Dositheus alone seems to imply the expiatory character of temporal chastisement inflicted on the soul after death, which is also implicit in a lesser measure in Kritopoulos. It is clear, then, that such teaching stands in need of interpretation and correlation, if it is to become consistent and unified. This has been the task of theologians subsequent to the time of the Symbolic Books.

At this point the facts suggest a comment which may not be out of place here. The progress and development of Orthodox teaching on the subject of the state of the departed apparently betrays the tendencies which would lead to a modified doctrine of Purgatory. The principle so often operative in conditioning the form of later Orthodox teaching seems here again to be in force: by reaction against Roman doctrine, Orthodox theologians have gone, as it were by instinct, as far as possible in a different direction. This has been apparent at many points in these Lectures. For example, we noticed that Dyobouniotes contended that the Orthodox theory of justification *could* not be the same as that of the Roman Church. Similarly, much of the Orthodox opposition to the term *transubstantiation* is due entirely to a reaction against the Roman use of the word, but not, as was pointed out, to the intrinsic doctrine involved in it. So in this case the prinicple which seems to have controlled the form (or the "formlessness"!) of later Orthodox teaching on the state of the departed, seems to be a violent reaction against the Roman doctrine of Purgatory—not on the basis of its intrinsic character so much as of its origin and its advocates—joined with a powerful reluctance inhibiting agreement with Rome on the subject. This repugnance to Roman teaching is clearly manifested in this matter: Dositheus' teaching *is* the Roman doctrine of Purgatory, yet without all the corollaries involved in the latter, and without the terminology. The term "Intermediate State" in Orthodox usage does not mean the state of the departed who are not good enough for heaven or bad enough for hell, but the state of all the departed, saint and sinner alike, from death to the Last Judgment. As we have seen, when the theologian delves more deeply into the question, three categories of persons are immediately discerned: the Saints, those who have attained perfection in this life; the sinners, the reprobate, unrepentant and incorrigible, who are damned to hell; and those who are imperfect penitents and potential saints, who stand in need of further purgation and development before being fit for heaven. In general the Orthodox repudiate a third *place* for the latter class. The Saints are in the hands of the Father; the damned in a place of torment; what of the imperfectly penitent? The Symbolic Books would seem to give them a term in hell, for purgation and expiation, and then admit them to blessedness. In this connection Androutsos says: "In general, Orthodox theologians repudiate unnecessary distinctions (such as the Latin *limbus puerorum, limbus patrum,* and the like), and not only these, but also that of a third or middle place between Paradise and Hell—the place or state of those who have not committed mortal sins and are not reprobate. Even though this distinction of itself is not devoid of truth (since the Orthodox theologians too distinguish between the Lost and those who are to be delivered from Hell), yet, on account of (the doctrine of) purgatorial fire with which this intermediate state is presented by Papist theologians, this theory is always strongly rejected by the Orthodox."[1] Androutsos, it may be noted, in lending even this little support to the doctrine of a "third or middle place", laid himself open to a sharp attack by Dyobouniotes,[2] and in his defense carefully disavowed any attempt to teach it.[3]

Modern theological opinion is divided on the questions of the state of the departed and on the relation of the prayers of the Church to them. Mesolora, as we have seen, held that the dead could receive forgiveness of sins by means of the good works and prayers of the Church. This implies that such souls had not received forgiveness in this life, and that they are capable of receiving it hereafter. The two great difficulties are these: If no progress or development is possible after death, how may any change occur in the state of the departed, and how may prayers assist or benefit the dead? If a progress or development is possible, then the verdict of the Particular Judgment is not final, and the life here is not what it is taught to be: the one and only place of probation, terminating with death. As we saw above, Mogila, for example, denied the possibility of development, yet allowed that of deliverance from hell. Subjective change is therefore impossible, but the Church's prayers may work a change in the soul's condition without its own initiation or coöperation. Kritopoulos and Dositheus both recognize the finality of the verdict of the Particular Judgment, but postpone its fulfilment (in the case of the imperfectly peni-

---

[1] *Op. cit.*, note 2, pp. 435-436.

[2] Ἡ Δογμ. ᾿Ανδρ. κριν., p. 63; ᾿Οφειλ. ἀπάντησις, pp. 156-159.

[3] Δογματικαὶ Μελέται Α´, pp. 132-133. He draws attention to the fact that Dyobouniotes himself had been driven practically to the recognition of a third place in acknowledging a distinction between the "higher" and the "lower" Paradise". Cf. Dyobouniotes, Ἡ μέση κατάστασις τῶν ψυχῶν, pp. 69-70: "The lower Paradise may well be in Heaven and at the same time belong to Hell."

tent), until these have been purged and chastised for a time. In view of the dilemma suggested above Androutsos says: "These prayers (for the dead) must be defined negatively within the limits in which the early Church determined them, excluding all theological speculation as to the manner or character of the 'relief' they afford the departed."[1]   The sufferings they undergo may not be thought to be expiatory, nor may it be held that the prayers of the Church dispense from certain of such sufferings.   They are, however, beneficial to the departed, as we believe.   The manner of the operation of such help and benefit is inscrutable, as is the whole larger question of answers to prayer.   These prayers, like all others, are subject to the laws and conditions of prayer in general; hence the limitation made by the Fathers as to the subjects of such intercession—those who have repented imperfectly, and not those who have sinned mortally—is reasonable and logical.[2]   "These prayers express the full fellowship of love on the part of the living with the departed, for death but changes location, and does not sever the bond of . . . love."[3]   Any attempt to fill the void in our knowledge by speculation about a third place for souls, or by the theory of the fire of Purgatory,[4] or the temporal character of punishments, are "efforts simply of human curiosity, since they serve no religious ends."[5]   Since we do not know who are lost and who have not sinned to the death, the prayers of the Church are made for all.[6]   "The general intercession for all the departed . . . is the expression of the communion between the living and the dead."[7]

On the contrary, Macarius and Dyobouniotes both hold to some sort of development and progress beyond the grave, which is assisted and promoted by the good works and prayers of the Church.   Says Macarius: "Our prayers are offered for those who have died in the true Faith and in true repentance. Since they departed in the Communion of the Church, they

---

[1] *Op. cit.,* p. 433.

[2] *Ibid.,* p. 434.

[3] *Ibid.,* p. 435.

[4] Cf. Mesolora on Purgatory, *op. cit.,* IV, pp. 105-117.

[5] Androutsos, *op. cit.,* p. 435.

[6] *Ibid.,* p. 436.

[7] *Ibid.,* p. 437.

have in them the beginnings of good, and the germ of the new life which they had not time to develop here. Under the influence of our fervent prayers by means of the offering of the Holy Liturgy, they are enabled gradually to develop and bring to fruition what they had here only in germ, just as a good seed grows on earth under the quickening influence of the sun. . . So, on the contrary, those who have died in impiety and have not repented, . . . are incapable of receiving such succor from the prayers of the living, since the influence of the sun . . . cannot quicken the seeds which have lost all power of growth."[1]   Such is the teaching also of Dyobouniotes,[2] who says that "if there can be no change after death in the Intermediate State, it follows that the prayers of the Church on behalf of the dead have no meaning."[3]   He acknowledges that the Early Church did not develop this teaching, but claims that its development is incumbent upon later generations in the Church.[4] He refuses to share Androutsos' reluctance to go beyond the negative limitations of the doctrine as found in early teaching, and says: "The Orthodox Church has the right . . . to engage upon the development and deeper understanding of dogmas not developed by the early Church. . . It is certainly no question of 'subverting the dogmas'[5] of the Faith."[6]   He holds that there is a development and progress in the state of the dead, helped and furthered by the Church's prayers, and that this theory does not militate against either of the truths of the Particular Judgment or the Orthodox teaching as to Repentance.[7]   In other words, no radical or absolute change may be effected after death. The direction and destination of the soul is fixed by the verdict of the Particular Judgment. But the realization of this destiny may be postponed, that the soul may be the better prepared to enjoy blessedness.

[1] Macarius, *op. cit.*, II. p. 714 ff. Souls lay the foundation in this life for the pardon which they may attain perfectly hereafter, thereby becoming worthy of the Church's good offices in their behalf, (*ibid.*, p. 719).

[2] Ἡ μέση κατάστασις τῶν ψυχῶν, pp. 98 ff.

[3] Ἡ Δογμ. Ἀνδρ. κριν., p. 63, Ὀφειλ. ἀπάντ., pp. 159-160.

[4] Ἡ Δογμ. Ἀνδρ. κριν., p. 62.

[5] As Androutsos says, Δογμ.. Μελέται Α', p. 139.

[6] Ὀφειλ. ἀπάντσις, p. 156.

[7] *Ibid.*, pp. 156-160.

2. The Consummation of All Things

The last topic of Orthodox dogmatic is discussed in three divisions, in accordance with the arrangement of the subject matter in the Creed. The first of these divisions is that on the Second Coming of our Lord, based on the words: "He shall come again, with glory, to judge both the quick and the dead; whose kingdom shall have no end." The next two sections treat of "the Resurrection of the dead" and "the Life of the world to come."

The Second Coming of our Lord is to be distinguished from His first Advent, when He came "in humility, for the emancipation of the human race from sin",[1] since He is to come in glory.[2] At this Coming He is to judge all, the righteous and the wicked, by a righteous and triumphant vindication of God's justice, in His rewarding of the good and His condemnation of the wicked. This Judgment is called the General or the Last Judgment.[3] The doctrine of our Lord's Coming in glory constitutes one of the fundamental Christian truths,[4] and is based on ample authority both of the Old[5] and New[6] Testaments in which His Coming in judgment is definitely predicted. All the creeds and the teaching of the Fathers combine to reiterate the conviction of the Second "Coming of the Lord and the expectation of the Resurrection of the dead and eternal life."[7] The time of the Coming has not been revealed, hence our Lord's injunction to His Apostles to watch, and their constant emphasis on this duty. "The mysterious hiddenness as to the day of Judgment is not illuminated by the signs which are to precede it, according to our Lord's and His Apostles words.[8] These 'signs' fall into five groups: (a) the preaching of the Gospel

[1] Mesolora, *op. cit.*, IV. p. 117.

[2] St. Matt. 24, 30.

[3] Mesolora, *ibid.*, p. 118.

[4] Androutsos, *op. cit.*, p. 437.

[5] Cf. Isaiah 66, 15, ff.; Joel 2, 30, ff.; 3, 2, ff.; Mal. 4, 1, 14, ff.; etc.

[6] Cf. St. Matt. 25, 3; St. Mark 13, 24, ff.; St. Luke 21, 27; Acts 10, 42; 17, 31; Rom. 2, 3, 5; 2 Thes. 1, 5, etc. For fuller references cf. notes 2 and 3, p. 118, Mesolora, *op. cit.*, IV.

[7] Androutsos, *ibid.*, p. 438.

[8] *Ibid.*, and cf. notes for references *ad loc.*

to all nations;[1] (b) the return of Israel to Christ;[2] (c) the coming of Elijah and Enoch in the last days;[3] (d) the coming of Antichrist; and (e) "the falling away from the Christian Faith . . . of many nations, under the influence of false teachers and false prophets, the great portents in external nature, and revolutions and wars among men. . ."[4] The coming of the Antichrist[5] has given rise to many speculations as to his person and character, but for lack of definite revelation we must confine ourselves to what is made known to us, in this matter as well as in that of the coming of Enoch and Elijah; these truths "are enshrouded in mysterious darkness."[6]

The Resurrection of the dead precedes the General Judgment, "which is followed by the end of the world, the separation of men into inheritors of eternal glory and sharers in eternal punishment."[7] This temporal sequence of the last things may not be understood literally, but presents simultaneous events as in a series.[8] Thus the Resurrection of the dead coincides with the end of the world, which in turn is not its extinction and destruction, but a change and renewal, consonant with the nature of renewed and glorified humanity.[9] Since the Last Things do not take place in a time sequence, there is no room in the Orthodox conception of them for *chiliasm*. According to the chiliastic theory—based on a misinterpretation of Rev. 20—"God will first raise up the righteous and with them will reign on earth for a period of a thousand years. In the various forms of this theory, a space of a thousand years

[1] Cf. St. Matt. 24, 14; St. Mk. 13, 10.
[2] Cf. Hosea 3, 5; Rom. II, 25-26.
[3] Rev. 11.
[4] Cf. St. Matt. 24, 4, ff; St. Mk. 13, 7-13; St. Lk. 21, 4-19; 2 Thes. 2, 2, 4, ff; etc. Androutsos, *op. cit.*, pp. 438-439. Mogila gives much this same enumeration, in Mesolora, *op. cit.*, I. pp. 406-407, cf. also Mesolora, IV. pp. 119-120.
[5] 1 St. John 2, 18; 2 Thes. 2, 3-4, 6-7. In this latter passage the words τὸ κατέχον involve difficulties of interpretation. Androutsos discusses them, *op. cit.*, note, pp. 440-441
[6] Androutsos, *op. cit.*, p. 439, and cf. note 5 (*ibid.*, and pp. 440-441) on Antichrist.
[7] Androutsos, *op. cit.*, p. 440.
[8] *Ibid.*
[9] Mesolora, *op. cit.*, IV. p. 123.

is to intervene between the Resurrection of the righteous and the General Resurrection and Judgment. . . " But chiliasm is in opposition to Holy Scripture, which knows but one Resurrection and Judgment, and Sacred Tradition, since early Fathers, such as Dionysius of Alexandria, Origen, and others, opposed it strongly.[1]

"By the Resurrection of the dead we understand the raising of all the bodies of those who have ever died and their reunion with their souls, through the might and operation of the Almighty God."[2] "The Resurrection is a complete reunion of soul and body, the second state of the living unit after dissolution. . . It is not impossible with Him who in the beginning made man of earth, after his dissolution and return to that from which he had been taken, again to restore him. If there be no Resurrection, let us eat and drink, let us live a life of pleasure and enjoyment. If there be no Resurrection, in what respect are we different from the beasts? If there be no Resurrection, there is no God, no Providence, and all things are driven mechanically."[3] St. John Damascene elsewhere says:[4] "If the soul alone exerted itself in the battle for virtue, then it alone should be crowned. If it alone was defiled with sensual pleasures, in justice it alone should be punished. But since neither soul nor body had existence the one apart from the other, nor did the soul apart from the body exercise itself in virtue or vice, quite rightly are both to receive their due reward together."[5] This notion of the unity of human nature, of the soul and body constituting the whole man, inhibits every dualistic conception of man's nature,[6] and affirms the truth that man is one, consisting of body and soul—a significant conception in view of the strong bias towards dualism of speculative thought. Androutsos conceives of the Resurrection as " a creative act of divine greatness and might, dissolving the rule of death and raising up all the dead along with the living before the divine bar of judgment. Just as God created all things of naught,

[1] Androutsos, *op. cit.*, pp. 441-442.
[2] Mesolora, *op. cit.*, IV. p. 120.
[3] St. John Damascene, Ἔκδοσις, IV. 104.
[4] In περὶ ἀναστάσεως, p. 209, quoted by Mesolora, *op. cit.*, IV, p. 121.
[5] An idea common in Rabbinic thought, cf. *Sanhedrin*, 91 b.
[6] Cf. Sec. 2, Lecture III, above.

thus through this same creative might He restores human bodies to their first essential form."[1]   This truth was suggested and taught more or less clearly in the Old Testament, but at the hands of our Lord and His Apostles it took definite form, and is "proclaimed as one of the most remarkable of the events connected with the consummation of the world, without which the whole edifice of the Christian Faith crumbles into ruin."[2]

According to Orthodox teaching, following St. Paul chiefly, the bodies of the dead will be transformed into incorruptible and spiritual bodies, the righteous rising to life eternal, and the wicked to punishment.   The bodies will be the same bodies, materially and essentially, though they will differ in their properties, since they are then to be spiritual; like the angels, they will not have the marriage relation; they are to be incapable of corruption, impervious to death, and "in general, conformed to the spiritual state of each individual after the general Resurrection."[3]   It is essential that the bodies of men be raised, "in order that they, as his organs, as an essential half of him, should attain to blessedness or receive the same condemnation as his soul."[4]   Some early heresies impugned the doctrine of the Resurrection of the Body, notably Origen and the Origenists, Carpocrates, Basilides, and certain Gnostics.[5]   According to one such early speculation, the soul possessed by nature a certain plastic principle or power (*forma corporeitatis*), by which it at the Resurrection could form a new body with which it would be hypostatically united.   Another speculation had it that the soul, after the Resurrection, acquires an ethereal and attenuated body, or by its nature already possessed an organ which was gradually to develop into such a body.   "Certainly the notion of bodies with spiritual properties is completely counter to the dictates of the physical sciences, nor is anyone able to reconcile the properties of the Resurrection bodies with the laws of physics, chemistry, and physiology, since the latter are based upon the principle that matter with its powers is

[1] *Op. cit.*, p. 442.

[2] *Ibid.*, *q. v.* for Old Testament references.

[3] Cf. 1 Cor. 15, 53; Androutsos, *op. cit.*, pp. 442-443; Mesolora, *op. cit.*, IV. pp. 120 ff.

[4] Cf. 2 Cor. 5, 10; Mesolora, *op. cit.*, IV, pp. 122-123.

[5] Mesolora, *op. cit.*, p. 122 note 1; Androutsos, *op. cit.*, p. 443.

something eternal and necessary. The whole question, however, becomes entirely different if one accepts in faith (the truth) that beyond the powers, energies, and phenomena of the empirical world there exist supernatural powers capable of changing and uplifting them."[1]

The well-known passages in the New Testament which have to do with the Resurrection and the General Judgment[2] do not give us all the facts about them, nor "must they be taken literally, since they are pictures portraying to us the inconceivable grandeur of that day." We do know this much: that it is our Lord who is to be the Judge; that "the basis and standard of the General Judgment will be the works of each individual or his faith as manifested in love. . . . according to the well-known intimate bond between faith and works."[3] Along with the Judgment will come the end of the world, which must not be conceived of as its destruction, but as its renovation and alteration according to a new pattern. Not only must nature share in the fruits of the final conquest and destruction of evil and death,[4] by becoming new and by being changed into a new entity, but man in glory will stand in need of a new habitation fit for his eternal life.[5] While the time and occasion are unknown to man, we are to watch and await its coming. The transformation of the world is to be accomplished by fire,[6] which is not to dstroy and annihilate, but to purify and purge the world and surviving humanity.[7] The Resurrection of the dead, the end of the world, and the General Judgment are to constitute the culmination and consummation of life in this sphere.[8]

"The result of the General Judgment is the eternal life of the righteous and the eternal punishment of the sinners—the

[1] Androutsos, op. cit., pp. 443-444, following Scheeben, Handbuch der katholischen Dogmatik, IV. pp. 918, 927.

[2] As e. g., St. Matt. 25, 31-46; St. John 3, 18; 5, 24; 1 Cor. 3, 13; Rom. 2, 6; 1 Cor. 3, 13, etc.

[3] Androutsos, op. cit., p. 444.

[4] Ibid., and p. 445.

[5] Mesolora, op. cit., IV. p. 123.

[6] Cf. 2 St. Pet. 3, 7, etc.

[7] Thus the Fathers, e. g., St. Clement Alex., Strom. VII; Origen, contra Celsum, V. 25; cf. Androutsos, op. cit., p. 445 note 3.

[8] For references, cf. op. cit., and notes; Mogila, in Mesolora, op. cit., I. pp. 406, 434-435.

former inheriting the Kingdom of God, and the latter being cast into hell fire."[1] Of the manner, place, and state of this blessedness or anguish we know little, for it is all a mystery inaccessible to us in this life.[2] Yet in certain general ways we may say that the bliss of those in Heaven is to consist in deliverance from pain, suffering, grief, corruption, and the like; in the enjoyment of the Beatific Vision; and in reunion and fellowship with all other righteous souls.[3] So the torment and suffering of the wicked will involve a deprivation of all good—joy and consolation—in their separation from the vision of God, in their torment of conscience, in remorse and regret, and in certain external punishments.[4] Both bliss and punishment are to be different in each instance, since judgment is meted out on the basis of individual acts of good or evil.[5] This graduated verdict is not only implied in Holy Writ, but is unanimously taught by the Fathers.[6]

The great difficulty in the Church's dogma on this subject is the eternal character of Heaven and Hell. "The theory of Origen and Gregory of Nyssa about the restoration of all and the conversion eventually of the demons and the impious, was condemned by the Church."[7] Any speculation which would lead to this type of universalism is in flat violation of the words of Holy Scripture. But if it be kept in mind that in God's plan for His world, life here is a definitely limited opportunity for ethical exercise and self-determination, the verdict passed on the results of this time of testing must be regarded as final. The objections brought against eternal blessedness and eternal punishment are chiefly of a rationalist origin and may be summarized as follows: eternal blessedness or punishment is inconsistent with the mercy, the justice, and the vision of God; with His mercy, in that this property demands that sinners should be brought through punishment to repentance and

---

[1] Androutsos, *op. cit.*, p. 445.

[2] *Ibid.*, pp. 447-448.

[3] Mesolora *op. cit.*, IV. p. 126.

[4] *Ibid.*, pp. 129-130; cf. on this, Kritopoulos, in Mesolora, I. pp. 353, 348; Mogila, *ibid.*, p. 410; etc.

[5] Androutsos, *op. cit.*, p. 447.

[6] *Ibid.*, note 1.

[7] *Ibid.*, pp. 445-446.

salvation; with His justice, in that small sins done in time cannot conceivably entail eternal punishment; and with His wisdom, in that the purpose of the creation of men being their happiness, it is brought to naught by eternal punishment. Others say, that since the soul still possesses its free-will, there must be provision for amendment and salvation. According to another view, the happiness of the Blessed is impossible, since they know that others of their own race are being punished eternally. So, others argue, God in His foreknowledge ought freely to have refrained from creating men who were destined to damnation. "But all these objections", says Androutsos, "are founded on the principle that reason is the standard and criterion of all things, and that in accordance with it even the divine wisdom and righteousness are to be estimated . . . If, on the other hand, reason be made subject to faith, then may come about the recognition of these truths, impossible of investigation by the human understanding, which lie beyond us."[1] "If the believer reason that (the wicked) have constituted themselves incapable of sharing in Blessedness, that no one can sanctify the free-will of man by force, nor coerce him into fellowship with God, he will sufficiently comprehend the possibility of alienation from God by the persevering act of man's free-will, and in consequence, the possibility of eternal punishment."[2] The dogma is fundamentally a mystery, apprehended through faith but not by reason alone, "for all these things are the object of our faith and hope, until the 'seeing through a glass, darkly' gives way to the Open Vision."[3] Then shall God be "all in all".

[1] Androutsos, *op. cit.*, note 4, pp. 446-447.
[2] *Ibid.*, (text) p 446.
[3] *Ibid.*, p. 448. Cf. Mesolora, *op. cit.*, IV. pp. 125-134; Mogila, in *ibid.*, I. pp. 407, 408-410, 435.

INDEX

A

B

C

S

T

PRINTED IN
THE UNITED STATES OF AMERICA
BY
MOREHOUSE PUBLISHING CO.
MILWAUKEE, WIS.